AMERICA AS A WORLD POWER

FOREIGN POLICY
IN A CONSTITUTIONAL FRAMEWORK

Also by the Author

The Making of International Agreements:
Congress Confronts the Executive

A Season of Inquiry: Congress and Intelligence

Through the Straits of Armageddon:
Arms Control Issues and Prospects
(coedited with Paul F. Diehl)

Decisions of the Highest Order:
Perspectives on the National Security Council
(coedited with Karl F. Inderfurth)

America's Secret Power: The CIA in a Democratic Society

Runoff Elections in the United States
(with Charles S. Bullock III)

AMERICA AS A WORLD POWER

FOREIGN POLICY IN A CONSTITUTIONAL FRAMEWORK

Loch K. Johnson

University of Georgia

McGRAW-HILL, INC.

New York   St. Louis   San Francisco   Auckland   Bogotá   Caracas
Hamburg   Lisbon   London   Madrid   Mexico   Milan   Montreal   New Delhi
Paris   San Juan   São Paulo   Singapore   Sydney   Tokyo   Toronto

AMERICA AS A WORLD POWER
Foreign Policy in a Constitutional Framework

1 2 3 4 5 6 7 8 9 0 DOC DOC 9 5 4 3 2 1 0

ISBN 0-07-032644-4

This book was set in Palatino by the College Composition Unit
in cooperation with General Graphic Services, Inc.
The editors were Bert Lummus and Tom Holton;
the production supervisor was Denise L. Puryear.
The cover was designed by Charles A. Carson.
R. R. Donnelley & Sons Company was printer and binder.

Library of Congress Cataloging-in-Publication Data

Johnson, Loch K., (date).
    America as a world power: foreign policy in a constitutional
  framework / Loch K. Johnson.
      p.   cm.
    Includes bibliographical references.
    ISBN 0-07-032644-4
    1. United States—Foreign relations—Law and legislation.
  2. United States—Constitutional law.   3. United States—Foreign
  relations—1945-   I. Title.
  KF4651.J64   1991
  342.73'0412—dc20   90-31902
  [347.302412]

ABOUT
THE AUTHOR

Loch K. Johnson, Regents Professor of Political Science at the University of Georgia, was born in Auckland, New Zealand, and holds a Ph.D. from the University of California—Riverside. He has been an American Political Science Association Congressional Fellow and has served on four U.S. House and Senate committees, including as staff director, Subcommittee on Oversight, House Permanent Select Committee on Intelligence.

Since joining the University of Georgia faculty in 1979, he has received numerous awards for outstanding teaching, including the 1988 Josiah Meigs Award (the university's highest teaching honor).

For Kristin, diplomat

Confidence is everywhere the parent of despotism—free government is founded in jealousy;...it is jealousy and not confidence which prescribes limited constitutions to bind down those we are obliged to trust with power....In questions of power, then, let no more be heard of confidence in man, but bind him down from mischief by the chains of the Constitution....

—Thomas Jefferson

CONTENTS

PREFACE   xiii

PART 1
AN INTRODUCTION TO
AMERICAN FOREIGN POLICY   1

CHAPTER 1
The Ends and Means of American
Foreign Policy   3

The Importance of American Foreign
    Policy   4
Why America Has a Foreign Policy   5
The Uses of American Foreign Policy   9
Summary   16

CHAPTER 2
Key Dimensions of the Foreign Policy
Milieu   21

The International Setting   21
The Domestic Setting   28
The Importance of the Individual
    Decision Maker   33
Summary   38

CHAPTER 3
The Past as Prologue   43

Nation Building, 1776–1865   43
Emergence as a Great Power, 1865–1920   53
America as a Reluctant Leader, 1920–   58
Summary   63

CHAPTER 4
The Contemporary Setting   69

The Nuclear Age   69
Peril Points   74
Detente   85
A Balance Sheet   90
Summary   92

CHAPTER 5
Remembering the Constitution   99

Shared Powers   99
The War Power   100
International Agreements   107
The Seeds of Acquiescence   111
The Purse Strings and Other Disputes   113
Marching to Different Drums   115
Conflict and Comity   120
Summary   122

CHAPTER 6
Institutional Dynamics   127

Fragments of Power   127
The Presidency   131
The Bureaucracy   134
The Congress   143
The Courts   149
Power: A Study in Cubism   152
Summary   154

CHAPTER 7
The Human Factor   161

Public Opinion and American Foreign
    Policy   161
Groups and American Foreign Policy   174
The Individual and American Foreign
    Policy   181
Summary   190

PART 2
THE USES OF AMERICAN
FOREIGN POLICY   197

CHAPTER 8
Strategic Intelligence: The
Foundations of Foreign Policy   199

The Origins of American Strategic
    Intelligence   200
Collection and Analysis   209
The Lure of Secrecy   218
Executive Privilege   221
Prior Restraint   223
Contractual Secrecy   224
Secrecy and Democracy   225
Summary   226

CHAPTER 9
America's Secret Power: The Hidden
Hand of the CIA   235

The Iran-Contra Affair   235
Covert Action   238
The Secret War against Chile   250
Covert Action: What Limits?   251
Intelligence Decision Making   253
Intelligence and Propriety   260
Summary   261

CHAPTER 10
The War Power: Resorting to the
Overt Use of Force   269

The Last Full Measure   269
The Uses of the War Power   270
Deciding to Use the War Power   274
Weapons of War in the Nuclear Age   283
Summary   296

CHAPTER 11
Diplomacy: The Art of Peaceful
Negotiations   303

Talking instead of Fighting   303
The Importance—and Ubiquity—of
   Diplomacy   305
The Making of International Agreements   306
America's Agreement Partners   313
The Pattern of American Diplomacy   314
The Hidden Side of Agreement Making   316
Military Agreements: Some Case
   Examples   318
The Dangers of Diplomacy by Executive
   Fiat   321
The Democratic Control of Diplomacy   322
Diplomacy's Far Reach   330
Summary   331

CHAPTER 12
Economic Statecraft: The Instruments
of Trade and Aid   341

Economic Goals: An Integral Part of
   American Foreign Policy   342
The Postwar International Economic
   Setting   342
Trade as an Instrument of American
   Foreign Policy   345

America's Trading Partners—and Rivals   350
America—No Longer the Solitary
   Economic Behemoth   353
Fragmentation of the International
   Economic Setting   356
The Fragmentation of Economic Power
   at Home   359
The Use of Trade Sanctions   363
Foreign Aid as an Instrument of
   American Foreign Policy   365
Trade and Aid: Stepchildren of American
   Foreign Policy   372
Summary   373

CHAPTER 13
Morality and Foreign Policy: On
Being Good in a Bad World   381

Prudence and Morality   381
Selected Ethical Dilemmas in Recent
   Foreign Policy Decisions   388
Charting a Moral Course   405
Summary   406

CHAPTER 14
American Foreign Policy in the
Twenty-First Century: A Normative
Epilogue   413

In Search of a New Foreign Policy   413
The Necessity for Better Citizen
   Awareness of Global Affairs   414
Overcoming the Centrifugal Forces of
   Domestic Political Institutions   415
A World beyond the Kremlin   417
An End to Compulsive Interventionism   421
Summary   423

APPENDIX   427
*Preamble to the United Nations
Charter, 1945*   427
*The Constitution of the United States:
Excerpts*   428

INDEX   433

FIGURES

3.1   Highlights in the Evolution of
      American Foreign Policy,
      1776–1945   44

4.1 Highlights in the Evolution of American Foreign Policy during the Nuclear Age   70

6.1 Organization Chart for the Department of Defense   138

6.2 Organization Chart for the Department of State   140

7.1 The High Cost of Weapons   180

7.2 A Comparison of Frank Church and Other Foreign Policy Leaders along Operational-Code Dimensions   188

8.1 The United States Intelligence Community   202

8.2 Organization Chart of the Central Intelligence Agency (CIA)   205

8.3 The Directorate of Operations   206

8.4 The Intelligence Cycle   209

9.1 Covert-Action Decision Process   255

11.1 International Agreement Making: A Continuum of Executive Discretion   307

11.2 Trends in the Content of U.S. International Agreements   310

11.3 America's Major Agreement Partners   315

12.1 The U.S. Trade Gap with Japan   351

12.2 Development Assistance Provided by the Industrialized Nations as a Percentage of GNP, 1987   368

10.5 NATO and Warsaw Pact Conventional Forces in Europe (1989)   293

11.1 Form of U.S. Foreign Agreements by Administration, 1946–1972   309

11.2 Form of U.S. Foreign Agreements by Content Areas, 1946–1972   312

11.3 Executive Agreement Index (EAI), 1946–1972   312

11.4 Regime Targets of U.S. Foreign Agreements by Administration, 1946–1972   314

11.5 The Use of Three Forms of Agreement Making within Six Global Regions   315

11.6 The Dominance of Executive Agreements over Treaties in the Making of Significant Military Commitments Abroad, 1946–1972   318

12.1 U.S.–Soviet Trade: Soviet Exports to and Imports from the United States, FOB   347

12.2 U.S. Trade Balances: 1960, 1976, and 1984   349

12.3 U.S. Trade Balances: 1985, 1986, and 1987   350

12.4 Institutional Fragmentation over International Economic Policy within the Executive Branch: A Partial Listing   360

12.5 Legislative Committees and Subcommittees with Jurisdiction over International Economic Policy: A Partial Listing   362

12.6 Instruments of International Economic Power: Trade Sanctions and Inducements   364

12.7 Foreign Economic and Military Assistance for Fiscal Year 1978   367

TABLES

2.1 Attitudes on the Use of U.S. Troops Overseas (1986)   29

7.1 The Most Important Problem Facing the Country, 1935–1985   163

7.2 Rally Events in American Foreign Policy   166

7.3 Survey Opinion on the Cambodian Invasion (1970)   172

10.1 Key International Incidents Relevant to the War Powers Resolution, 1973–1989   278

10.2 The Effects of Nuclear Weapons   284

10.3 The Effects of Whole-Body Radiation Doses   285

10.4 Strategic Warheads: A U.S. and Soviet Comparison (1986)   291

BOXES — "PERSPECTIVES ON AMERICAN FOREIGN POLICY"

1.1 Dean Rusk on the importance of information to foreign policy decision making   11

1.2 H. Bradford Westerfield on the "functional analysis" of American foreign policy   15

2.1 The Truman Doctrine (1947)   24

2.2 President Eisenhower on the "domino theory" (1954)   25

2.3 Paul Kennedy on the risks of fragmented government for America's external relations   33

3.1 President Washington's Farewell Address (1796)   46

3.2 The Monroe Doctrine (1823)   51

3.3 President Wilson's Fourteen Points (1918)   58

4.1 The Doolittle Report (1954)   74

4.2 President Kennedy's Inaugural Address (1961)   80

4.3 Clark M. Clifford on the war in Vietnam (1965)   82

4.4 Ronald Reagan on the war in Vietnam (1976)   85

5.1 Frank Church on presidential power   107

5.2 The Senate Foreign Relations Committee on international agreements   111

5.3 Laurence Tribe on foreign policy privatization   115

5.4 Hubert H. Humphrey on legislative participation in foreign policy   121

6.1 President Eisenhower's Farewell Address (1960)   136

6.2 Roger Hilsman on executive bureaucracy   142

6.3 Zbigniew Brzezinski on congressional micromanagement   147

6.4 Justice Sutherland's dicta in the *Curtiss-Wright* case   151

6.5 President Nixon on presidential power   153

7.1 Dean Rusk on public opinion and the war in Vietnam   164

7.2 James David Barber on foreign lobbying in the United States   177

7.3 Alexander George on Richard Nixon   186

8.1 Stansfield Turner on the National Security Agency (NSA)   204

8.2 A CIA analyst on the fall of the Iranian Shah (1979)   216

8.3 Charles W. Yost on secrecy   226

9.1 Vice Admiral John M. Poindexter on plausible denial   238

9.2 William Colby on CIA covert action   239

9.3 "Elimination by Illumination": A plan to depose Fidel Castro   241

9.4 John McCone on the CIA assassination plots against Fidel Castro   245

9.5 William Colby on supervising the CIA   260

10.1 Three legislators on Congress and the war power   277

10.2 Physicians for Social Responsibility depict a nuclear detonation in a U.S. city   287

11.1 President Truman's "Point Four" program   311

11.2 John Foster Dulles on the treaty power   324

11.3 Dick Clark on the Treaty Powers Resolution   329

12.1 Transnationalism versus *dependencia*   358

12.2 Furor over the export of U.S. oil equipment to the Soviet Union   361

12.3 Benjamin Constant contrasting economic statecraft and the war power   366

12.4 David D. Newsom on the Peace Corps   371

13.1 The realism of Georges Clemenceau   387

13.2 Kant and the consequentialist school of ethics: A hypothetical case   392

13.3 Roger Fisher on the ethics of covert action   399

13.4 Louis Halle on American foreign policy and medieval knighthood   404

13.5 Arthur M. Schlesinger, Jr., on international morality   406

14.1 Tom Teepen on a U.S. challenge in the developing world   420

14.2 Carl Rowan on the limits of power   422

PREFACE

Books traditionally begin with a preface and an introductory chapter. The purpose of the preface is to state the broad objectives of the book; it should provide the reader with a brief road map of the route the author intends to travel. The opening chapter then offers a more substantive and detailed guide to the author's subject, in this case American foreign policy in the aftermath of World War II. This sensible tradition is followed here.

OBJECTIVES

This book's objectives can be stated succinctly. In Part 1, the author introduces:

- the ends (or goals) of American foreign policy, as well as the means by which they are pursued (Chapter 1);
- the key dimensions of the foreign policy milieu and how they affect the conduct of America's external relations (Chapter 2);
- how U.S. foreign policy goals have been shaped by American and world history (Chapters 3 and 4);
- why the nation's constitutional framework continues to exert a strong and, from the author's point of view, a laudable influence over foreign policy making in the modern era (Chapter 5);
- the institutional frictions that arise from this constitutional framework (Chapter 6); and
- the human dimension of foreign policy, from the lofty decision making of presidents and legislators to the important role

that you, the reader, and other individual citizens can play in the fashioning of America's ties abroad (Chapter 7).

Then, in Part 2, the book examines:

- the conduct of American foreign policy across a range of important responsibilities, from gathering information about global threats and opportunities (Chapter 8) to the application of power and principle in the defense of the nation's interests and ideals around the world (Chapters 9 through 13)—that is, how the United States *learns* about events beyond its borders, and how it then *acts* upon this information—and
- new directions for America as a world power on the eve of the twenty-first century (Chapter 14).

Stated another way, the first half of this volume (Chapters 1 through 7) offers a primer on the fundamentals of American foreign policy—why this country must concern itself with the rest of the world and how America's external relations are forged. The second half (Chapters 8 through 14) moves from this backdrop to front stage, with a shift in focus toward U.S. foreign policy in action: the challenge of gathering and analyzing information collected from around the world (strategic intelligence), in an effort to guard against surprise attacks like the one that shook Pearl Harbor in 1941; the shadowy use of the Central Intelligence Agency (CIA) and its hidden hand to manipulate events overseas (covert action); the overt deployment of force—sending in the Marines—to achieve America's foreign objectives; the pursuit of more peaceful, diplomatic approaches to the settlement of international disputes; the application of economic inducements (trade and aid); and, last but not least, the evocation of moral principle to guide America's relations with other lands. Here, to draw upon the political scientist Harold D. Lasswell's spare yet venerable definition of politics (*Politics: Who*

Gets What, When, How, New York, McGraw-Hill, 1936), is where the book addresses the who gets what, when, and how of global affairs. Last, the concluding chapter examines ways in which citizens might choose to refashion and strengthen this nation's global ties as the world approaches a new century.

THEMES

A dominant theme unites this book: the drafters of the U.S. Constitution envisioned a sharing of authority for foreign policy across the institutions of government—the executive, the legislative, and the judicial branches. They sought, above all else, to guard against the dangers of tyranny; and—the central normative argument undergirding this book—their prescriptions are as valid today as they were in 1787. This sharing of authority across institutions has its frustrations. The power bestowed upon policymakers as a result of their positions of authority can become dispersed, Balkanized; overlapping jurisdictions may lead to inefficiencies and delay. Other countries, even America's allies, may become confused and dismayed by this open, sometimes unpredictable approach to international affairs. The nation's founders believed, nonetheless, that a concentration of power represented a far greater danger to the republic than whatever inefficiencies might be incurred under a system of shared authority. They opted for an imperfect democracy over attempts at perfect order. As Justice Louis Brandeis once put it,

> The doctrine of the separation of powers was adopted by the [Constitutional] Convention of 1787, not to promote efficiency but to preclude the exercise of arbitrary power. The purpose was, not to avoid friction, but, by means of the inevitable friction incident to the distribution of the governmental powers among three departments, to save the people from autocracy [*Myers v. United States*, 272 U.S. 52, 293 (1926)].

This constitutional blueprint for shared authority set loose powerful centrifugal forces within the government that continue to push the institutions of foreign policy making away from centralized control. By early design, the government of the United States consists of fragments of power that must be pieced together with skillful leadership—and luck—in order to make the parts move in harmony. Under such arrangements, Congress and the executive branch can find themselves in conflict over the proper direction of foreign policy—a system of governing quite different from dictatorships like the Soviet Union, where foreign policy is carved out with little consideration for public or legislative opinion; or even from Western parliamentary governments with their fused executive and legislative powers under the strong control of a prime minister or chancellor. Yet, a vigorous internal debate between the branches of government over the proper pathways for the United States to follow is precisely what the founders intended. They hoped for wisdom that would emanate from many heads, not just the president's; for open discourse, not regal command. Just as for the founders the nature of executive-legislative relations lay at the heart of foreign (and domestic) policy making, so, too, does it become the central focus of this book.

Embraced within the book's central theme, then, is the important notion extolled by the founders that the legislative branch has a vital, positive role to play in decisions of international affairs. Most volumes on American foreign policy are prone to exalt the presidency as the embodiment of those virtues often considered desirable for effective external relations: hierarchical organization, access to extensive information, quickness of decision, an intricate bureaucracy to carry out policy, and the like. This book, in contrast, maintains that no branch has a monopoly on wisdom for foreign policy. Rather, the government functions best when its various parts operate together, like an engine with all its cylinders at work. Comity between the executive and legislative branches, a spirit of good faith, a willingness to work shoulder to shoulder, even as each branch remains cautious about possible abuses of power by the other—here, argues this book, is the key to an effective foreign policy in a system of dispersed authority.

Despite the brilliance of the insights on governing offered by the founders, Americans lost sight of these basic principles during the first half of this century. The twin catastrophes of global war and economic depression spurred a trend toward the concentration of power within the executive branch. This dangerous aggrandizement, culminating in the "imperial presidency" of the Johnson and Nixon administrations, represented a radical departure from American traditions. It would take a souring war in Indochina, along with the Watergate and CIA scandals, to trim back burgeoning executive powers in the 1970s and awaken within the citizenry a renewed appreciation for the virtues in foreign policy of shared authority across the branches.

A primary purpose of this book is to explore the advantages, as well as the disadvantages, that America's constitutional framework holds for the conduct of foreign policy. Empirically, it attempts to shed light on the points of friction and cooperation in a system of shared authority; normatively, it tries to convey an appreciation for the safeguards put in place by the founders to protect the nation against one-man rule.

While the problems of power sharing between the branches occupy center stage in this book, a drama as large as American foreign policy has many subplots. An important secondary theme portrays the ambivalence of Americans toward their status as a world power—a persistent uncertainty about how to relate to the rest of the world. Citizens of this country have oscillated over the years between attitudes of isolationism, on the one hand, and interventionism, on the other.

Emphasized in this book, too, is the significance of the human factor in foreign affairs.

Some experts view foreign policy as essentially a product of broad historical or institutional forces. Certainly, these conditions must be taken into account, but the will or sometimes the whim of government officials and private citizens makes a difference as well and is given close attention throughout this volume.

An additional theme is the contention that the United States has been overly preoccupied with the "Soviet threat," transfixed by the unlikely event that Russian tanks will come rumbling through the Fulda gap in Europe, quickly overrunning Western military defenses. As a result of this fixation, Americans have been insufficiently attentive to greater long-term threats to their future—from global pollution and runaway population growth abroad to declining economic competitiveness and moral decay at home.

Other themes are woven through the book, among them: that U.S. external relations over the years have been a blend of realism and idealism; that the United States is only one of many nations on the globe, all of which exist in something of an anarchical state with no higher authority over them to adjudicate disputes or maintain order; and that the study of foreign policy is devoid of any single dominant theory or methodology.

A NEW PARADIGM

Despite the importance of these various themes, the essence of U.S. foreign policy lies in how and why decisions are made. Consequently, this book concentrates on decision processes and institutions, on the people who hold positions of authority, and on the foreign policy views of citizens as they affect deliberations in high office. Its further central intention is to understand the objectives of American foreign policy, and how they are carried out. Following a review of fundamentals, this volume in its second half illustrates the importance—and the difficulty—of acquiring good information (strategic intelligence) about the world in order to make informed foreign policy decisions. It examines how U.S. officials go about choosing which approaches to employ in the pursuit of America's goals from among the several means available—primarily, secret intervention abroad, open warfare, diplomacy, trade, aid, and moral suasion.

While most of this book is devoted to the scholarly marshaling of findings about how the United States makes its foreign policy decisions, the themes presented earlier indicate that normative undercurrents flow beneath the empirical analysis. This book calls for a new approach (or "paradigm," in social science jargon) to American foreign policy. The excessive deference paid to the president as an unerring architect of foreign affairs has failed (as the founders would have predicted); and so has the fixation of American officials on the threat of communism, as if the world were merely a Soviet-American chessboard. The new paradigm envisions a foreign policy based, institutionally, on an executive-legislative partnership and, ideologically, on a global perspective that extends beyond the shibboleths of the cold war. Whether this "fresh" approach (if a return to constitutional principles and a renewed friendship with the Russian people can be construed as fresh) is preferable to the formulas of the cold war era is for the reader to decide. The author hopes only that this work will contribute to the debate about how best to prepare the United States for its leadership responsibilities in the twenty-first century.

ACKNOWLEDGMENTS

I have had an opportunity to observe American foreign policy from vantage points within the government and, more recently, in the tranquillity of the ivory tower, to reflect upon this experience while immersed in the scholarly literature on this subject. Within the government, I served as assistant to the chairman of the Senate Select Committee on Intelligence; staff director of the Subcommittee on Oversight, House Permanent Select Committee on Intelligence; aide to the ranking majority member of the Senate Foreign Relations Committee; and senior aide on the Subcommittee on International Economic Policy and Trade, House Committee on Foreign Affairs. I have also had the privilege to serve as a consultant to the National Security Council and to the Department of State. Following these chances for close observation of how foreign policy is made, I have studied, taught, and written about foreign policy for the past decade as a professor of political science, traveling back to Washington periodically for interviews with officials, the presentation of testimony before Congress, and archival research. This book is a blend of impressions gained from these various "hands-on" and scholarly experiences.

Along the way, I have had the benefit of many wise tutors, beginning with the scholars Arthur C. Campbell, David S. McLellan, Vernon Puryear, and Lambert N. Wenner, and continuing, within the government, with Senators Frank Church and Wyche Fowler and Representatives Les Aspin and Jonathan B. Bingham, as well as David Aaron, James J. Angleton, William E. Colby, Stephen J. Flanagan, Arthur S. Hulnick, Karl F. Inderfurth, Thomas K. Latimer, William G. Miller, F. A. O. Schwarz, Jr., Gregory F. Treverton, and Stansfield Turner. More recently, I have had the chance to exchange foreign policy views with several thoughtful former government officials, researchers, and educators, including Richard Ball, former Ambassador W. Tapley Bennett, Gary Bertsch, former NSC director McGeorge Bundy, Paul F. Diehl, Dorinda Dallmeyer, I. M. Destler, Richard Falk, Peter Fenn, John Lewis Gaddis, Jerome Garris, Michael J. Glennon, former Secretary of State Alexander Haig, Alonzo L. Hamby, Glenn Hastadt, former Ambassador Martin Hillenbrand, George Kalaris, Charlotte Ku, former Senator George McGovern, Joseph S. Nye, Jr., Harry Howe

Ransom, George Rathjens, Jack Ruina, former Secretary of State Dean Rusk, Harry Sepp, Harold L. Sims, Robert Swansbrough, former Ambassador William Truehart, Garry Wenski, H. Bradford Westerfield, and David L. Williams. The bibliographic and footnote entries in this volume attest to my further indebtedness to an additional wide range of scholars. None of these good people should bear the blame for errors of fact or for the interpretations I have settled upon here; I thank them all sincerely, though, for their guidance, however poor a student I may have been.

I would also like to thank the following reviewers for their many helpful comments and suggestions: Richard Falk, Princeton University; David S. McLellen, Miami University; Robert Swansbrough, University of Tennessee, Chattanooga; Richard Weisfelder, University of Toledo; and H. Bradford Westerfield, Yale University.

Finally, I must thank New York University Press, the University Press of Kentucky, Oxford University Press, _Foreign Policy, International Journal of Intelligence and Counterintelligence_, and _International Studies Quarterly_ for allowing me to draw upon my work published by them; the Department of Political Science at the University of Georgia and John J. Kozak, Dean of the College of Arts and Sciences, for helpful support; David Price and Margaret Schuelke for research assistance; Bert Lummus and Tom Holton of McGraw-Hill, Inc. and copyeditor Richard K. Mickey for their sure guidance; and Leena, Kristin, and Roland Johnson for cheery encouragement, affection, and unfailing succor throughout the project.

Loch K. Johnson

PART 1

AN INTRODUCTION TO AMERICAN FOREIGN POLICY

THE IMPORTANCE OF AMERICAN FOREIGN POLICY

WHY AMERICA HAS A FOREIGN POLICY

    Peace and Security

    Economic Prosperity

    Quality of Life

    Human Dignity

THE USES OF AMERICAN FOREIGN POLICY

    Strategic Intelligence

    Covert Action

    The War Power

    Diplomacy

    Economic Statecraft

    Moral Suasion

SUMMARY

1

THE ENDS AND MEANS OF AMERICAN FOREIGN POLICY

Slash-and-burn agricultural methods in Latin America deplete rain forests. (Jacques Jangoux)

Colonel Park W. Tibbets pushed the throttles full forward on the B-29 bomber, a part of the 509th Composite of the 20th Air Force. Named *Enola Gay* in honor of Tibbets's mother, the plane lumbered down the runway on Tinian Island in the Pacific, lifted, and headed toward Japan. In the belly of the plane, its solitary cargo lay in darkness: ten feet long, two feet wide, nine thousand pounds in weight, packed with uranium. In ironic misnomer, the crew called it "Little Boy."

As dawn began to break, weather planes and two B-29 observer planes joined the *Enola Gay* over Iwo Jima. The weather reports were good for each authorized Japanese target: Nagasaki, Kokura, and, top priority on the list, Hiroshima. In his mind's eye the bombardier, Major Thomas W. Ferebee, could see the briefing maps of Hiroshima, with Aioi Bridge at the center of this city famous for its graceful willow trees.

The sky turned bright and clear as the bomber approached Hiroshima. Local time: 8:15 A.M., the sixth day of August, 1945. The speed of the *Enola Gay*: 200 miles per hour. Altitude: 31,060 feet. The Aioi Bridge moved swiftly into the cross hairs of the bombsight. Ferebee opened the belly of the plane and pressed the cargo-release button.

Fast as the shadow of a bird, the *Enola Gay* pulled upward, back, away, as Little Boy fell until its altimeter registered the correct height of 1890 feet above the unsuspecting city.

A burst, a blinding flash of light, tumbling helixes of white-hot mass rising in a glassy column, the sun come to earth—a world forever changed.

In an instant, an energy force equivalent to 12,000 tons of TNT struck Hiroshima. The city became an oven set at 50 million degrees centigrade. Above the maelstrom of death and destruction, a stately mushroom cloud rose 20,000 feet into the sky, its stem darkened by urban debris, at its top a white plume trailing off toward the horizon. Of Hiroshima's 255,000 population, 78,150 were killed by the blast and the fires that came in its wake, 100,000 more were seriously burned, and another 13,425 were never found.

Estimates by the Truman administration indicated that an invasion of Japan would have taken 18 months and cost the lives of anywhere from 40,000 to upwards of half a million GIs. Eager to end the war without further loss of life to American soldiers, Truman ordered the Air Force to use America's ultimate weapon against the Japanese: the atomic bomb, newly invented by government scientists. "You break your head and your heart to save one life," recalled President Truman. ". . . No man could fail to use the bomb and look his countrymen in the face."[1]

Three days following the destruction of Hiroshima, the United States dropped another atomic bomb on Japan, this time at Nagasaki, with 35,000 killed or lost and 40,000 injured— again all within seconds. The government of Japan surrendered and may have been preparing to give up the struggle even before the destruction of Nagasaki. A declaration of war against Japan by the Soviet Union probably contributed to this decision to surrender, and the march of the Red Army eastward may have also influenced Truman's decision to wind down the war quickly before the communists outraced the Americans to Tokyo. At long last, with a stunning use of a physical power that left the world in awe, the United States had brought the agony in the jungles of the Pacific to an end.

THE IMPORTANCE OF AMERICAN FOREIGN POLICY

The sudden destruction of Hiroshima and Nagasaki by atomic weapons marked the beginning of a new historical era, the nuclear age. The lives of human beings across the globe have been profoundly affected by the existence of nuclear weapons. Today, the explosive yield of sophisticated hydrogen bombs makes the thermal energy released by the atomic bombs

dropped on Japan seem like primitive fireworks. The United States and the Soviet Union have the capacity to annihilate one another if either were to start a full-scale war—perhaps destroying the rest of the world as well, as deadly radioactive clouds of dust and debris drifted with the prevailing winds without respect for national boundaries, or blocked out the sun's rays to begin a new ice age. As President Jimmy Carter once said (June 18, 1979), "In the age of the hydrogen bomb, there is no longer any meaningful distinction between a global war and global suicide."

At the beginning of the twentieth century, a young Winston S. Churchill (who would become prime minister of Great Britain during World War II) participated in a cavalry charge by the Twenty-first Lancers in Egypt against the fearsome Dervish warriors. As he later remembered, "Nobody expected to be killed. Here and there in every regiment or battalion, half a dozen, a score, at the worst thirty or forty, would pay the forfeit; but to the great mass of those who took part in the little wars of Britain in those vanished light-hearted days, this was only a sporting element in a splendid game. . . ."[2]

The global conflicts that soon followed brought an end to war as a genteel pursuit for the professional military. As became obvious from the staggering mass destruction and the unprecedented numbers of casualties among civilians and soldiers alike, war had assumed a more somber face. Nothing so poignantly revealed this change as the instant carnage at Hiroshima and Nagasaki. To a degree unseen in the prenuclear world, war as an instrument of foreign policy had become everyone's business. Each person—at least those living within the industrial nations of the world—now stood in the cross hairs of advanced weaponry, with no place to hide.

More than the nature of warfare has changed. The barriers that once impeded the international flow of capital, goods, services, information, and technology have begun to dissolve rapidly, allowing the emergence of a global market. The economic prosperity of every American is now more and more dependent upon the currents of world trade and finance. As one authority on foreign affairs has put it, "The American economy is increasingly tied to a world economy over which the United States exercises progressively less control."[3] The default of poor countries on international loans from U.S. banks has a harmful effect on interest rates at home for American citizens; the popularity of Japanese automobiles in the world marketplace sends the economy of Detroit reeling and injures other domestic industries that manufacture automobile components, from rubber and steel to glass and electronics; cheap labor costs in Korea, the Philippines, and elsewhere in the developing world draw American companies abroad and result in the loss of jobs at home for southern textile workers and northern manufacturers.

Threats from abroad are, of course, nothing new for the United States. The life of the new republic began—and almost ended at the hands of the British—in a perilous setting that saw the thirteen original states surrounded throughout their early years by hostile armies and navies from the rich and well-armed nations of Europe. Foreign policy today, though, has taken on a special urgency resulting from the acute dangers posed by modern weapons and the growing economic reliance of nations on one another. Now, more than ever, foreign policy warrants the attention of every thoughtful citizen.

WHY AMERICA HAS A FOREIGN POLICY

Though generally regarded as the strongest nation in the world, the United States faces severe limitations on its ability to act as it wishes in global affairs. When asked recently what U.S. strategy should be toward helping the Soviet Union liberalize its economic system (a policy called "restructuring" or *perestroika* in Russian),

a seasoned State Department official responded: "I don't think we should have a strategy, frankly, because most things we do we make such a mess of. Our ability to influence things diminishes greatly the farther we get from our shores."[4] A realization of the restraints on America's ability to mold the world to its liking is perhaps the most important legacy of this nation's tragic involvement in the Vietnamese civil war (officially, from 1964 to 1975, but also with U.S. intelligence officers and American military advisers unofficially supporting the South Vietnamese side from the Truman through the Kennedy administration). The South Vietnamese would eventually lose the war to the Marxist-communist North Vietnamese in 1975, at the cost to the United States of over 57,000 American lives and hundreds of billions of dollars, not to mention the disruptive political unrest and economic stagnation seeded within this country by the unpopular war.

Even closer to these shores, the success of the United States in controlling events in Central and South America has proven to be limited. This limitation has been demonstrated, for example, by America's inability in the 1960s to oust the communist leader of Cuba, Fidel Castro, or, in the 1980s, to dictate the outcome of the Nicaraguan civil war, where once again America backed a losing pro–U.S. faction (the contras, from the Spanish *contrarevolucionarios*) against a newly entrenched Marxist regime, the Sandinistas. Only in tiny Grenada was a large U.S. invasion force able, in 1983, to overcome a ragtag band of Marxist resisters, and in little Panama, in 1989, to overthrow the resident dictator. Closer still, America's very borders have seemed impossible to control, as illegal aliens and dangerous drugs pour in like water through fingers. Only about 10 percent of all the cocaine and heroin smuggled into the United States from abroad is intercepted by U.S. government authorities; the rest washes into the nation's back alleys and affluent suburbs alike, in an insidious attack on Americans that many observers view as a greater danger to the nation than the threat of Soviet missiles or communist insurgencies in the poor nations of the world.

Regardless of the inevitable limitations on foreign policy, few nations are willing to stand by passively and accept whatever fate and their adversaries may deal out to them. Instead, they actively try to shape their destiny (as best they can) in pursuit of their own objectives. What objectives does the United States seek in its relations with other countries? At the top of the list is the physical safety of this nation and its citizens, along with its allies and friends.

Peace and Security

During the Carter administration, the director of the influential Policy Planning Staff in the Department of State noted that "our first and most important foreign policy priority is peace—for ourselves and for others." Similarly, during the Reagan years, the State Department emphasized the importance of "seeking to protect the security of our nation and its institutions, as well as those of our allies and friends."[5]

So far humanity's record for peace and security has been uneven. Most of the time, most nations have been at peace with one another—a remarkable fact, given the bitter animosities that so often arise between nations. Yet, during the 5500 years of recorded history, the world has enjoyed only some 300 years in which no nation has been at war somewhere on the globe. During World War II, over 60 million people lost their lives, and more than 10 million have been casualties of armed conflict since then. In 1986 (heralded by the United Nations as the "Year of Peace"), 5 million combatants in forty-one nations were reportedly engaged in armed conflict. Around the world, nations purchase weapons at the cost of about $1 million every minute and, as these words are being written (1989), one out of every four countries is at war; just in the last twelve months, over 500,000 people lost their lives in violent conflicts in Central America, Sudan, Eritrea, the

Middle East, Northern Ireland, southern Africa, and Sri Lanka.[6]

"No diseases, no pestilence, no plagues have claimed as many lives as war," observes Dr. Bernard Lown, a recent Nobel Peace Prize recipient from the United States.[7] How has this happened? How can this earth—so beautiful in lake and mountain, a paradise among the barren planets of the solar system—be so smitten with hostility and bloodshed, when its inhabitants long for peace, when few people of any race or nationality wish to die prematurely on a battlefield? This question is vital, for the core objective of American foreign policy—the protection of the United States, its people, and its values, along with offering assistance for the security of its allies and friends—can be achieved only if this nation and others prove able to resolve their international disputes through nonviolent means.

The peaceful resolution of disagreements between nations becomes an even more compelling objective today as nuclear weapons begin to proliferate around the globe. These weapons are now openly maintained by five nations (the United States, the Soviet Union, Great Britain, France, and China); are held secretly by Israel (which reportedly has enough warheads to flatten every major Arab city); have been tested by India; and may soon be part of the arsenal of several other countries (Pakistan, Brazil, Argentina, and South Africa are high on the list of potential nuclear powers). Moreover, by the turn of the century, some fifteen developing nations will have, ready for firing or on the production line, ballistic missiles of their own. These rockets will be capable of reaching far beyond the traditional battlefield and with great velocity—possibly armed with chemical or biological warheads (twenty countries are at present developing the former, ten countries the latter, according to recent intelligence reports).[8] As we know from the outbreak of global war in 1914, and again in 1941, limited regional conflicts can spread quickly to engulf the major powers.

During the American Civil War (1861–1865),

An M-26 Pershing tank on display in front of a U.S. Army building in West Berlin. (Official U.S. Army photograph)

picnickers followed battlefield skirmishes across the Virginia countryside; today, neither the witchfire of a nuclear holocaust nor the deadly clouds of chemical-biological toxins will hold any attraction for curious observers. The study of American foreign policy has many dimensions, as the table of contents to this volume attests, but at its center is the challenge of preserving the globe for those who live now and for posterity. As acknowledged by the Reagan administration, a central foreign policy objective is to "contribute to a safer world by reaching equitable and verifiable arms reduction agreements with the Soviet Union."[9] This administration's ratification of the Intermediate Nuclear Force (INF) Treaty with Kremlin leaders in 1987, eliminating an entire class of U.S.–

Soviet medium-range nuclear missiles, is viewed by many as the crowning foreign policy achievement of the Reagan years.

Economic Prosperity

A second goal of U.S. foreign policy is the economic security of the American people. This security is closely tied to global economic conditions. The success of U.S. commodities in foreign markets translates into jobs for American workers. Spiraling oil-import costs mean inflation at home—indeed, a hemorrhaging of U.S. national wealth to oil-rich sheikhdoms in the Middle East. A rupture in U.S. relations with the Soviet Union can cost the American farmer dearly in the loss of grain sales abroad.

Economic woes in Brasilia and Caracas lead to handwringing among international loan officers within the American banking community. As this book is being written, U.S. warships patrol the waters of the Persian Gulf—at great cost to the taxpayer—in order to protect the access of the Western industrial nations to Middle East oil. Ironically, the nation that benefits most from this American armada is a major economic competitor of the United States—Japan, which obtains 55 percent of its oil from this region of the world.

Quality of Life

A third goal—one less uniformly supported by American citizens—has been to find solutions to a cluster of "lifestyle" issues that threaten the future of the United States and other nations. For most people around the globe, adequate health care, housing, and education—themselves important sinews of national strength—are sadly lacking. Two-thirds of the people who live in the developing countries are without clean water to drink—the cause of about 80 percent of the disease in these countries. Just a short distance from the United States, more people in Belize, Guatemala, Honduras, and even war-torn Nicaragua die of enteritis and diarrheal disorders—results of polluted water—than from any other cause. For an expenditure of roughly $300 billion (the amount of money spent by the United States on defense annually in recent years), international health experts estimate that the world's water supplies could be made pure.

Further, the world's rain forests are vanishing because of poor management. Nearly two-thirds of this precious resource has disappeared already in Central America; in Costa Rica, the rain forests are being overcome at a rate of 360 square miles annually. Farther south, in Brazil, the world's most magnificent rain forest, the Amazon, has shrunk from 140,000 square miles to just 4000 in the past two centuries. Worldwide, urban growth has swallowed up over a million acres of forested land in just the past ten years; and today, the rate of rain forest decline around the world is estimated at 50,000 square miles per year—an expanse larger than the state of Pennsylvania. Similarly, arable land in north Africa is being suffocated by spreading deserts. The depletion of the rain forests and the overheating of the earth's surface through the build-up of chemical pollutants in the atmosphere contribute to the "greenhouse effect," which—among other harmful environmental repercussions—retards the growth of farm crops.

The television images of starving children on the horn of Africa and in other poor regions, flies crawling across their dazed, unblinking eyes, are a grim reminder of the challenges faced by all nations. So are the terrorist attacks that occur on average over once a day around the world, often spawned by the resentment felt by desperate people who glimpse in magazines or on television the life of luxury in the industrial states while they experience only grinding poverty.

Human Dignity

A fourth objective, also lacking the widespread support accorded the goals of physical and economic security, has been the effort to eliminate global injustices—especially, the violation of human rights in other lands. The Carter administration elevated this concern to a high position on its foreign policy agenda; and in a list of international objectives issued by the Reagan administration during its last year in office, at the top stood a commitment to "uphold the principles of freedom, the rule of law, and observance of fundamental human rights."[10]

This is a monumental challenge, every bit as difficult as raising the level of health care, housing, and education within the poor countries. Fewer than 20 nations out of the total 180 are generally considered to be true democracies, with a high regard for civil liberties.[11] Yet, despite the difficulties, a large number of Americans would probably agree with an official in the Carter administration that "there is a simple moral imperative at the heart of our national identity. . . . Every individual has inherent rights and a special dignity. This belief has shaped our national purposes throughout our history."[12] For people around the world, freedom from government repression and a longing for democracy rank high in their hierarchy of personal aspirations. This feeling was vividly demonstrated in China during May 1989, when over 1 million people poured into Beijing's Tiananmen Square in a display of fervor for democratic reform—the largest public protest in the history of modern China, soon crushed by army tanks. Six months later another celebration of freedom broke out, in Berlin, as Germans on both sides of the Berlin Wall (erected in 1961 to seal off the East from the West) rejoiced together at its opening by the government of East Germany.

Beyond a sense of altruism, the United States has a clear stake in helping other countries address the problem of human dignity. With modern advances in communications, transportation, and weaponry, the world has simply become too small and dangerous for Americans to ignore the festering wounds of foreign people in distress. This lesson was illustrated vividly in December 1979 when Iranian citizens rose in revolt against their tyrannical ruler, the U.S.–backed shah, in course overrunning the American embassy in Tehran and holding its diplomats and staff hostage for over 400 days. This revolution caught the Carter administration by surprise, left it in a state of trauma throughout its final year in office, and contributed significantly (along with a slumping U.S. economy) to the president's electoral defeat in 1980.

Physical protection, economic prosperity, social well-being, freedom from coercion—these important objectives are more easily stated than achieved. Indeed, even their statement can lead to heated debate. Does America's physical protection depend upon routing the Marxists in Nicaragua? upon building the Strategic Defense Initiative (SDI, a proposed laser-beam shield against enemy missiles)? Does economic prosperity stem from free trade or protectionism? from exploiting the Third World or developing it? Should officials of the United States attempt to foster only democracy and capitalism, or can this nation coexist in peace and even friendship with other political and economic systems? Americans have been of two minds on such issues.

These few questions (and a host of others addressed in the book) suggest how complex the sorting-out of specific foreign-policy goals can be, once they have been expressed in the abstract. Then beyond the quandaries of defining and selecting goals stand a range of obstacles between what this country might want to do and what it is able to do. These further complications are introduced in Chapter 2, on the "foreign policy milieu," and are explored in detail throughout the subsequent chapters of Part I. First, though, this opening look at the ends of American foreign policy is augmented by an introduction to the central means (or instruments) used by policymakers in pursuit of the nation's global objectives.

THE USES OF AMERICAN FOREIGN POLICY

As the reader will note time and again in this book (and in the daily news reports), the United States faces many limitations on its ability to achieve foreign policy objectives. This country, like all others, is forced to accept a gap between its aspirations and what it can actually achieve in a world of competing nations. No nation has a monopoly on oil, technological innovation, or control of the seas, for example, and none has impermeable borders or foolproof military defenses. Still, large and resource-rich countries like the United States do enjoy a great advantage over less developed nations in the means at their disposal to achieve international objectives. They have available to them a wider and more imposing array of options in the conduct of their external relations than, say, poverty-stricken Haiti or, for that matter, wealthy but small Switzerland. While Part I of this volume focuses on key international, domestic, and individual influences that shape and limit American foreign policy, Part II explores the primary means available to decision makers in their efforts to fulfill foreign policy goals—the use of diplomats, spies, and soldiers, and the controversies that have surrounded these choices.

The range of approaches available for the pursuit of foreign policy goals is wide, either granted by the Constitution or fashioned over the years from the cloth of law and custom. This chapter next offers a brief introduction to the most important of these means, each of which is explored more comprehensively in the second half of the book. The starting place is the subject of intelligence, for nothing is so important to the success of foreign policy as a rational choice of means based on an accurate understanding of global opportunities and dangers.

Strategic Intelligence

Information about world events and personalities of significance to American foreign policy is often called *strategic intelligence* (or simply *intelligence*). Policymakers who must choose among various means—war, diplomacy, and trade, among others—to achieve their nation's foreign objectives will increase their chances for success if their decisions are grounded in the reality of accurate information. When they are forced to choose in a fog of ambiguous information (as is often the case)—or with no hard information at all—they become like blind men in a cave groping for direction.

The Japanese attack on the U.S. military base at Pearl Harbor, Hawaii, on December 7, 1941, stands as a reminder that a lack of good strategic intelligence can endanger a country's very survival. This surprise attack resulted in the destruction of an important part of America's Pacific fleet. It was the most disastrous intelligence failure in the history of the United States. Though U.S. intelligence agencies had broken the Japanese military codes and knew that Pearl Harbor might be bombed, this information was never provided to top officials in the form of a coherent analysis (though fragments of data filtered up to the Oval Office). The government lacked the necessary organizational channels to ensure a careful coordination of intelligence and its forceful dissemination to the highest levels of authority or to military commanders in the field (thus, the creation of the *Central* Intelligence Agency, or CIA, following the war). Moreover, the intelligence on the likelihood of a Pearl Harbor attack was ambiguous and contradicted by some evidence that a military strike would more likely occur in the Philippines or elsewhere closer to Japan.

The Cuban missile crisis further illustrates the importance of good intelligence for effective foreign policy decisions. American surveillance airplanes (high-flying U-2s) had the capacity to photograph the Soviet missile sites in Cuba. From the study of these detailed photographs, intelligence analysts were able to calculate that the missiles would not be ready for firing for about ten more days. This information gave the president and his aides more time to consider a broader range of responses than the military options that initially seemed most compelling. "If we had had to act on Wednesday [October 17, 1962] in the first twenty-four hours," President Kennedy later recalled, "I don't think probably we would have chosen as prudently as we finally did."[13]

The president ultimately decided on a naval blockade to prevent Soviet ships from bringing more missiles into Cuba. A blockade would signal to the Soviet premier, Nikita Khrushchev, that the United States would not tolerate the establishment of an offensive missile base in Cuba (the administration publicly and through diplomatic channels referred to the blockade as a "quarantine," to make it sound less warlike). Kennedy coupled this military option with diplomatic communications to the Soviet leader, telling him to dismantle the missiles already under construction. Prior to receiving the vital intelligence from the U-2 overflights, the president's advisers had leaned toward a quick, "surgical" bombing of the missile sites, which would have killed Soviet personnel and possibly led rapidly to war between the superpowers. Good intelligence (see Chapter 8) gave the president "breathing room" and an opportunity to consider more prudent alternatives.

In the selection of means to achieve international objectives, intelligence becomes the sine qua non for rational planning and implementation. With reliable information, a decision maker can better calculate which of the means available might be most advantageous with respect to the desired ends. Among the various paths the United States might choose to carry out its foreign policy, five of the most important ones are the focus of this book's second half. They include secret intervention (using the CIA and other clandestine agencies), an open deployment of military force, diplomatic negotiations, the inducements of trade and aid, and an evocation of moral principles. The central orienting question in this portion of the book is: On the basis of what America *knows* (intelligence), how does it *act*?

Covert Action

One method often used by the United States to advance its foreign policy interests is the secret operation—almost always, in the modern era, carried out by the CIA. These operations in-

---

Perspectives on American Foreign Policy   1.1

Secretary of State Dean Rusk on the importance of information to foreign policy decision making:

The ghost that haunts the policy officer or haunts the man who makes the final decision is the question as to whether, in fact, he has in his mind all of the important elements that ought to bear upon his decision or whether there is a missing piece that he is not aware of that could have a decisive effect if it became known.

I think we can be proud of the extraordinary improvement in our intelligence- and information-gathering activities in the last 20 years. The need for it has been multiplied many times by the fragmentation of the world political structure, and the breadth, character, and depth of the information we need mounts steadily. When I was assigned to G-2 [U.S. Army intelligence] in 1941, well over a year after the war had started in Europe, I was asked to take charge of a new section that had been organized to cover everything from Afghanistan right through southern Asia, southeast Asia, Australia, and the Pacific. Because we had no intelligence organization that had been giving attention to that area up to that time, the materials available to me when I reported for duty consisted of a tourist handbook on India and Ceylon, a 1924 military attache's report from London on the Indian Army, and a drawer full of clippings from the *New York Times* that had been gathered since World War I. That was literally the resources of G-2 on that vast part of the world a year after the war in Europe had started.

We have greatly improved our ability to gather relevant information. . . .

From Dean Rusk, testimony, *Hearings of the Government Operations Subcommittee on National Security Staff and Operations*, U.S. Senate, December 11, 1963, p. 390.

volve concealed transactions with other nations or, without their knowledge, intervention in their external and internal affairs. Such controversial means are known by practitioners as *covert action* or *"the quiet option"* (that is, less "noisy" or visible than sending in a Marine brigade). Covert action has been a vital part of American foreign policy since the founding of the republic. Benjamin Franklin secretly bought arms from the French to assist American rebels in the War of Independence, and President Thomas Jefferson covertly arranged a deal with foreign plotters to overthrow the Bashaw (or pasha) of Tripoli.

More recently, the United States has used secret operations of various kinds in an attempt to influence the behavior—sometimes terminally—of leaders abroad. Fidel Castro of Cuba became a target of a dozen or more assassination plots during the 1960s, all of which failed, concocted by the CIA in alliance with an unlikely partner for the government of the United States: mobster hit men. Patrice Lumumba of the Congo (now called Zaire) was another assassination target for the CIA, though he was killed by a rival African faction before "the Agency"—as insiders call the CIA—had its chance. In a further scheme, the CIA's "Health Alteration Committee" directed its agents to "incapacitate" with chemicals an uncooperative Iraqi colonel.

Salvador Allende of Chile, a freely elected president in a democratic regime, became a target during the 1970s of secret U.S. plans for a coup against his socialist government, perceived as a threat to American interests in the Western Hemisphere. Moreover, politicians in various countries have received money covertly from the CIA in exchange for taking pro–U.S. positions in their councils of government; and secret propaganda operations have been used worldwide to advance U.S. interests—including "disinformation" schemes that have fooled the American public as much as they have U.S. adversaries (a phenomenon known as "replay" or "blow-back").

The CIA has also sponsored large-scale "secret" wars—so-called overt-covert wars—most of which have become known to the public, simply because the din of war is impossible to conceal for long. They continue to be treated officially as covert actions, however, to avoid the formalities (and the more complicated legal requirements within the United States, discussed in Chapter 10) that attend overt warfare. Secret wars, or "paramilitary operations," have been supported by the United States in order to counter Soviet interests in, among other places, Asia (Laos, for example), the Middle East (Afghanistan), and Central America (Nicaragua). The Soviet equivalent of the CIA—the KGB—has been equally energetic in the conduct of similar operations designed to advance Soviet (and thwart U.S.) global objectives. This "back alley" approach to foreign policy is the subject of Chapter 9.

The War Power

When secret intervention fails, the United States sometimes threatens, or actually resorts to, open military intervention—the war power. When one thinks of this nation as a superpower, what readily comes to mind is its vast stockpile of nuclear warheads, its B-52 bombers, Trident submarines, aircraft carriers, and the like—the most tangible manifestations of America's might. Indeed, ever since its demonstration of impressive firepower during the Civil War, America's military prowess has been duly noted in the foreign policy councils of other nations.

A primary reason why President Kennedy was successful in persuading the Soviet Union to remove its offensive missiles from Cuba, just ninety miles off the Florida coastline, was the massive military force he had mustered near the southeastern seaboard of the United States (though not the only reason: the horror of a nuclear holocaust gave pause to both Khrushchev and Kennedy, causing them at the eleventh hour to reconsider the actual use of force). The president had the Soviets outgunned, which was relatively easy to do in a region so close to home. Moreover, at that time the United States enjoyed a great advantage (a 2-to-1 ratio) over the Soviet Union in the number of long-range missiles that could strike into the heartland of the adversary across the polar ice cap. As Secretary of State Dean Rusk said during the crisis, the superpowers had come "eyeball to eyeball" over Cuba, and the Soviets blinked—no doubt a result in part of the military imbalance that found the Soviets on the short end.

The power to make war represents the most extreme means that can be used by a nation in its pursuit of foreign policy goals. No decision is more fateful. The characteristics of modern weaponry, and how this nation decides to use the war power, are the subject of Chapter 10.

Diplomacy

The art of adjusting disputes between nations through negotiations, that is, *diplomacy*—talking instead of fighting—is a common means for achieving U.S. objectives in the world. Recently, the rising number of automobile exports from Japan to the United States has caused severe dislocations in this nation's automotive industry. In response, U.S. car manufacturers have lobbied strenuously for government relief from the vehicular deluge from abroad. Rather than resort to tough economic sanctions against Japan, now one of America's primary allies, President Carter turned instead to diplomatic negotiations in an effort to aid U.S. automakers without rupturing ties with the Japanese. This balancing act called for skillful bargaining.

In this instance, the Carter administration succeeded in persuading Japan to restrain, voluntarily, its shipment of autos to America. In the agreement, the Japanese promised to limit automobile exports into the United States to 1 million a year, a substantial reduction. By 1985, Japanese negotiators had persuaded the Reagan administration to raise the ceiling to 2.3 million cars a year—which remains the current ar-

rangement, despite persistent grumbling from Japan that the ceiling is still too low and represents a form of unnecessary U.S. protectionism. The Japanese have consented to this short-term solution no doubt in part because protectionist legislators in Congress threatened to advance stiffer economic sanctions against Japan if these initial diplomatic efforts failed. Moreover, the original agreement with the Japanese allowed them to ship higher-priced vehicles to the United States and thus earn greater profits (and ironically, in the process, deprived American consumers of the opportunity to purchase cheaper Japanese autos).

The power to make agreements with other countries has far-reaching implications. Military agreements, for example, are often harbingers of sweeping commitments that can draw the United States into war. As this book discusses in Chapter 11, Congress and the presidency have been engaged in a sometimes acrimonious struggle over how the power to make international agreements ought to be shared between the branches.

Economic Statecraft

Over the years, trade and aid—specific diplomatic approaches important enough to warrant separate treatment in this volume—have served as primary means used by the United States in pursuit of its global objectives. These approaches to foreign policy have been employed in two ways: as methods for applying negative coercion (punishments) or positive incentives (rewards). Policymakers, in other words, have economic sticks and carrots with which to deal with other nations. With respect to trade, the United States can resort to the negative sanctions of embargoes, boycotts, trade quotas, blacklisting, and the like; or this country can use such positive incentives as reducing tariffs, granting import licenses, and establishing favorable tariffs. During the Carter and Reagan administrations, for example, the granting of favorable tariffs helped to thaw America's relations with the People's Republic of China (the PRC, or mainland China, not to be confused with the offshore Republic of China, or Taiwan, a U.S. ally since the Chinese Nationalists fled from the mainland and founded their government there in 1947).

Neither negative sanctions nor positive trade incentives are guaranteed to work. As a form of punishment for its invasion of Afghanistan in 1979, an angry Carter administration refused to sell grain to the U.S.S.R. (reversing President Carter's long-standing opposition to the use of embargoes because of their harmful effect on America's own economy); but Argentina, Canada, and others soon filled the void with their own grain sales, sharply reducing the effectiveness of U.S. pressure on the Soviet Union. Sometimes, though, this approach does yield results (see Chapter 12). So do foreign aid inducements. The Marshall Plan is the most conspicuous example of a U.S. foreign aid success. America's economic assistance to Europe in the aftermath of the Second World War helped cement the Western democracies into a strong alliance.

Moral Suasion

Supreme Court Justice William O. Douglas once observed that the United States was admired abroad not "so much for our B-52 bombers and for our atomic stockpile, but we're really admired for the First Amendment and the freedom of people to speak and believe and to write, have fair trials." Here, in his view, was the "great magnet" that made America a great world leader.[14] As president, Jimmy Carter—a deeply religious man—placed a high premium on moral principles as a basic guide for the conduct of American foreign policy. This emphasis could be seen clearly in his criticism of unsavory covert actions (though he did not eschew this option altogether; see Chapter 9), and in his support of global human rights during his campaign for election in 1976 and after. He

sharply condemned the immorality of assassination plots and other "dirty tricks" carried out by the CIA, and following his inauguration as president, Carter reined in this agency. He also advocated (though inconsistently) trade and diplomatic pressures against regimes engaged in the degradation of human rights.

Other high government officials have been drawn to the power of principle, or *idealism*, in international affairs. A recent chairman of the Senate Foreign Relations Committee concluded: "... what have we lost [by using the CIA to manipulate foreign governments]? I suggest we have lost—or grievously impaired—the good name and reputation of the United States from which we once drew a unique capacity to exercise matchless moral leadership." More recently, a leading member of the House Foreign Affairs Committee has stressed that, in the conduct of America's relations abroad, "the best way to promote our interests is to promote our ideals."[15]

In contrast, some students of international politics—most notably a school of thought known as the *realists*—are skeptical of an emphasis on ethical considerations in international affairs. They believe that a nation's external relations should rest more prudently on a foundation of military might and economic strength. The roots of the realist tradition are long, extending back to the writings of Machiavelli (1469–1527) and even Thucydides (circa 460–400 B.C.), among others. More recently, a hard-boiled cynicism characteristic of the realist school enjoyed a resurgence in the aftermath of World War II, as an alternative to the interwar optimism and moralism of Wilsonian idealists (followers of President Woodrow Wilson, who held high hopes for world peace through the League of Nations). The League's failure to keep the peace, followed by British Prime Minister Neville Chamberlain's dashed hopes to satiate Hitler's appetite with a policy of appeasement, swelled the ranks of the realists.

"The horrors of Hitler's war made a post-war

generation of scholars worry about idealism in foreign policy," remarks Joseph F. Nye, Jr., "and the conventional wisdom in the professional study of international relations since 1945 has awarded the 'realists' a clear victory over the 'idealists.' "[16] Still, idealism continues to exercise a strong attraction for many Americans—indeed, the foreign policy views of public officials and private citizens are commonly a mixture of realism and idealism—and this approach to foreign policy merits an objective appraisal (see Chapter 13).

Rarely do the various foreign policy means stand alone, as suggested by the recent use of diplomacy by the United States to encourage voluntary Japanese automobile quotas. Behind this diplomatic approach stood the latent threat of formal economic sanctions and, as a further backdrop, the war power of the United States upon which the Japanese depend for their protection from potential adversaries like the So-

viet Union. Skillful presidents, legislators, and others with foreign policy responsibilities take into account the wide panoply of options available to the United States in its dealings with other nations. As Nash has noted with respect to arms negotiations, for instance, in order for diplomacy to succeed, U.S. officials must have "a sense of how military capabilities might be applied, deployed, or displayed for purposes of achieving a political advantage."[17]

The array of foreign policy means examined in this volume—secret intervention, war making, diplomacy, economic statecraft, moral suasion—comprises those most consistently used by policymakers in the day-to-day conduct of America's external relations. This book attempts to provide an understanding of how and why the different means are chosen, how well they work, and the political and constitutional controversies that have accompanied their use.

Perspectives on American Foreign Policy 1.2

H. Bradford Westerfield on the "functional analysis" of American foreign policy:

Contemporary America has a distinct fundamental foreign policy, one that is often challenged, periodically restyled, occasionally even subjected to major deviation, and frequently misunderstood by both its practitioners and its critics, yet one that has persisted at the core of the conduct of United States foreign relations since 1947. It is the policy of containment directed against totalitarian expansionism for the principal purpose of securing America's survival in freedom. In pursuit of containment, the country has been learning to utilize a variety of methods and instruments, includ-

ing military, economic, informational, and undercover interventionist practices. [A useful] organizing principle [for the study of American foreign policy] is *functional analysis*, directing attention to the ways and means by which the United States can exercise her influence overseas, and using examples of recent historical episodes in widely scattered geographical areas for comparisons and judgments about the utility of the various policy instruments available. . . .

H. Bradford Westerfield, *The Instruments of America's Foreign Policy* (New York: Crowell, 1963), pp. vii–viii.

SUMMARY

With the bombing of Hiroshima, the United States ushered in the nuclear age—an era unprecedented in its danger for the survival of humanity. Foreign policy now involves the ultimate question: whether its practitioners—here and in other nations—will have the wisdom to preserve the human species, which could be extinguished if nuclear warfare were to ensue. Foreign policy has become increasingly important for other reasons as well. As global competitiveness accelerates, the economic well-being of the United States now depends more than ever on its commercial ties with other nations. Modern transportation, communications, and other technological achievements have also brought in their wake the gray wash of global pollution and other environmental hazards that demand new levels of international cooperation for their solution.

The foreign policy of the United States, like that of other nations, has been a composite of ends and means. The ends (or goals) have included peace and security, that is, the physical safety of the nation and its citizens, as well as its allies and friends; economic prosperity; improvements in the quality of life (global advances in the eradication of disease, for example); and the advancement of human dignity—the pursuit of human rights and civil liberties for all the people of the world. How these goals are to be achieved, and what degree of America's finite resources should be dedicated to each, have been subjects of heated debate, now and throughout the nation's history.

Contentious, too, have been the debates over what means to use in the quest for America's global objectives. Among the most important means have been the collection and analysis of information about world conditions (strategic intelligence), the use of secret agencies to manipulate events abroad, and the overt use of military force, as well as a reliance on diplomacy, the inducements of trade and aid, and moral suasion. Seldom are these approaches used separately; instead, policymakers try to employ the range of options available to them, in combination and with varying degrees of success, as they pursue America's goals around the world. How and why each means is selected, how well each works, and (the string that threads together the chapters of this book) the political and constitutional controversies that have accompanied their use—here are the subjects that lie at the center of American foreign policy.

KEY TERMS

nuclear age
foreign policy goals
foreign policy ends and means
strategic intelligence
covert action
the war power

diplomacy
economic statecraft
moral suasion
realists
idealists
functional analysis

NOTES

1. Harry S Truman, interviewed in "Truman and the Atomic Bomb," a Learning Corporation film, 1969.

2. Winston S. Churchill, *My Early Life: A Roving Commission* (New York: Scribner, 1930), p. 180.

3. Richard J. Barnet, "Reflections: National Security," *New Yorker*, March 21, 1988, p. 104.

4. Quoted by Daniel Ford, "A Reporter at Large: Perestroika," *New Yorker*, March 28, 1988, p. 80.

5. See, respectively, Anthony Lake, *Managing Complexity in U.S. Foreign Policy* (Bureau of Public Affairs, Department of State, March 14, 1978), p. 1; and *Fundamentals of U.S. Foreign Policy* (Bureau of Public Affairs, Department of State, March 1988), p. 1.

6. These figures are from the Stockholm International Peace Research Institute, cited in "Institute Issues Tally of World Conflicts," *Boston Globe*, June 18, 1987; quoted by Joseph S. Nye, Jr., "International Security Studies," in Joseph Kruzel, ed., *American Defense Annual, 1988–1989* (Lexington, Mass.: Lexington Books, 1988), p. 242; and used in a speech by the president of the U.S. Institute of Peace, Samuel W. Lewis, Atlanta, May 9, 1989.

7. Public address, "Beyond War" Convocation, San Francisco, September 12, 1985.

8. The Israeli nuclear capability is described in a research report published by Leonard Spector, cited in the *New York Times*, March 4, 1987; the intelligence data on ballistic missiles and chemical-biological capabilities are from a speech by William H. Webster, director of Central Intelligence, before the Council on Foreign Relations, Washington, D.C., December 12, 1988.

9. *Fundamentals of U.S. Foreign Policy*, p. 1.

10. *Ibid.*

11. See Arend Lijphart, *Democracies* (New Haven: Yale University Press, 1984), p. 8.

12. Lake, *op. cit.*, p. 6.

13. Arthur M. Schlesinger, Jr., *A Thousand Days: John F. Kennedy in the White House* (Boston: Houghton Mifflin, 1965), p. 803. This crisis is examined in greater depth in Chapter 3.

14. Eric Sevareid, interview with William O. Douglas, *CBS Evening News*, January 19, 1980.

15. Senator Frank Church (D-Idaho), "Covert Action: Swampland of American Foreign Policy," *Bulletin of the Atomic Scientists*, vol. 32, February 1976, p. 11; Representative Stephen J. Solarz (D-N.Y.), remarks, C-Span Television, May 22, 1988.

16. *Ethics and Foreign Policy: An Occasional Paper* (Queenstown, Md.: Aspen Institute, 1985), p. vii.

17. Henry T. Nash, *American Foreign Policy: Response to a Sense of Threat* (Homewood, Ill.: Dorsey, 1973), p. 179.

RECOMMENDED READINGS

Brown, Lester R., et al. *State of the World, 1989* (New York: Norton, 1989). A report of the Worldwatch Institute, warning that the earth's forests are shrinking, its deserts expanding, and its soils eroding at record rates

Brown, Seyom. *New Forces, Old Forces, and the Future of World Politics* (Boston: Scott, Foresman, 1988). A call for a new global system based upon the increased use of diplomacy and other peaceful "transnational associations," in lieu of the present system founded on a narrow realism driven by self-serving calculations of national advantage and leading to widespread military confrontations.

Carr, E. H. *The Twenty-Years' Crisis, 1919–1939: An Introduction to the Study of International Relations* (London: Macmillan, 1939). An early, classic analysis of international politics by a leading realist.

Fisher, Roger. *International Conflict for Beginners* (New York: Harper & Row, 1969). A good introduction to foreign policy by a felicitous writer.

Galtung, Johan. *The True Worlds: A Transnational Perspective* (New York: Free Press, 1980). A sharp attack on large-power imperialism, coupled with a plea for a new world based on direct relations between peoples, nonterritorial organizations, and a central global authority to settle disputes peacefully.

Hoffman, Stanley. *Primacy or World Order: American Foreign Policy Since the Cold War* (New York: McGraw-Hill, 1978). A typically insightful study by a prolific analyst of international affairs, comparing realist and idealist perspectives.

Johansen, Robert C. *The National Interest and the Human Interest: An Analysis of U.S. Foreign Policy* (Princeton, New Jersey: Princeton University Press, 1980). A thoughtful argument in favor of a "global humanist framework" for American foreign policy, with the central objective of abolishing war, poverty, human rights violations, and ecological decay throughout the world.

Kennan, George F. *Memoirs* (Boston: Little, Brown, 1967). A rich, personal account of American foreign policy in the modern era by the nation's most heralded professional diplomat.

Keohane, Robert O. "Theory of World Politics: Structural Realism and Beyond," in Ada W. Finifter, ed., *Political Science: The State of the Discipline* (Washington, D.C.: American Political Science Association, 1983), pp. pp. 503–540. A useful review of realism and its alternatives.

Kissinger, Henry A. *American Foreign Policy* (New York: Norton, 1957). Valuable insights from America's most renowned scholar-statesman.

Morgenthau, Hans J. *Politics Among Nations* (New York: Knopf, 1973). First published in 1948, this classic realist perspective is probably the most widely read book ever published on international affairs.

THE INTERNATIONAL SETTING

    Balance of Power

    Geopolitics

    Idealism

    Interdependence

THE DOMESTIC SETTING

    The Mirror of the Past

    The Constitutional Matrix

    Institutional Fragmentation

    A Pluralist Politics

THE IMPORTANCE OF THE INDIVIDUAL DECISION MAKER

    Role-Playing

    Past Experience

    Distorted Perceptions

    Character

SUMMARY

2

KEY DIMENSIONS OF THE FOREIGN POLICY MILIEU

For purposes of analytical treatment, the conduct of American foreign policy may be thought of as taking place on three levels (or in three settings). On the international level, U.S. policymakers face many other strong-willed—and often well-armed—nations with goals of their own. On the national level, policymakers must deal as well with the vagaries of domestic politics and institutional conflicts within their own government (intentionally fostered by the Constitution). And least visible, on the level of the individual human mind, policymakers remain susceptible always to misperceptions and other psychological distortions of the world around them. Here are the key dimensions, intersecting in intricate ways, that bound and shape the course of America's foreign policy: the international setting, the domestic setting, and the personalities and attitudes of individual decision makers. Each has an important influence on the degree of America's success or failure in its search for well-being in a world of violence and disorder.

THE INTERNATIONAL SETTING

On one point virtually every scholar of foreign policy stands in agreement: the world is essentially anarchical, in the sense that "no central government exists with a range of authority compared to that found in contemporary states."[1] Currently and for the foreseeable future, nations are the basic entities in international affairs, as fundamental to an understanding of foreign policy as the atom is to an understanding of physics. A *nation* (sometimes referred to as a *state* or *nation-state*) may be defined as a gathering together of individuals under a common leadership, or government, in control of a well-defined territorial space.[2] Normally, the citizens of a nation share a cultural identity as well, including a common language and allegiance to a distinctive flag and national anthem. A nation thus has both territorial and psychological characteristics.

A network television cameraman follows U.S. Marines into battle near Hue, South Vietnam, in 1966. (AP/Wide World Photos)

If the existence of this gathering of people is widely recognized by other established nations, the geographical entity is widely known as a *sovereign* state. One authority defines sovereignty formally as "the legal capacity of an independent state to regulate its affairs as it pleases, without having to obtain permission from any outside source."[3] (In reality, of course, individuals within a nation make decisions on its behalf—often in conflict with one another; foreign policy is made by an abstract entity known as a "sovereign state" only in a legalistic sense.) To establish the sovereignty of the United States, free from British tyranny, the founders of this nation staged a revolution and by force removed its thirteen colonies from the empire of King George III. New nations are often born in blood, torn from some existing sovereign state by the force of arms.

As examined later in this book (Chapter 6), the international setting is crowded with many other entities in addition to sovereign states. Various governmental and nongovernmental organizations (NGOs) work with—and sometimes overarch—the nation-state. Examples include, respectively, the World Health Organization (WHO) and Amnesty International, a human-rights organization. With their cross-national bonds, some of these organizations help to dampen the tensions endemic in a system of competing and distrustful nations.

With this understanding of the term *nation*, combined with the outline of U.S. global objectives in the previous chapter, a more formal definition of foreign policy can now be presented. *American foreign policy* consists of those decisions and actions taken by the sovereign nation of the United States with respect to other sovereign nations, as well as various international groups and organizations, pursuant to the well-being of its citizens and allies and the advancement of their ideals.

The United States often finds itself in conflict with the international objectives of other sovereign nations. Photographs taken by astronauts portray the earth as a precious jewel beneath swirling clouds, lovely and serene in the blackness of space. Yet, as the newspaper headlines remind us each day, this planet is really not One World as it may seem through the porthole of a rocket ship, but rather a complex tapestry of disparate countries, trading blocs, and military alliances. Each nation has its own goals and ambitions, its own territory and culture, its own population and ideals to defend, and its own means of defense, from punji stakes dipped in primitive poisons (used against U.S. soldiers during the war in Vietnam) to modern intercontinental ballistic missiles (ICBMs) tipped with multimegaton warheads—the city busters that are a part of the Soviet and American arsenals.

Scholarly attempts to explain why nations behave as they do toward one another have been widely variant and often contradictory. No single theory of American foreign policy stands preeminent. Some explanations, though, have wider currency than others, and since the purpose of this chapter is to provide the reader with a broad orientation or overview, they are introduced briefly here and explored in greater detail during subsequent chapters. Among the most influential explanations of foreign-policy behavior are those that focus on the "balance of power" between nations, on their geographical opportunities and constraints (geopolitics), on the importance of morality and idealism, and, more recently, on the growing "interdependence" of nations in the contemporary world.

Balance of Power

In the balance-of-power "model" of foreign policy, the essential supposition is that if one nation becomes too dominant militarily it will attempt to manipulate—even conquer—others; therefore, nations have tried to form coalitions designed to prevent any single nation from achieving military superiority over the rest. In the Western world, nations have been unwilling to give any individual nation domination over the European continent, with its great industrial capacity for weapons production. When Adolf Hitler sent his tanks rolling into Poland in 1939, Great Britain reacted immediately by declaring war on the Third Reich; the British knew that this expansion of the German state would make Hitler a grave threat to the British Isles. When Hitler then turned against Britain, astute Americans similarly understood that the United States would soon have to resist his attempts to disrupt the equilibrium in Europe, because America might well be the next target of the Nazi war machine backed by the industrial might of all Europe in the Führer's hands.

A form of the balance-of-power perspective has shaped the American response to the global challenge of Marxist-Leninist ideology, espoused by communists in the Soviet Union and elsewhere—an ideology in obvious tension with fundamental American beliefs in democracy and free enterprise. As a check against the spread of communism, U.S. policymakers embraced "the central preoccupation of postwar national security policy—the idea of containment."[4] The containment policy rests on a conviction that the leaders of the Soviet Union are bent on the disruption of the international equilibrium—that they wish to dominate the globe just as Hitler had attempted, sometimes through the direct use of force (as in eastern Europe and Mongolia) but more often through subtler techniques involving propaganda operations and support for pro-Marxist "wars of liberation" (as in Vietnam and Angola).

To meet this perceived threat, the Truman administration vowed a steadfast resistance against totalitarian aggression in Greece and Turkey and, by implication, throughout the world (see Chapter 4). A great many U.S. foreign policy decisions since then—including most of the major ones—can be traced back to this core belief that the Soviets, though once America's allies in the war against Hitler, were really no better than the Nazis and had to be walled in by political, economic, and, if necessary, military means.

Geopolitics

Beyond acknowledging the importance of balance-of-power considerations, another proposition is rarely disputed among students of foreign policy: in the affairs of nations, geography often plays a significant role. Nicholas J. Spykman (1893–1943), a famous geopolitical thinker, no doubt overstated the case when he argued that geography was "the most fundamentally conditioning factor" in the shaping of foreign affairs. Nonetheless, this aspect of foreign policy remains prominent in the writings of scholars and statesmen and has been an important corollary to the balance-of-power approach.

"Poor Mexico," observed an unhappy President Porfirio Díaz (1830–1915) on the plight of his country's location, "so far from God and so close to the United States." Large nations with imposing arsenals have often insisted on a "sphere of influence" reaching out from their borders, into which other nations might tread only at the peril of triggering a military response. Since the proclamation of the Monroe Doctrine (see Chapter 3), the United States has officially claimed the Western Hemisphere as its sphere of influence. This is why Soviet assistance to Cuba beginning in the Eisenhower administration and, more recently, to Nicaragua has so deeply provoked American policymakers; such intervention is viewed by many as a serious affront to long-standing U.S. traditions, especially when backed by a superpower that has become America's major adversary around the world. As for the Soviet Union, it seems to view practically every weak country on its perimeter as within its sphere of influence. Finland, Estonia, and the other Baltic states, along with Afghanistan, Mongolia, and the nations of eastern Europe, have found themselves, like Mexico, in the shadow—and sometimes under the foot—of a military behemoth.

Some geopolitical analysts concerned about the future of the United States point to the importance of maintaining access to strategic min-

Perspectives on American Foreign Policy   2.1

The Truman Doctrine, *from a speech by President Truman before Congress on March 12, 1947, in which he requested $400 million for aid to Greece and Turkey to help them resist Soviet-backed guerrilla warfare—the most important early manifestation of America's commitment to the policy of containment:*

At the present moment in world history nearly every nation must choose between alternative ways of life. The choice is too often not a free one.

One way of life is based upon the will of the majority, and is distinguished by free institutions, representative government, free elections, guarantees of individual liberty, freedom of speech and religion, and freedom from political oppression.

The second way of life is based upon the will of a minority forcibly imposed upon the majority. It relies upon terror and oppression, a controlled press and radio, fixed elections, and the suppression of personal freedoms.

I believe that it must be the policy of the United States to support free peoples who are resisting attempted subjugation by armed minorities or by outside processes.

I believe that we must assist free people to work out their own destinies in their own way.

I believe that our help should be primarily through economic and financial aid which is essential to economic stability and orderly political pressures.

Public Papers of the Presidents, Harry S Truman, 1947 (Washington, D.C.: Office of the Federal Register, National Archives, 1952), pp. 178–179.

---

eral resources abroad: nickel and zinc in Canada; tin in Bolivia; bauxite in Jamaica and Guinea; platinum, industrial diamonds, and chromite in South Africa; and manganese ore in Brazil—among others. They warn, too, of another danger: the infectious spread of communism from one contiguous regime to another in what, using a different metaphor, has been widely referred to as the *domino theory*. First one domino would fall to the communists, then the next, toppling one after another as in the children's game until, at last, the chain reaction reached the last domino, the United States. (The first use of the domino analogy preceded America's adversial relationship with the Soviet Union, dating back to the appeasement of Hitler at Munich and the prediction of some observers that this British policy would lead to the collapse of the European "dominoes" under the onslaught of the Wehrmacht.)

In a revealing response to a correspondent's question in 1954, President Dwight David Eisenhower gave expression to these geopolitical anxieties. His comments bear reprinting at length, for they provide considerable insight into a world perspective shared by most Americans and their leaders in the decades immediately following the Second World War (see Perspectives on American Foreign Policy 2.2). Within the president's remarks are the key arguments that, a decade later, would pave the way for a major intervention into Southeast Asia by the American military establishment.

Sometimes the fear of falling dominoes can reach extremes. In his advocacy of covert U.S. military assistance to pro-West factions in Angola, then United Nations Ambassador Daniel P. Moynihan (now a Democratic senator from New York) said during a television interview in 1975: "The Communists will take over

Perspectives on American Foreign Policy   2.2

A news conference with President Dwight David Eisenhower (April 7, 1954):

Q. Robert Richards, Copley Press: Mr. President, would you mind commenting on the strategic importance of Indochina to the free world? I think there has been, across the country, some lack of understanding on just what it means to us.

A. President Eisenhower: You have, of course, both the specific and the general when you talk about such things.

First of all, you have the specific value of a locality in its production of materials that the world needs.

Then you have the possibility that many human beings pass under a dictatorship that is inimical to the free world.

Finally, you have broader considerations that might follow what you would call the "falling domino" principle. You have a row of dominoes set up, you knock over the first one, and what will happen to the last one is the certainty that it will go over very quickly. So you could have a beginning of a disintegration that would have the most profound influences.

Now, with respect to the first one, two of the items from this particular area that the world uses are tin and tungsten. They are very important. There are others, of course, the rubber plantations and so on.

Then with respect to more people passing under this domination, Asia, after all, has already lost some 450 million of its peoples to the Communist dictatorship, and we simply can't afford greater losses.

But when we come to the possible sequence of events, the loss of Indochina, of Burma, of Thailand, of the Peninsula, and Indonesia following, now you begin to talk about areas that not only multiply the disadvantages that you would suffer through loss of materials, sources of materials, but now you are talking really about millions and millions and millions of people.

Finally, the geographical position achieved thereby does many things. It turns the so-called island defensive chain of Japan, Formosa, of the Philippines and to the southward; it moves in to threaten Australia and New Zealand.

It takes away, in its economic aspects, that region that Japan must have as a trading area or Japan, in turn, will have only one place in the world to go—that is, toward the Communist areas in order to live.

So, the possible consequences of the loss are just incalculable to the free world.

Public Papers of the Presidents, Dwight D. Eisenhower, 1954 (Washington, D.C.: Office of the Federal Register, National Archives, 1960), pp. 382–383.

Angola and will thereby considerably control the oil shipping lanes from the Persian Gulf to Europe. They will be next to Brazil. They will have a large chunk of Africa and the world will be different in the aftermath...."[5] A majority in Congress remained unimpressed by this form of geopolitical ratiocination and rejected the covert assistance. Ten years later its members

would prove to be more sympathetic toward covert aid for Angola, though more out of a renewed political commitment to anticommunism on the African continent than to any geopolitical calculations that the future of "nearby" Brazil might be determined by events in Angola.

Some legislators remain highly critical of efforts to justify American foreign policy on the basis of a domino theory, as attempted by the Reagan administration in Central America. In its covert intervention against the Marxist government of Nicaragua, and its overt supply of military assistance and training to the anti-Marxist government of El Salvador, this administration cautioned that without these steps dominoes could fall throughout Central America toward the U.S. border. "When they [officials in the Reagan administration] get ready to send helicopters to El Salvador, they talk about saving the country from Communism," responded Representative (now Senator) Barbara Mikulski (D-Md.). "I want them to start talking about saving the country from birth defects. I'm talking about children in my district who are more likely to die of birth defects than from some communist who's going to come up the Chesapeake Bay."[6]

The chief weakness of the domino theory lies in its assumption that somehow the infection of one nation by a hostile ideology will inevitably lead to a spread of the disease to its neighbors. History would suggest, on the contrary, that there is nothing inexorable about anything, and that nations are often immunized against outside threats by their strong economies, potent military defenses, or simply a robust nationalism that finds colonialism, Marxism, or other attempts at outside domination utterly repellent, to be resisted in every way. Even the relatively weak African nations bordering the Cuban-backed Marxist state of Angola have successfully resisted communist expansion; they no more wish to be under the thumb of Cuban (or Soviet) influence than they did European colonial rule.

Dramatic changes in modern transportation, rapid delivery systems for ICBMs and other weapons, and additional technological changes have diminished to some degree the significance of geopolitical stratagems. Nevertheless—skepticism in Congress and elsewhere to the contrary—the domino theory and other geopolitical explanations of international affairs remain an important part of the debate over how to carry out America's external relations.

Idealism

One of the most famous phrases in American history, *manifest destiny* (see Chapter 3), stirred an idea popular in the nineteenth century that the United States had a clear mission on earth: first, to conquer the western territories of America and, then, to export this nation's God-given blessings of democracy and Christianity to the yet unenlightened backwaters of the world. Sometimes nations are motivated in their foreign policies by of a sense of idealistic mission, as when the British during their colonial period thought of themselves as bearing (in Rudyard Kipling's phrase) "the white man's burden" to bring civilization—or, at any rate, the British version of it, replete with the Anglican church, Shakespeare, cricket, and elaborate codes of administration—into the developing world.

At the beginning of this century, America's sense of global mission could be seen in the justifications for colonialism in Cuba following the Spanish-American War, as well as in the Philippines, Hawaii, and elsewhere. President Wilson, the most conspicuous moralist to occupy the White House, was among those to advance the philosophy that America should help sow democracy around the world. "We shall fight . . . for the rights and liberties of small nations," he declared in a war message to Congress (1917). The motive for America's participation in the First World War was, he often proclaimed, to "make the world safe for democracy."

In World War II, a prime reason for America's entry into the fray was to assist the Mother of Parliaments, Great Britain, in her struggle against the dark totalitarian forces of the Third Reich, a battle between democracy and tyranny, good and evil. In the 1960s, President Lyndon B. Johnson looked upon his ordering of U.S. troops into South Vietnam as, in part, an antidote to a communist-totalitarian assault against a struggling democracy. (Though he feared, too, that the right wing of the Republican Party would try to destroy him politically if the United States retreated from this war against communist insurgency.) As a college student writing in his campus newspaper, Johnson had extolled the virtues of Wilson's crusade to spread democracy, and now, as president, he was determined not to reward aggression with the same policy of "appeasement" that Prime Minister Neville Chamberlain of Great Britain had naively offered Hitler before the outbreak of World War II. "We will stay until aggression has stopped," stated President Johnson in 1966, "because in Asia and around the world are countries whose independence rests, in large measure, on confidence in America's word and in America's protection."[7]

As the slogan of manifest destiny suggests, the idealism promoted by some American leaders has had an evangelical side to it, as if the United States had been chosen by God to be the flag bearer for Christianity as well as for democracy around the world. An American diplomat at the turn of the century gazed toward China and envisioned a "shining cross on every hill and in every valley." In 1940, Senator Kenneth Wherry (R-Neb.) intoned: "With God's help, we will lift Shanghai up and up, ever up, until it is just like Kansas City."[8] Representative Mendel Rivers (D-S.C.), chairman of the House Armed Services Committee during the Vietnam era, declared that the struggle between democracy and communism represented nothing less than "a fight between Jesus Christ and the Hammer-and-Sickle."[9]

Interdependence

The approaches to foreign policy outlined above treat the nation-state as the central unit in international affairs. Some foreign policy specialists have recently called this assumption into question. They argue that global forces beyond the sovereign nation are transforming old ways of looking at the world.

The growth of multinational corporations and international organizations; a rising sense of common identity among groups in different nations (American and Soviet physicians who have issued joint statements against nuclear war, for example, or youth around the world joined by the bonds of common cultural tastes in rock music and fashion); the dependence of nations upon one another's market decisions; the effects of inflation in one country upon economic growth in another; cultural exchanges; rapid communications and transportation—indeed the entire intricate interplay among modern nations has made these "transnational" forces more important than the nation-state. Or so would argue proponents of this perspective on international affairs, often referred to as *complex interdependence* by contemporary scholars. "A new pattern of international politics is emerging," writes the political scientist Zbigniew Brzezinski, who served as President Carter's national security adviser. "The world is ceasing to be an arena in which relatively self-sustained, 'sovereign,' and homogeneous nations interact, collaborate, clash, or make war. . . . Transnational ties are gaining in importance, while the claims of nationalism, though still intense, are nevertheless becoming diluted."[10]

Global television linkages are a central part of this transnationalism. Television brought the Vietnamese war into the homes of millions of Americans, who from their dining room tables viewed the slaughter with a growing repugnance. It also brought into their homes the peace marches and the skeptical hearings on the war held by the Senate Foreign Relations Committee (1966), raising serious questions in the public mind about the wisdom of further U.S. involvement in this remote Asian battlefield. The pictures of combat that flickered across the TV screen made it clear that America's enemies, the North Vietnamese (and their guerrilla allies in South Vietnam, the Vietcong), were far stronger than the American people had been led to believe by the Johnson administration. Television had clearly become a factor of enormous importance for U.S. foreign policy. "If there had been live [television] coverage of the Civil War," suggests the political scientist Austin Ranney, "it would have ended in 1862 with the establishment of the Confederacy, because it was a terribly bloody war and the North was losing most of the early part of it."[11]

Abetted by new developments in satellite communications, television holds the potential for drawing the people of the world together as neighbors (in a "global village," in the media guru Marshall McLuhan's vivid characterization), instead of the distant and distrustful foreigners they have usually been. Some predict the nurturing of global peace through a worldwide emotional commitment to the same television images, the same soap operas, athletic events, and music concerts—that is, through a spreading visual awareness that human beings around the world have much in common, from an affection for comedy, sports, and music to a love of their children and a yearning for the next century to be free of war. In 1989, Americans were able to watch, live on television, the prodemocracy demonstrations of Chinese students in Beijing; rallies in support erupted in towns and on campuses across the United States—an expression of global solidarity among individuals embracing the ideals of human liberty and pulled together by an electronic net.

So-called world-order scholars see in this growing global communion of citizens an opportunity for a *new world order* superseding the anarchy and warfare common to the system of nation-states—a creation of transnational loyalties and commitments that would eventually bring peace to this planet. Others remain skeptical and emphasize the likely endurance of nation-state arrangements, basing their arguments on the power of vested interests and the fear of uncertainty that would accompany an abandonment of sovereign states.

Here, then, are four central and interwoven conceptual strands, briefly introduced, that help to explain the behavior of the United States and other nations on the international plane. They will be examined further and others will be considered as this book unfolds. Next this chapter offers an opening orientation to the significance for foreign policy of the national (or domestic) setting.

THE DOMESTIC SETTING

Just as the world has a collective history, so does each nation have its own story. "History is the memory of states," writes Henry Kissinger, who served as secretary of state during the Nixon and Ford administrations.[12] Of special interest in this look at forces within the nation that affect foreign policy are America's historical experiences, constitutional underpinnings, contemporary institutional arrangements, and pluralist politics.

The Mirror of the Past

The history of the United States in its relations with the rest of the world can be thought of as an attempt, marked by ambivalence, to determine the appropriate degree of involvement abroad. This country has alternated between two contradictory urges: *isolationism*, on the one hand (that is, a detachment from the affairs of other nations), and *interventionism*, on the other hand (that is, attempts to influence their affairs, openly or secretly). Though often unsure which impulse would better serve their nation, on balance Americans have preferred detachment. Yet, despite this escapist urge, the United States has been happy to accept friendly assistance from overseas in times of acute military danger and has always maintained a lively interest in foreign commercial opportunities.

Since the shock of World War II and the rise of the Soviet state, most Americans have concluded that a headlong retreat into isolationism—the nation's response following World War I—would be a prescription for disaster. Public opinion surveys indicate, however, that many still long "to be free from the wrangling world" (Thomas Paine's quaint phrase in 1776). Recently, a majority of Americans indicated opposition in a public opinion poll to direct U.S. military intervention in such trouble spots as Angola, Indochina, and Central America—though a large gap exists between the attitudes of the masses and their leaders on this question (see Table 2.1). Nevertheless, in the decades since 1945, the United States has often demonstrated a willingness to intervene in revolutions and other foreign upheavals—mostly in the developing world—in order to curb the rise of communist forms of government. Korea (1950–1953) and Vietnam (formally, 1964–1975) serve as the most conspicuous illustrations.

In its relations with the rest of the world, then, America has oscillated between retreat and involvement—an ambivalence of great con-sequence explored further in Chapters 3 and 4. A full understanding of American foreign policy today must be rooted in an awareness of these contradictory impulses that have been a part of the nation's history since its early stirrings.

The Constitutional Matrix

The constitutional blueprint for government drafted by the American founders has also had a profound influence on the conduct of foreign policy (the central thesis of this book). The venerable phrase usually invoked to describe this framework is the *separation of powers*. Richard E. Neustadt offers a more accurate description, depicting the government of the United States as an array of separate institutions required by the Constitution to share authority and its de-

TABLE 2.1   ATTITUDES ON THE USE OF U.S. TROOPS OVERSEAS (1986)

SITUATION	FAVOR SENDING TROOPS		OPPOSE SENDING TROOPS		DON'T KNOW	
	PUBLIC	*LEADERS*	*PUBLIC*	*LEADERS*	*PUBLIC*	*LEADERS*
1. Soviets invade western Europe	68%	93%	24%	5%	8%	2%
2. Soviets invade Japan	53	82	36	12	11	6
3. Nicaragua allows Soviets to set up missile base	45	67	42	27	13	6
4. Arabs cut off oil to United States	36	—	51	—	13	—
5. Arabs invade Israel	32	57	54	38	14	5
6. Soviets invade China	27	14	61	78	12	8
7. Iran invades Saudi Arabia	26	—	59	—	15	—
8. El Salvador government losing to leftist rebels	25	—	56	—	19	—
9. Nicaragua invades Honduras to destroy contra bases	24	17	60	74	16	9
10. North Korea invades South Korea	24	64	64	32	12	4
11. China invades Taiwan	19	—	64	—	17	—

From John E. Rielly, "America's State of Mind," Foreign Policy, *vol. 66, Spring 1987, p. 48. The poll was conducted by the Gallup Organization between October 20 and November 12, 1986, with a sample of 1585 (the "public") interviewed in person and another 343 leaders interviewed, either in person or by telephone, between mid-September and mid-November. A dash in the figure means "not asked." Table reprinted by permission. Copyright © 1987 by the Carnegie Endowment for International Peace.*

rivative powers. Put another way, the American government uniquely distributes foreign policy powers, and the authority to use them, across three branches of government.[13] The power to make war or to approve treaties, for example, requires participation by both the legislative and the executive branches (with occasional arbitration by the judicial branch; see Chapter 6).

This sharing of authority and power, with all the redundancy that comes with overlapping responsibilities, was no accident. As mentioned in the preface to this book, more than anything else the founders of the new republic wished to avoid a concentration of power in the hands of a single person or institution. They had dared a war of independence against one autocrat, King George III, and had no desire to see another tyranny established in the New World.

Yet, when power is shared, tensions and ambiguities are created within the government. Who ultimately will assume the responsibility to commit the nation to war, or to enter into agreements with other countries? By spreading the authority for such decisions across the branches of government, the new Constitution pitted one institution against another—precisely what many of the founders had in mind as a check against any one branch (especially the presidency) from becoming too strong. "Ambition must be made to counteract ambition," wrote James Madison in *The Federalist*, No. 51. While the sharing of authority had the virtue of keeping it under better control, this method carried with it as well the makings of a recipe for conflict and inefficiency.

Recently, in frustration over having to share foreign policy powers with a recalcitrant Congress, officials in the Reagan administration sought to bypass the legislative branch altogether. They sold weapons to Iran during 1985 and 1986 in exchange for its influence over the release of U.S. hostages in the Middle East—a secret deal with terrorists (Iran had repeatedly supported terrorist operations since the fall of its pro-American shah in 1979) that stood in sharp contradiction to the avowed foreign policy of the United States and in apparent violation of the Arms Export Control Act of 1976. These officials then used the profits from this sale to support the contras in Nicaragua. In addition, the administration sought funds for the contras from private, wealthy American citizens and from foreign potentates. This effort to skirt both the legal limitations against military aid to the contras (the Boland amendment, examined in Chapter 9) and the government's constitutionally based budget procedures—Article I, Section 8, of the Constitution lodges the power to spend in the hands of the Congress—precipitated the Iran-contra scandal of 1986–1987.

The scandal led to a series of investigations critical of the Reagan administration and to the indictment by a special prosecutor of top administration officials on the staff of the National Security Council (NSC)—some of whom were convicted in 1989 on felony counts. Officials in the administration evidently had sought nothing less than an "off-the-shelf, self-sustaining, stand-alone" capability to conduct secret foreign policy, free from the "interference" of Congress.[14] Had this scheme worked, the appropriations process would have become irrelevant and, as a result, so would a key element in the system of checks and balances established by the Constitution. These secret machinations represented a dangerous blow against constitutional government, carried out by misguided, self-professed patriots who, in the words of a leading senator who participated in the investigation of the scandal (Warren Rudman, R-N.H.), "wrapped themselves in the flag and go around spitting on the Constitution."[15]

Institutional Fragmentation

Just as the Constitution's insistence on shared authority leads to friction between the branches over the control of foreign policy, so, too, does its requirement for separate institutions. The sharing of authority across separated institutions means, in the day-to-day world of policy-

Lieutenant Colonel Oliver L. North in Marine Corps attire listens as his attorney, Brendan Sullivan, responds to a question from congressional investigators probing the Iran-contra affair in 1987. (UPI/Bettmann Newsphotos)

making, that a great many entities and individuals have a say in deciding whether this nation will tilt toward isolation or involvement in world affairs, as well as what means—dispatching the diplomats, filtering in spies, or calling out the Marines—will be used in the pursuit of specific foreign policy objectives.

According to some observers, the institutional arrangements for foreign policy within the American government have become excessively fragmented. With respect to relations between the legislative and executive branches, those critics unhappy over the active involvement of Congress in external relations complain of 535 would-be secretaries of state on Capitol Hill; too many investigative subcommittees and congressional hearings, each carrying a heavy surcharge on the time of the real secretary of state and other key officials appointed to foreign policy responsibilities by the president; and too many new statutes that require executive-branch reports to Congress on a vast array of plans and operations.

On the other side of this coin, those suspicious of power lodged too exclusively within the executive branch—the point of view that animated the nation's founders—complain of undue secrecy resorted to by agencies "downtown" as a means for concealing from legislators the faulty premises of misguided foreign policies. They complain, as well, about slippery grants of authority passed from the White House to the CIA, the Department of Defense (the Pentagon, or DOD), and other agencies in an elusive shell game within the executive branch that prohibits Congress from following the formulation of policy; and about attempts by the executive to detour around Congress by using groups outside the government as a means for achieving foreign policy goals blocked by law (as occurred with the "privatization" of secret operations abroad during the Iran-contra affair).

Even within each branch of government, the excessive friction and wear that result from too many movable parts in the policymaking machinery have become another sore point for critics. On Capitol Hill, a proliferation of subcommittees jostle over legislative jurisdiction and compete for the same witnesses from the executive branch for their legislative hearings. Junior members of Congress travel abroad to barter with heads of state over policy or try (as did Representative George Hanson, R-Idaho, in

1980) to gain the release of U.S. hostages in the Middle East, while professional diplomats in the Department of State look on in dismay.

Similarly, inside the executive branch, officials at times appear to be conducting their own foreign policies, not just beyond the purview of legislators but outside the supervision of the president and his cabinet as well. Operations that have been carried out evidently without the express approval of the White House include: contracts with organized crime for the murder of a foreign head of state (various CIA plots against Castro during the Kennedy administration); the establishment of Swiss bank accounts for the private funding of secret warfare in Nicaragua (staff members of the NSC during the Iran-contra affair); and, again as part of the contra counterinsurgency, the preparation of manuals by CIA field personnel in 1984 that seemed to advocate the assassination ("neutralization," a code word that meant murder in some previous CIA secret cables to its officers abroad) of political opponents in Nicaragua, despite a presidential ban against this extreme approach to foreign policy.

In light of these and other reckless operations, one can readily appreciate this observation from the historian Arthur M. Schlesinger, Jr.: "Students of public administration have never taken sufficient account of the capacity of lower levels of government to sabotage or defy even a masterful President."[16] The possibility also exists, of course, that presidents have actually known about these operations but their approval was concealed through a policy of "plausible deniability" in order to protect the reputation of the presidency (and their own political fortunes). In the instances cited above, however, top presidential aides have sworn under oath before congressional investigators that this was not the case (see Chapter 9).

The making of foreign policy in the American government is, in sum, a dispersed enterprise. The forces in the system tend to be centrifugal (pushing away from the center), not centripetal—precisely as the founders in-

tended. This means that presidents and congressional leaders face a difficult challenge: they must try to join the fragments together into some semblance of unity and purpose. Sometimes they succeed, most notably when the nation is endangered, say, by the great economic dislocations of a depression or by a sneak attack like the one that occurred at Pearl Harbor; but often, the whole unwieldy machine threatens to break down in what one keen observer has called a "deadlock of democracy."[17]

A Pluralist Politics

As if this institutional fragmentation within the government were an insufficient complication, the United States has in addition an open, pluralist society that further diffuses the number of groups and individuals able to influence foreign policy decisions. The term *pluralism* is used to characterize the existence of multiple centers of power within the United States. These power centers are found not only within the government but across the wide land, a bewildering assortment of organizations of various stripes and colorations—some with strong foreign policy beliefs which they press upon decision makers with marked success. Among the most prominent with concerns related to foreign policy are political parties (most prominently, the Democrats and the Republicans, who frequently disagree on foreign policy objectives), interest or "pressure" groups (like the influential American Israel Public Affairs Committee, or AIPAC), and occasional mass movements (like the pro-arms control freeze movement prominent in the mid-1980s).

Critics argue that the influence of these power centers has become too great, as they apply the salve of campaign funds to officeholders in exchange for foreign policy benefits. Moreover, critics maintain, the number of power centers has become so large—a condition sometimes referred to as *hyperpluralism*—that, added to the proliferating number of official agencies involved in foreign policy, the accumulation of

---

Perspectives on American Foreign Policy   2.3

Paul Kennedy on the risks of fragmented government for America's external relations:

. . . The country may not always be helped by the division of decision-making powers that was deliberately created when it was geographically and strategically isolated from the rest of the world, two centuries ago, and had time to find a consensus on the few issues that actually concerned foreign policy. This division may be less serviceable now that the United States is a global superpower often called upon to make swift decisions vis-à-vis countries that enjoy far fewer constraints. No one

of these obstacles prevents the execution of a coherent, long-term American grand strategy. However, their cumulative effect is to make it difficult to carry out policy changes that seem to hurt special interests and occur in an election year. It may therefore be here, in the cultural and political realms, that the evolution of an overall American policy to meet the twenty-first century will be subjected to the greatest test.

Paul Kennedy, "The (Relative) Decline of America," *Atlantic,* August 1987, p. 38. Reprinted by permission.

---

groups and organizations at the heart of the government threatens arteriosclerosis. The merits of this criticism are examined in Chapter 7.

THE IMPORTANCE OF THE INDIVIDUAL DECISION MAKER

The highly regarded American diplomat George F. Kennan complained in 1951 that foreign policy scholarship had been distorted by an "under-estimation of psychological and political reactions—of such things as fear, ambition, insecurity, jealousy, and perhaps even boredom—as prime movers of events."[18] More recently, a close observer of the Washington scene noted with reference to Congress: "The central truth about this place [is] that the chairman—whoever he is—of the committee—never mind which one—did not do that thing strictly and clearly for some ideological or partisan purpose. Five will get you ten that there was also at play a personal ambition, a head cold, a desire to catch a plane, a trade-off, a girl—or some combination of all the above."[19]

Influences of this kind are difficult, indeed often impossible, for the researcher to discover or document. Such emotions and needs, however, surely play a part in the making of both foreign and domestic policy. From among the many avenues of inquiry one might follow in analyzing the relevance of individuals to the shaping of foreign policy, four seem especially revealing: the extent of role-playing engaged in by the decision maker, the nature of his or her prior career experiences, the degree to which perceptual screens seem to block out factual information from the decision maker's mind, and the apparent effect on decision behavior of the individual's fundamental personality traits (character).

Role-Playing

The core idea behind the concept of *role* is that the particular office held by a decision maker will cause him or her to expound and implement views traditional to that office. This aspect of foreign policy behavior is related to the institutional influences discussed in the previous section, for role-playing represents a blend of both the domestic setting and the views of the individual holding a position of authority.

Illustrations of the interplay between the office and the officeholder are practically endless. If you were a dogcatcher, for instance, you would probably believe that the streets ought to be cleared of all unrestrained hounds. If your business were to catch foreign spies (a responsibility called counterintelligence), you would most likely have a highly negative attitude toward policies that permitted an increase in U.S. ports of call for Soviet ships (with their numerous "sailor" spies on board) or that led to an increase in the number of Soviet "diplomats" allowed here, many of whom are also really espionage agents. Lamenting the pernicious effects of role-playing in the Department of State, one experienced government official complains about an attitude he calls the *curator mentality*. Regardless of their personal views, State Department officials upon inheriting the job of a country desk officer are expected to keep established U.S. policy toward the nation intact, as they find it, carefully protected "under glass, untampered with, and dusted," as if the officials were but museum curators.[20]

Thus, the nature of the office itself, coupled with peer expectations about how the job ought to be conducted, becomes a critical influence on foreign policy behavior. As the late Senator Hubert H. Humphrey (D-Minn.) often put it, "How one stands depends upon where one sits." Role-playing is hardly an infallible predictor, though, of how officials will behave. During the Reagan years, for example, the Department of State—home of the diplomats—often advocated military intervention to achieve U.S. goals, while the Department of Defense, recalling the frustrations of the war in Vietnam, was apt to encourage a diplomatic approach (see Chapter 10).

Past Experience

Skill in a job usually depends upon prior experience. The robes of the neurosurgeon are not easily donned, nor are the controls of a Boeing 747 simple to command. Similarly, argue those who value a professional diplomatic corps, skills needed for the effective conduct of foreign policy require special training. "The art of diplomacy, as that of water-colours," wryly observed the seasoned British diplomat Harold Nicolson, "has suffered much from the fascination which it exercises upon the amateur."

Despite such criticism, the United States has often sent abroad to key foreign countries ambassadors who have not been experienced professional diplomats in the State Department's Foreign Service, but rather political appointees selected by a president because of their partisan connections—often as a reward for their help as fund-raisers in the last election. One study of U.S. diplomatic delegations concluded that major posts are often filled with Americans "trained in such dubiously relevant specialties as manufacturing, scientific research, teaching, singing, or organizing civic clubs."[21] The United States has had fewer professionals rise to the rank of ambassador and more inexperienced political appointees at this level (particularly during the Reagan administration) than any other democracy.

Further, America has been more inclined than any other major democracy to elect heads of state who have had limited international experience before arriving at the White House. Presidents Jimmy Carter and Ronald Reagan, former governors of Georgia and California, respectively, are two recent examples, while President George Bush—a man with extensive international experience before his election in 1988 (UN ambassador, chief envoy to China, CIA director)—stands as an exceptional case.

The clash between the professionals (the *pros*) in the foreign policy apparatus, with their long-term career perspectives, and the *amateurs*, who may serve in government for only a few years before returning to their previous jobs, has produced friction in the planning of this nation's external relations. The tensions have been particularly visible between the careerists in the Department of State and the so-called in-and-outers—academicians, businesspeople, and military personnel—who have served as assistants to the president for national security affairs on the staff of the National Security Council. The career diplomats usually bring to decision councils a longer time perspective, along with a more dispassionate analysis of foreign policy issues and a preference for the status quo; the national security advisers, in contrast, are often caught up in the political and ideological perspectives of the White House (where their office is located).[22]

With the coming and going of amateurs in high positions throughout the government, the political scientist Hugh Heclo suggests that policymaking in the United States often resembles "a sandlot pick-up game, with a variety of strangers, strategies, and misunderstandings."[23] America's European and Asian allies, not to mention the Soviet Union, are often bewildered by this ebb and flow of key policy officials, with the disjointedness it often lends to this nation's international relations; they themselves are more accustomed to leaving foreign policy to seasoned professional diplomats.

The place of the amateur in American foreign policy making has its defenders, however. "The Executive Branch of our Government is populated with specialists and experts," wrote Frank Church (D-Idaho), a chairman of the Senate Foreign Relations Committee. "These men have added greatly to the Government's skill in conducting foreign relations, but they have also shown a certain arrogance, purveying the notion that anyone who is not an expert, including Congressmen, Senators and ordinary citizens, is simply too uninformed to grasp the complexities of foreign policy. . . . This view is patently false: Clemenceau said that war was too important to be left to the generals; similarly, the basic decisions of foreign policy are too important to be left to the diplomats."[24] In comparable spirit, the historian Ruhl Bartlett has argued: ". . . there are no experts in wisdom concerning human affairs or in determining the national interest, and there is nothing in the realm of foreign policy that cannot be understood by the average American citizen."[25]

Amateurs have another advantage, from a White House perspective: presidents often like to place trusted friends and political allies at the controls of the bureaucracy in order to make sure that the policies preferred by the White House are honored and implemented by the "permanent government." The Reagan administration, which went to Washington with the avowed purpose of dismantling much of the federal government, realized it would face tough opposition by bureaucrats whose jobs were at stake. In an attempt to overcome this opposition, the administration penetrated the bureaucracy with its own political appointees to a deeper level than any other administration in the modern era.

Even this extensive "infiltration" seemed to have a minimal effect on forcing the government to abandon long-standing programs, however, in part because individual bureaucrats enjoyed strong alliances outside the government and on Capitol Hill with those who also opposed the so-called Reagan Revolution. John W. Gardner has commented on these *iron triangles*, a subterranean permanent government that has frustrated many a president: ". . . questions of public policy. . . are often decided by a trinity consisting of (1) representatives of an outside body [pressure groups], (2) middle level bureaucrats, and (3) selected members of Congress, particularly those concerned with appropriations. In a given field these people have collaborated for years. They have a durable alliance that cranks out legislation and appropriations on behalf of their special interests. Participants in such durable alliances do not want the department secretaries strengthened. . . ."[26] The hopes and plans of individual decision makers—even presidents—are frequently dashed by these counterforces in the national political arena.

Distorted Perceptions

As psychologists have long understood, how one perceives reality can be more important than reality itself. Foreign policy officials have often erred because of a failure to comprehend accurately the world around them. A variety of psychological distortions contribute to this common pathology of the policy process.

Self-delusion   Self-delusion is one important cause of misperception, as officials brush aside—or bend—facts that fail to conform to their worldview. Of Kaiser Wilhelm I (1797–1888), the king of Prussia and the first emperor of modern Germany, the historian Barbara Tuchman has observed: "[He] was interested in gold-plated news only and disliked above all else those tiresome visits from ministers with their reports of inconvenient facts that did not fit in with his schemes."[27] One of Hitler's close associates recalls how the Nazi leader "gladly sought advice from persons who saw the situation even more optimistically and delusively than he himself."[28]

Self-delusion is hardly just a Teutonic disorder. Looking back at the war in Vietnam, a high-ranking intelligence official regrets "that the policymakers did not better exercise their own power to listen," since the evidence against a quick American victory in Indochina was available, compelling—and ignored.[29] A former chief of CIA analysts, Dr. Ray S. Cline, remembers that in 1966 American policymakers began to "lose interest in an objective description of the outside world and were beginning to scramble for evidence that they were going to win the war in Vietnam." By 1969, the pathology had reached disease proportions, lasting through 1974, when, Cline concludes, "there was almost total dissent from the real world around us. . . ."[30]

Isolation   Sometimes leaders are cut off from reality because they become isolated from conflicting opinions. Before the secret invasion of Cuba by the CIA in 1961, analysts inside the Agency expressed skepticism in their reports (called "intelligence estimates") that Fidel Castro could be overthrown. The Cuban premier was "likely to grow stronger rather than weaker as time goes by," summed up a top-secret CIA estimate (since declassified) prepared for the agency's director. The study warned that Castro "now has established a formidable structure of control over the daily lives of the Cuban people."[31]

President Kennedy evidently neither saw this study nor spoke with a single CIA analyst regarding the Bay of Pigs scheme. Ambitious, persuasive, a member of Kennedy's social milieu, Richard M. Bissell, Jr., the CIA officer in charge of the invasion plans (as distinct from the CIA's analytic group), assured Kennedy that the irritant, Castro, could be removed by a swift covert operation—happy news for the moment, but soon to be proven disastrously wrong. The invaders were quickly defeated as they landed at the Bay of Pigs. A trained analyst from the CIA (or from the Department of State, whose Cuban specialists were also excluded from NSC planning sessions) presumably would have warned the president and his planners that, among other things, the contingency escape route to the Escambray Mountains was blocked by the impenetrable marshlands of the Zapata Swamp.[32]

Peer-group pressures   Moreover, reality can be distorted within the individual mind by a phenomenon of interaction within small groups that the Yale University psychologist Irving L. Janis has labeled *groupthink*. This term refers to a tendency for individuals in some groups to cast aside a realistic appraisal of alternative courses of action in favor of high cohesiveness among the group's members. It becomes more important for members to conform to group expectations than it is to be correct. On the basis of his study of the Bay of Pigs, Janis writes: "The failure of Kennedy's inner circle to detect any of the false assumptions behind the Bay of Pigs invasion plan can be at least partially accounted for by the group's tendency to seek concurrence at the expense of seeking information, critical appraisal, and debate."[33]

This "concurrence seeking" works against openness in decision making. An expert on modern governmental organizations notes that in bureaucracies "the average person who will *get along* with others and *go along* with the system is preferred."[34] Another organizational expert has observed this tendency within the government's intelligence agencies. "Like other bureaucrats, intelligence analysts have to conform to the regime's basic views, about the nature and morality of international relations if they wish to be treated as 'responsible' and 'serious,' " he suggests. "Therefore, they refrain from asking the really 'tough' but crucial questions such as the aggressiveness of the Soviet Union, the morality of the Vietnam War, and the validity of the 'domino theory.' "[35] A lack of opinion diversity can lead to disastrous results, as inaccurate Pollyannas force out accurate Cassandras and organizations drift farther and farther away from the moorings of reality.

Fatigue   The higher up the organizational ladder, the more harried an official is apt to be. This condition has an effect upon perceptions as well. A secretary of defense in the Reagan administration, Caspar W. Weinberger, was reportedly "swamped," "overwhelmed," "left with not enough time to think forward."[36] Similarly, a study of American policymakers during the war in Vietnam pointed to *executive fatigue* as an important influence on decision making. The fatigue resulting from too many responsibilities has a deadening effect on "freshness of thought, imagination, a sense of possibility and perspective. . . . The tired policymaker becomes a prisoner of his own narrowed view of the world and his own clichéd rhetoric."[37]

Character

A decision maker's basic personality traits, evolved from childhood, can have an important effect, too, on foreign policy outcomes. One recent study, for example, ties a willingness of some decision makers to use military force as a policy option to their "high-dominance" personalities, that is, their tendency to be individuals who "run the show" while in office, imposing their will forcefully on subordinates, berating them, often ignoring them altogether as they set policy directions by themselves— say, a Henry Kissinger compared with William P. Rogers (both secretaries of state for President Nixon, Kissinger considered active and Rogers passive).[38]

This list of psychological influences that can affect the views of policymakers is by no means exhaustive; it is offered in this early chapter merely to suggest the many forces that play on individual officeholders, high and low, and sometimes undermine their capacity to cope realistically with foreign policy challenges. The linkages between politics and psychology remain murky, in part because systematic research on this relationship is still in its infancy. Further, for day in, day out politics as usual, the effect of the individual decision maker on foreign policy is probably far less significant than role, institutional, and other constraints. As Greenstein notes, however, under certain conditions individual personality traits may become quite important, as when a person in a position of authority faces ambiguous, novel, complex, or contradictory situations.[39] The student of foreign affairs who ignores or rejects out of hand these influences of the mind risks the danger of overlooking strong undercurrents in the shaping of America's external relations.

The preceding survey has attempted to provide a broad, introductory orientation to the milieu in which U.S. foreign policy must find its place. In the next two chapters, this book briefly surveys how the currents of world and American history have buffeted and sometimes shifted this nation's course in its relations with other countries.

SUMMARY

American foreign policy is a complicated subject. As U.S. officials determine their objectives and consider what means to apply toward their fulfillment, they confront many obstacles in the world, at home, and within their own minds. On the international setting, this nation's goals may be affected at one time or another by the influences of balance-of-power considerations, geopolitics, idealism, and, among other forces, the growing trend toward global interdependence.

Trying to calculate the effects of these opportunities and dangers on America's foreign policy can be baffling enough, but, in addition, one must take into account influences from within the United States that stem from this nation's own history and traditions; from its Constitution and laws, which often pit the Congress against the executive branch for control over the direction of external policy; from the large number of institutions involved in the conduct of foreign affairs, which leads to a certain disjointedness; and from the wide range of groups in American society which are organized in an effort to mold this nation's international ties in their own interests—yet another centrifugal force.

Then, on the plane of the individual decision maker, one finds such microforces at work as role-playing, misperception, the isolation of leaders, groupthink, and other psychological pressures which can have the effect of undermining rational decision making. American for-

eign policy is more than global interactions and domestic lobbying; it can involve internal battles of the psyche, too.

The founders of the United States did not wish this country to go easily into war or other foreign entanglements. That is why they shared the powers for war and diplomacy (among others) with Congress and the presidency. The pursuit of America's foreign policy is complicated not only because the modern world is complex, but because the founders intentionally designed a government in which powers would be checked and used only after thorough deliberation by the legislative and executive branches, together, with further arbitration when necessary by the judicial branch.

But did the fear the founders had of centralized authority—a concern reinforced in the modern era by the war in Vietnam and by the Watergate, CIA, and Iran-contra scandals—lead to an excessive fragmentation of control over the instruments of foreign policy? Can the United States maintain its unique form of democracy and still compete successfully in a world of more strictly organized and disciplined totalitarian regimes? A central question throughout this book is whether, in the face of grave dangers from abroad, the constitutional arrangements designed over 200 years ago—in an era of sailing ships and covered wagons—can continue to serve the well-being of this nation in the nuclear age.

KEY TERMS

nation (state, nation-state)	new world order	curator mentality
sovereignty	isolationism	pros and amateurs
American foreign policy	interventionism	iron triangles
balance of power	power sharing	self-delusion
Truman Doctrine	institutional fragmentation	leadership isolation
geopolitics	pluralism	groupthink
domino theory	hyperpluralism	executive fatigue
complex interdependence	role-playing	

NOTES

1. See, for instance, Yale H. Ferguson and Richard W. Mansbach, *The Elusive Quest: Theory and International Politics* (Columbia: University of South Carolina Press, 1988), p. 187.

2. For elaboration, see David W. Ziegler, *War, Peace, and International Politics*, 2d ed. (Boston: Little, Brown, 1981), p. 96; Stephen D. Krasner, ed., *International Regimes* (Ithaca, New York: Cornell University Press, 1983), pp. 17–18 and 365–367; and Seyom Brown, *New Forces, Old Forces, and the Future of World Politics* (Boston: Scott, Foresman, 1988), pp. 3–4.

3. Hollis W. Barber, *Foreign Policies of the United States* (New York: Dryden, 1953), p. 9.

4. John Lewis Gaddis, *Strategies of Containment: A Critical Appraisal of Postwar American National Security Policy* (New York: Oxford University Press, 1982), p. viii.

5. Quoted by Graham Hovey, "Fog and Worse on Angola," *New York Times*, December 30, 1975, p. 25.

6. Quoted by Judy Mann, "Hunger," *Washington Post*, March 5, 1982.

7. Quoted by Stanley Karnow, *Vietnam: A History* (New York: Viking, 1983), p. 479; see, also, p. 321.

8. *Ibid.*, pp. 13, 14.

9. Quoted by Charles McCarry, "Ol' Man Rivers," *Esquire*, October 1970, p. 171.

10. *Between Two Ages: America's Role in the Technotronic Era* (New York: Viking, 1970), p. 275.

11. Quoted in *U.S. News & World Report*, July 15, 1985, p. 24.

12. *A World Restored* (Boston: Houghton Mifflin, 1957), p. 331.

13. Richard E. Neustadt, *Presidential Power* (New York: Wiley, 1960), Chap. 3. For a more elaborate theoretical discussion of power, influence, and authority, see these works by Robert A. Dahl: "Power," in David L. Sills, ed., *International Encyclopedia of the Social Sciences*, vol. 12, pp. 405–415; "The Concept of Power," *Behavioral Science*, vol. 2, 1957, pp. 201–215; and *Modern Political Analysis* (Englewood Cliffs, N.J.: Prentice-Hall, 1963).

14. *Hearings of the Congressional Committees Investigating the Iran-Contra Affair*, U.S. Senate Select Committee on Secret Military Assistance to Iran and the U.S. House of Representatives Select Committee to Investigate Covert Arms Transactions with Iran (chaired by Lee H. Hamilton, D-Ind., and Daniel K. Inouye, D-Hawaii), S. Rep. No. 100-216 and H. Rep. No. 100-433 (Washington, D.C.: U.S. Government Printing Office, November 1987): testimony, Lt. Col. Oliver L. North, July 13, 1987, and Vice Adm. John M. Poindexter, July 15, 1987.

15. Press conference, Washington, D.C., May 7, 1987, quoted in William S. Cohen and George J. Mitchell, *Men of Zeal: A Candid Inside Story of the Iran-Contra Hearings* (New York: Viking, 1988), p. 76.

16. *The Age of Roosevelt—The Coming of the New Deal* (Boston: Houghton Mifflin, 1958), p. 536.

17. James MacGregor Burns, *Deadlock of Democracy* (Englewood Cliffs, N.J.: Prentice-Hall, 1963).

18. *American Diplomacy: 1900–1950* (Chicago: University of Chicago Press, 1951), p. 11.

19. Meg Greenfield, *Newsweek*, August 1, 1977.

20. James C. Thomson, "Vietnam: An Autopsy," *Atlantic*, April 1968, p. 47.

21. "The Administration of Foreign Affairs," from *The Operational Aspects of United States Foreign Policy*, Study No. 6 in *United States Foreign Policy: Compilation of Studies*, prepared under the direction of the Senate Committee on Foreign Relations by the Maxwell Graduate School of Citizenship

and Public Affairs, Syracuse University, November 1959; reprinted in Andrew M. Scott and Raymond H. Dawson, eds., *Readings in the Making of American Foreign Policy* (New York: Macmillan, 1965), p. 523.

22. See Bert A. Rockman, "America's *Departments* of State," *American Political Science Review*, vol. 75 (December 1981), pp. 911–927.

23. *A Government of Strangers: Executive Politics in Washington* (Washington, D.C.: Brookings, 1977), p. 111.

24. "Of Presidents and Caesars: The Decline of Constitutional Government in the Conduct of American Foreign Policy," *Idaho Law Review*, vol. 6, Fall 1969, p. 12.

25. Testimony of Ruhl Bartlett, "U.S. Commitments to Foreign Powers," *Hearings of the Committee on Foreign Relations*, U.S. Senate, 1967, p. 20.

26. Testimony, John W. Gardner, Committee on Government Operations, U.S. Senate (1971), quoted by Jay M. Shafritz, *The Dorsey Dictionary of American Government and Politics* (Chicago: Dorsey, 1988), pp. 148–149.

27. *The Zimmermann Telegram* (New York: Viking, 1958), p. 26.

28. Albert Speer, *Inside the Third Reich* (New York: Macmillan, 1970), p. 243. See also a vivid account of Reichsmarschall Hermann Göring's dismissal of an intelligence report that might have upset the Führer (at p. 290).

29. Thomas L. Hughes, "The Power to Speak and the Power to Listen: Reflections in Bureaucratic Politics and a Recommendation of Information Flows," in Thomas M. Franck and Edward Weisband, eds., *Secrecy*

and Foreign Policy (New York: Oxford University Press, 1974), p. 28.

30. In Roy Godson, ed., *Intelligence Requirements for the 1980's: Analysis and Estimates* (Washington, D.C.: National Strategy Information Center, 1980), p. 79.

31. See Peter Wyden, *Bay of Pigs: The Untold Story* (New York: Simon & Schuster, 1979), p. 99.

32. See *ibid.*; Thomas Powers, *The Man Who Kept the Secrets: Richard Helms and the CIA* (New York: Knopf, 1979), p. 145; and Irving L. Janis, *Groupthink*, 2d ed. (Boston: Houghton Mifflin, 1982), p. 41.

33. Janis, *op. cit.*, p. 47.

34. Victor A. Thompson, *Modern Organization* (New York: Knopf, 1961), p. 91.

35. Steve Chan, "Intelligence of Stupidity: Understanding Failures in Strategic Warning," *American Political Science Review*, vol. 73, March 1979, p. 178.

36. Theodore H. White, "Weinberger on the Ramparts," *New York Times Magazine*, February 6, 1983, p. 24.

37. Thomson, *op. cit.*, p. 50.

38. Graham H. Shepard, "Personality Effects on American Foreign Policy, 1969–84: A Second Test of Interpersonal Generalization Theory," *International Studies Quarterly*, vol. 32, March 1988, pp. 91–123.

39. Fred I. Greenstein, "The Study of Personality and Politics: Overall Considerations," in Fred I. Greenstein and Michael Lerner, eds., *A Source Book for the Study of Personality and Politics* (Chicago: Markham, 1971), p. 14.

RECOMMENDED READINGS

Crabb, Cecil V., Jr. *Policy-Makers and Critics: Conflicting Theories of American Foreign Policy* (New York: Praeger, 1976). A solid critique of current theoretical debates on the study of foreign policy.

Falk, Richard. *The Promise of World Order: Essays in Normative International Relations* (Philadelphia: Temple University Press, 1987). A powerful explication of the global forces favoring a new world order over the traditional system of nation-states with its "violence-drenched orientations."

Jones, Howard. *"A New Kind of War": America's Global Strategy and the Truman Doctrine in Greece* (New York: Oxford University Press, 1989). A detailed history of America's first major test in the unconventional guerrilla warfare against communist aggression following the Second World War.

Kelman, Herbert C., ed. *International Behavior: A Social-Psychological Analysis* (New York: Holt, Rinehart & Winston, 1965). An early, still relevant display of efforts to borrow from the discipline of psychology for the study of international affairs.

Krasner, Stephen D., ed. *International Regimes* (Ithaca, New York: Cornell University Press, 1983). A selection of thoughtful essays by international relations specialists, exploring the tensions between realism and the prospects for a new world order.

Richardson, Lewis F. *Statistics of Deadly Quarrels* (Chicago: Quadrangle, 1960). Among the first of the important mathematical studies on international relations.

Rosenau, James N. *The Scientific Study of Foreign Policy* (New York: Nichols, 1980). First published in 1971, this work is one among many from this leading theorist.

Schelling, Thomas C. *The Strategy of Conflict* (Cambridge: Harvard University Press, 1960). An application of economic modeling to the international behavior of nations.

Singer, J. David, ed. *Quantitative International Politics* (New York: Free Press, 1968). A landmark in the quantitative approach to the study of international politics.

Waltz, Kenneth N. *Man, the State, and War* (New York: Columbia University Press, 1954). An early analytic study by one of the leading lights in the movement to theorize about the behavior of nations.

Wright, Quincy. *The Study of International Relations* (New York: Appleton-Century-Crofts, 1955). A pioneer contribution to the quantitative analysis of relations among nations.

Ziegler, David W. *War, Peace, and International Politics* (Boston: Little, Brown, 1981). An excellent critique of the literature on the causes of war.

Zinnes, Danna A. *Contemporary Research in International Relations: A Perspective and a Critical Appraisal* (New York: Free Press, 1979). A valuable examination of recent theoretical perspectives in the study of international affairs.

NATION BUILDING, 1776–1865

    Severing Ties with Europe

    Ambivalent Isolation

    Expansionist Stirrings

    Monroe Delivers a Lecture

    Westward Ho!

    North against South

EMERGENCE AS A GREAT POWER, 1865–1920

    The Spanish-American War

    American Imperialism

    Wilsonian Idealism

AMERICA AS A RELUCTANT LEADER, 1920–

    The Fascist Threat

    Internationalism Embraced—Gingerly

SUMMARY

3

THE PAST AS PROLOGUE

The conduct of contemporary American foreign policy has important antecedents in the early history of the republic. This country was born in the eighteenth century as a result of a momentous and daring foreign policy decision: the colonies of North America chose to sever their relations with a mother country whose rule had become intolerable. The founders established a representative democracy, a form of government in which policy decisions—foreign and domestic—would be subject to the influence of the nation's citizens, not just a royal court. Whether this experiment in democracy would work, allowing America to compete securely in a world of dangerous rivals who were unencumbered by the constraints of public accountability, was in doubt—and remains a subject of debate two centuries later.

The shots fired at Concord thus set this nation on a course sharply distinct from the monarchical rule practiced throughout Europe. This chapter surveys that course as revealed in key foreign policy decisions from 1776 to the dawning of the nuclear age in 1945. The purpose is to provide the reader with a quick overflight across the years, highlighting the uneasy vacillation by the United States between indifference and attraction toward other nations, depending upon the perceptions held by American leaders of the possible risks and rewards associated with foreign involvement. Major events in the development of American foreign policy to 1945 are listed in the form of a chart in Figure 3.1.

NATION BUILDING, 1776–1865

Nations, like people, may be characterized as introverted or extroverted. With human beings, this inner- or outer-directedness is often bound up with one's self-confidence. As a person becomes more self-assured, he or she is apt to be less introspective. While one must be careful about drawing analogies between individuals and nations, it nonetheless seems reasonable to

A crowd stands on the Rue Royale in Paris beneath an electric welcoming sign, awaiting the arrival of President Woodrow Wilson in December 1918. (U.S. Signal Corps)

FIGURE 3.1   Highlights in the evolution of American foreign policy, 1776–1945.

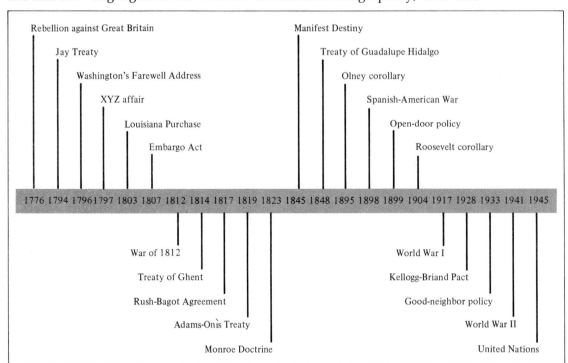

characterize the early United States as a country that—militarily weak, unsure of itself, groping for identity—for the most part looked inward. From the nation's birth in 1776 until its reluctant entry into World War I, the main goal of U.S. foreign policy was to distance this country from further trouble with the Europeans. The revolution against England had been trying enough. Now the new democracy needed a breathing spell, a chance to put its house in order, some time to find its identity, to think through what it stood for as a nation—beyond the initial impulse to be free from the tyranny of British monarchy.

Severing Ties with Europe

America was blessed with certain advantages to support its posture of aloofness from the affairs of other nations—a policy later generations would refer to as *isolationism*. Foremost among the advantages were those convenient moats, the Atlantic and Pacific oceans, "America's greatest liquid assets."[1] The Atlantic separated the nation from the upheavals of Europe by some six weeks of ocean travel, and the Pacific was vaster still. A second substantial advantage was the absence of strong, permanent rivals in the Western Hemisphere—though to be sure several European countries maintained a worrisome foothold in the New World. England had interests in Canada and the northwest; France had repossessed, by treaty with Spain in 1800, New Orleans and indeed the entire Louisiana territory (which had once been a French colony); Spain remained in Florida; and Russia cast a longing look at opportunities across the Bering Strait. Each of these nations had sobering military capabilities. Despite these potential threats, America's geographical good fortune was greatly envied by an early French ambassador to this country. "North and south, you have weak neighbors," he observed. "East and west, you have fish!"

A third stroke of good luck was the distraction of potential European foes by dangers on their own continent. The impertinences of a young America were insignificant compared with the threat of war at their very borders. While George Washington, Thomas Jefferson, and others remained wary of European disputes that could prove disastrous if America were drawn into them, the balance-of-power concerns on the Continent did offer a benefit: as distracted European strategists anguished over how to maintain a power balance close to home, Americans enjoyed the luxury of concentrating on their own national development, freer than most young nations from interference by strong external forces. The former colonists could nurture the fragile stems of republican government, promote a national identity, construct the home defenses (America had no navy at all and barely an army), strengthen weak financial institutions, and begin an exploration of the sprawling virgin territory to the west.

Ambivalent Isolation

To augment these happy circumstances, the founders advocated an arm's-length relationship with Europe—though they followed their own advice unevenly. In his famous farewell address in 1796, the nation's great revolutionary hero and first president, General Washington, cautioned against involvement in the "vicissitudes" of European politics. (See excerpts from this speech in Perspectives on American Foreign Policy 3.1.) Yet Washington himself had found it in the best interests of the Revolutionary War to forge an alliance with France against Britain. Indeed, without the participation of French military forces, the decisive victory over the English at Yorktown might have eluded the revolutionists. After the war of independence, however, Washington as president

allowed the relationship with France to cool, and he refused to assist the French revolutionary regime in its war against Britain. Washington issued his Proclamation of Neutrality in 1793, removing this country from a conflict that would have been an enormous drain on its meager treasury. Instead, America profited from the war by selling food to both sides.

Just two years before his farewell admonitions, Washington restored commercial ties with Britain, the very nation he had fought against so bitterly for independence. The president and his secretary of state, John Jay, were prepared to set aside earlier animosities in favor of trade opportunities that would benefit the frail American economy. This commercial agreement, known as the *Jay Treaty* of 1794, and the *rapprochement* (a diplomatic word meaning the healing of ruptured relations between nations) with Britain which it symbolized, stirred strong feelings among citizens of the young republic. Some sided emotionally with the French and others with the English. France itself reacted bitterly to President Washington's tilt toward Britain; American merchant ships were seized by the French and their sailors roughed up.

An undeclared war soon broke out between America and France, lasting for two and one-half years and provoked in part by the infamous *XYZ affair*. In an attempt to avert an open conflict with France, President John Adams (Washington's successor) sent a diplomatic mission to Paris in 1797. Upon arrival, the American diplomats were approached by a beautiful woman and three mysterious gentlemen identified only as Messieurs "X," "Y," and "Z." This exotic quartet, secretly financed by the French foreign minister, Talleyrand, quietly offered the Americans money to accept a negotiated settlement of differences favorable to France. In modern parlance, this kind of clandestine operation—in this case a bribe—is called *covert action*, that is, an attempt to influence foreign affairs through secret means (the subject of Chapter 9). The Americans rebuffed this ploy and reported the incident to President Adams.

Perspectives on American Foreign Policy   *3.1*

Washington's Farewell Address, 1796. In his most famous and final speech as president, George Washington advocated that America be faithful to its obligations with other nations, but that it stay clear of European intrigues. This was wise counsel for a young country hoping to pursue its own destiny free from great-power meddling.

Against the insidious wiles of foreign influence, (I conjure you to believe me, fellow-citizens) the jealousy of a free people ought to be constantly awake; since history and experience prove, that foreign influence is one of the most baneful foes of republican government. But that jealousy, to be useful, must be impartial, else it becomes the instrument of the very influence to be avoided, instead of a defense against it. . . .

The great rule of conduct for us, in regard to foreign nations, is, in extending our commercial relations, to have with them as little political connection as possible. So far we have already formed engagements, let them be fulfilled with perfect good faith:—Here let us stop.

Europe has a set of primary interests, which to us have none, or a very remote relation. Hence, she must be engaged in frequent controversies, the causes of which are essentially foreign to our concerns. Hence, therefore, it must be unwise in us to implicate ourselves by artificial ties, in the ordinary vicissitudes of her politics, or the ordinary combinations and collisions of her friendships or enmities.

Our detached and distant situation invites and enables us to pursue a different course. If we remain one people, under an efficient government, the period is not far off when we may defy material injury from external annoyance; when we may take such an attitude as will cause the neutrality we may at any time resolve upon, to be scrupulously respected; when belligerent nations, under the impossibility of making acquisitions upon us, will not lightly hazard the giving us provocation, when we may choose peace or war, as our interest, guided by justice, shall counsel.

Why forgo the advantages of so peculiar a situation? Why quit our own to stand upon foreign ground? Why, by interweaving our destiny with that of any part of Europe, entangle our peace and prosperity in the toils of European ambition, rivalship, interest, humor, or caprice?

It is our true policy to steer clear of permanent alliance with any portion of the foreign world; so far, I mean, as we are now at liberty to do it; for let me not be understood as capable of patronizing infidelity to existing engagements. I hold the maxim no less applicable to public than private affairs, that honesty is always the best policy. I repeat it, therefore, let those engagements be observed in their genuine sense. But in my opinion, it is unnecessary, and would be unwise to extend them.

Taking care always to keep ourselves by suitable establishments, on a respectable defensive posture, we may safely trust to temporary alliances for extraordinary emergencies.

Harmony, and a liberal intercourse with all nations, are recommended by policy, humanity, and interest. But even our commercial policy should hold an equal and impartial hand; neither seeking nor granting exclusive favors or preferences. . . . [We should keep] constantly in view, that it is folly in one nation to look for disinterested favors from another; that it must pay with a portion of its independence for whatever it may accept under that character; that by such acceptance, it may place itself in the condition of having given equivalents for nominal favors, and yet of being reproached with ingratitude for not giving more. There can be no greater error than to expect, or calculate upon real favors from nation to nation. It is an illusion which experience must cure, which a just pride ought to discard. . . .

He disclosed the operation to the American public, which immediately raised the level of hostility toward France and renewed demands for war to avenge this latest insult.

Thus, the splendid isolation enjoyed during this early period of the republic was neither fully splendid nor truly isolated. The operating rule was self-preservation, the fundamental law of man and nature. Isolation, yes—except when American security interests might be protected through a military alliance; isolation, yes—except when commercial ties abroad might buoy the new nation's struggling economy.

The next president, Thomas Jefferson, who had served as America's first secretary of state, advocated in his inaugural address "peace, commerce and honest friendship with all nations, entangling alliances with none" (a phrase often wrongly attributed to Washington). Like George Washington, though, Jefferson was no purist on neutrality; he was prepared to seek alliances if they would benefit this country. Even though he favored France, Jefferson fully intended to join with England in a military pact against the French if Napoleon I (Napoleon Bonaparte) refused to sell New Orleans to the United States. Greater than his affection for France was his concern that Napoleon might interfere with America's westward expansion.

Moreover, President Jefferson was not averse to the practice of covert action himself, despite his avowal of honest friendships and no entanglements. "In Washington, [William] Eaton, the U.S. Consul in Tunis, laid before Jefferson a scheme that had been developing among Americans in the Mediterranean for a couple of years," writes the historian Robert Wallace. "The Bashaw [pasha] of Tripoli was a usurper, having stolen the throne from an older brother who was now wandering forlornly somewhere in Africa. Eaton proposed to find the brother, give him sympathy and support, and install him as rightful head of state. Jefferson approved the idea and thus was launched the first, although not the last, Amer-

ican effort to overthrow an objectionable foreign ruler and put a cooperative one in his place. Jefferson also chose to have that plot proceed quietly, in twilight. He would send the would-be Bashaw, through Eaton, a few artillery pieces and 1,000 small arms. Eaton himself was to be given a vague title—'Navy agent of the United States for Barbary regencies'—and placed under the jurisdiction of the commodore of the Mediterranean squadron. If he could accomplish something, fine. If not, small loss."[2] Unfortunately, the scheme failed. The pasha's troops captured the older brother and again banished him into exile; and Eaton, wallowing in self-pity, drank himself into an early grave.

The primary objectives of American foreign policy in these early days were little different from today: the protection of the American people at home and the enhancement of their commercial interests abroad. Questions of human rights and the quality of life for people abroad were also part of America's foreign policy interests. The British trafficking in opium in China during the early 1800s, for example, outraged many Americans for its immorality. By and large, though, security and trade preoccupied the young and watchful nation.

The approaches to foreign policy adopted by the republic's first leaders were different from those used today, however, because early America was both militarily weak and diplomatically inexperienced. The nation's pursuit of its objectives rested on two basic propositions. First, the founders were opposed to American involvement in the great-power confrontations of Europe; and second, they resisted efforts by the great powers to encroach upon the Western Hemisphere, where they might become an immediate threat to American expansion. While hardly easy, keeping this country removed from direct involvement in European wars required less effort and risk than pushing European adventurers out of America's claimed sphere of influence in this hemisphere.

Expansionist Stirrings

The next try at dislodging the Europeans from the Western Hemisphere (the War of Independence had been the first) was another grand and, this time, bloodless success. In 1803, President Jefferson simply bought out the French interests in New Orleans and the Louisiana territory, in what he called a "noble acquisition." The $15 million price tag was, at the time, a great deal of money; but, in comparison with what a war might have cost to extricate the French, the sum seems paltry. The credit for this diplomatic coup was attributable less to American negotiating skills (which were still raw) than to Napoleon's desire to rid himself of unprofitable colonies in the Americas. The leader of France had larger designs: the conquest of Europe.

The Napoleonic wars (1795–1815)—during which Napoleon attempted to subjugate all of Europe and Russia to his will—fell short, though, of a full blessing for America. While this nation benefited initially by selling the French and the British commercial goods, Americans soon learned the danger of standing in the cross fire. Relations with Britain soured rapidly, as the British engaged in the impressment (naval recruitment by force—kidnapping, in essence) of American merchant sailors to man their warships against France; and Britain in turn complained of attempts by American shippers to recruit British sailors for commercial manpower needs. In 1807, the British fired upon the *USS Chesapeake*, an American frigate, killing three crew members. Jefferson responded by persuading Congress to pass the Embargo Act, prohibiting the export of goods to Britain.

When Jefferson left the White House in 1809, Congress overturned the Embargo Act. The embargo had failed to work well, and New England legislators—whose constituents in particular depended upon foreign trade for their livelihood—railed against it bitterly on Jenkins Hill (as Capitol Hill was then called). The hostility toward England continued throughout most of the country outside the New England border, however, and the new administration of James Madison—backed by a group of ultranationalist "War Hawks" (as those who demanded war against Britain were called) from the south and the west—proved to be highly belligerent. Especially grating to this faction were British violations of the free seas, even though the practice of impressment had tapered off. For them, British attempts to rule the Atlantic represented an unbearable insult to American national honor. Moreover, southern and western farmers feared British interference with agricultural exports. "Embargoes, nonintercourse, and negotiations, are but illy [badly] calculated to secure our rights," toasted War Hawks at a Fourth of July celebration in Kentucky in 1811. "Let us now try old Roman policy, and maintain them with the sword."[3] Another, far less glorious war of independence against the British was about to begin.

Part of the motivation for this war was the future of Canada, where Britain maintained a troubling military presence. Just as the early Americans wanted Europeans out of the southern reaches of the continent, so they wanted them out of the northern reaches, too—especially because the British were using Canada as a supply depot from which to arm and encourage Indians in their attacks against the expansionist aspirations of American settlers moving into the northwest territory. Besides, how could one fight the British at sea without a navy? Better to take them on with infantry in Canada. The British, unfortunately, proved less ready to abandon the New World than Napoleon had been.

Which country to declare war against—Britain or, equally annoying, France—had become a subject that caused bitter debate between the two major political parties, the New England Federalists (pro-British) and the rural Jeffersonian Republicans (pro-French). In the end, Republican arguments carried the day. By 1811, France, it was true, had become as deserving an opponent as Britain. The French had marauded American ships at sea just as mercilessly. Their practice, however, was to steal the ships far away from U.S. waters, imprison the crews, and then sell the ships—all entirely outrageous, but at least the French avoided the indignation of impressment and did their dirty work at a more polite distance from America's shores. Further, Britain had actually been responsible for the murder of American citizens (aboard the *Chesapeake*) and, moreover, was an old foe; France, in contrast, had helped the Americans during the War of Independence. Since the United States had insufficient resources to fight both countries at once, Britain thus received the honors of a declaration of war, with impressment the first article.

The War of 1812 was an embarrassment—"the greatest disgrace ever dealt to American arms," concludes one scholar.[4] The war was untimely, and America ill prepared. As the historian Thomas A. Bailey has noted, "The War of 1812 was a rash departure from the judicious policy of Washington, Adams, and Jefferson—of playing for time and letting America's booming birthrate and Europe's recurrent distresses fight the nation's battles."[5] Congress failed to appropriate moneys to block the British siege against Washington, and in the middle of the war, legislators chose to adjourn for the summer holiday! Cabinet members elected to remain in their home states during these torrid summer months. The governor of Vermont ordered his militia to desert, Massachusetts sought a separate peace with the British, and the other states of New England denounced what they referred to as "Mr. Madison's war." President James Madison roamed the Virginia countryside on horseback, almost being captured by the British at one point, while Admiral Sir George Cockburn of the Royal Navy set torch to the Capitol and the White House.

Andrew Jackson's stunning victory over the British at New Orleans accounted for one of the few bright spots on the American side during the war, along with Admiral Oliver Hazard Perry's success in the battle of Lake Erie ("We have met the enemy and they are ours," he reported). The invasion of Canada was a disaster, as British and Canadian forces pushed back American infantrymen across the border.

At last, by Christmas Eve of 1814, both sides—war-weary, tax-burdened, bloodied—were ready to call it quits. British and American diplomats signed the *Treaty of Ghent*, which restored the *status quo ante bellum*, delicately sidestepping any mention of open seas or impressment. Fearful that the outcome could have been much worse, the American people were pleased with the terms of the treaty; indeed, in Bailey's words, it was "the most popular peace pact with a major power ever concluded by the United States."[6] With Europe still in a state of turmoil, the British were also anxious to end this troublesome diversion so they could focus on a more immediate danger that would reach a climax with the Battle of Waterloo, where Wellington defeated Napoleon in 1815. The concentration of British, Canadian, and American naval ships on the Great Lakes left a potentially explosive situation. In a historic arms control negotiation (aided immeasurably by the British preference for a return of its ships to the high seas), the nations consented in the *Rush-Bagot Agreement* of 1817 to scale down sharply the number of armed vessels in these North American waters.

This calamity behind them, Americans returned to the happier task of nation building. Still, the problem of Florida remained. Farmers in Georgia and Alabama relied upon the river system of southeastern North America as a means for shipping their goods to seaboard ports, from where they would then be shipped abroad. The Spanish, and the Indians they supported, were sometimes a hindrance to this commerce. President James Monroe and his able secretary of state, John Quincy Adams, vowed to break this lingering European toehold. General Andrew Jackson (the "Hero of New Orleans") was sent to Florida in 1817 for the purpose of protecting backwoods settlements against the Indians. Interpreting his mandate broadly, Jackson deposed the Spanish governor, placed suspected British spies before a firing squad, and proclaimed American legal jurisdiction over the entire territory. Evidently impressed by this display of bravado, a weakened Spanish government decided to abandon the Florida territory (following Napoleon's example in Louisiana). America and Spain entered into protracted negotiations and eventually signed the *Adams-Onís Treaty* (1819). This treaty required Spain to exchange the Florida territory in return for unfettered Spanish rule over Texas and the southwest—a poor bargain for the United States, argued critics at the time.

Monroe Delivers a Lecture

Spain felt more than just the heat of the fiery General Jackson. Revolt was rife throughout the Western Hemisphere, as one after another of the Spanish colonies sought independence. President Monroe took this opportunity to proclaim what has become the most famous of all declarations in the annals of American foreign policy: the *Monroe Doctrine*. Fearful that Spanish armies, backed by France, were about to crush the newly independent nations of Latin America, Monroe posted a warning for the Europeans. In his annual message to Congress in 1823, the president declared that the nations of the Western Hemisphere were "henceforth not to be considered as subjects for future colonization by any European power." (See Perspectives on American Foreign Policy 3.2.)

This seemingly rash stance against the mighty military powers of continental Europe (Chancellor Otto von Bismarck of Germany would later call the message an "international impertinence") was assisted substantially by the knowledge that Great Britain was fully in support of the American position. Indeed, British leaders had proposed a joint statement to this effect, but Adams advised Monroe that the United States should avoid being merely a "cockboat in the wake of the British man-of-war" and, instead, lead the way. Britain had

not been suddenly overcome by a benevolent sense of mission to champion independence among the American republics, but rather sought to block Franco-Spanish economic competition in these lucrative markets.

The message from Monroe—a "lecture" to Europe, observed Adams (it was not considered a "doctrine" until the 1850s)—amounted to a second declaration of American independence (or a third, if one wishes to count the feeble efforts of 1812). Monroe put the Europeans firmly on notice that America would resist further attempts by them to colonize the Western Hemisphere. He also signaled the nation's special interest in its neighbors to the south as future friends and allies. These two principles have remained linchpins in American foreign policy ever since, even if corroded somewhat by Soviet intervention in Cuba (following Fidel Castro's Marxist revolution of 1959) and by periodic rough intrusions by the United States itself into the internal affairs of Latin American nations. The third principle invoked in Monroe's message—a repudiation of U.S. involvement in European politics—has been discarded as a contemporary principle of American foreign policy; but, at the time, this policy represented a natural continuation of the isolationism heralded in Washington's Farewell Address.

In 1823, Monroe's "lecture" carried far less weight than it does today. Europe's designs on Latin America were weak to begin with. (The rumors of a Franco-Spanish invasion proved to be false.) Asia and Africa seemed to hold out more lucrative opportunities for the Europeans. Moreover, the Europeans were soon able to establish profitable trade relations with the nations of Latin America without the threat of military conquest. The great importance of Monroe's statement lay in its legacy for the future. Subsequent presidents would be able to invoke the Monroe Doctrine and enjoy the sustained popularity of its underlying principles, buoyed by its "aura of antiquity" and the prestige of Monroe's famous name.[7]

Perspectives on American Foreign Policy 3.2

The Monroe Doctrine, 1823. In a bold state of the union message to Congress, President James Monroe announced a policy that, at its core, proclaimed the Americas for the Americans. This country would oppose further European meddling in the Western Hemisphere—a brash statement for a still weak nation, but a proclamation that appealed strongly to American patriotism then and through the years.

. . . The occasion has been judged proper for asserting as a principle in which the rights and interests of the United States are involved, that the American continents, by the free and independent condition which they have assumed and maintain, are henceforth not to be considered as subjects for future colonization by any European powers. . . . The citizens of the United States cherish sentiments the most friendly in favor of the liberty and happiness of their fellow-men on that side of the Atlantic. In the wars of the European powers in matters relating to themselves we have never taken any part, nor does it comport with our policy so to do. It is only when our rights are invaded or seriously menaced that we resent injuries or make preparation for our defense. With the movements in this hemisphere we are, of necessity, more immediately connected. . . . The political system of the allied powers is essentially different in this respect from that of America. This difference proceeds from that which exists in their respective Governments. And to the defense of our own, which has been achieved by the loss of so much blood and treasure, and matured by the wisdom of their most enlightened citizens, and under which we have enjoyed unexampled felicity, this whole nation is devoted. We owe it, therefore, to candor, and to the amicable relations existing between the United States and those powers, to declare that we should consider any attempt on their part to extend their system to any portion of this hemisphere as dangerous to our peace and safety. With the existing colonies or dependencies of any European power we have not interfered and shall not interfere. But with the governments who have declared their independence and maintained it, and whose independence we have, on great consideration and on just principles, acknowledged, we could not view any interposition for the purpose of oppressing them, or controlling in any other manner their destiny, by any European power, in any other light than as the manifestation of an unfriendly disposition toward the United States. In the war between these new governments and Spain we declared our neutrality at the time of their recognition, and to this we have adhered and shall continue to adhere, provided no change shall occur which, in the judgment of the competent authorities of this Government, shall make a corresponding change on the part of the United States indispensable to their security.

. . . Our policy in regard to Europe, which was adopted at an early stage of the wars which have so long agitated that quarter of the globe, nevertheless remains the same, which is, not to interfere in the internal concerns of any of its powers; to consider the government de facto as the legitimate government for us; to cultivate friendly relations with it, and to preserve those relations by a frank, firm, and manly policy, meeting, in all instances, the just claims of every power, submitting to injuries from none. But in regard to these continents, circumstances are eminently and conspicuously different. It is impossible that the allied powers should extend their political system to any portion of either continent without endangering our peace and happiness; nor can anyone believe that our southern brethren, if left to themselves, would adopt it of their own accord. It is equally impossible, therefore, that we should behold such interposition, in any form, with indifference. . . .

Westward Ho!

As Monroe turned the nation's attention inward again, the interest in continental expansion renewed. American farmers and trappers saw enticing possibilities to the west. Merchants dreamed of harbors on the Pacific coast and sea-lanes to the markets of Asia. American leaders worried—in the spirit of Monroe—about revived European or Russian interest in the western, southern, or northern territories, and argued that the nation should settle these regions before potential enemies arrived there first. Some Americans simply believed that their country had a calling to spread the fruits of its democratic and religious beliefs. Besides, it was argued on a more practical note, America needed more room for a growing population.

In 1845, the newspaper editor John L. O'Sullivan gave a name to these expansionist urges. It was "our *manifest* [read self-evident] *destiny*," he wrote, "to overspread and to possess the whole of the continent which Providence has given us."[8] The popular phrase was quickly adopted by politicians and soon took its place in the history books. The advance toward the Pacific Ocean was under way. Americans imagined limitless possibilities for themselves and their new republic.

This hunger for expansion would cost Americans, and those who stood in their way, considerable bloodshed. Settlers massacred Indians (and sometimes had the favor returned), crowded them onto reservations, or drove them farther westward to face their unhappy fate at a later date. In 1846, American expansionists were prepared to take on Great Britain in a third war, as they rallied behind their leader and presidential candidate, James K. Polk, under the banner "54-40 or Fight!" They wanted the United States to claim all of the Pacific northwest, which reached to 54°40′ north latitude. The existing joint U.S.–British control of this region since 1818 was no longer acceptable to them. President Polk proved able to settle this dispute with the British peaceably, through a diplomatic compromise dividing the territory at the 49th parallel.

Expansionist aspirations had contributed to the war against Britain in 1812 and against the Spanish in Florida. Next the nation would declare war against Mexico in 1846, acquiring in a peace treaty of 1848 (the *Treaty of Guadalupe Hidalgo*) all of New Mexico and California as well as an extension of the Texas boundary to the Rio Grande.

Arrival at the waters of the Pacific Ocean did little to weaken passions for further expansion. The prospect of selling clothes and other goods to several hundred million Chinese consumers was (as it continues to be today) an inspiring vision to American entrepreneurs, from southern cotton growers to western fur trappers. In 1844, the United States sent an emissary to China in a successful effort to secure formal access to markets for American goods, as well as to establish the right of *extraterritoriality* (which would allow American citizens accused of crimes in China to be tried before an American consular official, rather than face unpredictable Chinese judicial procedures—sometimes including torture). In 1854, Commodore Matthew C. Perry steamed into the Bay of Yedo (now Tokyo) with an impressive armada of U.S. naval ships. He carried with him a letter of friendship from the president of the United States (Franklin Pierce) to the emperor of Japan. Before his departure from Asia, the resourceful Perry managed also to visit China and make further inroads against its long tradition of isolationism. From 1850 to 1860, America's trade with China rose steadily.

Commodore Perry, however, was not the only white face to appear in this part of the world at mid-century. America soon discovered that it would have to contend with European rivals in the Far East who were similarly driven by commercial aspirations.

Beyond improved trade relations, the United States had a further interest in the Far East as a place where American missionaries might convert heathens to Christianity. As President

William McKinley would put it at the end of the century (with the Philippines in mind), it was the American duty to "uplift and civilize and Christianize."[9] Both objectives required the nurturing of friendly ties with the reigning powers. The results were contradictory: in Europe, America's policy was isolation; in the Far East, involvement. "Americans did not feel that a vigorous and far-reaching policy in the Pacific contradicted their basic isolationist premise," remarks a foreign policy analyst, "even though great-power intrigue complicated their every move."[10]

North against South

The nation had more on its mind in the 1860s, however, than tea, spices, and missionary work. The "United" States stood on the brink of disintegration. Nothing since the War of Independence so turned the country inward, while at the same time dividing it, as the War between the States. Yet, even at this time of acute domestic peril, the nation's leaders could ill afford to ignore America's external affairs. Indeed, both sides in the war hoped to attract outside military support. Great Britain came close to forming an alliance with the Confederate states, the source of 80 percent of the cotton used in British textile mills. "We do not like slavery," said Prime Minister Palmerston, "but we want cotton. . . . "[11] But when the Union armies showed unexpected strength in stopping General Robert E. Lee at Antietam, the British had second thoughts regarding intervention. Fearful of another troublesome war with the Americans, Great Britain soon chose the more prudent course of neutrality.

France saw an opportunity in America's distraction with civil war. Thumbing their noses at the Monroe Doctrine, French troops invaded Mexico and went about the business of establishing a monarchy under the control of Napoleon III. The French emperor imported an Austrian archduke, Ferdinand Maximilian, to sit on the Mexican throne; and although the U.S. government registered its protests and wrung its hands, President Abraham Lincoln was in no position at the time to do anything about this insolence. Immediately after the Civil War, however, the United States sent strong warnings to Napoleon that the French were to pack their bags and depart Mexico, posthaste. These thinly veiled threats, backed by a now impressive military prowess recently demonstrated in the victory over the Confederacy, doubtless gave the French emperor pause. Other considerations may have been more compelling still: the unpopularity in Paris of the Mexican venture, its expense, Napoleon's concern over rising German militarism in Europe, and the steady harassment of French soldiers by roving bands of resolute Mexican guerrilla forces. Napoleon withdrew; and poor, handsome Maximilian (the "archdupe") soon found himself in front of a Mexican firing squad.

Though a low tide in the ebb and flow of America's involvement abroad, the Civil War era paradoxically had a strong influence on how other nations viewed this country's position in the world community. The impressive firepower displayed by the North and the South signaled to the world that the United States had truly arrived as a genuine military force in global affairs. And American insistence, immediately after the Civil War, on the removal of French troops in Mexico confirmed the nation's tenacious adherence to Monroe's principles of 1823. The United States seemed prepared, if necessary, to push the French from the Americas at the point of bayonets. From this moment on, until the Cuban missile crisis of 1962, no foreign power would seriously challenge the Monroe Doctrine.

EMERGENCE AS A GREAT POWER, 1865–1920

After the Civil War, the still young republic returned once again to the preoccupation of nation building. Secretary of State W. H. Seward, a zealous expansionist, purchased the Alaskan territory ("Seward's Icebox") from the Russians for $7.2 million—in retrospect a genuine bargain at some two cents an acre. Yet this renewed expansionism represented only one impulse in the country. Many Americans were weary of the outward surge, and the Congress voted down efforts to buy the Virgin Islands and to establish a protectorate over Haiti. Like previous generations, Americans in 1865 were of two minds about their proper role in the world. "The nation lunged into the future at breakneck speed," notes an authority, "but with constant nostalgic glances to the simpler past it was leaving behind"[12]—a persistent ambivalence that remains with Americans to the present.

In the latter part of the nineteenth century, the United States reached farther outward for territorial gains now and then and became more confident of its own national strength. American officials informed the British flatly in 1895 that the United States would be the one to settle a diplomatic dispute between Britain and Venezuela. Magisterially, Secretary of State Richard Olney told the British that "the United States is practically sovereign on this continent, and its fiat is law upon the subjects to which it confines its interposition." As the historian Gaddis Smith writes, "this blustering affirmation quickly became known as the 'the *Olney corollary*'—the first of many expansions and interpretations of the original [Monroe] Doctrine."[13]

For the most part, however, America returned to its traditional policy of nonentanglement. At the feet of its citizens lay a vast continent to tame and draw together with roads, rails, and waterways; factories had to be built and new farmlands cultivated. Yet, this luxury of introversion was about to come to an end. Steadfastly aloof from European intrigue, consumed by the challenge of nation building, spoiled by the bounty of broad and fruitful lands, Americans remained provincials, still unaware—and unwilling to recognize—how inextricably bound this nation's destiny was to the rest of the world. Events in the critical year of 1898 would thrust the naive and ill-prepared republic into the role of a global power.

The Spanish-American War

"There can be little question that the year 1898 is a landmark in the development of American foreign policy," observes the historian Dexter Perkins; ". . . roughly, it can be said that up to 1898 the United States looked inward; after 1898 she looked outward."[14] The immediate cause of this watershed was the Spanish-American War, catalyzed by U.S. sympathy for the Cuban and Philippine rebellions against heavy-handed Spanish rule. This sympathy grew in intensity as Spanish troops dealt brutally with the insurrections. In Cuba, men, women, and children were herded into concentration camps where tens of thousands perished. Nonetheless, President McKinley, a pacifist, hoped to avoid war and directed his energies toward a diplomatic settlement.

A mysterious explosion that sank the U.S. battleship *Maine* in Havana harbor on February 15, 1898, killing more than 250 sailors aboard, sank McKinley's diplomatic overtures as well. The American public demanded intervention, their passions inflamed by warmongering, sensational headlines flowing from an unrestrained competition between rival newspaper publishers Joseph Pulitzer and William Randolph Hearst. "Remember the *Maine*! To hell with Spain!" became a popular rallying cry in the rising crescendo of war frenzy.

Though Spain suddenly seemed eager for a diplomatic settlement, events had gone too far. Congress passed a joint resolution in April 1898, demanding Spanish withdrawal from Cuba. Within days, Admiral George Dewey reported that he had destroyed the Spanish navy at Manila Bay in the Philippines. This stunning naval victory whetted American appetites not just for Cuban independence, but for the liberation of all the Spanish colonies. After assisting Cuban rebels to free their island from Spanish rule, U.S. troops overran Puerto Rico as well. As the nineteenth century wound down, America added to its list of fresh possessions Hawaii, the Philippines, Guam, Wake Island, and part of Samoa.

American Imperialism

Ironically, a war to dissolve Spanish colonialism had created a new colonial power, the United States. Yet, notes the historian Foster Rhea Dulles, this robust American expansionism "... did not constitute so sharp a departure from the isolationist tradition as has often been assumed. For the United States made no commitments to foreign nations as it emerged upon the international scene; it entered upon no entangling alliances with other powers."[15] What had changed most dramatically was the rest of the world's realization that the United States was now a great power, with global interests and responsibilities. For these new American imperialists to have believed they could manage a far-flung empire, yet sustain their hoary aversion toward foreign entanglements, required a miraculous ability to suspend the critical faculty. Their hopeful attitude was born, no doubt, of an innocence regarding world affairs rarely seen in powerful nations. The Europeans must have found this innocence both quaint and astonishing. As American officials began increasingly to confront powerful rivals in the Far East, they would soon learn the harder realities of international politics.

Marxists find the American expansion southward into the Caribbean and westward across the Pacific simple to explain: capitalists in the United States were merely in search of cheap foreign labor and overseas markets. One can certainly find some evidence for this brand of economic determinism. China provides one illustration. Americans, like the Europeans and the Japanese, were drawn to China as a vast marketplace. Yet, at the turn of the century, Europe and Japan seemed on the verge of dismembering China, in the process quite possibly severely disrupting U.S. commercial access to the world's most populous nation. Spurred by this concern for America's economic interests, Secretary of State John Hay advocated in 1899 an *open-door policy* in China, whereby each major power would agree to honor the commercial ties of the other powers in their particular spheres of influence within China. With varying degrees of evasiveness, the other nations responded to Hay with some sympathy for his proposal. Nevertheless, the immediate result was little more than a unilateral proclamation of America's self-interest in keeping this lucrative market relatively open. It would take the *Boxer Rebellion* a year later to shake the Europeans into action.

The Boxers were zealous Chinese xenophobes—terrorists, in today's lexicon—intent on ridding their country of foreigners. Their approach was straightforward: murder them all. Hay proposed that the United States and the Europeans agree to work toward defusing the Boxer Rebellion by assuring the Chinese of their territorial integrity. This compromise—along with the presence of European and American soldiers in China—helped calm the unrest, and the major European powers tacitly agreed to honor America's open-door policy. This settlement had an unfortunate upshot: the Japanese were angered by what they viewed as an interference in *their* sphere of influence. As the twentieth century began, John Hay had thus sown the seeds of bitterness toward the United States that would contribute to the Japanese decision favoring an attack against Pearl Harbor in 1941.

Some of America's interest in the Philippines was clearly motivated, too, by economic considerations. The U.S. business community had become persuaded that a presence in these islands would improve access to the Chinese market. As Foster Rhea Dulles relates, "the Philippines seemed to offer the United States an opportunity to secure a foothold in eastern Asia that would counteract these developments [foreign attempts to close China] by establishing a strategic base for American commercial operations in China."[16]

An overemphasis on economic matters, though, misses the influence of other forces propelling U.S. expansionism. Much of the interest in opposing the Spanish empire came from a genuine concern for the plight of human beings suffering under a tyrannical rule—the strain of idealism in American foreign policy.

As the United States found itself spread across the globe at the beginning of this century, interest also grew in the construction of a canal connecting the Atlantic and Pacific oceans. The idea seized the imagination of an extraordinary individual well suited for this season of further expansion: President Theodore Roosevelt, horseback hero of the Spanish-American War in Cuba. The President sided with insurgents in a civil war inside Colombia, which held title over a territorial expanse where Roosevelt wished to build the canal. When the insurgents gained control of this land, a new country—Panama—was established, one more favorably disposed toward the idea of Roosevelt's waterway than Colombia had been.

With construction of the Panama Canal under way, Roosevelt grew increasingly anxious that unrest and revolution in Latin America might disrupt shipping through his waterway, or tempt European powers to intervene in regional skirmishes for the protection of their economic interests. He therefore issued, in 1904, what would become known as the *Roosevelt corollary to the Monroe Doctrine*. Henceforth, the United States would not only continue to look upon European intervention in the Western Hemisphere with sharp disfavor, but would also take it upon itself to police the nations of Latin America. In Roosevelt's words: "Chronic wrongdoing, or an impotence which results in a general loosening of the ties of civilized society, may in America, as elsewhere, ultimately require intervention by some civilized nation, and in the Western Hemisphere the adherence of the United States to the Monroe Doctrine may force the United States, however reluctantly, in

flagrant cases of such wrongdoing or impotence, to the exercise of an international police power."

The president was fond of a West African proverb: "Speak softly and carry a big stick; you will go far." Here was *big-stick diplomacy* at its zenith. Roosevelt's pronouncement would provide the rationale for some thirty U.S. military interventions in South America over the next few decades. Several of these interventions (especially while Roosevelt's successor, William Howard Taft, was in office) were motivated by what critics would label *dollar diplomacy*, unbridled support from the government of the United States for American corporate interests in Latin America and elsewhere overseas.

Wilsonian Idealism

The next great figure in the annals of American foreign policy, the scholarly President Woodrow Wilson, was far less militant than Roosevelt, though, ironically, under his leadership the United States would enter into global warfare. An accomplished professor of political science and former president of Princeton University, Wilson was a thinker and a dreamer. He dreamed above all of world peace and labored diligently toward the goal of keeping the United States out of a brewing European conflict. Reverting to the basic instincts that had guided this nation throughout most of its history, the public wanted nothing to do with Continental intrigues. Isolationism—turning back the clock to a happier, more peaceful time—once again became the prevailing mood. But just as the sinking of the *Maine* had sparked anti-Spanish sentiment throughout the United States in 1898, the torpedoing by a German submarine of the British liner *Lusitania* in 1915 (with 128 Americans among the 1198 passengers killed) inflamed anti-German feelings.

Wilson remained optimistic, nonetheless, that diplomacy could still stem the growing war, and he continued to seek avenues for a negotiated peace. Following his reelection in November 1916 ("He kept us out of war," said the Democratic Convention keynote speaker, the former New York governor Henry Glynn, to thunderous applause from the delegates), Wilson stepped up his efforts to bring about a diplomatic settlement. An idealist, he proposed before Congress on January 22, 1917, "peace without victory" and called for a new "league of nations." He then sent a hopeful message to the Germans offering his help toward reaching a settlement that would reestablish the status quo ante, begin disarmament talks, and create a league.

The German response came within days: Berlin proclaimed unrestricted submarine warfare against every ship, including passenger liners, that entered the Atlantic war zone—American or otherwise. Here was the affront that thrust America into war, despite its longing for continued neutrality. Added to this insult was the Zimmermann message, secretly sent from the German foreign secretary, Herr Zimmermann, to his minister in Mexico. Intercepted by British intelligence and passed on to Washington, this communiqué ordered the German minister to seek a pact of aggression with Mexico against the United States, should the Americans enter the war against Germany; Mexico was to be promised the return of Texas, New Mexico, and Arizona. The American press printed the story, which seemed to stir up almost as much anti-German sentiment as Berlin's declaration of open season on U.S. shipping.

All this effrontery was too much even for the peace-loving Wilson, and he severed diplomatic ties with Berlin. "We shall fight . . . for the rights and liberties of small nations," Wilson told Congress in April 1917, and 2 million American servicemen went overseas to help tip the scales against the Kaiser. The war would be fought, in Wilson's words, to make the world "safe for democracy"—a global Monroe Doctrine. The German armies proved no match for the combined strength of the Allied powers, and the Kaiser was forced to abdicate. On November 11, 1918,

the First World War, which sent 6 million young men to the coldness of premature graves (including 116,516 Americans), came to an end. Wilson now turned to the task of preventing future wars through his *League of Nations* proposal, the capstone of his "Fourteen Points" peace initiative (see Perspectives on American Foreign Policy 3.3).

The Fourteen Points were a noble declaration of self-determination for all nations, a principle that remains dear to the American people. Unfortunately for Wilson and other idealists, however, the president had to contend with his own Senate and with the major powers of Europe. Key senators were clearly hostile toward the idea of a league of nations, and European leaders remained skeptical—notably the hardboiled realist Clemenceau of France. "God gave us his Ten Commandments and we broke them," he said. "Wilson gave us his Fourteen Points—we shall see."[17]

Undaunted, President Wilson sailed for Europe, the first American president to visit the Old World. The brilliant British economist John Maynard Keynes offered this elegant, if damning, observation on his contemporaries who gathered in Paris to negotiate the *Treaty of Versailles* and its provision for a league of nations. "These were the personalities of Paris—I forbear to mention other nations or lesser men: Clemenceau, aesthetically the noblest; the President [Wilson], morally the most admirable; Lloyd George [the British prime minister], intellectually the subtlest. Out of their disparities and weaknesses the Treaty was born, child of the least worthy attributes of each of its parents, without nobility, without morality, without intellect."[18]

In Paris, Wilson was forced to barter away most of his Fourteen Points in exchange for his beloved league of nations. When the president returned home, he found strong Senate opposition to the Versailles Treaty. The Republican leader and chairman of the Foreign Relations Committee, Henry Cabot Lodge (Massachusetts), disliked Wilson intensely on a personal

---

Perspectives on American Foreign Policy 3.3

Wilson's Fourteen Points, *January 8, 1918. In a speech before Congress, President Woodrow Wilson announced his plan for the peace to follow World War I. The Fourteen Points, especially Number 14, represented what Wilson called "the moral climax of this . . . final war for human liberty."*

1. Abolition of secret diplomacy

2. Freedom to navigate the high seas in peace and war

3. Removal of economic barriers among the nations

4. Reduction of armaments

5. Adjustment of colonial claims in the interest of both the inhabitants and the powers concerned

6. Restoration of Russia and a welcome for her in the society of nations

7. The return of Belgium to her people

8. Evacuation and restoration of French territory, including Alsace-Lorraine, taken by the Germans in 1871

9. Readjustment of Italian frontiers "along clearly recognizable lines of nationality"

10. Free opportunity for "autonomous development" for the peoples of Austria-Hungary

11. Restoration of the Balkan nations and free access to the sea for Serbia

12. Protection for minorities in Turkey

13. An independent Poland

14. "A general association [the League] of nations" to secure "mutual guarantees of political independence and territorial integrity to great and small states alike"

This summary is drawn from Thomas A. Bailey, *A Diplomatic History of the American People*, 9th ed. (Englewood Cliffs, N.J.: Prentice-Hall, 1974), p. 598.

---

level and was unwilling to support his league proposal, its merits notwithstanding. Lodge managed to stall the treaty in his committee for almost two months while he organized broader opposition. During this period, Wilson attempted to sell the idea of the League of Nations to Americans through an exhausting series of speeches across the country that ultimately broke the president's health. In the Senate, Lodge succeeded in so encrusting the treaty with reservations that Wilson himself chose to withdraw his support. The Senate rejected the treaty, as altered by Lodge.

America would not be a member of the League of Nations. Moreover, in the presidential election of 1920, the voters threw out the Democrats, who continued to support the concept. The voters turned to the Republican Warren G. Harding, handsome and vacuous, who promised a restoration of "normalcy." When Wilson first returned from Europe, the American public seemed to support his proposal for the League. Prodded by Lodge and the Republicans, however, an isolationist resurgence—a return to the vision of Washington, Jefferson, and Monroe—eventually carried the day.

AMERICA AS A RELUCTANT LEADER, 1920–

At this juncture in its history, though, the United States was finding it more and more difficult to retreat from the world. Wilson's quest for a league of nations had failed, but he did succeed in making the American people more aware of the necessity to address threats and opportunities beyond this nation's borders. The traditional attitude of ambivalence toward foreign commitments remained strong, but nevertheless, Wilson and the horrors of the world war had made Americans more concerned about the preservation of international peace.

In the spirit of Woodrow Wilson, American diplomats in 1922 convened a remarkably successful disarmament conference in Washington. They also assisted directly in the negotiations of war reparations and, in 1928, signed the *Kellogg-Briand Treaty* (or *Pact*) renouncing war "as an instrument of national policy." Yet the United States carefully avoided permanent, institutionalized arrangements with other nations. The goal of U.S. policymakers was to make the world a more secure and peaceful place so that Americans could be left alone—a dash of Wilsonianism in the isolationist stew.

This tentative reaching out to other nations was brought short by the Great Depression, a period of severe unemployment and financial chaos that began in 1929 with the crash of the American stock market. These domestic problems focused attention inward as much as ever before. Still, despite this renewed introspection, the United States did take the time in the aftermath of World War I to change its policies toward Latin America. President Herbert Hoover overturned the Roosevelt corollary to the Monroe Doctrine by declaring, in 1930, that nothing in the doctrine justified U.S. intervention in the internal affairs of its southern neighbors—a view the Soviet Union may have found inviting thirty-two years later when it placed missiles in Cuba.

His successor, Franklin D. Roosevelt, honored this view and withdrew all American troops south of the Rio Grande, with the exception of those stationed in the Panama Canal Zone. Following his inauguration in 1933, this Roosevelt spoke not of the Monroe Doctrine

(which many South Americans had begun to equate with Yankee imperialism), but of a *"good-neighbor"* policy. Most of the president's energies, though, remained directed toward his New Deal programs for economic recovery, with a wary eye on the totalitarian regimes beginning to amass arms in Germany, Italy, and Japan.

The Fascist Threat

Japan was the first to display an alarming militancy, invading Manchuria in 1931 and Shanghai the next year. The unchecked Japanese aggression demonstrated the feebleness of the League of Nations and further added to the sense of futility about involvement in international affairs—though critics of America's retreat from global responsibilities following World War I argued that if the United States had been a member of the League, Japanese aggression would have been less likely or at least dealt with swiftly through a collective military response. Instead, the Western democracies did nothing. So much for the Kellogg-Briand peace declarations.

By 1937, Japan had launched a full-scale invasion of China, its primary objective. Early signs of belligerency were evident in Europe as well. Italy's Mussolini invaded Ethiopia in 1936, and the next year he joined with Hitler to create the Rome-Berlin Axis under a fascist banner. Japan soon united with the European dictators in a formal alliance.

Still the United States stayed aloof. Already having been drawn into one global war by the Europeans, most Americans were determined to avoid a second, with all the loss of blood and treasure that another major conflict would entail. This country certainly did not like what was happening abroad, but Americans liked even less the idea of their own involvement in costly combat. Nor were Great Britain and France prepared to stop the Axis powers, even when Hitler marched his troops into Austria. In the view of most Americans, the Europeans and the Chinese would have to solve their own problems.

The clearest test of Britain's intentions came when Hitler's appetite for conquest turned toward Czechoslovakia. In 1938, he demanded that Czech officials turn over control of the Sudetenland, where a majority of the people were of German descent. With seven divisions massed on the Czech border, Hitler seemed prepared to invade his neighbor if this demand went unmet. Prime Minister Neville Chamberlain of Great Britain, desperate to maintain peace in Europe, believed that a policy of *appeasement*—giving in to Hitler's demands in an attempt to curb his appetite—would prevent the outbreak of a war that would engulf all of Europe. He met in Munich with Hitler, Mussolini, and Premier Daladier of France and signed a formal agreement to dismember the once-sovereign state of Czechoslovakia and hand over the Sudetenland to Hitler, all in exchange for a German promise not to invade Czechoslovakia. In a famous, soon tragic photograph published in British newspapers upon Chamberlain's return to London, the prime minister is shown descending the stairs from his airplane, umbrella in one hand, and in his other hand, held aloft, the four-power agreement. Chamberlain's face beamed with satisfaction. He had staved off the dictators. Europe would have, he announced proudly, "peace in our time."

Within six months, Hitler gobbled up the rest of Czechoslovakia by force of arms and thus revealed the true meaning of the agreement: it was a worthless scrap of paper. In the historian Bailey's felicitous phrase, Munich had proven to be "merely surrender on the installment plan."[19] The word *Munich* became forever synonymous with *appeasement* and the futility of trying to satiate fanatics by giving in to their demands—in short, "a lack of backbone in foreign affairs."[20]

A surprising pact of nonaggression signed by Hitler and the Russians, a people widely popular in the United States at the time (1939), left

Speaking at Heston Aerodrome in London, Prime Minister Chamberlain proudly holds a copy of the "No More War" Pact that he and Hitler had signed in Munich. (UPI/Bettmann Newsphotos)

Hitler free next to invade Poland—with a secret promise to turn over the eastern half of Polish territory to the Russians. On September 1, 1939, German panzer tanks crushed the brave Polish resistance, whose soldiers rode into battle on horseback. Two days later, the British and the French honored their defense pact with Poland and declared war on the Nazis. World War II had begun.

As these events took place in Europe, isolationist opinion continued to run high in the United States. President Roosevelt routinely announced American neutrality, and citizens across the land gathered around their radios with growing concern for the bleak news coming from the rest of the world. Reports of a brutal persecution of Jews in Germany brought forth protests from the Roosevelt administration, but no action. The Department of State said that its hands were tied; this was an internal German problem. Americans believed, or at any rate hoped, that the armies of Britain and France would now leash the German and Italian dogs of war.

This illusion was quickly shattered. France fell before the blitzkrieg in early 1940, and in May and June, Nazi troops ran British forces off the continent in a desperate evacuation at Dunkirk. His ambition swollen now by a sense of invincibility, Hitler brazenly opened a surprise second front in 1941 against his erstwhile ally, Russia. At last, Americans began to awaken to the possibility that the United States might appear on Hitler's wish list, too. President Roosevelt sensed this shift in attitudes and moved, slowly at first, to aid the beleaguered British. "We must be the great arsenal of democracy," he declared as 1940 came to a close; the United States would support the Allies "by all means short of war." The president traded fifty warships to the British in exchange for base rights in Bermuda and other locations in the Atlantic, and he pushed through Congress—over the steadfast objections of hardcore isolationists—a lend-lease bill to provide weapons cost-free to Britain. Neutrality was abandoned.

Senator Arthur H. Vandenberg (R-Mich.), leader of the isolationists, noted in his diary that this new direction amounted to suicide for the republic. "This is what I believe is the result," he wrote. "We have torn up 150 years of traditional foreign policy. We have tossed Washington's Farewell Address into the discard. We have thrown ourselves squarely into the power politics and power wars of Europe, Asia and Africa. We have taken the first step upon a course from which we can never hereafter retreat."[21]

While the Roosevelt administration was now prepared to support the antifascist cause, American citizens remained unwilling to enter the fray directly (though Roosevelt did introduce conscription in 1940, again over strong criticism from isolationists in Congress). This attitude would change dramatically on December 7, 1941, a day that in Roosevelt's famous words would "live in infamy." In a treacherous surprise attack on a Sunday morning, the Japanese struck the U.S. Pacific fleet at Pearl Har-bor, destroying seven battleships, crippling airplanes on the runways, and inflicting over 3000 casualties. American insistence that the Japanese withdraw from China, coupled with a U.S. ban against the sale of aviation fuel and scrap metal to Japan, had been perceived by the Japanese as an intolerable blow to their national pride and imperialist ambitions in the Far East.

Even the staunchest isolationists in the United States were now ready to fight. "The only thing now to do is lick hell out of them," declared Senator Burton K. Wheeler (R-Mont.), a leading voice among the isolationists.[22]

Over the next four years, this is precisely what the Allies did, joined by the Russians, who were now also fighting for their survival against Hitler. This combined military might was too much for the fascists. Italy capitulated first in 1943, then Germany in 1945, followed later in the year by Japan. With the closing of the war, the nuclear age had arrived and with it a realization that all nations could one day face the terror that fell without warning from the skies over Hiroshima and Nagasaki.

Internationalism Embraced—Gingerly

The horror of the Second World War, with Europe, Russia, and Japan smoldering in ruins and their graveyards filled by the corpses of some 60 million people, made even more poignant than the First World War the importance of global cooperation. Wilsonianism was resuscitated in the form of the *United Nations Charter*, signed in San Francisco in July 1945 by representatives from most of the nations in the world—"the boldest experiment in international organization yet adopted by man."[23] (See Appendix.) From the beginning, the UN was badly flawed by an inability to establish a workable international police force to halt military aggression by wayward nations; nonetheless, hopes remained high among idealists that this step toward global cooperation would vindicate Wilson and lead to a lasting peace.

The euphoria of international accord proved

short-lived. Subsequent chapters in this volume address in detail the politics and events of foreign policy in the turbulent postwar era, but it should be noted here that within a brief interval—some would say no interval at all—the United States and the Soviet Union entered into a protracted "cold war."[24] Although the American people maintained an affection for the Russian people in 1945, it became increasingly clear that their leader, Joseph Stalin, was as treacherous as Hitler and might well have designs of his own for world domination over the Western capitalist nations. Certainly his behavior toward the states on his borders (notably new Soviet "satellites" in eastern Europe and Mongolia) was aggressive, and his rhetoric toward the West was frequently hostile.

Winston Churchill, the British prime minister who had replaced Chamberlain and guided his country through the war with inspiring leadership, spoke of the new Soviet danger in a renowned speech delivered in 1946 at Westminster College in Fulton, Missouri. "From Stettin in the Baltic to Trieste in the Adriatic, an *iron curtain* has descended across the continent," he warned (emphasis added). "Behind that line lie all the capitals of the ancient states of Central and Eastern Europe. Warsaw, Berlin, Prague, Vienna, Budapest, Belgrade, Bucharest and Sofia, all these former cities and the populations around them lie in the Soviet sphere and all are subject in one form or another, not only to Soviet influence, but a very high and increasing measure of control from Moscow."

More than anything else, this domination of the Soviets over their neighbors aroused the American public to the disquieting possibilities of a fresh threat from abroad. Alarming, too, was the fall of China—half a billion people—to communist revolutionaries in 1949. The power of military force again seemed to be the prime mover in world affairs, not lofty principles and international organizations.

The stage was set for what would become the primary preoccupation of American foreign policy in the modern era: the competition for world influence between the United States and the communist nations—a conflict of basic philosophies. During the nineteenth century, relations between America and Russia had been cordial for the most part, though contact between the leaders of the two nations had always been infrequent. With the beginning of the twentieth century and the Bolshevik revolution (1917–1920), contact became more common but, at the same time, relations soon cooled at high government levels—even though the American people continued to express warm sentiments toward the Russian people, according to opinion polls conducted during the 1930s and early 1940s.[25]

Then, in the aftermath of World War II, the bonds of friendship that still existed between Russian and American leaders snapped altogether and, from Harry S Truman forward, every American president would place the Soviet Union at the top of his list of national security threats to the United States. Every president would have a confrontation of one kind or another with the communist nations. Not until 1972, under the leadership of President Nixon and his secretary of state, Dr. Kissinger, did a genuine thaw in the cold war begin (labeled *détente*, another French diplomatic term, meaning the relaxation of tensions between nations). This era of increased cordiality would last only a few years, however, unraveled in part by Nixon's fall from office over the Watergate scandal (1974).

Presidents Ford and Carter attempted, now and then, to rekindle the sparks of *détente* during their tenures, notably through arms control negotiations; but on the whole, superpower relations remained strained—especially when the Soviet Union invaded Afghanistan in December 1979, triggering a U.S. trade and Olympic boycott against the Soviet Union. Unpredictably, ironically, the arch-conservative President Ronald Reagan—whose anti-Soviet rhetoric had been the most strident of any president— would be the one to venture a major reversal of U.S.–Soviet relations. In 1988, he proclaimed that the Soviet Union was no longer an "evil empire," as he had originally maintained in 1983.

Perhaps President Reagan had become increasingly concerned about his historical legacy as his two terms in the White House came to an end. "The polls were showing Reagan's only vulnerability," reported one correspondent, "as lying in his bottomless hostility to the other superpower."[26] Whatever his motivation, Reagan was now prepared to enter into major arms control and other agreements with the Soviet Union, beginning with the Intermediate Nuclear Force (INF) Treaty of 1988 (examined in Chapter 10). Moreover, the American president seemed genuinely to like his Soviet counterpart, Mikhail S. Gorbachev. For many observers, the cold war appeared to be—if not over—at least thawing at a more rapid rate than ever before.

While East-West relations remained the primary preoccupation of the United States during the postwar period, the "north-south axis" of world affairs grew in importance. Accompanying the cold war as a dominant feature of international relations since 1945 has been the blossoming of new nations in the developing world, lying to the south of the established industrial nations. (This region is often called—

with a misleading lack of differentiation that is a common defect of all overarching labels—the Third World, or its poorest countries the Fourth World, with the Western industrialized nations and the Soviet bloc, respectively, the First and Second Worlds.) The dismantling of the old colonial empires has led to the creation of over a hundred new nations, most of them without wealth and searching for better military and economic security, their people often resentful of the creature comforts and life expectancy enjoyed by citizens in the industrialized societies. This "revolution of rising expectations" has been accelerated by television and other forms of modern communications technology that reveal vividly to those who are poor the bounty of the rich nations. From the south have come demands on the north for, among other things, a "new international economic order" designed to redistribute some of the global wealth to the poorer nations.

The response of the United States to these twin challenges of cold war and global inequities is a central focus in Part II of this book. The next step in Part I is to examine in greater depth the most significant historical forces that have shaped America's external affairs since the end of the Second World War.

SUMMARY

American foreign policy over the years has been like a roller-coaster ride, from occasional heady peaks of intervention abroad to quick rushes down into the longer stretches of isolationism. Though often ambivalent about which part of the ride has been best for the United States, Americans have felt more secure for the most part when distanced from the rest of the world—though never to the point of eschewing profitable commercial relations or useful assistance in times of military danger. As one essayist has put it: "Detachment—or, at the most,

rare moments of engagement—is America's natural state."[27]

Looking back on this nation's experience governing the Philippines, which the United States granted independence in 1946 chiefly because its administration had become a bother, the American diplomat and scholar George F. Kennan has similarly concluded, "the ruling of distant peoples is not our dish. . . . There are many things we Americans should beware of, and among them is the acceptance of any sort of a paternalistic responsibility to anyone, be it even in the form of military occupation, if we can possibly avoid it, or for any period longer than is absolutely necessary."[28]

Regardless of what might be America's "natural state," the United States since 1945 has maintained a comparatively high level of international involvement. Americans continue to feel ambivalent about this state of affairs. A report by the Chicago Council on Foreign Affairs, based on its 1983 opinion survey, noted that "only a bare majority of the public now holds the opinion that . . . international activism is best for the future of the country while over a third now say it would be better if the United States 'stayed out' of world affairs."[29] In 1986, a comparable poll indicated that supporters of "international activism" had risen in the United States to 71 percent, though more detailed follow-up questions on whether this nation ought to intervene with military power in trouble spots like Central America and the Middle East revealed little support among the public.[30]

Yet, however tempting on occasion, a plunge back into isolationism has been an option most Americans believe their nation can no longer afford—at least not the withdrawal displayed by the United States after World War I (despite the internationalist urgings of President Wilson). America is now one of the world's two superpowers, like it or not, and the noncommunist nations look toward America for leadership. How, and how well, the United States has gone about providing that leadership is what this book is about.

KEY TERMS

rapprochement
Jay Treaty
XYZ affair
Treaty of Ghent
Rush-Bagot Agreement
Adams-Onís Treaty
Monroe Doctrine
manifest destiny
Treaty of Guadalupe Hidalgo
extraterritoriality
Olney corollary
open-door policy
Boxer Rebellion

Roosevelt corollary
big-stick diplomacy
dollar diplomacy
League of Nations
Fourteen Points
Treaty of Versailles
Kellogg-Briand Treaty (or Pact)
good-neighbor policy
appeasement
United Nations
iron curtain
détente

NOTES

1. Nancy L. Hoepli, *A Cartoon History of United States Foreign Policy* (New York: Morrow, 1975), p. 1.

2. "The Barbary Wars," *Smithsonian*, January 1975, p. 91.

3. Thomas A. Bailey, *A Diplomatic History of the American People*, 9th ed. (Englewood Cliffs, N.J.: Prentice-Hall, 1974), p. 137.

4. James Sterling Young, *The Washington Community: 1800–1828* (New York: Columbia University Press, 1966), p. 184.

5. *Op. cit.*, p. 145.

6. *Ibid.*, p. 157.

7. The phrase is from Bailey, *op. cit.*, p. 189. For a recent evocation of the Monroe Doctrine by

the Reagan administration, see Stuart Taylor, Jr., "Washington Revival of Monroe Doctrine Gets Mixed Reviews," *New York Times*, November 13, 1984.

8. Cited by Richard N. Current, Alexander De-Conde, and Harris L. Dante, *United States History* (New York: Scott, Foresman, 1967), p. 234.

9. Quoted by Frances FitzGerald, "Reflections: Foreign Policy," *New Yorker*, November 11, 1985, p. 112.

10. Charles O. Lerche, Jr., *America in World Affairs* (New York: McGraw-Hill, 1963), p. 36.

11. Quoted in Hoepli, *op. cit.*, p. 27.

12. Lerche, *op. cit.*, p. 38.

13. "The Legacy of Monroe's Doctrine," *New York Times Magazine*, September 9, 1984, p. 46; emphasis added.

14. *The Evolution of American Foreign Policy* (New York: Oxford University Press, 1948), p. 58.

15. Foster Rhea Dulles, *America's Rise to World Power: 1898–1954* (New York: Harper & Row, 1954), p. 58.

16. *Ibid.*, p. 47.

17. W. A. White, *Woodrow Wilson* (Boston, 1929), p. 384, quoted in Bailey, *op. cit.*, p. 608.

18. *Essays and Sketches in Biography* (New York: Meridian, 1956), p. 180.

19. *Op. cit.*, p. 708.

20. Peter McGrath, "The Lessons of Munich," *Newsweek*, October 3, 1988, p. 37.

21. Arthur H. Vandenberg, Jr., and J. A. Morris, eds., *The Private Papers of Senator Vandenberg* (Boston, 1952), p. 10, cited in Dulles, *op. cit.*, p. 198.

22. Quoted by Bailey, *op. cit.*, p. 740.

23. *Ibid.*, p. 771.

24. On the roots of U.S.–Soviet hostility, see the balanced analysis by John Lewis Gaddis, *The United States and the Origins of the Cold War* (New York: Columbia University Press, 1972).

25. Cited in *ibid*.

26. John Newhouse, "Annals of Diplomacy: The Abolitionist," *New Yorker*, January 2, 1989, p. 51.

27. Philip L. Geyelin, "The Adams Doctrine and the Dream of Disengagement," in Sanford J. Ungar, ed., *Estrangement: America and the World* (New York: Oxford University Press, 1985), p. 197.

28. *American Diplomacy: 1900–1950* (Chicago: University of Chicago Press, 1951), p. 19.

29. Cited in Geyelin, *op. cit.*, p. 203.

30. See John E. Rielly, "America's State of Mind," *Foreign Policy*, vol. 66, Spring 1987, pp. 48, 51.

RECOMMENDED READINGS

Bailey, Thomas A. *A Diplomatic History of the American People*, 9th ed. (Englewood Cliffs, N.J.: Prentice-Hall, 1974). A classic, highly readable, and comprehensive study on the history of American foreign policy.

Barber, Hollis W. *Foreign Policies of the United States* (New York: Dryden, 1953). Another very readable survey of how American foreign policy has unfolded over the years, with a useful emphasis on key documents punctuating this evolution.

Dulles, Foster Rhea. *America's Rise to World Power: 1898–1954* (New York: Harper & Row, 1954). A valuable interpretive study of the tension between American instincts for expansionism and isolationism, with interesting photographs.

Hamby, Alonzo L. *The Imperial Years: The U.S. Since 1939* (New York: Weybright and Talley, 1976). This study by a noted Truman scholar provides clear insights into the cold war era.

Hoepli, Nancy L. *A Cartoon History of United States Foreign Policy: 1776–1976* (New York: Morrow, 1976). A fascinating portrayal of American foreign policy through the eyes of newspaper and magazine illustrators, accompanied by a succinct history in prose.

Kennan, George F. *American Diplomacy: 1900–1950* (Chicago: University of Chicago Press, 1951). America's most famous diplomat examines the Spanish-American War, the open-door policy, the world wars, and U.S.–Soviet relations.

Lerche, Charles O., Jr. *America in World Affairs* (New York: McGraw-Hill, 1963). A brief overview of American foreign policy, with an excellent capsule summary of its history.

Paterson, Thomas G. *Major Problems in American Foreign Policy*, 3d ed., Vol. I: to 1914; Vol. II: since 1914 (Boston: Heath, 1989). An excellent collection of essays and documents covering the span of America's external relations.

Perkins, Dexter. *The Evolution of American Foreign Policy* (New York: Oxford University Press, 1948). A gracefully written, succinct history by one of the country's premier historians.

Pratt, Julius W. *A History of United States Foreign Policy*, 2d ed. (New York: Prentice-Hall, 1965). A highly regarded, comprehensive treatment.

Ungar, Sanford J., ed. *Estrangement: America and the World* (New York: Oxford University Press, 1985). A collection of essays by several distinguished analysts of U.S. foreign policy, focusing on the traditional American mood of withdrawal from the world.

THE NUCLEAR AGE

    Containment and the Cold War

    A New Militancy

PERIL POINTS

    The Korean War

    Crises over Cuba

    Vietnam

DÉTENTE

    A Thawing in the Cold War

    Fresh Conflicts

    The Cold War Revisited

A BALANCE SHEET

SUMMARY

4

THE CONTEMPORARY SETTING

U.S. intelligence photo of a Soviet medium-range ballistic-missile site in Cuba, October 1962.

THE NUCLEAR AGE

Four events have been especially important in defining international politics since 1945: the invention of nuclear weapons with massive destructive force; the emergence of the United States as a world power; the growing confrontation between America and the Soviet Union as leaders of two armed and hostile camps, East and West—the condition known as the cold war; and the fragmentation of the globe into some 180 nation-states, as the old colonial empires disintegrated. None of these developments has made the world an easier place to live for Americans; on the contrary, foreign affairs have never been more difficult and dangerous—if only because humanity now has the capability of self-extinction, should its nuclear weapons ever be used in anger. (Highlights of U.S. foreign policy since World War II are listed in Figure 4.1.)

Containment and the Cold War

These events are tied one to another, and at their center churns the cold war. As the political scientist John Mueller has put it: "The predominant characteristic of international affairs over the last 40 years has been competition and confrontation between the United States and the Soviet Union."[1]

The U.S.–Soviet alliance against the Axis powers during the Second World War quickly unraveled once the war ended. The United States lost no time in demobilizing its troops and returning to a traditional posture of semi-isolation from world affairs. Despite its rhetorical embrace of the United Nations in 1945 and its willingness to have the UN headquarters located in New York City, the United States showed little inclination to remain deeply involved overseas—an attitude it would soon be forced to abandon.

The preoccupation of Soviet leaders during the immediate postwar period was to consolidate their control over eastern Europe and

FIGURE 4.1 Highlights in the evolution of American foreign policy during the nuclear age.

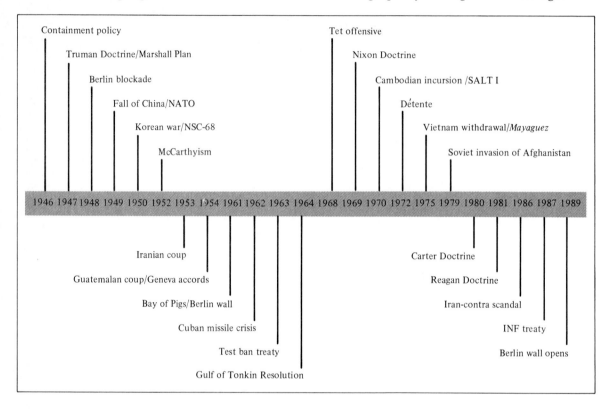

Mongolia by converting these once-free lands into satellites. Because Russia had been attacked too often in the past by armies from Europe, and because the loss of 20 million soldiers in the Second World War was fresh in mind, the Soviet leadership no doubt viewed this consolidation as a vital step to provide a buffer against future external threats. For western Europeans and Americans, however, this projection of Soviet power represented a dangerous turn in world affairs.

The entrenchment of the Red Army in eastern Europe, along with the uncivil behavior of the Soviet dictator Joseph Stalin and the string of agreements that he broke in succession, signaled to the West that an erstwhile friend might have become a foreboding adversary. Troubling, too, was the harsh Marxist-Leninist rhetoric coming out of Moscow. Among his many anti-Western statements, Stalin declared that the Second World War had been the inevitable result of "the capitalist system of world economy [that harbors] elements of general crisis and military clashes."[2] Nor was the peppery American president, Harry S Truman, in a conciliatory mood. "I do not think we should play compromise any longer," he told his secretary of state; ". . . I'm tired of babying the Soviets."[3]

As David S. McLellan notes in his history of this period, "Within six months after the war's end all pretense at friendship was being dropped. Henceforth each side would interpret all moves as basically hostile and therefore would act accordingly. The Cold War had begun."[4] This rude thump of reality compelled the United States to poke its head out from under its shell and face a new leadership role. No other country in the West could stand up to the

Soviets. Britain and the Continental powers had been wrecked by the war, their far-flung empires in a state of financial ruin, their armies exhausted.

Soon to be one of the most influential voices in this recognition of America's new place in the world was a U.S. diplomat stationed in Moscow, George F. Kennan, author of the now-famous containment doctrine. The doctrine took shape initially in a long cable Kennan sent to the Department of State in 1946 on the subject of Soviet motivations in external relations, but its outlines were first made public in an article he wrote anonymously for the journal *Foreign Affairs* a year later. "At the bottom of the Kremlin's neurotic view of world affairs," wrote Kennan (aged forty-three at the time) under the pseudonym "X," "is the traditional and instinctive Russian sense of insecurity. . . . " He warned that Soviet power "is a fluid stream which moves constantly, wherever it is permitted to move, toward a given goal. Its main concern is to make sure that it has filled every nook and cranny available to it in the basin of world power." To counter Soviet aggressiveness, Kennan recommended "a long-term, patient but firm and vigilant containment of Russian expansive tendencies." In a commemorative issue on the fortieth anniversary of the containment doctrine, the editor of *Foreign Affairs* looked back on the Kennan article as a hallmark of "the final collapse of nostalgia for prewar isolationism."[5]

This strategy of patience and firmness—with what soon became an emphasis on the latter—was most evident in the proclamation of the Truman Doctrine in March of 1947. Great Britain decided early in the year to withdraw its military and economic support for Greece and Turkey; the United States quickly moved to fill this power vacuum before the Soviets had a chance to fill it themselves. On top of this assistance to Greece and Turkey, the United States further provided billions of dollars of economic aid to other European countries, offered under the umbrella of the *Marshall Plan* (known more formally as the European Recovery Program, or ERP). Named after Secretary of State George C. Marshall, who had served with distinction as army chief of staff during World War II, this program of economic assistance was designed to make the limping economies of Europe sturdy and resistant to communist influence.

In his announcement of the Greek-Turkish aid package, Truman's ringing declaration that "it must be the policy of the United States to support free peoples who are resisting attempted subjugation by armed minorities or outside pressures" seemed to promise an expansion of American commitments far beyond Greece and Turkey. As the historian John Lewis Gaddis notes, the president's statement implied "a world-wide commitment to resist Soviet expansionism wherever it appeared."[6] This, at any rate, was the general perception. In reality, the Truman administration remained ambivalent about the extent to which the United States should shore up the perimeter around the Soviet Union. While the President's proclamation seemed to have no bounds, Secretary Dean Acheson (who had been the primary author of the Marshall Plan proposal while serving under Secretary Marshall, whom he succeeded as Secretary of State in 1949) explained to the Senate a week later that the Greek-Turkish aid carried no precedent for future policy. Subsequent needs would be examined individually, based on "whether the country in question really needs assistance, whether its request is consistent with American foreign policy, whether the request for assistance is sincere, and whether assistance by the United States would be effective in meeting the problems of that country."[7]

Some of the confusion over the proper direction of American foreign policy during this period stemmed from a misinterpretation of *Kennan's views on containment*. He advocated neither the use of military force to contain communism (except as a final recourse) nor resistance to communism everywhere in the world. In the first instance, he believed that one could successfully employ political, economic, and, especially, psychological pressure on the Soviets. Indeed, as Gaddis notes, "the very purpose of 'containment' had been to change the *psychology* of the Soviet leadership."[8] Toward this objective, Kennan urged the United States to align itself with the strongest of all anticommunist forces on the face of the globe: nationalism.

In the second instance, not all parts of the world were of equal importance to the United States. For Kennan, the freedom of western Europe and Japan—the great industrial centers—was crucial to America's own security. If the weapons production capabilities of these nations were to fall into the hands of an adversary, this could be disastrous for the United States. America, however, could not guarantee the protection of every region in the world. Financially, this nation could not afford such a universal approach. As Kennan put it, practically every leader around the globe would show up on America's doorstep "with his palm out and saying, 'We have some communists—now come across.'. . . That obviously won't work."[9]

The pursuit of U.S. foreign policy objectives in the aftermath of the Second World War reduced to two central questions: first, the appropriate means of implementation—military force, diplomacy, secret operations, and the like—and, second, the selection of geographic regions where these powers should be employed. For Kennan, the United States was better off emphasizing nonmilitary resistance to Soviet expansionist aspirations and carefully selecting limited regions of the world considered vital where Americans could concentrate their resistance. In his view, the Soviet challenge was basically political and concentrated in Europe. George Kennan, though, was but one man and here were great issues that could lead to differences of opinion. Increasingly Truman, Acheson, and others began to see the Soviet threat in even more ominous terms than Kennan: as essentially military in nature and global in scope.

A New Militancy

Further complicating this debate was the ongoing ambivalent attitude of Americans toward the role of the United States in world affairs. Like a mule placed equidistant between two bales of hay, undecided which way to turn, this nation continued to feel the tug of the isolationists, on the one hand, who wished to retreat once again from the entanglement of external relations, and individuals like Kennan and Churchill, on the other hand, who argued for U.S. global leadership against the new threat to world peace presented by the Soviet Union. Thickening the plot further still, another important group desired U.S. global leadership, too, but dedicated to the establishment of a single world government—not a fresh round of hostility and danger promised by a cold war with the Soviets.

Senator Robert A. Taft led the isolationists, and Secretary of the Department of Commerce (and former Vice President) Henry Wallace led the much smaller group of *one-worlders*. Though miles apart on most issues, these two camps both looked upon the prospects of a cold war with dismay. For Taft, it meant a continuation of twin evils: a large, spendthrift federal government to direct the cold war, and a further drain on American resources by foreigners. (Among the allies of the United States during the First World War, only Finland had fully paid its debts.) "Don't be Santa Claus!" was a popular slogan among the isolationists. And for Wallace, the cold war meant a continuation of nation-state rivalries that could lead to another global conflict. At every opportunity, he criticized Truman's new "get tough on the Russians" policy, overlooking the fact that he was secretary of commerce, not state, and that Harry Truman was his boss. Truman finally asked for his resignation and, in 1948, Wallace ran against his former boss for the presidency on the Progressive Party ticket.

Taft and Wallace, however, represented minority opinions. Most Americans seemed to support the idea of containment—especially after the Truman administration began to present its case for economic assistance to Turkey, Greece, and western Europe in stark cold war terms: the world had to choose between the United States and the Soviet Union, between freedom and enslavement.

President Truman (and his successors) carried the concept of containment far beyond what Kennan had originally espoused. The careful nuances in Kennan's State Department cable and *Foreign Affairs* article lost their refinement in the hands of high-level strategists who viewed his epistle as a convenient point of departure for a philosophy of military response against communism wherever it raised its ugly head. Truman and secretary of state Acheson resolved their ambivalence by abandoning the fine points that Acheson had briefly argued before Congress. "By presenting aid to Greece and Turkey in terms of an ideological conflict between two ways of life, Washington officials encouraged a simplistic view of the Cold War which was, in time, to imprison American diplomacy in an ideological straitjacket almost as confining as that which restricted Soviet foreign policy," writes Gaddis. "Trapped in their own rhetoric, leaders of the United States found it difficult to respond to the conciliatory gestures which emanated from the Kremlin following Stalin's death and, through their inflexibility, may well have contributed to the perpetuation of the Cold War."[10]

The sense of trust in the Russian people expressed by the American public in opinion polls before and during the Second World War declined precipitously in the postwar period. On the eve of the Japanese surrender, 54 percent of the respondents to a national public opinion poll indicated a willingness to trust the Russians in international affairs. Two months later, the figure had dropped to 44 percent; by the end of February 1946, it had plummeted further to 35 percent.[11]

The communist takeover in Czechoslovakia (1948), the Berlin blockade (1948) and other confrontations in this divided city, the fall of China to communists (1949), the successful Soviet test of a nuclear bomb (1949), and—the critical turning point—the war in Korea (1950–1953) would convert most of the isolationists (if not all the one-worlders) toward a cold war perspective on world affairs and an embrace of Truman's, rather than Kennan's, view of the Soviet threat. The red-baiting at the height of the McCarthy era (1952–1954), when Senator Joseph McCarthy (R-Wis.) made a national reputation by blaming (with flimsy evidence) the nation's foreign policy woes on unnamed phantom communists engaged in treason within the federal government, had a further stifling effect on those who might have questioned the militant form the containment doctrine had assumed. The unfair tactics of smear and innuendo used by the Wisconsin senator to charge his opponents with communist leanings resulted in a new word in American politics: *McCarthyism*.

By 1950, the Truman administration was prepared to state, in its most important decision document on national security (the top-secret National Security Council Paper No. 68, or simply *NSC-68*), that "the assault on free institutions is worldwide now, and in the context of the present polarization of power a defeat of free institutions *anywhere* is a defeat everywhere."[12] In response to the outbreak of communist aggression in Korea, lost was Kennan's sense of restraint; if necessary, the cold war would be fought across each longitude and latitude that measured out the globe. All communist powers, regardless how weak their allegiance to Moscow, were declared enemies of the United States.

The Eisenhower administration preached the same gospel, only with more fire and brimstone. "As there is no weapon too small, no arena too remote, to be ignored, there is no free nation too humble to be forgotten," declared Truman's successor, President Eisenhower.[13]

And his secretary of state, John Foster Dulles, a champion practitioner of inflamed rhetoric against the communists (unrivaled until the Reagan administration three decades later), warned that "already one-third of the world is dominated by an imperialist brand of communism; already the free world has been so shrunk that no further substantial parts of it can be lost without danger to the whole that remains."[14]

Neither the Truman nor the Eisenhower administration carried out its pronouncements to the point of staging war against every Soviet military move. Despite some blustering, Truman took no military action to assist Czechoslovakia in 1948. Both administrations poured forth buckets of heated verbiage threatening to "unleash" the Nationalist Chinese leader Chiang Kai-shek from his island fortress of Formosa (Taiwan) against the communists on the mainland (from whence he had been routed in 1949); but words are easier to speak than deeds to perform, and the two Chinas remained apart, staring sullenly across the Formosa Strait and firing verbal volleys and sometimes even artillery shells at one another.

Dulles often spoke with passion, too, about the "liberation" of the Soviet satellites, though,

as Gaddis points out, this posturing was motivated "more by determination to lure East European voting blocs [like the vocal colonies of Estonian exiles in New York City and Los Angeles] away from the Democrats than from any realistic expectations of 'rolling back' Moscow's sphere of influence."[15] Certainly the United States did little to assist the anticommunist uprisings in East Berlin (1953) or in Hungary (1956). Nevertheless, the escalation in rhetoric was accompanied by something more than mere shadowboxing. As Perspectives on American Foreign Policy 4.1 indicates, the Eisenhower administration was advised at the highest levels to take off its gloves in this struggle against the communists, and it did: with the vigorous use of the CIA to topple regimes in Iran and Guatemala (in 1953 and 1954, respectively), and with the dispatch of American combat troops to quell unrest and discourage Soviet intervention in Lebanon (1958).

PERIL POINTS

The most significant early response by the United States to the perceived Soviet threat was

---

Perspectives on American Foreign Policy   4.1

Top-Secret Recommendation of the General James Doolittle Committee, Hoover Commission, 1954.

It is now clear that we are facing an implacable enemy whose avowed objective is world domination by whatever means at whatever cost. There are no rules in such a game. Hitherto acceptable norms of human conduct do not apply. If the U.S. is to survive, long-standing American concepts of "fair play" must be reconsidered. We must develop effective espionage and counterespionage services.

We must learn to subvert, sabotage and destroy our enemies by more clever, more sophisticated and more effective methods than those used against us. It may become necessary that the American people will be made acquainted with, understand and support this fundamentally repugnant philosophy.

"Foreign and Military Intelligence," *Final Report of the Senate Select Committee on Intelligence* (the Church Committee), April 26, 1976, p. 9.

the establishment of a collective Western defense. The *Berlin blockade* implemented by the Soviets in 1948, and defeated by a dramatic U.S.–led airlift of food and other goods to the people of Berlin, clearly signaled that the U.S.S.R. was prepared to take extreme measures against the West. Reluctantly and against historical instincts, U.S. officials turned to a policy of remilitarization, first strengthening the European economy with the infusion of billions of dollars of economic aid provided through the Marshall Plan. America's business titans, sniffing profits in a healthy European market and aware as well of the need to bolster Europe's strength against the anticapitalists of the Soviet bloc, joined behind the Marshall Plan with unaccustomed support for the federal government. As McLellan notes, "The isolationists like Robert Taft and [former Republican President] Herbert Hoover and extreme laissez-faire opponents of foreign 'give-aways' were hopelessly outnumbered."[16]

Economic strength, though, was insufficient. Secretary of State Acheson, among others, was convinced that the only sure way to prevent Soviet encroachments into western Europe was to place a barrier of American military might before the Kremlin leaders. In the words of his biographer: ". . . Acheson believed that a workable American deterrence to Soviet seizure of western Europe depended upon the emplacement of American ground forces and the American strategic bomber wings as close to the Soviet industrial heartland as strategy would permit."[17]

In 1949, the United States joined with Canada and western Europe in the creation of America's first peacetime military alliance since the early days of the republic. Called the *North Atlantic Treaty Organization (NATO)*, this pact committed the United States to the placement of soldiers in Europe on a permanent basis. NATO would provide the muscle to protect the economic recovery in Europe. The Soviet Union responded in kind by forming the *Warsaw Pact*, comprising the nations of eastern Europe.

The Korean War

The most extreme outward probes by the Soviets came not in Europe, however, but first in Asia (Korea) and then in America's own backyard (Cuba). In 1948, elections were held in Korea, as a means for ending the military occupation and restoring self-rule to the Koreans. South of the 38th parallel on the peninsula (the American zone of occupation), the United Nations supervised an open election and Syngman Rhee was duly elected president of the "Republic of Korea"; however, in the Soviet zone north of the 38th parallel, UN officials found themselves barred from observing "elections" that put into power in this region the communist "Democratic People's Republic of Korea." The Western hopes for a free and democratic all-Korean government were dashed; in the place of one government stood two, each claiming authority over all of Korea—the government in the north clearly a Soviet satellite, the government in the south recognized by the UN. Two years later, in June 1950, the Soviet- and Chinese-backed army of the "People's Republic" suddenly advanced southward across all points of the demarcation line. An invasion was under way.

Though geographically distant from the shores of the United States, Korea represented a possible stepping-stone toward Japan for the communists and, moreover, had taken on added importance in light of the Truman and Eisenhower pronouncements that no nation was too remote in America's struggle against communist expansion.

McLellan accurately sums up the reasons why the United States decided to enter into this war, so far away, to help a country that under Syngman Rhee never had (and, to this day, never has) practiced democracy: "The Korean aggression was immediately interpreted in the light of Britain's experience at Munich. Dictators' appetites grow with eating and if allowed to get away with one aggression, they will be encouraged to perpetrate another. The integrity of America's pledge to defend its European allies would be judged by the resolution with which it acted to stem aggression in Korea. And it was felt that the strategical balance already shaken by the loss of China would be irretrievably upset should the United States fail to respond."[18] The strategist Thomas Schelling states the case even more succinctly: "We lost 30,000 dead [in the Korean war]... *to save face*... and it was undoubtedly worth it."[19]

The United States believed, in a word, that it needed to demonstrate determination. If it failed to take a stand against communist aggression, the West would be without leadership and the communist nations could march relentlessly forward, from one vulnerable nation to another, toppling each domino as they went. The memory of Neville Chamberlain's failed efforts to appease Hitler lingered ominously as a historical analogy—and remains today a powerful argument against those who would retreat in the face of aggression. The importance of the Korean war lay in the opportunity it afforded for a display of Western—chiefly American—resolve. The ensuing war—fought for almost three years, to a stalemate—was unpopular at home but had the tangible effect of forcing the communists to retreat back behind the 38th parallel bisecting Korea. The Western nations had demonstrated to the communist dictators that they would not be a pushover.

The war proved, too, that armed conflict between the superpowers could be kept limited, without an inexorable escalation to a third world war. A new school of thought arose on how to fight limited wars (*low-intensity warfare*, in the currently fashionable phrase). This approach to combat captured the imagination of the Kennedy administration, which developed a strategy of *flexible response* to replace Eisenhower's reliance on nuclear weapons to deter the Soviets by the threat of global war (a doctrine called *massive retaliation*). The Kennedy concept of flexible response emphasized preparation for limited war through the development of war-fighting capabilities below the level of nuclear weapons. As in Korea, America might be forced to join battle against the communists in other remote regions of the world, from the jungles of Asia and Africa to the deserts of the Middle East. The United States had to be prepared, according to this doctrine, to fight at every level of warfare, from guerrilla insurgencies to all-out nuclear war.

Crises over Cuba

As part of its flexible response to global challenges, the Kennedy administration established the "Green Berets," or Special Forces within the military—elite teams of highly trained personnel able to wage tactical warfare in virtually any part of the world. The administration also strengthened other nontraditional responses to Moscow-sponsored guerrilla insurgencies, including a reinforced CIA capability for paramilitary operations (PM)—secret warfare—and other covert actions.

Among the paramilitary operations carried out during the Kennedy years was the ill-fated attempt in 1961 to overthrow the regime of Fidel Castro in Cuba by landing a group of CIA-backed Cuban exiles on the beaches of the *Bay of Pigs*.[20] In theory, the people of Cuba were to have greeted these liberators with open arms and joined them in counterrevolution; in reality, however, most Cubans remained loyal to Castro, whose soldiers easily defeated the expeditionary force. The CIA-backed Cuban exiles had expected military air cover from the United States Air Force during the operation, if it became necessary, but the Kennedy administration rejected this overt use of force at the eleventh hour when the invasion began to falter. The administration decided that it did not wish to have its role in the war acknowledged publicly, for fear that world opinion might turn against the United States for bullying a small island neighbor.

The new range of military capabilities provided by the doctrine of flexible response placed the United States in a better position to respond to military situations around the globe, without escalating precipitously to the level of nuclear warfare. These capabilities would soon be put to use in America's longest and most tragic foreign conflict, the war in Vietnam.

First, though, the Kennedy administration faced a deepening hostility in U.S.–Soviet relations. On August 13, 1961, the Soviet-backed East German regime erected the *Berlin wall* to stop the flow of its citizens to the west in search of freedom and economic well-being. The Berlin wall stood as the most conspicuous symbol of the cold war. Then, in the next year, President Kennedy was forced into what some consider the nation's most perilous confrontation during the cold war: the *Cuban missile crisis* of 1962.

In 1957, the Soviets had lifted into space on the back of a powerful rocket a satellite (*Sputnik*) about the size of a basketball. This feat demonstrated impressive scientific advances in the field of rocketry, with all the implications that carried for a Soviet capacity to reach the United States with ICBMs carrying nuclear payloads. The long-range-missile race was on between the superpowers. Panicked, America poured enormous resources into its space and missile programs and tried to improve the teaching of the basic sciences in its schools. The effort paid off, and the United States soon moved ahead of the Soviets in the number and accuracy of its long-range (strategic) missiles.

In hopes of offsetting the American advantage (and to help Fidel Castro—his new Marxist ally in the Western Hemisphere—ward off renewed U.S. pressures), Soviet Premier Nikita Khrushchev attempted in October of 1962 to place *medium-range ballistic missiles* (*MRBMs*) on Cuban soil—less than 100 miles off the coast of Florida. Once operational, these missiles had the capability to strike with nuclear warheads any U.S. city east of the Mississippi River— hardly a happy prospect for President Kennedy to contemplate. Air cover for the Bay of Pigs operation in 1961 may have begun to look like a better idea now, but it was too late. Kennedy

and the United States at this point faced a dangerous confrontation with the Soviet Union. The chances of a third world war suddenly became more real than ever before.[21]

The president quickly convened a group to advise him on a course of action. Called the *Executive Committee* (or *Ex Comm*), the panel was made up of key officials from the departments of state and defense and from the CIA (now back in Kennedy's good graces after his short-lived pique following the Bay of Pigs debacle). A few other trusted individuals were also invited to attend the Ex Comm meetings, including the president's brother, Attorney General Robert Kennedy. The initial recommendation to the president—strongly supported by the military representatives and eloquently argued by former Secretary of State Dean Acheson (who was brought in out of retirement to lend his long experience to the crisis)—was to stage an air strike against the sites where the missiles were being installed. The majority of the civilians on the Ex Comm expressed reluctance, though, to employ this drastic option as a first step. Inevitably, Soviet troops and technicians would have been killed in an air strike, perhaps pushing the two superpowers directly to an all-out war. Moreover, argued Robert Kennedy, a military attack would be viewed as reprehensible in the eyes of world opinion: a ham-handed Uncle Sam delivering a crushing blow to a small Third World nation.[22]

Still, the threat posed to the United States by the Soviet missiles made a so-called surgical air strike (as if a bombing could be carried out with the precision of a surgeon's scalpel) an option that might have to be used—and soon. Fortunately, the reader may recall, fresh intelligence gave the president some breathing space to consider other possibilities: detailed photographs from U-2 reconnaissance aircraft revealed that the missiles would not be ready for launching ("operational") until about ten days later. The Ex Comm stepped up its search for additional options.

Some advisers, including Secretary of Defense Robert S. McNamara, argued that no response was necessary, because Americans already lived under the shadow of Soviet strategic missiles and a few more in Cuba did not change things that much; besides, the United States had encircled the Soviet Union with comparable missiles in Turkey and elsewhere and expected the U.S.S.R. to accept that condition. Others argued for a diplomatic settlement, perhaps swapping the Soviet missiles in Cuba for the American missiles in Turkey, or convincing Castro that he must either throw the Soviets out or else face a U.S. invasion. Some Ex Comm participants were ready to fight: a second Bay of Pigs invasion, only this time using the Marine Corps with the full support of the Air Force. "Go in there and take Cuba away from Castro," argued one short-fused committee member.[23]

As the days quickly passed, the Ex Comm and the president moved toward a decision that combined a show of strength and determination with a measure of prudence. The United States would establish a "quarantine" around Cuba to keep out further shipments of Soviet missiles. President Kennedy "consulted" with Congress (which amounted to telling key legislators a few hours in advance that the naval blockade was going into effect, like it or not), and, on October 22, informed the American people of the crisis over television. "The 1930s taught us a clear lesson," he said, evoking the memory of Munich. "Aggressive conduct, if allowed to go unchecked and unchallenged, ultimately leads to war."

The question now was whether the Soviets would turn back their missile-laden freighters or perhaps use their submarines, carrying nuclear weapons, to punch a hole through the blockade. It was High Noon. McNamara and Secretary of State Dean Rusk recall wondering if they would see the sunrise of a new day. Some Washington bureaucrats sent their families out of the capital and began to construct underground bomb shelters in their backyards.[24]

Then, on October 28, happy news came out of Moscow: Khrushchev would turn back all the freighters and dismantle the missiles under construction in Cuba. "We're eyeball to eyeball—and the other fellow just blinked," commented Rusk privately at the time. (This remark, unfortunately, was picked up by the press—a risky further humiliation to Khrushchev, who was already backed into a corner and would soon be deposed by opponents within the Politburo.) The superpowers had drawn back from the brink.

Vietnam

Albeit the most dramatic, Cuba was only one peril point for the United States in the developing world during the early 1960s. A more costly confrontation with the communists took place in Vietnam, a land most Americans had never heard of until their sons began to die there.

With its leadership in the Korean war, the United States had underwritten in blood a determination to respond to communist aggression in the Far East—though clearly this policy had its limits, as illustrated by the confrontation between President Truman and his top military commander in Asia. The imperious General Douglas MacArthur publicly advocated during the Korean war that the United States carry the conflict onto mainland China, striking at the roots of the communist aggression. Despite Truman's orders to drop the idea, MacArthur continued to speak out in favor of escalation. Incensed at this insubordination, Truman fired the brilliant but incorrigible general. Truman and his civilian—and most of his military—advisers were concerned that a direct attack against Communist China, which at that time was allied militarily with the Soviet Union, might precipitate a global war. A year after the Korean stalemate, events in Indochina would again test how far the United States was prepared to go in the pursuit of its policy of containment through military means.

In 1954, the French army suffered a humiliating defeat in its attempt to maintain colonial rule over Vietnam against indigenous communist revolutionaries operating out of the region which is now the country of Laos. The Vietnamese communists, under the leadership of Ho Chi Minh (pronounced "Ho Chee MIN"), sought to expel the French and unite all of Vietnam under their rule. After months of fierce jungle combat, the communists surrounded the French forces at *Dien Bien Phu*, a city in northern Vietnam. The Eisenhower administration refused a request from the government of France to provide its desperate soldiers with air cover from American aircraft carriers and, if necessary, ground troops—perhaps even the use of an atomic bomb. Despite his aggressive "domino theory" remarks (recall Perspectives on American Foreign Policy 2.2, in Chapter 2), President Eisenhower was reluctant to enter this war. In one of those rare occurrences for a modern American president, Eisenhower asked for and, more extraordinary still, actually followed the advice of senior members of Congress on a foreign policy issue. The legislators counseled that U.S. involvement in the Vietnam conflict would be ill-advised, especially since America's other European allies (other than France) appeared unwilling to join in the effort.[25]

American officials peered into this swampland and drew back—though the chairman of the Joint Chiefs of Staff, among others, urged the president to charge ahead. In the next decade, the United States would take the fatal plunge. In between times, diplomatic negotiations in Switzerland produced the *Geneva accords* of 1954. Vietnam was "temporarily" divided at the 17th parallel and general elections were scheduled for Vietnam in 1956. Instead, as in Korea, civil war broke out between the communists concentrated in the north and the anticommunists in the south. Within two months following the Geneva negotiations, the Eisenhower administration established the *Southeast Asia Treaty Organization*, or SEATO, along with several other formal alliances around the world (which led some critics to

charge Secretary of State John Foster Dulles with "pactomania"). The purpose of SEATO and similar alliances was to shore up the defenses against further communist expansion in Indochina and elsewhere.

In the period of transition between Eisenhower's reluctance to enter Indochina and Johnson's pell-mell escalation in 1965 came the Kennedy administration. Though the young Kennedy was viewed by some Americans as a vibrant new voice offering a departure from the cold war rhetoric of the Eisenhower-Dulles years, his worldview was little different from that of the Republican administration he had succeeded (note the language from his inaugural address in Perspectives on American Foreign Policy 4.2).

Though more restrained in his public rhetoric than John Foster Dulles, President Kennedy was—if anything—often tougher in his responses to the communists than Eisenhower and Dulles had been. The Kennedy administration approved and implemented the Bay of Pigs operation (though it had been planned during the Eisenhower years) and took the world to the nuclear brink during the missile crisis. Moreover, it was during the Kennedy administration that the attempts to assassinate Fidel Castro and Patrice Lumumba were carried out—though the record remains unclear whether the president himself actually authorized these murder plots (see Chapter 9).

This toughness of the Kennedy administration stemmed, in part, from the pressure of circumstances: Khrushchev's rash move to place nuclear missiles in the Western Hemisphere took place during Kennedy's watch, not Eisenhower's. But the toughness was also evidently an attempt on behalf of the inexperienced president to compensate for his sense of political and personal insecurity. Kennedy had barely won the presidency in 1960, and he no doubt realized that he brought little foreign policy experience or expertise to the job. He backed the Bay of Pigs scheme, according to one authoritative study, because he was afraid

Perspectives on American Foreign Policy   4.2

Inaugural address of President John F. Kennedy, January 20, 1961. The handsome young president sported liberal credentials as a former U.S. senator from Massachusetts. This address, however, reveals that his foreign policy represented a continuation of America's militant commitment to the doctrine of containment.

. . . I have sworn before you and Almighty God the same solemn oath our forebears prescribed nearly a century and three quarters ago.

The world is very different now. For man holds in his mortal hands the power to abolish all forms of human poverty and all forms of human life. And yet the same revolutionary beliefs for which our forebears fought are still at issue around the globe—the belief that the rights of man come not from the generosity of the state, but from the hand of God.

We dare not forget today that we are the heirs of that first revolution. Let the word go forth from this time and place, to friend and foe alike, that the torch has been passed to a new generation of Americans—born in this century, tempered by war, disciplined by a hard and bitter peace, proud of our ancient heritage—and unwilling to witness or permit the slow undoing of those human rights to which this Nation has always been committed, and to which we are committed today at home and around the world.

Let every nation know, whether it wishes us well or ill, that we shall pay any price, bear any burden, meet any hardship, support any friend, oppose any foe, in order to assure the survival and the success of liberty. . . .

---

he would be labeled "chicken" by the Republican Party if he refused, which could lead to "nasty" political repercussions—a "who lost Cuba" controversy like the "who lost China" debate that harmed the Democratic Party during the Truman years.[26]

During campaigns for the presidency in the postwar period, the conservative wing of the Republican Party has frequently leveled a "soft-on-communism" charge against the Democrats, beginning with criticism over the fall of Chiang Kai-shek in China, continuing with the reversals in Korea during the Truman administration, and reaching a fever pitch throughout the witch-hunts of the McCarthy era. Kennedy (and subsequently Johnson) hoped to avoid this accusation, along with all the other political shrapnel that vocal right-wingers in the GOP were capable of exploding; the Democrats would prove they were as *macho* as the Repub-

licans in combating communism. (Virtually every postwar administration has alloyed its anticommunism, however, with some attempts at U.S.–Soviet cooperation; in 1963, for example, President Kennedy signed with the Soviets an important *nuclear test ban treaty*, forcing nuclear weapons tests to be conducted underground and thereby removing harmful radioactive materials from the earth's atmosphere—not much of a curb on the arms race, as it turned out, but certainly a significant health and environmental achievement.)

When SEATO members began to feel the strains of communist insurgencies in southeast Asia during the Kennedy years, the president—true to his inaugural address (see Perspectives on American Foreign Policy 4.2)—responded to the challenge by bolstering the American military presence in that part of the world. In a display of toughness, he raised the ante. The historian Arthur M. Schlesinger, Jr., reports that President Kennedy told one of his advisers: "... Eisenhower could stand the political consequences of Dien Bien Phu and the expulsion of the west from Vietnam in 1954 because the blame fell on the French." In the President's words: "I can't take a 1954 defeat today."[27] A member of the President's brain trust, Walt W. Rostow, recalls: "Kennedy said that if we walked away from Southeast Asia, the Communist takeover would produce a debate greater than the loss of China to Communism."[28]

At Kennedy's direction, U.S. military advisers in South Vietnam expanded their role, occasionally flying sorties against the Vietcong (South Vietnamese communists allied with the North) and returning ground fire on patrol throughout South Vietnam. By 1963, the Kennedy administration found itself deeply involved in the political machinations of internal South Vietnamese politics, even seeming to condone a military coup against President Ngo Dinh Diem, who was eventually murdered (along with his brother) by South Vietnamese generals. Fewer than 700 U.S. military advisers were stationed in South Vietnam when John Kennedy entered the White House; at the time of his death in 1963, the figure had swollen to some 16,500. His successor, Lyndon Baines Johnson, would increase the number to over 72,000 by the spring of 1965. The United States had grabbed hold of the civil war in Vietnam and, like a tar baby, the war refused to let go. America's intervention in Indochina would become, for President Johnson, a Bay of Pigs in slow motion.[29]

Lyndon B. Johnson came into office as a highly experienced legislator, having served as majority leader in the Senate before assuming the vice presidency in the Kennedy administration. His interests and orientation were essentially domestic; his dream: to rebuild the decaying cities of America and establish a "Great Society" founded on a life of justice and well-being for all citizens. In place of this aspiration, he soon found himself consumed by events in Vietnam. Here was the tragedy of President Johnson: that he was so well prepared to advance his Great Society programs on Capitol Hill, yet so dragged down by a distant war that increasingly robbed him of resources, personal energy, and, most important, his standing with the electorate. "The Great Society has been shot down on the battlefield of Vietnam," lamented the civil rights leader Dr. Martin Luther King, Jr.

Congress precipitously passed the Gulf of Tonkin Resolution in August of 1964 (a foreign policy decision of great significance examined in detail in Chapter 5). President Johnson interpreted this resolution as a legislative blank check for him to protect U.S. military advisers in Vietnam and ships in the South China Sea. He began an escalation of the war in Vietnam, both in rhetoric and—more important—in the number of troops sent to the battlefield. What was at first supposed to be a limited operation designed to protect U.S. advisers soon became, in the president's speeches, a fundamental test of America's national will to thwart global communist expansion. The 72,000 American troops sent to South Vietnam by Johnson in the spring of 1965 were joined by 128,000 more before the end of the year.

Johnson alternated between threatening Ho Chi Minh with military power ("America wins the wars it undertakes. Make no mistake about it.") and trying to woo him with pork-barrel promises—a technique he had refined to a high art in Congress as majority leader. In a speech delivered at Johns Hopkins University during the war, the president promised a TVA for North Vietnam—patterned after the Tennessee Valley Authority project sponsored by the federal government in the 1940s that had done so much to revitalize the economies of Tennessee and surrounding states. (President Truman, too, had once dreamed of "TVAs in the Euphrates Valley to restore that country to the fertility and beauty of ancient times; of a TVA in the Yangtze Valley and the Danube."[30]) An adviser to Johnson, Bill Moyers, once noted: "If Ho [Chi Minh] had been George Meany [the

---

Perspectives on American Foreign Policy   4.3

Letter from presidential adviser Clark M. Clifford to President Lyndon Baines Johnson, dated May 17, 1965, raising one of the few voices of opposition within the administration against a widening of the war in Vietnam.

Dear Mr. President:

I am returning herewith the letter of the Director of Central Intelligence, dated May 8, 1965, together with enclosures. I wish to make one major point.

I believe our ground forces in South Vietnam should be kept to a minimum, consistent with the protection of our installations and property in that country. My concern is that a substantial buildup of U.S. ground troops would be construed by the Communists, and by the world, as a determination on our part to win the war on the ground. This could be a quagmire. It could turn into an open end

commitment on our part that would take more and more ground troops, without a realistic hope of ultimate victory.

I do not think the situation is comparable to Korea. The political posture of the parties involved, and the physical conditions, including terrain, are entirely different.

I continue to believe that the constant probing of every avenue leading to a possible settlement will ultimately be fruitful. It won't be what we want, but we can learn to live with it.

Respectfully yours,

Clark

From Leslie H. Gelb and Richard K. Betts, *The Irony of Vietnam: The System Worked* (Washington, D.C.: Brookings, 1979), p. 371. Reprinted by permission.

American labor leader], President Johnson would have had a deal."

Instead, Ho was a revolutionary (who, ironically, looked upon George Washington as a historical mentor and early in his career was aided by the Office of Strategic Studies, or OSS, the precursor of the CIA). The North Vietnamese leader was committed to driving foreigners out of his country and unifying the north and the south into one nation. He could not be bought. He was willing, however, to accept weapons and moral support from Peking and Moscow, if that is what it took to throw out first the French and then the Americans—a Faustian bargain that he, like Castro, would come to view with growing uneasiness.

The war went badly for the United States. American soldiers found the jungle terrain alien, and their South Vietnamese allies in the

Army of the Republic of Vietnam (ARVN) looked disconcertingly like their enemies in the Vietcong (VC) and from the North. Moreover, guerrilla warfare was still something of a novelty for Americans, not at all like the head-on clashes and distinguishable fronts of the Second World War and the Korean war. Here was combat in which the innocent-looking seventy-year-old woman in a rice paddy might have a hand grenade tucked under her black pajamas, where every turn on the jungle trail might hold a booby trap, where VC would appear and disappear like deadly phantoms in the thick underbrush.

Tim O'Brien's recollections of his days as a soldier in Vietnam capture the haunting fear and bewilderment of a war so different from any that GIs had been called upon to fight before:

Should you put your foot to that flat rock or the clump of weeds to its rear? Paddy dike or water? You wish you were Tarzan, able to swing with the vines. You try to trace the footprints of the man to your front. You give it up when he curses you for following too closely; better one man dead than two. The moment-to-moment, step-by-step decision-making preys on your mind. The effect is sometimes like paralysis. You are slow to rise from rest breaks. You walk like a wooden man . . . with your eyes pinned to the dirt, spine arched, and you are shivering, shoulders hunched.[31]

For ten years the fighting went on. Over 57,000 Americans lost their lives. Some 200,000 more required hospitalization from battle wounds; among these, thousands were badly maimed, physically and mentally. Many soldiers returned home with serious drug addictions, for the strain in Vietnam was great and drugs were plentiful.

Disputes persisted throughout the war over how America ought to proceed. One school of thought—prevalent within the U.S. military—argued that if America was going to be involved at all, its political and military leaders ought to do whatever it took to win. Some advocates of this view believed that the president should seek a declaration of war against the North Vietnamese, rallying Congress and the people into a frontal attack against the enemy, instead of subtly engaging in a war of hidden escalation and slow attrition. Others of this school urged the use of more sweeping military measures than the Johnson administration had yet taken, including the bombing of dikes in North Vietnam to flood the enemy's countryside; employing air strikes directly and heavily against the urban population centers of the north; possibly invading the north, as well as Cambodia and Laos (the other nations that made up Indochina, where VC and North Vietnamese regulars maintained sanctuaries); or perhaps even, as "mused" upon by some military men, resorting to the use of nuclear weapons—the complete destruction of communism in

Indochina, not merely its containment, checkmate for once, rather than the stalemate America had settled for in a divided Europe and Korea.[32]

An opposing school of thought rejected this "win" objective, with its provocations that might trigger World War III. They preferred instead a withdrawal from the jungles of Indochina before the United States lost still more lives in a struggle that seemed to have no end.

The Johnson administration chose a middle course: fearful, on the one hand, that dramatic escalation might bring in the Chinese (or even the Soviet) armies, yet unwilling, on the other hand, to retreat and incur the political wrath of those who would blame the Democrats again for being soft on communism. Johnson worried also that the "loss" of Vietnam would turn Congress against his greatest ambition as president: passage of the Great Society legislation.[33] As in Korea, the United States would attempt to contain communism, yet steer clear of a global war against the Chinese and the Soviets. Two thoughtful political-military analysts, Gelb and Betts, argue that this was exactly the course preferred by most Americans; therefore, "the system worked."[34]

The end result was a bloody war of attrition leading to another stalemate, with a spiraling increase in the number of dead American soldiers shipped home in pine boxes, often under the cover of darkness to avoid media reporting. Accompanying these tragic loses came a widening public disenchantment with the conflict. Virtually every evening, television news carried gruesome pictures of the death and destruction in Vietnam: villages engulfed in napalm; wounded GIs evacuated by helicopter, their faces contorted in pain; the rag-doll figures of men, women, and children massacred at the village of My Lai—a sickening mass murder of Vietnamese civilians by American soldiers; the profusion of bomb craters that had become the pockmarks of the distress infecting Vietnam; the chaos of Saigon, with protesting Buddhist monks aflame in suicidal self-immolations; and the wanton killing so dramatically symbolized by the impassive street execution of a suspected VC by Colonel Nguyen Ngoc Loan, the police chief of South Vietnam. On television, too, came the incessant count of American soldiers killed each week; Army generals speaking of victory around the corner—with always another corner; and the demonstrations on American college campuses, often erupting into violent clashes with the police.

Never before had an entire nation stood as a daily witness to the agony of war. As the number of coffins from Vietnam became too many to ignore, as the American people were surfeited with bad news from Saigon and the battlefields beyond, opinion shifted against the war. The *Tet offensive* of January 1968, during which the VC mounted attacks against U.S. troops throughout Vietnam, served as a poignant demonstration that—contrary to the assurances of American generals—the enemy was strong and capable (even though the VC were repelled and suffered large numbers of casualties in this bold and unexpected initiative).

At home, press and congressional criticism of the Johnson administration mounted, and serious political opposition to the president's reelection arose within his own political party. In the 1968 presidential contest, Senator Eugene McCarthy of Minnesota entered the New Hampshire primary against Johnson. Even though Johnson won, McCarthy tallied an impressive second-place finish, revealing the weakness of the incumbent president. These results encouraged Robert Kennedy (the brother of President Kennedy and, at the time, a U.S. senator representing the state of New York) to enter the race—an even more formidable foe.

This opposition, coupled with Johnson's steady decline in the polls, led to a surprising political decision: on March 31, 1968, the president announced in a dramatic television statement that he would not seek a second term. McCarthy and Robert Kennedy immediately stepped up their campaigns. In June, on the eve of Kennedy's stunning victory in the California primary, a Jordanian-born Arab murdered him in a Los Angeles hotel. Hubert H. Humphrey, the vice president in the Johnson administration, was able to capture the nomination over McCarthy, as antiwar protesters (mainly college students) clashed violently with police in the streets of Chicago outside the convention arena. The Republican nominee, Richard M. Nixon, narrowly won the general election, no doubt in large part because of Humphrey's identification with the failing war in Vietnam and the unwillingness of many McCarthy and Kennedy supporters to vote for him.

Prominent in Nixon's campaign rhetoric was a promise to end the war in Vietnam (just as Eisenhower, for whom Nixon had served as vice president, had promised during the 1952 election to end the war in Korea). His much heralded—but always secret—"plan" worked poorly. The negotiations between Nixon's top foreign policy aide, Dr. Henry Kissinger, and the North Vietnamese; the bombing of Hanoi and other cities in the North; the mining of enemy harbors; an invasion of Cambodia in May 1970 (at the time allegedly to clean out VC and North Vietnamese bases, but in reality to help the Cambodians resist a takeover by communist insurgents[35]); and various public efforts to threaten and cajole the enemy—all failed. The Cambodian invasion (which the president preferred to call an "incursion") served only to incite the public further against the war in Vietnam—more so than any other single event during this tragic era. Protests erupted across the country. National Guardsmen at Kent State University in Ohio, and police at Jackson State University in Mississippi, gunned down protesting students. An avalanche of antiwar mail fell upon the Congress from an outraged citizenry.[36] Soon after, the Nixon administration decided at last to bring the soldiers home.

Before Nixon could complete this withdrawal (a period during which another 20,000 Americans perished in Vietnam), he was caught up in the Watergate scandal. *Washington Post* reports revealed the president's attempt to cover up criminal evidence implicating his aides in a burglary of the Democratic national headquarters, located in the Watergate office building in Washington. Members of Congress further investigated the charges and, in August of 1974, Nixon was forced to resign—or risk almost certain impeachment. The final retreat from Vietnam fell to his vice president and successor, Gerald R. Ford. In April of 1975, as VC and North Vietnamese troops closed the noose on Saigon, those Americans still in the capital waited nervously on the roof and grounds of the American embassy (along with a few lucky South Vietnamese) for evacuation by helicopter to U.S. Navy ships anchored in the South China Sea. It was America's Dien Bien Phu.

For the first time, the United States had lost a war. The cost in blood and treasure had been enormous, and the long conflict had ripped the country asunder like nothing else since the Civil War. Never had the United States experienced such massive street protests. As the Great Society programs faltered, blacks rioted and torched cities. Students burned American flags, their draft cards, and even banks supposedly implicated in the financing of the war. Young men fled to Canada, avoiding the draft

for a war many believed to be immoral and illegitimate. A few young men and women joined radical antiwar groups like the Weathermen, resorting to terrorism against their own government. Across the land campuses closed down. At the height of the protests, the White House encircled itself with Washington's city buses for protection against youthful dissenters, like settlers braced for an attack by rampaging Indians. The White House, the CIA, the Federal Bureau of Investigation (FBI), and the military prepared and implemented—in violation of various laws—Orwellian spy plans to monitor the domestic unrest.[37] The country seemed in a state of siege.

DÉTENTE

The war in Indochina called into doubt the most fundamental tenets of American foreign policy in the nuclear age. Above all, as Gelb and Betts conclude, it "brought an end to the consensus on containment."[38] In 1933, Dean Rusk—three decades later secretary of state during the buildup of American troops in Vietnam—had been a Rhodes scholar at Oxford University in England. At the time, he had witnessed a vote by the student members of the

---

Perspectives on American Foreign Policy 4.4

Ronald Reagan in 1976 on the war in Vietnam:

The plain truth of the matter is that we were there [in Vietnam] to counter the master plan of the Communists for world conquest, and it's a lot easier and safer to counter it 8,000 miles away than to wait until they land in Long Beach [California]. . . . The Communist master plan, as we know it from published sources and from our own painful experience, is to isolate free nations,

one by one, stimulating and supplying revolution without endangering their own troops. What they did in Vietnam was simply to follow the plan they have pursued in many countries around the world. . . . There is a Communist plan for world conquest, and its final step is to conquer the United States."

From Charles D. Hobbs, *Ronald Reagan's Call to Action* (New York: Nelson, 1976), p. 42. Reprinted by permission.

Oxford Union in opposition to fighting "for King and country" against the Nazis. He sharply disagreed with this vote, and the further aggressive behavior of Hitler would soon prove him correct. Rusk carried back to the United States a conviction that aggression had to be stopped wherever it occurred, a principle he would apply during the Kennedy and Johnson administrations.[39]

A Thawing in the Cold War

But with the American retreat from Vietnam, the traditional policy of containment took on a new and less strident character. The *Nixon Doctrine* (1969) had already made it clear that nations in the developing world would be expected to use their own—not U.S.—troops to defend themselves (though the United States would continue to sell, or sometimes give, them arms). Moreover, the Sino-Soviet schism (which first opened in 1962) had deepened, and President Nixon and Dr. Kissinger skillfully set out to edge China farther away from the influence of Moscow. Even America's cold war confrontations with the Soviet Union underwent a remarkable thaw during the Nixon years. The president and Kissinger ushered in a period of relaxed tensions between the superpowers, punctuated by arms control accords and increased trade agreements—the powers of diplomacy and economic inducements at a time when Americans had become skeptical about the power of war.

This brief experiment with détente, blossoming in the years from 1972 to 1974, made the harsh rhetoric of the Dulles era seem antediluvian. The purpose of the thaw was to attempt, by means of a calmer dialogue, the managing of U.S.–Soviet disagreements at, as Spanier writes, *"a lower level of tension and lower cost than those required by the policy of cold war confrontation and frequent crisis."*[40] The Nixon-Kissinger approach involved several tactics. Among the most important were the negotiation of mutually beneficial agreements on trade and arms

control with the Soviets, in an attempt to tie their interests more closely to those of the United States; playing China off against the U.S.S.R. (the so-called China card), by hinting at the possible establishment of closer Sino-American relations if the Soviets failed to be more cooperative; and punishing the Soviets in one area (say, trade) if they refused to show conciliation in another (say, arms control)—an approach often referred to as policy *linkage*.

America's withdrawal from Vietnam, along with these fresh overtures to Moscow and Beijing, signaled that in the future the United States intended to be more circumspect about where it intervened to protect the world against communism; Vietnam had demonstrated that the policy of containment would not work everywhere. As General Maxwell D. Taylor (once a strong proponent of U.S. involvement in Vietnam) would put it after the retreat from Saigon, "Until we know the enemy and know our allies and know ourselves, we'd better keep out of this kind of dirty business. It's very dangerous."[41] Senator Gary Hart (D-Colo.), a presidential candidate in 1984 and 1988, looked upon the year 1973 as a turning point in American foreign policy: "Nixon proved that big government is not necessarily a benign government [a reference to the Watergate scandal]; OPEC [the Organization of Petroleum Exporting Countries] proved that our economy was vulnerable to international influences; and the Vietnam War proved that we couldn't have our way in the world."[42] In each case, it was a rude awakening.

By 1975, when the United States departed from Vietnam, the North Vietnamese and the Chinese had already entered into a bitter rivalry for military and political influence in Indochina. The Chinese extended to Cambodia a billion-dollar, interest-free aid package to resist Vietnamese expansion. The Soviets supported the Vietnamese. And eventually, the United States—uncomfortably, ironically—backed a coalition of anti-Vietnamese rebels in Cambodia, led for many years by a radical communist (!)

named Pol Pot, a murderous autocrat responsible for the death of at least 1 million citizens in his country who were deemed ideologically "contaminated" by either Vietnamese or Western views. Indochina had proved to be more complicated than theoreticians of the domino principle envisaged. Docile Laos did fall quickly to the Vietnamese, as predicted; but Cambodia, backed by two major powers (China and the United States, odd bedfellows indeed at this time), was a more steadfast piece, not easily toppled. This struggle continues, as the people of Cambodia pay the high price of protracted fighting in lives and dislocation.

Fresh Conflicts

Détente turned out to be a disappointment to many Americans, especially those who had confused the term with *entente*—that is, genuine friendship, not just an attempt to relax tensions between nations. The world was not so easily transformed. From the American point of view, the Soviets continued to be mischievous, sponsoring surrogate warfare in Angola and elsewhere and, among other things, preparing (it seemed) to enter the Israeli-Egyptian Yom Kippur war in 1973—which led to the placement of U.S. forces on their first major nuclear alert since October of 1962. And from the Soviet point of view, the United States no doubt appeared to be dragging its feet on economic agreements, moving slowly on arms control, and, in 1974, turning inward as the nation became mesmerized by the Watergate scandal. On both sides, détente rapidly lost its glitter.

President Ford turned out to be less attracted to the use of diplomatic initiatives (central to détente) than Nixon had been. With the ignominious withdrawal from Saigon fresh in mind, Ford struck quickly with military force when Cambodian communists intercepted an American merchant vessel, the *Mayaguez*, off their coast a few weeks following the U.S. retreat from Saigon. This farcical rescue mission, which cost the lives of forty-one marines, oc-

curred after the Cambodians had already released the American sailors, who were steaming happily homeward as the marines landed on Cambodian soil. The operation, which included the bombing of Cambodia with the largest nonnuclear bomb in the American arsenal, apparently had the effect at least of making the Ford administration feel better about itself, and the president's leap upward ten points in the opinion polls indicated public support for the operation—though neither the public nor the Congress was privy to the details of the operation at the time, including the number of marines who died or the fact that the *Mayaguez* sailors had already been released before the marines arrived.[43]

Ford was ready for battle in Africa, too, in this case to thwart Soviet adventurism in Angola, the nation that had so worried Senator Moynihan because of its "threat" to Brazil (Chapter 1). The president sought funding for a CIA covert action in Angola, designed to assist pro-Western forces in the south against Moscow-backed Angolan Marxists and Cuban soldiers in the north. The Congress refused, signaling both its new assertiveness in the post-Vietnam period and a fresh wariness about more "Vietnams" elsewhere in the developing world—a restraint sometimes referred to as the *Vietnam syndrome* (a dangerous flirtation with appeasement, in the eyes of conservative critics). The Ford administration, though, was prepared to cooperate with the Soviets on some matters and successfully continued negotiations with Moscow on a few arms control measures.

The Ford administration enjoyed only a short life (1974–1976), and the Carter administration that followed exhibited a more complex view of foreign affairs. President Carter, less experienced in foreign policy than any president since Calvin Coolidge, seemed prepared to continue along the pathway of détente. He expressed special concern about the dangers of nuclear war and dedicated himself to winning Senate approval of a second *SALT* [Strategic Arms Limitation Talks] *Treaty* between the United States and the Soviet Union, as an extension of Nixon's SALT I, which placed a cap on the number of strategic weapons in the superpower arsenals. Though never approved by the Senate (largely because of a Soviet invasion of Afghanistan in 1979), the SALT II provisions were honored by both nations until 1986, when the Reagan administration decided to exceed the arms ceiling. President Carter concentrated, too—more than any president since Woodrow Wilson—on the moral aspects of American foreign policy, perhaps a reflection of his personal experience as a "born-again" Christian.

Carter's secretary of state, the Wall Street lawyer Cyrus Vance, enthusiastically supported the president's warming relations with the Soviets as well as his human rights initiatives. Carter's national security adviser, Dr. Zbigniew Brzezinski, was, however, more of a conservative "hard-liner" on relations with the Soviets. A confidant of the president's before Vance and a dynamic, persuasive advocate of his own views, Brzezinski often won Carter's ear over the more reserved secretary of state. Vance was an architect of diplomacy, Brzezinski of less subtle forms of power—quick to propose the use or threatened use of military force or covert action. The Brzezinski stamp was clear on the *Carter Doctrine* (1980), a policy which the president applied to the Middle East with these words: "Any use of outside force to try to gain control of the Persian Gulf oil area will be regarded as an assault on the vital interests of the United States and will be repelled by American military force." Here was a Monroe Doctrine for the Middle East—a region of the world rather more difficult to defend than America's closer neighbors in the Western Hemisphere.

The outcome of this awkward staffing arrangement in the Carter administration was often a vacillation by the president between the Vance and the Brzezinski worldviews, leading to an internal confusion that soon spilled out into the public as the two presidential advisers appeared on television talk shows to speak on

behalf of the administration—or, at least, to present their views on what the administration ought to be doing. Traditionally, the secretary of state is supposed to speak for the nation on foreign policy. Brzezinski brushed aside this custom, however, and was the first national security adviser to have his own press assistants in the White House. Criticism of this cacophony of voices from the Carter administration mounted in the media, on Capitol Hill, and in foreign capitals.

During the Carter years, Soviet officials demonstrated anew that they have their doctrines, too: during this period, the so-called *Brezhnev Doctrine*, after the Soviet leader Leonid Brezhnev, who crushed an uprising in Czechoslovakia in 1968 that was supposedly instigated by outside agitators. The Brezhnev Doctrine proclaimed the Soviet right to protect communist nations from outside interference, through the use of force if necessary. In accordance with this doctrine, the Soviet Army invaded Afghanistan with 85,000 troops in December of 1979 to assist the new and teetering Afghan Marxist regime. This surprise move drove Carter further toward the views advocated by Brzezinski. Weary of the infighting with Brzezinski and, more specifically, opposed to the military option advanced by Carter and Brzezinski in April 1980 for the rescue of American diplomats taken hostage in Iran (in November of 1979), Vance tendered his resignation after the rescue attempt failed.

The president said at the time of the Soviet invasion into Afghanistan that this attack had changed his "opinion of the Russians . . . more dramatically in the last week than over the previous two and one-half years"—revealing, critics thought, an astounding naiveté. Carter embargoed grain shipments bound for the U.S.S.R., imposed a boycott of the 1980 Moscow Olympics, and stopped the shipment of high-technology exports to the Soviet bloc. With the Afghan invasion, notes an observer of American foreign policy, "Cold War II had begun."[44] In the next presidential election, the newly militant Carter was no match for a Republican candidate, the former California governor Ronald Reagan, who had been on the far right when it came to the Soviet Union for most of his political career. Slumping economic indicators at home and stalled hostage negotiations abroad provided the coup de grâce, and, winning only six states, Carter limped home to Georgia in defeat.

The Cold War Revisited

Under President Reagan, the renewal of cold war rhetoric reached a level of intensity unseen since the Eisenhower years. The Soviet Union was an "evil empire," the president told the American people in 1983 as he sharply increased spending on military weapons (in the process, driving the national deficit to unprecedented heights). Covert actions by the CIA proliferated: in Cambodia, Nicaragua, Angola, Libya, Afghanistan, and other spots around the world where Marxists and communists posed, or seemed to pose, a threat to the United States or its friends. The so-called *Reagan Doctrine*, not a formal policy statement but an appellation applied by the media to the Reagan administration's new aggressiveness, envisaged the robust use of covert intervention abroad to assist nations in their resistance against communist aggression. Like the Brezhnev Doctrine, the "Reagan Doctrine" represented a rationale for superpower intervention into the affairs of third world nations. The United States seemed to return to the 1950s in both rhetoric and action, though this time with a divided consensus as members of Congress wary of a renewed cold war voted—sometimes by a winning majority—against funding for the Reagan approach to foreign affairs.

Legislators, for example, limited expenditures for covert paramilitary operations against the Sandinista regime in Nicaragua. For several members of Congress, the proposed recipients of the funds—the anticommunist, CIA-backed contra rebels (who, in Reagan's view, embod-

ied the spirit of America's founding fathers in their fight for freedom)—appeared to be an unsavory group of mercenaries no better than the Sandinistas. Efforts by the Reagan administration to bypass congressional bans against further aid to the contras led to the president's most significant foreign policy crisis: the Iran-contra scandal of 1986. Legislators and the media charged White House officials with selling arms improperly to Iran in exchange for assistance in the release of American hostages, as well as funneling the profits through a secret Swiss bank account to the contras, in apparent violation of law (the Boland amendment, examined in Chapter 9). "If a White House can decide that a law passed by Congress is inconvenient, and simply set out to circumvent it," concluded a Washington correspondent, "then our constitutional system is finished."[45]

As the Reagan administration suffered through the embarrassment of the Iran-contra scandal, the president himself began to show an astonishing change of heart with respect to the main plank of his foreign policy platform—his unalloyed distrust of the Soviet Union. For many observers, President Reagan—once King of the Cold Warriors—actually seemed to be trying to wind down the cold war. The first important sign of change occurred in 1985, when the new, reform-minded Soviet leader, Mikhail S. Gorbachev, met with Reagan in Geneva for a spirited exchange of goodwill on the prospects for the reduction of nuclear weapons. The two appeared to connect on a personal level.

A second meeting occurred in October 1986, in Reykjavík, Iceland, where—to the amazement of Reagan's aides—both men openly expressed a desire to abolish all nuclear weapons. Then, in December of 1987, Gorbachev traveled to the United States and the two leaders agreed on the INF treaty to remove intermediate nuclear forces—medium-range missiles—in Europe (an agreement approved by the Senate and ratified by the president the next year).[46] In 1988, Gorbachev announced he would withdraw within the next year all 115,000 Soviet sol-

With their respective flags in the background, Soviet President Mikhail S. Gorbachev and U.S. President Ronald Reagan shake hands at the superpower summit meeting held in Reykjavík, Iceland, in 1986. (UPI/Bettmann Newsphotos)

diers from Afghanistan—the end of Moscow's Vietnam. He kept this promise; and he also proposed significant cuts on both sides in European conventional forces, a step subsequently endorsed by President Bush in 1989.[47]

As the twenty-first century approaches, the superpower competition continues for minds and marketplaces around the globe. Now, though, the sharp edges have been blunted. Signs are evident that President Bush will further pursue the startling opening to a new era of détente initiated by the unlikely duo of Reagan and Gorbachev; and the Soviet leader seemed prepared to discard the Brezhnev Doctrine. In light of this apparent easing of the military and ideological threat from the Soviet bloc, symbolized most graphically in November, 1989, by the opening of the Berlin wall, Western analysts began to question the relevance of America's postwar containment doctrine.[48]

A BALANCE SHEET

The years since 1946 have been filled with global strife and tension. Though—fortunately— nuclear weapons have never been fired in anger

after World War II, anywhere from 10 million to 20 million people have perished in conventional conflicts around the world (precise numbers on this grisly subject are hard to come by, as combatants prefer to keep their losses secret). Weapons have also become ever more dangerous, as inventors discover how to make them more powerful and at the same time smaller and, therefore, easier to conceal. Their range, speed, and evasiveness have increased dramatically as well.

The world has been plagued, further, by a rash of new conflicts beyond the U.S.–Soviet confrontation. Fundamentalist Muslims, for example, view both superpowers as enemies and, in strident terms, have declared the superiority of their own ideology. "We are not socialist, we are not capitalist, we are Islamic," states one of their leaders, and another adds: "Islam is a faith and a ritual, a nation and a nationality, a religion and a state, spirit and deed, holy text and sword."[49] The television images of demonstrations in Tehran by supporters of the Ayatollah Khomeini in 1980, burning American flags and boasting over the capture of American hostages, recall the fervor of Islamic zealotry. The continuing bloodshed between Cambodians and Vietnamese, white and black South Africans, north and south Angolans, Sandinistas and contras, Irish rebels and British soldiers, Afghan rebels and Soviet-backed Afghan Marxists, Iranians and Iraqis, Israelis and a host of Arab enemies—all further testify (among other examples) to the still primitive capacity of human beings to resolve their disputes peaceably.

Yet, not all the news is bad. Relations between the United States and the Soviet Union, while far from friendly, have arguably achieved a higher level of cooperation in the past twenty years than in the preceding twenty years—and the unexpected warm relations between Reagan and Gorbachev promised hope for a new era of cordiality between the superpowers. "The Cold War, with all of its rivalries, anxieties, and unquestionable dangers," writes the historian John Lewis Gaddis, "has produced the longest period of stability in relations among the great powers that the world has known in this century; it now compares favorably as well with some of the longest periods of great power stability in all of modern history."[50]

Keeping the world's nuclear weapons in check has been no small achievement in itself. That they have not been fired in war is perhaps the most important observation one can make about the nuclear age. Deterrence—the nuclear standoff—has replaced defense, and with deterrence has come a fear of mutual annihilation that helps to keep the superpowers at bay. The ability of the major powers to spy on one another from the skies and with electronic listening posts on the ground and beneath the seas— the so-called surveillance revolution—has been equally important for maintaining stability; surprise attacks are far less likely than they used to be. The "hot line" communications system that was established between Moscow and Washington following the Cuban missile crisis, with many improvements in its efficiency over the years, and other efforts to improve crisis management represent further significant steps that have made this planet a safer place.

Moreover, while disease and hunger continue to haunt the developing world (where most of humanity lives in squalor), great strides forward have occurred in the use of technology to conquer threats against basic human well-being. New high-yield grains have allowed India, for instance, to achieve what not long ago was thought impossible: self-sufficiency in the feeding of its people (though food distribution remains a serious problem). New medicines have helped to eradicate many dangerous diseases, like smallpox and tuberculosis. Much more could be done with the new technologies, if the political will—and, in its wake, the money—were present. High on the agenda of American foreign policy will continue to be the subject of political economy: how to cope with the demands of the developing world for a greater share of the global wealth while, at the same time, protecting the economic interests of the United States and its allies—from access to oil in the Persian gulf to fair trade arrangements with Japan and other nations. This represents an enormous challenge requiring this country to find from among its citizens a few more George Marshalls and Dean Achesons in the coming years.

Thus, Americans live in a world of great danger, but also of great challenge and promise. Looking back at the Cuban missile crisis, the foreign policy analyst Graham Allison writes: "The event symbolizes a central, if only partially thinkable, fact about our existence. That such consequences could follow from the choices and actions of national governments obliges students of government as well as participants in governance to think hard about these problems."[51] That is a central objective of this book: to encourage thought about the challenges America faces as but one of many nations on a small and insecure planet.

In the next chapter, the discussion turns to America's constitutional framework for the making of foreign policy. Nothing has so steadfastly affected this nation's approach to world affairs from 1787 to the present as the language and underlying philosophy of the U.S. Constitution.

SUMMARY

American foreign policy since the Second World War has had to cope with a world more complicated and dangerous than ever before— more complicated because the United States is now a world power in a fragmented globe of 180 nations, more dangerous because the nuclear age holds the prospect that a spreading war could engulf the superpowers and lead to the extinction of the human race. In the psychologist Erik Erikson's expression, "We have become a species mortally dangerous to itself."

America's competition with the Soviet Union—a rivalry known as the cold war—has been the predominant preoccupation of U.S. foreign policy during the nuclear age. In the protection of America's global interests, the response of U.S. officials to this rivalry has been primarily a reliance on nuclear deterrence and on the containment doctrine. Deterrence, coupled with dramatic improvements in technical surveillance capabilities, has contributed significantly to the maintenance of stability between the superpowers—indeed, a longer epoch of great power stability than the world has seen before in this century and one of the longest at any time.

Yet, while the superpowers have avoided direct warfare between themselves, they have fought limited wars indirectly against one another in various developing nations. The United States has engaged in costly overt warfare in Korea, Indochina, and elsewhere, in order to shore up the perimeter defense against the threat of communist expansion, and this nation has pursued an even larger number of covert operations (the Bay of Pigs, for one) toward the same objective. At the same time, the Soviet Union has similarly entered into a series of overt and covert wars in an effort to thwart, indirectly, U.S. influence around the globe.

Occasionally, the United States and the Soviet Union have tried to accommodate one another's needs through less severe forms of foreign policy, such as diplomacy (the nuclear test ban treaty of 1963, for example) and economic trade. The period of détente during the Nixon administration (1972–1974) represented a notable experiment in this direction. Détente led to disappointments on both sides, however, and a new round of bickering began. When the Soviet Union invaded Afghanistan in 1979, relations plummeted even further and led to what some observers viewed for a time as a full-scale revival of the cold war. Under President Reagan, U.S.–Soviet relations further cooled; yet, ironically and unpredictably, the final years of the Reagan administration and the beginnings of the Bush administration witnessed efforts in Washington and Moscow to stem the cold war.

The poor nations of the world are in desperate need of assistance from the older and wealthier nations. The anger of the poor has led to new global tensions, seen most conspicuously in the proliferation of terrorist incidents during the past decade. While some American presidents have focused on this problem (especially Jimmy Carter), most have remained preoccupied with the U.S.–Soviet rivalry. As the twenty-first century approaches, the superpowers remain locked in a competition for minds and marketplaces around the world; but, as a result of the Reagan-Bush-Gorbachev initiatives, both nations seem less gripped by a fear and total distrust of one another.

KEY TERMS

Marshall Plan	Ex Comm
Kennan's views on containment	Dien Bien Phu
one-worlders	Geneva accords
McCarthyism	SEATO
NSC-68	nuclear test ban treaty
Berlin blockade	Tet offensive
NATO	Nixon Doctrine
Warsaw Pact	linkage
low-intensity warfare	*Mayaguez*
flexible response	Vietnam syndrome
massive retaliation	SALT Treaty
Bay of Pigs	Carter Doctrine
Berlin wall	Brezhnev Doctrine
Cuban missile crisis	Reagan Doctrine
MRBMs	

NOTES

1. "Containment and the Decline of the Soviet Empire: Some Tentative Reflections on the End of the World As We Know It," paper presented at the Annual Convention of the International Studies Association, Anaheim, Calif., March 25–29, 1986, p. 1.

2. Cited by Robert D. Warth, *Soviet Russia in World Politics* (New York: Twayne, 1963), p. 320.

3. Harry S Truman, *Memoirs*, vol. I (New York: Doubleday, 1955), pp. 551–552.

4. David S. McLellan, *The Cold War in Transition* (New York: Macmillan, 1966), p. 6. For evidence that the cold war had deeper roots, see John Lewis Gaddis, *The United States and the Origins of the Cold War: 1941–1947* (New York: Columbia University Press, 1972).

5. See "Containment: Forty Years Later," *Foreign Affairs*, vol. 65, Spring 1987, p. 829. Kennan's "X" article was published under the title "The Sources of Soviet Conduct," *Foreign Affairs*, vol. 25, July 1947, pp. 566–582, reprinted in George F. Kennan, *American Diplomacy, 1900–1950* (Chicago: University of Chicago Press, 1951), pp. 89–106, with the quotes used in this text drawn from pp. 98–99.

6. John Lewis Gaddis, *Strategies of Containment: A Critical Appraisal of Postwar American National Security Policy* (New York: Oxford University Press, 1982), p. 22; see, also, Howard Jones, *"A New Kind of War": America's Global Strategy and the Truman Doctrine in Greece* (New York: Oxford University Press, 1989).

7. Quoted by Joseph M. Jones, *The Fifteen Weeks* (New York: Viking, 1955), p. 190.

8. "The Long Peace," *International Security*, vol. 10, Spring 1986, p. 130, original emphasis.

9. Cited by Gaddis, *Strategies of Containment*, p. 41.

10. Gaddis, *The United States and the Origins of the Cold War*, p. 352.

11. See *ibid.*, p. 288. The polls were conducted by the American Institute of Public Opinion.

12. Quoted by Gaddis, *Strategies of Containment*, p. 91, emphasis added.

13. *Ibid.*, p. 130.

14. *Ibid.*, pp. 130–131.

15. *Ibid.*, p. 128.

16. McLellan, *op. cit.*, p. 13.

17. *Ibid.*, p. 18.

18. *Ibid.*, p. 23.

19. Thomas C. Schelling, *Arms and Influence* (New Haven: Yale University Press, 1966), p. 124, emphasis added.

20. On the Bay of Pigs, see Peter Wyden, *The Bay of Pigs: The Untold Story* (New York: Simon & Schuster, 1979).

21. On September 11, the Soviets warned the United States that, in one White House adviser's recollection, "any U.S. military action against Cuba would unleash nuclear war." Theodore C. Sorensen, *Kennedy* (New York: Harper & Row, 1965), p. 680.

22. See the account in Robert Kennedy, *Thirteen Days* (New York: Signet Books, 1969), pp. 38–39. For more recent retrospectives on this crisis, see James G. Blight, Joseph S. Nye, Jr., and David A. Welch, "The Cuban Missile Crisis Revisited," *Foreign Affairs*, vol. 66, Fall 1987, pp. 170–188; and Peter S. Usowski, "John McCone and the Cuban Missile Crisis: A Persistent Approach to the Intelligence-Policy Relationship," *International Journal of Intelligence and Counterintelligence*, vol. 2, Winter 1988, pp. 547–576.

23. Quoted by Sorensen, *op. cit.*, p. 682.

24. See, for example, Amos Yoder, *The Conduct of American Foreign Policy since World War II* (New York: Pergamon, 1986), p. 31, note 1.

25. See Chambers M. Roberts, "The Day We Didn't Go to War," *Reporter*, September 14, 1954, pp. 31–35. "You boys must be crazy," said Eisenhower to those advisers who wanted him to use atomic weapons to help the French at Dien Bien Phu. "We can't use those awful things against Asians for the second time in less than ten years. My God." Quoted by Stephen E. Ambrose, *Eisenhower: The President* (New York: Simon & Schuster, 1984), p. 184.

26. Peter Wyden, *op. cit.*, p. 100. According to Wyden, the presidential adviser Ted Sorensen inferred in a conversation about the invasion plans with the president that Kennedy "thought the project's opponents were chicken. The president was not going to be chicken" (p. 165).

27. President Kennedy to W. W. Rostow, cited in Arthur M. Schlesinger, Jr., *A Thousand Days: John F. Kennedy in the White House* (Boston: Houghton Mifflin, 1965), p. 339.

28. W. W. Rostow, *The Diffusion of Power* (New York: Macmillan, 1972), p. 270.

29. This Bay of Pigs analogy is from James C. Thomson, Jr., "How Could Vietnam Happen? An Autopsy," *Atlantic Monthly*, April 1968, p. 52.

30. Quoted in Alonzo L. Hamby, *Beyond the New Deal: Harry S. Truman and American Liberalism* (New York: Columbia University Press, 1973), p. 371.

31. Tim O'Brien, *If I Die in a Combat Zone, Box Me Up and Ship Me Home* (New York: Dell, 1973), cited by Stanley Karnow, *Vietnam: A History* (New York: Viking, 1983), p. 472.

32. See Leslie H. Gelb and Richard K. Betts, *The Irony of Vietnam: The System Worked* (Washington, D.C.: Brookings, 1979), p. 265.

33. See Fox Butterfield, "The New Vietnam Scholarship," *New York Times Magazine*, February 13, 1983, p. 28.

34. *Op. cit.* The trouble with this argument is that "the system" actually failed to inform the American people about the reality of the war. In a democracy, the sine qua non for success is an informed electorate; yet, both the Johnson and Nixon administrations were notorious for refusing to discuss the war candidly with Congress or the American people. As Kissinger puts it in his memoirs (with specific reference to the military operations carried out by the Nixon administration against Cambodia): "We were wrong, I now believe, not to be more frank with congressional leaders" (*White House Years*, Boston: Houghton Mifflin,

1979, p. 253). As the lack of candor became apparent, congressional opposition to these administrations increased. A well-informed public might well have turned against the war long before so many Americans died. At least for the system truly to have worked, this opportunity should have been available. Misguided efforts within the executive branch to conceal information from Congress and the public led ultimately to the distrust of the presidency that became the hallmark of the 1970s.

35. Robert Shaplen, "A Reporter at Large: The Captivity of Cambodia," *New Yorker*, May 5, 1986, p. 90.

36. Loch K. Johnson and Jerome Garris, "Public Opinion and Ideology in the Senate: The Cambodian Incursion as a Critical Incident," *Southeastern Political Review*, vol. 14, Spring 1986, pp. 35–61.

37. See Loch K. Johnson, *America's Secret Power: The CIA in a Democratic Society* (New York: Oxford University Press, 1989), Chap. 7.

38. *Op. cit.*, p. 368.

39. See Stanley Karnow, "Vietnam as an Analogy," *New York Times*, October 4, 1986.

40. John Spanier, *American Foreign Policy since World War II*, 10th ed. (New York: Holt, Rinehart & Winston, 1985), p. 171, original emphasis.

41. Quoted by Karnow, "Vietnam as an Analogy."

42. *Washington Post*, May 17, 1981.

43. For an account, see Richard J. Barnet, *Real Security: Restoring American Power in a Dangerous Decade* (New York: Simon & Schuster, 1981), pp. 66–68.

44. Lloyd C. Gardner, *A Covenant with Power: America and World Order from Wilson to Reagan* (New York: Oxford University Press, 1984), p. 213.

45. Elizabeth Drew, "Letter from Washington," *New Yorker*, March 3, 1987, p. 111.

46. On the Reagan-Gorbachev relationship, see the two-part series by the arms control expert John Newhouse, "Annals of Diplomacy: The Abolitionist," *New Yorker*, January 2 and 9, 1989, pp. 37–52 and 51–72, respectively.

47. See the *New York Times*, May 30, 1989, pp. 1, 7.

48. See, for example, Paul H. Kreisberg, "Containment's Last Gasp," *Foreign Policy*, vol. 75, Summer 1989, pp. 146–163.

49. The Malaysian leader Anwar Ibrahim, quoted in the *New York Times*, March 28, 1980; and the founder of the Muslim Brethren organization, Hasan al-Banna, *al-Mutamar al-khamis*, p. 10, quoted in Richard P. Mitchell, *The Society of the Muslim Brothers* (London: Oxford University Press, 1969), p. 233—both cited in Daniel Pipes, "Fundamentalist Muslims between America and Russia," *Foreign Affairs*, vol. 64, Summer 1986, p. 944.

50. "The Long Peace," p. 142.

51. "Conceptual Models and the Cuban Missile Crisis," *American Political Science Review*, vol. 63, September 1969, p. 689.

RECOMMENDED READINGS

Acheson, Dean. *Present at the Creation: My Years in the State Department* (New York: Norton, 1969). A lively, eloquent testimony from a central figure in the postwar planning of American foreign policy, President Truman's secretary of state.

Barnet, Richard J. *Real Security: Restoring American Power in a Dangerous Decade* (New York: Simon & Schuster, 1981). A brief, highly readable, and strongly critical analysis of American foreign policy during the 1970s.

Figley, Charles R., and Seymour Leventman, eds. *Strangers at Home: Vietnam Veterans since the War*

(New York: Praeger, 1980). A series of essays on the effects of the Vietnamese war on those who felt them most directly: the soliders sent there to fight.

Gaddis, John Lewis. *The United States and the Origins of the Cold War, 1941–1947* (New York: Columbia University Press, 1972). A balanced treatment of how the United States and the Soviet Union became adversaries.

———. *Strategies of Containment: A Critical Appraisal of Postwar American National Security Policy* (New York: Oxford University Press, 1982). A detailed examination of American security policy from NSC-68 through détente, with special attention throughout to Kennan's perspectives on containment.

Gelb, Leslie H., with Richard K. Betts. *The Irony of Vietnam: The System Worked* (Washington, D.C.: Brookings, 1979). A full account of why and how the United States decided to try to prevent the loss of Vietnam to communism, with many insights into the political pressures on the government to sustain the war.

Karnow, Stanley. *Vietnam: A History* (New York: Viking, 1983). A fascinating and exhaustive account of this tragedy.

Kegley, Charles W., Jr., and Eugene R. Wittkopf. *Perspectives on American Foreign Policy: Selected Readings* (New York: St. Martin's, 1983). A useful collection of essays on relations between the United States and other nations since 1945.

McLellan, David S. *The Cold War in Transition* (New York: Macmillan, 1966). One of the best short histories on the beginnings of the cold war.

Pogue, Forrest C. *George C. Marshall: Statesman 1945–1959* (New York: Viking, 1987). A detailed examination of Marshall as secretary of state, concentrating on the plan which bears his name—in the view of many, the high point of American diplomacy in the modern era.

Schlesinger, Arthur M., Jr. *The Cycles of American History* (Boston: Houghton Mifflin, 1986). An excellent discussion of the cold war and the question of American imperialism.

Spanier, John. *American Foreign Policy since World War II*, 10th ed. (New York: Holt, Rinehart & Winston, 1985). This excellent survey of the cold war years has become a classic.

Talbott, Strobe. *Deadly Gambits* (New York: Random House, 1984). A revealing study of U.S.–Soviet jostling over arms control in the nuclear age.

Walworth, Arthur. *Wilson and His Peacemakers: American Diplomacy at the Paris Peace Conference* (New York: Norton, 1986). The best study on the failed peace of 1918 and its important influence on the rest of twentieth-century American foreign policy.

Wyden, Peter. *Bay of Pigs: The Untold Story* (New York: Simon & Schuster, 1979). How the United States planned and carried out the secret attack on Cuba in 1961, and why it failed.

Yoder, Amos. *The Conduct of American Foreign Policy since World War II* (New York: Pergamon, 1986). An interesting survey of postwar policy by an experienced diplomat and political scientist.

SHARED POWERS

THE WAR POWER

   Defensive versus Offensive Warfare

   Inherent Presidential Authority

   War by Blank Check

INTERNATIONAL AGREEMENTS

   The Destroyers Deal

   Creeping Commitments

THE SEEDS OF ACQUIESCENCE

THE PURSE STRINGS AND OTHER DISPUTES

   Money

Diplomatic Recognition, Confirmation, and Oversight

MARCHING TO DIFFERENT DRUMS

   Contrasting Constituencies

   Pressures of Office

   Career Cycles

   Structural Differences

   Modern Communications

   Unequal Information

CONFLICT AND COMITY

SUMMARY

5

REMEMBERING THE CONSTITUTION

President Franklin D. Roosevelt asks a Joint Session of Congress on December 8, 1941, for a declaration of war against Japan. (AP/Wide World Photos)

SHARED POWERS

The government of the United States comprises *separate institutions sharing power*. The nation's founders devised this arrangement intentionally, for they hoped above all else in creating a new government to avoid a concentration of power in the executive. King George III had taught them, vividly, the perils of centralized authority. America's early leaders, with fresh memories of their recent subjugation under British rule, were "imbued with antipower values."[1] By distributing power across institutions, they hoped to limit its abuse. With responsibilities and prerogatives spread over the executive, legislative, and judicial branches of government, the constitutional framers sought to ensure that no branch would grow so mighty as to dwarf the others or dictate to the American people.[2] "The greatest insight of our Founding Fathers," concluded a modern-day senior member of the Senate Foreign Relations Committee, "was their recognition of the dangers of unlimited power exercised by a single man or institution. Their greatest achievement was the safeguards against absolute power which they wrote into our Constitution."[3]

While a sharing of powers across institutions held an obvious attraction to a young republic still reeling from a war against British tyranny, the new arrangements also contained the seeds of inefficiency—especially the fundamental problem of coordinating dispersed units of government, each with formidable powers. How could these separate entities be truly made to share power and work together for the good of the nation? The answer remained in doubt, particularly since the very Constitution that gave the three branches their authority seemed—with its silences and ambiguities—to present, in Professor Edward S. Corwin's memorable phrase, "an invitation to struggle."[4]

Those who drafted the Constitution were wise to concern themselves with the dangers of concentrated power. Few observers of history would deny the truth of Lord Acton's famous aphorism, "power corrupts, and absolute power corrupts absolutely." Yet, in their headlong escape from tyranny had the founders embraced another serious threat to democracy: a paralysis resulting from a government excessively fragmented? If at one end of a power continuum stood the dangers of absolute power, at the other stood anarchy.

The purpose of this chapter (and Chapter 6) is to examine the foreign policy strains that have evolved from the constitutional blueprint devised by America's early leaders, men with strongly negative attitudes toward the exercise of power. At the heart of these two chapters, and indeed this entire book, is the question of governability: Do America's institutions, as they presently stand, permit sound foreign policy decisions? Can collaborative government work, especially when dealing with the often tangled and perilous challenges of international affairs? Sometimes the institutions of American government appear to be chaotic and unmanageable. "The executive branch," writes a leading political scientist, "is so divided, so fragmented, and its parts are often so autonomous that the President's power of command over them is often little more than a fiction."[5]

Have the precautions against the abuse of power taken by the founders led to a government that, more than two centuries later, lacks sufficient centralized authority to react with the necessary quickness and coherence to contemporary global threats? Or are their concerns and prescriptions as valid today as they were at the beginning of the nation's history?

In a search for answers to these vital questions, this chapter offers an overview of the problems associated with power sharing between Congress and the executive branch, especially in the use of military force (the war power) and the making of international agreements (diplomacy). These two instruments of foreign policy have produced the most friction between the branches. The second part of this book will examine the contemporary use of these instruments; the objective of this chapter

(and Chapter 6) is to set the stage with examples of institutional sparring that have occurred over the years, as different parts of the government interpreted their constitutional responsibilities in different ways.

This chapter focuses on the basic constitutional sources of conflict over power sharing, while Chapter 6 takes a look inside the branches of government to see how they shape the course of modern foreign policy. The purpose of both chapters is to evaluate the consequences for America's external affairs that flow from the decision of the founders to distribute powers across the institutions of government.

THE WAR POWER

The Constitution shares the treaty power equally between the executive and legislative branches (see the next section, International Agreements). In contrast, the *war power* is lodged predominantly in Congress. In the Constitution's first article (Section 8), the founders gave Congress the right to declare war; to raise and support armies; to provide and maintain a navy; to make rules for the government and regulation of the armed forces; to provide for calling forth the militia to execute the laws, suppress insurrections, and repel invasions; to provide the organizing, arming, and disciplining of the militia; and to make all laws necessary and proper for executing the foregoing powers. In Article II, Section 2, the founders addressed the role of the executive during war and designated the president as commander in chief of the Army and Navy. (See the Appendix.)

The founders were more concerned about the war power than any other, and with good reason. As colonists, they had viewed with great alarm how easily George III could commit Great Britain—and therefore the American colonies—to war. In their new republic, the founders were determined to remove the momentous decision of war making from the hands of a single individual. Even Alexander Hamilton—a champion of executive power—remained wary of a concentrated authority to make war. "The President is to be commander in chief of the army and navy of the United States," he wrote in *The Federalist*. "In this respect his authority would be nominally the same with that of the king of Great Britain, but in substance much inferior to it. It would amount to nothing more than the supreme command and direction of the military and naval forces, as first General and Admiral of the Confederacy, while that of the British king extends to the *declaring* of war and to the *raising* and *regulating* of fleets and armies—all which, by the Constitution under consideration, would appertain to the legislature."[6]

The constitutional framers worried further that the widespread predisposition toward monarchy throughout the world (and certainly across most of Europe) might arise in time within their own nation. Consequently, the prospect of a large standing army in America—with its potential for military defiance of republican rule—troubled them deeply. Thomas Jefferson, James Madison, and others had no interest in turning over the weapons of war to the discretion of a solitary individual; better to keep this power harnessed within a popular assembly. "We have already given in example one effectual check to the Dog of war," wrote Jefferson to Madison in 1789, "by transferring the power of letting him loose from the Executive to the Legislative body, from those who are to spend to those who are to pay."[7]

Defensive versus Offensive Warfare

A misinterpretation of Article II, Section 2, sometimes leads to the unwarranted conclusion that the president enjoys preeminent authority over the war power. Properly understood, this section gives to the president the right and obligation as commander in chief to make use of the armed forces to *repel* sudden attacks against the United States, when a delay to consult with

Congress would be foolhardy, even suicidal. As commander in chief, the president is responsible as well for leading the armed forces in ways specified by the Congress. The president, however, was not to *initiate* hostilities. The renowned constitutional authority Senator Sam Ervin, Jr. (D-N.C.), once emphasized the difference:

> . . . a distinction must be drawn between *defensive warfare* and offensive warfare. There is no doubt whatever that the President has the authority under the Constitution, and, indeed, the duty, to use the Armed Forces to repel sudden armed attacks on the Nation. But any use of the Armed Forces for any purpose not directly related to the defense of the United States against sudden armed aggression, and I emphasize the word "sudden," can be undertaken only upon congressional authorization.[8]

During the first hundred years of the nation's history, presidents for the most part honored this original understanding between the two branches. An important illustration is President Jefferson's handling of the Barbary pirates, who jeopardized American shipping in the Mediterranean Sea. He dispatched a naval squadron to protect U.S. commerce in these waters. Upon deciding that defensive action was insufficient, however, the president prudently turned to the Congress for permission to employ offensive measures against the pirates. He acknowledged that he himself was "unauthorized by the Constitution, without the sanction of Congress, to go beyond the line of defense," and requested permission to "place our force on an equal footing with that of its adversaries"—an offensive decision "confided by the Constitution to the legislature exclusively."[9]

In an exhaustive analysis of the war power's early use, the Senate Foreign Relations Committee noted in 1969 that even President James Monroe, well known for his aggressive foreign policy views (Chapter 3), drew a careful distinction between the enunciation of his major statement of policy (the Monroe Doctrine), on the one hand, and, on the other hand, its implementation, which would have required authority from Congress. His secretary of state, John Quincy Adams, replied to an inquiry from Colombia in 1824 (regarding what steps the United States would take against possible European intervention in Latin America) with this prudent notice: "With respect to the question, 'in what manner the Government of the United States intends to resist on its part any interference of the Holy Alliance for the purpose of subjugating the new republics or interfering in their political forms' you understand that by the Constitution of the United States, the ultimate decision of this question belongs to the Legislative Department of the Government. . . ."[10]

The Foreign Relations Committee noted further, and again with obvious approval, a speech by Abraham Lincoln when he was a member of Congress from Illinois and critical of presidential power. (The committee chose to overlook President Lincoln's subsequent disregard for the prerogatives of Congress during the Civil War.) In 1846, at the time of President Polk's war against Mexico, Lincoln was convinced that the president had acted unconstitutionally when he ordered American forces into disputed territory along the Rio Grande without the permission of Congress. Wrote Representative Lincoln:

> . . . Allow the President to invade a neighboring nation, whenever *he* shall deem it necessary to repel an invasion, and you allow him to do so, *whenever he may choose to say* he deems it necessary for such purpose—and you allow him to make war at pleasure. Study to see if you can fix *any limit* to his power in this respect, after you have given him so much as you propose. . . .
>
> The provision of the Constitution giving the warmaking power to Congress, was dictated, as I understand it, by the following reasons. Kings had always been involving and impoverishing their people in wars, pretending generally, if not always, that the good of the people was the object. This, our convention undertook

to be the most oppressive of all kingly oppressions; and they resolved to so frame the Constitution that *no one man* should hold the power of bringing this oppression upon us.[11]

Such distinguished protests notwithstanding, the erosion of legislative control over the war power accelerated, slowly at first, and then in this century with increasing speed. With congressional acquiescence, presidents during the late 1800s used military force abroad for limited—though sometimes clearly offensive—purposes, including the "hot pursuit" of criminals across international borders and operations against piracy and the slave trade. Presidents confined this use of force chiefly to missions involving individuals or bands of renegades, not sovereign states; in the twentieth century, however, presidents would claim constitutional authority to direct military force against other nations.

While men like Theodore Roosevelt, William Howard Taft, and Woodrow Wilson never declared the right to launch full-scale war on behalf of the United States, they nonetheless did use the military to intervene repeatedly in the affairs of Mexico and other sovereign states in Central America and the Caribbean. Again, Congress either stood by passively, or sometimes enthusiastically cheered this use of the war power. The precedents—and temptations—mounted for presidents to exalt the commander-in-chief clause of the Constitution (Article II, Section 2) over those passages which spelled out the right of Congress to declare war, raise armies, and the like (Article I, Section 8).

Then early in the twentieth century arrived the twin catastrophes of the Great Depression (1929–1942) and the Second World War, both powerful catalysts for a further concentration of powers in the White House. In this time of great risk for the nation, the American people were prepared to accept—even demanded—aggressive leadership from the president. This suited the temperament of Franklin D. Roosevelt. In the worthy battle against the Axis powers, not only was he willing to usurp the treaty power through his destroyers-for-bases deal with Britain (discussed later in this chapter), but he also sought a more exclusive control over the war power than any president since Lincoln.

Strictly on his own authority and without meaningful consultation with Congress, President Roosevelt in 1941—a time when the American people held strong isolationist sentiments—offered U.S. forces for the protection of Greenland and Iceland against a Nazi invasion; assigned warships to accompany (all the way to Iceland) American convoys loaded with supplies for war-wrenched Britain, provided only that one or more of the ships in each convoy fly an American or Icelandic flag; and announced (after an American destroyer assisted in a British military operation and was fired upon by a German submarine) that American naval ships would shoot on sight against any German or Italian vessels of war discovered in the western Atlantic.

With these decisions, the executive branch—by itself—had done nothing less than push the United States into undeclared naval warfare in the Atlantic Ocean. While few would dispute the merits of his cause, the president by avoiding Congress had established a dubious precedent for war making that his successors could draw upon for purposes less noble.

Inherent Presidential Authority

Each of the presidents in the postwar period from Harry S Truman to Ronald Reagan has tended to view the war power more from the vantage point of Franklin Roosevelt than of Jefferson or the other founders—though, as discussed in Chapter 10 ("The War Power"), the degree of presidential independence in the exercise of this instrument has varied widely. For each, the belief has endured that only Congress had the right to declare war formally; many executive officials, however, have seemed to think that—short of a formal declaration of

war—the president as commander in chief enjoys the prerogative of using the military as he sees fit, as if America's soldiers and sailors were so many chess pieces and the president the grandmaster.

In 1950, President Truman made the decision to commit American troops to the war in Korea (a "police action," in the administration's phrase) without congressional authorization—a war that would eventually result in the death of over 30,000 GIs. Truman's only public explanation regarding this use of the war power appeared in the *Department of State Bulletin*. "The President, as Commander in Chief of the Armed Forces of the United States, has full control over the use thereof," he opined, adding that there existed a "traditional power of the President to use the Armed Forces of the United States without consulting Congress."[12]

In the institutional struggle over the war power, Truman had taken off the gloves. For the first time, a president of the United States had espoused a doctrine that claimed an *"inherent" constitutional right* of presidential dominance over the decision to make war. The president's designation as commander in chief, and the constitutional injunction that "he shall take Care that the Laws be faithfully executed," allowed him—so went the claim—the implicit right to use U.S. troops as he saw fit. This accretion of presidential power was allowed, once more, to pass with hardly a murmur from Capitol Hill—though by 1951 the conservative Republican leader of the Senate, Robert Taft of Ohio ("Mr. Republican," as he was often called) lamented that "the President simply usurped authority, in violation of the laws and the Constitution, when he sent troops to Korea to carry out the resolution of the United Nations in an undeclared war."[13]

Truman's secretary of state, Dean Acheson, would have none of Taft's interpretation. Indeed, he found the reference to constitutional questions quite improper: "We are in a position in the world today where the argument as to who has the power to do this, that, or the other thing, is not exactly what is called for from America in this very critical hour." Acheson declared, imperiously: "Not only has the President the authority to use the Armed Forces in carrying out the broad foreign policy of the United States and implementing treaties, but it is equally clear that this authority may not be interfered with by the Congress in the exercise of powers which it has under the Constitution."[14]

War by Blank Check

Perhaps mindful of Taft's views on the misuse of the war power by the Truman administration, President Eisenhower (now, like Taft, serving under the GOP banner) proved to be more ambivalent than either Franklin Roosevelt or Truman had been about executive claims to broad, inherent war powers. He turned instead to an approach that would become almost as controversial: permission to use military force by way of a *congressional resolution* (requiring a majority vote in both legislative chambers). Eisenhower asked on several occasions for authority from Congress to use the armed forces in various parts of the world, and Congress complied—indeed, provided sweeping authority to employ force "as [the president] determines necessary."

Caught up in the exigencies of the moment, legislators lost sight of the constitutional question. They left the unfortunate impression (in the critical view of an analysis offered by the Senate Foreign Relations Committee in 1969) that Congress had accepted presidential authority over the use of the military as he saw fit, and that the role of legislators was merely to express a sense of national unity behind the president as he sought to protect America's "vital interests" abroad. In its postmortem, the committee expressed a fear that "an authorization so general and imprecise amounts to an unconstitutional alienation of its war power on the part of the Congress."[15]

Congress had passed several resolutions of the kind found repugnant to the Foreign Relations Committee in 1969, at the request of President Eisenhower to defend, first, Formosa (Taiwan) and the offshore islands located between Formosa and mainland China in 1955, and, second, the Middle East in 1957; of President Kennedy, for Cuba and Berlin in 1962; and of President Johnson, for Vietnam in 1964. Written with a broad brush, the resolutions steadily evolved toward an advance approval by Congress for virtually any military operations the president might see fit to take.

Initially, the Eisenhower administration was cautious in its dealings with Congress on foreign policy. When the Chinese communists shelled the offshore island of Quemoy in 1955 and an invasion from the mainland against Formosa seemed imminent, President Eisenhower asked the Congress "to participate now, by specific resolution, in measures designed to improve the prospect of peace," including "the use of the Armed Forces of the United States if necessary to assure the security of Formosa and the Pescadores." A senior senator asked the secretary of state, John Foster Dulles, if it would be "fair to describe this resolution as a predated declaration of war." Dulles prudently replied, "The president does not interpret this as a declaration of war, and if there were a situation to arise which in his opinion called for a declaration of war, he would come back again to the Congress."[16]

Calmed by such assurances, Congress quickly approved the *Formosa Resolution* with little thought to the shift in constitutional prerogatives it implied. As the historian Arthur M. Schlesinger, Jr., has written, the Formosa Resolution—unlike prior resolutions in American history—failed either to order a specific action or even to name an enemy: "Rather it committed Congress to the approval of hostilities without knowledge of the specific situation in which the hostilities would begin."[17]

Two years later, in 1957, the Eisenhower administration again came to Capitol Hill armed with a resolution on foreign policy, this time aimed at the Middle East, where U.S. strategists feared that the recent British withdrawal had created a power vacuum that the Soviet Union might find enticing. In January, the president appeared before Congress with a request for authority to use American armed force if necessary to protect the national sovereignty of Middle East nations against Soviet encroachment. Again, a senator posed the question of whether such a resolution would amount to a "predated declaration of war." Secretary Dulles objected: "I would call it a declaration of peace rather than a declaration of war, because I think that without this we are in great danger of getting into war."[18]

The secretary of state soon discovered, however, that key members of the U.S. Senate were now prepared to match his more brazen attitude with an equal dose of strong skepticism of their own (the House at this stage remained content to ally itself with the president). The Formosa Resolution had slipped through Congress with relative ease; but now the Middle East Resolution—dubbed the *Eisenhower Doctrine* by the press—faced rough sledding in the Senate.

The Senate floor debate clearly revealed a new skepticism among senators who had sup-

ported the Formosa Resolution. J. William Fulbright (D-Ark.), chairman of the Foreign Relations Committee, complained that there had been "no real prior consultation with Congress, nor will there be any sharing of power. The whole manner of presentation of this resolution—leaks to the press, speeches to specially summoned Saturday joint sessions, and dramatic secret meetings of the Committee on Foreign Relations after dark one evening before the Congress was even organized, in an atmosphere of suspense and urgency—does not constitute consultation in the true sense. All this was designed to manage Congress, to coerce it into signing this blank check."[19]

The transcript of closed hearings on the Middle East Resolution, held jointly by the committees on Foreign Relations and Armed Services, indicates that Fulbright's views were shared by other stalwarts of the Senate leadership. "In my opinion," said Richard Bevard Russell (D-Ga.), widely regarded at the time as the most influential member of the Senate on military issues, "the Congress of the United States is being treated as a group of children, and very small children, and children with a very low IQ at that, in the manner that this resolution has been presented to us. . . . I think that the Con-

Secretary of State Dean Acheson (right) of the Truman administration at a San Francisco airport press conference with John Foster Dulles, who would succeed him in the Eisenhower administration. (UPI/Bettmann Newsphotos)

gress, if it is going to preserve its own self-esteem, ought to have more information than we have on it." Russell believed that the resolution left the legislative branch "as an appendage of the executive branch in dealing with this very vital and important matter," and predicted that if the Senate passed the resolution (as it finally did on March 12) ". . . from here on out we will never get back in control of your program in this area. . . . It may be going for the next 25 or 30 years, and the Congress will never regain control of it. It will from here on out be in the hands of the executive branch of the Government."[20]

Senator Wayne Morse (D-Ore.) concurred: "You have got a resolution here which, for the first time, suggests that the President of the United States can exercise discretion to proceed to protect the territorial integrity of some other country somewhere in the world attacked by some Communist country, because he thinks that eventually that may involve the security of the United States, and I think that is an absurd stretching of that alleged emergency power on the part of the President, and I think it would be a clear violation of the constitutional power of the president."[21] Senator Sam Ervin noted that the Constitution "contemplates that the Armed Forces of the United States will not be put into an offensive war . . . without the consent of Congress; and here this first part of this resolution says that the president can put our Armed Forces against some enemy which has not yet been selected, in the Middle East. The resolution is not directed against Russia; it is directed against the nations which we fear will become Communist in the Middle East. . . and it is a perfect invitation for another Korea, with Russia furnishing arms, and us furnishing the boys to do the dying."[22]

For several weeks, the two Senate committees agonized over the language of the resolution, stumbling around in what Russell referred to as the "shadowland" that fell between the commander-in-chief and the declaration-of-war clauses of the Constitution. At last they decided to strike from the resolution the concept of legislative authorization; instead, the language would simply represent a statement of American policy on the Middle East.

The effect was untoward. According to Schlesinger, President Eisenhower became convinced "less of the need for serious consultation with Congress than of his inherent authority to employ armed forces at presidential will."[23] When the president sent American troops into Lebanon in the next year (1958), he neither invoked the Middle East Resolution nor requested authority from Congress, but merely pointed to his authority as commander in chief.

The most fateful of the foreign policy resolutions passed by Congress in the postwar era was undoubtedly the so-called *Gulf of Tonkin Resolution*, approved in August of 1964. Reacting to intelligence reports provided by the executive branch claiming that American naval vessels off the coast of Vietnam had come under enemy fire, legislators declared precipitously in this resolution: ". . . the Congress approves and supports the determination of the President, as Commander in Chief, to take all necessary measures to repel any armed attack against the forces of the United States and to prevent further aggression."

During the legislative debate, a colleague asked Senator Fulbright (as a leading sponsor of the resolution, evidently willing on this occasion to give a blank check to the president) whether "looking ahead, if the President decided that it was necessary to use such force as could lead into war, we will give that authority by this resolution." Responded Fulbright: "That is the way I would interpret it."[24]

The erosion of legislative control over the war power had reached an extreme; Congress seemed to acknowledge practically unlimited presidential control over the use of military force. Subsequently, the Johnson administration's under secretary of state, Nicholas Katzenbach, would point to the Gulf of Tonkin Resolution as the "functional equivalent" of a declaration of war by Congress—even though, according to a senior member of the Foreign Relations Committee who participated in the original debate, "Congress neither expected nor even considered at the time of the debate on the resolution that the President would later commit more than half a million American soldiers to a full-scale war in Vietnam."[25]

INTERNATIONAL AGREEMENTS

The Congress and the executive branch share, through the power of diplomacy, the authority to establish American commitments abroad. The only explicit reference to international agreement making in the Constitution of the United States is the *treaty provision* of Article II, Section 2. This passage states that the president "shall have power, by and with the Advice and Consent of the Senate, to make Treaties, provided two-thirds of the Senators present

concur. . . ." These words convey the idea of a partnership between the legislative and executive branches. As one prominent legal analyst of the treaty clause concludes: "The Founders made unmistakably plain their intention to withhold from the President the power to enter into treaties all by himself. . . ."[26]

The executive branch obviously plays a central role in the treaty procedure. Another authority offers these observations on the president's involvement: "It is on his initiative and responsibility that the treaty-making process is undertaken; he determines what provisions the United States wishes to have embodied in the treaty; he decides whether reservations or amendments that the Senate attaches to a draft treaty are acceptable to him and should be submitted to the other parties to the treaty; and, even if the Senate by two-thirds vote approves a treaty that he has negotiated, he may, influenced by change of heart or political conditions,

---

Perspectives on American Foreign Policy 5.1

Senator Frank Church (D-Idaho), an outspoken member of the Senate Foreign Relations Committee (and later its chairman), commenting in 1970 on the aggrandizement of presidential power over the use of overt military force:

One hears it argued these days—by high officials in the Executive Branch, by foreign policy experts, and by some political scientists—that certain of our Constitutional procedures, including the power of Congress to declare war, are obsolete in the nuclear age. This contention, in my opinion, is without merit. Nothing in the Constitution prevents—and no one in Congress would ever try to prevent—the President from acting in a genuine national emergency. What is at issue is his authority to order our military forces into action in foreign lands whenever and wherever he judges the

national interest calls for it. What is at issue is his right to alter Constitutional processes at his option, even in the name of defending those processes.

I do not believe that the Constitution is obsolete; I do not believe that Congress is incapable of discharging its responsibilities for war and peace; but, if either of these conditions ever should arise, the remedy would lie in the amendment process of the Constitution itself. As George Washington said in his farewell address, ". . . let there be no change in usurpation; for though this in one instance may be the instrument of good, it is the customary weapon by which free governments are destroyed."

Congressional Record, April 30, 1970, p. 13566.

decide not to ratify it and at the last minute file it in his wastebasket."[27]

Despite the president's considerable powers, the wording of Article II, Section 2, undeniably provides the Senate a central role in decisions regarding commitments overseas. Yet, the historical record reveals that presidents—and even middle-ranking officials in the executive branch—have involved the United States in major foreign obligations without the requisite advice and consent of two-thirds of the Senate membership. Thomas Jefferson argued: "On the subject of treaties, our system is to have none with any nation, as far as can be avoided."[28] His advice has come close to being honored; treaties are rarely used as an instrument of American foreign policy. The irony lies in the reason why: this constitutional procedure has simply been bypassed. In its place have arisen either loosely worded statutes granting permission for international agreements (so-called *statutory agreements*) or hidden transactions with other nations carried out by the executive branch without meaningful consultation with the Congress (*executive agreements*).

Originally designed to be the solemn means by which the United States would enter into agreements with other nations, the treaty has been mostly abandoned by presidents in the modern era. From 1946 through the Carter administration, for example, a scant 6 percent of the total number of international agreements were approved through the treaty procedure—though, among these, a few (like the Panama Canal Treaty of 1978) were of substantial importance.

The Destroyers Deal

The most pronounced insult to the treaty process in this century occurred during the presidency of Franklin Roosevelt. In the summer of 1940, Great Britain faced imminent invasion by the Nazis. France had already fallen, and the English Channel no longer seemed an adequate barrier in light of the formidable prowess dis-

played by the German general staff. The hour was late, the fate of Britain dark. To assist the British, President Roosevelt entered into a major agreement. The United States would lend the British fifty somewhat antiquated American destroyers for their defense against the Germans, in exchange for leasing rights to certain naval bases in the Western Hemisphere belonging to Great Britain. This "lend-lease" arrangement had far-reaching implications, providing legal grounds for a possible declaration of war against the United States by the Germans. While one might have expected such a serious commitment to be joined by way of the constitutional treaty provision, Roosevelt used instead an approach that has come to be known as the *executive agreement*. He simply consummated the pact between the United States and Great Britain by his own signature, without even the slightest nod to Congress—let alone a request for a two-thirds vote of support within the Senate.

The president's motives were, without doubt, of the highest order. He quite properly wished to help turn back the totalitarian assault against Western democracies, and to move quickly before it was too late. A debate in the Senate might have prolonged an American response; London could have fallen before the British received the ships they needed. Critics have subsequently contended, however, that the president exceeded his constitutional authority by failing to use the treaty process. The Senate Foreign Relations Committee singled out the lend-lease agreement (in its 1969 report) in assessing the decline of the treaty power:

> More serious in the long run than the President's action [the lend-lease agreement] was the preparation of a brief by the Attorney General contending that the action was constitutional. Had the President publicly acknowledged his incursion on the Senate's treaty power and explained it as an emergency measure, a damaging constitutional precedent would have been averted. Instead, a spurious claim of constitutionality was made, com-

pounding the incursion on the Senate's authority into a precedent for future incursions.[29]

The destroyer agreement ushered in an era
that witnessed many other international commitments arrived at outside the explicit procedural requirements stated in the Constitution.
The treaty process, indeed, has been largely
pushed aside by executive agreements and statutory agreements (which, recall, are foreign
commitments based on law, that is, requiring
approval by majority vote in both legislative
chambers, rather than by a two-thirds vote in
the Senate). Roosevelt's deal with the British,
reached in a time of emergency, came to be
seen by the executive branch as a precedent to
draw upon following the Second World War.

Creeping Commitments

In 1962, for example, Secretary of State Dean
Rusk joined with the foreign minister of Thailand to issue a statement in which the secretary
announced "the firm intention of the United
States to aid Thailand, its ally and historic
friend, in resisting Communist aggression and
subversion." This pledge passed far beyond the
language of the SEATO treaty, signed in 1954,
which provided only that member nations
would "consult" in times of military peril and
act to meet the common danger in accordance
with their own "constitutional processes." The
collective security arrangement established under SEATO was suddenly transformed by joint
communiqué into a bilateral U.S.–Thai defense
pact.

Under the new relationship, the United
States Military Assistance Program (MAP) for
Thailand rose from $24 million in 1960 to $88
million in 1962. This dramatic leap in funding
required congressional approval, but, as a part
of MAP, only from the House and Senate
armed services committees. These two panels
have the authority (granted by Congress) to dis-
guise, for purposes of national security and secrecy, specific military requests within the overall annual Pentagon budget. Thus, for some

programs, all the executive branch has to do is
persuade two committees in Congress, not a
majority of each chamber; and often, the legislators on these committees have deferred this
authority to the chairmen and their minority-
party counterparts.

Through this approach, the executive branch
was able in 1962 to avoid a full-fledged debate
in Congress on the merits of the Thai relationship, relying instead on support from a few
strategically located and sympathetic legislators
at the helm of the armed services committees.
By the end of the decade, the United States—
or, more accurately, the executive branch—had
assured the Thai government through a secret
joint-contingency agreement that America
would intervene in the event of a conventional
military attack against Thailand. The secret
agreement also established the payment of special bonuses to Thai troops in Vietnam—in essence, the hiring of mercenaries to fight on behalf of the United States in the Vietnamese
war.[30]

During this period, the executive branch
never requested treaty—or even statutory—approval from the Congress to authorize the stationing of 5000 U.S. combat troops in Thailand,
a portion of whom were actively engaged in
counterinsurgency operations in the jungles;
yet, it did manage to forward to the Senate for
approval a far less significant tax treaty with
Thailand. This (and similar experiences) led
frustrated members of the Senate Foreign Relations Committee to conclude in 1969: "In some
instances we have come close to reversing the
traditional distinction between the treaty as the
instrument of a major commitment and the executive agreement as the instrument of a minor
one."[31]

Whether or not the military pacts with Thailand were appropriate is a separate question;
what concerned constitutional experts was the
procedure used to arrive at the commitments.
The original intent of SEATO, a military alliance
approved through the rigorous and solemn
treaty procedure laid out in the Constitution,

had been altered by communiqué and secret executive agreements.

In 1966, Secretary Rusk cast his net more broadly still. As the war in Vietnam heated up and threatened to boil over into Thailand, he warned that "no would-be aggressor should suppose that the absence of a defense treaty, congressional declaration, or U.S. military presence grants immunity to aggression." Again, as with Franklin Roosevelt, the secretary's motive appears laudable enough; but members of the Congress saw the declaration as yet another blow to their constitutional prerogatives. It "put Congress on notice," remarked a prominent senator, "that, with or without its consent, treaty or no treaty, the Executive will act as it sees fit against anyone whom it judges to be an aggressor. . . . It is indeed nothing less than a statement of intention on the part of the Executive to usurp the treaty power of the Senate."[32]

In the eyes of international law, executive agreements carry the weight of treaties; so do statutory agreements. All three forms of agreement making represent official commitments by the United States to other nations. Given their importance, the realization that executive agreements are sometimes made in secret—without debate in the Congress—has made them a subject of controversy. Legislators accept the value of the executive agreement when used for minor commitments; good management sense would argue against congressional involvement in the hundreds of routine understandings reached each year between the United States and other nations, on everything from trade in strawberries to the protection of migratory birds whose flight carries them across international borders. Legislators balk, though, when new and far-reaching commitments are pursued through this instrument of diplomacy, as occurred with the establishment of U.S. military bases in Spain.

During the 1960s, the United States entered into a series of secret commitments with Spain over military base rights. Once again Secretary Rusk laid the groundwork with a public joint declaration signed in 1963 with the Spanish minister for foreign affairs. The document, which read like a treaty, asserted: "The United States Government reaffirms its recognition of the importance of Spain to the security, well-being and development of the Atlantic and Mediterranean areas. The two governments recognize that the security and integrity of both the United States and Spain are necessary for the common security. A threat to either country, and to the joint facilities that each provides for the common defense, would be a matter of common concern to both countries, and each country would take such action as it may consider appropriate within the framework of its constitutional processes."

On top of this public pronouncement came a series of secret understandings, including a memorandum signed between high-ranking military officers in both nations which committed the United States to defend Spain against third countries. Another memorandum, written by the chairman of the Joint Chiefs of Staff to his Spanish counterpart, offered the assurance that U.S. troops stationed on Spanish soil represented "a far more visible and credible security guarantee than any written document."[33]

For the Senate Committee on Foreign Relations, this pronouncement epitomized yet again the penchant of the executive branch for *commitment by accretion* and an abandonment of constitutional procedure. "The making of such a commitment by means of an executive agreement, or a military memorandum," the committee argued, "has no valid place in our constitutional law, and constitutes a usurpation of the treaty power of the Senate." The committee referred to the Spanish bases agreement as a "quasi-commitment, unspecified as to exact import but, like buds in springtime, ready, under the right climatic conditions, to burst into full bloom."[34]

The full Congress remained yet unwilling to join the Senate Foreign Relations Committee in a challenge to the executive branch on either the Thai or Spanish military arrangements. The

---

Perspectives on American Foreign Policy   5.2

The Senate Foreign Relations Committee in 1972 on the importance of keeping Congress informed about international agreements:

. . . the principle of mandatory reporting of agreements with foreign countries to the Congress is more than desirable; it is, from a constitutional standpoint, crucial and indispensable. For the Congress to accept anything less would represent a resignation from responsibility and an alienation of an authority which is vested in the Congress by the Constitution. If Congress is to meet its responsibilities in the formulation of foreign policy, no information is more crucial than the fact and content of agreements with foreign nations.

"Transmittal of Executive Agreements to Congress," Senate Report No. 92–591, 92nd Cong., 2d Sess., January 19, 1972, p. 3.

---

agreements stuck, and Congress provided the necessary funding. Within the next few years, however, attitudes toward executive agreements would change sharply on Capitol Hill. Fed by disillusionment over the Watergate scandal and the souring war in Vietnam, a legislative rebellion against executive dominance in foreign affairs began to run full tide. Presidential insensitivity to the constitutional underpinnings of the war power, coupled with a growing concern among legislators over the demise of the treaty power, stoked long-smoldering congressional grievances toward the executive branch. A key objective in this congressional resurgence was the restoration of a meaningful involvement for legislators in the making of American commitments abroad (examined more fully in Chapter 11).

THE SEEDS OF ACQUIESCENCE

If the war and treaty powers rightly belong to Congress, as claimed by the Senate Foreign Relations Committee (and other critics) at the height of the Vietnamese war, why had they been abdicated by legislators in the first place? In the early days of the republic, the answer can be found in a willingness of legislators, first, to give presidents free rein to chase pirates and bandits who threatened U.S. interests and, second, to defend the Monroe Doctrine and its corollaries. In more recent times, the surface answer for the passage of the Tonkin Gulf Resolution appears to be that legislators were simply responding rapidly to a perceived emergency and never anticipated President Johnson's later interpretation of their temporary grant of authority as a "blank check" from Congress to expand the war in Vietnam through a massive troop buildup. After all, the president was promising audiences around the country during the 1964 presidential election that ". . . we are not about to send American boys 9,000 or 10,000 miles away from home to do what Asian boys ought to be doing for themselves."[35]

The Senate Foreign Relations Committee had trusted the Johnson administration during its early years (the president and Chairman Fulbright, from the adjacent states of Texas and Arkansas, had been close friends in the Senate for decades) and that trust had backfired, first over the president's invasion of the Dominican Republic in 1965 (which he had promised Fulbright he would never undertake) and then in his steady escalation of the war in Vietnam.

"In adopting a resolution with such sweeping language. . . ," concluded the repentent committee in 1969 (still under Senator Fulbright's leadership), "Congress committed the error of making a *personal* judgment as to how President Johnson would implement the resolution when it had a responsibility to make an *institutional* judgment, first, as to what *any* President would do with so great an acknowledgment of power, and, second, as to whether, under the Constitution, Congress had the right to grant or concede the authority in question."[36]

Yet, since congressional acquiescence in the postwar era began long before 1964, one must search for deeper explanations. One important source was the preoccupation of Congress with the cold war. Just as the depression and World War II had the effect of centralizing power in the government, so, too, the enduring conflict between the United States and the Soviet Union has been a centripetal force in Washington. Some legislators have expressed the belief that Americans must now live in a constant state of war readiness. During an exchange between senators at a hearing in 1975, for example, Frank Church argued that some CIA intelligence operations that might infringe upon civil liberties ought to be prohibited in peacetime. In response, John Tower (R-Tex.) objected to Church's distinction between "war" and "peace."

> Church: I think that we should recognize the distinction between war and peace. It poses the question whether this country in peacetime wants to live always under the customs of war. . . .
> Tower: I think that we cannot draw this in strict terms of war and peace, in terms of whether or not the United States is actually at war. We are in effect in a war of sorts. That is a war of the preservation of the climate in this world where national integrity will be respected.[37]

Legislators have been reluctant to question the president and his aides on matters of foreign policy, for fear that it might be misinterpreted as a lack of patriotism or proper support for the nation in an age of continuous crisis. A careful consideration of constitutional questions was often abandoned in the face of emergencies (real or imagined) like the Cuban missile crisis or the *Mayaguez* rescue attempt. In their rush to buttress the president against the pressures of the cold war, legislators have often failed, in sum, to weigh the effects of this uncritical support on their constitutional obligation to serve as an independent check on the use of power by the executive branch in its conduct of foreign policy.

Important, too, has been the ghost of the Treaty of Versailles. Some legislators continued to wear a hair shirt because the Senate failed to approve the treaty. Had it been accepted, the League of Nations might have worked and the Second World War might have been avoided—questionable "mights," to be sure, in light of the UN's inauspicious record of peacekeeping around the globe since 1945. Whatever the validity of this causal linkage between the failure of the Versailles treaty and the outbreak of totalitarian aggression, it had the effect of inhibiting some members of Congress who otherwise may have urged a clearer separation between the two branches on matters of external affairs.

Moreover, the pressures of *bipartisanship* intimidated some legislators. "Politics stops at the water's edge" is a venerable adage in the lore of U.S. foreign policy. According to this prescription, Congress is supposed to eschew partisanship and rally behind the White House for the sake of national unity. The world had become too dangerous to reveal foreign policy disagreements before the eyes of America's adversaries; politics would have to be reserved strictly for disputes over domestic policy. While this argument has some obvious merit, legislators began to realize during the 1960s that one of its end results was to concentrate foreign policy powers further in the hands of the president by stifling dissent on Capitol Hill. The pill "bipartisanship" became, all too often, merely a soporific to lull the "loyal opposition" in Congress.

The war in Vietnam provided a rude awakening for legislators. "The myth that the Chief Executive is the fount of all wisdom in foreign affairs today lies shattered on the shoals of Vietnam," proclaimed a leading member of the Foreign Relations Committee at the height of the war.[38] Unpopular uses of presidential power in Vietnam, and the even clearer expression of presidential arrogance in the Watergate scandal, would turn the attention of legislators back to forgotten questions of constitutional authority.

THE PURSE STRINGS AND OTHER DISPUTES

By constitutional design, then, foreign policy authority and the power that flows from it—that is, control over this nation's external relations—are shared within the government of the United States. The question of the proper distribution of power in a country that has grown from an isolated agrarian society to a mighty industrial state with global commitments has been a source of ongoing debate, fueled by the ambiguities and omissions of the Constitution. The war and the treaty powers have produced the most frequent and acrimonious disagreements between the branches, but other constitutional provisions have led to conflict, too. Chief among them is the power of the purse.

Money

The Constitution places the power to spend directly in the hands of the Congress. "No Money shall be drawn from the Treasury, but in Consequence of Appropriations made by Law," reads Article I, Section 9. The importance of money to foreign and domestic policy is self-evident. Virtually everything a country might wish to do requires financial resources. So ubiquitous is the spending power that, rather than consider it separately, this aspect of American foreign policy is considered throughout Part II of this book. A few examples are offered here, though, to provide a sense of how the spending power has been a further source of tension between the branches.

Although the Constitution clearly lodges the spending power with the legislative branch, executive officials have established methods to bypass Congress. One technique is *impoundment*, the freezing of funds in the federal treasury despite the passage of an appropriations law requiring the money to be spent. Presidents Truman, Eisenhower, and Kennedy (among others) all refused to spend funds appropriated by Congress for various weapons systems.[39] Presidents have often opposed the military hardware recommended by Congress in favor of their own shopping list; but, rather than veto the congressional recommendations, presidents have taken the less visible (and therefore easier) course of simply never spending the appropriated funds. The rationale used by the executive branch to justify impoundment has often been that conditions change between the passage of a law and its implementation. Inflation, for example, may suddenly spiral upward, making additional expenditures unwise. Further, the absence of presidential authority for a line-item veto presents the White House with the choice of either vetoing an omnibus (and perhaps popular) bill in order to omit a single weapons proposal within it which the president opposes, or accepting the weapon as a bitter pill immovably lodged within the larger and more palatable statute. Impoundment becomes a tempting alternative.

In 1974, Congress passed the Budget and Impoundment Control Act in an effort to tighten controls over the executive use of impoundment. Now the executive branch must openly report its intention to impound funds, providing legislators with an opportunity to accept or dismiss its rationale. While a significant piece of legislation, this 1974 Budget Act is sufficiently ambiguous, according to one authority, to allow "the executive ample room for interpretations."[40] Institutional jockeying over the nature of permissible impoundments is likely to continue.

Secret spending by the executive branch has caused friction as well. Burying appropriations in the Defense Department's annual budget bill under secrecy provisions, with the cooperation of just the two armed services committees—often only their leaders—is just one way to bypass legislative debate. This approach may be legitimate at times, because vital, secret military missions may necessitate special measures; but such legerdemain can be abused, as critics contend was the case with funding to Thai mercenaries (discussed earlier in this chapter) and with funding for the hidden escalation of U.S. forces in Vietnam from 1964 to 1966.

Moneys for the CIA and other intelligence agencies are also handled in secrecy. Though this is understandable, the practice leads to a situation of limited accountability, with reliance again on only a few legislators and staff to monitor the spending. In the early days of the CIA (established in 1947), key legislators proved willing to let the agency handle its financial affairs with minimal congressional involvement. Closer controls might have prevented the channeling of resources to the Bay of Pigs operation and other misfortunes. Moreover, in the past, administrations sometimes diverted funds from one foreign policy account to another without legislative approval—or even awareness, as when funds for foreign aid to Laos were used for covert warfare against communist guerrillas in its northern region.[41]

Today, controls over intelligence funding are tighter; but, as the 1986–1987 Iran-contra scandal revealed, an administration can seek support from outside sources when Congress shuts off the money spigot for a particular program. In this instance, Congress had set a ceiling on funds for covert warfare against the Sandinista regime in Nicaragua. As the reader will recall, officials on the National Security Council then arranged (in cooperation with personnel in the CIA) to sell arms to Iran and divert the profits through Swiss banks to finance the anti-Sandinista contras. In addition, the Reagan administration sought to finance the war with funds from private citizens and foreign governments—the "privatization" of American foreign policy. This approach to foreign policy would, as the constitutional scholar Louis Fisher has observed, "destroy the system of checks and balances. Executive use of funds obtained outside the appropriations process would create a government the framers feared the most: union of sword and purse."[42]

Diplomatic Recognition, Confirmation, and Oversight

The Constitution grants to the president the power to receive foreign diplomats ("he shall receive Ambassadors and other public Ministers"). President George Washington relied upon this portion of the founding document to bestow diplomatic recognition on foreign nations that otherwise Congress might have failed to acknowledge as legitimate, as in the case of revolutionary France. Washington successfully converted a seemingly insignificant constitutional clause into a potent executive prerogative in foreign affairs.

The Senate similarly has used its right to confirm ("with the Advice and Consent of the Senate") selected presidential appointments as a means of cross-examining candidates for high office in the executive branch—to see if they are fit, in the view of the Senate, for a position of high authority and are willing to cooperate with the Congress. In the early 1970s, for instance, the Foreign Relations Committee rejected an ambassadorial candidate who displayed during confirmation hearings an appalling ignorance about the country where he was going to serve. The 1974 Budget and Impoundment Control Act established the right of the Senate to confirm the president's budget director—clearly a key official—and in recent years legislators have proposed a law, still under debate, that would require confirmation hearings for another important executive official: the president's adviser for national security affairs, the top NSC staff aide.

Perspectives on American Foreign Policy 5.3

Laurence H. Tribe, professor of constitutional law at Harvard University, on President Ronald Reagan's attempts to privatize American foreign policy during the Iran-contra episode:

. . . The carefully crafted requirement of Article I, Section 9 [of the Constitution], that all funds raised by the Government or its agents must enter and leave the Federal Treasury, and must do so only pursuant to laws passed by Congress, would be rendered utterly meaningless if the President, seeing himself not as an agent of the Government but as an outsider, could preside freely over the creation of a shadow treasury designed to aid his shadow intelligence network in pursuit of his private schemes.

Congress's control over the purse would be rendered a nullity if the President's pocket could conceal a slush fund dedicated to purposes and projects prohibited by the laws of the United States. . . .

Laurence H. Tribe, "Reagan Ignites a Constitutional Crisis," *New York Times*, May 20, 1987, p. 31. Reprinted by permission.

Moreover, Congress has evolved into an institution which, more and more, emphasizes its role as overseer of the executive branch. Legislators have realized that if they are to make sound laws, they must conduct serious *oversight*, that is, monitor and review the executive branch's implementation of existing laws. In this capacity, Congress has become the watchdog that James Madison envisioned. In *Federalist* Paper No. 51, Madison wrote:

> . . . If men were angels, no government would be necessary. If angels were to govern men, neither external nor internal controls on government would be necessary. In framing a government which is to be administered by men over men, the great difficulty lies in this: you must first enable the government to control itself. A dependence on the people is, no doubt, the primary control on the government; but experience has taught mankind the necessity of auxiliary precautions.[43]

Informal discussions with officials in the executive branch, field inspections, legislative hearings, and, most formal, full-scale investigations provide such precautions—though these methods are imperfect and sometimes Congress has abused its oversight power (as with the McCarthy hearings in 1954 when Senator McCarthy of Wisconsin accused witnesses of subversion and attempted on national television to browbeat them with flimsy evidence and innuendo).

MARCHING TO DIFFERENT DRUMS

The disputes between the Senate Foreign Relations Committee and the executive branch during the Vietnam era offer a line graph registering the institutional frustrations over decision making in a system where power is supposed to be shared across separate institutions. Just as Americans have been ambivalent about the correct degree of involvement for the United States abroad—fluctuating between isolationism, on the one hand, and intervention, on the other hand—so, too, have they been ambivalent about the ideal mix of control over foreign affairs between Congress, the executive, and the judiciary. Nor is this debate likely to end in some golden resolution, for it is a by-product of the constitutional matrix established by the founders and reinforced by subsequent events. Beyond the tension between the branches that results from this uneasy sharing of foreign policy powers, additional provisions of the Constitution dealing with such matters as electoral constituencies, terms of office, and related subjects guaranteed that the president and the Congress would often march to different drums.

Contrasting Constituencies

To begin with, the framers of the Constitution designed the executive and legislative branches so that they would serve different constituencies. Legislators, particularly members of the House of Representatives, tend to be more parochial in their orientation than presidents, who serve a national constituency. A House member represents about 500,000 people, a president over 245 million. The House member may have a homogeneous district, say, almost completely rural in eastern Idaho or urban in eastern Massachusetts; the president's "district" will always be a heterogeneous mixture of rural and urban, conservative and liberal, prairie and pavement. The congressional perspective on policy, then, can be much more fragmented than the president's—conceivably 535 times more fragmented. This can translate into legislative obstructionism against presidential proposals, as members of Congress put the good of the part—their part—before the good of the whole. Home constituency may come first, the nation second. In times of genuine national emergency, though, legislators are strongly inclined to shed their parochialism and rally behind the president.

With the need to be responsive to such different voting electorates, the president and Congress are bound to attract different constellations of interest groups in support of (or against) their policies. The question of interest groups was never addressed in the Constitution, but they have come to have a significant influence on foreign policy. These groups (examined more closely in Chapter 7, "The Human Factor") are fully aware of how the Constitution shares powers, and as a result they concentrate their attention on key officials in both branches. On any one foreign policy decision, a legislator's comparatively small district may or may not have groups affected by the decision; a president, however, will almost always draw praise or blame for the decision from some groups somewhere within the United States. With a broader constituency, the president has no escape from the steady pressures of domestic lobbying on foreign affairs.

Jewish and Greek lobbying organizations within the United States provide two examples. Few legislative constituencies have significant numbers of Jewish or Greek-American voters; yet, Americans with these affiliations have established effective lobbying groups in Washington. Over the years, these organizations have scored many successes in targeting key institutions like the White House and the Senate Foreign Relations Committee with persuasive information on the needs of their members (foreign aid for Israel and for Greece has always been high on the list). To improve their access to the president and leading members of Congress, lobbying groups have skillfully directed campaign funds toward individuals holding (or likely to hold) influential foreign policy posts affecting Israel and Greece. No country has received more American foreign aid than Israel (at a rate of $7 million a day!); and Greece has always been among the top recipients, too. While legislators from Wyoming, Utah, Iowa, and most other states will only occasionally hear the drumbeat of the Jewish and Greek lobbies, for the president—and for the heads of the foreign affairs and armed services committees on Capitol Hill—the drumming will be steady, and at times intense, on issues of foreign policy, for these prominent officials are in a position to push through the government important aid programs for Israel and Greece.

Pressures of Office

President Kennedy once commented poignantly on an even more compelling reason why a chief executive is forced to concentrate on foreign affairs (even if initially elected on the basis of his or her domestic policy promises): the danger that the United States could be extinguished by a sudden nuclear attack. "Domestic policy...can only defeat us," he observed; "foreign policy can kill us."[44]

Since 1954, the Soviet Union has held the capacity to strike at this nation across the polar cap with intercontinental ballistic missiles (ICBMs). Today, most ICBMs are tipped with at least 1-megaton warheads (the primitive bomb dropped by the United States on Hiroshima in 1945 carried a "meager" 12-kiloton warhead). Close off the American coastline, Soviet submarines have the ability to hit Washington, D.C., within ten minutes or so with submarine-launched ballistic missiles (SLBMs). Land-based, and thus more accurate, American Pershing-II missiles placed in western Europe during the 1980s had a comparable ability to strike rapidly against Soviet territory. (These Pershing missiles were dismantled by the INF Treaty, in exchange for concessions by the Soviets to dismantle a percentage of their comparable missiles arrayed along their western border.) The sense of urgency created by the presence of nuclear weaponry lends credence to the argument that the United States must be able to make decisions quickly. In the fashionable phrase, the world has shrunk; therefore, so has the time available for U.S. leaders to respond to international crises. In this setting, the presidency with its organizational attributes of hierarchy gains favor over Congress with its multiple centers of power ("polycentrism," in social science jargon). The red telephone that could begin the Third World War sits in the Oval Office, not on Capitol Hill.

In contrast to the president's concentration on foreign affairs, most legislators usually feel less responsibility for events overseas; their gaze turns homeward. In the middle of a Senate hearing on secret operations against Chile concocted by the executive branch, a senior legislator stood and departed with these telling words: "I have to go now. I am trying to get jobs for 400 people in Minnesota today. That is a great deal more important to me right now than Chile."[45] Moreover, much of what the United States does in its external relations remains confidential, for often involved are secret intelligence operations or sensitive diplomatic negotiations. Legislators, even if they took the time to become well versed in these matters, would be unable to tell their constituents about the good work they have done. This is hardly a formula for enhancing one's reelection opportunities. As the legislative scholar David Mayhew has written, "In general, members [of Congress] intervene effectively in the bureaucracy on matters where they can claim credit for intervention."[46] This intervention is more likely to occur within the domain of domestic policy.

Career Cycles

The constitutionally based difference in terms of office for the president and for legislators has important implications for foreign policy as well. Presidents are limited (by the Constitution's Twenty-second Amendment) to a maximum service of ten years (and thus can be *elected* to the office a maximum of two times); in contrast, legislators often serve two, three, even four decades in Congress. Given their relatively brief time in office, presidents are in a hurry; they must achieve their goals quickly. Legislators, however, can afford a longer time perspective in their consideration of policy initiatives; most legislators will long outlast the incumbent president as central players in Washington politics. "Congress and the Presidency are like *two gears*, each whirling at its own rate of speed," notes the political scientist Nelson Polsby. "It is not surprising that, on coming together, they often clash."[47] Further, the president's presumed institutional allies, the bureaucrats, enjoy a length of tenure more compatible with legislators', and they often develop closer ties over the years with members of Congress than with any president (recall the "iron triangles" relationship discussed in Chapter 2).

Structural Differences

The sheer size of Congress with its 535 members makes decision making on the Hill inevitably slower than in the White House. As Chapter 6 explores more fully, Congress does its work in subcommittees and committees—over 300 of them, each led by a chairperson from the chamber's majority party. These individuals guard their prerogatives jealously and fight for policy jurisdiction, staff allotments, travel budgets, and the like. They must contend with divisions within their own party on the subcommittee, and with minority-party members across the aisle. The very fact that the Congress is bicameral means that each chamber might be controlled by a different party, as was true for the first six years of the Reagan administration, with the Democrats the majority in the House and the Republicans in the Senate (an advantage lost again by the GOP in the 1986 elections).

This internal division on Capitol Hill leads to an organization all the more unwieldy. During his second term, President Reagan attempted to increase funding for the contras in Nicaragua. The Senate accepted the proposal, but the House initially rejected it. Subsequent compromise legislation took two years to fashion before the House finally authorized the funding proposal. The president was forced to delay his war plans in Central America as the two chambers, led by opposite parties, worked out their differences. Beginning in 1987, with both houses controlled by Democrats, President Reagan faced an even more hostile Congress on the contra question, particularly in light of the

scandal over the questionable diversion of funds to the rebels by the National Security Council aide Lieutenant Colonel Oliver L. North. Despite the normally slow movement of legislation on Capitol Hill, however, it bears repeating that in times of real emergency the Congress can pass policy measures with alacrity—especially when the United States or its soldiers abroad have been attacked or threatened by a foreign power.

Modern Communications

Its large membership makes it difficult, also, for the Congress to speak with unity. The Capitol often resembles a tower of Babel, while the executive branch has a better chance of speaking with a single voice through the president. As the president speaks while sitting before a crackling fireplace in the West Wing of the White House, each word and gesture is carried by television cameras to practically every living room in America. Recent efforts allowing legislators an opportunity to respond after some presidential addresses have usually resulted in the presentation of a lifeless homogenization of conflicting views among congressional leaders. Nothing in the modern era has done more to provide the president with leverage over the Congress, in foreign and domestic policy, than the ability to sway public opinion through the use of direct appeals over television. Like the influence of interest groups, television represents another extraconstitutional development in the United States that has profoundly affected the struggle over power sharing between the branches.

A vivid illustration of an effective presidential use of television on a foreign policy issue occurred in 1975. During that year, Congress undertook an exhaustive investigation into the nation's secret intelligence operations. The revelations from Senate and House investigative committees portrayed an executive branch engaged in covert operations to overthrow foreign leaders, regardless of whether they had been duly elected by the people of their country (as was the case with one target, President Salvador Allende of Chile). These operations included assassination plots against Fidel Castro and Patrice Lumumba, as well as the shipment of weapons to various pro-American factions around the world. In an attempt to reverse the tide against this congressional criticism, the White House successfully turned the tragic murder (in December of 1975) of an American intelligence officer stationed in Greece into a media event designed to blame the death, at least implicitly, on the legislative investigators.

Two days before Christmas, masked terrorists gunned down the erudite CIA chief of station in Athens, Richard S. Welch, in front of his home. His body was flown back to Washington and honored with unprecedented fanfare. President Ford waived restrictions to permit his burial in Arlington National Cemetery. Thirty-one CIA officers had died in the service of their country before Welch, but his coffin was the only one ever met by an Air Force color guard and the nation's highest officials. The White House carefully staged the ceremony from beginning to end, "a show of pomp," observed the *Washington Post*, "usually reserved for the nation's most renowned military heroes."[48] As a member of Congress recalls, "The air transport plane carrying his body circled Andrews Air Force Base for three-quarters of an hour in order to land live on the 'Today Show.' "[49] One journalist who had followed the investigations closely concluded that the ceremony surrounding the Welch burial had been "a political device . . . to arouse a political backlash against legitimate criticism."[50]

The ploy worked. Public opinion shifted against the investigations, even though the congressional committees had been careful during their inquiries never to mention the name of Welch (or any other CIA officer on active duty) and had never uttered a word about CIA operations in Greece.

Presidents cannot rely unerringly on television to amplify their powers. Sometimes its unblinking eye turns against the president, as Lyndon Johnson discovered during the war in Vietnam. His assurances to the American people that the United States was winning the conflict failed to match the television images brought home by network cameramen. President Johnson soon developed a "credibility gap" between his promises of victory and the brutal television pictures of dying American soldiers.

In 1986, President Reagan's air strike against Libya created ambiguities in the minds of Western observers. The retaliation against terrorism was applauded, but the television pictures of innocent Libyan children killed or maimed in the attack raised questions about the administration's claim of a clean, "surgical" bombing against terrorists. Moreover, the attack stirred a certain cynicism about President Reagan's attitude toward the law. At the beginning of his administration, he renewed a legally binding executive order that prohibited U.S. involvement in assassination attempts against foreign leaders. The F-111 bombing of the Libyan leader Col. Muammar al-Qaddafi's home during the raid (he was unexpectedly away at the time) raised doubts about Reagan's credibility. Nevertheless, television remains a potent tool in the hands of a skillful president and White House staff; today, media consultants are as vital to a president in the handling of foreign affairs as are experts on international relations.

Unequal Information

Another powerful resource for the White House unanticipated by the Constitution has been the information-gathering capabilities the president enjoys through the vast bureaucracy at his command. Congress finds it particularly difficult to compete with the president's sources of information about foreign events. Although the *New York Times* and other newspapers provide legislators with reliable news from around the globe, a president or CIA director who claims to have special inside information based on secret espionage sources or sophisticated satellite photography has a unique advantage in the dialogue that leads to decision around the conference tables of the powerful in Washington.

The executive branch has thousands of the most advanced computers for information handling; the CIA alone has computers that fill half of its spacious headquarters in Langley, Virginia. In contrast, Congress has only a few outdated computers, and little interest in this technology for improving its analysis of policy or its monitoring of executive-branch operations. The executive branch has thousands of experts with advanced academic degrees, trained in the nation's best graduate and law schools; Congress has a much more youthful and (with some exceptions) less well-educated staff. Moreover, members of Congress seem to have even less time for reading policy reports than their executive counterparts. The turnover rate on Capitol Hill for staff is greater than in the executive branch, too, which means less of a corporate memory in Congress at the level of detailed staff work. This disadvantage is offset to some degree by the long service of legislators; the leaders of Congress have a record of experience in foreign affairs that normally exceeds that of the president and the cabinet.

Congress attempts to counterbalance these informational deficiencies in various ways. Among the most important is to invite expert witnesses to educate the Congress (and the public) through the medium of legislative hearings. During the antiballistic missile (ABM) debate in 1972, scientists from MIT and elsewhere opposed to this missile defense (on grounds of its technical impracticality) provided legislators with valuable data to counter the views of pro-ABM scientists employed by the Department of Defense. Sometimes Congress will send its own staff into the field to gather information, as a check against executive-branch testimony be-

fore legislative committees. At the peak of the war in Vietnam, the Senate Foreign Relations Committee dispatched two experienced staffers to Saigon periodically; they returned with reports that questioned fundamentally the roseate prognosis offered by the White House and the Department of Defense.

Legislators themselves will occasionally seek information directly by traveling abroad to examine programs in the field. Sometimes these trips are abused and thus labeled "junkets" by the press, as when one U.S. senator toured England in a Rolls-Royce at government expense in 1982 on the eve of his retirement. More typically, legislators who travel abroad pay serious attention to the study and evaluation of executive-branch field operations. Throughout the 1980s, groups of legislators traveling to Central America have returned with a better understanding of the complexity of politics in these countries, which in turn has made their evaluation of executive initiatives wiser.

Congress, though, has neither the intention nor the capacity to match the information-gathering bureaucracy of the executive branch. To the extent that information is power (the focus of Chapter 8, "Strategic Intelligence"), the executive branch will always have an edge on the legislative branch—unless a credibility gap arises or this information is misused in some way that becomes known to the public (as when the Nixon administration tried unsuccessfully to conceal its bombing raids against Cambodia).

CONFLICT AND COMITY

While disputes over power sharing have always been a central feature of American foreign policy, not by any means are all the relations between the executive and legislative branches conflictual. Widespread agreement exists among legislators, presidents, and bureaucrats on many topics, like the need to combat terrorism and drug trafficking—though the appropri-

Perspectives on American Foreign Policy   5.4

Senator Hubert H. Humphrey (D-Minn.) in 1959 on the importance of legislative participation in foreign policy:

Since Hitler's march into Poland two decades ago, foreign policy has been the dominant concern within the Senate itself. The primacy of the Executive Branch in foreign affairs in no way lessens the moral and legal responsibility of the Congress to work for national policies which come to grips responsibly and realistically with urgent demands of the world crisis. In this connection the Senate's activities go far beyond scrutinizing treaties and Presidential appointments. Former Secretary of State Dean Acheson has correctly observed that in one "aspect of foreign affairs Congress is all-powerful. This is in the establishing and maintaining of those fundamental policies, with their supporting programs of action, which require legal authority, men and money. Without these foundations—solidly laid and kept in repair—even wise and skillful diplomacy cannot provide the power and develop the world environment indispensable to national independence and individual liberty for ourselves and others."* Parliamentary bodies cannot govern, and our Congress is no exception. But with its power of the purse, and through the right to investigate, to criticize and to advocate, the Congress does exert a significant influence on the quality and direction of United States foreign policy, and it usually does so without violating the integrity of the Executive Branch.

. . . If the "unique, deliberate—and, to me, agreeable—disarray of the American Government," to use [*New York Times* correspondent]

William S. White's words, is to function properly, the foreign policy committees of Congress must have the resources to enable them to question, review, modify or reject the policies of the Executive Branch. The information, intelligence and insight available to the Executive Branch are vast and continue to expand. This is a natural development in an era of total diplomacy. . . . But in contrast, [countervailing expertise is missing] in Congress. Such independent expertise is absolutely necessary if the House and Senate are to fulfill their Constitutional responsibility of surveillance and initiative. Without competent independent sources of fact and wisdom they cannot make discriminating judgments between alternative programs and proposals. Faced with an impressive case by the Administration, and unarmed with counter facts and arguments, even a conscientious Senator sometimes vacillates between giving a grudging consent and opposing for the sake of opposing. . . .

The Foreign Relations Committee needs a much larger and more specialized staff, loyal to the Legislative Branch, and equal in competence to the best talent in the State Department. . . . Adequate staffing will alone enable Congress to escape from uninformed acquiescence on the one hand and irresponsible obstruction on the other. . . .

New York Times Magazine, January 6, 1957

"The Senate in Foreign Policy," *Foreign Affairs*, vol. 37, July 1959, pp. 532–535. Reprinted by permission.

---

ate methods may lead to strong disagreements. Moreover, presidents will always have some vocal support on Capitol Hill, especially within their own party or with legislators who believe it their duty for the sake of national unity to ac-

cept without question the president's position on foreign affairs.

Conflict, though, will continue to be a hallmark of the American form of government. What else would one expect from a system willfully devised by the nation's founders to thwart the facile and, therefore, dangerous use of power? As Madison argued in *The Federalist*, ". . . the great security against a gradual concentration of the several powers in the same department, consists in giving to those who administer each department the necessary constitutional means and personal motives to resist encroachments of the others. . . . Ambition must be made to counteract ambition."[51] The founders adopted this prescription.

The result, doubtless, is a government less prone to tyranny. But critics argue that the costs may be too high, that the United States is unable to compete effectively in the global arena with nations more streamlined and autocratic in their decision making. The world is too small, events move too fast, weapons have become too dangerous for the luxury of checks and balances, or, at any rate, for Congress to do anything more than support executive decisions on foreign matters. This important argument is examined further in the last two chapters of Part I, where a closer examination is made of both the institutional tensions that make up an integral part of American foreign policy and the effects of public opinion and individual personalities on these institutions.

SUMMARY

The Constitution of the United States established a government in which authority and its derivative, power, were to be shared between the branches, in an attempt to guard against their dangerous concentration in the hands of one person or institution. "Ambition must be made to counteract ambition," reasoned James Madison, one of the most influential founders. This sharing of power, however, has led to tensions between the branches resulting from the explicit intention of the drafters to create institutional opposition, as well as from ambiguities and silences in the Constitution.

Chief among the sources of tension have been the war and the treaty powers. Over the years, the executive branch has gained dominance over the war power and has largely discarded the treaty procedure in favor of statutory and executive agreements. The executive agreement as a form of diplomacy has been especially controversial, because it has been used at times for sweeping commitments abroad without legislative participation in the decisions. Presidential aggrandizement of the war power has been controversial, too, especially the conduct of war based upon an assumed inherent constitutional right of the commander in chief. Controversial, as well, has been the use of open-ended congressional resolutions, passed in times of perceived emergency and subsequently used by presidents to escalate military conflict. Critics point to the Gulf of Tonkin Resolution, voted by Congress during the early days of the war in Vietnam, as a classic example.

Further tension between the branches in the making of foreign policy arises from their contrasting constituencies, different pressures in office, career cycles that are out of phase with one another, organizational differences, and advantages enjoyed by the presidency over mass communications and access to information. While relations between the branches are often carried out in a spirit of comity, particularly during national emergencies, America's institutional arrangements for foreign affairs will continue to be characterized by an uneasiness over the sharing of power—precisely what the founders intended. Whether or not the world has become too dangerous a place for this form of decision making remains a subject of debate explored throughout this volume.

KEY TERMS

power sharing	Eisenhower Doctrine	legislative acquiescence
war power	Gulf of Tonkin Resolution	bipartisanship
defensive warfare	treaty provision	impoundment
inherent constitutional authority	executive agreement	oversight
congressional resolution	statutory agreement	two-gears analogy
Formosa Resolution	commitment by accretion	

NOTES

1. James Sterling Young, *The Washington Community: 1800–1828* (New York: Columbia University Press, 1966), p. 81.

2. See James Madison's important theoretical exposition in Nos. 10 and 51 of *The Federalist* (New York: Modern Library, 1937), pp. 53–62, 335–341.

3. Frank Church, "Of Presidents and Caesars: The Decline of Constitutional Government in the Conduct of American Foreign Policy," *Idaho Law Review*, vol. 6, Fall 1969, p. 14.

4. *The President: Office and Powers, 1787–1957,* rev. ed. (New York: New York University Press, 1957), p. 171.

5. Grant McConnell, *The Modern Presidency* (New York: St. Martin's, 1967), pp. 52–53.

6. No. 69, *The Federalist*, p. 448.

7. Julian P. Boyd, ed., *The Papers of Thomas Jefferson*, vol. 15 (Princeton, N.J.: Princeton University Press, 1955), p. 397.

8. "U.S. Commitments to Foreign Powers," *Hearings of the Committee on Foreign Relations,* U.S. Senate (1967), p. 194, emphasis added.

9. James D. Richardson, ed., *Compilation of Messages and Papers of the Presidents*, vol. 1, Joint Committee on Printing, U.S. Congress (New York: Bureau of National Literature, 1897), p. 314.

10. John Quincy Adams to Don José María Salazar (August 6, 1824), quoted by Ruhl J. Bartlett, ed., *The Record of American Diplomacy*, 3d ed. (New York: Knopf, 1954), p.

185, cited in "National Commitments," Committee on Foreign Relations, Report No. 91–129, U.S. Senate, April 16, 1969, p. 12. This useful document provides the foundation for much of the historical analysis in the first part of this chapter.

11. Letter to William H. Herndon (February 15, 1848), in *The Collected Works of Abraham Lincoln* (New Brunswick, N.J.: Rutgers University Press, 1953), vol. 1, pp. 451–452, cited in *ibid.,* pp. 12–13, the committee's emphasis.

12. *Department of State Bulletin* 23, July 31, 1950, pp. 173–177.

13. *Congressional Record*, 101, January 24, 1955, p. 601.

14. Testimony, "Assignment of Ground Forces of the United States to Duty in the European Area," *Hearings before the Committees on Foreign Relations and Armed Services*, U.S. Senate, February 28, 1951, p. 306. More recently, in 1987, an aide to President Ronald Reagan argued that laws passed by Congress to bar U.S. aid to the contras in Nicaragua failed to affect the president's "constitutional and historical power" to manage American foreign policy (quoted by Steven V. Roberts, "Aide Cites Reagan Foreign Policy Power," *New York Times*, May 15, 1987, p. 5).

15. "National Commitments," p. 20.

16. *Executive Sessions of the Senate Foreign Relations Committee (Historical Series)*, Committee on Foreign Relations, U.S. Senate, Vol. 7, 1955 (Washington, D.C.: Government

Printing Office, 1978), pp. 87, 104; cited by Senator Robert Byrd (D-W. Va.), *Congressional Record*, April 28, 1986, p. S4963, the primary source for this discussion of the Formosa and Middle East resolutions.

17. Arthur M. Schlesinger, Jr., *The Imperial Presidency* (Boston: Houghton Mifflin, 1974), pp. 159–160.

18. Cited by Byrd, *Congressional Record*, April 28, 1986, p. S4963.

19. *Ibid.*, p. S4964.

20. *Executive Sessions of the Senate Foreign Relations Committee Together with Joint Sessions with the Senate Armed Services Committee (Historical Series)*, Committee on Foreign Relations, U.S. Senate, vol. 9, 1957 (Washington, D.C.: Government Printing Office, 1979), pp. 1, 245–246, 267.

21. *Ibid.*, p. 310.

22. *Ibid.*, p. 297.

23. Schlesinger, *op. cit.*, p. 162.

24. *Congressional Record*, August 6, 1964, p. 18409.

25. Senator Frank Church, *op. cit.*, p. 10. For Katzenbach's testimony, see "U.S. Commitments to Foreign Powers," p. 82.

26. Raoul Berger, "The Presidential Monopoly of Foreign Relations," *Michigan Law Review*, vol. 71, 1972, p. 39.

27. Hollis W. Barber, *Foreign Policies of the United States* (New York: Dryden, 1953), p. 30. Note how the final ratification of a treaty lies within the power of the president and not the Senate, as commonly misconceived.

28. Cited by Louis Henkin, *Foreign Affairs and the Constitution* (Mineola, New York: Foundation Press, 1972), p. 372. This classic study includes an excellent discussion of the treaty process, pp. 129–171.

29. "National Commitments," p. 27. Looking back on the Roosevelt years, the famous American journalist James Reston observed recently that the president had done a "ter-

rible thing" by creating "a politburo in the White House for the conduct of foreign policy" (*New York Times*, November 5, 1989, p. 22).

30. See "U.S. Security Agreements and Commitments Abroad: Laos and Thailand," *Hearings of the Subcommittee on United States Security Agreements and Commitments Abroad*, Committee on Foreign Relations, Part 6, U.S. Senate, 1969–1970 (the Symington Subcommittee, after its chairman, Stuart Symington, D-Mo.).

31. "National Commitments," p. 28.

32. Frank Church (D-Idaho), *op. cit.*, p. 4.

33. For these memoranda, see the *Washington Post*, October 14, 1976; and "Spain and Portugal," Hearings of the Symington Subcommittee, p. 2356.

34. "National Commitments," pp. 28, 29.

35. For example: remarks in Memorial Hall, Akron University, Akron, Ohio, October 21, 1964.

36. "National Commitments," p. 23, original emphasis.

37. See Loch K. Johnson, *A Season of Inquiry: Congress and Intelligence* (Chicago: Dorsey, 1988), p. 113.

38. Frank Church, *op. cit.*, p. 11.

39. See Allen Schick, *Congress and Money* (Washington, D.C.: Urban Institute, 1981).

40. Louis Fisher, *Constitutional Conflicts between Congress and the President* (Princeton, N.J.: Princeton University Press, 1985), p. 238.

41. See "Kingdom of Laos," *Hearings of the Subcommittee on United States Security Agreements and Commitments Abroad*, Senate Foreign Relations Committee, Part 6, 1969–1970.

42. Louis Fisher, "Foreign Policy Powers of the President and Congress," *Annals of the American Academy of Political and Social Science*, vol. 499, September 1988, p. 156.

43. *The Federalist*, p. 337.

44. Cited by Aaron Wildavsky, "The Two Pres-

idencies," *Trans-Action*, vol. 4, December 1966, p. 2.

45. *New York Times*, March 16, 1975.

46. *Congress: The Electoral Connection* (New Haven: Yale University Press, 1974), p. 125.

47. *Congress and the Presidency* (New York: Prentice-Hall, 1964), p. 115, emphasis added.

48. December 26, 1975.

49. Les Aspin (D-Wis.), *Congressional Record*, February 19, 1976, p. H1179.

50. Anthony Lewis, *New York Times*, January 8, 1976.

51. No. 51, *The Federalist*, p. 337.

RECOMMENDED READINGS

Corwin, Edward S. *The President: Office and Powers* (New York: New York University Press, 1957). An exhaustive examination of the presidency, sharing with most works on the subject a sympathy for the chief executive in the conduct of foreign affairs.

Crabb, Cecil V., Jr., and Pat Holt. *Invitation to Struggle: Congress, the President and Foreign Policy* (Washington, D.C.: Congressional Quarterly, 1980). Presents a useful set of case studies illustrating the conflict between the two branches, with a rare sensitivity to the positive role Congress can play in American foreign policy.

Fisher, Louis. *Constitutional Conflicts between Congress and the President* (Princeton, N.J.: Princeton University Press, 1985). A close legal analysis of the tensions between these two branches, with excellent references to the constitutional sources of this uneasy partnership.

Franck, Thomas M., ed. *The Tethered Presidency* (New York: New York University Press, 1981). A collection of essays on executive-legislative relations, some in favor of executive dominance in foreign affairs and others supportive of a partnership between the branches.

——— and Edward Weisband. *Foreign Policy by Congress* (New York: Oxford University Press, 1979). The most thorough look yet at congressional efforts to be more assertive in foreign policy during the 1970s and 1980s, with unfortunate results in the view of these two experienced observers.

Fulbright, J. William. *The Crippled Giant* (New York: Random House, 1972). One of several thoughtful books by the former chairman of the Senate Foreign Relations Committee and leading intellectual light of the legislative resurgence in the midst of the war in Vietnam.

———, with Seth P. Tillman. *The Price of Union* (New York: Pantheon Books, 1989). A distillation of the former Senator's half-century of foreign policy experience.

Hamilton, Alexander, John Jay, and James Madison. *The Federalist* (New York: Modern Library, 1937). Essays written in 1787 in support of the Constitution, providing insights into the philosophy of government guiding the nation's founders.

Henkin, Louis. *Foreign Affairs and the Constitution* (New York: Norton, 1972). A detailed legal analysis and, for many, the bible on the subject.

Rossiter, Clinton. *The American Presidency* (New York: Harcourt, Brace & World, 1956). A highly readable exaltation of the president's powers in foreign affairs.

Schlesinger, Arthur M., Jr. *The Imperial Presidency* (Boston: Houghton Mifflin, 1973). Another gracefully written study of the presidency, but one sharply critical of the aggrandizement of power in the White House.

U.S. Senate Foreign Relations Committee. "National Commitments," Report No. 91–129, April 16, 1969. A key document in the congressional resurgence in foreign policy, presenting a constitutionally based argument in favor of a greater role for Congress in the treaty and war powers.

Wilcox, Francis O. *Congress, the Executive, and Foreign Policy* (New York: Harper & Row, 1971). A widely praised overview of executive-legislative relations in foreign affairs.

FRAGMENTS OF POWER
    Efficiency versus Freedom
    Presidents versus Legislators
    A Foreign Policy Compact
THE PRESIDENCY
    The Limitations of Power
    Time and Information
    Permissibility
    Resources
    Previous Commitments
    Formal Powers
THE BUREAUCRACY
    Behemoth
    Subgovernments

    Complex Wiring
    Turf Battles
    Command and Control
THE CONGRESS
    Fissures on Capitol Hill
    Reformist Zeal
    Minnows and Whales
    Legislative Watchdogs
THE COURTS
    Emerging Judicial Activism
    Tilt toward the Presidency
POWER: A STUDY IN CUBISM
SUMMARY

6

INSTITUTIONAL DYNAMICS

A sign at a construction site in New York City reminds passersby that as of November 3, 1980, American hostages had been held captive for 366 days in Iran. (UPI/Bettmann Newsphotos)

FRAGMENTS OF POWER

Given the experiences of the founders with the tyranny of Great Britain, their disenchantment with centralized power is understandable. Yet, is their original design workable for the conduct of foreign policy in today's threatening world—indeed, some would say, today's condition of global anarchy—where national cohesion rather than fragmentation, dispatch rather than delay, decision rather than debate, are necessary for the very survival of the United States? Does the sharing of power, in short, permit the efficiency necessary to respond to contemporary crises?

Efficiency versus Freedom

In the minds of those who crafted the Constitution, efficiency was hardly the cardinal virtue of good government. If efficiency had been their goal, they would have placed greater power in the hands of the president. On the contrary, as one constitutional specialist has noted, "the framers were unwilling to give the President anything resembling royal prerogative."[1] Through their rejection of sweeping executive powers, they sought to protect themselves—and posterity—against the risks of autocracy.

By rejecting royal prerogative, however, the constitutional framers created a government that often displays signs of sluggishness, parochialism, and disarray. The premium placed by the Constitution on power sharing drives hierarchists to distraction, turns proponents of tidy organizational charts grim-faced, and sends twitching those whose chief goal is to make the trains run on time. The founders had established precisely what Winston Churchill once said a democracy would always be: the worst possible form of government—except for all the others that have been tried from time to time.

The shortcomings of democracy become magnified on matters of foreign policy. With domestic policy, one can arguably afford to muddle through, moving incrementally for the

127

most part with slight changes at the margins of existing policy when necessary—an approach that many political scientists have argued is the signature of domestic policymaking in the United States.[2] But with foreign policy the dangers from abroad may be too dire for politics as usual. Protection against thermonuclear annihilation, terrorist attacks, oil embargoes, and other potential calamities may require special attention and bold initiatives.

Events overseas often appear to move more quickly than those at home—in part no doubt because they are farther away and, therefore, less familiar and closely watched. This potential for surprise from abroad might require the government to react with greater speed than it normally displays. The need for quick response is hardly a new phenomenon; the founders drafted the commander-in-chief clause of the Constitution as a means for providing the president with authority to repel a sudden attack against the nation, without waiting for a congressional declaration of war. The ten-minute flight time of Soviet SLBMs off the American coastline has, however, added an exclamation mark to the principle.

Such reasoning leads some to advocate a different approach to foreign policy from what they would tolerate for domestic policy. For external affairs, because of the acute dangers and the need for rapid decision, they turn to hierarchy, secrecy, deliberations by the few—chiefly the president and a few very close advisers. The hallowed traditions of democracy—openness, debate, the careful consideration of a wide range of options, the testing of public opinion—are sacrificed on the altar of national security.[3]

Others argue, in contrast, that the debate and openness characteristic of domestic policy can and must be maintained for foreign policy, too, with the exception of a few necessary secrets (such as the blueprints for a new weapons system). To surrender foreign policy to a small group of officials in the executive branch, they argue, is to risk the making of decisions con-

trary to the will of the people, thereby undermining in the name of national security the very essence of democracy and the American form of government.[4]

Presidents versus Legislators

A central issue in any appraisal of American foreign policy, then, is whether it ought to be an executive function—indeed, narrowly defined to encompass only the top officials in the executive branch—or, as in domestic policy, the United States can afford the luxury of a wider range of participants, to include the representatives of the American people in Congress. From an institutional point of view, one can imagine two extreme approaches to foreign policy: first, a *presidential model*, in which global decisions would be left exclusively to the president and his or her top aides, and, second, a *legislative model*, in which these decisions would be left primarily to members of Congress. (The judicial branch is seldom a part of this discussion, though as explored later in this chapter its involvement in foreign policy matters can sometimes have lasting consequences.)

The first, presidential model enjoys widespread support for the reasons of urgency mentioned earlier, and because of the far-flung intelligence apparatus within the executive branch that presumably provides the president with better information about foreign affairs than Congress may have at its disposal. Moreover, a strong sense exists that in order to be taken seriously in world affairs the nation must speak with one voice. Some legislators have also been more than happy to pass responsibility to the White House for knotty and controversial foreign problems that might spell trouble in the next election.

Not everyone, though, has been enthusiastic about foreign policy by executive fiat. Even before Vietnam and Watergate raised serious doubts about presidential power, a pro-Congress viewpoint could be frequently heard—especially from the conservative side of the political spectrum. Economic conservatives lamented the centralism that Franklin Roosevelt had brought to the marketplace. States-rightists fretted over international agreements signed by presidents that might lead indirectly to a further strengthening of authority in Washington. Southerners, for example, feared that the federal government might establish new civil rights regulations by way of executive agreements with African nations (see Chapter 11). Isolationists looked upon the presidency as the agent of interventionism abroad, which so often had led to a drain on American resources— or to a complete sellout of American interests, as conservatives argued Roosevelt had done in 1945 through executive agreements negotiated with Stalin at Yalta.

Ironically, many conservatives in more recent times—with one of their own in the White House, Ronald Reagan—argued quite differently. Now they favored broad authority for the president in foreign policy. The president should be allowed, they reasoned, to do whatever was necessary to halt communist aggression in Central America—even if that meant rising above laws like the Boland amendments (named after their sponsor, Edward P. Boland, D-Mass.; see Chapter 9), which between 1982 and 1987 placed limits on military assistance to the CIA-backed contras. The Boland laws were "unconstitutional," argued the arch-conservative Senator Barry Goldwater (R-Ariz.). "It's another example of Congress trying to take away the constitutional power of the President to be Commander in Chief and to formulate foreign policy."[5] A majority of legislators in both chambers disagreed with Goldwater, however, and steadily tightened the Boland legislative restrictions.

Regardless of political leanings, some students of democratic theory have felt that legislators are closer to the grass roots—especially members of the House with their perpetual re-election pressures—and, as a result, have a better comprehension of what the people in Pocatello and Tuscaloosa really want. Are the

citizens back home willing to send their sons to combat in Nicaragua? Do they favor more vigorous arms control accords? Are they prepared to support costly defense programs with tax increases? Members of Congress, continues this argument, are like raw nerve endings reaching into each of the 435 congressional districts across the land, sensing the likely response to vital foreign policy and national security issues. The president cannot possibly visit each district; members of Congress usually visit their respective districts every week—some each day if their districts are close to Washington. This makes Congress a unique, continuous forum of timely public opinion, even though efforts by legislators to gauge opinion back home are far from perfect (discussed in Chapter 7).

During his second term, President Reagan was inclined initially to resist, on ideological grounds, the subsidized shipment of wheat to the Soviet Union. Legislators complained vociferously, however, that he ought to spend more time listening to the plight of American farmers out in the congressional districts and less time playing cold war politics. In light of this criticism from Capitol Hill, led by then majority leader Robert Dole (R-Kan.), the president allowed the wheat to be sold to the Soviets. This episode provides an illustration of how complex foreign policy decisions can be. By authorizing the sale, the president mollified farm-state legislators, but in the process irritated the hawkish right wing of the GOP (which frowns upon any trade deals that might help the Soviet economy). Moreover, this decision undercut the sale of Australian wheat to the U.S.S.R. and triggered angry protests by Australian farmers in front of the American embassy in Canberra.

A Foreign Policy Compact

In between these presidential and legislative models of foreign policy making lies a third, which can be called the *model of constitutional balance*—the perspective favored in this book. Here the emphasis is on a healthy cooperation between coequal branches—an engine with all its cylinders at work, not just one or another. A classic example of constructive cooperation between the branches occurred in 1954. As the reader will recall from the previous chapter, Secretary of State John Foster Dulles, a strong proponent of the domino theory, proposed to President Eisenhower the introduction of U.S. forces into Vietnam in order to assist French troops surrounded by communist troops at the city of Dien Bien Phu. Before making his decision, Eisenhower asked Dulles to consult with leading members of Congress regarding their opinions on how the United States should proceed. Invited to the White House for a meeting with Dulles and other top officials, the legislators asked several probing questions that uncovered an important fact: neither the Joint Chiefs of Staff nor key American allies supported the plan. This discovery caused much skepticism about the plan among members of the congressional delegation (some of whom were normally strong administration supporters) and they advised against it. President Eisenhower backed away from Dulles's proposed use of force in Indochina.[6]

More recently, the Bush administration has demonstrated the value of close executive-legislative cooperation. During his first months in office, President Bush patiently and quietly negotiated with Congress an interbranch agreement favoring nonlethal aid for the contras in Nicaragua, successfully defusing the most controversial foreign policy issue of the 1980s. In June of 1989, when Chinese troops attacked pro-reform students in Beijing, Bush immediately called top legislators to the White House and worked out with them a strategy of criticism and sanctions against the PRC government for ordering the barbarous murder of hundreds of peaceful demonstrators.

President Carter's under secretary of state, Warren Christopher, casts the argument for interbranch cooperation in terms of an *executive-legislative compact*. "As a fundamental precept," he writes, "the compact would call for restraint on the part of the Congress—for Congress to recognize and accept the responsibility of the Executive to conduct and manage foreign policy on a daily basis." He stresses that, in return, the executive branch must be prepared to provide Congress "full information and consultation," and "broad policy should be jointly designed." For its part, Congress should only rarely, in extreme circumstances, attempt "to dictate or overturn Executive decisions and actions. . . ."[7]

Employing a different image, Senator J. William Fulbright often suggested (while chairman of the Foreign Relations Committee) that the Congress and the president should jointly chart the desired global routes for the American ship of state. Then it would be up to the president to perform as an able captain and safely steer the ship to port, making periodic adjustments as necessary in consultation with experienced hands in Congress.

Real life, though, falls outside the confines of tidy theoretical models. Prescriptions like Christopher's can sound platitudinous in light of the divided institutional relations and fragmented power that actually characterize U.S. foreign policy making. Still, models do serve to highlight a sense of where, in the opinion of various observers, the institutional "center of gravity" ought to be when decisions are made: with the president, with the Congress, or, as Christopher and Fulbright (and this book) would have it, somewhere between the two.

What ought to be and what is, of course, are two different matters. As this chapter attempts to illustrate, something resembling each of these models can be observed at different times as one looks at the institutional side of foreign policy. Sometimes the president is able to gather and assemble enough of the fragments of power to achieve ascendancy over a decision, sometimes the Congress does, and sometimes they share the fragments. The challenge is to understand why no single model is sufficient in itself to explain America's relations with other countries. The previous chapter examined the constitutional wellsprings of institutional tension over foreign policy—the theory of separate institutions sharing power; this chapter turns to the actual practice of this theory in the modern era, beginning with a look at the presidency.

THE PRESIDENCY

The Limitations of Power

As political scientists have shown, the powers of the presidency are often grossly exaggerated. A prominent scholar once examined high school and college texts on government and discovered an image of the president as someone who can do no wrong, who has all the information and skilled advisers necessary to make wise decisions.[8] One text went so far as to call Lincoln "the martyred Christ of democracy's passion play."[9] This same text, widely used in college courses on the presidency in the 1950s and 1960s, suggested further that "there is virtually no limit to what the President can do if he does it for democratic ends and by democratic means. . . . "[10] Even the astute journalist Theodore H. White lapsed into unfettered adulation of the presidency in his best-selling *The Making of the President 1960*. "So many and so able are the President's advisors of the permanent services of Defense, State, Treasury, Agriculture," wrote White, "that when crisis happens all necessary information is instantly available, all alternate courses already plotted."[11]

In contrast to this distorted *textbook presidency* stands a starkly different reality. Despite the fabled red telephone on the president's desk that could ignite a third world war, despite his guaranteed access to the people of the United States through television and radio, and despite a common belief that he is (as Nelson Rockefeller once put it in overstatement) "the unifying force in our lives," scholarly studies of the presidency show that nothing so defines the nation's highest office as its limitations.[12]

As the earlier chapters in this volume have emphasized, one of the primary limitations on the president is the international setting in which the United States finds itself. Regardless of how skilled a chief executive may be, the demands of events can be simply unmanageable. Reflecting back on the problems of the Carter administration soon after its electoral defeat in 1980, the president's national security adviser, Zbigniew Brzezinski, expressed dismay at the inability of this nation to control events abroad—particularly the fate of American hostages held in Tehran by Iranian insurgents from November of 1979 until the end of the Carter administration (a total of fourteen months). "History is much more the product of chaos than of conspiracy," observed Brzezinski. "The external world's vision of internal decision-making in the Government assumes too much cohesion and expects too much systematic planning. The fact of the matter is that, increasingly, policy makers are overwhelmed by events and information."[13] The ill-fated rescue mission attempted by the Carter administration to free the hostages is replete with further examples of events that defied careful planning, including a crash of rescue helicopters in the Iranian desert and a series of military communications snafus.

Time and Information

Brzezinski's stress on the problem of information overload is well warranted. Policymakers can be inundated by too much information. Paradoxically, this becomes a limitation on their powers, as illustrated by the early warning predicting a Japanese attack on Pearl Harbor in 1941. American intelligence agencies had intercepted coded Japanese messages about the impending attack, but this information was lost in the "noise" of several conflicting reports from other sources. The key messages floundered in the lower bureaucracy and President Roosevelt never received the warning.

The opposite phenomenon is probably even

more common, that is, insufficient information. Research on surprise military attacks makes it plain that all too often nations are caught unprepared because of a lack of information about their enemies.[14] Though reconnaissance satellites and other sophisticated intelligence-gathering equipment have reduced this danger, no administration has a crystal ball, and unexpected events will continue to occur as part of the human condition.

When one speaks of information (the focus of Chapter 8), one must also recognize that time is a limitation faced by all decision makers. Information and time are intimately related. Without sufficient time to gather data and comprehend their meaning, the decision maker must act with an incomplete understanding of events and conditions. President Kennedy's reflections on the Cuban missile crisis bear repeating: "If we had had to act in the first twenty-four hours, I don't think... we would have chosen as prudently as we finally did."[15]

Permissibility

To this list of restraints on the president, Theodore C. Sorenson (a top aide to President Kennedy) has underscored the further limits of permissibility, available resources, and previous commitments.[16] The Constitution, statutes, court decisions, and international law all define what the president is allowed to do (though ambiguities, as we have seen, certainly exist). Presidents are further hemmed in by what others within the government, and in other nations, are prepared to let them do. Kennedy's use of a naval quarantine during the Cuban missile crisis was facilitated by formal support from the Organization of American States (OAS, made up of most of the governments in the Western Hemisphere), which voted to endorse the military blockade. This support gave added authority to Kennedy's decision in the eyes of world opinion; it was now sanctioned by international law through the required two-thirds vote of the OAS for such actions. "What

is clear is that a President's authority is not as great as his responsibility," concludes Sorenson, "and that what is desirable is always limited by what is possible or permissible."

Resources

How would you fill in this blank: "The official most likely to loom largest in the president's thinking when a key decision must be made is _____"? Would you say the secretary of defense? the secretary of state? the speaker of the House? the vice president? These would be good guesses, and each might be true on specific occasions. Overall, though, Sorensen suggests a different person: the director of the Office of Management and Budget, the top financial officer in the executive branch.

Almost all government programs cost money. Yet a president confronts limits on how much money can be spent or how high taxes can be raised without wreaking havoc on the economy or stirring a rebellion among taxpayers. Thus, for each program, a president will have to consult closely with the budget director and will always feel the pressure to control spending. Lyndon Johnson's simultaneous attempt to rebuild the cities of America and fight a war in Vietnam proved too costly, fueling inflation and leading to the unpopularity that drove him from office. Ronald Reagan's unprecedented spending deficit, equivalent to the *combined* deficits of all presidents who served before him, is viewed by most experts as an economic time bomb likely to go off with devastating effects in the 1990s, when the bills come due.

Money is only one governmental resource. Others include the number of soldiers available to fight a war, the quantity and quality of weapons in a nation's ordnance, the will or determination of a populace to pursue a difficult course (like the war in Vietnam), the credibility of a president, the frequency of television appeals the president can make directly to the public without losing their attention, the industrial output of a nation, the supply of brilliant generals and civilian advisers, and more. As with money, presidents have rarely felt that they had enough of these resources. During the Johnson years, media experts concluded that the president used television appeals too often in his efforts to muster support for the Vietnamese war. The media saturation, combined with the president's lack of candor about the poor progress of the war, led the public to either tune him out or view his remarks with increasing skepticism.

Previous Commitments

Sorenson reminds us, as well, that "no President starts out with a clean slate before him." Principles set down by earlier presidents and other officials have to be honored, as do statements the new president has made on the election trail. It would be difficult for any new president to decide suddenly to withdraw from NATO; too many of his or her predecessors have promised America's commitment to this defense pact. Nor could a president easily abandon in midstream a major weapons system already placed into production by the previous administration, for it would prove difficult to justify the waste of money that had been invested in the development of the prototype.

Formal Powers

Even the formal powers of the presidency are less potent than often believed by the general public. Truman's classic prediction about the experience that his successor, General Eisenhower, would have in the Oval Office serves as a poignant reminder of this fact. "He'll sit here," said Truman, "and he'll say, 'Do this! Do that!' And nothing will happen. Poor Ike—it won't be a bit like the Army. He'll find it very frustrating."[17] Expressing his own sense of frustration, President Johnson once exclaimed: "Power? The only power I've got is nuclear—and I can't use that."[18]

During the Cuban missile crisis, President Kennedy decided it would be prudent to move his naval blockade closer to Cuba. This would give the Kremlin more time to evaluate the danger and then order those Soviet ships approaching the blockade to return home. The U.S. Navy, though, had different ideas about how to conduct this operation, as the secretary of defense, Robert S. McNamara, soon discovered.

McNamara drove from the Ex Comm meetings at the White House over to the Pentagon in order to inquire about the blockade plans. Inside a heavily guarded section of the building, he confronted Navy officials with incisive questions about their management of the operation.

Finally, the chief of naval operations waved the *Manual of Navy Regulations* in the secretary's face and shouted: "It's all in there!"

"I don't give a damn what John Paul Jones would have done," McNamara responded. "I want to know what you are going to do, now."

At the end of this angry exchange, the chief of naval operations concluded brusquely, "Now, Mr. Secretary, if you and your Deputy will go back to your office the Navy will run the blockade."[19]

Even mundane matters can bog down in bureaucratic resistance. It took two weeks, and presidential intervention, just for the Kennedy administration to convince the CIA that it should remove its sign from alongside the George Washington Parkway in Virginia, after Attorney General Robert Kennedy decided it was indiscreet to advertise the location of America's foremost secret service.

The president's bureaucrats, in short, often have their own agenda, which may be quite distinct from White House objectives. Comments one recent former secretary of the navy in the Reagan administration on the difficulty of making the Pentagon responsive to presidential programs: "No matter who is Secretary of Defense, it is not a rational decision-making organization. It is too big. It is big, big, big; . . . it makes any management person laugh out loud."[20]

At least when it comes to dealing with Congress, the president has one strong, constitutional prerogative: the veto. Legislators have to muster a two-thirds majority in both chambers in order to override the veto, and such an extraordinary majority is difficult to achieve. Moreover, the War Powers Resolution of 1973 gives the president even greater authority to use military force than the commander-in-chief clause of the Constitution (Article II, Section 2). Under this controversial law (a focus of Chapter 10), the president is permitted to use troops for up to forty-eight hours in order to protect American interests without formal notification of Congress, though the White House is urged to consult with legislators in advance—a provision largely ignored by presidents of both parties. The right to appoint ambassadors (with confirmation by the Senate), to choose the nation's national security adviser (without confirmation), and to recognize foreign regimes gives the president additional formal powers of importance.

Nevertheless, these centralizing prerogatives are few in number and largely outmatched on most occasions by the limitations on the office, even when coupled with the advantage of ready access to the media enjoyed by the chief executive. As President Kennedy remarked a few months before his death: "The President . . . must wield these powers under extraordinary limitations—and it is these limitations which so often give the problem of choice its complexity and even poignancy."[21] A examination of the executive bureaucracy corroborates this observation.

THE BUREAUCRACY

Behemoth

Perhaps nothing so impresses a student of government who tours the nation's capital as the vastness of its public institutions. The Department of Agriculture—which has its own foreign service—spreads out over several large city blocks, reaching across streets with walkways to connect its various parts; the Department of Commerce takes a half hour to walk around; the Department of State has a seemingly endless number of windows in its many-storied complex; the Department of Defense, the giant of them all, is a honeycomb of corridors that would baffle the most accomplished orienteer. These are merely a few of the enormous government buildings that dominate the streets of Washington like so many feudal fortresses, none with moats but all nonetheless difficult if not impossible for anyone—even a president—to subdue.

Though ostensibly, at least, in charge of some 3 million workers in the executive branch and responsible for seeing to it that they obey the thousands of laws and regulations guiding their departments, agencies, bureaus, and offices, in reality the president has direct control over very few. The president appoints only a thin layer of officials at the top. These include the highest position in a department—the "secretary"—as well as under secretaries, assistant secretaries, deputy assistant secretaries, and a number of other top officials without the designation of secretary in the job title, such as the chief trade negotiator, who goes by the formal title of special trade representative (STR)—altogether some 1500 so-called Schedule C jobs, out of about 9000 upper-level slots.

The president must rely on these appointees to imbue their civil service subordinates with a sense of loyalty to the White House. Often the submerged mass of the iceberg refuses to support those perched on the tip. This can be especially true when a Republican president occupies the White House. The *Hatch Act* (1939) prevents most officials in the executive branch from involvement in partisan politics; but, of course, they are allowed to vote, and studies have shown that on Election Day bureaucrats tend to support the Democratic Party—probably because this party views the government as a positive force and is more willing to finance

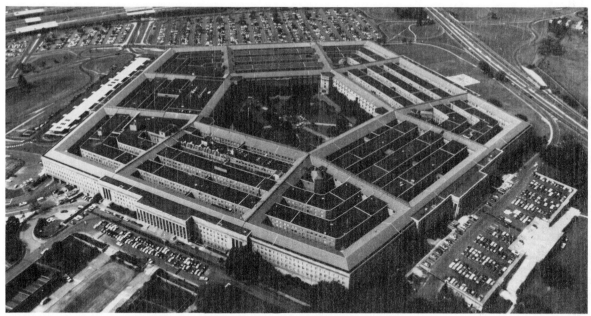

The Pentagon (Department of Defense). (Official U.S. Navy Photograph)

various agency programs. In contrast, the GOP (in theory) seeks to curtail government programs—though few were actually dismantled during the Reagan antigovernment "revolution."

Subgovernments

The difficulties of presidential control over the bureaucracy have long been observed by political scientists. Every respectable textbook on American government devotes space to the concept of *iron triangles* (or "subgovernments"), that is, the alliance in Washington that joins together bureaucrats, legislators (and their aides), and interest-group lobbyists, discussed in Chapter 2. Presidents come and go, but this bond endures.

The defense industry obviously has a vested interest in new weapon systems, and this interest is shared by corporate managers and stockholders as well as by labor organizations. In 1985, the United Auto Workers lobbied vigor-

ously on behalf of the MX missile, because it meant jobs for blue-collar workers. Legislators also receive substantial campaign contributions from defense-industry political action committees (PACs), and military brass often seek employment after retirement with the same corporations they provided with contracts while in the Pentagon. Thus, presidents will have their own views on weapons systems; but the White House must contend with these subterranean governments devoted to more weapons (the generals), more contracts (labor and management), and more PAC money and jobs back home—read "votes" (the legislators). This is a powerful force by any reckoning.[22]

For the sociologist C. Wright Mills (in his influential book entitled *The Power Elite*), a troika—made up of generals, corporate executives, and their handmaidens, legislators—represented the controlling authority in American government for foreign and domestic policy.[23] While Mills's view is no doubt simplistic (as Part II of this book illustrates, American politics

---

Perspectives on American Foreign Policy   6.1

A notorious example of an iron triangle is the so-called military-industrial complex. In a famous passage from his farewell address, President Dwight David Eisenhower warned:

This conjunction of an immense military establishment and a large arms industry is new in the American experience. The total influence—economic, political, even spiritual—is felt in every city, every State house, every office of the Federal government. We recognize the imperative need for this development. Yet we must not fail to comprehend its grave implications. Our toil, resour-

ces, and livelihood are all involved; so is the very structure of our society.

In the councils of government, we must guard against the acquisition of unwarranted influence, whether sought or unsought, by the military-industrial complex. The potential for the disastrous rise of misplaced power exists and will persist.

Public Papers of the President, Dwight D. Eisenhower, 1960–1961 (Washington, D.C.: Office of the Federal Registrar, National Archives, 1961), p. 1038.

---

is more complicated than a theory based on iron triangles alone would suggest), this alliance sometimes does represent a formidable barrier to presidential aspirations. In times of war, presidents give great deference to the judgment of their generals in the field and the weapons manufacturers at home; and even in times of peace, the generals and the corporate titans have easy access to officials in high places. Their skills, their expertise, and their service to the nation are valued in the White House; so are their defense contracts and, in the case of the corporate leaders, their political campaign funds. And what they fail to win from the president, they have another (often better) chance of winning from key members of Congress.

Complex Wiring

The sheer complexity of the government machinery in Washington presents an additional barrier to presidential aspirations. Take, for example, the intricacy of the national security establishment. At its pinnacle stands the *National Security Council* (NSC), since 1947 the central entity within the executive branch for the for-

mulation of foreign policy recommendations to the president. While the NSC itself is a simple enough structure (recall that it has only four statutory members: the president, the vice president, the secretary of state, and the secretary of defense), its history has been rife with controversy.[24]

The director of the NSC, known more officially as the *assistant to the president for national security affairs* or simply the *national security adviser*, has often been a keen competitor with the secretary of state for the ear of the president and the title of chief foreign policy aide. As discussed earlier, the competition between the two offices grew particularly acrimonious during the Carter years, with the aggressive NSC director, Brzezinski, often edging out the more restrained secretary of state, Cyrus Vance.

As a rule, presidents will gravitate for foreign policy advice toward the dominant personality in their administration, the individual who displays a solid understanding of the political and policy needs of the White House—regardless of his or her institutional slot. Still, national security advisers have advantages over secretaries of state in winning the president's favor. For starters, the office of the national security adviser is located in the West Wing of the White House, a short stroll from the Oval Office; this propinquity allows quick and easy access to the president. In contrast, the secretary of state is often out of the country and, when home, has offices in the State Department, a mile away from the White House.

Moreover, by virtue of being located in the West Wing, the national security adviser often has a better sense of the political leanings of the president and the president's top aides. The secretary of state, in comparison, is more involved in the pursuit of diplomatic initiatives than in reading the domestic political tea leaves that preoccupy the attention of White House officials. "The irrepressible ethos of the building [the Department of State]," writes one authority, "is to look outside the United States, not inward."[25] Presidents have often felt that in its recommendations the State Department has been insufficiently sensitive to potential political repercussions at home. In the Iranian hostage situation during the Carter years, for example, the Department of State argued for a long-range view based on patient diplomatic negotiations; the White House and the national security adviser, though, worried more about the immediate political problem at home if President Carter failed to take decisive measures in an attempt to free the hostages.

The NSC staff is also relatively small and sheltered from public attention; unlike the Department of State, it can operate swiftly and in tight secrecy. These features are offset by its superficial depth; compared with the State Department, it has limited global expertise and operational reach. Still, speed and secrecy are attractive attributes to presidents, and it was precisely because of these advantages that the Reagan administration turned to the NSC staff in 1985–1986 as an operational, not just an advisory, group (an important subject taken up further in Chapter 9).

The fragmentation of power advocated by the nation's founders has been carried out in practice to an extreme, argue some critics. The tensions between the NSC staff and the Depart-ment of State are just one illustration of the institutional friction that is present throughout the government. Beneath the president sprawl a multiplicity of organizational charts that in themselves easily fill a volume. The *United States Government Manual*, the official handbook of the federal government that contains organizational blueprints and the *raison d'être* for most agencies, is over 800 pages long. The "wiring diagrams" in these pages are static drawings of what, in reality, are offices in competition with one another for support from their department chiefs, the White House, and Congress. The size of the departments, along with their vast and complicated array of bureaucratic rivalries, makes them all but impossible for presidents to manage.

Consider just two important departments: Defense and State. The Department of Defense (DOD), responsible for providing the military strength required to deter war and protect the security of the United States, employs some 2 million men and women in uniform (including 50,000 at sea and 434,000 on foreign soil) as well as 1 million civilians. Within the Pentagon, the world's largest office building, are layers upon layers of administrative organization, topped by the office of the secretary of defense. The secretary is assisted by two deputy secretaries of defense, nine assistant secretaries, and a host of other directors, chiefs, and assistants (see Figure 6.1).

Among other officials in the Pentagon are the *Joint Chiefs of Staff*—the principal military advisers in the government, headed by a chairman selected from one of the military services. The JCS, among other things, is responsible for the preparation of strategic planning. In addition to the chairman, the JCS consists of the chief of staff, United States Army; the chief of naval operations; and the chief of staff, United States Air Force. The commandant of the Marine Corps is an equal participant on the JCS when it addresses subjects germane to the Marines. The JCS is assisted by a Joint Staff composed of 400 officers selected in equal numbers from the Army, the Navy (including the Marine Corps), and the Air Force.

FIGURE 6.1   Organization chart for the Department of Defense.

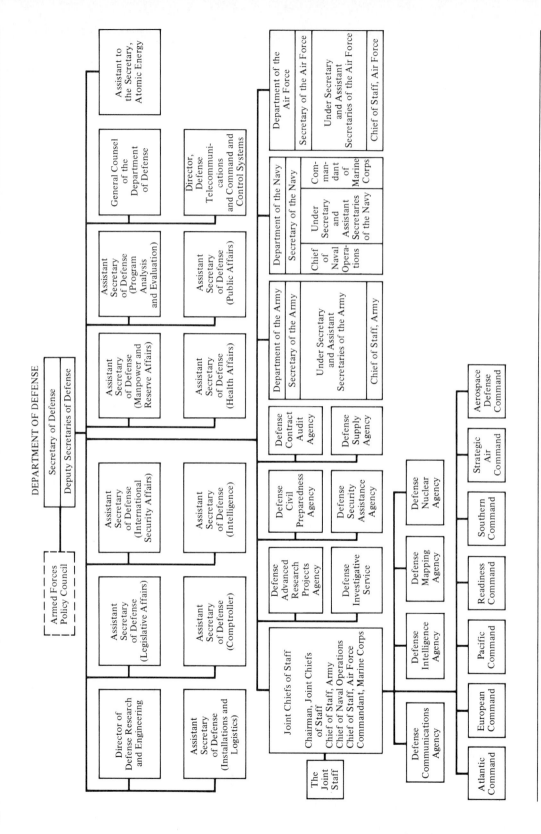

Source: Department of Defense.

138

The military intelligence agencies alone within the Defense Department account for about 85 percent of the federal intelligence budget (some $13 billion annually). This side of the DOD includes a worldwide network of electronic surveillance equipment, coordinated by America's largest intelligence organization, the National Security Agency (NSA), as well as more classic forms of spying (espionage) conducted by units within each of the military services.

The Department of State is practically as intricate. The secretary of state, at least officially the chief foreign policy adviser to the president, is assisted by a deputy secretary of state and four under secretaries: one each for political affairs, economic affairs, security assistance (the overall coordinator of the U.S. military aid program), and management. The secretary also has on call one or more "ambassadors at large" who may be dispatched to conduct special negotiations anywhere around the world. In addition, five assistant secretaries direct geographic bureaus for African Affairs, European Affairs, East Asian and Pacific Affairs, Inter-American Affairs, and Near Eastern and South Asian Affairs (see Figure 6.2). They are in turn assisted by *country directors*, who serve as the key point of contact in Washington for ambassadors and the rest of the "country teams" at U.S. missions abroad. The department also has several functional bureaus: for Educational and Cultural Affairs, Economic and Business Affairs, Intelligence and Research (INR), International Organization Affairs, Public Affairs, Security and Consular Affairs, Politico-Military Affairs, and Oceans and International Environmental and Scientific Affairs.

At the heart of the State Department lies the Foreign Service, responsible for the day-to-day conduct of America's relations with other countries. The men and women of the Foreign Service, selected through perhaps the most rigorous screening examinations in the government, serve overseas in 134 embassies, 10 missions, 68 consulates general, 47 consulates, and a few other offices. Their reports provide valuable information for the shaping of foreign policy decisions (remember the influence of George Kennan's reporting). The Agency for International Development (AID) is also located within the Department of State. Its job is to guide America's economic assistance programs for the less developed countries of the world (see Chapter 12).

As if their size alone were an insufficient management challenge, the Departments of State and Defense make life all the more complicated for presidents by often advocating quite separate views of the world and how to respond to foreign threats. The Department of State traditionally has been predisposed, as one might guess, to advocate the power of diplomacy. Here is the home of the peacemakers. The Department of Defense, in contrast, has traditionally been predisposed toward the war power. The Cuban missile crisis is illustrative. The pressures for an air strike against Cuba came from the Department of Defense; the Department of State advocated a more cautious approach, relying on diplomatic channels in the United Nations and elsewhere. During the Reagan administration, however, these departmental views were sometimes reversed, with State advocating the use of force and Defense moving more cautiously—an apparent reaction by the armed services to the experience in Vietnam and an unwillingness to become involved in military ventures abroad without the full and clear support of America's political leaders in both the executive and legislative branches.

The Department of State has also been a greenhouse for the nurturing of détente with the Soviet Union. In contrast, the Department of Defense is notorious for its "worst-case" analysis of Soviet military intentions, projecting a more negative view of future U.S.–Soviet relations. (After all, if the cold war is over, how can the huge DOD budgets be justified?) These different perspectives became all the more divisive in the Carter and Reagan administrations because of personality conflicts between the two departmental secretaries (discussed in the next chapter, "The Human Factor").

FIGURE 6.2 Organization chart for the Department of State.

Department of State

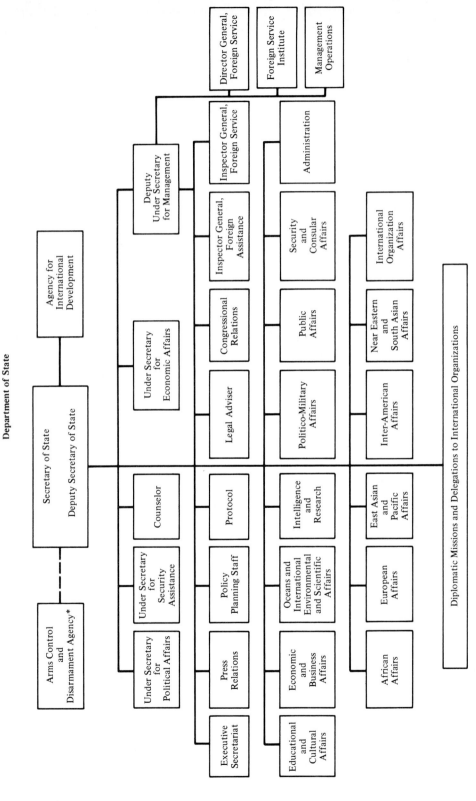

*A separate agency with the director reporting directly to the secretary and serving as principal adviser to the secretary and the president on arms control and disarmament.

Source: Department of State.

The magnitude and number of foreign programs and operations conducted by the Departments of State and Defense would alone be enough to keep a conscientious president burning the midnight oil. Yet these behemoths represent only a fraction of the leadership challenge. Almost every major agency in the government seems to have an international component, involved in negotiations of one kind or another with other nations—often with little or no guidance or control from the White House, the State Department, or Congress (see Chapter 11, on diplomacy). As one observer has noted, "With over 700 international conferences a year, transnational collegiums of professionals in agriculture, atomic energy, meteorology, satellites, and health tend to work directly with one another with little supervision by the foreign policy agencies (basically State) in staffing conferences, drawing up technical guidelines or reaching consensual decisions."[26] James Madison may well wonder if the seeds of institutional division he and his colleagues sowed in 1787 have borne too much fruit!

Part II of this book presents many examples of this fragmentation of power with respect to intelligence policy, the conduct of war, the making of international agreements, the allocation of foreign aid, and other foreign policies. Suffice it to say here that organizations like the Departments of Defense and State are like Chinese puzzles, with boxes inside of boxes. No mere mortal, president or not, can fully comprehend how they all operate together—or in pursuit of their own agendas.

Turf Battles

And, indeed, it is frequently their own agendas, not the president's, which these agencies pursue. "Career officials, including those who will come to head organizations such as the Joint Chiefs of Staff, often develop their position largely by calculating the national interest in terms of the organizational interests of the career service to which they belong," writes Morton Halperin, an expert on the national security bureaucracy.[27] The Air Force, for instance, steadfastly resisted efforts to develop ICBMs at the expense of manned bombers (considered to be the heart and soul of the Air Force mission). "Sitting in [missile] silos just cannot compare to flying bombers," observes Halperin, summing up the Air Force view. White House and Department of Defense priorities be damned; the Air Force generals wanted to *fly*! Advocacy of narrow bureaucratic interests can lead to considerable strife within the executive branch. Another experienced observer of American politics sees in the nation's capital "a *Balkanization* of our own government, with little groups putting as much energy into planning against each other as into planning how to deal with the Soviet Union."[28]

Command and Control

Legislators in recent years have been vocal in their criticism of the looseness in the executive chain of command. Operations carried out by the Central Intelligence Agency provide an example. In 1983, Representative Boland, chairman of the House Committee on Intelligence, observed that the CIA was "almost like a rogue elephant, doing what it wanted to."[29] This verdict stemmed from Boland's exasperation over CIA efforts to circumvent his amendments limiting the CIA's warlike (paramilitary) operations in Nicaragua.

Within the CIA, instances have occurred in which units have planned and implemented aggressive operations abroad without the approval or even the awareness of authorities outside the agency. In one widely reported example, James Angleton, chief of the CIA counterintelligence staff from 1954 to 1974, is said to have doctored the famous "secret speech" of Soviet Premier Nikita Khrushchev.[30] By adding deceptive paragraphs to the speech, then circulating it in eastern Europe, Angleton apparently hoped to stimulate an uprising against the Soviet regime by painting an even more venal portrait of the Stalinist era than did the unadulterated speech itself.

Individuals working for the CIA, like any other organization, may also simply ignore properly authorized policies, guidelines, directives, orders, and laws promulgated by the president, the CIA director, and the Congress. A CIA manual advocating assassinations in Nicaragua in 1984, apparently never approved by the president or even high officials within the agency, is one recent illustration.[31] Another is the secret sale of arms to Iran in exchange for hostages in 1986, an operation never reported to Congress (as required by law); the director of the CIA at the time, William J. Casey, advised against informing Congress and, evidently, personally guided the covert action in collusion with NSC staff aide Lieutenant Colonel North, outside authorized channels. (Earlier, Casey fired his deputy, John McMahon, who objected to the involvement of the CIA in the Nicaraguan civil war in ways that seemed to violate the restrictions of the Boland amendments.)

McGeorge Bundy, who chaired the NSC panel responsible for the approval of clandestine operations during the Kennedy years (the 303 Committee), has testified: "It can happen and I think it has happened that an operation is presented in one way to a committee [the NSC] and executed in a way that is different from what the committee thought it had author-

ized."[32] The hiring of organized-crime figures by a middle-ranked CIA official in the 1960s as a means for killing Fidel Castro is a further, striking example of this possibility. According to sworn testimony before a Senate investigative committee in 1975, members of the NSC knew nothing of the murder plot—let alone a CIA-mob alliance.

A constant quandary in the CIA (as in every bureaucracy) has been how to control overzealousness or plain unlawfulness, not just at the apex of the organization but at lower echelons even less visible to the public, to Congress, or to the bureau chiefs themselves. This difficulty is magnified in the national security apparatus, where agencies are virtually invisible to the public throughout, top to bottom. Commenting on this problem during the Carter years, a senior CIA official said with some anguish and with special reference to his officers trained in paramilitary operations: "What do you do with the firehorses when there's no fire!"[33] Ruthless former Nicaraguan National Guardsmen in the contra army, mobster hit men, and ideologically fervent Cuban exiles have numbered among the CIA agents who have proved difficult—sometimes impossible—for even the CIA to control, not to mention more distant White House officials.

Bureaucrats, then, sometimes appear as forbidding aliens resistant to the charms and blan-

---

Perspectives on American Foreign Policy   6.2

The political scientist Roger Hilsman, once a high official in the Department of State, on the dilemma of bureaucratic control:

... in action after action, responsibility for decision [within the executive branch] is as fluid and restless as quicksilver, and there seems to be neither a person nor an organization on whom it can

be fixed. At times the point of decision seems to have escaped into the labyrinth of governmental machinery, beyond layers and layers of bureaucracy.

From Roger Hilsman, *To Move a Nation* (New York: Delta, 1967), p. 7.

dishments of presidents. And they are supposed to be on the president's side; at least, they are in the same branch of the government. More forbidding still are those who have an obligation to be skeptical about the president's objectives and methods, who by virtue of the Constitution, the law, and historical tradition are separated from the executive branch and inclined toward a more open form of resistance: the Congress and the courts.

THE CONGRESS

"The Congress looks more powerful sitting here [in the White House] than it did when I was . . . one of a hundred in the Senate," President Kennedy once reflected. "From here I look . . . at the collective power of the Congress; . . . there are different views, different interests [and] perspectives . . . from one end of Pennsylvania Avenue to the other. . . . There is bound to be conflict."[34] Presidents spend a good deal of time feeling exasperated about the Congress. Eisenhower once referred to its members as "those damn monkeys on the Hill."[35] Most presidents probably think this, or worse, but usually keep it under their hats to avoid retaliation against their programs by aggrieved legislators.

Fissures on Capitol Hill

A primary reason presidents find members of Congress difficult to deal with is that there are so many of them. Moreover, the legislators view themselves as separate sovereign entities, answerable neither to the president nor even to congressional leaders, but rather to the voters on Election Day in each of their far-flung consituencies. "This is a Senate; a Senate of equals; of men of individual honor and personal character, and of absolute independence," declared Senator Daniel Webster in 1830, adding: "We know no masters; we acknowledge no dictators."[36] That same spirit of independence exists today in both chambers,

probably in a more acute form than at any other time in this century as a result of reforms spearheaded by freshmen legislators in the "class of 1974."

Elected during the Watergate scandal, these legislators came to Congress with what they considered to be a mandate to clean up the government. They started with their own house, insisting in party caucuses held at the beginning of the new session of Congress that power be more widely shared. Sounding like the Founding Fathers, they argued that in the Congress as well as in the White House the concentration of power—symbolized by Watergate—led to abuse and was therefore dangerous to the republic. The Democrats, who were in control of both chambers at the time (that is, a majority of legislators in each house had been elected under the Democratic party label), yielded to these demands for reform. They established several new subcommittees to give new members a greater opportunity for participation in important decisions, without waiting the two or more decades it normally took legislators to rise into an important full-committee chairmanship under the old system. In the Senate, the number of subcommittees increased to 174 in 1975 (later reduced to 90); in the House, the figure climbed to 141. Meanwhile, the number of staff aides steadily mushroomed.

The proliferation of legislative subcommittees has led to tangled lines of jurisdiction. Attention in the House of Representatives to the issue of Japanese automobile imports offers an example. During recent congressional hearings on this subject, several subcommittees scrambled to protect their turf. Two joined forces to hold joint hearings: the Subcommittee on International Economic Policy and Trade and the Subcommittee on Asian and Pacific Affairs (both part of the Committee on Foreign Affairs). Meanwhile, the Subcommittee on Trade of the Ways and Means Committee decided to hold its own separate hearings. Staffers on these various units eyed one another suspiciously and competed for top witnesses and newspaper headlines. Competition has its virtues, but the duplication of effort brought about by subcommittee proliferation strikes many critics as wasteful.

Reformist Zeal

In the post-Watergate enthusiasm for reform, the Democrats also tampered with the most sacrosanct tradition within the modern Congress: the *seniority system*. Before Watergate, a legislator, once assigned to a committee, progressed steadily up its party seniority ladder as more senior members of his or her party retired, died, were defeated at the polls, or voluntarily transferred to another, more prestigious committee (to start at its bottom rung). Health and the voters willing, a committee member could look forward to the day when he or she might arrive at the top rung and, at last, lead the committee. While the system had certain defects (by the time an individual headed a committee, he or she might be—and occasionally was—senile), it worked better than the earlier, nineteenth-century method of throwing key positions up for election in the party caucus, with all the disruption of partisan intrigue encouraged by that kind of free-for-all.

The Watergate "class," however, wanted to make sure that committee chairmen would be less autocratic than had been the case with some in the past. During the 1950s, for example, Otto Passman (D-La.) ruled the Appropriations Subcommittee on Foreign Operations like a dictator. He had risen through the House hierarchy to become head of this subcommittee responsible for foreign aid. Coming from a small town and with little personal sympathy for international relations, Passman routinely took a meat cleaver to the U.S. foreign aid program, stifling the objections of younger and more cosmopolitan members by tightly controlling their use of staff, travel funds, and the like.

The reformists demanded, and won, the opportunity to vote on each committee chairman during the party caucus at the start of every session. While most chairmen kept their positions and most senior ranking members ascended to the top committee position as they would have anyway under the old system, a few were displaced. Indeed, in 1984, Representative Les Aspin (D-Wis.) leaped over seven rungs to become chairman of the Armed Services Committee, backed by reformers who believed the top six men were unlikely to be responsive to the broad party membership. Ironically, the reformers soon found Aspin, who as chairman attempted the difficult task of satisfying his champions while healing the wounds of the older members, insufficiently attuned to their agenda and seriously considered voting him out in 1986. He skillfully won back their support by assuring them greater adherence to their views in the future. The reformers were willing to give him another try and Aspin now continues his delicate balancing act.

One thing is certain about the new rules: all committee chairmen have gained a fresh respect for the novel idea of listening to views expressed by junior members. The changes represented a bracing tonic for the morale of the Young Turks, while the more senior members grumbled over the reforms but lacked the votes to stop them.

Minnows and Whales

Whatever the merits regarding this devolution of power within Congress, one main result has been a politics much more complicated for the president and others engaged in foreign policy within the executive branch. "When I was a young assistant secretary of state," remembers Dean Rusk, who served in that capacity during the 1950s, "the Department had only to consult five 'whales' on the Hill to gain an accurate reading on how the Congress would react to our foreign policy initiatives." The five whales included Senators Everett Dirksen, the minority leader (R-Ill.), Lyndon Johnson, the majority leader (D-Tex.), Hubert H. Humphrey (D-Minn.), and Richard B. Russell (D-Ga.); and, in the House, Speaker Sam Rayburn (D-Tex.).

"Today," Rusk concludes, "you have 535 minnows."[37]

This movement toward the splintering of power on Capitol Hill accelerated as Rusk was named secretary of state in 1961. Lyndon Johnson left the Senate to become vice president in the Kennedy administration and Rayburn died that same year. Then, with the profusion of new subcommittees in 1975, the spawning of the minnows ran wild.

Dialogue between the executive branch and Congress has been greatly complicated by the reforms of 1974–1976. Lobbying five individuals on behalf of the president's foreign policy was clearly a much simpler task than trying to lobby virtually the entire membership. President Reagan seems to have responded more effectively to this challenge than did President Carter. Perhaps Carter's weakest personnel appointment was the man he named White House liaison to the Congress, a fellow Georgian, Frank Moore. While a likable fellow, he was a stranger to Washington, unknown to most legislators and unsure of how to work with Congress. Others in the Carter administration from Georgia (including the president) also seemed to bring with them to Washington an antipathy toward members of Congress, perhaps a holdover of attitudes stemming from their unhappy experience trying to work with the Georgia state legislature when Carter was governor.

Carter's idea of lobbying the Congress often seemed to pass little beyond issuing an invitation to 125 or so legislators for breakfast at the White House. In contrast, the Reagan administration proved more adept at providing attention to the needs of individual legislators, from providing Speaker of the House Thomas P. ("Tip") O'Neill, Jr. (D-Mass.) a box of his favorite cigars (though such blandishments seemed to have little effect on this Speaker, so ideologically opposed was he to the Reagan agenda) to plying members with special invitations to social galas at the White House.

While Reagan and his team exuded more charm than the Carter administration on Capi-tol Hill, both faced a paucity of powers available to persuade legislators that they ought to adopt those foreign policy initiatives favored by the White House. Boxes of cigars, invitations to the ball, and other so-called *side payments* (political science jargon for rewards and punishments) can only go so far—even threats or promises regarding major federal pork-barrel projects over which the president has some control.

Once after Senator Frank Church of Idaho had criticized President Johnson's war policy in Vietnam, he received an invitation to visit with the president at the White House.

"Who helped you write that speech on Vietnam?" Johnson inquired, his huge arm around Church's shoulder as they walked through the White House rose garden.

"Walter Lippmann [a prominent journalist] gave me some ideas," Church replied.

"Well, Frank," said the president, "the next time you need a dam out in Idaho, you go see Walter Lippmann."[38]

Despite this thinly veiled threat, Church continued—indeed, stepped up—his criticism of the war. The state of Idaho seemed to survive regardless, and Church was reelected.

Legislative Watchdogs

Added to the constitutionally derived sovereignty of individual legislators, and the further scattering of power in the Congress by recent reforms, stand other features of the legislative branch that make it a natural rival for the executive on matters of foreign policy. The previous chapter briefly discussed the war and the treaty powers (probed in greater detail in Chapters 10 and 11); here we offer only the reminder that each of these powers *requires* the Congress to take a close look before the president moves the country toward major commitments abroad. And in recent years the Congress has passed a spate of statutes that further require executive-branch reports to legislators on a range of policy proposals. Burned by the executive branch over Vietnam, Watergate, and abuses by the intelligence agencies, members of Congress are now twice shy. Or, to change metaphors, they no longer want to be kept in the dark, and these *reporting requirements* are designed to shed light on the intentions of those in the White House and the bureaucracy.

This is a main reason why Congress became so incensed over the Iranian arms scandal. This scheme represented a clear violation of their demand, in law, to be kept informed of significant foreign policy initiatives (in this case, an important covert action).

The War Powers Resolution (1973), for example, requires the president to report within forty-eight hours after moving troops into areas of hostility; the Hughes-Ryan Amendment (1974) requires the president to report "in a timely fashion" on the use of the CIA for covert action; the Nelson-Bingham Amendment (1974) requires reporting on foreign military sales agreements; the Nuclear Non-proliferation Act (1974) requires reports on all plans to ship fissionable materials abroad; the Harkin Amendment (1974) requires annual reports from the Department of State on the status of human rights in other lands; and, among others, the Comprehensive Anti-Apartheid Act (1986)—approved over President Reagan's veto—prescribes, in detail, U.S. policy toward South Africa.[39] In an attitude of defiance, Representative Carl Vinson (D-Ga.), chairman of the House Armed Services Committee, informed the secretary of defense in 1949 that "Congress won't be bypassed, and we will be conversant with what goes on."[40] A similar spirit has pervaded many members of the legislative branch in the wake of Vietnam and Watergate.

Moreover, Congress has gone beyond simple reporting requirements to employ the *legislative veto* as a control against abuses of power by the executive branch. The legislative (or congressional) veto is commonly defined as "a statutory provision that delays an announced administrative action, usually for a specified number of days, during which time Congress

may vote to approve or disapprove the action without further Presidential involvement."[41] Sometimes legislative vetoes have had the objective of halting specific executive actions altogether. As with statutes designed to solicit advance notification (like the ones outlined in the preceding paragraph), the legislative veto has been used—according to a report issued by the House Committee on Foreign Affairs—"as a basic device for insuring effective prior consultation by the executive branch."[42] Before a 1983 Supreme Court ruling called the veto technique into question (discussed below), Congress used it as a check on a wide variety of foreign policy proposals involving the war powers, arms transfers, nuclear nonproliferation, international trade, and foreign aid, among others.[43]

The Trade Act of 1975, for instance, contained a provision giving Congress the right to disapprove within sixty days any international agreement made pursuant to the legislation. Similar language was written into the Nelson-Bingham law on arms sales (an amendment to the 1974 Foreign Assistance Act). Under this law, any intended sale of defense items or services worth $25 million or more had to be reported to the Congress. In turn, the Congress could disallow any sale by a majority vote in both chambers within twenty days. In 1976, Congress amended this act to include the sale of any major defense item costing $7 million or more, and legislators lengthened the review time to thirty days. Since then, a procedure has been worked out between the executive branch and the Congress whereby a total of fifty days of congressional review is allowed—twenty days of "informal notification" and thirty days of "formal notification." In 1983, the Supreme Court decided against the constitutionality of the legislative veto imbedded in immigration laws and, by implication, in other statutes as well (see page 150).

Congress's new insistence on a full role for itself in foreign policy has led to the development of its own bureaucracy on Capitol Hill, designed to compete to some extent with the executive bureaucracy. This match is highly uneven. The executive branch, for example, has some 10,000 large computers for storing and processing information, operated at a cost of $10 billion a year; the legislative branch operates six medium-sized computers at $29 million a year. Still, Congress has shown some determination to join the twentieth century and now concentrates increased resources toward improving its capacity for vigorous monitoring of executive-branch programs.

More oversight has meant more staff, and few statistics so vividly chronicle the rise of the "new" Congress as its swelling personnel figures. The Senate has over 1100 staff aides serving on committees, the House over 2000—roughly double the number before the reformist mood set in during the mid-1970s.[44] Some committee staffs have more than quadrupled in size during the period from 1970 to 1985.[45] The personal staffs of legislators have grown even more dramatically, doubling to almost 30,000 in the past fifteen years. Among the Hill staffers are many highly trained attorneys, researchers, and former bureaucrats—all well equipped to conduct meaningful oversight (though some have become entrapped within the iron triangles and subtly co-opted into the service of one or another agency).

Those who take their job—and the concept of coequal branches—seriously have grown skillful at playing one agency off against another. In 1988, the CIA alone gave over 1000 briefings on Capitol Hill.[46] Such briefings provide Congress with ammunition for the critique of executive-branch programs. These days during hearings one is likely to find staff aides whispering to legislators: "That testimony is wrong, and you can cite CIA document such-and-such."

The growth in congressional staff has been a mixed blessing. Posing the question "Is anyone in charge on Capitol Hill?," several Congress-watchers have marshalled strong evidence on behalf of a resounding "no!" According to one Hill aide: "The staffs are so large everybody wants to have his say and leave his own little stamp. Pretty soon the weight of people wanting attention becomes greater than the force moving the legislation, and the whole thing grinds to a halt."[47]

Congress has not relied on its committee staffs alone to monitor the executive on foreign affairs. Legislators have created such research arms as the Congressional Budget Office (CBO, which, among other things, provides independent forecasts on the domestic and international economy) and the Office of Technology

---

Perspectives on American Foreign Policy   6.3

Zbigniew Brzezinski, a political scientist and national security adviser in the Carter administration, comments on what he perceives to be an excessive involvement of legislators in foreign policy decisions:

. . . Today, the decision-making process at the very top [the presidency] is institutionally more fragmented than at any point since World War II. . . . This condition is made worse by the continuing and expanding intrusion of Congress into

the tactics of foreign policy. Almost every congressman sees himself as a putative secretary of State, surrounded by personal staffers who make it their business to make the life of the secretary of State as miserable as possible. . . .

From Zbigniew Brzezinski, "Reagan May Be a Great Leader, but His Foreign Policy Is a Shambles," *Washington Post*, national weekly edition, October 20, 1986, p. 23. Reprinted by permission.

Assessment (OTA, which in 1985 presented a highly critical assessment of President Reagan's Strategic Defense Initiative—the proposed "Star Wars" umbrella against nuclear attack). Legislators have also upgraded the quality of the Library of Congress research staff and Congress's team of auditors and investigators in the General Accounting Office (GAO).

The conduct of oversight by these organizations—and by the scores of new subcommittees, most led by individuals not at all shy about making the evening news—has led to an expensive surcharge on the time of ranking officials in the executive branch. According to one report, Secretary of State George P. Shultz of the Reagan administration testified formally before Congress twenty-five times in 1983, or every other week; and other senior State Department officials appeared an additional 375 times the same year.[48] During Senate and House investigations (the most extreme form of oversight) of the CIA in 1975, the agency director, William E. Colby, recalls spending at least half of his time preparing for hearings and testifying on Capitol Hill.[49]

Congressional inquiries have become one of the chief means used by legislators to review the foreign policy initiatives of the executive branch. The investigative findings often lead to new legislation designed to make the government work more effectively. Senate and House committees in 1975, for example, uncovered several instances of wrongdoing in the intelligence agencies. In light of this evidence, legislators created permanent intelligence-oversight committees in both chambers, with the mandate to watch more attentively the future operations of the CIA and its companion services. Congressional and executive-branch probes into the Iran-contra scandal in 1987 led to reforms limiting the operational authority of the NSC staff.

"You see, the way a free government works," President Truman once remarked, "there's got to be a housecleaning every now and then." This is the primary purpose of congressional investigations. When it becomes clear that the government house has fallen into disarray, Congress reacts in an effort to restore lawfulness and propriety. At least, that is the ideal. Sometimes the investigative power has been abused by Congress, as, recall, with Senator McCarthy's witch-hunt against the Truman administration for its foreign policy reversals in China and Korea.

The power of legislative oversight has been misused in other ways by members of Congress—as power may be wherever it is lodged. In 1980, for example, Representative George Hanson (R-Idaho) rushed off to Iran during the hostage crisis in an attempt to gain release of the Americans single-handedly, as if he were the secretary of state; in 1984, Senator Jesse Helms (R-N.C.), a member of the Foreign Relations Committee, enlisted the public endorsements of U.S. ambassadors for his reelection bid, an unseemly involvement of the diplomatic corps in domestic politics; in 1986, Joseph Biden (D-Del.) threatened to disclose certain secret intelligence operations if the executive branch failed to halt them; also in 1986, David Durenburger (R-Minn.), chairman of the Senate Intelligence Committee, clumsily disclosed information about highly classified U.S. intelligence operations against Israel. Moreover, sometimes well-intentioned oversight can lead to a meddlesome, excessive involvement by legislators in the day-to-day conduct of international affairs by the executive branch—so-called *micromanagement*, in a damning phrase that has become a favorite of bureaucrats opposed to virtually any congressional participation in foreign policy decisions.

And, frequently, the Congress simply proves unable or unwilling to engage in serious oversight. A seasoned Hill observer once described the House of Representatives as, like a dinosaur, "a large, slow-witted, thin-skinned, defensive composite that wants to stay out of trouble. Its real passion is reserved for its creature comforts: salaries, recesses, office space, allowances, ever more staff to help it reach its timid decisions."[50]

At its best, though, the Congress can play an indispensable role in the protection of democracy in the United States and in the improvement of America's foreign policy decisions. Stephen K. Bailey has stated the possibilities:

> Congress defends freedom by asking rude questions; by stubbornly insisting that technology be discussed in terms of its human effects; by eliciting new ideas from old heads; by building a sympathetic bridge between the bewildered citizen and the bureaucracy; by acting as a sensitive register for group interests whose fortunes are indistinguishable from the fortunes of vast numbers of citizens and who have a constitutional right to be heard.
>
> Congress defends freedom by being a prudent provider; by carefully sifting and refining legislative proposals; by compromising and homogenizing raw forces in conflict; by humbling generals and admirals—and, on occasion, even Presidents.[51]

The capacity of Congress to test the programs and proposals of the executive branch through independent means, coupled with its grip on the purse strings, makes it the strongest legislative branch not only in the world today but at any time in history since the golden days of the Roman senate.

THE COURTS

Emerging Judicial Activism

Rarely do books on American foreign policy address the role of the third branch of government: the judiciary. This branch has been overlooked largely because its involvement in issues of foreign policy has been relatively infrequent. Indeed, the Supreme Court had little to say on this subject for the first 150 years of the nation's existence. Yet, beginning with the administration of Franklin Roosevelt, the courts have sometimes had a profound influence on the directions and methods of foreign policy.

Soon after its establishment, the Supreme Court insisted on the right to rule on the constitutionality of laws (in the famous case *Marbury v. Madison*, decided in 1803), a practice known as *judicial review*. Throughout the stretch of American history, the Court usually refrained from involvement in executive-legislative disputes over foreign policy—especially if they were controversial or dealt with political or military matters. When it did enter the fray, the Court was normally careful to state that foreign policy is shared by Congress and the presidency as coequals—though sometimes justices have sided with the president.

The Court's long period of dormancy in foreign affairs, followed by occasional pro-executive decisions, may now be a relic of the past. With the emergence of individuals in Congress and elsewhere prepared to challenge the president's once-exclusive dominion, the judiciary has become more aggressive and important as an arbiter, sometimes finding against the executive branch. This new activism spells an additional complication for executive dominance over foreign policy decisions. "The probable result," suggests one authority, "is an opening-up of the foreign policy process to a variety of societal actors, for taking a case to court and acquiring 'standing' is much more easily accomplished than attempting to penetrate Congress or the executive branch."[52]

Tilt toward the Presidency

The judiciary's first major venture into the foreign policy field came in the celebrated case *United States v. Curtiss-Wright Export Corp.* [299 U.S. 304 (1936)], often misconstrued as an affirmation of presidential preeminence in external affairs. The case gained further attention in 1987, because a principal in the Iran-contra scandal (Lieutenant Colonel Oliver L. North) invoked *Curtiss-Wright* as a justification for his secret operations bypassing the Congress.[53] In this case, a lower court convicted Curtiss-Wright (an American weapons-manufacturing company) for the sale of machine guns to Bolivia. The conviction was based on grounds that the sale violated a presidential embargo of arms and munitions to both Bolivia and Paraguay, which were at war against one another at the time. Franklin Roosevelt had based his embargo on authority derived from a congressional joint resolution, which permitted the use of an embargo—at presidential discretion—if such action might "contribute to the reestablishment of peace between [the warring] countries." On appeal to the Supreme Court, Curtiss-Wright argued that the wording of the resolution was too vague and represented an unconstitutional delegation of legislative power to the president.

Writing the majority opinion for the Supreme Court, Justice George Sutherland (himself a former member of the Senate Committee on Foreign Relations) rejected the appeal. Congress could delegate its own powers to the president, if it wished—more so in foreign than in domestic affairs. At the heart of the case stood the prerogatives of Congress, not whether the president possessed independent powers in foreign affairs. "The power at issue was legislative, not executive," emphasizes the constitutional expert Louis Fisher.[54] Nor does *Curtiss-Wright*, in the opinion of another expert, have "anything to do with 'plenary' presidential power—the authority of the President to act in the face of congressional disapproval."[55]

What has confused the issue and allowed the *Curtiss-Wright* case to be used selectively by those attempting to advance the independent powers of the executive is the pages of obiter dicta (a legal term from the Latin, meaning incidental comments and therefore not binding) added by Sutherland, going far beyond the scope of the decision before the Court. In these dicta, Sutherland opined that the president had an inherent right to exercise authority in foreign affairs, over and above existing statutory inhibi-

tions (see Perspectives on American Foreign Policy 6.4)—a position the Court had never dared to propose on domestic policy.

A legal specialist refers to Sutherland's added commentary as "the most extreme interpretation of the powers of the national government. It is the farthest departure from the theory that the United States is a constitutionally limited democracy."[56] Here was an invitation for President Roosevelt and his successors, along with adventurous NSC staffers like North, to let their powers swell on matters of foreign policy. Far more important than Sutherland's dicta, concludes Fisher, is this unaltered fact: "the Constitution effectively provides that the power of foreign affairs is allocated between Congress and the president."[57]

In more recent years, justices on the Supreme Court have sometimes taken additional positions in favor of the presidency. One illustration comes from President Carter's decision in 1979 to end—without Senate consultation—the mutual defense treaty with Taiwan. Initially, a federal district court came close to siding with the Congress ("the power to terminate treaties is a power shared by the political branches of this government," said the presiding judge, "namely the President and the Congress"), but ultimately declined on technical grounds. The Supreme Court, in turn, proved unsympathetic to the view of many senators that the Senate's advice and consent should have been sought. By a vote of 7 to 2, the Court held in *Goldwater v. Carter* [444 U.S. 996 (1979)] that the president had the constitutional authority to terminate the Taiwan defense pact by himself.

Legislators suffered a more serious setback in 1983, when the Supreme Court declared the legislative veto unconstitutional, in *U.S. Immigration and Naturalization Service v. Chadha* [77 U.S. 317 (1983)]. Ruling on an obscure immigration statute containing a legislative-veto provision, the Court seemed to strike a blow at such devices in hundreds of laws, including some highly important ones like the War Powers Res-

Perspectives on American Foreign Policy   6.4

Mr. Justice Sutherland's opinion on presidential authority in foreign affairs, offered in the Curtiss-Wright *case (1936):*

... The two classes of powers [foreign and domestic] are different, both in respect of their origin and their nature. The broad statement that the federal government can exercise no powers except those specifically enumerated in the Constitution, and such implied powers as are necessary and proper to carry into effect the enumerated powers, is categorically true only in respect of our internal affairs. ...

Not only, as we have shown, is the federal power over external affairs in origin and essential character different from that over internal affairs, but participation in the exercise of the power is significantly limited. In this vast external realm, with its important, complicated, delicate and manifold problems, the President alone has the power to speak or listen as a representative of the nation. He makes treaties with the advice and consent of the Senate; but he alone negotiates. Into the field of negotiation the Senate cannot intrude; and Congress itself is powerless to invade it. As Marshall said in his great argument of March 7, 1800, in the House of Representatives, "The President is the sole organ of the nation in its external relations, and its sole representative with foreign nations." *Annals*, 6th Cong., col. 613 ...

It is important to bear in mind that we are here dealing not alone with an authority vested in the President by an exertion of legislative power, but with such an authority plus the very delicate, plenary and exclusive power of the President as the sole organ of the federal government in the field of international relations—a power which does not require as a basis for its exercise an act of Congress, but which, of course, like every other governmental power, must be exercised in subordination to the applicable provisions of the Constitution. It is quite apparent that if, in the maintenance of our international relations, embarrassment—perhaps serious embarrassment—is to be avoided and success for our aims achieved, congressional legislation which is to be made effective through negotiation and inquiry within the international field must often accord to the President a degree of discretion and freedom from statutory restriction which would not be admissible were domestic affairs alone involved. Moreover, he, not Congress, has the better opportunity of knowing the conditions which prevail in foreign countries, and especially is this true in time of war. He has his confidential sources of information. He has his agents in the form of diplomatic, consular and other officials. Secrecy in respect of information gathered by them may be highly necessary, and the premature disclosure of it productive of harmful results. ...

United States v. Curtiss-Wright Export Corporation, 299 U.S. 304 (1936).

olution (examined in Chapter 10), which allowed the Congress to terminate U.S. military involvement abroad by a concurrent resolution (that is, a bicameral majority vote free of a possible presidential veto).

Debate continues over whether *Chadha* truly applies to all other laws beyond immigration statutes, especially those in the realm of national security. While accepting that it does apply in some instances, Congress has nonetheless enacted over 100 new legislative vetoes since *Chadha*—mostly without objections from the executive branch (whose agencies prefer to maintain cordial relations with legislators insofar as possible). Further, Congress has resorted to a number of other methods in an attempt to maintain control over specific executive actions, from oversight hearings and "gentlemen's agreements" with individual agencies to thinly veiled threats of budgetary retaliation against recalcitrant bureaucrats. As Fisher notes, *Chadha* has become a target of "open defiance and subtle evasion on Capitol Hill."[58]

Occasionally—and this is what distinguishes the present era of judicial involvement from earlier eras—the courts have trimmed back the president's authority. In the so-called Pentagon Papers case (*New York Times Co. v. United States*, 403 U.S. 713, 719), for example, the Supreme Court decided in 1971 against the president's request to prevent the *Times* and other papers from publishing the Pentagon's classified, in-house history of the war in Vietnam, on grounds that nothing within these papers, if published, would lead to "irreparable harm" to the United States.[59] In another case, handed down in 1984, a federal district court ordered the CIA to release fifteen classified documents on its operations in Nicaragua because, the Court argued, their contents had been already discussed openly by the president and his advisers.

In these cases, the courts signaled that limits existed on what the president could keep concealed from the public (discussed further in Chapter 8). And, on various occasions, federal district and appeals courts have ruled against the U.S. Immigration and Naturalization Service on questions related to the deportation of refugees from Cuba and Haiti. In light of these and other rulings,[60] presidents are apt to long for the less ambiguous ruminations of George Sutherland.

POWER: A STUDY IN CUBISM

The key institutions involved in American foreign policy resemble more a study in cubism than a harmonious and pleasantly arranged landscape portrait, for in truth the various parts of the U.S. government hold but fragments of power and are often set one against the other. Participants in the democratic process within this country are faced with the difficult task of piecing together these fragments in an effort to build coalitions supporting their policy objectives. As historians and political scientists have emphasized, leadership in the United States relies primarily on the skills of persuasion and bargaining—and only rarely on simple command.[61] "All the President is," wrote Truman in a letter to his sister, "is a glorified public relations man who spends his time flattering, kissing, and kicking people to get them to do what they are supposed to do anyway."[62]

Sometimes, though, presidents do find themselves in a position of command. They may even find it necessary to elevate themselves above the law—or so some presidents have argued and even done. President Lincoln's eleven-week "dictatorship" is a close case in point. As Rossiter summarizes, "he called out the militia, clamped a blockade on the South, enlarged the regular army and navy beyond their statutory limits, advanced public moneys to persons unauthorized to receive them, pledged the credit of the United States for a sizable loan, closed the mails to 'treasonable correspondence,' authorized the arrest of potential traitors, and, in defiance of all precedent, suspended the writ of habeas corpus along the line of communication between Washington and New York."[63] Lincoln justified these actions, in a message to Congress (July 4, 1861), in terms of his obligation to exercise the power of self-preservation for the government of the United States—even if that meant breaking the law. "Are all the laws but *one* to go unexecuted, and the Government itself go to pieces lest that one be violated?" he asked, rhetorically. "Even in such a case, would not the official oath be broken if the Government should be overthrown when it was believed that disregarding the single law would tend to preserve it?"

Former President Nixon has expressed his views regarding the prerogative of presidents to violate the law in their "higher" calling to protect the nation's security. Nixon's response, which glosses over the distinction between times of war and peace, is presented in Perspectives on American Foreign Policy 6.5.

When behaving in this extreme manner, presidents presumably are facing dire circumstances (unlike President Reagan during the Iran-contra operations, critics contended): a national crisis, probably associated with military conflict. In such rare circumstances, one might well expect presidents to conduct themselves with less constitutional restraint than under normal conditions—at least if they truly believe the preservation of the nation is at stake. As has been said—in terms that would have appealed to Lincoln—the Constitution is not a suicide pact.

If it turns out that the president has misled the public or badly misread the situation, the Congress can subsequently respond through the ultimate power available to it in its dealings with the executive: the impeachment procedure. This power is unwieldy, however, and—against someone as broadly popular as the affable Ronald Reagan—politically impractical, unless the offenses mount to the level of indisputable high crime. Instead, the legislative response traditionally has been to teach the president and his aides a lesson by exposing their mischief in hearings before the embarrassing glare of television cameras and by opposing their policy objectives on Capitol Hill through the power of the purse.

What the observations by Lincoln and Nixon suggest is the notion that the ability to exercise power (that is, to persuade others to follow a particular course) will depend upon the partic-

---

Perspectives on American Foreign Policy   6.5

Former President Richard M. Nixon on presidential power and the rule of law:

It is quite obvious that there are certain inherently governmental actions which if undertaken by the sovereign in protection of the interests of the nation's security are lawful but which if undertaken by private persons are not. . . . [I]t is naive to attempt to categorize activities a president might authorize as "legal" or "illegal" without reference to the circumstances under which he concludes that the activity is necessary. Assassination of a foreign leader—an act I never had cause to consider and which under most circumstances would be abhorrent to any president—might have been less abhorrent and, in fact, justified during World War II as a means of preventing further Nazi atrocities and ending the slaughter. Additionally, the opening of mail sent to selected priority targets of foreign intelligence, although impinging upon individual freedom, may nevertheless serve a salutory purpose when—as it has in the past—it results in preventing the disclosure of sensitive military and state secrets to the enemies of this country.

In short, there have been—and will be in the future—circumstances in which presidents may lawfully authorize actions in the interests of the security of this country, which if undertaken by other persons, or even by the president under different circumstances, would be illegal.

From "Supplementary Detailed Staff Reports on Foreign and Military Intelligence," Appendix, Book IV, *Final Report of the Select Committee to Study Governmental Operations with Respect to Intelligence Activities* (the Church Committee), Report No. 94-755, U.S. Senate, April 23, 1976, pp. 157–158.

ular role the president is playing in the White House and the perceived level of crisis faced by the nation. By *role*, analysts mean "that set of expectations by other political elites and the citizenry which defines the scope of presidential responsibilities within a given sphere of action."[64] Presidents, to put it another way, wear different hats from time to time. As Tatalovich and Daynes observe, when acting as commander in chief, the president is most powerful—especially when the nation is threatened from abroad. Next, in the role of chief diplomat the president's powers remain considerable, for according to the Constitution and custom the president has clear prerogatives in this realm. The president has progressively weaker authority, however, while wearing the hats of chief executive, legislative leader, and, the least powerful of all, public opinion and party leader— roles that rely less on constitutional or statutory authority than on the president's abilities to bargain and persuade. By having unparalleled access to information on international affairs, the president gains an added advantage as commander in chief and as chief diplomat.

Thus, at times, despite President Truman's emphasis on the president as persuader, presidents may find themselves in the role of commander. Truman himself, after all, integrated the Army in 1948 by executive order—the stroke of a pen—without trying to persuade anyone. On other occasions, though (and these will no doubt be more common), the president will be forced to try to assemble fragments of power in the nation's capital, flattering, kissing, and kicking as Truman described, in competition with the rest of the power brokers in Washington.

Sometimes the officials the president would try to persuade on foreign policy will follow, instead, advice from pressure groups or take their cues from the public opinion polls. Sometimes they will rely on their own judgment, a practice urged upon members of Parliament in the eighteenth century by the famous British conservative Edmund Burke. These additional sources of foreign policy conduct—the human factor— are the subject of the next chapter.

SUMMARY

American foreign policy is guided by a host of different entities within the government: the presidency, a large array of bureaucratic agencies, a proliferation of legislative subcommittees, shifting coalitions of "subgovernments" beneath the patina of official organizational charts, and, occasionally, the courts. At the top of this vast domain sits the president, whose hand ostensibly guides the ship of state through safe passage in the treacherous seas of international affairs. In reality, the powers of the president are limited by inadequate time and information for thoughtful decision, by disagreement over what is permissible for him or her to do, by a lack of adequate resources, by the ties of previous commitments,

and—except in times of national emergency— by fewer grants of formal authority than often supposed.

The president must contend with a bureaucracy within the executive branch that is huge and complex. Various agencies often have closer ties with outside interest groups and legislative subcommittees (the subgovernments or "iron triangles" of government) than with the president and his or her top-level appointees. Sometimes the executive agencies seem to devote more attention to the protection of their own interests than to the policy agenda set by the president and the Congress; and, sometimes, command and control problems arise in which it becomes clear that parts of the bureaucracy have subverted the will of their elected overseers, even to the point of breaking the law or drawing the country into unsavory operations abroad.

As if the bureaucratic behemoth were not enough for the president to contend with, the Constitution ensures that Congress has a major role in the making of foreign policy. Moreover, the practice of congressional oversight—the monitoring of the executive branch by legislators—has evolved from an implicit constitutional duty into a formal and extensive scrutiny of the presidency and the bureaucracy through the use of hearings, investigations, and the like. Reforms on Capitol Hill in the 1970s dispersed authority over lawmaking and oversight, which has further complicated the foreign policy duties of the president. In the past two decades, the Congress—no longer content passively to follow leadership from the White House—has increasingly demanded a legislative-executive partnership in the charting of this nation's international course. The courts, too, have become more actively engaged in foreign policy issues, with an inclination toward favoring the presidency—though less predictably so in recent years.

The complex institutional arrangements for arriving at foreign policy decisions within the United States present a far different picture from the one the simplistic organizational diagrams would suggest. Presidents and others with responsibility for external relations must work with the fragments of power given to them by custom and the Constitution. It is up to their ingenuity to sum these fragments into workable policy initiatives. Much depends upon circumstances facing the nation (in crisis, greater deference is shown to the presidency), as well as the skills and attitudes of key officeholders.

KEY TERMS

presidential model
legislative model
constitutional-balance model
executive-legislative compact
textbook presidency
Hatch Act
military-industrial complex
National Security Council
national security adviser
Joint Chiefs of Staff
country directors

seniority system
side payments
reporting requirements
legislative veto
micromanagement
judicial review
Curtiss-Wright case
Goldwater v. Carter
Chadha case
president's role

NOTES

1. Professor Laurence H. Tribe, Harvard Law School, quoted by Stuart Taylor, Jr., "Reagan's Defenders Arguing He Can Defy Congress's Ban," *New York Times*, May 17, 1987.

2. See Charles E. Lindblom, *Intelligence of Democracy* (New York: Free Press, 1965).

3. See, for example, the arguments in H. H. Wilson, *Congress: Corruption and Compromise* (New York: Rinehart & Co., 1951); Harold Laski, *The American Presidency* (New York: Harper & Row, 1949); and William F. Mullen, *Presidential Power and Politics* (New York: St. Martin's, 1976).

4. See, for example, Ernest S. Griffith, *Congress: Its Contemporary Role* (New York: New York University Press, 1961).

5. Quoted in *U.S. News & World Report*, May 2, 1983, p. 29.

6. Chalmers M. Roberts, "The Day We Didn't Go to War," *The Reporter*, September 14, 1954, pp. 31–35.

7. Warren Christopher, "Ceasefire between the Branches: A Compact in Foreign Affairs," *Foreign Affairs*, vol. 60, Summer 1982, p. 999.

8. Thomas E. Cronin, "Superman, Our Textbook President," *Washington Monthly*, vol. 2, October 1970.

9. Clinton Rossiter, *The American Presidency*, rev. ed. (New York: New American Library, 1960), p. 108.

10. *Ibid.*, p. 69.

11. Theodore H. White, *The Making of the President 1960* (New York: Atheneum, 1961), p. 441.

12. See, for example, Richard E. Neustadt, *Presidential Power: The Politics of Leadership from FDR to Carter* (New York: Wiley, 1980); Raymond Tatalovich and Byron W. Daynes, *Presidential Power in the United States* (Belmont, Calif.: Brooks/Cole, 1984); Richard M. Pious, *The American Presidency* (New York: Basic Books, 1979); Theodore C. Sorensen, *Decision-Making in the White House: The Olive Branch or the Arrows* (New York: Columbia University Press, 1963); and Richard P. Nathan, *The Administrative Presidency* (New York: Wiley, 1983).

13. *New York Times*, January 18, 1981, p. 3.

14. Richard K. Betts, *Surprise Attack: Lessons for Defense Spending* (Washington, D.C.: Brookings, 1982).

15. Quoted by Sorensen, *op. cit.*, p. 30.

16. *Ibid.*

17. Quoted by Neustadt, *op. cit.*, p. 9.

18. Remarks by Senate Hubert H. Humphrey (D-Minn.), Congressional Fellows Program, American Political Science Association, Washington, D.C., February 21, 1977.

19. See Elie Abel, *The Missile Crisis* (Philadelphia: Lippincott, 1966), pp. 154–156.

20. John F. Lehman Jr., quoted by John H. Cusman, Jr., "Ex-Insider Who Elects to Remain on Outside," *New York Times*, January 6, 1989, p. 11.

21. Quoted in preface to Sorenson, *op. cit.*, p. xii.

22. See Loch K. Johnson, "Three Windows on Armageddon," in Paul Diehl and Loch K. Johnson, *Through the Straits of Armageddon: Arms Control Issues and Prospects* (Athens, Ga.: University of Georgia Press, 1987), pp. 241–259.

23. New York: Oxford University Press, 1959.

24. On the NSC, see Karl F. Inderfurth and Loch K. Johnson, *Decisions of the Highest Order: Perspectives on the National Security Council* (Belmont, Calif.: Brooks/Cole, 1988).

25. Leslie H. Gelb. "Why Not the State Department?" *Washington Quarterly*, Autumn 1980, p. 27.

26. Raymond Hopkins, "The International Role of 'Domestic' Bureaucracy," *International Organization*, vol. 30, 1976, p. 424.

27. "Organizational Interests," in Daniel J. Kaufman, Jeffrey S. McKitrick, and Thomas J. Leney, eds., *U.S. National Security: A Framework for Analysis* (Lexington, Mass.: Heath, 1985), pp. 201–232.

28. Elizabeth Drew, *New Yorker*, February 14, 1983, original emphasis.

29. Quoted by Don Oberdofer, *Washington Post*, August 6, 1983, p. A13.

30. Seymour M. Hersh, "The Angleton Story," *New York Times Magazine*, June 25, 1978, p. 13.

31. On this manual, see the *New York Times*, December 6, 1984. Entitled *Psychological Operations in Guerrilla Warfare*, the document has been published by Random House (New York, 1985).

32. Quoted by Norman Kempster, *Washington Star*, November 12, 1975.

33. Remarks, CIA headquarters, Langley, Va., February 24, 1978.

34. Cited by Theodore C. Sorenson, *Kennedy* (New York: Harper & Row, 1965), p. 346.

35. Cited by James David Barber, *The Presidential Character: Predicting Performance in the White House* (Englewood Cliffs, N.J.: Prentice-Hall, 1972), p. 157.

36. From "Second Speech on Foote's Resolution," delivered in the Senate, January 26, 1830, reprinted in *The Writings and Speeches of Daniel Webster*, Vol. 6 (Boston: Little, Brown, 1903), p. 7.

37. Interview with Dean Rusk, Athens, Ga., May 22, 1980.

38. Interview with Senator Church, Boise, Idaho, October 22, 1974.

39. See Thomas M. Franck and Edward Weisband, *Foreign Policy by Congress* (New York: Oxford University Press, 1979); and the *New York Times*, December 12, 1988, p. 13.

40. Hearings cited by Vance Packard, "Uncle Carl, Watchdog of Defense," *American Magazine*, vol. 149, April 1950, p. 123.

41. "Studies on the Legislative Veto," prepared by the Congressional Research Service for the Committee on Rules, House of Representatives, Committee Print, February 1980, p. 1.

42. "Congress and Foreign Policy," *Report of the Special Subcommittee on Investigations*, 1977, p. 10.

43. See "Executive-Legislative Consultation on Foreign Policy: Strengthening the Legislative Side," House Foreign Affairs Committee Print, prepared by the Congress Research Service (Congress and Foreign Policy Series no. 5), April 1982, pp. 61–62.

44. Norman J. Ornstein, Thomas E. Mann, Michael J. Malbin, Allen Schick, and John F. Bibby, *Vital Statistics on Congress, 1984–85 Edition* (Washington, D.C.: American Enterprise Institute for Public Policy Research, 1984), p. 120.

45. Gregg Easterbrook, "What's Wrong with Congress?" *Atlantic*, December 1984, p. 59.

46. Remarks, William H. Webster, Director of Central Intelligence, before the Association of Former Intelligence Officers, April 10, 1989, reprinted in *Periscope*, Spring 1989, p. 21. A CIA official claimed this same number of briefings for 1983, too; see Robert Gates, Deputy Director for Intelligence, CIA, "Conference on U.S. Intelligence: The Organization and the Profession," Central Intelligence Agency, Langley, Va., June 11, 1984.

47. Easterbrook, *op. cit.*, pp. 57–84. In the view of political scientist James A. Thurber, "Too many people mucking around . . . slowed the place down" [quoted by Burt Solomon, "Pendulum of Power," *National Journal* (November 18, 1989), p. 2817].

48. Easterbrook, *op. cit.*, p. 65.

49. Author's interview with William Colby, Washington, D.C., March 21, 1979.

50. *Washington Star*, March 9, 1976.

51. *Congress in the Seventies*, 2d ed. (New York: St. Martin's, 1970), p. 109.

52. Jerel A. Rosati, "A Neglected Actor in American Foreign Policy: The Role of the Judiciary," *International Studies Notes*, vol. 12, Fall 1985, p. 14.

53. Testimony of Lt. Col. Oliver L. North, Iran-contra hearings, July 13, 1987, U.S. Congress, Washington, D.C.

54. Louis Fisher, "Foreign Policy Powers of the President and Congress," *Annals of the American Academy of Political and Social Science*, vol. 499, September 1988, p. 152.

55. Michael J. Glennon, "In Foreign Policy, the Court Is Clear: President Is Subject to Will of Congress," *Los Angeles Times*, July 19, 1987, sec. 5, p. 3.

56. D. M. Levitan, "The Foreign Relations Power: An Analysis of Mr. Justice Sutherland's Theory," *Yale Law Journal*, April 1946, p. 493, cited by Arthur M. Schlesinger, Jr., *The Imperial Presidency* (Boston: Houghton Mifflin, 1973), p. 104.

57. Fisher, *op. cit.*, p. 154.

58. Louis Fisher, *Constitutional Dialogues: Inter-pretation as Political Process* (Princeton, N.J.: Princeton University Press, 1988), p. 225. See, also, Frederick M. Kaiser, "Congressional Control of Executive Actions in the Aftermath of the *Chadha* Decision," *Administrative Law Review*, vol. 36, Summer 1984, pp. 239–276; and Michael J. Glennon, "The Good Friday Accords: Legislative Veto by Another Name," *American Journal of International Law*, vol. 83, 1989, pp. 544–546.

59. See Sanford J. Ungar, *The Papers and 'The Papers,'* (New York: Dutton, 1972). This case is discussed at greater length in Chap. 8.

60. See Rosati, *op. cit.*, pp. 11–12.

61. Neustadt, *op. cit.*

62. November 1947, Truman Archives, Truman Presidential Library.

63. Rossiter, *op. cit.*, p. 94.

64. Tatalovich and Daynes, *op. cit.*, p. 16.

RECOMMENDED READINGS

Burns, James M. *The Deadlock of Democracy* (Englewood Cliffs, N.J.: Prentice-Hall, 1963). A superbly written account of institutional strains in the American political system by a president of the American Political Science Association with a pro-executive bias.

Commission on the Organization of the Government for the Conduct of Foreign Policy. Multivolume reports (Washington, D.C.: U.S. Government Printing Office, June 1975). This commission, known as the Murphy Commission, was established by Congress to submit findings and recommendations on how to make the conduct of foreign policy in the United States more effective.

Cronin, Thomas E. *The State of the Presidency* (Washington, D.C.: Brookings, 1974). A comprehensive examination of the literature on the presidency, augmented by Cronin's own original research on how the American people glorify the office.

Destler, I. M., Leslie H. Gelb, and Anthony Lake. *Our Own Worst Enemy: The Unmaking of American Foreign Policy* (New York: Simon & Schuster, 1984). A critique of the present creakiness in our foreign policy machinery, with suggestions where to oil and retool from three experienced foreign policy experts.

Fisher, Louis. *Constitutional Conflicts between Congress and the President* (Princeton, N.J.: Princeton University Press, 1985). An exhaustively documented legal analysis of the strains between these two branches of our government.

Griffith, Ernest S. *Congress: Its Contemporary Role* (New York: New York University Press, 1961). A thoughtful defense of a full role for Congress in matters of public policy.

Hargrove, Erwin C., and Michael Nelson. *Presidents, Politics, and Policy* (New York: Knopf, 1984). An original analysis of the presidency employing a cyclical approach based upon alternate periods of policy preparation, achievement, and consolidation.

Inderfurth, Karl F., and Loch K. Johnson. *Decisions of the Highest Order: Perspectives on the National Security Council* (Pacific Grove, Calif.: Brooks/Cole, 1987). A selection of readings on the nation's most important decision-making entity for foreign and defense policy.

Neustadt, Richard E. *Presidential Power* (New York: Wiley, 1960). A classic on the subject, emphasizing that the president is a persuader, not a commander.

Pious, Richard M. *The American Presidency* (New York: Basic Books, 1979). A comprehensive treatment, stressing the formal ("prerogative") powers of the office.

Polsby, Nelson W. *Congress and the Presidency*, 2nd ed. (New York: Prentice-Hall, 1971). An excellent introduction to this subject, to-the-point and highly readable.

Smith, Hedrick. *The Power Game: How Washington Works* (New York: Random House, 1988). Written by one of America's most distinguished journalists, a lively account of institutional dynamics in Washington, D.C., with the fragmentation of power a central theme.

Sorensen, Theodore C. *Decision-Making in the White House: The Olive Branch or the Arrows* (New York: Columbia University Press, 1963). An excellent little book on the limitations of presi-dential power, with a foreword by President Kennedy.

Tatalovich, Raymond, and Byron W. Daynes. *Presidential Power in the United States* (Belmont, Calif.: Brooks/Cole, 1984). A comprehensive and useful study of the presidency, with a role orientation.

PUBLIC OPINION AND AMERICAN
FOREIGN POLICY

Democracy versus Demoscopy

The President and Public Opinion

The Opinion-Leadership Hypothesis

The Congress and Public Opinion

Presidential Deference

The Cambodian Incursion

Vox Populi

GROUPS AND AMERICAN FOREIGN
POLICY

Squeaky Wheels

Foreign Lobbies

A Kaleidoscope of Domestic Pressures

A Diversity of International Pressure
Groups

"En Masse" versus Group Opinion

THE INDIVIDUAL AND AMERICAN
FOREIGN POLICY

The Importance of Character

The Lasswellian Hypothesis

Ego Defense versus Statecraft

The Barber Typology

Operational Codes

The Worth of the Individual

SUMMARY

7

THE HUMAN FACTOR

"Political science without biography," wrote Harold Lasswell, "is a form of taxidermy." A pioneer in the analysis of personality and politics, Lasswell understood that although a thorough knowledge of political institutions was important to the study of public policy, one also had to consider the behavior of individual citizens—whether in the voting booth, as members of pressure groups, or in high office. This chapter presents an introduction to the place of individuals in the making of American foreign policy, beginning, like the Constitution, with "we the people" ("*en masse*" public opinion) and then moving to people in organized groups and, finally, to the significance of individual policymakers.

PUBLIC OPINION AND AMERICAN FOREIGN POLICY

Democracy versus Demoscopy

"Public opinion is like the castle ghost," Sigmund Graff has said. "No one has ever seen it, but everyone is scared of it." While indeed often ghostlike in its elusiveness, the public (or, at any rate, that percentage who take the time to vote—barely over 50 percent in the last two presidential contests) does express itself with an audible voice on election day. Elections seldom turn on issues of foreign policy, though, unless the nation is at war; voters are usually most concerned about the state of the domestic economy—basic pocketbook issues. (See the polling responses in Table 7.1.) While the ballot box remains the most important means of public expression in a democracy, few successful politicians have been willing to ignore voters between elections.

Yet, sometimes elected officials—who may have access to secret information unavailable to the general public—must make foreign and domestic policy decisions that they believe are best for the country, even if initially unpopular. "Democracy is not equivalent to *demoscopy* [the

Street demonstration in Austin, Texas, against the U.S. invasion of Cambodia in May of 1970. (AP/Wide World Photos)

161

scientific analysis of public opinion polls]," declared the West German chancellor Helmut Kohl in defending his government's acceptance of American intermediate-range nuclear missiles on German soil in 1983, even though poll findings indicated overwhelming public opposition in his country.[1] Political leaders in the United States have found this distinction valid as well. "Men of integrity find it necessary, from time to time, to act contrary to public opinion," wrote John F. Kennedy. "The true democracy . . . puts its faith in the people—faith that the people will not condemn those whose devotion to principle leads them to an unpopular course. . . ."[2] In deciding on foreign policy, how have presidents and legislators coped with this tension between "devotion to principle" and a healthy respect for public opinion?

The President and Public Opinion

Public opinion seldom exerts a strong tug on presidents when it comes to foreign policy decisions. This is true because the American people remain in a state of blissful ignorance about most aspects of foreign affairs and so are largely inert. The important U.S.–Canadian trade negotiations of 1987, for example, passed virtually unnoticed by most American citizens and received little attention in U.S. newspapers (though the topic dominated Canadian news for months). Even when the public is aroused, as occurred in May of 1970 when the Nixon administration expanded the Vietnamese war into Cambodia, opinion can be so diverse and conflicting that no clear signal comes to the president or to legislators in the Congress. As a result, policymakers are freed to rely on their own predispositions. The Cambodian invasion is examined later in this chapter as an illustration of the ambiguities that can accompany even the most vociferous expressions of public opinion. Leaders remain wary, nonetheless, that the sleeping giant of public opinion might awake one day and speak with a clear voice.

Then the world—or at least their constituency—may tremble.

While it is true that most voters have little *specific* information about foreign policy, they are able to express significant views on (as one researcher has put it) "*overall* policy directions."[3] The polling data presented in Table 7.1 reveal the public's perception of the most important overall problem facing the United States in each year from 1935 through 1985. In 1968, for example, the American public made plain enough its dislike for President Johnson's Vietnam policies. Johnson's precipitous decline in the polls no doubt contributed to his decision to withdraw his reelection bid that year. The distinguished political scientist V. O. Key, Jr., draws the conclusion that, in this broad sense, the nation's electorate is "responsible."[4]

As suggested by the data in Table 7.1, two conditions are most likely to stir public opinion into awakening: prolonged military conflict with no victory in sight, and bleak economic news—inflation, rising interests rates, a dramatic plunge in the stock market (like the record drop of 508 points in October of 1987), high unemployment, or an unfavorable Consumer Price Index. The lives of U.S. soldiers and the family checkbook—peace and prosperity—these count most in the public eye. Wisely, Americans are unwilling to squander either. The rising price of meat sent President Truman on a slippery downhill slide in the opinion polls following World War II; and war-induced inflation, coupled with the spiraling loss of American lives in Vietnam (with no end in sight), cost Lyndon Johnson the presidency in 1968.

A question of considerable interest to students of international affairs is how the public responds, as indicated by opinion polls, to the most extreme form of foreign policy power: the use of overt military force. Presidents Truman and Johnson both suffered greatly in the polls as a result of their unpopular wars; but researchers have noted a tendency in briefer mil-

TABLE 7.1   THE MOST IMPORTANT PROBLEM FACING THE COUNTRY, 1935–1985

Since 1935, the Gallup organization has polled Americans several times each year asking what they think is the most important problem facing the United States. Gallup's list of the most frequent responses by year shows that the public's concern has alternated over time between issues of war and peace and issues pertaining to the economy. The only other issues that aroused the nation were labor unrest at the end of the 1940s, race relations in the late 1950s and early 1960s, and Watergate and energy issues in the 1970s. Over the last decade, the public has been mainly concerned with the high cost of living (inflation) and unemployment.

1985	Fear of war; unemployment	1959	Keeping peace
1984	Unemployment; fear of war	1958	Unemployment; keeping peace
1983	Unemployment; high cost of living	1957	Race relations; keeping peace
1982	Unemployment; high cost of living	1956	Keeping peace
1981	High cost of living; unemployment	1955	Keeping peace
1980	High cost of living; unemployment	1954	Keeping peace
1979	High cost of living; energy problems	1953	Keeping peace
1978	High cost of living; energy problems	1952	Korean war
1977	High cost of living; unemployment	1951	Korean war
1976	High cost of living; unemployment	1950	Labor unrest
1975	High cost of living; unemployment	1949	Labor unrest
1974	High cost of living; Watergate; energy crisis	1948	Keeping peace
1973	High cost of living; Watergate	1947	High cost of living
1972	Vietnam	1946	High cost of living
1971	Vietnam; high cost of living	1945	Winning war
1970	Vietnam	1944	Winning war
1969	Vietnam	1943	Winning war
1968	Vietnam	1942	Winning war
1967	Vietnam; high cost of living	1941	Keeping out of war; winning war
1966	Vietnam	1940	Keeping out of war
1965	Vietnam; race relations	1939	Keeping out of war
1964	Vietnam; race relations	1938	Keeping out of war
1963	Keeping peace; race relations	1937	Unemployment
1962	Keeping peace	1936	Unemployment
1961	Keeping peace	1935	Unemployment
1960	Keeping peace		

itary engagements for presidents to enjoy a strong surge upward in the polls. The polls reflected support (albeit slight) for President Nixon's order to invade Cambodia in 1970, for instance, as well as for President Ford's use of the Marines to rescue the crew of the *Mayaguez*, and, more recently, for President Reagan's invasion of Grenada (a small island in the Caribbean Sea north of Venezuela) in opposition to pro-communist forces there. To what degree does military conflict involving the United States inflate or deflate a president's standing with the public (as measured by the pollsters), and why?

Perspectives on American Foreign Policy   7.1

Former Secretary of State Dean Rusk (1961–1969) on public opinion and the war in Vietnam:

... there is a problem in the conduct of our foreign relations stemming from the very nature of our society and its constitutional system. We had very detailed and careful reports on the attitudes of the American people at the grassroots throughout the Vietnam experience, and it was not until 1967 or the first half of 1968 that we began to see real evidence that the people at the grassroots, not the demonstrators on campuses and a few Nobel Prize winners here and there, had finally come to the conclusion that if we could not tell them when this war was going to be over, we might as well chuck it. ...

But there is a problem because in an open society such as ours, where debate is free and must

be free, a good many of the things that were said in 1966, 1967, and 1968 went to Hanoi as a message, in effect saying, "Just hang in there fellows, and you will win politically what you have not been able to win militarily."

Now, that is a heavy price to pay, but I think it's the price we must gladly pay for our kind of system. However, it does complicate, at times, the conduct of our foreign relations because the North Vietnamese never had any incentive to negotiate. They were told that if they persisted, they would get what they wanted. They made that judgment and they were right in that judgment, from their point of view.

From *1983 Annual Report of the Former Secretaries of State* (Atlanta: Southern Center for International Studies, 1985), pp. 15–16. Reprinted by permission.

The *rally-round-the-flag hypothesis* provides one answer. This hypothesis (or research "hunch") states that a perceived threat to the United States and its citizens will result in a display by the American public of strong patriotic support for the president, sending his (one day, her) standing sharply upward in the public opinion ratings on job performance. This rallying response seems to occur, however, only with certain kinds of events. Research indicates they must be international in nature (for domestic political events remain too divisive in most cases for a clear rally phenomenon, even in times of crisis); they must directly involve the United States and, therefore, the president; and they must be "specific, dramatic, and sharply focused."[5]

Five types of international events meet these criteria: rapid intervention by the United States in another nation (say, Korea in 1950 or Grenada in 1983); significant military develop-

ments in an ongoing war (the Gulf of Tonkin incident in 1964, or the accidental Iraqi attack on the American naval ship *Stark* in the Persian Gulf in 1987, which provided public backing for a U.S. buildup of military force in this tense region); major diplomatic initiatives (the Truman Doctrine in 1947); startling new technological developments (*Sputnik*, 1957); and, because of wide media coverage accorded formal gatherings of the two superpowers, virtually any U.S.–Soviet summit meeting.

Examples of the rally response are abundant. Among the most conspicuous is the *Mayaguez* confrontation with Cambodia (Chapter 4). Use of the Marines in this abortive rescue attempt led to an eleven-point surge in President Ford's approval rating in the polls. The shooting down of the American U-2 spy plane by the Soviets in 1960 pushed President Eisenhower three points upward in the polls. The presidential dispatch of the Marines to Lebanon in 1958, and to the

Dominican Republic in 1965, stimulated a rise of six percentage points each for Eisenhower and Johnson, respectively. The Grenada invasion in 1983 and an air strike against Libya ordered by President Reagan in 1987 boosted his standing in the polls thirteen and twenty-five points, respectively.

What researchers have found most intriguing about the rally hypothesis is its apparent validity regardless of how poorly the president happens to handle the crisis. Why is it that, according to one researcher, "invariably, the popular response to a president during [an] international crisis is favorable, regardless of the wisdom of the policies [he] pursues"?[6] After all, the *Mayaguez* "rescue" can hardly be considered a successful use of force by the president: forty-one Marines died, fifty more were wounded—and no one was rescued. Nor was the U-2 shoot-down exactly a high point in the history of American foreign policy, for it led to the collapse of a potentially important arms control summit meeting between the United States and the Soviet Union.

Unwilling to accept this hypothesis at face value, or the argument that the rally response is simply an outpouring of patriotic sentiment from the public, researchers have begun to examine the phenomenon more closely. Skepticism toward the conventional explanations grew out of a series of events fitting the assumed rally criteria but actually leading to a decline in presidential standing in the polls. For example: the *Pueblo* incident of January 23, 1968, when an American spy ship was captured by North Koreans off their coastline, has some similarity to the *Mayaguez* incident, but the public displayed no rallying response in support of President Johnson. Then, in 1969, another American spy plane was downed (by the North Koreans); yet, unlike Eisenhower in the aftermath of the U-2 shoot-down, President Nixon enjoyed no surge in the polls. And, unlike the U.S. military interventions in Lebanon (1958) and the Dominican Republic (1965), the Cambodian intervention in 1970 afforded Nixon only a

modest rise in the polls (barely one percentage point; see Table 7.2).

The Opinion-Leadership Hypothesis

In the sixty-five instances of "rally events" presented in Table 7.2, forty-two led to an increase in presidential popularity, as the rally hypothesis would predict. But what about the other twenty-three cases, which were clearly significant events (six involved major military encounters in an ongoing war)? The missing ingredient in the rally hypothesis, according to the *opinion-leadership hypothesis*, may be the availability of information to the public that could call into question the merits of a presidential deicision.[7] In many crises, the broad, inattentive public—and even the attentive public opinion leaders in Congress and elsewhere—will have little access to information about fast-breaking events. In the *Mayaguez* rescue, for instance, most people (even most members of Congress) remained unaware of the details of the operation until after it was over.

Without reliable information, individuals who might be critical of the president—say, congressional leaders in the opposition party—are in a weak position to offer a critique; therefore, they are inclined to be supportive. Or, at least, they remain quiet. And when these opinion leaders are quiescent, the general public has no source of information or guidance from respected officials as to why, or in what way, they should question a presidential decision. Safe from criticism (at least for the time being), the decision rises in public esteem as the president maintains the monopoly over information about unfolding events—a telling illustration of the power of secrecy, examined in Chapter 8.

That many of the exceptional cases are related to protracted wars seems to strengthen the public-information hypothesis. In such instances, the public—and certainly opinion leaders in Congress—have had a longer opportunity to evaluate a president's use of force and have been able to accumulate more information

TABLE 7.2   RALLY EVENTS IN AMERICAN FOREIGN POLICY

	% change in approval
Truman	
Truman Doctrine (March 1947)	+12
Berlin blockade (April 1948)	+3
Soviet A-bomb announced (September 1949)	−6
Korean invasion (June–July 1950)	+9
Inchon landing (September 1950)	−4
China crosses the Yalu River (November–December 1950)	−3
Korean peace talks begin (July 1951)	+4
Eisenhower	
Korean truce signed (July–August 1953)	+1
Big Four Geneva conference (July 1955)	+4
Sputnik I launched (October 1957)	+3
U.S. Marines land in Lebanon (July 1958)	+6
Khrushchev visit at Camp David (September 1959)	+5
U-2 shot down by Soviets; Paris summit (May 1960)	+3
Kennedy	
Bay of Pigs incident (April 1961)	+5
Vienna summit (May 1961)	−3
Berlin wall (August 1961)	+1
Test ban treaty (August–September 1961)	+4
Berlin crisis (October 1961)	+2
Cuban missile crisis (October 1962)	+12
Johnson	
Gulf of Tonkin incident (August 1964)	−5
Start of North Vietnam bombing (February 1965)	−2
Invasion of Dominican Republic (April–May 1965)	+6
Extension of North Vietnam bombing (July 1966)	+8
Glassboro summit (June 1967)	+8
Pueblo incident (January 1968)	−7
Tet Offensive; U.S. embassy invaded (January–February 1968)	−7
North Vietnam agrees to peace talks (April 1968)	+4
Bombing halt (November 1968)	+1
Nixon	
"Vietnamization" speech (November 1969)	+11
Invasion of Cambodia (May 1970)	+1
China trip (February 1972)	+4
Haiphong harbor mined (May 1972)	−3
"Peace is at hand" speech (October–November 1972)	+6

TABLE 7.2 (Continued)   *RALLY EVENTS IN AMERICAN FOREIGN POLICY*

	% change in approval
Nixon *(cont.)*	
Christmas bombing (December 1972)	−8
Vietnam peace agreement (January 1973)	+16
Washington, D.C., summit (June 1973)	−5
Arab-Israeli cease-fire (May 1974)	+3
Moscow summit (July 1974)	−2
Ford	
Cambodia falls to communists (April 1975)	−5
Mayaguez incident (June 1975)	+11
Helsinki summit (July 1975)	−7
Egypt-Israel treaty (August 1975)	+1
Carter	
Panama Canal treaty (August 1977)	+6
Neutron bomb deferred (March–April 1978)	−8
Mideast summit at Camp David (September 1978)	+3
Mideast treaty (March 1979)	+6
Vienna summit (June 1979)	−1
Embassy seized in Tehran (November 1979)	+6
Soviet invasion of Afghanistan (December 1979)	+2
Hostage rescue attempt fails (April 1980)	+4
Reagan	
U.S. downs Libyan fighters (August 1981)	−8
Falklands war (April 1982)	−2
Bombing at U.S. embassy in Lebanon (April 1983)	+2
South Korean passenger plane shot down by USSR (September 1983)	+4
Bombing of Marine compound in Beirut; invasion of Grenada (October 1983)	+4
Truck bombing of U.S. embassy in Beirut (September 1984)	−3
Kuwait airline hijacking (December 1984)	+3
TWA hijacking (June 1985)	+3
Palestinians seize cruise ship; U.S. intercepts jet with hijackers (October 1985)	+3
Geneva summit (November 1985)	−2
U.S. attack on Libya (February 1986)	−1
U.S. jets attack Libyan targets (March 1986)	−1
Daniloff detention in USSR; Pan Am jet hijacking (August–September 1986)	+ 1
Nicaragua shoots down U.S. plane, captures Hasenfus; Reykjavik summit (October 1986)	+4
Iran-contra affair (November 1986)	−21

Reprinted from Richard A. Brody and Catherine R. Shapiro, "A Reconsideration of the Rally Phenomenon in Public Opinion," in Samuel Long, ed., Political Behavior Annual, *Vol. 2 (Boulder, Colo., and London: Westview, 1989), pp. 85–86. Copyright 1989 by Westview Press, Inc.*

with which to judge new developments. As a consequence, opinion leaders are less inclined to be tentative, more willing to speak their personal views. In turn, these views are reported by the media. As media consumers, the public then has an opportunity to select from among different viewpoints—not just the president's—and is, therefore, in a better position to arrive at a negative judgment of an event than if forced to rely on limited information controlled by the executive branch alone. The public, in a word, is less likely under these circumstances to rally blindly behind a president.

The effect which public information can have on the rallying phenomenon points to a necessary modification in a venerable explanation about public opinion: the *two-step flow of communications*. This widely accepted hypothesis suggests that information travels from the media to society's opinion leaders (step one), and then from the opinion leaders down to the general public (step two).[8] The public-information hypothesis points to an important potential distortion in this linkage. When the executive branch withholds information from the media, or monopolizes the kind of information the media are able to obtain, then opinion leaders hear only what the executive branch wants them to hear. Under these conditions, the result is a three-step flow of communications: (1) the executive branch to the media; (2) the media, as a conveyor belt of government-controlled information, to the opinion leaders outside the executive branch (in the Congress and at various levels of society); and (3) from these leaders, as the final conveyor of executive-branch information, to the public.

In essence, then, the views of the executive branch can be translated to the public with little or no intermediary correction, criticisms, or other filtering by outside opinion leaders. The public knows of no reason to rail against the president and therefore rallies instead. "In aggregate terms, a lack of critical opinion leadership can outweigh even relatively unambiguous evidence of policy failure and hence pave the way for positive evaluations of presidential performance," conclude Richard A. Brody and Catherine R. Shapiro, the authors of the opinion-leadership hypothesis. "A corollary of this hypothesis is that when opinion leadership is both divided and vocal such that it offers contradictory evaluations of presidential performance [through the media], the public's response will be tied in greater measure to the indications of policy success or failure evinced by the events themselves."[9]

The effects of the media on public perceptions of foreign policy are still poorly understood, and to complicate matters further, recent research suggests that often the people are far from empty vessels waiting passively to be filled with facts and opinions from print and electronic news outlets. In the linkages between government information, opinion leaders, and the public, the media can become a distorting filter of some consequence; but apparently the filtering is designed more to make the news conform with the expectations of what the public wants to hear than to try and change their views. Media managers are evidently disposed, for example, to reinforce those positive or negative stereotypes about presidents which they believe match images acceptable to consumers—say, the perception of an "incompetent" Jimmy Carter unable to free American hostages in Iran or a "Teflon-coated" Ronald Reagan (who emerged without a scratch from the press in 1983, despite the loss of over 200 U.S. Marines in Lebanon in a terrorist bombing of their barracks).[10]

The Congress and Public Opinion

As discussed in earlier chapters, the Congress is now much more involved in decisions of foreign policy than once was the case before the war in Vietnam. What can be said about the relationship between legislators and public opinion? Political theorists often discuss this subject in terms of a classic dichotomy: on the one hand, the legislator as "trustee" making decisions strictly on the basis of his or her own judgment; and on the other hand, the "instructed delegate" who attempts to mirror the opinion of constituents back home.

While in the Senate, John F. Kennedy wrote derisively about legislators content simply to be "a seismograph recording shifts in popular opinion."[11] Similarly, the British conservative Edmund Burke, in a speech to his constituents at Bristol in 1774, dismissed the *instructed-delegate model of representation* with the famous rebuke: ". . . Your representative owes you, not his industry only, but his judgment; and he betrays, instead of serving you, if he sacrifices it to your opinion."[12]

Despite the acclaim for this independence from the whims of public opinion—often referred to as the *Burkean model of representation*—most elected officials in the United States read the tea leaves of public opinion as well as they can. (Perhaps Burke should have, too, for he was soon defeated after his famous speech at Bristol.) Legislators on Capitol Hill (as well as White House officials) try to gauge "en masse" or "grass roots" opinion on foreign policy in a variety of ways, including their mail, visits from citizens, travels around their constituencies, articles and letters to the editor in newspapers in their state, and opinion polls. In the importance members of Congress attached to these sources of opinion, "mail outweighs every other form of communication."[13]

Yet, peering into their mailbags for instructions on how to handle a crisis in Berlin or Iranian threats to American shipping in the Persian Gulf can be a perilous way to judge constituency opinion, chiefly because the mail contains many distortions. Relatively few people write to public officials (about 17 percent[14]), for instance, and those who do tend to write repetitively. Letter writers are also apt to be significantly above the average citizen in terms of education, income, and status. Moreover, they are disposed to write legislators who already share their views. Finally, almost half the mail received in congressional offices is orchestrated by pressure groups (who have their members write similarly worded messages to legislators or simply sign their names to form letters); for that reason, it may not necessarily reflect the views of a true cross section of the constituency.

Aware of these shortcomings, most officials monitor additional sources of opinion on foreign policy. Research indicates that letters published in newspapers may also influence political decision makers.[15] Although only about 3 percent of the public write letters to the editor,[16] congressional staffs (and their White House counterparts) monitor this source, too. Newspapers are examined to determine the drift of public thinking on America's covert wars in the developing countries, arms negotiations with the Soviet Union, and the like. Sometimes letters printed on the editorial page are answered by officials.

In the 1940s, a series of interviews with legislators revealed that public opinion polls ranked last behind mail, visits to constituents, newspapers, and visits from constituents as a source of constituency opinion.[17] A more recent study found that polls continued to rank last among opinion sources.[18] Part of the problem with polls is their broad focus. With some exceptions (like the statewide Field Poll in California), they are national or regional in scope; therefore, a legislator must make a considerable extrapolation to assume that the opinions on foreign affairs expressed in these polls are reflective of views held by citizens in his or her smaller constituency. Some legislators conduct their own polls; but, since accurate, scientific polling is expensive, most simply send unsophisticated questionnaires to a small percentage of citizens on their mailing lists. The response rates are uniformly low and unreliable. Thus, while legislators (like presidents) do keep track of available polls—even if they are inclined to be skeptical about their accuracy—researchers confirm that most members of Congress continue to believe that "their mail provides them with the single best indicator of constituent attitudes on legislative issues."[19]

Presidential Deference

The question of how—and how well—legislators gauge the will of their constituents may well be irrelevant most of the time. Several studies have concluded that representatives rarely face the task of accepting or rejecting the demands of constituents, for the simple reason that "the people" seldom articulate their views.[20] This appears to be doubly true with foreign policy, which rarely generates much public awareness.

For foreign affairs, the political scientists Miller and Stokes have suggested a modern twist to the Burkean model of representation: a *model of presidential deference*. Writing in the era before the war in Vietnam, they argued that in the case of foreign policy, legislators are freed from constituent pressures, because on such matters the public is ill informed and inattentive. Yet, rather than exercise their own judgment in a Burkean fashion, legislators were inclined (at the time the research was conducted in 1962) to defer to presidential leadership—a kind of "father knows best" attitude.[21] Since the Vietnam era, however, representatives have been far less trustful of presidential leadership—a skepticism reinforced by Watergate, spy scandals, and no doubt in 1987 by the congressional testimony of high-ranking officials in the Reagan administration that they had lied to Congress during the Iran-contra affair. Nevertheless, as evidence for the rally-round-the-flag hypothesis indicates, under some circumstances the model of presidential deference remains alive and well.

That most Americans have limited knowledge regarding international affairs, or world geography, is a common finding few would gainsay. In a poll taken during the 1960s, for example, a majority of Americans expressed a willingness to use military force against the Soviet Union in order to protect the freedom of West Berlin. Follow-up questions revealed that the respondents had little or no knowledge about the location of West Berlin and the tactical difficulties posed for the U.S. Army of protecting a city surrounded by East Germany, a highly garrisoned nation controlled by Soviet troops.

In 1984, when pollsters asked a national sample of Americans whether the United States was supporting, or fighting against, the government of Nicaragua (the Marxist Sandinista regime), 73 percent said they did not know—even though U.S. support for the anti-Sandinista contras had been widely reported in the newspapers for well over a year. In 1986, 43 percent responded affirmatively to the statement that the Reagan administration "has been supporting the government of Nicaragua," with another 25 percent "not sure." Only 32 percent of those polled answered correctly that the administration opposed the Sandinistas.[22]

On another issue, about 50 percent of the American public is unaware that this country imports almost half the oil it uses—indeed, a poll in 1978 found that most Americans thought their nation was strictly self-sufficient from its lush oil fields in Texas and Alaska. And while U.S. consumers often extol a "buy American" attitude, their knowledge of what is made where can be shallow. A 1986 poll, for instance, found that 43 percent of those U.S. consumers in the survey thought that General Electric (GE) microwave ovens were made entirely within the United States, yet actually this product is produced almost completely overseas.[23]

Even when it comes to governmental matters at home, most Americans appear to be poorly informed. Most, for instance, are unaware how many representatives they have in Washington (let alone their names)—or even their length of terms; and fewer than one out of five Americans can refer to *any* vote or action taken by their representative in Congress.[24] Only 32 percent of the American people had the foggiest idea what the Electoral College was, according to a Gallup Poll. The others surveyed thought it might be, among other fanciful notions, "[a place] where they train the politicians how to vote," "some kind of college around here," and, "[something that] helps people to live comfortably. . . . "[25] In 1986, a poll found that 69 percent of those sampled thought the U.S. Constitution established English as the national language; and only 43 percent identified William Rehnquist as the Chief Justice of the Supreme Court.[26]

The research findings summarized here suggest that the instructed-delegate model of representation may be difficult to carry out; accurate "en masse" instructions are simply too hard, if not impossible, to obtain (the mail is clearly not a representative sample of broad constituency opinion, for instance). Moreover, this form of representation may be foolish to adopt anyway, since the public at large seems so poorly informed. Sometimes, though, a foreign policy will attract close public attention—even a strong outburst of opinion. On these occasions, public "instructions" to their delegates may make this seismographic form of representation more workable. To examine this possibility, this chapter explores the most conspicuous example since 1945 of a loud public clamor over a foreign policy decision: the nation's response to President Nixon's invasion of Cambodia in May of 1970.

The Cambodian Incursion

Nixon's decision to send U.S. troops into Cambodia ignited a storm of controversy. In the days immediately following the invasion (which Nixon, the reader will recall, chose to call euphemistically an "incursion"), antiwar demonstrations erupted across the United States. Constituents paraded by the hundreds through the halls on Capitol Hill and demonstrated in front of the White House, as the mass media focused public attention on the president's dramatic decision. For many, the invasion signaled a shocking escalation of the war in Vietnam, despite reassurances to the contrary from the White House that the operation was intended merely to wipe out North Vietnamese and Vietcong hiding places ("sanctuar-

ies") across the border in Cambodia. Public attitudes were further inflamed a few days after the invasion, when the Ohio National Guard gunned down student protestors at Kent State University and police in Mississippi killed students at Jackson State University.

For seven weeks, the Senate debated the wisdom of the military action, to the exclusion of nearly all other business. According to a Senate Post Office official, in the three weeks following the invasion, senators received over 2 million letters and telegrams—the largest outpouring of direct constituent communication on a single issue in the history of the Senate. Thus, the Cambodian episode represents an unusual case, an exception to the conclusion of researchers that the public lacks interest in foreign affairs. How did legislators react to this extraordinary outburst of public opinion on a foreign policy issue?

An answer to this question can be found in an analysis of the downpour of letters that fell like a tropical storm on the U.S. Senate after the invasion.[27] This mail revealed little support for the president's decision. On the average, letters to Democratic senators ran 10 to 1 against the invasion, while letters to Republicans averaged about 4 to 1 against. The south was the only region showing significant support for Nixon's decision. Of the nine senators who reported preponderantly "hawkish" mail, seven represented southern states. Yet, even the mail sent to all the southern senators (as a whole) opposed the decision to intervene, by a ratio of 2 to 1.

In contrast, the overall frequency distribution of "hawk" and "dove" letters to the editor in each state's major newspaper was relatively balanced. The ratios ranged from 6 to 1 in opposition to 6 to 1 in favor of the attack. Thus, senators who examined letters to the editor on Cambodia received a substantially different view of constituent attitudes from that conveyed by the mail arriving in their own offices.

Further, if a senator studied the Harris poll on the invasion, he or she would have found a plurality supporting the decision—a significantly divergent pattern from the mail received by most senators. This poll, taken soon after the attack, found that 49 percent of those surveyed believed that the president was right in sending American troops into Cambodia, 43 percent had serious doubts about the decision, and the rest were undecided.[28] Examined by region (see Table 7.3), the figures are similar to the other sources of opinion, in that the east displayed the greatest reservations and the south the most support for the "incursion."

A senator who hoped to gauge the nature of "true" grass roots opinion back home consequently faced a kaleidoscope of images. Each of three significant indexes of "en masse" opinion—mail, letters to the editor, and opinion polls—presented a different picture of public opinion on the Cambodian military action. One scholar's contention that "when an issue does evoke a sizable response from [a] senator's constituents, its meaning is highly ambiguous" was borne out.[29] Each Senate office resolved the mixed signals presented by these conflicting opinion sources just as earlier research would have predicted: staff aides relied upon the mail as the most accurate source of constituency opinion.

Did the enormous ground swell of citizen

mail on Cambodia guide the response of senators to the crisis, as the instructed-delegate model of representation would prescribe? Were senators guided chiefly by their own convictions, the Burkean model? Or did they bow to the president as commander in chief, implicitly adopting the model of presidential deference?

A statistical analysis discloses the association between measures of these models of representation and Senate votes on the Cooper-Church Amendment, a legislative proposal designed to halt a continued military presence in Cambodia. An amalgam of earlier votes cast by senators in support of the president on previous foreign policy issues showed little association with their votes on the Cooper-Church Amendment, calling into question the use of the presidential-deference model in this instance. In contrast, the ratios of pro and con constituency mail on Cambodia were significantly associated with the voting pattern on this amendment. Stronger still, though, was the relationship between voting on the Cooper-Church Amendment and measures of each senator's general philosophical orientation (broadly, liberal versus conservative), as derived from a range of votes on foreign and domestic issues in the previous session of Congress.

Thus, despite the efforts of unprecedented numbers of Americans to write their senators in May of 1970, the strongest correlation with a senator's vote for (or against) legislation to withdraw from Cambodia was not the mail or a senator's past record of deference to the president, but rather established ideological predilections—a senator's broad philosophical outlook, as revealed by earlier votes on a wide constellation of issues.[30] Senators with a consistently "dovish" voting record tended to support the Cooper-Church Amendment for withdrawal from Cambodia, and senators with a consistently "hawkish" record were inclined to oppose the amendment.

Rather than bowing to the icon of presiden-

TABLE 7.3   SURVEY OPINION ON THE CAMBODIAN INVASION, 1970*

REGION/ PARTY	RIGHT DECISION	SERIOUS DOUBTS	UNCERTAIN
National	49%	43%	8%
East	45	47	8
Midwest	48	45	7
West	51	43	6
South	57	34	9
Republican	62	31	7
Democrat	43	47	10

Harris Survey taken from May 8 to May 10, 1970.

tial deference, voting on the Cooper-Church Amendment reflected instead the characteristics of the Burkean model, as senators rebuffed White House pleadings and endorsed the views of Senators Cooper and Church. The focus of the Cambodian debate in the Senate was expansive, with constitutional—not constituency—arguments raised by participants. As Senator Church stated early in the debate: "Basic constitutional questions are at stake here. Are we going to permit our government to slide relentlessly toward all power being concentrated in the hands of one Chief Executive? Are we going to permit our government to become a Caesardom, or are we going to reassert the authority that the Constitution placed in the Congress? That is the fundamental issue. . . ." For Senator Clifford Hansen (R-Wyo.), "What the argument is all about is, in fact, the role that the United States should play in the world today."

For most senators, the Cambodian vote was an example of representatives pursuing their own foreign policy preferences, making their own assessment of the national interest, and voting as their convictions dictated. How are these preferences derived? The political scientist Robert A. Dahl has described their origins: "The Congressman's preferences are shaped by his loyalties, his attitudes of deference and respect, his view of a desired future for himself and for those with whom he identifies himself, for his constituency, for his society, his country, the world, posterity."[31]

As the Cambodian case illustrates, these personal preferences can be of overriding importance on foreign policy issues. One must avoid making too much of a single (albeit important) case; the Cambodian invasion came at a time when senators had grown increasingly wary of the U.S. combat role in Indochina. It may be that in some foreign policy crises, constituency mail or deference to the president might override a legislator's own predispositions—especially, one would hypothesize, if a president's decision were unrelated to a prolonged and un-

popular war like the one in Vietnam. Nonetheless, the reaction of senators to the Cambodian crisis emphasizes the need for students of foreign policy to understand more about the philosophical orientations of individuals in Congress and in the White House—a subject addressed later in this chapter.

Vox Populi

In light of the inattention paid by most citizens to international affairs, coupled with their lack of specific knowledge about events abroad, one might be tempted to dismiss public opinion altogether as an inconsequential influence on American foreign policy. This would be an error. "The point isn't that the heads of 'We the People' are full of Jell-O and that they should be ignored," writes Everett C. Ladd, an expert on public opinion. "The public brings to the controversy some basic values and expectations that are firm enough."[32] Here is the hard lesson that President Johnson learned from the war in Vietnam. Most of the time, the public's views on foreign affairs will be as invisible as the castle ghost; but when officials go beyond the boundaries of what the public finds acceptable—especially in terms of lost blood and treasure—here is one ghost who can suddenly become quite real for presidents and legislators who must stand for reelection.

As we have seen, Americans can make their opinions on foreign policy known through various means, among them letters, opinion polls, and, most important, the ballot box. On most occasions, however, the foreign policy views of the general public are less likely to be taken into account than those of citizens who have organized themselves into cohesive groups for the purpose of protecting and promoting their own special interests. The Department of State, like other government agencies, conducts few public opinion polls; but its officials meet regularly with a wide range of interest-group leaders. Here are "the people" we turn to next.

GROUPS AND AMERICAN FOREIGN POLICY

Squeaky Wheels

In and around the branches of government move an astonishing array of interest (or pressure) groups. They enjoy the constitutional right to advocate their views in the councils of power; the First Amendment grants Americans the privilege "peaceably to assemble, and to petition the Government for a redress of grievances." Every conceivable interest seems to be represented, from the mighty International Brotherhood of Teamsters to the obscure Southwest Peanut Shellers Association. The oil companies, the textile industries, the veterans, the peace movement, the trade associations, shipping interests, airline interests, farmers, human rights activists—the list goes on.

The groups may hope to convince decision makers that they should support policies designed to help the economic needs of the group members—in the case of Detroit auto workers, relief from the flood of Japanese cars streaming into the United States, or, for American farmers, assistance in locating foreign markets for wheat, corn, and potatoes. Or they may seek to fulfill political and ideological objectives, be they support for the existence of Israel, funds for the anticommunists in Nicaragua, or freedom for political dissenters in Chile. The range of goals, and the lobbying methods, are as diverse as the groups themselves. Legitimate lobbyists and the people they represent not only have a right to be heard, but, further, many of them bring to the government useful information and opinions that often elevate the quality of decisions. Most scholarly studies of lobbyists conclude that they are an excellent source of data for policymakers who seek to understand the problems confronting the nation and their constituencies.[33]

Thus, the Congress and agencies throughout the executive branch experience a steady parade of group advocates who pass through their corridors each day in search of access to decision makers. Nor is this improper (except in those infrequent instances when a few lobbyists violate the law in an attempt to bribe their way to success). Yet, this system of representation is hardly perfect, as every critique of American pluralism has recognized. Simply put, groups in American society are unequally blessed with the resources—money, membership, Washington contacts, and the like—which they can bring to bear on their lobbying efforts.

A typical lobbying experience of a staff aide on the Senate Foreign Relations Committee illustrates the inequities. During the Carter administration, two young lobbyists—fresh out of college and representing a poorly funded solar-energy group—met with an aide who worked for a senior committee member. Over Cokes in the Senate cafeteria, the lobbyists requested help from the committee to establish a solar-energy project in a developing nation.

In sharp contrast, during the next week the Westinghouse International Corporation invited the same staff aide out to dinner. Its team of lobbyists included a distinguished former U.S. ambassador and a garrulous former member of Congress. Together, they dined at Washington's most expensive French restaurant. After a few days, the Westinghouse group visited the staff aide again, this time armed with impressive charts and briefing materials to support their case for legislative assistance. The Foreign Relations Committee, they argued, ought to help their corporation obtain federal subsidies for the revamping of its expensive nuclear plant in South Carolina. The plan was to develop a reprocessing facility designed to convert radioactive "spent fuels" (nuclear waste products) into fissionable materials, which could then be sold overseas.

The aide dutifully passed on to his senator the arguments of both lobbying groups. It was obvious, however, that Westinghouse—with its well-known lobbyists, large expense account, and sizable treasure chest of campaign funds—was going to have far greater success in bringing its case to key legislators and their aides. Eventually, in this instance, both groups failed to achieve their objectives. Despite the considerable clout of Westinghouse, the Carter administration opposed the reprocessing concept in principle, and when a president opposes a bill in Congress its chances for passage diminish significantly. The failure was a rarity for Westinghouse, a routine event for the solar-energy neophytes.

Foreign Lobbies

Some of the groups that descend upon the government with foreign policy demands represent the interests of other nations, toward which the group members may feel a strong identification and sympathy. Among these groups, some have been remarkably adept in achieving their goals. Sometimes a group has extraordinary skills of persuasion, with leaders of high intellect, eloquence, and reputation; sometimes its cause seems so just as to require little lobbying at all; and sometimes the muscle that money represents can convince legislators—always in need of campaign contributions—that they should stop and listen. A brief look at a few of the major foreign policy lobbying groups in the United States will provide a sense of their diversity.

The American Jewish community has been successful in lobbying the U.S. government for large sums of money earmarked for Israel—funding levels "without precedent in international philanthropy," notes Zbigniew Brzezinski.[34] The community's chief lobbying arm is the *American Israel Public Affairs Committee* (*AIPAC*), which works with allied organizations around the country. These groups skillfully channel campaign contributions to important legislators—especially those on the foreign affairs, armed services, and appropriations committees—and to the president (or, in election years, to those who seem to have a good chance of entering the White House). This careful nurturing of the powerful pays off. In 1987, the

American aid package to Israel was worth over $3 billion—the largest for any country. (When Egypt agreed to a peace treaty with Israel in 1979, it too found itself amply rewarded by becoming second on the list of U.S. aid recipients, at $2.3 billion.) In 1984, the United States decided to provide outright economic and military grants to Israel, instead of loans, so that Israel would not have to pay back anything.

Not all of this success is attributable singly to the lobbying prowess of AIPAC, considerable as that may be. Policymakers are pleased to have a pro-American stalwart like Israel in the Middle East—an oil-rich location of obvious strategic importance to the United States and its allies. Moreover, most Americans are sympathetic to the claim of Israel—one of the world's few democracies—for the right of self-determination in a region of hostile nations, and are prepared as a matter of fairness to help this small country protect itself with sophisticated American weapons against opponents vastly superior in number.

Even so, Israel sometimes loses its bid for favorable treatment in Washington's corridors of power. Occasionally U.S. officials, sensitive to the dependence of America and its allies on Arab oil, and appreciative of the help from nations like Saudi Arabia and Jordan in maintaining peace in the Middle East, will sell advanced weapons to Israeli's opponents—over AIPAC's loud objections. A conspicuous example involved the sale of the AWACS (Airborne Warning and Control System), a modern radar-equipped communications airplane, to Saudi Arabia in 1980. The Saudis told American officials they wished to use the airplane as part of their defense against a Soviet attack, but Israelis feared that the plane might be used some day in a war against them. In 1985 and 1986, AIPAC was more successful. It led the opposition against congressional support for the sale of forty F-15 jet fighters and 800 Stinger missiles to the Saudis (who then took their $25 billion shopping list to the British, where the pro-Israel lobby is weaker).[35] American sympathies for the Israeli cause began to diminish somewhat during 1988 and 1989, as U.S. television news cameras revealed instances of brutality directed toward Palestinians (including women and children) by Israeli soldiers attempting to quell rock throwing and other manifestations of unrest in disputed territories.

The Greek-American lobby has proven to be effective as well—with Greece ranked consistently among the top three or four recipients of U.S. aide over the years. Just as AIPAC has been helped by Jews in key political positions (such as the late Senator Jacob Javits, R-N.Y., who served on the Foreign Relations Committee for years), so has the Greek-American lobby accrued the benefits of Greek-Americans in high office, including presently one of the most important members of the Foreign Relations Committee, Senator Paul Sarbanes (D-Md.). In 1988, a Greek-American stood as a Democratic presidential candidate: Michael Dukakis, governor of Massachusetts.

Not to be outdone, Turkey—often a bitter rival of Greece in the Mediterranean and in Washington—has established an impressive lobbying effort of its own in the United States. The Turkish embassy, a magnificent building along Embassy Row in Washington (built at the turn of the century by the inventor of the bottle cap), is the site of sumptuous feasts hosted by Turkish diplomats as part of their effort to win friends among the powerful (and their aides) in the nation's capital.

The Washington skies have been further brightened by additional constellations of foreign lobbies that, until recently, had displayed only a distant twinkle. Arab nations, for instance, have begun to understand the importance of political lobbying in America and have hired well-connected individuals in Washington able to open the right doors—and the public purse strings—on their behalf. Senator Fulbright, now retired, former CIA director and ambassador Richard Helms, and former Representative James Symington (D-Mo.) are examples of individuals who, for the right fee, can gain admission for outsiders into the inner sanctums of Capitol Hill and the Department of State.

The Japanese lobbying effort in Washington—possibly the most well-heeled of all the foreign lobbies, with an annual budget reported to be in excess of $40 million—has become more sophisticated, too, over the past decade. It often uses an approach successfully employed by several interest groups in the nation's capital: a trio of three American lobbyists. First a bright and attractive blonde, not easily forgotten, drops by staff offices on the Hill or in the executive branch to discuss an issue of importance to the Japanese, say, fishing rights in U.S. waters. Next a former member of Congress telephones to see if he, the blonde, and another colleague could continue the discussion over lunch at a chic Washington restaurant. Staff aides are unaccustomed to saying no to present, or former, members of Congress. The third lobbyist turns out to be the expert. The blonde perks up attention, the former congressman adds prestige, and then comes the expert to make the pitch for legislation with a finely honed set of statistics and some well-oiled arguments. "Look, here are the facts: the oceans off the American coastline have enough fish to go around for everyone." Enter reams of data. "And this will help U.S.–Japanese relations immensely."

It can be a persuasive combination—though always within limits. After all, members of Congress have *American* fishermen to worry about, and these fishermen—not the Japanese—get to vote. Still, the Japanese lobby has been able to increase the share of fishing opportunities for Japan by exercising a persuasive presence in the right places.

Since the end of World War II and the beginning of America's global competition with the Soviet Union, anticommunist emigrants in the United States have also enjoyed good access to the powerful. During the 1950s, for example, refugees from the Baltic states living in New York and California proved effective fund-raisers for Republican candidates (favored because of their strong anti-Soviet rhetoric) and, as a result, won the ear of GOP leaders. Eisenhower's secretary of state, John Foster Dulles, tightened the relationship with his hyperbolic pledge to "roll back the Iron Curtain."[36]

Gaining influence recently has been another group of anticommunist émigrés, the Cuban-American lobby. For most of the thirty years since the exodus of Cubans to the United States (when Fidel Castro established his dictatorship on the island), the voice of Cuban-Americans "was heard but faintly."[37] Now, though, several members of this community have achieved positions of status and distinction in American society; they are successful businesspeople—millionaires in some instances—as well as politicians, lawyers, and physicians. Spearheading

the effort to influence U.S. policy toward Cuba has been the Cuban American National Foundation (CANF), established in 1981 by prosperous business leaders in south Florida. The foundation has raised enough funds to open a lobbying office in the prestigious Georgetown area of Washington, D.C., with a staff of five. The objective of the foundation, according to its literature, is to promote "an independent and democratic Cuba" and to "enlighten and clarify public opinion on problems of Cuban concern." Among its successes have been Radio Martí, a radio station established by Congress to transmit propaganda into Cuba from the Cuban-American community in Florida, and legislative hearings in Congress to highlight claims that Castro is presently involved in drug trafficking directed toward the United States.

Perspectives on American Foreign Policy 7.2

The political scientist James David Barber on foreign "mega-lobbies":

... Some of the biggest [foreign lobbies] make their headquarters in the United States. They hire themselves out to countries with shocking and offensive records on human rights. And so great is their skill and influence that they tempt Congress to forget that two years ago [1984] both houses passed, and President Reagan signed, the Congressional Resolution Against Torture, officially committing the Government to fight torture wherever it persists. In the face of these new mega-lobbies, it is going to take all the concentration Congress and the public can muster to keep that commitment in mind. ...

Turkey is a particularly flagrant example. This year, the Turkish Government will receive hundreds of millions in economic and military aid from the United States, a package ranking third

after Israel and Egypt. Turkey pays its public-relations company hundreds of thousands of dollars to brighten its image and to obscure its continuing practice, documented in detail, of secret arrest and systematic torture of men and women.

American-based companies representing foreign governments clearly outspend the human rights movement, but the larger point is this: when governments torment and butcher humans violating the principles our nation was founded upon, Americans ought not permit themselves to be distracted by hired propagandists. We should insist that United States foreign policy put first for other people what we put first for ourselves: the dignity and liberty of the individual.

James David Barber, "Lobbies Can't Erase Rights Violations," *New York Times*, June 9, 1986, p. 19. Reprinted by permission.

A Kaleidoscope of Domestic Pressures

Some altruistic groups within the United States are less concerned about the fortunes of a particular interest at home or government abroad than they are about the well-being of needy people everywhere in the world. At times (as with many American groups having an interest in foreign affairs), their goals can run counter to the official policy of the U.S. government. Such a conflict occurred in 1986 with the Boston-based private relief organization called Oxfam America. This group wanted to ship to nongovernment organizations in Nicaragua some $41,000 worth of supplies, including hammers, chain saws, water pipes, shovels, wrenches, rakes, seeds, and books on agriculture. The purpose, according to Oxfam's director, was to alleviate food shortages in a country ravaged by civil war. A year earlier, however, the Reagan administration had instituted a trade embargo against Nicaragua as part of its squeeze on the Sandinista regime. The administration refused permission for Oxfam to ship the materials. "We are dealing with the politics of hunger," complained an Oxfam official. "This is a clear example of the government playing politics with the poor overseas."[38]

One long-established organization in the United States with foreign policy interests is the *Council on Foreign Relations*, an elite club of well-educated, affluent, often pedigreed, and mainly east coast members. Founded in 1921 and supported by leading U.S. foundations and corporations, the CFR has become an important recruitment reservoir for top-level foreign policy officials of both major parties. It also publishes the widely read journal *Foreign Affairs*, as well as numerous reports and studies (several of which are commissioned by the government). Through its publications and study groups, the council attempts to lobby decision makers by way of intellectual reason. The CFR has been criticized by outsiders (and an occasional insider[39]) for its tepid writings and cold war outlook (during the war in Vietnam, its members were largely in support of a strong U.S. combat role down to the last gasp of retreat), though in recent years its membership has been younger and somewhat less tied to the status quo.

Significant as lobbying interests, also, have been the so-called *nonstate actors*, that is, various global corporations and international organizations that have been on the rise for a few decades. One U.S. corporation, International Telephone and Telegraph (ITT), demonstrated its clout at the White House during the 1960s by applying strong direct pressure upon the Nixon administration to intervene on its behalf in Chile. The corporation wanted the government to overthrow the socialist leader, Allende, who (ITT worried) might expropriate its holdings in Chile. As a means for encouraging the adoption of an anti-Allende policy by the Nixon administration, ITT provided $1 million of its own funds to be used by the CIA in carrying out the operation—a form of "lobbying" seldom discussed in civics books.[40] The role of multinational corporations (MNCs) in American foreign policy is examined at greater length in Chapter 12, "Economic Statecraft".

Even individual American states sometimes adopt their own foreign policies. The California State Assembly, for instance, passed a statute in August 1986 that required the state's pension system to dispose of stocks in companies conducting business with South Africa, a policy called *divestment*. At the time, this law represented one of the strongest blows against apartheid (as racial segregation is called in South Africa) yet taken by any organization within the United States, involving some $11.3 billion worth of investments. Seventeen other states had already taken modest steps toward divestment, but, as the *New York Times* reported, "in the scope of its divestment legislation and the amounts involved, California's action dwarfs any previous effort in this country to use economic pressure on multinational corporations as a lever to persuade South Africa to change."[41]

Even mayors of American cities can be found pursuing their own brand of international affairs. Sam Yorty, for example, the mayor of Los Angeles during the 1960s, spent much of his time traveling abroad seeking markets for California goods and singing the praises of those nations willing to enter into economic relations with his city. Mayor Andrew Young of Atlanta (former U.S. ambassador to the UN during the Carter years) also traveled abroad frequently, dabbling in foreign policy. In August of 1986 on a visit to Angola, Mayor Young proclaimed his undying friendship to the Marxist regime there, causing conservative interest groups in Washington close to the Reagan administration to ask the mayor in newspaper letters to the editor: "Which side are you on?"[42]

Some groups can provide all the comfort of a political buzz saw for officials who fail to endorse their positions. When President Eisenhower fought John Bricker (R-Ohio) over his efforts in the Senate to trim back—or even eliminate—the use of executive agreements, arrayed against the White House in hearings before Congress were, among others, the Vigilant Women for the Bricker Amendment, the American Legion, the Daughters of the American Revolution, the Veterans of Foreign Wars, Kiwanis International, and the Chamber of Commerce of the United States. Eisenhower had his backers, too, including the American Federation of Labor, the League of Women Voters, and the American Veterans' Committee; but Bricker's allies comprised a formidable listing by any reckoning.[43] (The tense denouement of this historical confrontation is presented in Chapter 11.)

During his tenure, President Carter also discovered the potency of aroused foreign policy interest groups. Conservative organizations, spurred to new heights of cold war rhetoric by the Soviet invasion of Afghanistan in 1979, pounded away at what they perceived to be deficiencies in the president's conduct of external affairs. Among the chorus of voices to be heard from the right during this period were the "Madison Group" (conservative legislators meeting weekly at the Madison Hotel in Washington); the Committee for the Survival of a Free Congress; the Committee on the Present Danger; the Advanced International Studies Institute at Bethesda, Maryland; the Ethics and Public Policy Center in Washington; the Institute for Foreign Policy in Philadelphia; the Institute for Foreign Policy Analysis in Cambridge, Massachusetts; the National Strategy Information Center in New York; and the Institute for Contemporary Studies in San Francisco.[44] One of these bees alone would have only stung a little; together, their swarm of criticism grew to a political threat of some magnitude and likely damaged the president's standing with the public.

Accompanying these groups, with their primary focus on one foreign policy issue or another, are others that are essentially domestic in their orientation but whose objectives, nonetheless, have definite implications for America's relations abroad. High on this list is the military-industrial complex. Weapons manufacturers, and the network of consultants, think tanks, and laboratories that surround them, have a clear economic stake in raising the budget for national defense. So do politicians, labor unions, and a host of other beneficiaries in many states (the Saudi arms deal lost to Britain, referred to earlier, carried with it some 50,000 new jobs for the weapons-manufacturing sector[45]). As Figure 7.1 illustrates, weapons like the laser-beam shield advocated by the Reagan administration (the Strategic Defense Initiative, or "Star Wars") can mean large sums of federal funds for a state's economy.

Specialists at a Harvard-MIT roundtable held on this topic agreed that laboratories engaged in the designing of weapons (the Lawrence-Livermore Laboratory in California and the Los Alamos Scientific Laboratory in New Mexico, for instance) may well represent a stronger influence in Washington over increased military expenditures than even the defense corporations themselves.[46] The roundtable participants

FIGURE 7.1   The high cost of weapons.

Billion-dollar weapons

Weapons programs in the Pentagon's proposed 1987 budget that would cost $1 billion or more. Amounts for classified programs, such as the Stealth aircraft, are not available. Rounded figures in billions.

Strategic Defense Initiative $4.8
F-16 Falcon Air Force fighter plane 3.9
F/A-18 Hornet Navy fighter plane 3.5
Trident II submarine-launched ballistic missile 3.1
DDG-51 destroyer 2.6
SSN-688 attack submarine 2.4
F-15 Eagle Air Force fighter planes 2.3
M-1 tank 2.2
CG-47 Aegis cruiser 2.1
C-5B Galaxy transport plane 2.0
MX missile 1.8
Trident nuclear-missile submarine 1.7
Midgetman ballistic missile 1.4
AH-64 attack helicopter 1.4
Bradley fighting vehicle (armored troop carrier) 1.2
Patriot surface-to-air missile 1.1

Source: Based on data from the Department of Defense.

concluded, however, that these components of the military-industrial complex are really of secondary importance for understanding the large U.S. defense expenditures. The more fundamental driving force was, in their view, the ongoing attitude of unalloyed fear and distrust toward the Soviet Union held by the American public and, at the time (1985), by the Reagan administration. On a day-to-day basis, broad public opinion is rarely as influential on foreign policy makers as are opinions expressed by specific organized groups; still, this public backdrop of anticommunism—so firmly a part of "en masse" opinion in the United States—stands as an influence of considerable weight in decision councils.

A Diversity of International Pressures

In addition to the formidable array of pressure groups within the United States, the world has over 300 *intergovernmental organizations* (IGOs) and some 2400 *international nongovernmental organizations* (INGOs), many of which have an affect upon the conduct of U.S. foreign policy.[47] Examples of IGOs include the UN, NATO,

OAS, the League of Arab States (LAS), the European Economic Community (EEC), the World Health Organization (WHO), the International Labor Organization (ILO), and the International North Pacific Fisheries Commission.

The INGOs, comprising about 90 percent of all international organizations, also include political parties like the Social Democrats in western Europe. The Social Democrats have separate parties within many of the nations of western Europe, but these parties also reach across national boundaries in an attempt to maintain financial and policy ties based on shared ideological interests. Moreover, INGOs encompass organizations like the International Olympic Committee, certain terrorist groups, religious groups (the Roman Catholic church, for one), professional organizations like the global network of Physicians for Social Responsibility, and a wide range of groups established to foster commercial relations between nations.

"En Masse" versus Group Opinion

"En masse" public opinion, as we have seen, is rarely a danger to foreign policy elites. This is true in part because the elites share many of the same views held by the public (an anticommunist philosophy, for example) and, further, because on controversial issues elites can usually adjust their policies quickly to stay within the anticipated boundaries of public tolerance. When polls in 1986 indicated that the public wanted tougher curbs on the flow of illicit drugs into the United States, Republicans and Democrats, conservatives and liberals alike, rushed to support increases in government spending on border interdiction and to establish the death penalty against drug pushers. Policymakers clearly understand, too, that in the post-Vietnam era the public is reluctant to engage in what could become a prolonged military conflict abroad. A quick attack on Grenada, Libya, or an Iranian oil rig in the Persian Gulf (as carried out by the Reagan administration) seems acceptable—even popular—but polls consistently indicate a widespread reluctance to take on more serious and protracted engagements, say, an overt U.S. combat presence in Nicaragua, El Salvador, or Angola.

More organized public opinion—that is, group opinion—can present an immediate and palpable danger, however, because it may be directed toward individual policy makers. Public officials who fail to respond to these more specific demands may soon face the loss of PAC money, mounting public criticism, and threats of retaliation at the polls by dedicated group members. This opinion can hurt, especially when groups with sizable resources of money and membership are involved, just as it can help propel forward the careers of more sympathetic politicians. One result of this attention to organized groups by public officials is a further fragmentation of power among those responsible for American foreign policy (the central theme of the preceding chapter). These groups attempt—many, like AIPAC, with considerable success—to place their specific objectives high on the foreign policy agenda of national leaders. This can have the effect of dividing the attention and the resources of government officials, which might otherwise be dedicated to broader, national objectives.

As the case of the Cambodian invasion illustrates, though, perhaps more important to foreign policy than public opinion or even group opinion are the philosophies and beliefs of individual decision makers themselves. This leads us to the microlevel of foreign policy analysis: the behavior of individuals in high office—what the international relations scholar J. David Singer refers to as the "psycho-political process" in foreign affairs.[48]

THE INDIVIDUAL AND AMERICAN FOREIGN POLICY

The Importance of Character

"Character is destiny," wrote the Greek historian Heraclitus. But how is character formed?

What makes the individual foreign policy maker tick? He or she may be alert to public opinion, on those rare occasions when it registers an unambiguous signal; he or she may be sensitive to group demands, particularly when the group has the capacity to help or hurt the policymaker's career in a significant way. A burgeoning research literature makes clear, however, that the policymaker is far more than a cork bobbing on the broad gulf streams of "en masse" opinion or even the usually stronger currents of group pressure. Each policymaker has a unique set of life experiences and psychological perspectives that can affect policymaking in vital ways. This is what Edmund Burke, Chancellor Kohl, and John F. Kennedy understood and appreciated when they dismissed mere demoscopy.

In an effort to comprehend the effects of an individual's experience and personality on decision making, scholars have turned to a wide variety of approaches and produced a rich lode of findings and hypotheses.[49] This chapter reviews only some of the most prominent research in an attempt to suggest how the relatively new discipline of "personality and politics" illuminates the importance of the individual in American foreign policy.

The Lasswellian Hypothesis

The political scientist Harold Lasswell was sensitive to the influence that early, private events in the life of a political leader could exert on his later, public decisions. He defined political man (*homo politicus*) as a power seeker, driven primarily by a desire to overcome feelings of inferiority engendered by unhappy experiences early in life. "Power," Lasswell wrote, "is expected to overcome low estimates of the self."[50] With obvious Freudian antecedents, Lasswell's hypothesis attempted to link the low self-esteem of the youth to power seeking in the adult. Here in outline form is Lasswell's causal chain:

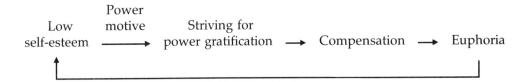

Employing the Lasswellian hypothesis, studies have explored the life of Woodrow Wilson, tracing his intransigence with senators over the League of Nations dispute back to the president's early childhood relationship with his father, a prominent clergyman in Virginia.[51] In odd emotional outbursts, Wilson flatly refused to compromise with the Senate—especially Henry Cabot Lodge, the chairman of the Foreign Relations Committee. The president would have the League his way, or no way at all.

Searching through his early record, scholars find evidence of low self-esteem in the young Wilson. The son of a domineering father, he seemed stymied in his maturation, fearful that he might be unable to reach his father's lofty example or high expectations. The father did little to allay these misgivings, and indeed exacerbated them with harsh criticism of the boy's schoolwork. According to this research, Wilson later sought political power as a means for proving his worth to himself and to his father. When confronted by opponents like Lodge, Wilson lashed out irrationally at what he perceived to be a manifestation of attempts to dominate him as his father had done. Through Lodge and other enemy "fathers," Wilson—now a powerful adult—had the opportunity to settle the score, indirectly, with his real father.

This "victory," as Lasswell predicted, gave Wilson only a fleeting sense of euphoria before the more deeply flowing sense of inferiority would once again well up in his psyche. Again the cycle would begin, as Wilson set out to prove his worth against the next impediment, the next manifestation of that source of childhood frustration and anxiety: the domineering father. As Lasswell himself observed, in an approving comment on this research: "[it calls] at-

tention to the significance of Wilson's relationship to his father, noting the inner necessity for over-reacting against any subsequent authority figure who reawakened incompletely resolved unconscious conflicts."[52]

According to theorists, a physical impairment can be the origin of low self-esteem in some political figures. The candid autobiography of Kurt Schumacher, a German Social Democrat in the 1930s, speaks convincingly, for example, about his sense of inferiority which resulted from a physical loss (a war-wound amputation). He testifies to his subsequent attempts to gain power as a means of compensating for his perceived loss of manhood inflicted by the amputation—a startlingly frank affirmation of the Lasswellian hypothesis.[53]

Ego Defense versus Statecraft

The Freudian approach lacks appeal to many students of political behavior. One major objection is the theory's inherently unscientific nature, in the sense of failing to provide an opportunity for testing and disproving ("falsifying") the central hypothesis in a laboratory—as one has, for instance, with Einstein's famous equations on relativity. The Freudian explanation of behavior requires a leap of faith. One can only evaluate in one's mind whether the explanation seems to fit the available facts, a less satisfying test than the rigors of modern scientific empiricism demand.

Moreover, sometimes this form of analysis can be rather farfetched. Two political scientists once plucked from the historical record a letter written by Richard Nixon to his mother when he was ten years old. In the letter, Nixon pretends he is the family cocker spaniel:

My Dear Master

The two boys that you left me with are very bad to me. Their dog, Jim, is very old and he will never talk or play with me. One Saturday the boys went hunting. Jim and myself went with them. While going through the woods one of the boys triped [sic] and fell on me. I lost my temper and bit him. He kiked [sic] me in the side and we started on. While we were walking I saw a black round thing in a tree. I hit it with my paw. A swarm of black thing [sic] came out of it. I felt a pain all over. I started to run and as both of my eys [sic] were swelled shut I fell into a pond. When I got home I was very sore. I wish you would come home right now.

Your good dog
Richard

The political scientists saw in these youthful jottings an early indication of Nixon's later tendency in the White House toward brooding introspection, especially during times of foreign policy crisis. "The sense of loneliness, bad treatment and impotent rage expressed in this letter, whatever its immediate context, seems too powerful to be of only passing importance," they write, with a degree of speculation that many scholars would find hard to accept.[54]

Despite the Wilson, Schumacher, and other examples that seem to fit the theoretical frameworks of Freud and Lasswell, critics of psychoanalytic and psychological theory (sometimes referred to as *psychohistory* when applied to historical biography) would readily agree with Stanley Hoffman: ". . . it partakes of the fascination of adventure stories: it is the search for the missing clue and the missing link, a search in which everything revealed is treated as a sign of something concealed, and things expressed are deemed the revelation of things repressed."[55] In contrast, Hoffman prefers to emphasize the centrality of politics and *statecraft*—"the way in which the leader conceives of and carries out his role as statesman, his relations with and impact on his followers or opponents." From this perspective, the League of Nations failure can be explained in simpler terms of poor lobbying on Capitol Hill by the executive branch, coupled with faulty draftsmanship of the Versailles treaty and a political tide running against Wilson for a variety of reasons having nothing at all to do with his relationship with his father during adolescence.

The Barber Typology

A psychological approach relying on events less hidden in the mists of early childhood experience has been developed by James David Barber for the analysis of presidential behavior. Barber is especially interested in the origins of presidential style and character, that is, "the political habits [a president] brings to the office" and "his basic orientation toward his own life." For instance, a president who is faced with a major foreign policy crisis, Barber suggests, is apt to draw upon a style of decision making that worked well in an earlier period of life—not childhood (like the Freudian school), but rather "his *first independent political success,* usually in early adulthood, when he developed a personal style that worked well for him."[56]

Barber uses the term *political success* broadly to mean the first sign of high competence and accomplishment against whatever major challenge a person may face in life, from a first electoral victory (Nixon in 1946) to high achievement on the battlefield (Truman in the First World War) or some other field of endeavor. The methods that seemed to succeed in this early period—say, Harry Truman's "take-charge" style as a combat commander in Europe—are turned to again. The essense of Truman's decisiveness as president, exemplified by his bold use of atomic bombs against Japan and his integration of the U.S. armed services by executive order, could already have been seen (Barber suggests) in his behavior as a resolute young infantry officer.

As for character, Barber offers a fourfold classification for typing presidents according to whether, first, they are active or passive (a personal energy dimension) and, second, positive or negative—that is, happy and optimistic in their work, or sad and pessimistic. For Barber, the *active-positive* president is the ideal (Truman, for instance). Here is the adaptive, rational individual, confident and flexible, prepared in times of foreign policy crisis to react coolly, reaching out to consult with a range of advisers, searching for the best facts (intelligence) available before making a final decision.

Most troubling to Barber is the active-negative type, because people of this sort tend to be compulsive and aggressive, and likely to rely on themselves to the point of isolation from others. As another researcher who concentrates on the personalities of presidents has noted: "Those, like Woodrow Wilson, Lyndon B. Johnson and Richard M. Nixon [all active-negative in the Barber framework], who dug in and lashed back like rattlesnakes, exemplify the sorts of temperaments that spell trouble."[57] Less dangerous—but also unlikely to produce vigorous leadership—are the passive-positive types (Taft), inclined to be compliant, and the passive-negative types (Eisenhower), inclined to be withdrawn.

A central characteristic of the active-negative foreign policy maker seems to be his or her tendency toward isolation from objective facts about the world. Barber portrays Presidents Johnson and Nixon as classic illustrations. Both men displayed incredible stamina; their level of involvement in their jobs made most of their contemporaries seem like so many cowpokes ambling languidly across the landscape. Johnson and Nixon were, by all accounts, indefatigable. This is arguably an admirable trait, an embodiment of the work ethic revered in American culture (though with all the hazards of "burnout" and a deadening of the mind to fresh ideas). Both men, though, also exhibited Barber's "negative" qualities. They were discouraged much of the time, and felt as though the world had turned against them.

In their conduct of the war in Vietnam, both Johnson and Nixon have been accused of shutting themselves off from all information regarding the war that failed to conform to their preconceptions (or to the like-minded views of the small coterie of advisers surrounding them). In response to outside criticism, they closed themselves off from a hostile environment, choosing to rely on the loyal band of staffers surrounding them—several of whom were all too ready (like the king's aide in the drawing reprinted here) to provide them with comforting reassurance. This phenomenon appears to have occurred during the Reagan administration, too, as the president's immediate advisers urged him take steps (trading weapons for hostages and failing to report this covert action to Congress, among others) that a less enclosed and compliant president (Reagan was "passive-positive" in Barber's classification) might have realized would eventually reap widespread criticism outside the confines of the White House.

A former press secretary to President Johnson has commented on this danger, noting that a president's aides prefer to avoid uncomfortable truths: "every effort must be made to relieve [the president] of the irritations that vex the average citizen; . . . no one ever invites him to 'go soak your head.' "[58] Why? Because no one wants to upset his or her access to the Great Leader. Other seasoned Washington observers have similarly criticized this trap of foreign policy *sycophancy*: "The President, needing 'access to reality,' in order to govern effectively, too often has access, instead, only to a self-serving court of flunkeys." They concluded that, "In a thousand conference rooms, where the smell of moral sterility is as strong as ether in a hospital corridor, the new courtiers do their minuet each day and [government] organizations slip further and further from reality."[59] The end result of organizational servility can be a foreign policy based not on fact but on fantasy.

A need for reassurance will be a part of any leader's personality, and every organization is apt to have some servile flatterers on the roster; but, Barber would argue, the active-positive leader—more self-confident and questioning—

"Oh, no, sir. I'm not just saying it because you're king. I think it's really very, very good."

is less likely to need or want this blind allegiance, because he or she will better understand the hazards of making foreign policy decisions while wearing blinders. Barber's approach remains rudimentary (the entire discipline of personality and politics is still in its infancy) and subject to criticism for oversimplifying.[60] Nonetheless, it stands as a significant early step toward the application of psychology to the study of leadership in both foreign and domestic policy. His intriguing research invites a new generation of scholars to improve upon the results.

Operational Codes

More direct (and more readily researched) than these various psychological approaches is the *operational code* ("op-code") method for exploring the attitudes and behavior of individual foreign policy leaders. As explained by Alexander L. George, the op-code approach provides a framework for the systematic investigation of a "political leader's beliefs about the nature of politics and political conflict, his views regarding the extent to which historical developments can be shaped, and his notions of correct strategies and tactics. . . ."[61] According to George, a leader's answers to such philosophical and instrumental (ends-means) questions provide important clues to how he or she "may perceive different types of situations and approach the task of making a rational assessment of alternative courses of action." In short, the explanation and prediction of leadership *behavior* are improved by understanding the leader's political *beliefs*. The researcher will still be unable to predict with certainty the precise responses of the decision maker in any specific circumstance, but he or she will have an improved understanding of the probable range of choices acceptable to the leader.

Each leader's operational code comprises several fundamental philosophical and instru-

---

Perspectives on American Foreign Policy 7.3

A Fable

At the palace, the Emperor's tailors presented him with garments said to be woven from the finest silk.

The Emperor's advisers praised the garments, fearful of telling the Emperor that he had been deceived: neither the silk, nor the garments, were real. The Emperor's subjects joined the praise. Until one young lad, unaware that most Emperors prefer praise to candor, shouted out the truth. "The Emperor," he said, "has no clothes!"

        *   *   *

The political scientist Alexander George on Richard Nixon:

Nixon's pronounced sense of aloneness and privacy, his thin-skinned sensitivity and vulnerability were not conducive to developing a collegial model of management. . . . [His] preference for a highly formalistic system was reinforced by other personality characteristics. He was an extreme "conflict avoider"; somewhat paradoxically, although quite at home with political conflict in the broader public arena, Nixon had a pronounced distaste for being exposed to it face-to-face. Early in his administration, Nixon tried a version of *multiple advocacy* in which leading advisers would debate issues in his presence. But he quickly abandoned the experiment and turned to structuring his staff to avoid overt manifestations of disagreement and to avoid being personally drawn into the squabbles of his staff, hence, Nixon's need for a few staff aides immediately around him who were to serve as buffers and enable him to distance himself from the wear and tear of policymaking.

Alexander L. George, *Presidential Decisionmaking in Foreign Policy: The Effective Use of Information and Advice* (Boulder, Colo.: Westview, 1980), pp. 153–154, emphasis added. Reprinted by permission.

---

mental dimensions. Among the most significant are those dealing with his or her views on the nature of politics and political conflict. Does the leader approach political goals from a moralist-ideological or a pragmatic, problem-solving perspective? Does he or she look upon foreign adversaries in "zero-sum" terms (that is, as a life-and-death struggle between nations with only one winner), or in "positive-sum" terms with a more cooperative attitude and a willingness to bargain (nations can work together)? In the pursuit of global objectives, does the leader believe in the use of armed intervention or in less intrusive forms of power? These are vital questions, the answers to which can provide valuable insights into the beliefs and likely decisions of foreign policy officials. A look at the contrasting belief systems of a few key decision makers affords a sense of the insights that can be gleaned through use of the operational-code approach.

Conciliators and Crusaders Senator Frank Church, a former chairman of the Foreign Relations Committee, was an important leader of the resurgence in foreign policy participation on Capitol Hill during the war in Vietnam, as well as a leading spokesman for a noninterventionist approach to international affairs.[62] His operational code is illustrative of one important perspective on America's proper external relations. Presented here are two of its dimensions, the first philosophical and the second instrumental. Each dimension consists of a cluster of basic foreign policy beliefs.

Image of the Opponent (Philosophical)

Belief 1: Neither the Russians nor the Chinese are inherently evil.

Belief 2: Nationalities do not differ markedly one from another.

Belief 3: Communist nations have shown no greater tendency toward aggression than the United States.

Belief 4: Under certain circumstances and certain leaders, nations will be carried into adventures of aggression.

Belief 5: Moral judgments must be discounted on many questions of international relations, since spheres of influence and the hegemony of large nations over their smaller neighbors have been historical facts of life.

Church rejected the idea that historical events could be interpreted from the standpoint of aggressive tendencies in one people as compared with another. He found other countries no more aggressive than the United States. "Our history is one of conquest," he once observed. "Beginning at Plymouth Rock in 1620, and proceeding to conquer an entire continent, we drove the aboriginal people into reservations by force of arms." One of the most important principles to remember about relations between nations, Church believed, is that "big countries have always tended to behave aggressively toward their smaller neighbors." When the Russians have done this in eastern Europe, Westerners have called it naked aggression; yet, Church emphasized, the United States has insisted at the same time upon maintaining a very large hegemony in its own region of the world. This insistence goes back to the early days of the republic when America declared in the Monroe Doctrine that it would exercise the dominant political, economic, and military influence in the western hemisphere. Even before really becoming a world power, this nation

staked out a sphere of influence that consisted of half the globe.

The Monroe Doctrine was only the beginning, in Church's view. As the United States grew to power, it was no longer content with that limited hegemony. In his words: "In the years following the Second World War, we extended our sphere of influence to the middle of Europe, incorporating the whole of the Atlantic and Pacific Oceans; and not content with the Pacific Ocean—the widest moat on earth—we extended our hegemony on to the mainland of Asia itself and established permanent American military bases on the mainland of Asia." Church looked upon Asia as China's "natural sphere of influence." He saw no chance for good relations with the most populous nation in the world until adjustments were made on mainland Asia "that will give to China what large nations are accustomed to demanding for themselves."

Utility of Means (Instrumental)

Belief 6. The United States must abandon its propensity to intervene in the affairs of other nations around the globe.

"We not only can live with a great deal of ferment and change," Senator Church once stated, "but there is no reason why we cannot allow a relationship to develop between countries that we need not dominate." He often pointed to Asia as an illustration, noting that were it not for the insistent intervention of U.S. military power in this region following the Second World War, a "natural equilibrium" would have developed there between Russia, China, and Japan in the north (the "triangle of power") and India and Indonesia in the south, both bulwarks of resistance against foreign adversaries. "The smaller countries were really incidental," he argued, "and would develop relationships with the larger countries as was natural to their situation, as they had done historically through the ages." The unnatural element injected into Asia was the American presence, with its insistence upon establishing alliances that made no sense and depended on the presence of U.S. military forces. America's alliances with Taiwan, the Philippines, and Thailand did not really forge "a circle of steel" around China at all. "It was only to the extent that the United States was willing to commit her own sons and her own money to fight wars in Asia that a circle of steel existed."

For Church, the argument that the United States had a moral obligation to protect the oppressed peoples of Asia represented a "perversion of morals." "Protect them from what?" he once asked. "What we end up giving them is Thieu [the South Vietnamese president during the last years of the Vietnamese war] and a corrupt dictatorship in South Vietnam." He wondered how it was possible to justify the sacrifice of over 50,000 American lives, 300,000 wounded and maimed, and $175 billion lost in a war that divided and demoralized our own people. "For what? For the day that we inevitably have to leave, when the indigenous forces once more will determine the destiny of these areas?" Church thought the invasion of Southeast Asia with a Western army was looked

upon by most Asians who lived in that part of the world as "the last gasp of Western imperialism." Moreover, he added, "the people we engulfed in the very act of protecting them are dismissed as contemptible puppets of Western power."

Church believed, above all, that the United States must "live with the world and not try so feverishly to control it." Throughout his career, he emphasized that "nationalism—rather than preference of the great powers—is the engine of change in modern history." He cautioned against overseas involvement "except when the national security of the United States was under 'clear and present danger.' "[63]

As a way of placing Senator Church's views in a broader context, they are contrasted in Figure 7.2 (Church is designated by "C") with the operational codes of some other leading spokesmen of American foreign policy in the postwar period: Secretaries of State Dean Acheson ("A," 1949–1952), John Foster Dulles ("D," 1953–1959), and Dean Rusk ("R," 1961–1968), as well as two other chairmen of the Senate Foreign Relations Committee, Arthur H. Vandenberg ("V," 1946–1948) and J. William

FIGURE 7.2   A comparison of Church and other foreign policy leaders along operational-code dimensions.

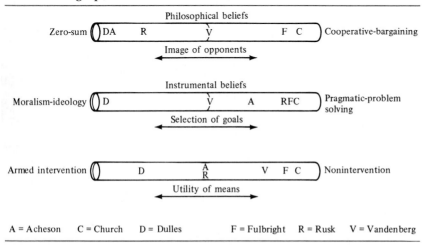

A = Acheson   C = Church   D = Dulles   F = Fulbright   R = Rusk   V = Vandenberg

Source: Loch K. Johnson, "Operational Codes and the Prediction of Leadership Behavior," in Margaret G. Herman, ed., *A Psychological Examination of Political Man* (New York: Free Press, 1977), p. 102.

Fulbright ("F," 1959–1974). The placement of these individuals along the two key belief dimensions—image of opponents and utility of means—is based on a number of op-code studies; it represents an approximate "center of gravity" for the worldview of each leader.[64]

As illustrated in Figure 7.2, the foreign policy philosophies of Church and Fulbright differed markedly from the secretaries of state; both senators displayed a much stronger belief in the possibility of cooperation with U.S. adversaries. Instrumentally, Church, Fulbright, and (to a lesser extent) Vandenberg also stood apart from the secretaries in their greater reluctance to intervene abroad with overt military power. On both dimensions, Church and Fulbright exhibited more affinity for one another's beliefs than for those held by the secretaries, with Vandenberg in the middle (though leaning toward his colleagues in the Senate).

The contrast between the belief systems of Church and Dulles is dramatic. According to the political scientist Ole Holsti's op-code analysis, Secretary Dulles saw a "world dominated by bold strokes of black and white"—a zero-sum outlook that pitted communism against Christianity, atheism against spiritualism, Marxist economic doctrine against the free-enterprise system.[65] The United States faced, in Dulles's view, a titanic struggle against evil, where military power—not diplomatic persuasion—was the only approach the Soviets would understand and respect. Victory would require, in Dulles's words, a "crusading spirit" in defense of America's spiritual and economic values. The United States had to do whatever it could to sow dissension within the U.S.S.R.; and in the Korean war, China would have to be given "one hell of a licking." In his zealous effort to shore up communist expansion, Dulles is reputed to have offered the French three atomic bombs in 1954 to use in their failing armed struggle against Vietnamese communists at Dien Bien Phu.

Dulles would probably have considered Church and Fulbright naive and immoral—or worse—in their willingness to try negotiation and compromise (the power of diplomacy) with the Soviets and the Chinese. As this comparison between Church and Dulles suggests, a leader's basic philosophical views may have a decided effect upon how he or she approaches the problems of foreign policy. This is why the operational-code approach, which concentrates on the policymaker's fundamental set of beliefs about the world, can be a useful analytic tool.

The Worth of the Individual

Foreign policy decisions reflect not only the forces of history, constitutional principles, institutions, and the other influences examined earlier in this book, but the force of the individual mind as well. Political man is driven by private motives displaced onto public objects and rationalized in terms of the public interest—so argued Harold Lasswell in his classic formulation of the effect that private battles of the psyche may have on public decisions.[66] Who can deny the importance of private motives, even though the attempts of researchers to understand them

Senator J. William Fulbright (D-Ark.), chairman of the Senate Foreign Relations Committee, cross-examines an executive branch official in 1966 on President Lyndon B. Johnson's Vietnam policies. (AP/Wide World Photos)

remain primitive? Consider for a moment the importance of individual emotions in the following descriptions of relations between high-ranking officials in the Reagan administration.

"Think of someone you really hate," said a foreign policy specialist during the Reagan years. "Multiply that by twenty and raise the answer to the fourth power, then you will have an idea of how Shultz and Weinberger [the secretaries of state and defense] feel toward one another."[67] According to a senior official in the Reagan administration, the assistant secretary of state for Latin American affairs and a key NSC staff aide "fought like cats and dogs and would not speak to each other."[68] Another observer reports that Secretary Shultz "had come to loathe [CIA Director William J.] Casey."[69]

Such conflicts of personality at the loftiest levels of the government likely have some effect upon the course of foreign policy. How well individuals relate to one another (and how well they cope with the stresses of their own psychic civil wars) will always influence the quality of policy-making. "The real organization of government at higher echelons is not what you find in textbooks or organization charts," Secretary of State Dean Rusk once remarked. "It is how confidence flows down from the President."[70] Government is in large part a matter of personal relations and bonds of trust.

Presidents, legislators, diplomats, bureaucrats, lobbyists—all are made of flesh and blood. They are moved by the often contradictory emotions of trust and suspicion, love and hate, altruism and avarice, toughness and charity, fatigue, anger, idealism, fear, ambition, pride, zeal, restraint, and all the other feelings that give humanity its character and complexity. How these emotions are balanced in the foreign policy official can be a matter of consequence to the republic. As John Stuart Mill understood, "The worth of a State, in the long run, is the worth of the individuals composing it."

SUMMARY

Individuals have an effect upon American foreign policy as members of the general public, in smaller groups, and in their capacity as officials in government office. As one moves from this macro- to the microlevel, that is, from broad public opinion to the individual decision maker, the significance of the individual is magnified. At the macrolevel, the foreign policy views of individuals as aggregated into "the public" are frequently discounted by policymakers. Presidents and legislators normally prefer to think of themselves as "trustees" exercising their best judgment on behalf of their electors, rather than mere "instructed delegates" registering the ups and downs of public whim. During the crisis surrounding the Cambodian invasion of 1970, for instance, U.S. senators were guided less by the phenomenal outpouring of constituency mail on this issue than by their own policy predispositions.

In foreign policy, this trustee form of representation is encouraged by the lack of instructions from the electorate; the level of knowledge about foreign affairs tends to be low among the general public. What instructions or opinions do exist are often difficult for leaders to gauge; accurate barometers of "en masse" sentiment are largely nonexistent. Moreover, key sources of public opinion—the polls, letters, and the like—can be contradictory. This lack of reliable instructions from the public frees public officials from the instructed-delegate role most of the time, allowing them to rely on personal judgment. For legislators, this freedom has often been less a matter of self-reliance than a deference to the president on foreign affairs—

though distrust on Capitol Hill toward the presidency in the wake of the Vietnamese war and the Watergate scandal (and, more recently, the Iran-contra scandal) has encouraged legislators to be more skeptical about a complacent reliance on executive leadership.

As with domestic policy, organized groups within the broad public have learned that with foreign policy, too, the government of the United States responds to pressure from those who band together in order to make their needs known. By pooling their resources—money, advertising, organizational skills, the threat of votes against uncooperative elected officials—individuals have a better chance of gaining the attention and favor of decision makers than those who remain as only a part of a faceless, fragmented mass. As the process of American politics has often been described colloquially, "the squeaking wheel gets the oil." Large corporations with foreign policy interests have developed their approaches to lobbying into a high art form, as have groups concerned about the fate of specific countries abroad (such as the American Israel Public Affairs Committee, AIPAC). As a pluralist democracy, the United States consists of diverse pressure groups that attempt to shape foreign policy according to their own goals. Government leaders are inclined to pay more attention to group than to "en masse" opinion. The instructions from groups are clearer, and groups are often well organized to intervene in the electoral fortunes of public officials.

The destiny of the nation depends in part upon the character of its individual leaders—a central lesson of government carried down from Greek antiquity. The character of American foreign policy makers, like that of the rest of us, is shaped by many influences during the life span. Freudian analysis emphasizes the importance of the early years in the formation of the leader's political personality. Woodrow Wilson's failure to achieve congressional support for the League of Nations, according to this perspective, can be traced to an emotional turmoil rooted in his unhappy relationship with his father—a psychic eruption released from the depths of time by the figure of Senator Henry Cabot Lodge, whom Wilson in his adult life may have perceived as a threatening figure reminiscent of his own father. Scholars with Freudian antecedents stress the importance of low self-esteem as a significant influence on leadership behavior, a condition hypothesized to trigger emotional responses and feelings of paranoia.

Researchers skeptical about Freudian and other psychological approaches have preferred to analyze the influence of the individual foreign policy official in the more straightforward terms of "statecraft," that is, the acquired leadership skills of the individual. Others have found it useful to probe the official's system of beliefs (his or her "operational code"), particularly basic views about the Soviet Union. The study of political psychology as it applies to foreign policy remains in its infancy, but few would deny the relevance of a leader's personality traits for understanding behavior in office.

KEY TERMS

demoscopy
rally-round-the-flag hypothesis
opinion-leadership hypothesis
two-step flow of communications
instructed-delegate model
Burkean model
presidential-deference model
AIPAC

Council on Foreign Relations
nonstate actors
divestment
IGOs
INGOs
homo politicus
psychohistory
statecraft

first independent
  political success
active-positive
sycophancy
multiple advocacy
operational code

NOTES

1. Press conference, August 26, 1983, reported in *German Press Review*, August 31, 1983, Embassy of the Federal Republic of Germany, Washington, D.C. (emphasis added).

2. *Profiles in Courage* (New York: Harper & Row, 1956), p. 208.

3. Fred I. Greenstein, *The American Party System and the American People*, 2d ed. (Englewood Cliffs, N.J.: Prentice-Hall, 1970), p. 11, original emphasis.

4. V. O. Key, Jr., *The Responsible Electorate* (Cambridge, Mass.: Harvard University Press, 1966).

5. John Mueller, *War, Presidents and Public Opinion* (New York: Wiley, 1973), pp. 208–213, upon which this discussion of the rallying effect is based.

6. Nelson W. Polsby, *Congress and the Presidency* (Englewood Cliffs, N.J.: Prentice-Hall, 1964), p. 25.

7. Richard A. Brody and Catherine R. Shapiro, "A Reconsideration of the Rally Phenomenon in Public Opinion," in Samuel Long, ed., *Political Behavior Annual*, Vol. 2 (Boulder, Colo.: Westview, 1989), pp. 77–102; see, also, Richard A. Brody and Catherine R. Shapiro, "Policy Failure and Public Support: Reykjavik, Iran and Public Assessments of President Reagan," paper, Annual Meeting of the American Political Science Association, Chicago, September 3–6, 1987.

8. See Paul F. Lazarsfeld, Bernard Berelson, and Hazel Gaudet, *The People's Choice*, 3d ed. (New York: Columbia University Press, 1968), pp. 151–152.

9. Brody and Shapiro, "A Reconsideration of the Rally Phenomenon," p. 100.

10. George C. Edwards III, *Presidential Influence in Congress* (San Francisco: Freeman, 1980), p. 159; Bruce Buchanan, *The Citizen's Presidency* (Washington, D.C.: Congressional Quarterly, 1987), pp. 12–13.

11. *Profiles in Courage*, p. 208.

12. Sir Philip Magnus, ed., *Selected Prose* (London: Falcon, 1948), p. 40.

13. Lewis A. Dexter, "What Do Congressmen Hear: The Mail," in Nelson W. Polsby, Robert A. Dentler, and Paul A. Smith, eds., *Politics and Social Life* (Boston: Houghton Mifflin, 1963), p. 486.

14. Fred I. Greenstein, *The American Party System and the American People*, 1st ed. (Englewood Cliffs, N.J.: Prentice-Hall, 1963), p. 11. See, also, Malcolm E. Jewell and Samuel C. Patterson, *The Legislative Process in the United States*, 3d ed. (New York: Random House, 1977), Chap. 14.

15. Philip E. Converse, Aage R. Clausen, and Warren E. Miller, "Electoral Myth and Reality: The 1964 Election," *American Political Science Review*, vol. 59, June 1965, pp. 321–336.

16. *Ibid.*

17. Martin Kriesberg, "What Congressmen and Administrators Think of the Polls," *Public Opinion Quarterly*, vol. 9, Fall 1945, pp. 33–37.

18. Warren E. Miller, "Policy Preferences of Congressional Candidates and Constituents," paper presented at the 1961 Annual Meeting of the American Political Science Association.

19. Donald R. Matthews, *U.S. Senators and Their World* (Chapel Hill: University of North Carolina Press, 1960), p. 221. For a more recent reiteration of this point from Capitol Hill, see the study conducted by the *Congressional Staff Journal* and printed in vol. 6, November–December 1981, pp. 1–8.

20. V. O. Key, Jr., *Public Opinion and American Democracy* (New York: Knopf, 1961), p. 482; and John C. Wahlke, Heinz Eulau, William Buchanan, and Leroy C. Ferguson, *The Legislative System* (New York: Wiley, 1962), p. 273.

21. Warren E. Miller and Donald E. Stokes, "Constituency Influence in Congress," *American Political Science Review*, vol. 57, March 1963, pp. 45–56.

22. See Everett C. Ladd, "Where the Public Stands on Nicaragua," *Public Opinion*, vol. 10, September–October 1987, p. 2.

23. *Ibid*.

24. Greenstein, *The American Party System*, 2d ed., p. 11.

25. Greenstein, *The American Party System*, 1st ed., p. 14.

26. Ladd, *op. cit.*

27. See Loch K. Johnson and Jerome Garris, "Public Opinion versus Ideology in the Senate: The Cambodian Incursion as a Critical Incident," *Southeastern Political Review*, vol. 14, Spring 1986, pp. 35–62, from which this discussion is drawn. The data, collected by the authors in interviews with each Senate office, represent ratios on the mail related to Cambodia received during the three weeks following the president's announcement of the "incursion" on April 30, 1970.

28. The question asked a cross section of 1281 households across the nation from May 8 to May 10 was: "Taking everything into consideration, do you think President Nixon was right in ordering the military operation into Cambodia, or do you have serious doubts about his having done this?" The results of the Harris Survey are printed in the *Washington Post*, May 25, 1970.

29. Matthews, *op. cit.*, p. 224. This finding is supported as well by the research of Raymond A. Bauer, Ithiel de Sola Pool, and Lewis A. Dexter, *American Business and Public Policy*, 2d ed. (New York: Atherton, 1963).

30. A simple dichotomous variable was used to examine the extent of party-line voting on the Cambodia-related amendments. Senators were rank-ordered on the two measures of presidential leadership, as reported in the *Congressional Quarterly Weekly Report*, February 20, 1970, p. 569. The ideological scores were derived by subtracting the score given each senator by the conservative Americans for Constitutional Action (ACA) from the scores of the liberal Americans for Democratic Action (ADA), both of which are printed in the this same *CQ Weekly Report*, p. 569. This edition of *CQ* is the source as well for the "Conservative Coalition" index, another standard measure of a representative's philosophy on public policy. For an account of the Senate roll-call votes on Cambodia, see the *Washington Post*, June 12, 1970, and the *Congressional Quarterly Weekly Report*, June 12, 1970, p. 1516.

31. Robert A. Dahl, *Congress and Foreign Policy* (New York: Harcourt, 1950), p. 12.

32. Ladd, *op. cit.*, p. 59.

33. See, for example, Donald R. Matthews, *U.S. Senators and Their World* (Chapel Hill: University of North Carolina Press, 1960); Lester W. Milbrath, *The Washington Lobbyists* (Chicago: Rand McNally, 1963); and Terry M. Moe, *The Organization of Interests: Incentives and the Internal Dynamics of Political Interest Groups* (Chicago: University of Chicago Press, 1980).

34. "Reagan May Be a Great Leader, but His Foreign Policy Is a Shambles," *Washington Post*, National Weekly Edition, October 20, 1986, p. 23.

35. See Jeffrey Record, "AIPAC's Extremism Serves Israel Badly," *Los Angeles Times*, August 8, 1988, sec. 2, p. 13.

36. See John Lewis Gaddis, *Strategies of Containment* (New York: Oxford University Press, 1982), p. 155.

37. See Stuart Taylor, Jr., "Rising Voice of Cuban-Americans," *New York Times*, March 7, 1984, upon which this account is based.

38. Quoted in an Associated Press story, *Athens (Georgia) Banner-Herald*, September 4, 1986, p. 101.

39. See John Kenneth Galbraith, "Staying Awake

at the Council on Foreign Relations," *Washington Monthly*, September 1984, pp. 40–43. For a history of the council, see Robert D. Schulzinger, *The Wise Men of Foreign Affairs* (New York: Columbia University Press, 1984).

40. On the ITT-Chile case, see "Covert Action in Chile, 1963–1973," staff report of the Senate Select Committee on Intelligence (the Church Committee), December 18, 1975.

41. Robert Lindsey, "California's Tough Line on Apartheid," *New York Times*, August 31, 1986, p. 2E.

42. See, for example, the *Atlanta Constitution*, September 7, 1986.

43. On these groups, see Stephen A. Garrett, "Foreign Policy and the American Constitution: The Bricker Amendment in Contemporary Perspective," *International Studies Quarterly*, vol. 16, June 1972, pp. 197–198; and "Treaties and Executive Agreements," *Hearings of the Committee on the Judiciary*, U.S. Senate, May 21–June 9, 1952.

44. See Gillian Peele, *Revival and Reaction: The Right in Contemporary America* (New York: Oxford University Press, 1984), pp. 171–172. In the 1976 presidential elections, right wing religious groups supported Jimmy Carter for president, viewing him as one of them: a born-again Christian; they soon turned against the president, because of his "giveaway" of the Panama Canal and his support for a range of social issues that were anathema to the right. See Loch K. Johnson and Charles S. Bullock III, "The New Religious Right and the 1980 Congressional Elections," in Benjamin Ginsberg and Alan Stone, eds., *Do Elections Matter?* (Armonk, N.Y.: Sharpe, 1986), pp. 155, 163 (note 25).

45. Record, *op. cit.*

46. "Assessing Strategic Arms Control," roundtable, MIT-Harvard Summer Program on Nuclear Weapons and Arms Control, June 27, 1985.

47. These figures are cited by Charles W. Keg-

ley, Jr., and Eugene R. Wittkopf, *World Politics: Trend and Transformation* (New York: St. Martin's, 1981), p. 104.

48. See, for example, Singer's remarks in "Sarajevo and Arms Control," *In Brief . . .* (the United States Institute of Peace Newsletter), vol. 5, March 1989, pp. 2–3.

49. For important efforts to examine the effects of "personality" on politics, see Harold D. Lasswell, *Psychopathology and Politics* (Chicago: University of Chicago Press, 1930); M. Brewster Smith, "Opinions, Personality, and Political Behavior," *American Political Science Review*, vol. 52, March 1958, pp. 1–17; Jeanne N. Knutson, "Personality in the Study of Politics," in Jeanne N. Knutson, ed., *Handbook of Political Psychology* (San Francisco: Jossey-Bass, 1973), pp. 28–56; James MacGregor Burns, *Leadership* (New York: Harper & Row, 1978); Irving L. Janis, *Groupthink*, 2d ed. (Boston: Houghton Mifflin, 1982); Alexander L. George, "The Case for Multiple Advocacy in Making Foreign Policy," *American Political Science Review*, vol. 66, September 1972, pp. 751–785; Fred I. Greenstein and Michael Lerner, eds., *A Source Book for the Study of Personality and Politics* (Chicago: Markham, 1971); Fred I. Greenstein, *Personality and Politics: Problems of Evidence, Inference and Conceptualization* (Chicago: Markham, 1969); James David Barber, *The Presidential Character: Predicting Performance in the White House*, 3d ed. (Englewood Cliffs, N.J.: Prentice-Hall, 1985); Bruce Buchanan, *The Presidential Experience: What the Office Does to the Man* (Englewood Cliffs, N.J.: Prentice-Hall, 1978); and Joseph H. DeRivera, *The Psychological Dimension of Foreign Policy* (Columbus, Ohio: Merrill, 1968).

50. Harold D. Lasswell, *Power and Personality* (New York: Norton, 1948), p. 223.

51. See, for instance, Alexander L. George and Juliette L. George, *Woodrow Wilson and Colonel House: A Personality Study* (New York: Dover, 1964).

52. Harold D. Lasswell, "Political Systems, Styles and Personalities," in Lewis J. Edinger, ed., *Political Leadership in Industrialized Societies: Studies in Comparative Analysis* (New York: Wiley, 1967), p. 320.

53. See the account in Lewis J. Edinger, *Kurt Schumacher: A Study in Personality and Political Behavior* (Stanford, Calif.: Stanford University Press, 1965).

54. Michael Rogin and John Lottier, "The Inner History of Richard Milhous Nixon," *Transaction*, November–December 1971, p. 21.

55. "Heroic Leadership: The Case of Modern France," in Edinger, ed., *Political Leadership*, p. 109.

56. "Analyzing Presidents: From Passive-Positive Taft to Active-Negative Nixon," *Washington Monthly*, vol. 1, October 1969, p. 34, emphasis added; for book-length treatment, see Barber's *Presidential Character*.

57. Bruce Buchanan, "Open All Candidates before Election," *New York Times*, October 2, 1987, p. 25.

58. George E. Reedy, *Twilight of the Presidency* (New York: World, 1970), p. 4.

59. Russell Baker and Charles Peters, "The Prince and His Courtiers: At the White House, the Kremlin, and the Reichschancellery," *Washington Monthly*, vol. 3, March 1971, pp. 34, 44.

60. See the book review by Arnold A. Rogow, *American Political Science Review*, vol. 70, December 1976, pp. 1299–1301.

61. Alexander L. George, "The 'Operational Code': A Neglected Approach to the Study of Political Leaders and Decision Making," *International Studies Quarterly*, vol. 13, 1969, pp. 197, 200.

62. See Loch K. Johnson, "Operational Codes and the Prediction of Leadership Behavior: Senator Frank Church at Midcareer," in Margaret G. Hermann, ed., *A Psychological Examination of Political Leaders* (New York: Free Press, 1977), pp. 80–119, from which these observations by Senator Church are drawn (based on interviews in 1972, Washington, D.C.).

63. For an elaboration of Church's philosophy of foreign affairs, see his remarks in the *Congressional Record*, February 21, 1968, pp. 3803–3813.

64. See the operational-code studies on Acheson, Dulles, Fulbright, Rusk, and Vandenberg cited in Johnson, "Operational Codes," p. 102.

65. Ole R. Holsti, "The 'Operational Code' Approach to the Study of Political Leaders: John Foster Dulles' Philosophical and Instrumental Beliefs," *Canadian Journal of Political Science*, 1970, pp. 123–155.

66. Harold Lasswell, *Psychopathology and Politics* (Chicago: University of Chicago Press, 1930): see pp. 124, 262.

67. The political scientist Michael Nacht, Harvard-MIT Summer Program, 1985.

68. John Felton, "Testimony Sheds New Light on North's Role," *Congressional Quarterly Weekly Report*, vol. 45, August 29, 1987, p. 2107.

69. Bob Woodward, "The Man Who Wasn't There," *Newsweek*, October 5, 1987, p. 66.

70. Dean Rusk, quoted in *Life*, January 17, 1969, as cited by I. M. Destler, "National Security Advice to U.S. Presidents: Some Lessons from Thirty Years," *World Politics*, vol. 29, January 1977, pp. 143–176.

RECOMMENDED READINGS

Barber, James David. *The Presidential Character*, 3d ed. (Englewood Cliffs, N.J.: Prentice-Hall, 1985). Presents an intriguing typology of presidential character, relating early adulthood experiences to behavior in the White House.

Bauer, Raymond A., Ithiel de Sola Poole, and Louis Anthony Dexter. *American Business and Public Policy*, 2d ed. (Chicago: Aldine-Atherton, 1972). One of the most exhaustive efforts to study the influence of interest groups on American foreign policy.

Burns, James MacGregor. *Leadership* (New York: Harper & Row, 1978). A comprehensive and gracefully written review of the findings on this subject by a president of the American Political Science Association.

Edinger, Lewis J., ed. *Political Leadership in Industrialized Studies in Comparative Analysis* (New York: Wiley, 1967). An excellent collection of articles on leadership, balanced between the perspectives of statecraft and psychohistory.

George, Alexander L., and Juliette L. George. *Woodrow Wilson and Colonel House: A Personality Study* (New York: Dover, 1956). An application of the Lasswellian hypothesis on the power seeker to President Woodrow Wilson.

Greenstein, Fred I., and Michael Lerner, eds. *A Source Book for the Study of Personality and Politics* (Chicago: Markham, 1971). A useful resource book for an orientation toward the discipline of personality and politics, with essays by M. Brewster Smith, Alexander George, Erik Erikson, Harold Lasswell, and others.

Hermann, Margaret G., ed. *A Psychological Examination of Political Leaders* (New York: Free Press, 1977). A collection of essays that explore, using a wide range of methodologies, the connection between politics and psychology.

———. *Political Psychology* (San Francisco: Jossey-Bass, 1989). This recent anthology surveys the current state of research on personality and politics.

Mueller, John E. *Presidents and Public Opinion* (New York: Wiley, 1973). A thoughtful tracing of the relationship between presidential behavior and "en masse" opinion, emphasizing the rally-round-the-flag phenomenon in times of military conflict.

Rogow, Arnold. *James Forrestal* (New York: Macmillan, 1963). An illustration, based upon the life of a secretary of defense, of how psychopathology can intrude upon the public policy process.

Rustow, Dankwart A., ed. *Philosophers and Kings: Studies in Leadership* (New York: Braziller, 1970). Another useful set of essays on leadership, emphasizing the importance of the individual.

Tucker, Robert C. *Politics as Leadershup* (Columbia: University of Missouri Press, 1981). A succinct summary of the scholarly research on leadership.

Wolfenstein, E. Victor. *The Revolutionary Personality* (Princeton, N.J.: Princeton University Press, 1967). An examination of why some individuals are inclined toward participation and leadership in revolutions, written by a political scientist with training in psychoanalysis.

PART 2

THE USES
OF AMERICAN
FOREIGN POLICY

THE ORIGINS OF AMERICAN STRATEGIC INTELLIGENCE

    The Coordination of Intelligence

    The Structure of Intelligence

    The Intelligence Missions

COLLECTION AND ANALYSIS

    Planning and Direction

    Collection

    Processing

    Production and Analysis

    Dissemination

THE LURE OF SECRECY

    Good Secrets

    Bad Secrets

EXECUTIVE PRIVILEGE

    A Cloak of Executive Secrecy

    Delay and Deceit

PRIOR RESTRAINT

CONTRACTUAL SECRECY

SECRECY AND DEMOCRACY

SUMMARY

8

STRATEGIC INTELLIGENCE: THE FOUNDATIONS OF FOREIGN POLICY

The execution of Nathan Hale (portrait by F. D. C. Darley). (Historical Pictures Service)

At the gateway to Part 2 of this book stands the subject of *strategic intelligence*: the use of America's secret agencies to gather and analyze information on foreign affairs (Chapter 8), as well as to carry out covert actions (Chapter 9). The collection and analysis of information from around the globe (the first definition of strategic intelligence) is fundamental to the successful conduct of foreign policy, for without an accurate understanding of the world around them policymakers are forced to make decisions blindfolded. Reliable information can improve their vision—although the planet is so vast and the decisions of most nations are so secretive that an unobstructed view into the capabilities and intentions of America's foes, or even its friends, remains unattainable. As this chapter reveals, many shadows (ambiguous data, misperceptions, and secrecy among them) fall across the latitudes and longitudes, diminishing the chances for 20/20 vision.

Moreover, as if the collection and analysis of information were insufficiently difficult for U.S. policymakers, they face a further difficulty when it comes to the proper sharing of information between the branches. Who should get what information—and when—has proven to be a contentious issue, adding to the deep-seated constitutional frictions as legislators rub against presidents and other officials in the executive branch. The institutional ill feelings stem chiefly from attempts by the executive to monopolize information about world events, sometimes in an effort to avoid legislative criticism or interruption of its policy plans. When this hoarding of intelligence succeeds (as is frequently the case), America's constitutional framework for foreign policy is knocked out of kilter.

This chapter explores these problems: first, the difficulties of gathering and analyzing intelligence and disseminating it among key foreign policy officials; and, second (in a continuation of this book's central theme), the conflict that has arisen between the branches over the sharing of information. Part 2 has an additional focus: what policymakers do on the basis of the information they possess. Action follows knowledge. In their pursuit of U.S. foreign policy ends, how do officials go about choosing the appropriate means from among those at their disposal—primarily, covert action, the overt use of armed force, diplomacy, economic statecraft, and moral suasion? As anticipated in Part 1, these choices are shaped by a collision of events, institutions, and personalities.

THE ORIGINS OF AMERICAN STRATEGIC INTELLIGENCE

Strategic intelligence had its origins at the very birth of the nation.[1] Even at these early stirrings, the leaders of the revolution were well aware of the vital role intelligence operations would play in a successful revolutionary war. In 1776, the Continental Congress established America's first intelligence service, the Committee of Secret Correspondence; and General George Washington (who had his own secret code, "711") made use of an effective network of spies, led by Paul Revere. Perhaps the most famous officer in this network was young Nathan Hale, who in 1776 uttered his memorable declaration "I only regret that I have but one life to lose for my country" moments before being hanged by the British for espionage.

The interest of the founding fathers in matters of intelligence went well beyond *espionage* (that is, the secret collection of information by spies), or the interpretation of both secrets and more openly derived information (what modern practitioners would call *analysis*).[2] Benjamin Franklin and Thomas Jefferson, among others, vigorously encouraged the use of secret operations for another objective: to influence other nations toward a favorable regard for American foreign policy objectives (covert action, or *special activities*, in current parlance). Franklin urged the government of France to join with the colonists in the creation of a secret conduit for the supply of military aid in support of the Revolutionary War. To conceal this relationship from the British, a front (or proprietary) was formed, the Hortalez Company, ostensibly a private commercial enterprise.[3] As president, recall, Jefferson approved a covert action to supply arms for a coup designed to place on the throne of Tripoli a man friendlier toward the United States than the ruling pasha had become (though the effort failed).[4] The American revolutionaries were concerned, too, about protecting their army and the new nation from foreign spies, an important and difficult responsibility known today as *counterintelligence* (CI).

These three types of operations—collection (espionage, when the information is secretly acquired) and analysis, covert action, and counterintelligence—have constituted the nation's primary intelligence missions since 1776.[5] This chapter concentrates on the collection-and-analysis mission, which has been drastically revamped in the modern era as a result of that unforgettable day, December 7, 1941, when Japanese air units struck Pearl Harbor.[6]

Almost 100 Navy ships and some 300 airplanes were based at Pearl Harbor at that fateful hour. The Japanese hit all eight battleships moored in the harbor, and five sank. So did two destroyers and several other ships. Over 200 aircraft were damaged and many destroyed. Luckily, the two aircraft carriers in the Pacific Fleet happened to be at sea and escaped. Less fortunate were the 2330 service personnel killed and the 1145 wounded (along with 100 civilian casualties) who were stationed at Pearl Harbor.

The blow stunned the nation. It represents the most disastrous intelligence failure in American history. The United States had failed to appreciate both the capabilities and the intentions of the enemy. Government officials did not realize that the Japanese had developed aerial torpedos that, when dropped into the sea, could navigate in the relatively shallow waters of Pearl Harbor. The greatest damage to U.S. warships came from these weapons.[7] Officials also thought that a Japanese attack in the Philippines was infinitely more likely,[8] and they were confused by the buzz of ambiguous, often inconsistent and irrelevant, information about Japanese military plans—the "noise" that frequently engulfs and sometimes drowns out the important information U.S. officials need to know.[9] Moreover, policymakers failed to analyze thoroughly the fragments of data that were available regarding the possibility of a Japanese attack on Hawaii.

Most inexcusably, the government—evidently including President Roosevelt—failed to comprehend what was known and to distribute this information in a timely way to key naval officers. The president was under great stress and may have misperceived the significance of the information; and apparently lower officials kept key data bottled up, for fear that Operation Magic (the U.S. intelligence program that cracked the Japanese military codes) might be revealed—"compromised," in spy argot—if shared too widely.[10]

The Coordination of Intelligence

This last contribution to the failure at Pearl Harbor—the poor sharing and coordination of intelligence—was a problem Harry S Truman (who became president upon Roosevelt's death in 1945) vowed to address. The exigencies of war, however, delayed his intentions to overhaul the American approach to intelligence—not that much existed to overhaul. "On the eve of Pearl Harbor the United States had no strategic intelligence system worthy of the name," conclude two foreign policy specialists.[11] At the time, funding for U.S. intelligence was only about $3 million a year. America had to make do during the war with a loosely defined intelligence apparatus called the Office of Strategic Services (OSS).

Despite various notable accomplishments by the fledgling OSS, American intelligence continued to suffer after the war from uneven coordination as well as from poorly defined lines of authority. During this period, President Truman was especially perturbed by the downpour of intelligence reports that fell on his desk from different parts of government—sometimes directly contradicting one another. He preferred to have a single report from one central organization.

"So I got a couple of admirals together," Truman once recalled, "and they formed the Central Intelligence Agency for the benefit and convenience of the President of the United States. . . ." As a result, Truman continued, "instead of the President having to look through a bunch of papers two feet high, the information was coordinated so that the President could arrive at the facts."[12]

Initially, in 1946, Truman established by executive order the Central Intelligence Group (CIG), patterned after the OSS. Then, on July 26, 1947, the National Security Act gave statutory authority to this idea, replacing the CIG with the upgraded *Central Intelligence Agency* (CIA). This law placed the CIA under the control of a new White House structure that would henceforth coordinate American foreign policy: the National Security Council (NSC). The NSC would soon become the most important forum in the government for the discussion of major intelligence proposals and the formulation of advice to the president on other national security issues.

The CIA failed to achieve undisputed dominance over intelligence policy in the government, as its advocates hoped it would. As Harry Howe Ransom writes, "the principle of federation prevailed over the concept of tight centralization in shaping the structure of the intelligence community."[13] One of the deputy directors of the CIA, Admiral Rufus Taylor, ruefully described the various intelligence agencies in the late 1960s as little more than a "tribal federation."[14]

The centrifugal forces in the intelligence system were now less intense, however, than in the years preceding the establishment of the CIA. The other intelligence agencies accepted the *director of the CIA (DCIA)* as at least the titular head of the intelligence establishment (or "community," in the accepted mythology). In this role, the DCIA is known as the *director of Central Intelligence* (*DCI*), with the primary mission of trying to coordinate information from the different agencies for presentation to the principal decision makers in the government.

The Structure of Intelligence

Just how difficult the job of DCI is can be appreciated by a glimpse into the way intelligence is structured in the United States (see Figure 8.1). Beneath the DCI, in theory, are the mili-

FIGURE 8.1   The United States intelligence community.

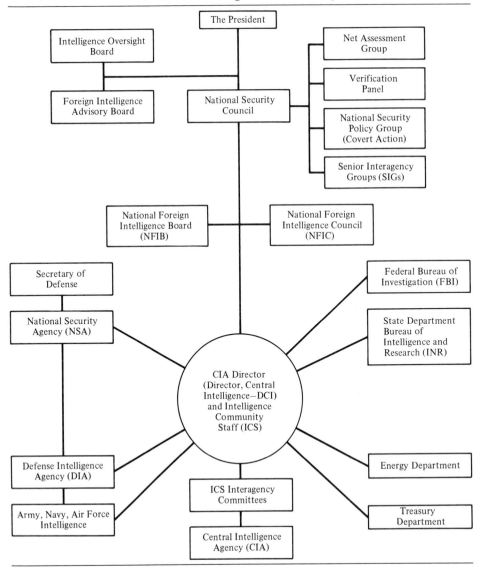

tary intelligence agencies, yet they have another boss, too: the secretary of defense, who outranks the DCI in the language of the 1947 National Security Act and in Washington protocol. (President Ronald Reagan appointed his first DCI, William J. Casey, to the cabinet in 1981, a practice discontinued in 1987 when his second DCI, William H. Webster, preferred to avoid the hint of politics that comes with membership in the cabinet.) Moreover, imagine any DCI attempting to tell the longtime head of the Federal Bureau of Investigation (FBI)—the imperious J. Edgar Hoover, with his host of close ties in the Washington political community—how to run bureau intelligence operations. The few forays ventured by DCIs into this perilous territory so angered Hoover that his relations with the CIA plummeted. Although CIA-FBI relations have improved in the post-Hoover era, the centralism under a DCI sought by reformers in 1947 remains a distant objective. Today, this "ideal" (if indeed a strong DCI is a desirable goal—rather than a dangerous concentration of power) must be balanced against what is bureaucratically possible, as secretaries of defense and others resist a loss of authority over strategic intelligence.

Additional centrifugal forces come from the sheer number of intelligence agencies under the DCI's titular leadership—over forty in the federal government. The military intelligence units are predominant from a budgetary point of view, absorbing over 80 percent of the total U.S. intelligence budget. Much of this funding goes toward the collection and analysis of tactical intelligence used by commanders in the field and admirals at sea (in contrast to broader strategic intelligence used by policy planners in the nation's highest decision councils); and a large portion supports the vital work of the largest U.S. intelligence entity, the military's *National Security Agency* (*NSA*).

The National Security Agency has the most floor space, the longest corridors, the most electrical wiring, the largest computers, and the biggest budget of any agency in the intelligence community. Atop the NSA building at Fort Meade, Maryland, are enormous antennas and odd-looking shapes that provide instantaneous communications throughout the world. The NSA is the nation's cryptological, or codebreaking, center. Nations communicate with their diplomats—and their spies—overseas through elaborate codes. Within this great beehive of technology at Fort Meade, NSA cryptologists, computer programmers, mathematicians, engineers, interpreters, electronic and radar experts, and communications specialists practice the science and art of breaking codes and intercepting communications throughout the world. While the CIA receives more publicity—in large part because of its controversial involvement in plots to overthrow foreign regimes—the NSA and other military units account for the hidden bulk of the intelligence iceberg.

Combined, the agencies within the intelligence community account for the employment of some 150,000 individuals and an annual budget in 1989 of around $13 billion. Also counted among these agencies are units within the FBI; intelligence components of the Drug Enforcement Agency (DEA); the Department of State's highly regarded Bureau of Intelligence and Research (INR); the Department of the Treasury's Customs Bureau, Secret Service, and Internal Revenue Service (IRS); and the Department of Energy's International Security Affairs division (which monitors nuclear testing and the international transfer of nuclear material)—to name only a few (see Figure 8.1).[15]

As DCIA, the director of Central Intelligence is preoccupied enough, for the CIA is a large, complex, and controversial organization in its own right (see Figure 8.2). In a strongly fenced and guarded, heavily forested region of Langley, Virginia, twelve miles from downtown Washington, stands the CIA, hidden by trees from the busy George Washington Memorial Parkway a few hundred yards away. The "Pickle Factory," "the Company," or "the Agency" (as CIA headquarters is often called by insiders) rises seven stories high and is topped

---

Perspectives on American Foreign Policy   8.1

The director of Central Intelligence (DCI) during the Carter administration, Admiral Stansfield Turner, on the difficulties he experienced in trying to maintain his statutory authority over the National Security Agency (NSA):

Teamwork in both collection and analysis [of intelligence] is impeded today by the NSA's insistence on doing analysis, which is neither its mission nor its forte, and by its penchant for withholding information from the rest of the Community so as to be able to give it directly to the President or the National Security Council. Scooping the rest of the Community is the game;

the NSA plays it well and the overall intelligence effort suffers. The NSA can get away with this in part because there is ambiguity as to whether the DCI or the Secretary of Defense has jurisdiction over these aspects of its work. The President can eliminate that ambiguity by stating in an Executive Order that the DCI has the authority to control the dissemination of the NSA's product and to limit the NSA's analytic efforts to what is necessary for the effectiveness of its collection efforts.

From Stansfield Turner, *Secrecy and Democracy: The CIA in Transition* (Boston: Houghton Mifflin, 1985), pp. 275–276. Copyright © 1985 by Stansfield Turner. Reprinted by permission of Houghton Mifflin Company.

---

by elaborate radio antennas for worldwide communications.

On the seventh floor is the director's office, with windows opening to a panoramic view of the Potomac River. On the floors beneath are a seemingly endless maze of hallways with doors of different colors. Behind these doors sit the thousands of country analysts, scientists, clerical assistants, computer technicians, cartographers, and others who make up the work force of the agency. Organizationally, the CIA is divided into five sections: the office of the director and, under this office, four functional directorates. The directorates are known as the Operations Directorate, headed by the *deputy director of operations*, or *DDO*; the Directorate of Science and Technology, headed by the *deputy director of science and technology*, or *DDS&T*; the Directorate of Administration, with its chief, the *deputy director of administration*, or *DDA*; and the Directorate of Intelligence, headed by the *deputy director of intelligence*, or *DDI*.

The Operations Directorate   The largest and most controversial is the Directorate of Opera-

tions (known early in its history as the Clandestine Services). Roughly two-thirds of the personnel in the Operations Directorate are involved in espionage, counterintelligence, and liaison work with intelligence services in allied nations. The rest are engaged in some form of covert action, such as mounting paramilitary operations or secretly financing friendly politicians overseas (the focus of Chapter 9). The Operations Directorate is subdivided by geographical responsibilities and into specialized staffs (see Figure 8.3). The former include the Soviet bloc, western Europe, the Western Hemisphere, the Far East, the Near East, and Africa. Separate staffs within the directorate are in charge of covert action, counterintelligence, and a few other tasks such as counterterrorism and counternarcotics.

Each of the area divisions at headquarters is organizationally tied into apposite CIA personnel in the field. The European division, for instance, is responsible for the CIA's officers and agents in each European nation, from Norway to Spain and Greece. The top CIA man or woman in each country is called the *chief of station*, or *COS*, the DDO's country spymaster and

FIGURE 8.2 Organization chart of the Central Intelligence Agency (CIA).

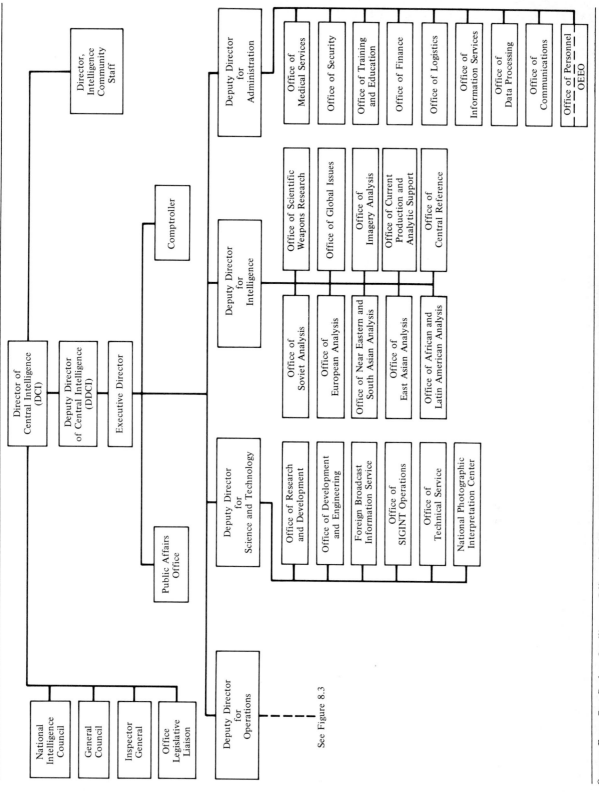

Source: From *Fact Book on Intelligence*, Office of Public Affairs, Central Intelligence Agency, April 1983, p. 9.

FIGURE 8.3   The Directorate of Operations.

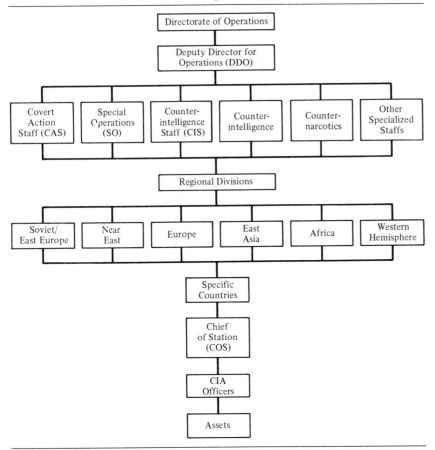

Source: Loch K. Johnson, *America's Secret Power: The CIA in a Democratic Society* (New York: Oxford University Press, 1989), p. 46.

the CIA's equivalent of an ambassador. Beneath the COS serve the American CIA *case officers* and their native agents. The COS reports to his or her country desk housed in one of the geographic divisions of the Operations Directorate at CIA headquarters, supposedly without bypassing the U.S. ambassador (the chief of mission), to whom the COS is, in theory at least, subordinate. The link between the COS and the ambassador in the field has often been delicate and has led to considerable tension at times between the CIA and the Department of State.

The CIA emphasis overseas is placed on the recruitment of spies from the so-called hard targets like the USSR and other leading communist states. Over half of the time case officers spend abroad is devoted, first, to observing (technically referred to as "spotting and assessing"), gaining access to, then recruiting, and, finally, handling an agent from one of these hard targets. Simply meeting and becoming better acquainted with a potential recruitment can be a painstaking task, with exorbitant personnel requirements. As one DDO has commented: "Often, when we target a person and say, 'All right, there is an individual who has access to information we want,' often our case officer doesn't have a direct approach to him, so he may have to recruit several 'access agents' in order to finally develop [the situation] to the point where he can engage in a dialogue with that individual and hopefully bring him around to recruitment."[16] One former CIA officer has referred to these "confidential collaborators around the globe" as "the main day-in-day-out instruments of covert political action."[17]

The S&T Directorate   The Directorate of Science and Technology, the newest and smallest of the CIA's major divisions, is devoted to the improved application of technology to espionage—notably in spying with satellites and high-altitude airplanes. The S&T Directorate does the research and development on James Bond gadgetry used by indigenous "agents" in the field (a commonly used name for what the CIA usually refers to as *assets)*, experiments with drugs and other chemicals, constructs such handy objects as fake rocks and trees with hollowed out spaces for hiding messages, and handles some of the agency's computer processing tasks. The DS&T is also the home of the Foreign Broadcast Information Service (FBIS), charged with the responsibility of monitoring foreign radio and television broadcasts, and the National Photographic Interpretation Center (NPIC), which analyzes satellite photography.

The Administration Directorate   The Directorate of Administration carries out agency housekeeping chores, hiring, training, computer processing, worldwide communications and logistics, and various other administrative duties. While on the surface this shop may seem the most innocuous of all, its provision of training, logistical, and communications support for clandestine and covert operations abroad has brought this directorate close to the Operations Directorate and forced upon it some share of the "dirty tricks" stigma. Together, these two directorates have formed, in the words of two authorities, "an agency within an agency, . . . [which] like the largest and most

dangerous part of an iceberg, floats along virtually unseen."[18]

Located within the Directorate of Administration is the Office of Security, a key element in the agency's counterintelligence defenses. This office is responsible for the physical protection of agency facilities at home and abroad from infiltration by foreign spies or American traitors. It also administers the polygraph (lie detector) tests given to all new CIA recruits and, at least every five years, to seasoned agency employees.

The use of the polygraph by the Office of Security has received much criticism. Its opponents have argued that the lie detector machines are often used merely to harass and intimidate employees and that they fail to uncover genuine spies—several of whom have passed polygraph tests while in the service of foreign intelligence agencies. Secretary of State George P. Shultz, skeptical over the reliability of this technique, flatly refused to have employees in his department polygraphed, even when President Reagan endorsed this approach as a means for sealing off leaks within the government. Advocates of the polygraph admit the method is not foolproof but maintain that it has helped to catch some spies and may contribute to the honesty of those with access to sensitive national security information.

The Intelligence Directorate   The Directorate of Intelligence is where the CIA conducts the sorting and interpretation of data about world events and personalities—in a word, analysis, the primary purpose for which the agency was established. Only about 20 percent of the agency's employees are engaged in information processing and analysis, accounting for less than 10 percent of the total CIA budget. In contrast, two-thirds of the CIA's personnel and monetary resources are dedicated to covert—or clandestine—operations (terms used interchangeably to encompass secret intelligence collection, counterintelligence, and covert action). Despite its modest percentage of total agency resources, those who founded the CIA in 1947 meant this directorate to be the center of the intelligence universe around which all the other entities and activities would revolve. Its importance becomes more obvious with a closer look at the purposes of American intelligence.

The Intelligence Missions

The founders of the CIA confronted two major challenges at the end of World War II: first, to establish greater centralism within the intelligence community as a means for improving the coordination of information within the government on foreign threats, and, second, to define more precisely the intelligence mission in the modern era. This second challenge required planners to address the question: What tasks was the new CIA expected to accomplish?

An examination of the 1947 National Security Act and the accompanying legislative history indicates that, as President Truman insisted, the CIA was established above all else to collect, evaluate, and coordinate intelligence, and to provide for its proper dissemination within the government. The CIA would be a clearinghouse for the various American intelligence agencies. The agency would also be expected, in the words of a DCI, Allen Dulles, "to weigh facts, and to draw conclusions from those facts, without having either the facts or the conclusions warped by the inevitable and even proper prejudices of the men whose duty it is to determine policy. . . ."[19] In a phrase, espionage and analysis would be the primary responsibility of the CIA—hardly a new venture but one that reformers hoped would now be carried out more effectively and efficiently.

The National Security Act gave the CIA (under the direction of the NSC) five specific authorities, of which the last gestured—in slippery language—toward duties beyond espionage. The statute charged the CIA with responsibilities to: advise the NSC on intelligence activities related to national security; make rec-

ommendations to the NSC for the coordination of such activities; correlate, evaluate, and disseminate intelligence within the government; carry out services for existing agencies that the NSC decides might be best performed centrally; and, in the ambiguous catchall phrase of the act, "perform such other functions and duties related to intelligence affecting the national security as the National Security Council may from time to time direct."[20] While the founding statute overwhelmingly emphasized intelligence collection and interpretation, the door was left ajar nonetheless to use the CIA for "other functions and duties"—an invitation quickly accepted by the NSC for launching the new agency on a wide range of covert actions around the world.

Like covert action, counterintelligence went without specific mention in the 1947 act but, by the early 1950s, had also achieved a status of considerable importance as a mission within the CIA. Counterintelligence (CI) specialists soon waged nothing less than a secret war against antagonistic intelligence services around the world. Explaining why this warfare evolved, a CI specialist points out that "in the absence of an effective U.S. counterintelligence program, [adversaries of democracy] function in what is largely a benign environment."[21] Led by the mysterious James Jesus Angleton, the Idaho-born, Harvard-educated CIA chief of counterintelligence from its beginnings until 1974, the CI staff developed its own global network of assets. Rather than merely settle for catching spies as they tried their handiwork against the United States, this staff began to conduct aggressive operations to confuse and thwart hostile intelligence services.

Collection and analysis, covert action, and counterintelligence thus were soon established as the core missions of the intelligence community in the postwar era. At the center of this hidden side of American foreign policy lies the collection-and-analysis mission, driven by the so-called intelligence cycle.

COLLECTION AND ANALYSIS

As emphasized in the preceding discussion, the essential purpose of the intelligence community is to gather, analyze, and coordinate information for policymakers, so that their decisions will be based on a more accurate understanding of the world they confront. Just as the collection and analysis of strategic intelligence make up the foundations of American foreign policy, so is the *intelligence cycle* central to collection and analysis. The CIA defines this cycle as "the process by which information is acquired, converted into intelligence, and made available to policymakers."[22]

The intelligence cycle has five phases: planning and direction, collection, processing, production and analysis, and dissemination (see Figure 8.4), though, as a former CIA analyst notes, the cycle is really less a series of discrete phases, one leading to another, than it is a matrix of steady interactions between producers and consumers of intelligence, with multiple feedback loops.[23] These interactions are simplified here and treated as discrete, however, both for analytic purposes and in conformity with common practice among intelligence officials.

Planning and Direction

The first phase of the intelligence cycle entails the identification of what kinds of data need to be gathered and the assignment of specific agencies to accomplish the gathering—that is, the management of the mission. The chief responsibilities for the collection of intelligence fall upon the NSA and the CIA. The CIA, the State Department's Intelligence and Research division (INR), and the Defense Intelligence Agency (DIA, under Pentagon leadership) are

FIGURE 8.4   The intelligence cycle.

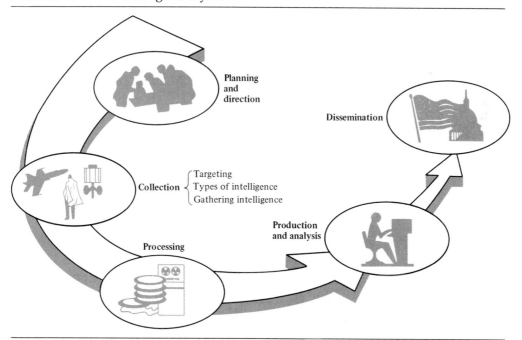

Source: Adapted from *Fact Book on Intelligence*, Office of Public Affairs, Central Intelligence Agency, April 1983, p. 16.

the top analytic organizations in the intelligence community. For purposes of illustrating the intelligence cycle, this chapter concentrates on the CIA—though in reality each of the major agencies has an important part to play in this process.

Within the CIA, the deputy director of intelligence is the chief analyst; this official more than anyone else deserves the credit, or the blame, for the quality of the completed ("finished") intelligence products presented to those who make decisions on behalf of the United States. The whole purpose of the cycle is to provide useful knowledge to U.S. policymakers—especially the president, but also presidential advisers ranging from the secretaries of state and defense to the scores of deputy assistant secretaries throughout the executive branch—in advance of their decisions. As the CIA puts it, "intelligence is knowledge and foreknowledge of the world around us—the prelude to Presidential decision and action."[24]

Major difficulties arise, however, in this seemingly straightforward relationship between the CIA (the producer of knowledge) and the policymakers (the consumers). The informational needs of policymakers are sometimes never made known, or never made clear, to the producers; the needs may extend beyond the capabilities of the CIA; or the information provided may be disbelieved and ignored by the consumer.

Thus the management problems can grow complex, as the DDI and the staff of the Directorate for Intelligence attempt, on the one hand, to obtain the best information available and, on the other hand, to make sure that the right people at the right time know about it. What may appear at first glance to be a simple and smoothly flowing process in Figure 8.4, with essential and accurate data swept along from agent to analyst to consumer, is instead a complicated series of interactions among men and women and their organizations that often result in the loss or distortion of vital information.

Collection

This planet may be but a tiny speck in the universe from a cosmological point of view, but its dimensions seem vast for an agency trying to keep up with events in the 180 nations of the world. No agency can be omniscient; priorities must be set. The managers in the intelligence cycle must decide, in consultation with policymakers, which countries to target, what kind of information about the targets is most important, and what means of gathering the information will be employed.

Targeting   American defense officials have all echoed the centrality of the U.S.S.R. in our national security planning. "The most obvious and most significant [threat to the United States] is the global challenge posed by the only nation that rivals us in military power—the Soviet Union," stated Harold Brown, secretary of defense during the Carter administration.[25] Discussing the American defense budget, Caspar Weinberger, secretary of defense in the Reagan administration, observed: "It's the threat that makes the budget. You've got to build your budget on the Russian budget."[26] Similarly, the Soviet Union has been the target that has attracted most of our intelligence resources.

In the past decade, though, an evolution has taken place in CIA targeting priorities, as this excerpt from a CIA memorandum suggests:

The traditional idea of intelligence is the spy who provides the enemy's war plans. Actually, intelligence is concerned not only with war plans, but with all the external concerns of our government. It must deal with the pricing debates of OPEC and the size of this year's Soviet crop (and here our foreknowledge comes from CIA's pioneering in new analysis techniques). It is concerned with Soviet strength along the Sino-Soviet border, with the intricacies of Chinese politics, with the water supply in the Middle East, with the quality of Soviet computers and its impact on our own export controls, with the narcotics trade in Southeast Asia, even with the struggle for control of Portuguese Timor.[27]

According to CIA officials, the Soviet Union continues to attract about one-half of the U.S. intelligence budget for collection, but the remaining half is much more broadly distributed. Now a host of other targets—less countries than topics—crowd in line for limited budget resources. Among them: debt financing in the developing countries and other economic questions, international energy shortages, science and technology, international terrorism, narcotics, agriculture, natural resources, immigration flows, water supplies, population projections, and arms control.

As the Carter administration turned beyond traditional issues of East-West confrontation to address issues of North-South reconciliation between rich and poor nations, the policymaker's list of new intelligence needs grew rapidly and both the executive and the legislative branches became increasingly dependent upon CIA data for a wide range of subjects.

Arms control is a conspicuous example. American diplomats relied almost entirely upon a CIA data base on the number of Soviet strategic weapons for their successful negotiations leading to the first Strategic Arms Limitations Treaty between the United States and the Soviet Union (SALT I, ratified in 1972). Assessments offered by the CIA have been vital as well to U.S. negotiators in the mutual and balanced force reduction (MBFR) talks in Vienna on conventional weapons. Before diplomats, legislators, and the American public are prepared to accept arms control agreements, they must be satisfied that the government, first, knows how many weapons are in the hands of the Soviets and, second, can monitor whether or not the U.S.S.R. is honoring its side of the arms agreements (an objective called *verification*).

Through satellite reconnaissance and other technical means, as well as with human spies, the CIA and other U.S. intelligence agencies have been able to provide these assurances. Any dangerous violations by the Soviets can be detected with confidence by U.S. surveillance methods, just as the Soviet Union can now detect American violations. This ability to watch one's adversary from afar has contributed immeasurably to the sense of security that undergirds the long, if troubled, peace that has characterized superpower relations so far in the nuclear age—the most important contribution to American foreign policy made by the power of intelligence. Verification, though, promises to become increasingly complex as strategic weapons become smaller and more mobile. The monitoring of mobile missiles requires on-site inspections in addition to the use of satellite and other remote surveillance. The INF Treaty permitted the United States to conduct on-site inspections at 117 Soviet facilities; a successful treaty dealing with long-range strategic missiles would probably require as many as 2500 inspection sites.[28]

The selection of intelligence targets ("setting requirements," or *tasking*) is a job involving many hands, sometimes including even the president. "When I became President," remembers Jimmy Carter, "I was concerned, during the first few months, that quite often the intelligence community, itself, set its own priorities as a supplier of intelligence information. I felt that the customers—the ones who receive the intelligence information, including the Defense Department, myself and others—ought to be the ones to say this is what we consider to be most important."[29] The White House, the Department of State, and especially President Carter's DCI, Admiral Stansfield Turner, took a more active role than had recently been the case in assigning intelligence-collection requirements to the CIA and other agencies—especially shifting attention toward the gathering of global economic information and data on developments within the smaller nations of the third world.

When the Reagan administration came to

town in 1981, it too was unhappy with certain omissions. As this administration's CIA director, William J. Casey, recalled, the intelligence community was excessively country-oriented. Reports were available on Nicaragua, Honduras, and El Salvador, but "no one was looking at the regional interplay." Moreover, Casey continued, "no one was concentrating on the economic component of these situations."[30] Also, in twenty years, the CIA had produced only five major evaluations of the Soviet economy. Casey took steps to correct these perceived shortcomings and, in addition, created two new analysis centers on subjects of high interest to the Reagan administration: technology transfer and "insurgency and instability." This latter interest went hand in glove with the so-called Reagan Doctrine, a geopolitical scheme resting upon the use of covert action to take the offensive against Marxist-communist "wars of liberation" in the poorer nations of the world.

Members of Congress have had their own suggestions for intelligence tasking, too, but here the intelligence community has drawn the line. "We don't seek input from the Hill on collection requirements, but sometimes we get it anyway," says a DDI, ruefully. "We definitely don't want 535 new taskers; serving the executive branch is tough enough."[31]

Types of Intelligence   Often the issue of debate between consumer and producer is less about the proper targets of intelligence operations than the types of intelligence one thinks ought to be produced from the collected data. Policymakers might like to know—ideally— what has occurred in, say, Monrovia in the past two hours, or what is apt to occur in Nicaragua over the next year. In the first instance, the policymaker desires current intelligence—up-to-the-minute information often vital in times of crisis; in the second instance, what is needed is more thoroughly researched and analyzed, longer-range predictions—known as *estimates* in the intelligence business. And, in a third instance, the policymaker might require a truly in-depth study on a specific subject, perhaps a definitive examination of Soviet oil reserves. Respectively, these three categories are often referred to as *current, predictive,* and *research intelligence*.

While these are the most common packages of intelligence sought by consumers, others exist. Sometimes a policymaker will simply ask for a brief response to a query in the form of a typed memorandum. In one page, what can you tell me about the Chinese coal industry? About West German Chancellor Helmut Kohl's agenda for his approaching visit to the United States? The effect of U.S. bombing of Col. Muammar Qaddafi's headquarters in 1986 on damping down Libyan terrorism?

On other occasions, the consumer will prefer a quick oral briefing, perhaps on the run between meetings or in a limousine on the way to the airport (practices discouraged by intelligence security personnel for fear of eavesdropping by hostile intelligence services). "Policymakers will accept fifteen-minute briefings over the investment of five minutes to read a report," observes a recent DDI.[32] Frequently, policymakers come from a political background; they are often less comfortable reading than talking and listening—or viewing: the president and other top officials in the Reagan administration liked to have intelligence reports presented in a videotape format, especially personality profiles on Qaddafi and various Soviet leaders. Regardless of what form they may want the collected intelligence to assume, the policymaker usually wants it *now*, wants it perfectly accurate, and wants it without too many nuances—demands that usually defy human capabilities and protective instincts or even technological feasibility.

Gathering Intelligence   The intelligence community relies upon three approaches to the gathering of information vital to our national security: overt collection, and two forms of covert collection: classical espionage using spies ("human intelligence," or *HUMINT*) and modern technical surveillance ("technical intelligence," or *TECHINT*, especially using satellites). Ransom estimates that "80 per cent or more of intelligence material in peacetime is overtly collected from nonsecret sources such as newspapers, libraries, radio broadcast, business and industrial reports, or from accredited foreign service officers. . . ."[33] Nonetheless, a well-placed HUMINT asset may be able to steal a key document from a safe in the middle of the night, or may overhear foreign leaders discuss impending military operations; and satellites can photograph the number and location of Soviet missiles—topics that fall outside the public domain.

To assist the efforts of analysts to sift through open sources of intelligence, the CIA maintains vast library holdings, and the agency's Foreign Broadcast Information Service (FBIS) monitors global radio and television emissions, which are translated and circulated to the offices of country analysts. While overt collection provides the bulk of information gathered by the CIA, covert HUMINT and technical collection often unearth the most important knowledge for decision making. Two celebrated HUMINT successes reveal how important this approach to intelligence collection can be. One example is Major Popov of Soviet Military Intelligence (GRU). During the 1950s, he provided secret documents to the CIA that revealed the inner workings of the GRU and saved the United States an estimated half billion dollars in military research. In the 1960s, Colonel Oleg Penkovsky (also with the GRU) smuggled to the West thousands of documents on Soviet missilery. Both men were eventually discovered and executed by Soviet authorities. Most recent HUMINT successes remain classified; but, absent a human source within the Soviet Union, the Reagan administration would have been unable to reveal to the American public in 1988 the existence of vast and deep subterranean bomb shelters which the Soviets have constructed beneath Moscow and other cities in case of nuclear war.

Calculating the cost-effectiveness of HUMINT is difficult. For every Popov or Penkovsky, the intelligence community may have hundreds of agents who produce little more than snippets of gossip. Often HUMINT reports are unreliable. Prior to the Cuban missile crisis of 1962, intelligence from CIA agents in Cuba proved notoriously inaccurate; of 200 reports of missile sightings, only six proved accurate.[34] Then one always faces the possibility that an asset is actually a double agent through whom a deception operation is being conducted by an adversary.

The costliest phase of the intelligence cycle is collection (especially the collection of intelligence through technical means, like satellites), and budgeteers from the various intelligence agencies engage constantly in a tug-of-war over the distribution of these large dollars. The end result of the budget battles over the years has been for HUMINT to come up with the short straw when compared with technical intelligence (with all of its expensive hardware), by a ratio of about 1 to 7.[35] "Is this the right balance?" asks one experienced intelligence analyst. "We don't know for sure; we're not that smart."[36] Nobody is. HUMINT defies evaluation by normal budgetary criteria, for one Penkovsky makes the deficits column—however lengthy—suddenly appear insignificant.

As the 1-to-7 ratio of HUMINT to TECHINT indicates, though, the Penkovsky argument is difficult to sell in budget councils. As researcher after researcher has discovered, the people who make decisions about national security priorities prefer "to concentrate on things that can be 'scientifically' measured."[37] Just as counting missiles, and—the favorite—warheads, becomes the fascination of strategic planners, so are intelligence planners drawn to the counting of mechanical devices for surveillance, with their glittering, awesome technology. A spy plane is something tangible: it takes pictures; its appurtenances can be demonstrated with slides before the members of the congressional appropriations subcommittees in closed session. In a word, the hardware is impressive and promises immediate results (cloud cover willing).

In contrast, the nameless spy, who for security reasons can never be discussed explicitly in budget meetings (indeed, his or her true identity will be known only to the case officer and perhaps one or two others at headquarters), may, or may never, obtain information of great significance. Moreover, the giant aerospace corporations and laboratories persistently lobby for surveillance hardware contracts, with skills finely tuned through experience in weapons contracting through the Department of Defense. HUMINT has no such external advocate and, despite occasional coups like Penkovsky, remains the stepchild of the collection process.

Satellites and aircraft have their limits (half the world remains cloud-covered at any mo-

ment); but, coupled with HUMINT and open-source intelligence, America's capabilities for knowing about the world have increased dramatically. Surprises will continue to occur, for neither U.S. officials nor the Soviets are all-knowing; but surprises are now fewer.

Processing

The third step in the intelligence cycle (after collection) is the least disputatious. Here the collected information undergoes various refinements for closer study by analysts. Coded data will be decrypted, foreign languages translated, photographic material interpreted, and the like, to make the information readable and understandable for the analyst. "The major problem during the processing stage is information overload," reports a CIA official. "Fortunately, the

The National Security Agency (NSA), located at Fort George C. Meade in Maryland. (Courtesy National Security Agency)

use of computers offsets this to a large degree."[38]

The processing procedures, nevertheless, can be time-consuming. A professional photo-interpreter may require four hours to decipher fully a single frame of satellite photography. The art of "cratetology"—interpreting the often obscure markings on crates aboard ocean freighters—can also require hours of careful study by experts. In November of 1984, the "cratelogists" at the CIA failed to agree on what the markings indicated on boxes unloaded from a Soviet cargo vessel in Nicaragua: the presence of MIG-21s, antiaircraft missiles, attack helicopters, or something more benign. A reliable HUMINT asset on board ship would have been valuable.

After processing comes the central purpose of the entire cycle: the conversion of raw information into usable intelligence. Here is the marriage of data, overtly and covertly gained, with thoughtful assessment—in a word, analysis.

Production and Analysis

The individuals responsible for the conversion of "raw" (unevaluated) information into "finished" intelligence are called *analysts*—men and women, highly educated, who are experts on a single country such as Zaire, or on broad topics, such as the flow of petrodollars, or quite narrow (albeit important) topics, such as the efficiency of Soviet rocket fuels. Within the CIA alone are several hundred specialized analysts with such skills. Each, ideally, has the characteristics advocated by Sherman Kent, for years the dean of analysts in the CIA: "the best in professional training, the highest intellectual integrity, and a very large amount of worldly wisdom."[39]

The job of the analysts, who (recall) are often called the "producers" of intelligence, is to supply policymakers—those who actually make the foreign policy decisions on behalf of the United States—with accurate interpretations of global threats and opportunities facing this nation.

The policymakers, or "consumers" of intelligence, include the president, the vice president, the secretaries of state and defense, the president's national security adviser, the chairman of the Joint Chiefs of Staff, and hundreds of other top-ranking officials with national security responsibilities—from assistant and deputy assistant secretaries in the executive branch to key legislators and their aides on Capitol Hill. As discussed below, the relations between analysts and policymakers are ambiguous and sometimes strained, for they have different backgrounds and outlooks.

For current intelligence, the CIA produces (in coordination with the larger intelligence community) a number of daily documents among which the *President's Daily Brief* (*PDB*) is preeminent. The PDB is the most tightly held document in Washington. It arrives early in the morning, via CIA courier, and is placed on the desktops of five individuals: the president, the vice president, the secretaries of state and defense, and the president's special assistant for national security affairs (who directs the NSC staff). This top-secret "newspaper" briefs these officials on major political developments throughout the world that have occurred in the last twenty-four hours; it often sets the agenda for early morning discussions among the five and with aides.

The PDB is supplemented with other daily reports, similarly designed for limited distribution. The Situation Room in the White House, the president's communications center, pulls together up-to-the-minute intelligence materials (mostly cables and NSA reports), summarizes them, and forwards them to the national security adviser for possible presentation to the president. Usually a few of these items make it to the Oval Office. Also, the Department of State's morning intelligence report, prepared for the secretary of state by INR, goes to the national security adviser and, almost always, on to the president.

More difficult to prepare are predictive and research intelligence. The key documents for this production task have been, for short-range projections, the *Interagency Intelligence Memoranda (IIM)* and, the showpiece of mid- to long-range projections, the *National Intelligence Estimates (NIEs)*, prepared routinely on different parts of the world, and *Special National Intelligence Estimates (SNIEs)*, prepared in response to specific subjects requested by senior policymakers. Lyman Kirkpatrick, former executive director of the CIA, offers this definition of the NIE: "a statement of what is going to happen in any country, in any area, in any given situation, and as far as possible into the future."[40]

Though the amount of resources devoted to collection and analysis is great, the intelligence community—like every other human enterprise—will never be free of mistakes. As Richard K. Betts has emphasized, "some incidence of failure [is] inevitable." He urges a higher "tolerance for disaster."[41] Even the last phase of the intelligence cycle—dissemination—has proven to hold more potential for error than one might expect.

Dissemination

"Being right isn't enough," stresses Donald Gregg, a seasoned intelligence professional. "You have to inject that 'rightness' into the policy process. Unless a particular concern is actually raised at the correct moment during one of the key meetings, say, the NSC, the good analysis done by the intelligence community is often lost. The chip must be put in the pot at this stage—and forcefully."[42] As Gregg's observation reminds us, there is nothing preordained or automatic about good intelligence being heard and accepted in high places. Remember that a central explanation for the successful Japanese surprise at Pearl Harbor was the faulty dissemination of sound intelligence regarding the possibility of an attack.

The key to success for the CIA during the dissemination phase may be summed up in one word: dialogue. Senior intelligence officers and senior policymakers must talk to each other if this transfer of intelligence is to work. This sounds simple enough, until one considers several barriers that arise. Perhaps the toughest assignment for an intelligence agency, notes a recent DDI, is "to give honest assessments and still keep the policymaker reading."[43] A former senior CIA analyst draws this conclusion: "Many of the consumers are ideologues. It is hard to work with them—especially when we're usually dealing with highly ambiguous

---

Perspectives on American Foreign Policy   8.2

A senior DDI analyst on the difficulty of estimating events in Iran preceding its revolution in 1979:

We knew the Shah was widely unpopular, and we knew there would be mass demonstrations, even riots. But how many shopkeepers would resort to violence, and how long would Army officers remain loyal to the Shah? Perhaps the Army would shoot down 10,000 rioters, maybe 20,000. If the ranks of the insurgents swelled further, though, how far would the Army be willing to go before it decided the Shah was a losing proposition? All this we duly reported; but no one could predict with confidence the number of dissidents who would actually take up arms, or the "tipping point" for Army loyalty.

Author's interview, August 28, 1984, Washington, D.C.

data. When consumers criticize our product, it is often on grounds that it fails to support their suppositions."[44]

This rejection by policymakers of objective intelligence became particularly controversial during the Reagan administration. Reportedly, the Reagan White House rejected the conclusions of CIA analysts calling into question the administration's convictions that Syria was a puppet of the Soviet Union; that Nicaragua aggressively exported arms to Marxist guerrillas throughout Central America; that a Soviet oil pipeline to western Europe would significantly increase the vulnerability of U.S. allies to Soviet pressure; that the shooting down of a South Korean passenger airliner in 1983 was not misidentification of it by the Soviets as a hostile spy plane but rather an intentional murder of civilians; and, among other examples, that the assassination plot against the pope in 1981 had been concocted in Moscow.[45]

Critics charged the administration's CIA director himself, William J. Casey, the former presidential campaign manager for Ronald Reagan in 1980, with "cooking" (slanting) some intelligence reports to suit the ideological predilections of the White House. In 1983, congressional staffers on the intelligence committees claimed that the CIA under Casey's direction had prepared reports for the president that purported to confirm—on skimpy evidence—the administration's suppositions that the pro-Marxist Sandinistas intended to eliminate through a policy of genocide the Miskito Indians in the northern provinces of Nicaragua, and that the Catholic church in Central America was sympathetic to the Marxist regime.[46]

On other occasions, the policymaker may like the intelligence provided by the CIA; it may agree with his or her predispositions or political hopes. Yet, according to a former DDI, this happy situation can be short-lived: "We always get new information, and we may have to change our original assessments."[47] In the meantime, the policymaker may have already delivered a widely reported speech or press comment based on the first evaluation. President Carter spoke strongly in favor of pulling U.S. troops out of South Korea in the early days of his administration; he had to reverse his position when the intelligence community began to report increases in the number of North Korean fighting forces.

Moreover, Congress is now part of the dissemination phase, and this has exacerbated relations between analysts and policymakers in the executive branch. During the CIA's carefree days from 1947 to 1974, when it was relatively free from congressional monitoring, little information was asked for by legislators and little was offered by the CIA. Today, legislators demand a greater share of the intelligence product. "Few intelligence documents went to the Hill before 1976," a DDI has reported. "Now only a tiny percentage of intelligence that goes to the executive doesn't go also to the two Intelligence Committees of Congress."[48] In 1983, the Intelligence Directorate alone gave 500 briefings on Capitol Hill. All this provides Congress with ammunition for the critique of executive-branch programs, a favor unlikely to endear the CIA to administration policymakers.

And, of course, sometimes the intelligence agencies are just plain wrong in their judgments. During the Carter administration, the most conspicuous miscalculation was the failure to predict the fall of the shah in Iran. Another embarrassment, noted above, occurred when CIA analysts underestimated the number of North Korean troops, encouraging President Carter to endorse a reduction of U.S. troop strength in South Korea—a position he was forced to abandon, red-faced, when military intelligence analysts reappraised the figures and found them to be incorrect.[49] Such mistakes do little to nurture the consumer-producer relationship.

Despite such hazards, intelligence officials have become quite sophisticated in ways of nurturing ties with policymakers. "We use to throw things over the transom," remembers a senior analyst. "Now we *market*."[50] The chief manager of current intelligence in the CIA once emphasized the importance of packaging, timing, and building rapport. "Good packaging is vital," he states. "You must focus the policymaker's attention. They are busy. They like pictures and graphs. Videotapes have been a big hit with the Reagan team, especially in portraying international personalities like [the late Soviet premier] Brezhnev."[51]

To improve the chances of access to the office in the first place, the CIA now encourages the growth of closer personal ties between analysts and policymakers—easier said than done, given the particularly harried existence of the latter. (One CIA analyst calculates that policymakers spend about fifteen minutes a day on intelligence at best.[52]) This "personal chemistry" may be the most important aspect of the entire intelligence cycle, a senior CIA analyst emphasizes. But even when the chemistry is good, "getting on the policymaker's calendar is hard," complains a senior DIA manager.[53]

"The purpose of the intelligence cycle is to find the best minds available to produce the best one-page report on subject x," concludes a CIA official. "After that, it's all technique."[54] As these remarks on the dissemination phase indicate, the best minds and the most brilliant reports will be of little use without the skillful management of interpersonal relations between producer and consumer during this last phase of the cycle.

As the preceding portion of this chapter indicates, U.S. officials face a variety of challenges in their efforts to understand global threats and opportunities. On top of these challenges comes a further complication: internal disputes over the proper sharing of intelligence between the branches. When one considers the time and energy consumed by these political travails, the task of monitoring the Soviet Union often seems to pale in comparison.

THE LURE OF SECRECY

Secrecy has obvious advantages in the planning and execution of foreign policy. Leaders of the republic have acknowledged this from the earliest days. Commenting on the importance of good military intelligence during the Revolutionary War, General George Washington observed: "The necessity of procuring good Intelligence is apparent and need not be further urged. All that remains for me to add is that you keep the whole matter as secret as possible, for upon Secrecy Success depends in most enterprises of the kind, and for want of it, they are generally defeated, however well-planned or promising of favorable issue."[55]

Good Secrets

The sailing dates and destinations of troopships during time of war; the sophisticated technology of the radar-elusive Stealth bomber and other advanced weapons systems; the names of espionage agents operating on behalf of the United States in foreign lands; the bargaining positions of U.S. negotiators at arms control sessions in Geneva—each depends upon the element of secrecy for success. Sometimes, too, secret (or so-called back-channel) dialogues with the leaders of other nations can persuade them to change their positions more readily than public criticism. In the glare of public light, foreign leaders may be unwilling to back down under pressure from the United States, for fear they may lose face with their own people.

During the Carter administration, for example, the leader of South Korea was apparently on the verge of executing his chief political opponent. President Carter moved to intercede, but South Korean diplomats warned Carter's emissary that if the United States made a public issue of the matter, the president of South Korea would order the execution rather than have it seem he was an American lackey. Carter quietly negotiated a stay of execution through back-channels. During the Nixon and Ford administrations, Secretary of State Henry Kissinger maintains that he achieved his greatest successes through private diplomacy with foreign ministers and heads of state. In his memoirs, he levels his sharpest criticism at Congress for meddling in this private diplomacy and, through publicity, sometimes upsetting finely tuned understandings with foreign officials. Kissinger is especially critical of legislative pronouncements during the war in Vietnam that called for a quick U.S. withdrawal at the same time he was trying to negotiate a settlement with North Vietnamese representatives in Paris.[56]

For proponents of secret diplomacy, a classic illustration of the advantages of this approach is the Jackson-Vanik Amendment of 1974. Sponsored by Senator Henry Jackson (D-Wash.) and Representative Charles Vanik (D-Ohio), this law attempted to use open trade inducements as a method to stimulate the emigration of Soviet Jews. The idea seemed logical enough: the more Jews the Soviets would permit to leave their country, the more trade and credit advantages the United States would give to the U.S.S.R. The Soviets, though, resented this unveiled attempt to manipulate their emigration policies, and the number of Jews allowed to leave the Soviet Union actually went into a decline after the passage of the Jackson-Vanik law. Only when the fervor for this approach dissipated and U.S. diplomats returned to back-channel negotiations for the release of individual Jews who wished to leave the Soviet Union did the emigration rates begin to climb again.

Bad Secrets

Yet, all too often, the arguments of the executive branch for secrecy rest on less firm grounds. Frequently, its officials prefer to conduct foreign policy in secret simply because this approach avoids the necessity for defending their policies before legislators, reporters, and the American people. During the investigation into the Iran-contra scandal in 1987, a key witness, Vice Admiral John M. Poindexter (President Reagan's national security adviser), admitted: "I simply did not want any outside interference."[57] Constitutional checks and balances were merely a hindrance, to be bypassed in secret. Poindexter said he believed in tight *compartmentation*, the practice within the executive branch of maintaining operational security through the establishment of special channels which limit the access of individuals to information.

Responded the co-chairman of the investigative committee, Representative Lee H. Hamilton (D-Ind.): "You compartmentalized not only the President's senior advisers [neither Secretary of State George P. Shultz nor Secretary of Defense Caspar Weinberger knew of the contra diversion], but, in effect, you locked the President himself out of the process."[58] If the top appointed officials of the Reagan administration who testified before Congress under oath were telling the truth, not a single elected official in the government knew of this reckless foreign policy venture that ran directly counter to the Boland amendments prohibiting military assistance to the contras (as well as other legal strictures against dealing with terrorists in the Middle East; see Chapter 9).

The American people and their representatives in Congress have become wary of secret foreign policy because of the many instances when they have been misled by officials in the executive branch. As the reader will recall from Part 1 of this book, during the Johnson administration the president lost credibility with the public—and his bid for reelection in 1968—when his statements about the success of U.S. military operations in Vietnam proved hollow and the number of American casualties continued to mount, with victory nowhere in sight. The lies of the Nixon administration raised further alarm, first over the president's management of the war in Vietnam (Nixon promised an end to the struggle, yet the war went on, punctuated by extensive bombing in North Vietnam and Cambodia) and, then, Watergate. The word *Watergate* quickly became synonymous with deception in the lexicon of American politics. The president himself had tried to cover up the second-rate burglary of Democratic campaign files perpetrated by his overzealous staff (though evidently without his knowledge) and was driven from office.

On the heels of Watergate came the revelations of CIA intrigues, disclosed by legislative inquiries in 1975. Investigators discovered the use of intelligence operations against American antiwar protesters (Operation Chaos), assassination plots against foreign leaders, and attempts to topple democratically elected officials whom the U.S. government disliked (Salvador Allende of Chile, among others)—all done in secrecy.[59]

Then, during the Reagan administration, officials not only lied to the Congress about the Iran-contra affair, but evidently misled legislators (and the public) about other matters as well. The administration falsely attributed the shooting down of a South Korean passenger airliner in 1983 (KAL flight 007), recall, to brutal and trigger-happy Kremlin officials, whereas the incident appears to have been a tragic error of judgment by a Soviet fighter pilot who thought he had engaged a spy plane that refused to land.[60]

Further, the administration reportedly attempted to blacken the image of Sandinista leaders by accusing them of drug trafficking (after the NSC staff aide Lieutenant Colonel North helped lure one minor official into a drug deal) and by planting Soviet weapons in Central America in order to "verify" the claim that Nicaraguan Marxists were spreading weapons to leftist guerrillas in the region. In 1983, the Reagan administration also seems to have exaggerated the threat of a Marxist takeover in Grenada, rationalizing a U.S. troop invasion (see Chapter 10); and in 1986, the administra-

tion approved a propaganda campaign against Colonel Qaddafi, which portrayed him as a madman about to employ widespread violence against the United States and other nations. The purpose of the propaganda attack against Qaddafi was to turn world opinion even more against the Libyan leader. When word of the operation leaked to the media, Secretary of State George P. Shultz defended the activity as legitimate psychological warfare; his chief spokesman (Bernard Kalb) resigned in protest, however, over this attempt to mislead the public in the United States and elsewhere. Moreover, the administration blamed Qaddafi, without evidence, for the terrorist bombing of a disco in Berlin (by all accounts a Syrian-backed operation), clearing the way for a U.S. bombing raid against his home and government buildings.[61]

Over the years, secrecy has bred corruption and a contempt for traditional American values. Open debate—the very anchor of democracy—has often been abandoned. As the thoughtful television commentator Bill Moyers observes,

> . . . [to abandon] these basic values out of fear, to imitate the foe [communism] in order to defeat him, is to shred the distinction that makes us different. In the end, not only our values but our methods separate us from the enemies of freedom in the world. The decisions we make are inherent in the methods that produce them. An open society cannot survive a secret government.[62]

Moreover, though sometimes excessive congressional involvement in foreign policy can be harmful to American objectives (as with the Jackson-Vanik initiative), participation by legislators can provide at other times just the publicity needed to bring about useful change. The betterment of human rights throughout the world, advocated by the Carter administration, offers an example. As two authorities conclude: ". . . the highly visible, public pursuit of human rights that is the consequence of the 1975 and 1976 human rights laws on balance has probably done more to help than hinder the achievement of the human rights policy's objectives. ... It has transformed human rights from a U.S. diplomatic concern into a global popular issue."[63]

Regardless of the lessons drawn from recent scandals and the strong democratic arguments in favor of openness ("open covenants, openly arrived at," advocated President Woodrow Wilson, naively in the view of his critics), secrecy continues to hold an almost irresistible temptation for officials in the executive branch. The frequent evocation of the so-called doctrine of executive privilege offers additional insight into their attempts to bypass Congress through the control of information.

EXECUTIVE PRIVILEGE

In the eyes of executive-branch officials, a central attraction of America's secret intelligence agencies is the opportunity they afford to chart a foreign policy course with little or no public debate. In its covert shipment of arms to Iran during 1985–1986, the Reagan administration carried the goal of exclusion to an extreme, refusing not only to inform Congress but keeping the operation strictly within the limited confines of a few NSC staffers, some field operatives, and a narrow slice of the CIA—beyond the purview evidently of even the president and the NSC's other principal members.

A Cloak of Executive Secrecy

Sometimes this goal of exclusion is achieved through the use of *executive privilege*, defined as an assertion by the president of constitutional authority to withhold information from the legislative and judicial branches of government. Appearing before the Ervin committee, established by the Senate in 1973 to investigate the Watergate scandal and chaired by Sam Ervin, Jr. (D-N.C.), President Nixon's attorney general, Richard Kleindienst, claimed that "the constitutional authority of the President in his discretion" allowed the president to withhold information in his possession "or in the possession of the Executive branch" if the president concluded disclosure "would impair the proper exercise of his constitutional functions."

This implied that Congress could be prohibited from speaking to any of the millions of employees in the executive branch! Kleindienst's statement represented a sweeping extension of the traditional notion that only the closest White House aides could hide behind the president's cloak. The Watergate crisis was coming to a head, however, and Nixon soon fired Kleindienst for his inept efforts to head off a legislative inquiry.

President Nixon went further in his attempt to use executive privilege as an escape from the Watergate inquiry. Without precedent, he stated in 1973 that not only could current members of the president's staff refuse to appear before congressional committees, but so could past members—a position senators sarcastically labeled the "doctrine of eternal privilege." Among other things, Nixon also extended executive privilege to cover "presidential papers," which he defined magisterially as "all documents, produced or received by the President or any member of the White House staff in connection with his official duties."[64] In a case that went to the Supreme Court in 1974, Nixon argued that the doctrine protected the tapes and records of sixty-four White House conversations that had been secretly recorded and were then being sought by Watergate investigators. The Court rejected the contention (*United States v. Nixon* 418 U.S. 683) that the president had an absolute executive privilege. Nixon had to relinquish the tapes relevant to the Watergate trial. The Court noted, however, that great deference would be given to the doctrine if foreign policy or military secrets were involved.

In response to the Ervin committee's hot criticism, the president's aides eventually consented to appear in executive (secret) session, but not in public hearings. Chairman Ervin remained unimpressed.

"What do they eat that makes them grow so great?" he asked. "I am not willing to elevate them to a position above the great mass of the American people. I don't think we have any such thing as royalty or nobility to let anybody come down at night like Nicodemus and whisper something in my ear that no one else can hear. This is not executive privilege. It is executive poppycock."[65]

As evidence regarding the Watergate break-in began to surface in the press, a refusal to testify in open hearings became an increasingly untenable position for those aides implicated in the cover-up. This portion of Nixon's wall of executive privilege started to crumble.

The Ford administration stretched the cloak of executive privilege to another extravagant length. At issue were a number of secret activities, including Operation Shamrock, an intelligence operation involving the National Security Agency and private communications companies. Operation Shamrock was designed to intercept cables and telegrams sent abroad or received by Americans. Initially at the request of the Truman administration, RCA, Global Corporation, and ITT World Communications began to store their international paid message traffic on magnetic tapes, which were then turned over to the NSA. The NSA studied the messages for possible hints of espionage activity. The operation may have been a violation of the Federal Communications Act provisions protecting the privacy of communications, and so Shamrock became a subject of legislative investigations in 1975–1976.

When a House subcommittee called the corporation presidents as witnesses in 1976, they turned to the Ford administration for guidance. President Ford through his attorney general, Edward H. Levi (former dean of the University of Chicago School of Law), claimed that the corporations were immune from congressional appearances in this case, since Shamrock was a sensitive, top-secret project ordered by the White House. The doctrine of executive privilege was now extended to the private sector!

The chairperson of the subcommittee, Bella S. Abzug (D-N.Y.), expressed dismay over the assertion of executive privilege by a private corporation. Her colleague, Representative John E. Moss (D-Utah), put the matter directly. "The Attorney General is without any authority," he declared. "It is the most outrageous assumption, the most arrogant display by the Attorney General I have ever seen. Some damn two-bit appointee of the President is not the law-making body of this country."[66] The House subcommittee, like the Ervin committee, was disinclined to accept extensions of executive privilege that blocked what it thought was its constitutional duty to provide a check on the executive branch. When the subcommittee called for contempt of Congress citations against the corporate executives if they refused to testify, the CEOs decided that wisdom lay in appearing before Congress—regardless of the attorney general's advice.

Delay and Deceit

Usually, though, the conflicts between the branches over information are less clear-cut. The more common response of the executive branch is simply to *stonewall*, that is, to delay, delay, and then delay some more in response to congressional requests for information. "Bureaucrats engage in interminable stalling when asked for information," notes an expert on executive privilege, the Harvard University professor of law Raoul Berger.[67]

This seems to have been the initial strategy used by the Reagan administration to avoid the Iran-contra scandal. "The charge has been made that the United States has shipped weapons to Iran as ransom payment for the release of American hostages in Lebanon, that the United States undercut its allies and secretly violated American policy against trafficking with terrorists," stated President Reagan at one of his rare press conferences (November 13, 1986), concluding unequivocally: "Those charges are utterly false."

Less than a week later (November 16), the following exchange with the press took place:

> Reporter: Mr. President, I don't think it's still clear just what Israel's role was in this. Could you explain what the Israeli role was here?
>
> President Reagan: No, because we, as I say, have had nothing to do with other countries or their shipment of arms, or doing what they're—they are doing.

The President's statements were false; America had shipped the weapons to Iran, and the Israelis had helped.

Executive privilege, either in its formal manifestation or through the tactics of delay and deceit, represents a potent force in foreign affairs for concealing information from the Congress. President Reagan said in 1986 that he might invoke the doctrine to prevent his top aides from testifying before Congress on the covert shipment of arms to Iran; only when the media discredited his earlier misleading statements and the outrage grew on Capitol Hill did the president retreat from this position. His retreat was fortuitous for Congress; the legal obstacles it faced in forcing the aides to testify would have been, according to legal opinions gathered by the *New York Times*, "formidable."[68] Contempt of Congress charges would have resulted in criminal prosecution only if brought to court by the U.S. attorney in Washington—a Reagan appointee.

As the time came in February of 1989 for the trial of Lieutenant Colonel North and other Iran-contra principals, their defense attorneys resorted to so-called graymail—a subtle form of blackmail, in the view of critics—as a means for thwarting the proceedings. The attorneys argued that a trial would reveal sensitive national security information and therefore should not be held. Secrecy had to be preserved above all else. On these grounds, the U.S. district judge dismissed four charges against North, but insisted on moving forward with twelve others in which the secrecy argument seemed less compelling. Following a lengthy trial, a jury found North guilty of three felony crimes: obstructing Congress by providing its investigators false and misleading chronologies, "mishandling" (a euphemism for shredding) top-secret White House files, and receiving an illegal gratuity (an expensive security system for his home, provided by arms dealers involved in the Iran-contra operation).

The executive branch will no doubt continue to resist full disclosure of its activities to Congress, let alone to the American people (one of the most alarming examples has been the secrecy surrounding the harmful effects of nuclear waste at government facilities, concealed over the years by officials more concerned with nuclear weapons production than with public health[69]). And no doubt members of Congress will continue to berate the practices of stonewalling and executive privilege. Clearly, many legislators share the conclusion reached by Professor Berger. "At bottom, the issue concerns the right of Congress and the people to participate in making the fateful decisions that affect the fortunes of the nation," he has written. "Claims of presidential power to bar such participation or to withhold on one ground or another the information that is indispensable for intelligent participation undermine this right and sap the very foundations of democratic government."[70]

PRIOR RESTRAINT

As a further attempt to bottle up information within the executive branch, officials sometimes try to curb the publication of materials deemed sensitive. This withholding by the government of the right to publish information is often referred to as *prior restraint*. The health of a democracy depends upon an adequate flow of information to the people regarding public affairs. Only in this way can the electorate make informed decisions about the quality of their representatives. Without good information, elections become a farce because voters have no way to evaluate the merits of those who hold office. Truth is the sine qua non for successful democracy, but truth can only be arrived at through an open flow of information. This is why courts in the United States have been loath for the most part to permit the enforcement of prior restraint. "Any system of prior restraints of expression comes to this Court bearing a heavy presumption against its constitutional validity," stated the Supreme Court in the celebrated case *New York Times Co. v. United States* (1971). "The government thus carries a heavy burden of showing justification for the imposition of such restraint."[71]

In *New York Times v. United States* (known less formally as the "Pentagon Papers" case), the government failed to convince the justices that prior restraint was necessary in this instance. The Nixon administration sought to prevent publication of a secret Department of Defense history of the war in Vietnam, on grounds that it contained information that could be harmful to American foreign policy. The man responsible for the leak, a Defense Department analyst named Daniel Ellsberg, believed the contrary to be true: that Americans would benefit from knowing the facts about U.S. involvement in the war. This would make the debate over further involvement more meaningful and accurate. He was personally convinced, moreover, that no secrets of real significance were in the documents; rather, the materials were being kept secret because officials wished to hold from public view a record of the various mistakes that had been made, leading the United States deeper into the Vietnam conflict. Ellsberg's critics looked upon his decision as close to treason, for he revealed classified information without proper authorization.

Responding to the dictates of his own conscience and at great personal legal risk, Ellsberg leaked the documents to the *New York Times* and the *Washington Post*. As soon as officials in

the Nixon administration picked up their morning newspapers and realized what had happened, they moved to stop further publication of the leaks by bringing an injunction against the *Times*, the first newspaper to publish excerpts from the Pentagon Papers. Joined by the *Washington Post*, the *Times* appealed a lower-court injunction, and given the great importance of the issue and the key figures involved, the case moved quickly to the Supreme Court.

The justices decided against the government, in the spirit expressed by Mr. Justice Potter Stewart: "We are asked, quite simply, to prevent the publication by two newspapers of material that the Executive Branch insists should not, in the national interest, be published. I am convinced that the Executive is correct with respect to some of the documents involved. But I cannot say that disclosure of any of them will surely result in *direct, immediate, and irreparable damage* to the Nation or its people. That being so, there can under the First Amendment be but one judicial resolution of the issues before us. I join the judgments of the Court."[72]

CONTRACTUAL SECRECY

Still another way for the executive branch to keep information from the Congress and the public is to require that its officials sign contractual secrecy agreements, pledging silence regarding any sensitive information they have come across in office. Once the official leaves public office, he or she must allow the government to review any subsequent writings or lectures by the individual in order to guard against the inclusion (inadvertent or otherwise) of classified material. While it may seem reasonable to require such contracts with people who will have access to classified information, critics argue that these agreements have been too broadly interpreted, stripping employees and former employees of their First Amendment rights to discuss and write about topics which would help inform the citizenry without jeopardizing the national interest.[73]

SECRECY AND DEMOCRACY

Clearly, concern about the protection of certain information within the executive branch makes sense. No American wants to endanger the lives of public servants in the U.S. intelligence agencies, for instance, and no one wants to reveal the other "good" secrets. The record indicates, however, that these secrets have been fairly well contained. As one U.S. senator has observed, "secrets that ought to be kept are being kept. For example, with the single exception of the book by Philip Agee [a CIA officer who defected and wrote a book, entitled *Inside the Company*, which revealed the names of some agency officers abroad]. . . there has been little or no disclosure of CIA sources or methods; or of the confidentiality of sensitive negotiations, such as preceded the partial test ban treaty, SALT I, and the release of the Pueblo crew [a U.S. spy ship captured by North Korea]."[74]

The most egregious security breaches have come from within the executive branch itself, not from former employees, investigative reporters, legislators, or other "outsiders." The Department of State leaked highly classified information to a writer preparing a favorable profile on then-Secretary of State Henry Kissinger in 1975, for instance, with no legal action taken against the leaker.[75] In the same year, at a briefing for the American Institute of Aeronautics and Astronautics, CIA officials disclosed intelligence estimates that Israel possessed ten to twenty nuclear weapons "ready and available for use"—another highly classified subject.[76] More serious still, the CIA and other intelligence agencies have had personnel who sold secrets to the KGB; Edward Lee Howard, the Walker family, and William Kampiles number among these traitors.[77] Improved counterintelligence within the executive branch—that is, closer supervision of its own personnel—would do more to protect the "good" secrets than measures taken against the First Amendment rights of reporters and other scribblers.

Most worrisome is the use of secrecy to conceal information necessary for the electorate to evaluate their leaders. Study after study on the classification system concludes that the government classifies too many documents, and at too high a level of secrecy. Sometimes this is done simply to remove embarrassing policy errors from the purview of the public; at other times it may involve bureaucratic gamesmanship—piquing the interest of the boss with the titillation "Top Secret." Whatever the reason, the end result has been to keep mountains of information away from the public which might be necessary for them to make an informed judgment about future foreign policy directions. The Pentagon Papers, in the opinion of a Supreme Court majority, held out little prospect for true damage to the United States—despite their top-secret classification—but did serve to inform Americans about the course of U.S. involvement in Indochina. Other government secrets have been equally dubious: the files on illegal FBI, CIA, and NSA domestic operations, the Watergate tape transcripts, reports on atrocities committed by GIs in Vietnam (the My Lai village scandal), and the secret bombing missions in Cambodia, among others.

This form of secrecy, usually evoked in the name of "national security," has been designed more to keep a "meddlesome" public and their representatives in Congress out of the policy process, and to ensure executive domination over the government—sometimes at the agency level against even the will of the president. As the historian Arthur Schlesinger has noted: "By the 1960s and 1970s, the religion of secrecy had become an all-purpose means by which the American Presidency sought to dissemble its purpose, bury its mistakes, manipulate its citizens, and maximize its power."[78]

The executive branch has developed to a high art various methods of evading legislative and public scrutiny over its conduct of foreign affairs. The sale of arms to Iran during the Reagan administration revealed anew how simple it is for the executive branch to carry out policy without legislative consultation, despite the existence of laws to the contrary. First, the president merely "waived" the existing arms

---

Perspectives on American Foreign Policy   *8.3*

Former Department of State senior official Charles W. Yost on secrecy:

"National security" is a godsend. It enables a government official to justify keeping his actions and intentions secret even when they might lead the nation into war.

Genuine considerations of national security may require secrecy in regard to the character and deployment of certain weapons. In my thirty-five years in foreign affairs, however, I almost never found that the public disclosure of political measures or plans could be truthfully said to jeopardize national security or be more than temporarily inconvenient.

Once "national security" has come to be accepted as a cloak for the conduct of foreign affairs, it is all too likely that public officials will find it irresistibly convenient for cloaking also some of their more far-out domestic activities. In fact, once they slip into the national security psychosis, they easily begin to equate, as we have so often seen, the nation's security with their own political power or their partisan aims.

From "Security Cloak Has Way of Deceiving the Deceiver," *Baltimore Sun*, November 3, 1973, p. 17, cited by Raoul Berger, *Executive Privilege: A Constitutional Myth* (Cambridge, Mass.: Harvard University Press, 1974), p. 369. Reprinted by permission.

---

embargo against Iran by signing a secret executive order. Then the president refused to inform the Congress of the shipment, despite laws mandating a report (among them, the 1980 Intelligence Oversight Act). His national security adviser, Vice Admiral Poindexter, lamely explained to the press that "there will always be special circumstances . . . involving human lives . . . [when the executive branch might have to ignore the law]."[79]

In the aftermath of Watergate and Vietnam, the intention of government reformers was to gain greater access to information held within the tight grasp of executive officials. Put simply, an increasing number of people outside the NSC, the CIA, and other inner sanctums of the executive domain wished to know which way America was headed. To know would place them in a better position to advise, and perhaps to help avoid disasters like the Bay of Pigs, as well as questionable practices like assassination plots, the secret sale of weapons to terrorists, and other ill-fated covert actions—the subject of the next chapter.

SUMMARY

Since the War of Independence, the use of secret agencies to gather and analyze information and to carry out secret operations—strategic intelligence—has been an integral part of American foreign policy. At the heart of the collection-and-analysis mission is the intelligence cycle, a sequence of procedures followed by the secret agencies to provide the best information available for policymakers. The cycle consists of five major phases: planning, collection, processing, production and analysis, and dissemination. Each phase has revealed imperfections, especially the dissemination phase, in which policymakers (the "consumers" of intelligence reports) may discard the findings of the analysts (the "producers") on ideological grounds—or simply fail to even consider the findings for lack of time or interest.

Strategic intelligence has been a vital part of American foreign policy—most notably in its capability to keep an eye on U.S. adversaries through satellites and other methods of surveillance. This mutual ability to watch one another has allowed the United States and the Soviet Union a sense of assurance that they would not be the victims of a surprise attack and, as a result, has dampened down the dangers of a world war.

The control of strategic intelligence, however, has led to bitter disputes between the branches of government. Secrecy in the pursuit of American foreign policy has been attractive to executive officials since the nation's earliest days. Some "good" secrets need to be kept closely guarded, such as the names of U.S. intelligence agents abroad, advanced weapons designs, and strategies for international negotiations. Other secrets are less defensible, such as efforts to conceal mistakes within the government and attempts to bypass constitutional procedures like the formal appropriations process (as occurred during the Iran-contra scandal of 1985–1986).

Other forms of obfuscation used by the executive branch to avoid public debate over its policies have included the use of executive privilege, delay and deceit, prior restraint, and contractual secrecy. In general, the Congress and the courts have sought openness, while the executive branch has preferred the shadowy world of secrecy. For a democracy to function properly, the citizenry must be informed; yet, paradoxically, the republic itself could be endangered by foreign threats if all its external relations were conducted in the open. The challenge for democracy is to determine and maintain the proper balance between necessary secrecy, on the one hand, and open debate—the lifeblood of democracy—on the other hand.

KEY TERMS

strategic intelligence
espionage
analysis
special activities
Central Intelligence Agency (CIA)
director of the Central Intelligence Agency (DCIA)
director of Central Intelligence (DCI)
National Security Agency (NSA)
deputy director for operations (DDO)
deputy director for science and technology (DDS&T)
deputy director for administration (DDA)
deputy director for intelligence (DDI)
chief of station (COS)
case officer
"assets"
intelligence cycle
verification

tasking
estimates
current intelligence
predictive intelligence
research intelligence
HUMINT and TECHINT
analysts
President's Daily Brief (PDB)
Interagency Intelligence Memo (IIM)
National Intelligence Estimate (NIE)
compartmentation
executive privilege
U.S. v. Nixon
stonewalling
prior restraint
Pentagon Papers

NOTES

1. See *Intelligence in the War of Independence,* Central Intelligence Agency, Washington, D.C., 1975.

2. For a useful lexicon of modern intelligence terms, see "Foreign and Military Intelligence," *Final Report of the Select Committee to Study Governmental Operations with Respect to Intelligence Activities* (hereafter the Church committee), Book I, U.S. Senate Report No. 94-755, April 23, 1976, pp. 617–629.

3. Statement by Senator John Tower (R-Tex.), Church committee hearings, May 21, 1975, Washington, D.C.

4. See Robert Wallace, "The Barbary Wars," *Smithsonian,* January 1975, p. 21.

5. See William R. Corson, *The Armies of Ignorance: The Rise of the American Intelligence Empire* (New York: Dial, 1977), Chap. 2.

6. See Roberta Wohlstetter, *Pearl Harbor: Warning and Decision* (Stanford, Calif.: Stanford University Press, 1962).

7. The necessary fin adjustment was devised by the Japanese less than 2 months before the Pearl Harbor attack. See *ibid.,* p. 369; also, John Deane Potter, *Yamamoto: The Man Who Menaced America* (New York: Viking, 1965), p. 53.

8. See Seth W. Richardson (general counsel for the Joint Congressional Investigating Committee on Pearl Harbor), "Why Were We Caught Napping at Pearl Harbor?" *Saturday Evening Post,* May 24, 1947, pp. 79–80.

9. See Wohlstetter, *op. cit.,* pp. 55–56, 225, 387.

10. On Roosevelt's state of mind at this time, see Edward S. Barkin and L. Michael Meyer, "COMINT and Pearl Harbor: FDR's Mistake," *International Journal of Intelligence and Counterintelligence,* vol. 2, Winter 1988, pp. 513–532. On the hoarding of intelligence data, see Alvin D. Coox, "Pearl Harbor," in Noble Frankland and Christopher Dowling, eds., *Decisive Battles of the Twenti-*

eth Century (New York: McKay, 1976), p. 148; Edwin T. Layton (with Roger Pineau and John Costello), *"And I Was There": Pearl Harbor and Midway—Breaking the Secrets* (New York: Morrow, 1985); and Wohlstetter, *op. cit.,* p. 394.

11. Richard C. Snyder and Edgar S. Furniss, Jr., *American Foreign Policy* (New York: Rinehart, 1954), p. 229.

12. Cited by Merle Miller, *Plain Speaking: An Oral Biography of Harry S. Truman* (New York: Berkley, 1973), p. 420, note.

13. Harry Howe Ransom, *The Intelligence Establishment* (Cambridge, Mass.: Harvard University Press, 1970), p. 81.

14. Quoted by Victor Marchetti and John D. Marks, *The CIA and the Cult of Intelligence* (New York: Knopf, 1974), p. 70.

15. On the structure of the intelligence community, see Jeffrey T. Richelson, *The U.S. Intelligence Community* (Cambridge, Mass.: Ballinger, 1985); on the National Security Agency, see James Bamford, *The Puzzle Palace: A Report on America's Most Secret Agency* (Boston: Houghton Mifflin, 1982).

16. Author's interview with intelligence official, September 12, 1979, Washington, D.C.

17. Harry Rositzke, *The CIA's Secret Operations* (Pleasantville, N.Y.: Reader's Digest General Books, 1977), p. 208.

18. Marchetti and Marks, *op. cit.,* p. 90.

19. Quoted by Senator Frank Church, *Congressional Record,* January 27, 1976, p. 1165.

20. National Security Act of 1947, signed on July 26, 1947 [50 U.S.C. 401 note].

21. These remarks on counterintelligence draw upon the author's research (with John Elliff) conducted for the Church committee (*Final Report,* Book I, pp. 163–173).

22. *Fact Book on Intelligence* (Washington, D.C.: Central Intelligence Agency, April 1983), p. 17.

23. See Arthur S. Hulnick, "The Intelligence Producer–Policy Consumer Linkage: A Theoretical Approach," *Intelligence and National Security*, vol. 1, May 1986, pp. 212–233.

24. *Fact Book on Intelligence.*

25. Report of the Secretary of Defense to the Congress of the FY 1982 Budget, January 19, 1981.

26. Quoted in Theodore H. White, "Weinberger on the Ramparts," *New York Times Magazine*, February 6, 1983, p. 19.

27. Written by a senior CIA analyst, February 21, 1974, mimeograph, and provided to the Church committee in September 1975.

28. Remarks by DDI Robert M. Gates, "Developments in the Soviet Union: Implications for U.S. Intelligence," Security Affairs Support Association, Fall 1988 Symposium, Washington, D.C.; Gates warns that new advances in Soviet weaponry may necessitate increased funding for collection and analysis against the USSR, especially in order to monitor the status of Soviet directed-energy weapons, mobile weapons, chemical and biological warfare potential, and advanced telecommunications capabilities. See, also, Gates, "The CIA and American Foreign Policy," *Foreign Affairs*, vol. 66, Winter 1987–1988, pp. 215–230.

29. Press conference, November 30, 1978, answer to question 16.

30. Quoted by Suzanne Garment, "Casey's Shadows: A Greater Emphasis on CIA Analysis," *Wall Street Journal*, July 16, 1982, p. 16.

31. Robert M. Gates, *Conference on U.S. Intelligence: The Organization and the Profession*, Central Intelligence Agency, Langley, Va., June 11, 1984.

32. *Ibid.*

33. Ransom, *op. cit.*, p. 20.

34. See Thomas Powers, *The Man Who Kept the Secrets: Richard Helms and the CIA* (New York: Knopf, 1979), p. 447, note 6. On the weakness of U.S. HUMINT estimates regarding the number of Soviet troops in Cuba during the missile crisis, see Raymond L. Garthoff, "Cuban Missile Crisis: The Soviet Story," *Foreign Policy* 72 (Fall 1988), p. 67.

35. Interview with CIA officer, June 11, 1984.

36. Interview with CIA officer, June 12, 1984.

37. Gary D. Brewer and Paul Bracken, "Some Missing Pieces of the C^3 Puzzle," *Journal of Conflict Resolution*, vol. 28, September 1984, p. 453.

38. Gates, *Conference on U.S. Intelligence*, June 11, 1984.

39. *Strategic Intelligence for American World Policy* (Princeton, N.J.: Princeton University Press, 1949), pp. 64–65.

40. *Military Review*, May 1961, p. 20, cited by Ransom, *op. cit.*, p. 147.

41. Richard K. Betts, "Analysis, War and Decision: Why Intelligence Failures Are Inevitable," *World Politics*, vol. 31, October 1978, p. 78.

42. *Conference on U.S. Intelligence*, June 13, 1984.

43. Gates, *Conference on U.S. Intelligence*, June 11, 1984.

44. Arthur S. Hulnick, *Conference on Intelligence, Policy and Process*, U.S. Air Force Academy, Colorado Springs, Colo., June 6, 1984.

45. Based on remarks by senior CIA officials, *Conference on Intelligence, Policy and Process*, and *Conference on U.S. Intelligence* (June 11, 1984), as well as (on the Korean airline shoot-down) Seymour M. Hersh, *"The Target Is Destroyed"* (New York: Vintage, 1987). For additional complaints about a Reagan administration bias toward "intelligence to please," see Lee H. Hamilton (chairman of the House Permanent Select Committee on Intelligence, D-Ind.), "View from the Hill," in *Extracts from Studies in Intelligence* (Langley, Va.: Central Intelligence Agency, September 1987), p. 68; and the testimony of Secretary of State George P. Shultz, *Hear-*

ings of the Joint Select Committee to Investigate Covert Arms Transactions with Iran (the Inouye-Hamilton committees, after cochairmen Senator Daniel K. Inouye, D-Hawaii, and Representative Lee H. Hamilton), U.S. Congress, July 1987, hereafter the Inouye-Hamilton committees.

46. Author's interviews with government officials, Washington, D.C., December 19–20, 1978.

47. Gates, *Conference on U.S. Intelligence*, June 11, 1984.

48. *Ibid.*

49. CIA analyst Arthur S. Hulnick, public lecture, University of Georgia, Athens, November 20, 1984.

50. Gates, *Conference on U.S. Intelligence*, June 11, 1984, original emphasis.

51. *Conference on U.S. Intelligence*, June 11, 1984.

52. *Ibid.*

53. *Ibid.*

54. *Ibid.*

55. Letter written by George Washington (1777), private collection, Walter Pforzheimer, Washington, D.C., reprinted in the *Yale Alumni Magazine and Journal*, December 1983.

56. Henry A. Kissinger, *Years of Upheaval* (Boston: Little, Brown, 1982).

57. Testimony, *Hearings before the Inouye-Hamilton Committees*, vol. 8, p. 159.

58. Hamilton, *ibid.*, July 21, 1987.

59. See Loch K. Johnson, *A Season of Inquiry: Congress and Intelligence* (Chicago: Dorsey, 1988).

60. See Hersh, *op. cit.*

61. On questionable propaganda operations carried out by the Reagan administration, see Robert Parry and Peter Kornbluh, "Iran-Contra's Untold Story," *Foreign Policy*, vol. 7, Fall 1988, pp. 3–30, as well as the exchange of letters in subsequent issues between the authors and defenders of the administration. For an account of the bombing raid on Libya, see Seymour M. Hersh, "Target Qaddafi," *New York Times Magazine*, February 22, 1987, p. 16.

62. Bill Moyers, "Moyers: The Secret Government—The Constitution in Crisis," Public Affairs Television, November 4, 1987.

63. Thomas M. Franck and Edward Weisband, *Foreign Policy by Congress* (New York: Oxford University Press, 1979), p. 160.

64. Arthur M. Schlesinger, Jr., *The Imperial Presidency* (Boston: Houghton Mifflin, 1973), p. 251.

65. Herb Altman, ed., *Quotations from Chairman Sam* (New York: Harper & Row, 1973), p. 31.

66. *New York Times*, February 26, 1976.

67. Raoul Berger, *Executive Privilege: A Constitutional Myth* (Cambridge, Mass.: Harvard University Press, 1974), p. 7.

68. *New York Times*, November 17, 1986, p. 7.

69. See John H. Glenn, "The Mini-Hiroshima near Cincinnati," *New York Times*, January 24, 1989, p. 27.

70. Berger, *op. cit.*, p. 14.

71. 403 U.S. 713, 91 S.Ct. 2140, 29 L.Ed.2d 822 (1971).

72. Emphasis added; on this case, see Sanford Unger, *The Papers and "The Papers"* (New York: Sutton, 1972).

73. See Frank Snepp, "Protect Rights of All Privy to U.S. Secrets," *New York Times*, February 22, 1984, p. 27.

74. Interview with Senator Frank Church, Washington, D.C., October 16, 1976; see, also, Frank Church, "Which Secrets Should Be Kept Secret?" *Washington Post*, March 14, 1977. The Agee book is *Inside the Company: CIA Diary* (Harmondsworth, England: Penguin, 1975).

75. See William Safire, "Henry's Leaked Secrets," *New York Times*, March 8, 1976.

76. See the *Washington Post*, March 15, 1976, and the *New York Times*, March 16, 1976.

77. See, for example, David Wise, "The Spy Who Got Away," *New York Times Magazine*, November 2, 1986, p. 18.

78. Quoted in Alistair Buchan, "Questions about Vietnam," in Richard Falk, ed., *The Vietnam War and International Law*, Vol. 2 (Princeton, N.J.: Princeton University Press, 1969), p. 345.

79. Interview, *ABC Evening News*, November 18, 1986.

RECOMMENDED READINGS

Barron, John. *KGB: The Secret Work of Soviet Secret Agents* (Pleasantville, New York: Reader's Digest General Books, 1974). A standard work on Soviet intelligence operations.

Berger, Raoul. *Executive Privilege: A Constitutional Myth* (Cambridge, Mass.: Harvard University Press, 1974). A comprehensive and strongly critical legal history on the use of executive privilege.

Berkowitz, Bruce D., and Allan E. Goodman. *Strategic Intelligence for American National Security* (Princeton, N.J.: Princeton University Press, 1989). A sophisticated examination of the central role that strategic intelligence now plays in America's external relations.

Betts, Richard K. "Analysis, War and Decision: Why Intelligence Failures Are Inevitable," *World Politics*, vol. 31, October 1978. An essay with the thesis that every nation will have intelligence failures, because human beings make mistakes.

Cline, Ray S. *Secrets, Spies, and Scholars: Blueprint of the Essential CIA* (Washington, D.C.: Acropolis, 1976). A look inside the CIA by a former deputy director for intelligence.

Colby, William F., and Peter Forbath, *Honorable Men: My Life in the CIA* (New York: Simon & Schuster, 1978). Former CIA Director Colby's memoirs.

Corson, William R. *The Armies of Ignorance: The Rise of the American Intelligence Empire* (New York: Dial, 1977). A good history of the U.S. intelligence establishment.

Flanagan, Stephen J. "The Coordination of Intelligence," in Duncan L. Clarke, ed., *Public Policy and Political Institutions: United States Defense and Foreign Policy: Coordination and Integration* (Greenwich, Conn.: JAI Press, 1985). A sophisticated study of the bureaucratic strengths and weaknesses within the U.S. intelligence organization.

Franck, Thomas M., and Edward Weisband, ed. *Secrecy and Foreign Policy* (New York: Oxford University Press, 1974). An excellent compilation of essays in search of the proper balance between secrecy and openness in the conduct of American foreign policy.

Godson, Roy, ed. *Intelligence Requirements for the 1990s: Collection, Analysis, Counterintelligence and Covert Action* (Lexington, Mass.: Heath, 1989). A collection of essays on intelligence issues, with distinct cold war overtones.

Halperin, Morton H., and Daniel N. Hoffman. *Top Secret: National Security and the Right to Know* (Washington, D.C.: New Republic Books, 1977). A discussion of the ill effects of overclassification in the government, which, the authors maintain, deprives decision makers of the important advantages accrued from public debate.

Johnson, Loch K. *A Season of Inquiry: The Congress and Intelligence* (Chicago: Dorsey, 1988). An account of the Church committee investigation into the intelligence agencies in 1975.

Karalekas, Anne. "History of the Central Intelligence Agency," *Supplementary Detailed Staff Reports*, Book IV, the Church committee, U.S. Senate, April 23, 1976. A detailed tracing of the evolution of intelligence within the U.S. government, with an emphasis on decision-making patterns and attempts at oversight.

Knight, Amy W. *The KGB: Police and Politics in the Soviet Union* (Winchester, Mass.: Unwin Hyman, 1989). A valuable updating of John Baron's work on Soviet intelligence.

Marchetti, Victor, and John D. Marks. *The CIA and the Cult of Intelligence* (New York: Knopf, 1974). Two disgruntled intelligence officers provide a revealing and critical look inside the CIA.

May, Ernest R., ed. *Knowing One's Enemies: Intelligence Assessments before the World Wars* (Princeton, N.J.: Princeton University Press, 1985). An excellent collection of articles on intelligence issues.

Powers, Thomas. *The Man Who Kept the Secrets: Richard Helms and the CIA* (New York: Knopf, 1979). A fascinating account of the CIA, written in a lively fashion by a journalist with access to the elusive former CIA Director Richard Helms.

Ranelagh, John. *The Agency: The Rise and Decline of the CIA* (New York: Touchstone, 1987). The most comprehensive history of the CIA, especially valuable for its treatment of the early years.

Ransom, Harry Howe. *The Intelligence Establishment* (Cambridge, Mass.: Harvard University Press, 1970). A reliable study of the workings and problems of U.S. intelligence, written by a leading light among intelligence scholars.

Richelson, Jeffrey T., and Desmond Ball. *The Ties That Bind* (Boston: Allen & Unwin, 1985). An exhaustive inventory of differences and likenesses among the intelligence services of the United States, Great Britain, Australia, and New Zealand.

Rositzke, Harry. *CIA's Secret Operations: Espionage, Counter Espionage, and Covert Action* (Pleasantville, New York: Reader's Digest General Books, 1977). A lively and balanced account written by a former CIA insider.

Turner, Stansfield. *Secrecy and Democracy: The CIA in Transition* (Boston: Houghton Mifflin, 1985). Former CIA Director Admiral Turner's reflections on his watch at the agency—and his self-confessed failure to bring the organization under control.

THE IRAN-CONTRA AFFAIR

   Congress and the Contras

   The Privatization of American Foreign Policy

   The Contra Diversion

COVERT ACTION

   Propaganda

   Political Covert Action

   Economic Covert Action

   The Paramilitary Option

   Accountability versus Micromanagement

THE SECRET WAR AGAINST CHILE

COVERT ACTION: WHAT LIMITS?

INTELLIGENCE DECISION MAKING

   Congress Seeks Tighter Controls over Intelligence Policy

   Decision Procedures within the Executive Branch

   Reporting to Congress

   Legislative Prerogatives

INTELLIGENCE AND PROPRIETY

SUMMARY

AMERICA'S SECRET POWER: THE HIDDEN HAND OF THE CIA

Cuban exiles trained by the CIA practice their paramilitary skills in the Florida Everglades in anticipation of their ill-fated Bay of Pigs attack against Cuba in 1961. (Camera Press)

THE IRAN-CONTRA AFFAIR

In its conduct of foreign affairs, nothing so captured the Reagan administration's attention as the machinations of the Soviet Union—an "evil empire," said the president in 1983, whose aggressive intentions around the world had to be thwarted. Not since the 1950s had the government of the United States aimed such harsh rhetoric at its chief adversary. And, soon, no country was deemed more important to the administration as a test of U.S. will in this global struggle against communism than Nicaragua in Central America. America would not practice appeasement; Reagan would not be Neville Chamberlain; Managua would not be Munich.

Congress and the Contras

Yet, Congress had a different view of the civil war in Nicaragua, fought between the Marxist Sandinista regime and, operating chiefly out of jungle sanctuaries in neighboring Honduras, the contras—counterrevolutionaries backed by the CIA. Though few, if any, members of Congress trusted the Sandinistas, with their ties to the Soviet Union, most found the contras equally unattractive. A sizable percentage of the contras had been members of the corrupt, often brutal, National Guard in the previous Somoza regime, which—to the joy of most Nicaraguans—the Sandinistas had overthrown. An official in the Reagan administration observed in an internal memorandum (later disclosed by congressional investigators) that several of the contra leaders were "not first-rate people. They're liars, greed- and power-motivated. This war has become a business to many of them."[1] Moreover, the contras seemed to have little chance for success in their hopes to dislodge the revolutionary government. The Congress was further concerned about a negative reaction throughout Latin America if the United States intervened too blatantly. Those nations south of the American border harbored bitter memories of the many invasions carried out against their homelands by the U.S. Marine Corps earlier in the century.

Members of Congress were troubled, though, by the possible export of Marxist revolution to other countries of Central America and, eventually, to Mexico—a domino theory for the western hemisphere. Therefore, reluctantly, a majority supported early initiatives in the Reagan administration to interdict alleged shipments of arms from the Sandinistas to Marxist rebels in the jungles of El Salvador. Few weapons shipments were ever discovered. "We did not find a mouse," remembers a high-ranking official in the CIA.[2]

A more ambitious agenda soon emerged, however, in the Reagan administration: nothing less than the overthrow of the Sandinistas. The contras turned from interdiction missions to the use of explosives against power lines, the bombing of airports, and other tactics designed to disrupt the regime. At first, this escalation remained hidden from Congress and the American people; but fact-finding trips to Nicaragua by legislators, coupled with press reports from the region, uncovered the real agenda. Congress then moved to place tougher legislative restrictions on the contras, beginning in 1982 and growing more restrictive over the next several years, eventually resulting in a ban on all funding of lethal assistance. This series of *Boland amendments* (named after their chief sponsor, Edward P. Boland, D-Mass.) soon became the bugaboo of the Reagan administration. In frustration over legislative interference in its holy war against communism, the president's men resorted to more secretive methods that would eventually rock the administration with scandal.

The Privatization of American Foreign Policy

Blocked by Congress from supplying the contra "freedom fighters" (in the expression of the president, who said he viewed the contras as the "moral equivalent" of America's Founding Fathers) through the normal appropriations process, officials in the CIA and on the NSC staff began a "privatization" of Reagan's foreign policy. Funds would be raised through private, extraconstitutional means. Wealthy conservatives and foreign nations—Israel, South Africa, and oil-rich Saudi Arabia and Brunei, among others—were quietly asked to provide funds to the contras in exchange for an audience with the president in the Oval Office, in the case of private citizens, as well as undisclosed foreign policy favors for cooperative nations.

Some of the deals have since come to light. Then Vice President George Bush offered, for example, secret assurances to the leaders of Honduras: if they cooperated by allowing the contras to use their country as a military staging area for attacks against neighboring Nicaragua, the United States would increase its foreign aid to Honduras. The American beer tycoon Joseph Coors contributed $65,000 toward the purchase of an airplane for the contras; the king of Saudi Arabia provided $1 million a month, later doubling the figure for several months; and the sultan of Brunei sent $10 million to a designated Swiss bank account.

The Congress of the United States could be bypassed. When it disagreed with the president, its dissent would be as irrelevant to foreign policy as the appendix to the digestive system. According to Lieutenant Colonel Oliver L. North, the NSC staff official at the center of the fund-raising, through these efforts (known by insiders as "the Enterprise") the director of the CIA, William J. Casey, hoped to establish—out of sight from Congress and the American people, free from the constraints of debate and the formal appropriations process, unfettered by the nay-sayers on Capitol Hill—an "off-the-shelf, self-sustaining, stand-alone entity, that could perform certain activities [read secret operations abroad] on behalf of the United States."[3] At last: foreign policy by the president—or the CIA—alone.

Growing out of the administration's concern

over the well-being of American hostages held by various terrorist groups in the Middle East came another "Enterprise" idea for contra funding. Among the hostages was William Buckley, the CIA's top man (COS) in Lebanon. Director Casey was prepared to move heaven and earth to rescue this officer, and the president also wanted to see him and the other hostages brought home. A possible solution seemed to be the sale of weapons to Iran in return for this nation's influence over the terrorists holding the hostages.

Yet, Congress might well have found this deal unacceptable—providing arms to, of all places, Iran, a country itself known as a haven for terrorists which had kept fifty-two Americans captive for over 400 days during the Carter administration. Arms for hostages, legislators might reasonably argue, would lead only to the taking of more hostages when terrorists needed additional arms. The administration did not want a national debate, however; it wanted William Buckley. The plan, therefore, had to be concealed from Congress, even though existing laws (the Hughes-Ryan Act of 1974 and the Intelligence Oversight Act of 1980) clearly required the president to report to the House and Senate intelligence committees on all secret arms sales and other covert actions.

The Contra Diversion

Enter the next "Enterprise" venture. If Iran would pay cash for weapons, why not divert the profits to the contras? How splendid and ironic, thought North and his close circle of confidants: Iran's leader, the Ayatollah Ruhollah Khomeini, who had caused so much grief to the United States in the past, could now help pay for the cold war! "The Enterprise" sprang into action, and with retired Air Force General Richard V. Secord acting as a go-between, the government of Iran was told to place its money in a Swiss bank account, from where it was later forwarded to the contras—after Secord and his operatives skimmed off large

"agent fees" for themselves. (Meanwhile, another retired officer, Army general John Singlaub, relieved of his command for insubordination in 1977, was busily raising additional funds for the contras from private groups through his World Anti-Communist League.)

And to make sure that Congress would never know about the arms sales and the diversion, North would shred all the telltale documents. Moreover, he and other officials would lie to inquisitive legislators, if necessary.[4] Despite all these precautions, news of the arms sale leaked via a Middle East magazine, leading to a full-scale investigation by the U.S. Congress and the resulting scandal.

Even the president, according to his national security adviser John Poindexter, was never told of the diversion, so that later he could credibly disclaim any knowledge of the operation if the Congress somehow found out about it (a doctrine known as *plausible deniability* and roundly criticized by reformers in the 1970s for fuzzying the lines of accountability between the White House and the bureaucracy). Whether or not the president was truly unaware of the diversion, as he claimed when the operation came to light in 1986, or was relying on deniability to protect the office of the presidency (and his own political standing) remains a topic of conjecture and debate.

Less murky than the question of who within the administration knew what about the Iran-contra diversion was a central feature of the scandal: a contempt for Congress which led, in turn, to foreign policy by utmost secrecy. Officials in the Reagan administration seemed to have been driven by a shared obsession: the global war against communism. "I think it is very important for the American people to understand that this is a dangerous world," testified Lieutenant Colonel North before legislative investigators, in an attempt to justify his covert activities, "that we live at risk, and that this nation is at risk, in a dangerous world." Yet, the end result of the administration's approach to foreign policy was, according to a critic in the

---

Perspectives on American Foreign Policy   9.1

Vice Admiral John M. Poindexter, President Ronald Reagan's assistant for national security affairs, on plausible deniability during the Iran-contra operation:

The President was bound and determined and still is, that he will not sit still for the consolidation of a Communist government on the mainland of America. And in order to prevent that, he feels that the most effective way, with which I also agree, is to keep pressure on the Communist Sandinista Government. And the most effective way to do that, given all of the factors considered and because we don't want to send U.S. soldiers to Nicaragua, is to provide support to the contras and keep them alive until we can get the $100 million [in congressional appropriations]. . . .

And so after weighing all of these matters— and I also felt that I had the authority to approve it because I had a commission from the President which was in very broad terms. My role was to make sure that his policies were implemented. In this case, the policy was very clear, and that was to support the contras. After working with the President for five and a half years, the last three of which were very close and probably closer than any other officer in the White House except the chief of staff, I was convinced that I understood the President's thinking on this and that if I had

taken it to him that he would have approved it. [Note: This assertion was later denied by the president.]

Now I was not so naive as to believe that it was not a politically volatile issue; it clearly was because of the divisions that existed within the Congress on the issue of support for the contras. And it was clear that there would be a lot of people that would disagree, that would make accusations that indeed have been made. So although I was convinced that we could properly do it and that the President would approve if asked, I made a very deliberate decision not to ask the President so that I could insulate him from the decision and provide some future deniability for the President if it ever leaked out. Of course, our hope was that it would not leak out.

Q: When you say deniability, are you saying that your decision was not to tell the President so that he would be able to deny that he knew of it?

A: That's correct. . . .

Source: "The Iran-Contra Affair," *Hearings before the U.S. Senate Select Committee on Secret Military Assistance to Iran and the Nicaraguan Opposition and U.S. House of Representatives Select Committee to Investigate Covert Arms Transactions with Iran,* July 1987, Washington, D.C.

Senate, "the very thing that James Madison and others feared most when they were struggling to put the Constitution together, which was to create an accountable system which didn't have runaway power, which didn't concentrate power in one hand, so that you could have one person making a decision and running off against the will of the American people."[5]

The use of secret means to achieve America's foreign policy ends—the second half of what we mean by the phrase *strategic intelligence*—has been an attractive option to policymakers since

the founding of the republic, as mentioned in the preceding chapter. In the modern world, how is the hidden hand of the CIA brought into play by the United States in pursuit of its global objectives? Here is the central question of this chapter.

COVERT ACTION

The government initially established the Central Intelligence Agency, recall, in order to improve the coordination of intelligence collection and analysis; but almost immediately, covert action became a central preoccupation of officials within the agency and the White House. Former Secretary of State Henry Kissinger has explained why: "We need an intelligence community that, in certain complicated situations, can defend the American national interest in the gray areas where military operations are not suitable and diplomacy cannot operate."[6]

The main concern of covert-action practitioners has been, in the words of a former chief of the CIA Covert Action Staff (CAS), "the global challenge of communism . . . to be confronted whenever and wherever it seemed to threaten our interests."[7] Covert action (CA) has taken four major forms: propaganda, political, economic, and paramilitary (PM—secret warfare). These forms account, respectively, for about 40, 30, 10, and 20 percent of the total number of covert actions over the years—though paramilitary operations have been by far the most expensive and controversial. This chapter first briefly examines the forms of covert action, then traces the decision process by which this means is selected.

Propaganda

No form of covert action is used more extensively than *propaganda*. To supplement the flow of official information from U.S. embassies abroad, the CIA provides a flood of supportive material distributed secretly through its vast network of "media assets": reporters, newspaper and magazine editors, television producers—the whole range of media personnel. Whatever the White House may be pushing at the time, the CIA will likely be advancing the same themes through its covert channels—say, during the Carter administration, the glory of neutron bombs or Pershing missiles for Europe or, during the Reagan administration, perhaps, the political blackmail that could arise from European dependence on a Soviet oil pipeline or the pernicious influence of the KGB on the peace movement in western Europe.

In addition to this support for Department of State propaganda themes, the CIA will use its media assets to help or harm foreign political leaders or aspirants, depending upon how these individuals are apt to affect the interests of the United States. The classic example is the

---

Perspectives on American Foreign Policy **9.2**

DCI William E. Colby on covert action:

In a number of instances, some quiet assistance to democratic and friendly elements enabled them to resist authoritarian groups in an internal competition over the future direction of their countries. Post-war Western Europe resisted communist political subversion and Latin America rejected Cuban-stimulated insurgency. They thereby thwarted at the local level challenges that could have escalated to the international level. . . . That there can be debate as to the wisdom of any individual activity of this nature is agreed. That such a potential must be available for use in situations truly important to our country and the cause of peace is equally obvious.

Pacem in Terris IV Convocation, December 4, 1975, Washington, D.C.

CIA's effort to discredit the Chilean socialist leader, Salvador Allende.[8] In an unsuccessful attempt to halt his rise to power, the White House under President Nixon directed the CIA to use its assets against Allende. To help protect their own interests in Chile, the International Telephone and Telegraph (ITT) corporation and other American businesses threw $1.5 million of their own into the CIA pot (an example of foreign policy privatization preceding the Iran-contra affair)—indeed, the corporations strongly encouraged Nixon to intervene covertly in the first place, for fear that Allende might nationalize their holdings.

In the 1964 election alone, the CIA spent $3 million secretly in Chile to blacken the name of Allende and his party. Between 1963 and 1973, the CIA spent over $12 million in Chile on propaganda alone, not to mention additional moneys spent on other forms of covert action. The Church committee described the forms of propaganda employed in the 1964 election: "Extensive use was made of the press, radio, films, pamphlets, posters, leaflets, direct mailings, paper streamers, and wall paintings. It was a 'scare campaign,' which relied heavily on images of Soviet tanks and Cuban firing squads and was directed especially to women. Hundreds of thousands of copies of the anticommunist pastoral letter of Pope Pius XI were distributed by Christian Democratic organizations. . . ."[9]

The extensive CIA propaganda capability produces a great tide of information flowing unseen from Washington into hundreds of hidden channels around the world. Once released, the information cannot be bottled up or directed to only one spot on the globe, as one might apply an antiseptic to a sore. Rather, it is free to drift here and there, and even back to the United States. This can lead to *blow-back*, or *replay*, whereby false information directed toward America's enemies can find its way back home to deceive our own citizens—precisely the concern that led the State Department official Bernard Kalb to resign over the anti-

Qaddafi covert propaganda operations of the Reagan administration (Chapter 8).

Political Covert Action

Sometimes covert action takes the form of secret financial aid to friendly politicians and bureaucrats abroad—bribes, if one wishes to put a harsh light on the practice, or stipends to advance the cause of democracy, if one prefers a rosier interpretation. Whatever one wishes to call this assistance ("King George's cavalry" is the expression used in British intelligence), the record is clear that through the CIA the United States has provided substantial sums of money to various political parties, leaders, and would-be leaders around the world—*political covert action*.

At times the Covert Action Staff at CIA headquarters has resembled nothing so much as a group of political campaign consultants, producing slick materials for favorable foreign candidates: brochures, bumper stickers, speech drafts, placards, even campaign buttons for remote regions of the world where they have never been seen before. The CIA sent to an anticommunist faction in one African civil war 50,000 political lapel buttons proclaiming the partisan affiliation of the wearer: "I am a member of the —————— Party." Battlefield results proved more significant than lapel buttons, however, and the CIA's side retreated to the hinterland.[10]

Economic Covert Action

Another approach is to disrupt the economies of America's enemies through secret means—*economic covert action*. In one instance during the Kennedy years (though without the knowledge of the president), the CIA tried to damage Cuban-Soviet relations by lacing sugar bound from Havana to Moscow with an unpalatable, though harmless, chemical substance. A White House aide caught wind of the operation and informed the president, who rejected the idea

---

Perspectives on American Foreign Policy 9.3

The covert-action project "Elimination by Illumination," proposed by the CIA to depose Fidel Castro of Cuba:

This plan consisted of spreading the word that the Second Coming of Christ was imminent and that Christ was against Castro [who] was anti-Christ. And you would spread this word around Cuba, and then on whatever date it was, that there would be a manifestation of this thing. And at that time—this is absolutely true—and at that

time just over the horizon there would be an American submarine which would surface off of Cuba and send up some starshells. And this would be the manifestation of the Second Coming and Castro would be overthrown.

Testimony of a senior Operations Directorate officer to the Church committee; see *Alleged Assassination Plots Involving Foreign Leaders: An Interim Report*, November 20, 1975, p. 181, note.

---

and quickly had the 14,125 bags of sugar confiscated before they left for the Soviet Union.[11]

During the efforts to undermine Allende, the CIA used various overt and covert measures to disrupt the Chilean economy. By heightening the level of unrest in the regime, the U.S. government hoped that the local military forces would finally decide to strip Allende of his power. Inciting labor strikes was one proposal considered by the CIA. Senior agency officials eventually rejected this option; but the CIA nonetheless continued to provide moneys to groups in Chile directly involved in strike tactics, especially within the trucking industry, in an attempt to impede the flow of commerce. As part of the Reagan administration's efforts to overthrow the Sandinista regime, the CIA-supported contras carried out a range of secret attacks against the Nicaraguan economy, including the mining of piers in the nation's main harbors to disrupt international shipping and the blowing-up of power lines throughout the countryside. Other economic operations have reportedly included the counterfeiting of foreign currencies, depressing the world price of sugar to undermine the Cuban economy, and the preparation of parasites to destroy foreign crops.

The Paramilitary Option

The most severe method of secret intervention has been *paramilitary covert action*. This approach to foreign policy encompasses the concealed use of U.S. military force overseas (for example, the covert war waged by the CIA against communist guerrillas in Laos during the 1960s); the unacknowledged sale of weapons abroad (like the Iranian arms scandal); the training, advising, and supplying of foreign surrogate troops—mercenaries—to fight on behalf of America's external interests (the contras and the Afghan mujahedeen, among others); antiterrorist and security training for foreign intelligence services; and assassination plots (Fidel Castro of Cuba was one CIA target). However convenient for presidents, the paramilitary approach has been fraught with controversy. It personifies, in extreme form, America's secret foreign policy and, argue critics who recoil from the CIA's murder plots and coups against foreign governments, the ultimate perversion of American ideals.

Paramilitary Authority The War Powers Resolution of 1973 establishes the procedures to be employed by the government in its use of overt military force short of a formal declaration of war (see Chapter 10); this important statute is silent, however, on the question of secret paramilitary operations. America's covert warfare is subject to a different set of legislative checks—namely, the Hughes-Ryan Act of 1974 and its strengthening successor, the Intelligence Oversight Act of 1980.[12] Before passage of these statutes, the executive branch enjoyed a freedom of discretion over paramilitary operations and the other covert actions that, in contrast, makes the much lamented "blank check" of the Tonkin Gulf Resolution (see Chapter 5) look like a finely embroidered contract.

In the days before Hughes-Ryan, officials drew upon the brief "catchall" passage of the 1947 National Security Act for paramilitary authority. This passage, recall, directed the CIA to "perform such other functions and duties related to intelligence affecting the national security as the National Security Council may from time to time direct."[13] Contemporary CIA attorneys have conceded that this language represents a questionable legal basis for paramilitary operations. They have turned instead to the Hughes-Ryan Act, in which the Congress officially recognized covert action as a policy option. At the very first meeting of the National Security Council in December of 1947, however, NSC officials relied upon the catchall passage to adopt NSC Directive No. 4/A, which ordered the CIA to engage in a variety of covert actions designed to combat international communism.[14]

From this moment until the enactment of the Hughes-Ryan legislation twenty-seven years later, decisions on the paramilitary option required only a brief meeting between the CIA director and the four statutory members of the NSC (the president, the vice president, and the secretaries of state and defense). Sometimes, according to one legislative inquiry, all that was necessary was a telephone call over a secure line from the CIA to NSC members or their designated staff aides for these matters.[15] Rarely was Congress in the decision loop. The CIA did

not want to tell, and, conveniently, the Congress did not want to know. The political risks might be too high for legislators if an operation went awry and became public; it was safer to remain untutored. One could then claim innocence and pillory the CIA for its poor judgment.

That the NSC was consistently apprised of paramilitary and other covert-action operations, let alone the Congress, proves to be a fiction. In 1975, a congressional committee found that out of the thousands of covert-action projects from 1949 to 1968, only 600 went before the NSC for approval.[16] The tendency seems to have been for the CIA to ask the NSC for broad grants of authority that would then become the sire of subsidiary operations—many arguably warranting separate and specific approval. One member of the NSC, Dean Rusk, the secretary of state for Presidents John Kennedy and Lyndon Johnson, apparently was in the dark on most CIA operations. "I never saw a budget of the CIA, for example, . . . " he remembers.[17] Nor does he or any other NSC official recollect any decisions or briefings on CIA assassination plots. All denied, under oath, knowledge of presidential authority for these PM operations—though clearly they took place.[18]

Today, with the Hughes-Ryan legislation and the 1980 Intelligence Oversight Act, the decision pathway for covert action (traced below) is much more comprehensive, requiring formal written authorizations from the president and reports to the legislative committees on intelligence. Paramilitary operations—indeed, all covert-action proposals—are expected by law to run this tougher decision gauntlet. The failure of the Reagan administration to honor these reporting requirements during the Iran-contra operation inflamed the scandal of 1986–1987.

Secret Wars   No covert actions have held higher risk or been subject to more controversy than paramilitary operations. While these operations have accounted for only 20 percent of the total number of covert actions in the postwar period, they can consume a much greater percentage of the CIA budget—over 50 percent during the height of the war in Vietnam. Sometimes called *special operations* or, simply, special ops (especially when carried out by the Department of Defense rather than the CIA), the paramilitary mission often involves nothing less than large-scale "secret" wars—as if anything of that magnitude could remain secret for long. From 1963 to 1973, the CIA backed the Meo hill tribes of northern Laos in a war against the North Vietnamese puppets, the Pathet Lao, in what was essentially a draw until the United States withdrew from the struggle.[19] The CIA has sponsored other guerrilla wars, providing support for insurgents in the Ukraine, Poland, Albania, Hungary, Indonesia, China, Oman, Malaysia, Iraq, the Dominican Republic, Venezuela, North Korea, Bolivia, Thailand, Haiti, Guatemala, Cuba, Chad, Mauritius, Lebanon, South Yemen, Cambodia, Suriname, Greece, Turkey, Vietnam, Afghanistan, Angola, and Nicaragua, to recall some operations on the public record.[20]

In addition to support for groups engaged in insurgency fighting, the CIA has funded various paramilitary training activities, including counterterrorist training. It has provided military advisers (usually "sheepdipped," that is, borrowed from the Pentagon and dressed in nonofficial battlefield gear); and has shipped abroad, directly or indirectly, arms, ammunition, and other military equipment. Further, the CIA paramilitary program has included assistance to the Department of Defense in the development of its own unconventional warfare capability.[21] During the Carter administration, when paramilitary and other covert actions were sharply curtailed because of the president's aversion to their unsavory moral implications, the specialists in this trade spent most of their time—partly in an attempt to justify their existence—in training, equipment maintenance, and (the overwhelming workload) support to intelligence-collection programs, particularly those involving specialized equipment and delivery techniques.

The Soviet invasion of Afghanistan in December of 1979 changed President Carter's views on covert action. He was so shocked and appalled by the use of brutal force by the Soviets that he began to endorse the wider use of paramilitary operations and the other range of covert actions throughout the world against Marxist-communist regimes, shedding his skin of moral qualm. When the Reagan administration came to office in 1981, paramilitary operations received a still larger slice of the CIA's budget as the cold war heated up to temperatures unseen since the 1950s. The Reagan Doctrine, the reader will remember, envisioned vigorous support for anticommunist insurgencies throughout the world, with covert action as the most viable and prudent modus operandi.

In Afghanistan and Nicaragua, among other Third World countries, paramilitary operations—chiefly the supply of weapons to indigenous guerrillas—attracted rising attention and funding from the Reagan administration, whose members remembered the "glory days" of covert action in the 1950s, when the CIA helped curb communist expansion in Europe and placed malleable pro-American officials in power in Iran (1953) and Guatemala (1954). Critics raised serious questions, however, about the value of the paramilitary option. They pointed to the disaster at the Bay of Pigs in 1961 when CIA-backed insurgents were defeated by Cuban regulars, and noted how the CIA-supported shah of Iran had been driven from office in 1979.[22] They also decried the blackening of America's name in the world as a result of CIA assassination attempts against foreign leaders during the 1960s.

Assassination Plots   The murder of individual enemies of the United States represents a special category of paramilitary activity. Over the years, the CIA developed a lethal storehouse of chemicals and several inventive delivery systems. The poisons, which included shellfish toxin ("saxitoxin") and cobra venom, were extensive and deadly enough to eliminate the entire population of a small city. One delivery system entailed first applying poison to a tiny dart the size of a sewing needle ("a nondiscernible microbioinoculator," it was called by an imaginative scientist in the CIA Directorate of Science and Technology), then using an electric dart gun (a "noise-free disseminator"), resembling a large .45 pistol with a telescopic sight, to propel the dart silently toward the victim. The gun was reputed in CIA documents to be accurate up to 250 feet—the ultimate murder weapon, able to kill without sound and with barely a trace.

Murder High Insofar as legislative investigators have been able to ascertain, the United States has resorted to assassination plots only infrequently and, at least with heads of state, never successfully—despite a goodly amount of trying in the instance of Fidel Castro. The Cuban president received the full attention of the CIA's Covert Action Staff: propaganda, political, economic, and paramilitary operations. The agency directed drugs and poisons his way through various ingenious, if unsuccessful, methods: depilatory powder in his shoes (meant to enter Castro's bloodstream and make his charismatic beard fall off), LSD and botulinum toxin in his cigars (to disorient in the first instance, kill in the second), Madura-foot fungus in his diving suit (causing a debilitating disease), and the deadly poison Blackleaf-40 readied for injection into his skin through the extraordinarily fine tip of a special ballpoint pen.

When these and similar efforts failed (for Castro is elusive and well protected by a KGB-trained corps of bodyguards), the CIA upped the ante. It hired organized crime figures, who still had contacts in Cuba from pre-Castro days when Havana was a world gambling center, to kill Castro. The mobster John Rosselli went to Florida on behalf of the agency in 1961 and

Senator Frank Church (D-Idaho), chairman of the Senate Select Committee on Intelligence, holds a CIA "dart gun" during hearings on September 16, 1975, as the committee's vice-chairman, Senator John Tower (R-Texas), looks on. Church said that orders from President Richard Nixon to destroy lethal toxins for use in this and other CIA weapons "were evidently directly disobeyed" by personnel in the secret agency. (UPI/Bettmann Newsphotos)

1962. His task was to assemble assassination teams of Cuban exiles who would infiltrate their homeland and try to take Castro's life. Rosselli in turn called upon two other crime figures: the Chicago gangster Sam Giancana and the Cosa Nostra chieftain for Cuba, Santos Trafficante. Giancana's role was to find someone in Castro's entourage who could drop poison pills into his food, and Trafficante was expected to serve as courier to Cuba and, once on the island, would help make arrangements for the murder. Several assassins were dispatched; none came close to fulfilling the mission.

A second major target for the CIA, during the final months of the Eisenhower administration, was the Congolese leader Patrice Lumumba. In the fall of 1960, the CIA's chief of station in the Congo (now called Zaire) received from headquarters via diplomatic pouch an unusual assortment of items: rubber gloves, gauze masks, a hypodermic syringe, and lethal biological toxins. As one CIA officer remembered with dark humor: "I knew it wasn't for somebody to get his polio shot up to date."[23] The enclosed instructions explained how to inject the poison into Lumumba's food or toothpaste to bring about his quick death.

As an alternative to poisoning Lumumba, the CIA station officer in the Congo recommended that the leader be shot, and cabled his request that a weapon be sent via diplomatic pouch: RECOMMEND HQS POUCH SOONEST HIGH POWERED FOREIGN MAKE RIFLE WITH TELESCOPIC SCOPE AND SILENCER. The cable ended cryptically: WOULD KEEP RIFLE IN OFFICE PENDING OPENING OF HUNTING SEASON, which meant (according to testimony before the Church committee by the CIA's African chief) that the weapon would not be used until final approval had been received from CIA headquarters. Before the COS was able to carry out any of these operations, however, Lumumba was killed at the hands of a rival Congolese faction.

Rafael Trujillo of the Dominican Republic, Ngo Dihn Diem of South Vietnam, and General Rene Schneider of Chile were actually killed by assassins who had once had connections with the CIA; but congressional investigators concluded after an exhaustive inquiry in 1975 that, at the time when each was murdered, the CIA no longer had control over the killers. The CIA also gave weapons to dissidents who then may have plotted murder against President Sukarno

---

Perspectives on American Foreign Policy   9.4

Former CIA Director John McCone (1961–1963) on Operation Mongoose, *the code name for a series of attempts to remove Fidel Castro from power in Cuba:*

Here was a man [Castro] who for a couple of years would seize every opportunity before a microphone or television to berate and criticize the United States in the most violent and unfair and incredible terms. Here was a man that was doing his utmost to use every channel of communication of every Latin American country to win them away from any of the principles that we stood for

and drive them into Communism. Here was a man that turned over the sacred soil of Cuba in 1962 to the Soviets to plant nuclear warhead shortrange missiles, which could destroy every city east of the Mississippi. This was the climate in which people had to think what to do. And before criticizing anything that was done, whether I knew of it or not—and I did not—I would think a little bit about the conditions of the time.

Press conference, Washington, D.C., June 6, 1975.

of Indonesia and François "Papa Doc" Duvalier of Haiti, but again the plots did not have the clear imprimatur of the CIA. Nevertheless, though the fingerprints of the CIA were missing, the agency seemed to have at least encouraged others to carry out its wishes on their own behalf.

In no instance, then, was a CIA finger actually on the trigger of any weapon aimed at a foreign leader. Technically, neither the CIA nor any other U.S. government agency had committed murder; but, through others, the government certainly tried. Whether the CIA acted on its own as a *rogue elephant* in these operations, off on a rampage of its own making, as a Senate critic once declared,[24] or followed presidential orders remains a subject of dispute.

For many reasons, congressional investigators on the Church committee found it incredibly difficult in 1975 to pinpoint responsibility for these murder plots. The presidents who might have been involved in the plots—Eisenhower, Kennedy, and Johnson—and several of their top aides were no longer alive to speak for themselves. Among the living, memories had faded, conveniently or otherwise; testimony conflicted; and some individuals seemed to yield to their sense of presidential loyalty and to instincts of self-protection. High on the list of obstacles between the committee and the truth was the system of decision making itself, particularly the doctrine of plausible deniability (which Vice Admiral Poindexter had resorted to during the Iran-contra affair), along with ambiguous grants of authority.

The purpose of plausible deniability (then as in the Reagan administration) was to sweep away footprints in a covert operation to prevent anyone from following the tracks back to the United States and, especially, to the Oval Office. Above all, the virtue of the nation was to be protected by shielding the reputation of the president. His office was to be disassociated—in memoranda, minutes, or other records—from the foul deeds that might be necessary in the rough-and-tumble world outside the United

States. If the CIA or other agencies found it necessary to discuss an "extralegal" or unsavory operation with the president in order to obtain his approval, euphemisms and doubletalk were to be used. This would leave the chief executive free to deny, plausibly, that he had granted authority for its execution. It was decision making by a wink and a nod.

This effort to escape from potential embarrassment—and responsibility—at the highest level of government led to vague directives from above and unpredictable responses from below. When high officials said they longed for some way to "get rid of" Castro (a phrase often found in the minutes of cabinet meetings during the Eisenhower and Kennedy eras), did they mean only that the CIA should encourage Cubans to demonstrate and hound him from office, or was this a wink and a nod to have the CIA arrange for his murder?

Uncertain, too, was how long the authority for a covert action, once so loosely granted, could last. The CIA was reluctant to discuss the black arts with the president and other high officials; consequently, authority once received often drifted or "floated" from year to year and from administration to administration, without explicit renewal—even within the agency itself. John McCone, successor to Allen Dulles as CIA director, was never told of agency ties to the underworld, for example, on the grounds that this was unnecessary since Dulles had approved the relationship.

In the face of these obstacles, congressional investigators remained unsure which of three theories regarding the origins of authority for the assassination plots might be true. Was "the theory of the rogue elephant" most accurate, in which the CIA had concocted plots on its own without higher authority? Or, perhaps, "the theory of presidential authority," in which the CIA had simply carried out the will of the president? Or had there been confusion over what the president had really intended the CIA to do, a "theory of misunderstanding"? In questioning a key witness, the former secretary of defense during the Kennedy administration, Robert S. McNamara, the chairman of the Senate investigative committee (Frank Church) expressed the growing frustration of his colleagues as they sought to pin down responsibility for the plots:

> Now, you see what we are faced with in this dilemma. Either the CIA was a rogue elephant rampaging out of control, over which no effective direction was being given in this matter of assassination, or there was some secret channel circumventing the whole structure of command by which the CIA and certain officials in the CIA were authorized to proceed with assassination plots and assassination attempts against Castro. Or, the third and final point that I can think of is that somehow these officials of the CIA who were so engaged misunderstood or misinterpreted their scope of authority.
>
> Now, it is terribly important, if there is any way that we can find out which of these three points represented what actually happened. That is the nature, that is the quandary.
>
> Now, is there anything that you can tell us that would assist us in finding an answer to this central question?

McNamara directly rejected the theory of misunderstanding, but was unable to reconcile the remaining possibilities. On the one hand, he firmly believed that the CIA was under the control of the president; on the other hand, he had never heard of any assassination attempts approved by the president. Still, the fact remained: plots had been devised. "So," he testified, "I frankly can't reconcile . . . and I understand the contradiction that this carries with respect to the facts."[25]

The trouble was that evidence seemed to abound for each of the theories. Former CIA Director Richard Helms (1966–1973) expressed his belief to a congressional committee that the agency did have presidential authority for its intrigues against Castro—through an authority heavily clothed in ambiguity and the doctrine of plausible denial. Senator Charles Mathias

(R-Md.) questioned Helms with a historical analogy:

> Senator Mathias: Let me draw an example from history. When Thomas Beckett was proving to be an annoyance, as Castro, the King said, "Who will rid me of this man?" He didn't say, go out and murder him. He said, who will rid me of this man, and let it go at that. . . . [Is] that typical of the kind of thing which might be said, which might be taken by the director or by anybody else as presidential authorization to go forward?
> Mr. Helms: That is right. But in answer to that, I realize that one sort of grows up in the tradition of the time and I think that any of us would have found it very difficult to discuss assassinations with a president of the U.S. I just think we all had the feeling that we're hired out to keep those things out of the Oval Office.
> Senator Mathias: Yet at the same time you felt that some spark had been transmitted, that that was within the permissible limits.
> Mr. Helms: Yes, and if he had disappeared from the scene they would not have been unhappy.[26]

Though Helms—who was responsible for covert action at the CIA during the Kennedy years after the Bay of Pigs fiasco in 1961—admitted he was never told directly by President Kennedy to kill Castro, nevertheless "no member of the Kennedy Administration . . . ever told me that [assassination] was proscribed,⁻ [or] even referred to it in that fashion. . . . Nobody ever said that [assassination] was ruled out."[27]

Yet, the Senate investigators remained plagued by doubts over the validity of the presidential-authority theory. Perhaps Helms and other CIA officials had misinterpreted the signals being sent by Kennedy and his advisers. John McCone told the investigators that he, too, had often heard the Cuban problem discussed in such terms as "dispose of Castro" or "knock off Castro," but he interpreted this language to mean the "overthrow of the Communist Government in Cuba," not assassination.[28]

Sometimes the evidence on assassination

plots seemed to suggest nothing less than the CIA as rogue elephant. The presidential adviser and noted historian Arthur M. Schlesinger, Jr., wrote to President Kennedy in 1962: "One of the most shocking things which emerged after the last Cuban episode [the Bay of Pigs] was the weakness of top-level CIA control—the discrepancy between what high CIA officials thought their operatives were saying and doing in the field, and what these operatives were actually saying and doing."[29] All the former presidential advisers testifying before the Church committee in 1975 denied under oath any knowledge of White House or cabinet-level orders to assassinate foreign leaders. At the agency level, William Harvey, the CIA officer who worked with the mob to plan the assassination of Castro, admitted that he failed to tell the incoming director, McCone, about the murder plans. According to McCone's successor, Richard Helms, Harvey kept the entire arrangement with the underworld "pretty much in his back pocket"—that is, hidden out of view of his superiors in the White House and, apparently, within the CIA itself.[30]

The CIA out of control, a wink and a nod, a misunderstanding—where was the truth? It was unlikely to be found in writing. "I can't imagine any Cabinet officer wanting to sign off on something like that," Helms told the Congress. "I can't imagine anybody wanting something in writing saying I have just charged Mr. Jones to go out and shoot Mr. Smith."[31] Unable to learn the truth for certain, the Congress simply reported all the facts it had found and left the matter there, embracing none of the three theories in its report.[32]

Murder Low   Less well understood than high-level assassination plots is CIA involvement in the incapacitation or murder of lower-level officials. Here the public record is largely blank, though some indications exist that such activity has occurred. In 1975, Congress discovered a cable sent to CIA headquarters from a Middle East division chief regarding an obstreperous Iraqi colonel with Soviet connec-

tions. The division chief recommended that the colonel be disabled for several months by exposing him to an incapacitating chemical. "We do not consciously seek subject's permanent removal from the scene," read the cable. "We also do not object should this complication develop."[33]

The most well-known operation to remove large numbers of lower-level officials from the scene is the *Phoenix program*, an operation carried out in South Vietnam as part of the U.S. war effort to subdue the influence of the communists in the South Vietnamese countryside, that is, the Vietcong Infrastructure (VCI). According to former CIA Director William Colby, who for a time was the agency's field officer in charge of the project, some 20,000 VC leaders and sympathizers were killed as a result of Phoenix; but, Colby stresses, about 85 percent of those killed were engaged in military or paramilitary combat with South Vietnamese or American soldiers. Another 12 percent died at the hands of South Vietnamese security forces, and none died through an authorized plan of "assassination." Critics, though, find this a thin line, and even Colby has conceded that assassinations might have taken place at the hands of overzealous Vietnamese, or even American, participants in the Phoenix program.[34]

As repugnant as the Phoenix project was, at least it took place in a war zone where the United States had openly and massively committed itself to an overt (though undeclared) war. More recently, in Nicaragua CIA personnel distributed a manual which instructed its guerrilla fighters (the contras) in the arts of "neutralizing" local civil officers.[35] In its investigation of CIA assassination plots, Congress discovered that the verb *neutralize* in agency cables often seemed to mean *murder*.[36] Despite a strong public reaction against assassination plots when they were revealed by Congress, despite executive orders by every president from Gerald Ford forward to prohibit assassination, despite the lack of a strong commitment by Congress or the American people to a war against Nicaragua (though there was some modest support for covert action there), the CIA seemed to advocate through this manual a Phoenix-like plan of systematic assassinations. Once the manual was revealed in the press, the leadership of the agency denied they had authorized its use and, as in the case of Phoenix excesses, laid the blame at the feet of over-zealous officers in the field. The director of the CIA, William Casey, publicly apologized for the manual and reprimanded five officials near the bottom of the agency hierarchy for allowing its distribution. President Reagan concluded that the whole matter had been "much ado about nothing."[37]

Guns for Sale　In addition to its concoction of assassination plots, the paramilitary wing of the CIA's Covert Action Staff has distributed weapons throughout the Third World. In March of 1961, pro-Western dissidents in the Dominican Republic requested weapons from the CIA. Information about the dissidents and their request traveled through Department of State and CIA communications channels disguised with references to a picnic: ". . . the members of our club [that is, the dissidents] are now prepared in their minds to have a picnic [coup]. Lately they have developed a plan for the picnic, which just might work if they could find the proper food [weapons]. They have asked us for a few sandwiches [guns]. . . . Last week we were asked to furnish three or four pineapples [fragmentation grenades] for a picnic in the near future. . . ."[38]

Congress has uncovered, in addition to the several tons of weapons provided to Iran by the Reagan administration during the Iran-contra affair, a wide variety of CIA arms shipments to pro-Western dissidents in various developing nations. These shipments have included high-powered rifles with telescopes and silencers, suitcase bombs, fragmentation grenades, rapid-fire weapons, 64-mm antitank rockets, .38 caliber pistols, .30 caliber M-1 carbines, .45 caliber submachine guns, tear gas grenades, and

enough ammunition to equip an army. This ordnance was merely for small dissident groups here and there. For the major paramilitary operations, like those involving the Meo tribesmen of Laos and the Kurds of Iraq, the ordnance provided would have dwarfed that affordable to most countries in the world.[39]

Large-scale Paramilitary Operations　As mentioned at the beginning of this chapter, beyond assassination plots and logistical support for friendly foreign intelligence services lie paramilitary operations of a much broader scope. These covert wars are normally supported by the entire panoply of covert action. Former CIA Director William Colby points to two major successes in the use of these combined techniques during the postwar period: western European resistance to communist political subversion, and Latin American rejection of Cuban-stimulated insurgency.[40] Certainly among the most conspicuous early successes (at least over the short term) were the paramilitary operations waged in 1953 and 1954 that brought to power pro-American leaders in Iran and Guatemala. Hardly a shot was fired in either coup; the operations seemed to flow with the ease of a silk handkerchief from a magician's sleeve.

Coming as they did on top of earlier good fortune in Greece and elsewhere in Europe, these coups encouraged the view that the CIA could orchestrate events throughout the world, remaking its image more in our likeness. Such quick and unobtrusive results gained through the use of this "quiet option" held strong appeal over the frustration of diplomacy and the dangers of overt military conflict. In the global chess game with the Soviets, the United States now had a wonderful "third option" between diplomacy and calling out the Marines, and—so it seemed—the option worked quite well.

The national security establishment began to rely on paramilitary operations and other forms of covert action as a panacea for Marxist infection practically wherever and whenever it occurred. Similar pressure came from the CIA's worldwide network of foreign agents known as the *infrastructure* (or the "plumbing"). These individuals, admits a CIA insider, are not beyond concocting various schemes "to make themselves appear busy and worth their keep."[41]

The short list of early covert-action successes grew into a long list of failures: the Bay of Pigs, Indonesia, Laos, Vietnam, among others, as well as the bungled assassination plots. Some schemes were written for the theater of the absurd: the plan (described in Perspectives on American Foreign Policy 9.3) to incite rebellion against Castro with fireworks shot from submarines off the coast of Havana; or a recommendation from a CIA consultant, initially approved and only at the last minute squelched by Director Allen Dulles, that American scientific journals be laced with false research findings to fool Soviet scientists (and only "inconvenience" America's own).[42] Others, though less foolish in conception, failed nonetheless. A classic example, which also illustrates how PM operations are usually employed as part of a synchronous use of several covert-action methods, is the secret American intervention in Chile.

THE SECRET WAR AGAINST CHILE

From 1958 to 1973, the United States resorted to a wide array of covert-action operations in Chile in an attempt to undermine the rule of the socialist leader Salvador Allende.[43] At first, the purpose was to use "spoiling operations" or "dirty tricks" during Chile's presidential elections to foil Allende's candidacy; then, when these tactics failed, plans for a military coup accelerated.

In the 1964 presidential elections, recall, the CIA spent more than $3 million, financing over half of the campaign expenses incurred by the anti-Allende Christian Democratic Party; about $1 million of these funds came from American corporations, funneled through CIA conduits. To put this in context, this amount of money is equivalent to about $60 million if a foreign government had spent a comparable sum in the 1964 American presidential election—$35 million more than the candidates, Lyndon Johnson and Barry Goldwater, spent combined.

In 1964 the CIA, under orders from the White House, secretly subsidized Chilean media willing to project an anti-Allende slant to their news broadcasts. The agency also disseminated anti-Allende leaflets and wall posters (3000 a day). The Christian Democrats won the election by 56 percent of the vote.

In 1970, Allende stood as a candidate for the presidency once more, and, again, the CIA instigated a series of political and propaganda operations against him, though with reduced intensity compared with 1964. Agents were recruited to scrawl slogans on walls throughout the country designed to evoke images of communist firing squads, which presumably the left-leaning Allende would convene and use against the people of Chile. Posters warned of the end of religion and family life if the Allende forces came to power. This time, though, the covert actions failed; Allende won a plurality in the presidential election. Since no candidate had achieved a majority, Chilean law required the national congress to choose between the first- and second-place finishers.

The Nixon administration then began to focus more seriously on the Chilean situation. Two plans were proposed: "track I" and "track II." The first included more propaganda and political covert action, supplemented now with increased covert economic pressure. The second consisted of a plot to stage a military coup that would prevent the accession to power of Allende, should track I fail. Neither track succeeded and, in October of 1970, Allende was elected by a vote of 153 to 35 in the congress of Chile.

The Nixon administration then turned to the work of undermining the Allende regime. On the eve of Allende's victory, the U.S. ambassador in Chile warned the incumbent Christian Democratic president, Eduardo Frei, that "once

Allende comes to power we shall do all within our power to condemn Chile and the Chileans to utmost deprivation and poverty." In an attempt to cripple the Allende government, the White House resorted to an assortment of CIA covert actions meant, in the words of the U.S. ambassador, to "make the [Chilean] economy scream."

The NSC immediately approved the expenditure of $7 million to strengthen the anti-Allende operations, with most of this money going into the coffers of the Christian Democratic Party and other groups opposed to the new government, as well as toward the incitement of antigovernment strikes. Over the next three years, additional moneys were approved by the NSC. Between 1963 and 1973, the CIA spent $8 million in Chile on anti-Allende propaganda, another $900,000 trying to influence various groups in Chile (students, labor organizations, peasant women), and $200,000 promoting a military coup d'état. Then, on September 11, 1973, President Allende was murdered in a military coup whose perpetrators apparently had no connection with the CIA—though, earlier, a group armed by the CIA had killed the Chilean military chief of staff, General Rene Schneider, when he refused to participate in a coup attempt and resisted his captors.

With the death of Allende and the establishment of a military junta, U.S. covert actions in Chile were cut back dramatically. News reports by the *New York Times* correspondent Seymour Hersh on the CIA's operations in Chile encouraged passage of the Hughes-Ryan Act in December of 1974 as Congress, shocked by the scale of the operations, attempted for the first time since the creation of the CIA to place firmer controls on intelligence activities.

COVERT ACTION: WHAT LIMITS?

Critics contend that in America's obsession to preserve the global status quo, the United States turned its intelligence apparatus more to-

ward intervention abroad than its original purpose of gathering and assessing information. Frank Church, the chairman of a Senate investigative committee, declared in 1976 that paramilitary operations and other covert actions were increasingly directed against "leaders of small, weak countries that could not possibly threaten the United States; . . . no country was too small, no foreign leader too trifling, to escape our attention."[44]

To criticize covert intervention abroad is to miss the point altogether, retort practitioners. Turning aside hostile questioning by a congressional panel in 1975, then CIA Director Colby concluded simply: "What we are really talking here is policy, not covert action."[45] Covert action was just one form—the most invisible—of U.S. intervention around the world that had become part and parcel of the containment doctrine since the Truman administration. If the Congress could persuade presidents to adopt a less interventionist stance, was Colby's implication, then a decline in covert action would follow; but as long as the U.S. government sought to influence events abroad, America's secret power would remain an arrow in its quiver. "What does everybody think we've really been doing all these years?" asks a CIA man with a ready answer: *Fighting the Cold War!*[46]

Thirty years ago, this meant adopting tough measures "in the back alleys of the world" (former Secretary of State Dean Rusk's phrase[47]). Despite the controversy these measures have stirred over the years, CIA officialdom continues to advocate covert action in support of policy. As a high-ranking CIA official put it in 1978: "I am not thinking of returning to those days when CA was a large percentage of the CIA budget; but, I do feel that the present very small percentage [less than 5 percent in 1978] is below minimum. It is an assignment that is a lawful part of the Agency's duties." The official continued: "As soon as we can improve the understanding of it and clear up the controversies that surround it, I think this area should be given more resources if we are to carry out effectively a mission given to us by the president."[48]

Though some CIA officials may remain enthusiastic about the quiet option, critics inside and outside the agency have posed serious reservations about its value. For some observers, paramilitary operations and other covert actions have summed to rather limited harassments of perceived foes, modest help here and there for a few (chiefly Third World) friends, and some efforts to curb terrorism and narcotics trafficking (with limited success—recall, 90 percent of the illicit drugs smuggled into the United States go uncaught). Overall, since 1947 covert actions seem most often to have been modest—as in Nicaragua, where the contras have been little more than an annoyance to the Sandinista regime—or even trivial, on the one hand, or wildly overdrawn (the Bay of Pigs), on the other hand.[49] That the United States could have gotten by without the modest ones is plausible; that it would have been better off without the overdrawn ones is persuasive. The latter have failed most of the time, opponents argue, at the cost of much money and—more important still—America's reputation as a country more honorable than its foes.[50]

Yet, the temptation to resort to America's secret power remains strong. "As you look ahead to the next ten or twenty years, we don't know when another kind of political crisis might arise in the world, . . ." William Colby has said, "and I think it is better that we have the ability to help people in these countries where that will happen, quietly and secretly, and not wait until we are faced with a military threat that has to be met by armed force."[51]

The plans of the Ford administration, in 1975, to assist the pro-Western side in the Angolan civil war illustrate a common argument in favor of covert action. According to a senior CIA official, the motivation for entry into this war (eventually blocked by Congress through a law sponsored by Senator Dick Clark, D., Iowa, prohibiting covert action in Angola; the *Clark Amendment*, later repealed in

1986) was twofold. The first objective was to prevent the Soviet Union from expanding its presence and influence in Africa. Especially worrisome was the perceived strategic or geopolitical threat; the Soviets had already gained a toehold in Guinea and Somalia, and now Angola offered them valuable port facilities on the Atlantic seaboard. Second, the Ford administration hoped to achieve a negotiated settlement of internal differences in Angola, one that would place moderate groups in power. "Ultimately, the purpose was to throw the Soviets out," concludes the CIA official, "at which point we would leave, too."[52]

Appearing before a congressional committee when he was still CIA director, Colby offered a justification of the quiet option. Paraphrasing the conclusion of the Murphy Commission on Foreign Policy, he told the senators on the panel that "there are many risks and dangers associated with covert action. . . . But 'we must live in the world we find, not the world we might wish.' Our adversaries deny themselves no forms of action which might advance their interests or undercut ours. . . . In many parts of the world a prohibition on our use of covert action would put the U.S. and those who rely on it at a dangerous disadvantage; . . . therefore . . . covert action cannot be abandoned. . . ."[53]

Other witnesses appearing before Congress have also accepted the necessity of a covert action capability, but for use only in carefully restricted circumstances. "The guiding criterion," advised Clark Clifford, former secretary of defense and an author of the National Security Act of 1947 which created the CIA, "should be the test as to whether or not a certain covert project truly affects our national security." Cyrus Vance, who would soon become secretary of state in the Carter administration, told the committee that he believed "it should be the policy of the United States to engage in covert actions only when they are absolutely essential to the national security."[54]

In the Senate's 1975 investigation of the CIA, just one witness opposed covert action altogether. "Such operations," testified Morton H. Halperin, a former NSC staffer, "are incompatible with our democratic institutions, with Congressional and public control over foreign policy decisions, with our constitutional rights, and with the principles and ideals that this Republic stands for in the world."[55] The chairman of the Senate panel, after months of investigation, offered an ambiguous prescription. He was willing to support covert action only if it were "consistent with either the imperative of national survival or with our traditional belief in free government."[56]

Normative views aside, Colby seems correct on the fundamental point: the lines of argument about covert action return to policy—the containment doctrine, the domino theory, and the other postulates advanced to reinforce the anticommunist theme that has dominated American foreign policy since 1945. If the use of covert action has been indiscriminate, then perhaps this is because America's reaction to tumult and revolution in other lands has been indiscriminately driven by an obsessive fear of communism—regardless of how distant the bayou in which it might arise or how feeble its effects upon the United States. Yet, the very secrecy of the decisions to use paramilitary and other covert operations has prevented adequate debate about the wisdom of intervention. All too often, Congress, public opinion, media opinion, and other important voices in a democracy become inconsequential as the NSC and the CIA rely upon their secret power to pursue foreign policy as they alone see fit.

Arguably, some covert actions have been useful and should be maintained. Perhaps the best case can be made for selected propaganda operations to spread the truth where America's adversaries would sow lies, and operations designed to combat genuine terrorism and the narcotics trade. Even more arguably, the United States must have a paramilitary capability for extreme circumstances, say, to thwart a terrorist nuclear attack against this nation. The critics of America's secret power are persuasive,

however, in their central theme: to resort to covert action whenever someone, somewhere, is a nuisance to this nation runs counter to America's democratic beliefs in fair play and usually ends in a waste of lives, money, and esteem. It can also lead to the decline of constitutional government within the United States, as demonstrated by the attempts of NSC and CIA officials in the Reagan administration to bypass Congress—and evidently even the president—in their conduct of the Iran-contra operation.

Despite their failure in the Iran-contra affair, the intelligence oversight procedures put in place during the past fifteen years represent a dramatic improvement in the supervision of America's hidden foreign policy. These new procedures are examined in the next section of this chapter.

INTELLIGENCE DECISION MAKING

Routine intelligence decisions are made within the various intelligence agencies, according to their traditions and executive orders. Major decisions, though, that affect the strategic relations of the United States with other nations have required the participation of the NSC—at least since 1974–1975, when the earlier, looser controls over intelligence were criticized by Congress and a presidential commission.[57]

Congress Seeks Tighter Controls over Intelligence Policy

Since the passage of the *Hughes-Ryan Act* in December of 1974, the president is expected to approve in writing all important covert actions and inform the Congress of these decisions. Its provisions required that "no funds appropriated under the authority of this or any other Act may be expended by or on behalf of the [CIA] for operations in foreign countries, other than activities intended solely for obtaining necessary intelligence, unless and until the

President finds that each such operation is important to the national security of the United States and reports, in a timely fashion, a description and scope of such operations to the appropriate committees of the Congress. . . . "

From the verb *finds* came the term of art *finding*, that is, the written document of approval bearing the president's signature. The "appropriate committees" to whom this finding was to be delivered in a timely fashion (within twenty-four hours came to be the understanding) were initially three in the House of Representatives and three in the Senate: the committees on appropriations, armed services, and foreign affairs. In 1976, legislators added a Senate intelligence committee to the list, and, in 1977, a House intelligence committee; then, in 1980, legislators trimmed back the list to the two intelligence committees with the Intelligence Accountability Act (usually referred to less formally as the *Intelligence Oversight Act*).

This 1980 statute, the most important formal measure taken by Congress to strengthen its control over intelligence operations, further had the effect of clarifying that Congress wanted to be informed of *all* important covert actions—not just those sponsored by the CIA. This language sought to close a loophole in the Hughes-Ryan Act that made it possible for the president to call upon other agencies—presumably within the military—for covert-action operations in order to avoid the Hughes-Ryan reporting requirements. Moreover, with this legislation the Congress took a firm stand in favor of prior notification on covert actions—not after the fact as the Hughes-Ryan phrase "timely fashion" allowed.

In emergency situations, the new law allowed the president to limit prior notice to eight leaders in Congress (the so-called *Gang of Eight*). The language of the statute is quite clear on this point: ". . . if the President determines it is essential to limit prior notice to meet extraordinary circumstances affecting the vital interests of the United States, such notice shall be limited to the chairmen and ranking minority members of the intelligence committees, the Speaker and minority leader of the House of Representatives, and the majority and minority leaders of the Senate. . . . " Yet, in spite of this language, at least one recent CIA director, Admiral Stansfield Turner, who served under President Carter, has rejected the obligation of prior notice. Moreover, the Iran-contra scandal revealed that President Reagan actually ordered the CIA not to report to Congress on his finding that approved a controversial sale of arms to Iran. The matter remains unsettled, as does much of the relationship between the intelligence community and Congress in the wake of the investigations of 1975 and the stringent new control procedures.

Decision Procedures within the Executive Branch

About 85 percent of all covert-action proposals originate from CIA stations overseas—though occasionally important ones, like the Iran-contra operations, germinate within the White House itself. From the stations abroad, the typical covert-action recommendation advances through the CIA hierarchy (see Figure 9.1). Prior to gaining final approval within the agency, covert-action proposals in the Carter administration were reviewed by a variety of offices within the CIA, including the Comptroller, the Office of General Counsel, the Legislative Counsel, and the Intelligence Directorate (called the National Foreign Assessment Center under Carter). The proposals were also reviewed by two organizations outside the agency before going to the DCI for his imprimatur: the Department of State and a special NSC panel called the Special Coordination Committee (SCC—renamed the National Security Planning Group during the Reagan administration).

Directly beneath the Special Coordination Committee in the Carter administration stood a working group of staff aides from each government organization represented on the National Security Council. This group had the responsi-

Figure 9.1 Covert action decision process.

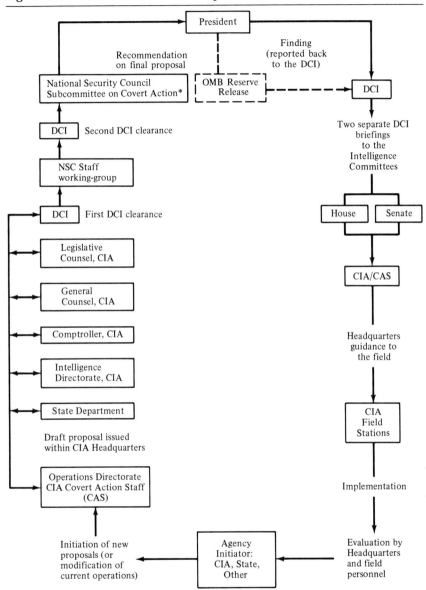

*Known as the Special Coordination Committee (SCC) during the Carter Administration and the National Security Planning Group (NSPG) during the Reagan Administration.

Source: Loch K. Johnson, "Covert Action and Accountability: Decision Making for America's Secret Foreign Policy," *International Studies Quarterly*, vol. 33, March 1989, p. 95.

bility for giving each covert-action proposal an acid bath of criticism. At this staff level, a high percentage of the proposals were rejected outright, or, in most cases, at least sent back to the CIA for clarifications or modifications. In preparation for this review before SCC staffers, the CIA had to make sure that its proposal addressed several points: justification of the project, expense, alternatives, risks, prior coordination, past related activities, and whether the proposal was important enough to warrant presidential review and congressional reporting. Consideration of covert-action proposals, then as now, depended greatly upon the attitudes of individual reviewing officers; but risk, compatibility with American foreign policy goals, likelihood of success, value of outcome, cost, and the prevailing political climate all weigh in the balance.

The SCC's "working group" was not a decision committee; only the president himself has the authority to approve important covert actions. Rather, the working group acted in a staff advisory relationship to the principals on the SCC—the vice president, the secretaries of state and defense, and the president's national security adviser—and as a conduit back to the initiating agency (usually the CIA). Its job was to ensure that full and complete deliberations, including supporting and dissenting opinions, were reported to the SCC and to the director of the agency which generated the proposal.

If a covert action were supported at the level of the SCC working group (typically following one or more revisions) and then by the director of Central Intelligence, the full SCC would examine its merits and submit a policy recommendation to the president, along with comments and dissents (if any) from individual members of the Committee. An affirming decision by the president (the finding) would then, as now, be reported to Congress. This last provision applied only to the CIA until passage of the 1980 Intelligence Oversight Act, at which time it applied to all government agencies; no report is required during times of declared war or when the president is operating under the War Powers Resolution.

Reporting to Congress

Once the congressional intelligence committees know about a finding (its invariably succinct wording bearing the president's signature is hand-carried to the Congress), they must decide if and when they wish to receive details on the covert action. If either committee wishes to learn more, the practice has been for the committees to listen to an oral briefing. The quality of these briefings has varied, usually depending upon how interested the legislators are in asking questions and how well informed these questions (and follow-ups) prove to be.[58]

The most egregious example of a poor briefing (and evidently poor questioning by committee members, too) occurred in April of 1984. In a briefing to the Senate Committee about CIA covert action in Nicaragua, DCI William J. Casey slid over the fact—all too quickly—that the agency had escalated its operations to include the mining of Nicaraguan harbors. The president had approved this finding in February, but at least some members of the Senate committee—probably most—remained unaware of the risky operation (which endangered not only Nicaraguan vessels but international shipping, including that of our allies). Apparently, the CIA had briefed the House committee reasonably well (thanks to persistent questioning by a few members of that committee), and some individual members of the Senate committee; but, when the full Senate committee met, only one sentence in a briefing lasting over an hour dealt with the mining. In the days that followed, the DCI tried to deflect questions on the subject by flatly denying that *harbors* had been mined. Only later did senators discover this was merely a subterfuge. Casey had relied on a technical distinction: the CIA had mined *piers* within the harbors.[59]

Not even the committee's chairman, Barry Goldwater (R-Ariz.), usually highly supportive of each and every CIA project, heard and understood the reference to mining. Later, when he learned of the project from a member of his committee who had requested an additional individual briefing, he was furious and sent a letter to Casey, which said, in part, "It gets down to one, little, simple phrase: I am pissed off!"[60] It may be true that Casey, with his succinct reference to mining, had honored the letter of the law, but, as former DCI Turner has concluded, "hardly the intent. . . . The CIA did go through the motions of informing, but it wasn't speaking very loudly."[61]

With the secret arms sale to Iran in 1985 (and the funneling of profits to the contras), the CIA failed to speak at all. Despite the 1980 Oversight Act, the executive branch provided no report to the Congress—indeed, by presidential order.[62] The president evidently hoped to guarantee the secrecy of the arms deal by taking refuge in the ambiguous escape hatch found in the preamble to the 1980 Oversight Act, with its fleeting reference (among other ambiguities) to the right of the president to remain "consistent" with his constitutional authorities and duties.[63] The refusal to report was doubly disconcerting for the Senate Intelligence Committee, because after the mining flap Casey had entered into a series of "understandings" with the panel (communicated by letters) that henceforth he would report promptly and fully on all new covert actions, as well as on any notable changes in those already reported.[64]

The arms-for-hostages deal came as a shock to legislative overseers in another important respect: for the first time, a finding had been based on an oral approval from the president with no written documentation—precisely the slippery accountability Hughes-Ryan had been designed to overcome. "The oversight process has been fractured," concluded the vice chairman of the Senate Intelligence Committee,

Patrick Leahy (D-Vt.), in the wake of the Iran-contra disclosures.[65]

Legislative Prerogatives

The CIA's covert-action briefings are supposed to be provided (by law) whenever a "new" covert action is approved or (by custom) when a "significant change" to an existing program is made. Following a briefing, committee members face a decision: how to react to the covert action already approved by the president and on the brink of implementation—if not already under way. Under current law, the committees are not required to approve or disapprove a finding. The CIA must only report the finding to the committees and, by custom, then inform the White House of any dissent. Failure to dissent, however, is widely regarded within the executive branch as tacit approval of the finding by Congress. The briefing on a finding, therefore, takes on greater significance than other CIA briefings; the committees, which meet in their separate chambers, must decide whether to place their tacit authority and reputation behind each covert action.

If members of the intelligence committees are displeased with a covert action, they have a number of possible responses available to them. One or more members may voice reservations during the briefing and ask the CIA to make these objections known to the president. Obviously the greater the number of those objecting, the more serious the negative response is taken in the White House. Exactly who is objecting can be important, too; if it is the chairman of the committee, or, worse yet for the executive branch, the chairman *and* the ranking minority member, here is a force to be reckoned with. To emphasize the seriousness of their opposition, one or more members of the committees might formally write—or even visit—the president to stress why the project is ill-advised. A committee may even decide to take a formal vote on a finding to register clearly its feelings, as the Senate has done on a few occasions. At least four times a negative formal vote by the Senate committee has caused a president to rescind his approval of a covert action. One instance reportedly involved the renewal of funding for the Christian Democratic Party in Italy in 1976 and, in a more recent example, a coup plot aimed at the Panamanian dictator, General Manuel Antonio Noriega in 1988.[66]

Thus, even though the Congress has no legal role in the approval of findings, it clearly has a tacit opportunity to veto an operation. This "veto" may be ignored by the president, but there may be a heavy political price to pay. The president must work with these committees in the future, and the CIA must come to them many times each year for budgetary requests as well as other items of business now that the Congress has insisted on greater involvement in the making of intelligence policy. The members of the intelligence committees, especially the senior ones, are not good enemies for the White House and the director of Central Intelligence to make. The power of the purse held by Congress remains a particularly potent corrective to uncooperative behavior in the executive branch. In 1978, the Senate Intelligence Committee terminated one covert action during the panel's review of the CIA's annual budget request simply by striking the moneys designated for it.[67]

Either of the committees may also take its opposition to the full house, which by the rules can meet in secret session to hear the case—though it is unlikely the project would remain "covert" with so many people hearing about it. Explicit resolutions to terminate a covert action before the parent chamber in open session suffer the same drawback: they lead to public exposure of a supposedly secret operation; nevertheless, as the Clark Amendment to prohibit covert action in Angola (1976) and the Boland amendments to limit covert action in Nicaragua (1983–1987) illustrate, Congress occasionally reaches a point of sufficient frustration over some policies that a majority of its members are prepared to hold a debate in the chamber and vote on a "covert" action—one then apt to become an *"overt-covert" action*. Finally, a legislator could telephone the press about the proposed operation—a "leak item veto" that could stop the operation dead in its tracks. Legislators have rarely stooped to this unauthorized release of classified information.

Accountability versus Micromanagement

Despite its invisibility to the general public and to most elected representatives as well, the covert-action decision process has nonetheless matured since 1974 into a complex matrix of checkpoints and overseers—too much so from the perspective of most intelligence professionals. "What we have is covert action by national consensus," complains a recent deputy director for operations in the CIA.[68]

Covert-action decisions can be time-consuming, exhausting, and nerve-racking. In one recent instance involving a terrorist hijacking of an airplane, a counterterrorist team in a NATO country requested help from the CIA. The team sought expert advice from the United States on how to blow out the door of the airliner without harming passengers inside, a skill the CIA and only one other Western intelligence agency had developed to a high degree. The CIA station in the NATO country cabled headquarters for permission to help in this covert action. Hours passed, and soon turned into days. Finally, two days later, with still no decision from the United States, the NATO nation turned to the other Western intelligence agency, which responded affirmatively over the telephone on the first call. Within a few hours, paramilitary commandos from this agency were en route to the hijacked plane and soon successfully blew off the door for the counterterrorist team.[69]

For intelligence professionals, the conclusion to be drawn is self-evident: U.S. intelligence has been paralyzed, or at least maimed, by oppressive layers of decision makers and overseers brought on by congressional inquiries and investigative journalism run wild. The intelligence bureaucrats make a strong case against what they call *micromanagement*—that is, too many executive and legislative policymakers enmeshed in the small wheels of covert action and other delicate intelligence operations best left to the pros.

A strong case can be made, too, however, that too much discretion has existed in some parts of the chain of command. Recall how, in 1975, Senator Church concluded at one point in his exhaustive investigation of the CIA that the agency had lost control of its clandestine operations; it had become, in his words, "a rogue elephant on a rampage."[70] In 1983 (the reader may recall from Chapter 6), Representative Boland observed similarly, after chairing the House Intelligence Committee for six years, that the CIA was "almost like a rogue elephant, doing what it wanted to do."[71]

These harsh judgments come from a deep sense of frustration over what these key legislators found to be dangerous CIA excesses: in the instance of Church, the assassination plots with the underworld connections, domestic spying (Operations Chaos and HQ Lingual), and sequestered shellfish toxins despite a presidential order to destroy them (among other things); and in the instance of Boland—well before he learned of the Iran-contra end run—the CIA efforts to circumvent his amendment limiting paramilitary operations in Nicaragua.

The past and present validity of the "rogue elephant" hypothesis remains a subject of lively debate, stirred anew by the Iran-contra scandal. As the siphoning of funds to the contras outside the view of legislative overseers demonstrates, opportunities clearly exist to encourage intelligence operations even when they have been expressly prohibited by law. As the reader will remember from earlier in this chapter, in pursuit of its goal to overthrow the Sandinista regime—despite the Boland Amendment to limit further spending on paramilitary operations in Nicaragua—the Reagan administration

engaged in a variety of improprieties related to intelligence operations. Among other things, the administration persuaded Israel, Saudi Arabia, South Africa, Brunei, and other nations to supply weapons and funding to the contras; lobbied wealthy American civilians to fund the contras; assigned an NSC staffer experienced in guerrilla warfare—Lieutenant Colonel North— to provide guidance for the operations; and lied repeatedly to Congress in order to conceal these activities. With respect to the secret arms sale to Iran, the administration back-dated the president's approval (an innovative—and improper—"retroactive finding"), ordered the director of Central Intelligence not to report the operation to the intelligence committees (as required by the 1980 Oversight Act), and, from the president on down, misled the American people about the existence of the arms sale.[72]

In *Perspectives on American Foreign Policy* 9.5, a thoughtful former CIA director offers his prescription for controlling the abuse of power by America's secret intelligence agencies. The Iran-contra revelations remind us that the control system he extols is far from perfect. Nevertheless, the checks now in place—plus the added warnings to future administrations that have come from the 1987 Iran-contra investigations and the indictments handed down by a special prosecutor in 1988 to Poindexter, North, and others involved in the scandal—sum to a vastly more serious effort to cope with the supervision of covert action than was even remotely attempted before Congress came to grips with the hidden side of America's government in 1974–1975.

The Congress, in summary, has no direct authority to approve covert actions and other sensitive intelligence operations; still, the very requirement of reporting on these projects serves as a strong deterrent against madcap proposals which surfaced within the intelligence bureaucracy more easily in the past. A major force of congressional influence over covert action is the *law of anticipated reactions* that the political scientist Carl Friedrich knew to be so important in all

---

Perspectives on American Foreign Policy   9.5

William Colby on supervising the CIA:

With today's supervision, and with the command structure trying to keep things straight, the people in CIA know what they should do and what they should not do—as distinct from the Fifties, in which there were no particular rules. If CIA people today are told to violate their limits, or if they are tempted to violate those limits, one of the jun-

ior officers will surely raise that question and tell the command structure, and, if not satisfied there, he will tell the Congress, and, if not satisfied there, he will tell the press, and that is the way you control it.

"Gesprach mit William E. Colby," *Der Spiegel* [a West German newsmagazine], January 23, 1978, p. 114, author's translation.

---

executive-legislative relations; the potential for negative legislative reaction can have a sobering effect on bureaucrats who must obtain annual funding from the Congress.

Thus, while the two intelligence committees do not have the authority formally to approve (or disapprove) covert actions, they do hear about them; and they may argue and even symbolically vote against them in closed meetings with CIA officials. The covert action may be short-lived if the executive branch senses strong legislative opposition. Committees have no formal veto, but they have the power—or, at any rate, the opportunity—to persuade. If a sufficient number on an intelligence committee (presumably a majority, or at least an intense minority) object to a particular operation, a prudent chief executive will doubtless have second thoughts about what was expected to be a "quiet option."

INTELLIGENCE AND PROPRIETY

Few, if any, observers of intelligence policy deny the value of rigorous intelligence collection and analysis. No one wants another Pearl Harbor. Yet even with this most widely accepted of the intelligence missions, limits must

exist if democracy is to survive in the United States. In 1970, President Nixon authorized a master domestic spy plan, the Huston plan, named after the overzealous White House aide who recommended it, Tom Charles Huston—a precursor of Lieutenant Colonel Oliver North. The purpose of the plan was to spy on American citizens opposed to the war in Vietnam. The White House felt sure that these protesters were being funded by the Soviet Union or other communist powers. (No evidence to support this allegation was ever found.) Laws prohibiting domestic spying were brushed aside as the administration, in its paranoia over mounting student demonstrations, mobilized the CIA and other intelligence agencies to watch their every move. Nixon soon rescinded his support for the spy plan when the FBI director and the attorney general learned of his approval and complained; only five years later did congressional investigators discover that the agencies continued the illegal domestic spying, despite the presidential rescission.[73]

Like the Iran-contra scandal, the Huston plan demonstrates how easily power can be abused at the highest levels of the government. In the case of the Huston plan, the Nixon administration turned the secret intelligence agencies against America's own citizens; in the case of the Iran-contra scandal, the Reagan administration violated the nation's fundamental constitutional arrangements. In both instances, a fear of communist influence—on the campuses for Huston, in Nicaragua for Lieutenant Colonel North—led to a disregard for the rights of Americans and their representatives in Congress. The communist bugbear has been a primary stimulant for the overzealous use of the U.S. intelligence agencies, from the secret hiring of Nazi war criminals immediately after the war to provide intelligence on the Soviet Union (when these men—Klaus Barbie, for one—should have been standing trial for wartime atrocities) to the assassination plots, the Huston plan, and the Iran-contra operations.

Important, too, in deciding how far to push the boundaries of propriety has been the degree to which top government officials have adopted a "realist" or an "idealist" approach to world affairs. Dr. Ray Cline, formerly a high CIA official, represents the realist school. During a forum on the uses of covert action by the United States, his philosophy took on sharp definition. "We are already engaged in a protracted secret war against the Soviet Union," he said. As a result, America needed to get on with the business of winning the war, using covert action wherever and whenever it might aid this objective. "The United States is faced with a situation in which the major world power opposing our system of government is trying to expand its power by using covert methods of warfare," Cline continued, asking rhetorically: "Must the United States respond like a man in a barroom brawl who will fight only according to Marquis of Queensberry rules?"[74]

In contrast, George W. Ball, under secretary of state during the Kennedy and Johnson administrations, represents the idealist school, with its emphasis on world public opinion, image, and morality. "In principle I think we ought to discourage the idea of fighting secret wars or even initiating most covert operations," he argued. ". . . When the United States violates those principles—when we mine harbors in Nicaragua—we fuzz the difference between ourselves and the Soviet Union. We act out of character, which no great power can do without diminishing itself. . . . When we yield to what is, in my judgment, a childish temptation to fight the Russians on their own terms and in their own gutter, we make a major mistake and throw away one of our great assets."[75]

The dispute between the realists and the idealists over the uses of strategic intelligence (discussed further in Chapter 13, "Morality and Foreign Policy") is a manifestation of a more fundamental debate in the United States over when and where to intervene abroad. As so often in the nation's history, Americans have felt ambivalent about the use of secret power. While the debate on this basic question continues, reformers take comfort in the new executive-legislative arrangements for strategic intelligence decisions. Judgments about sensitive intelligence operations, they argue, are now more apt to be made with the participation of elected representatives in Congress—and not by the president or an intelligence agency alone.

SUMMARY

In addition to the gathering, analysis, and coordination of information, strategic intelligence involves the use of covert action. This approach to American foreign policy objectives entails secret interference in the affairs of other countries, usually by the Central Intelligence Agency (CIA) at the order of the White House. Covert action may take the form of secret propaganda, political assistance or manipulation, economic disruption, and paramilitary (warlike) operations.

The paramilitary operations of the CIA illustrate the widespread resort by presidents over the years to America's secret power. The United States has carried out paramilitary operations throughout the world, to include assassination plots against Fidel Castro of Cuba and Patrice Lumumba of the Congo, arms shipments to a host of insurgents, training to foreign intelligence services, and, among other operations, large-scale secret wars like the one against communist guerrillas in Laos during the 1960s. In combination with other forms of covert action, the United States has used the paramilitary option in an attempt to topple unfriendly regimes. The most widely documented case is Chile, where from 1958 to 1973 the CIA carried out extensive operations tailored to discredit the democratically elected president, Salvador Allende.

In the years since 1974, the decision process for covert action has grown complex—with many checks and balances and a new, vigorous role for Congress. Criticism has arisen within the intelligence agencies that this process has become too complicated and, therefore, has crippled the ability of America's secret agencies to act with speed and success. Reformers maintain, however, that the checks are necessary to keep the CIA and other agencies within the boundaries of the law.

The Iran-contra affair (1986–1987) revealed anew the risks for constitutional government of hidden operations. Officials within the National Security Council (NSC) staff and the CIA secretly diverted funds from a covert arms sale agreement with Iran to finance paramilitary operations in Nicaragua. Contrary to law, neither the arms sale nor the diversion of funds to Central America was reported to Congress. Even the president was apparently excluded from an awareness of the diversion, so that he could plausibly deny knowledge of the operation (if it came to light). Moreover, the NSC staff sought funding for the Nicaraguan counterrevolutionaries (the contras) from private sources, including wealthy conservative Americans and friendly foreign countries. This "privatization" of American foreign policy raised serious questions of propriety in the minds of critics who viewed this approach to foreign policy as tantamount to an attack against the constitutional underpinnings of American government. The debate over how to balance the effectiveness of the nation's secret agencies with their accountability continues today.

KEY TERMS

Boland amendments
plausible deniability
propaganda
blow-back (replay)
political covert action
economic covert action
paramilitary option
special operations
Operation Mongoose
rogue elephant

Phoenix program
CIA infrastructure
Clark Amendment
Hughes-Ryan Amendment
finding
1980 Intelligence Oversight Act
Gang of Eight
"overt-covert" action
micromanagement
law of anticipated reactions

NOTES

1. Testimony of Robert Owen, "Iran-Contra Affair," *Hearings before the U.S. Senate Select Committee on Secret Military Assistance to Iran and the Nicaraguan Opposition and U.S. House of Representatives Select Committee to Investigate Covert Arms Transactions with Iran* (hereafter the Inouye-Hamilton committees, chaired by Senator Daniel K. Inouye, D-Hawaii, and Representative Lee H. Hamilton, D-Ind.), Washington, D.C., July 1987.

2. Bob Woodward, *Veil: The CIA's Secret Wars* (New York: Simon & Schuster, 1987), p. 266.

3. *Hearings of the Inouye-Hamilton Committees*, July 1987. The figures on private contributions come from this source, too. For the Bush promises to Honduras, see the *New York Times*, June 25, 1989, p. 13.

4. *Hearings of the Inouye-Hamilton Committees.*

5. Senator John Kerry (D-Mass.), on *Moyers: The Secret Government—The Constitution in Crisis*, Public Affairs Television, November 4, 1987, moderated and written by Bill Moyers.

6. *NBC Evening News*, January 13, 1978.

7. B. Hugh Tovar, "Strengths and Weaknesses in Past U.S. Covert Action," in Roy Godson, ed., *Intelligence Requirements for the 1980s: Covert Action* (Washington, D.C.: National Strategy Information Center, 1981), pp. 194–195.

8. See "Covert Action in Chile: 1963–1973," *Staff Report of the Select Committee on Intelligence Activities* (the Church committee), U.S. Senate, December 1973.

9. *Ibid.*, p. 15.

10. Author's interview with CIA official, June 11, 1984, Washington, D.C.

11. Tom Wicker et al., "C.I.A. Operations: A Plot Scuttled," *New York Times*, April 28, 1966, p. 1.

12. For the Hughes-Ryan law, see Section 662 of the Foreign Assistance Act of 1974 (22

U.S.C. 2422); for the Oversight Act, more formally known as the Accountability for Intelligence Activities Act, see Title V of the National Security Act of 1947 (50 U.S.C. 413).

13. Section 101 [50 U.S.C. 402 (b) (2)].

14. On this early history, see Anne Karalekas, "History of the Central Intelligence Agency," *Supplementary Detailed Staff Reports on Foreign and Military Intelligence*, Book IV, the Church committee, U.S. Senate, April 23, 1976.

15. See the Pike committee report (House Select Committee on Intelligence, chaired by Otis Pike, D-N.Y.), reprinted in "The CIA Report the President Doesn't Want You to Read: The Pike Papers," *Village Voice*, February 16, 1975, pp. 69–92.

16. Church committee, investigative files, 1975.

17. Dean Rusk, Oral History No. 86, taped by Hughes Cates, Richard B. Russell Library, University of Georgia, Athens, February 22, 1977.

18. See *Alleged Assassination Plots Involving Foreign Leaders: An Interim Report*, Church committee, November 20, 1975.

19. See Theodore Shackley, *The Third Option: An American View of Counterinsurgency* (Pleasantville, New York: Reader's Digest General Books, 1981).

20. See Victor Marchetti and John D. Marks, *The CIA and the Cult of Intelligence* (New York: Knopf, 1975); William Colby and Peter Forbath, *Honorable Men: My Life in the CIA* (New York: Simon & Schuster, 1978); Stansfield Turner, *Secrecy and Democracy: The CIA in Transition* (Boston: Houghton Mifflin, 1985); Shackley, *op. cit.*; and Loch K. Johnson, *America's Secret Power: The CIA in a Democratic Society* (New York: Oxford University Press, 1989).

21. See Marchetti and Marks, *op. cit.*, and Shackley, *op. cit.*

22. See Thomas Powers, *The Man Who Kept the Secrets: Richard Helms and the CIA* (New York: Knopf, 1979); John Prados, *Presidents' Secret Wars* (New York: Morrow, 1986); Johnson, *America's Secret Power, op. cit.*; Marchetti and Marks, *op. cit.*; and Frank Snepp, *Decent Interval* (New York: Random House, 1979), especially the Postscript, pp. 573–580.

23. *Alleged Assassination Plots*, p. 41.

24. Senator Frank Church, press conference, Washington, D.C., July 19, 1975.

25. *Alleged Assassination Plots*, p. 158.

26. *Ibid.*, p. 149.

27. *Ibid.*

28. *Ibid.*, p. 154.

29. Memorandum from Arthur M. Schlesinger, Jr., to President John F. Kennedy, September 5, 1962, Church committee files, U.S. Senate.

30. *Alleged Assassination Plots*, pp. 151, 154.

31. *Ibid.*, p. 151.

32. See Loch K. Johnson, *A Season of Inquiry: Congress and Intelligence* (Chicago: Dorsey, 1988).

33. *Alleged Assassination Plots*, p. 181, note.

34. See Colby and Forbath, *op. cit.*, p. 272; and "Gesprach mit William E. Colby," *Der Spiegel*, January 23, 1978, pp. 69–115.

35. *New York Times*, December 6, 1984.

36. *Alleged Assassination Plots*, p. 41.

37. *New York Times*, December 4, 1984, p. 3. For an account of CIA backing for what appear to be assassination squads in Lebanon during the Reagan administration, see Woodward, *op. cit.*, pp. 396–397. Recall, as well, the U.S. military air strike against Muammar Qaddafi's home in 1986, which—though denied by President Reagan—is difficult to view as anything less than an assassination attempt against the Libyan leader (despite an executive order prohibiting assassination, signed by the president).

38. *Alleged Assassination Plots*, p. 199.

39. See Shackley, *op. cit.*

40. Pacem in Terris IV Convocation, Washington, D.C., December 4, 1975.

41. Interview, Washington, D.C., January 1976.

42. See Stuart H. Loory, "The CIA's Use of the Press: A 'Mighty Wurlitzer,' " *Columbia Journalism Review*, vol. 13, September–October 1974, p. 13.

43. See "Covert Action," *Hearings of the Church Committee*, October 23, 1975.

44. Senator Frank Church, "Covert Action: Swampland of American Foreign Policy," *Bulletin of the Atomic Scientists*, vol. 32, February 1976, p. 9.

45. U.S. Senate, Washington, D.C., October 24, 1975.

46. Quoted in Powers, *op. cit.*, p. 266, original emphasis.

47. Interview, Athens, Georgia, May 22, 1980.

48. Interview, Washington, D.C., August 18, 1980.

49. See, for example, Richard Helms's apparent disgust with covert propaganda operations "of no consequence" (Powers, *op. cit.*, p. 101) and his skepticism about covert action generally (at p. 28).

50. For former Senator Church, this remained the central argument against covert action. "If we have gained little [from covert action], what then have we lost?" he once asked. His answer: ". . . our good name and reputation." "Covert Action: Swampland," p. 11.

51. "Gesprach mit William E. Colby," p. 101, author's translation.

52. Interview, Washington, D.C., December 16, 1975.

53. "Covert Action," *Hearings of the Church Committee*, October 23, 1975.

54. *Ibid.*, December 4, 1975.

55. *Ibid.*

56. Senator Frank Church, Pacem in Terris Convocation, *op. cit.*

57. Johnson, *Season of Inquiry.*

58. Loch K. Johnson, "The U.S. Congress and the CIA: Monitoring the Dark Side of Government," *Legislative Studies Quarterly*, vol. 4, November 1980, pp. 477–499.

59. Interviews, staff, congressional intelligence committees, April 1984 and July 1986.

60. The letter was dated April 9, 1984; see the *Washington Post*, April 11, 1984.

61. Turner, *op. cit.*, p. 170.

62. *Report of the President's Special Review Board* (the Tower commission) (Washington, D.C.: Government Printing Office, February 26, 1987, B39), p. 67.

63. See the *New York Times*, January 15, 1987; on these ambiguities, see Loch K. Johnson, "Legislative Reform of Intelligence Policy," *Polity*, vol. 17, Spring 1985, pp. 549–573.

64. See David B. Ottaway and Patrick E. Tyler, "New Era of Mistrust Marks Congress' Role," *Washington Post*, May 19, 1986.

65. Interview by David Brinkley, *This Week with David Brinkley*, ABC Television, December 14, 1986.

66. Interviews, senior intelligence officials, November 1980, Washington, D.C.; see, also, Senate Select Committee on Intelligence Annual Report No. 95-217, May 18, 1977, p. 2; and Leslie H. Gelb, "Overseeing of CIA by Congress," *New York Times*, July 7, 1986. Former DCI Turner has said that, under congressional pressure, "three times Rea-gan signed, then cancelled, covert action operations" (Stansfield Turner, interview, WGST Radio, Atlanta, July 30, 1985). On the cancelled coup against Noriega, see the *New York Times*, October 23, 1989, p. 5.

67. Interview, staff aide, Senate Select Committee on Intelligence, December 12, 1980, Washington, D.C. Most of the time, though, the intelligence committees have been supportive of the intelligence agencies, whose budgets have reportedly tripled in the past decade (see Gelb, *op. cit.*).

68. Interview, Washington, D.C., June 11, 1984.

69. Interviews, CIA officials, Washington, D.C., November 17–18, 1980.

70. Press conference, U.S. Capitol, Washington, D.C., July 19, 1975.

71. Quoted by Don Oberdofer, *Washington Post*, August 6, 1983, p. A-13.

72. See Stansfield Turner, "Has Reagan Killed CIA Oversight?" *Christian Science Monitor*, September 26, 1985, p. 14; *Report of the Inouye-Hamilton Committees*, Washington, D.C., November 1987; *Report of the Tower Commission*; and, Dan Morgan and Walter Pincus, "Somehow, the Irangate Story Still Doesn't Add Up," *Washington Post*, National Weekly Edition, September 28, 1987, pp. 23–25.

73. See Loch K. Johnson, *America's Secret Power*; and *Church Committee Report*, vol. III.

74. "Should the CIA Fight Secret Wars?" *Harper's*, September 1984, pp. 39, 44.

75. *Ibid.*, p. 37.

RECOMMENDED READINGS

Church Committee. *Alleged Assassination Plots Involving Foreign Leaders: An Interim Report*, Senate Select Committee on Government Operations with Respect to Intelligence Activities, U.S. Senate, November 20, 1975. A history of the plots against Fidel Castro (Cuba) and Patrice Lumumba (the Congo), and the murder of Gen. Rene Schneider (Chile).

———. "Foreign and Military Intelligence," *Final Report*, Book I, U.S. Senate, April 23, 1976. The Church committee's summing up of its findings on paramilitary operations and other covert actions.

Church, Frank. "Covert Action: Swampland of American Foreign Policy," *Bulletin of the Atomic Scientists*, vol. 32, February 1976. A skeptical look at covert action by the chairman of a Senate panel that examined the CIA and other intelligence agencies in 1975–1976.

Jeffreys-Jones, Rhodri. *The CIA and American Democracy* (New Haven: Yale University Press, 1989). An examination of the CIA through the eyes of a leading British scholar.

Johnson, Loch K. *America's Secret Power: The CIA in a Democratic Society* (New York: Oxford University Press, 1989). An examination of recent attempts to place controls on the CIA without undermining its effectiveness.

Pike Committee. "The CIA Report the President Doesn't Want You to Read," *Village Voice*, February 16, 1976. A damning portrait of the CIA's use of covert operations, originally a top-secret study which was leaked to the press.

Prados, John. *Presidents' Secret Wars: CIA and Pentagon Covert Operations since World War II* (New York: Morrow, 1986). A comprehensive review of U.S. covert actions in the modern era.

Shackley, Theodore. *The Third Option: An American View on Counterinsurgency* (Pleasantville, N.Y.: Reader's Digest General Books, 1981). A description of the theory and method of covert action by a former practitioner.

Snepp, Frank. *Decent Interval* (New York: Random House, 1979). A firsthand remembrance of the CIA's last days in Vietnam as the United States military evacuated in 1975, written by a then-CIA officer appalled by the agency's lack of concern for the fate of those South Vietnamese who had assisted U.S. intelligence during the war.

Treverton, Gregory F. *Covert Action: The Limits of Intervention in the Postwar World* (New York: Basic Books, 1987). A thoughtful appraisal of CIA covert actions since 1947 by a former staff aide on the Church committee.

Woodward, Bob. *Veil: The CIA's Secret Wars* (New York: Simon & Schuster, 1987). An absorbing account of paramilitary and other covert actions conducted by the Reagan administration, with the enthusiastic encouragement of the CIA director, William J. Casey.

THE LAST FULL MEASURE

THE USES OF THE WAR POWER

The Dimensions of Strategy

In Search of Security

No More Vietnams?

DECIDING TO USE THE WAR POWER

Sending In the Marines

The War Powers Resolution

Flies in the Ointment

Wrestling over the Resolution

A House of Cards

The Use of Nuclear Weapons

WEAPONS OF WAR IN THE NUCLEAR AGE

Backpacks and City Busters

The Effects of Nuclear Weapons

Star Wars

Deterrence and the Triad

Command and Control

The Arsenals

Arms Control

SUMMARY

10

THE WAR POWER: RESORTING TO THE OVERT USE OF FORCE

The Vietnam War Memorial in Washington, D.C. (Courtesy National Parks Service)

THE LAST FULL MEASURE

. . . ROY W PEAGLER • FRANK M RHODES • LAVLE J HALL • ROBERT G ROBERTSON • THOMAS QUICHOCHO SABLAN • ROBERT V THOMAS • RICHARD V THOMPSON • LAWRENCE S VOGEL • JOHN S WOOL-HEATER . . .

Here are a few of the 58,156 names on the Vietnam War Memorial in Washington, D.C. The death roster, carved in sleek, black marble, stirs a strong emotional response in most visitors old enough to remember the war in Indochina. Reading—touching—the row after row of names brings back painful images of GIs being evacuated from the battlefield on armored half-tracks, bandages over their eyes, their legs twisted and bloodied, plasma tubes jabbed into their arms. These soldiers were youngsters for the most part, with worried moms and dads back home, romances put on hold, jobs to resume, schooling to complete, careers and families ahead—the American Dream interrupted, or, for those with names now etched in marble, lost forever. The memorial, the most visited site in the nation's capital, stands above all as a reminder of the human costs that accompany warfare.

Without doubt, the war power—defined broadly in this book to mean the actual or potential use of overt military force—represents the most extreme and hazardous means for the pursuit of foreign policy ends. The importance of the war power stems from the fundamental fact that international politics remains in a primitive state, with force as the final arbiter between sovereign and contentious nations. When diplomacy seems ineffectual, when covert action fails (or if insufficient time is available for either negotiations or the use of secret instruments), or when this country chooses to display its full strength, the armed services may be used to secure U.S. objectives. Whatever means America's leaders may select, from secret power to the use of moral suasion (the range of options discussed in Part 2 of this book), the success of each usually depends upon a convincing reserve of military strength. The security of American citizens will always be the government's first obligation, and in the final analysis, this security depends upon the nation's capacity to defend itself with effective weaponry and well-trained soldiers.

The war power is preeminent for another reason: high stakes accompany its use, as symbolized by the rows of names on the Vietnam War Memorial. The decision to use armed force has always been the most fateful a nation can make. The war power may require, as Lincoln so movingly stated in his Gettysburg Address, a citizen's "last full measure of devotion." And with the dawning of the nuclear age, the dangers of armed conflict have dramatically escalated. New weapons of mass destruction hold the prospect of extinction for the human race. "The central fact of life in the nuclear age," write two authorities, "is the unquestioned and unambiguous ability of nations possessing nuclear weapons to destroy each other."[1]

In its appraisal of overt military force as a foreign policy means, this chapter has three objectives. First, it considers the various uses of the war power; second, it examines recent controversies surrounding the decision to use the military option; and third, it explores the ways in which the sophisticated weapons of the nuclear age have changed the face of war. This book's primary concern—how well America's 200-year-old constitutional framework fits the needs of contemporary foreign policy—lies at the core of this chapter, for no topic better reveals the disputes that haunt the Constitution's sharing of authority across the branches than the war power.

THE USES OF THE WAR POWER

The Dimensions of Strategy

The war power has been important to nations as a support for diplomacy and the other foreign policy instruments explored in the second part of this book; as a method of intimidation—a show of force ("saber rattling"); and for direct operations against other nations or groups.[2] These uses frequently overlap, as illustrated by events in Korea from 1950 to 1953. Following an invasion into the South by communist North Koreans, the Truman administration decided it was necessary to employ military force in order to set the stage for a diplomatic settlement of the conflict. The use of diplomatic negotiations designed to end the war rested squarely on the capacity of American-led UN forces to repel the communist invaders and prevent their military takeover of the entire peninsula. The war power, calculated the administration, had to precede the power of diplomacy.

Viewed from another perspective, the involvement of U.S. troops in the Korean conflict also represented a show of force to other communist nations, notably the Soviet Union and mainland China, intended to demonstrate that attempts at communist aggression in the Far East would be resisted with fierce determination by America and its allies. And, of course, the use of the war power in Korea represented, further, a direct military operation against aggressors: the Korean communists and their allied Chinese soldiers.

The war power involves more than just the application of force ("firepower") against the enemy. *Military strategy*, that is, the overt use of armed force to achieve American foreign policy goals, depends upon a complex interplay of operational, logistical, social, and technological variables.[3] The *operational dimension* consists of the skill displayed by a nation's battlefield commanders and war-room planners, particularly the flexibility and imagination with which they handle their troops and arms. Having a Napoleon or a Robert E. Lee at the helm clearly can be of immeasurable importance when a nation turns to the war power.

Yet, as reflected in the experiences of the American Civil War (among other conflicts), a General Lee may be insufficient alone for success. The North won, even with generals of lesser talent, in part because the Northerners were able to deploy an overwhelming physical force against the South. The superior roads and riverways enjoyed by the North, plus its greater industrial capacity to produce rifles and cannonballs—the *logistical dimension*—relegated operational skills to a secondary, perhaps even irrelevant, plane.

Yet, transportation systems and factories are also in themselves insufficient to ensure victory. Political will, as the great military thinker Clausewitz emphasized, is indispensable for military success. When it came to the massive production of weapons, North Vietnam had no hope of matching the United States during the Vietnamese war, even with the help of the Soviet Union and China; however, missing from the American side was a resolute desire to win the war, to go the distance, regardless of time and cost. In contrast, the North Vietnamese (and their Vietcong allies in the South) seemed prepared to fight on indefinitely. During the American Civil War, leaders in the South had hoped that the Northerners would soon tire of the conflict and quit. This proved a fatal miscalculation, too, and, as the military historian Michael Howard points out, once both sides displayed equal degrees of resolution—the *social dimension* of strategy—"the capacity of the North to mobilize superior forces ultimately became the decisive factor in the struggle."[4]

Moreover, the fourth strategic dimension, *weapons technology*, can be important in some instances (though not during the American Civil War, where both sides had arms of comparable sophistication). The longbow, the breech-loading rifle, steel breech-loading artillery, and, to leap forward a century, the atomic bomb are examples of weapons that have given one nation a decided edge over another in military combat.

In Search of Security

In the use of the war power, the United States has a range of alternatives between the extremes of surrender, on the one hand, and the initiation of nuclear war, on the other hand. This nation has periodically used overt military force for each of the purposes discussed above. General Andrew Jackson's bold military forays into Florida (territory claimed by the Spanish) were no doubt indispensable for persuading the government of Spain to negotiate a diplomatic settlement over the contested region. Teddy Roosevelt's imperious show of force by sailing America's great battleships in convoy around the world made a memorable impression on observers who, as a result, realized that the United States was now a military force to be reckoned with.

And America's history has been punctuated by the direct use of soldiers abroad. Since 1798, the United States has been involved in more than 200 military actions overseas. Congress formally declared war in only five of these instances, and gave some other form of legislative approval (from the appropriation of moneys to the passage of resolutions in support) on sixty-two occasions. Fully 140 engagements—the overwhelming majority—were the result of decisions reached by the executive branch alone to employ the war power.[5]

The reasons for the overt use of force have varied, to include protecting America's trading opportunities abroad (recall Jefferson's operations against the Barbary pirates and, a century later, U.S. intervention in the Boxer Rebellion in China), chasing European powers out of the western hemisphere, and President Wilson's promise, in his stirring war message to Congress, to defend "the rights and liberties of small nations." More recently, U.S. military strategy since the end of the Second World War has been based on the containment of communism (Chapter 4), a policy backed up by an imposing arsenal of nuclear and conventional weapons as well as a ring of global military alliances that encircle the Soviet Union. Throughout this period, the essential purpose of the war power has been to deter the Soviet Union and other communist nations from using their own war powers in ways that might endanger the vital interests of the United States and its allies. At first, this goal of *deterrence* was meant to be achieved through the threat—usually implicit but, early in the Eisenhower administration, quite explicit—of a massive, retaliatory nuclear attack against Moscow or Peking if their troops dared to invade western Europe, Korea, Japan, or other regions considered important to America's interests abroad.

Deterrence, it should be stressed, is essentially a psychological concept. The United States might not be able immediately to halt a Soviet invasion of West Germany; but the prospect of a subsequent triggering of U.S. nuclear weapons against the Russian homeland is designed to give leaders in the Kremlin pause. By 1957, the Soviets had achieved their own capacity to strike the United States with nuclear warheads; a condition of mutual deterrence now existed. Both superpowers were able to deter the outbreak of an attack against themselves, or their major allies, through the threat of *mutual assured destruction* (*MAD*). In theory at least (and so far in practice), this prospect of mutual suicide stood as a potent psychological barrier against the initiation of a third world war. As Richard Smoke observes, during the early years of the nuclear age "containment and deterrence reigned supreme" in American strategic thinking.[6]

In a key National Security Council document prepared in 1950 (NSC-68), strategic thinkers in the Truman administration raised early doubts, however, about an exclusive reliance on massive retaliation to protect U.S. interests. "Limited" wars against communist aggression might become common in the future (the war in Korea would immediately give substance to this theorizing), and a huge nuclear arsenal—while perhaps holding World War III at bay—might be irrelevant for smaller regional conflicts. Moreover, as the Soviet nuclear stockpile mushroomed, the prospect of relying on nuclear weapons—even as a bluff—became increasingly less palatable. Strategists began to shift

their attention back to the importance of nonnuclear, "conventional forces" (tanks, howitzers, mortars, rifles, and the like), which would soon account for the overwhelming proportion of U.S. weapons costs—some 85 percent of the total.

In a strategic policy developed during the Kennedy administration and labeled "flexible response" (Chapter 4), the United States would prepare itself to contain communism around the world with a variety of conventional and nuclear weapons for use at different levels of engagement. On the nonnuclear side, these flexible forces would comprise everything from the Green Berets in the 1960s and the Rapid Deployment Force in the 1970s to a flotilla of Navy ships in the Persian Gulf in the 1980s—a conventional deterrent to augment MAD, the nuclear deterrent. Nuclear weapons continued to remain the backbone of America's deterrence, though, as illustrated by the NATO military pact. As one analyst puts it, "the strategy of the North Atlantic Treaty Organization is based on nuclear retaliation, because it is cheaper than fielding a non-nuclear defense, be it high technology or trench variety infantry."[7]

Following its failed attempt in 1962 to gain an improved nuclear balance vis-à-vis the United States through the placement of medium-range missiles in Cuba, the Soviet Union also turned toward a massive buildup of its nuclear and conventional forces. By the mid-1970s, the United States and the Soviet Union had reached a level of essential equivalence in nuclear weaponry—a standoff little affected by occasional arms control negotiations. Employing the latest technology, both sides searched for new armaments to strengthen the credibility of their deterrence posture, with the prospect of the superpowers deploying advanced laser and nuclear weapons in orbit around the earth sometime early in the twenty-first century.

According to some experts, the future also held the dark possibility of limited nuclear wars that might have to be fought. Improved missile accuracy led the Carter administration to draft a controversial plan (Presidential Directive No. 59, or PD 59) that envisioned a tit-for-tat exchange of pinpointed nuclear strikes against specific military targets in the Soviet Union. Subsequently, officials in the Reagan administration spoke further of a nuclear *war-fighting doctrine* beyond deterrence: a capacity to "prevail" in a "protracted" nuclear war. These statements stirred a revival of the peace movement in Europe and America, leading to mass demonstrations in support of a bilateral "freeze" on warhead production and a favorable climate of public support for arms control measures. With this condition of rising public anxiety as a backdrop, the superpowers agreed in 1988 to a Treaty on Intermediate Nuclear Forces (INF), removing an entire class of medium-range missiles from European and Soviet soil (although these missiles accounted for only 4 percent of the world's total number of nuclear weapons, and the treaty left in place thousands of shorter-range nuclear missiles on the Euro-Soviet frontier).

No More Vietnams?

As both superpowers strengthened their military arsenals, each also turned to the war power in a variety of overt military actions. The Soviet Union invaded Hungary (1956), Czechoslovakia (1968), and Afghanistan (1979), among other examples; and the United States used overt military force about as many times (if usually for nobler reasons), including in Lebanon (1958), Cuba (1962), the Dominican Republic (1965), Vietnam (1964–1975), and, most recently during the Reagan administration, Lebanon, Grenada, Libya, and the Persian Gulf—more than two dozen limited, conventional wars and military skirmishes since the end of the Second World War.[8]

Although President Reagan often drew the sword, some of his leading advisers began to express a sense of caution about using the war power. This new restraint was evident in Secretary of Defense Caspar W. Weinberger's so-

called six commandments, which he presented in the form of a major policy statement on U.S. armed intervention abroad. Drawing upon what he said were lessons derived from the American experiences in Korea and Vietnam, Secretary Weinberger offered the following guidelines for U.S. military engagement:

- The military action had to involve vital national interests.
- The United States must intend to win.
- The operation had to have clear-cut political-military objectives.
- These objectives had to be subjected to a continual reassessment.
- The American people had to be in support (the social dimension of military strategy discussed earlier).
- All alternatives to the use of overt force—the other foreign policy powers examined in this book—had to have been tried first and found wanting.

The secretary said that his intention was to "sound a note of caution" against the rash use of military personnel in dangerous situations. While many generals welcomed the guidelines as an assurance against future unpopular wars of attrition like the Vietnam conflict, others raised questions about whether the six tests would in effect bind the military from any action at all short of a third world war.[9]

Despite this interest in limits on the use of the war power, both superpowers continue to spend billions of dollars and rubles on weapons. The enormous expenditures have brought little sense of security to either nation. Such is the central paradox of modern weaponry, examined later in this chapter. First, though, two important questions are considered: How does the United States decide to use the war power, and has the politics of war changed with the new face of modern weaponry? As one authority notes, the decision to use overt military force as an instrument of foreign policy has been "without question the greatest source of friction and misunderstanding in executive-legislative relations."[10]

DECIDING TO USE THE WAR POWER

Sending in the Marines

"When and where to go to war," once observed Senator Thomas Eagleton (D-Mo.), "is the most solemn and fateful decision a free nation can make."[11] Yet, as shown in Part 1 of this book, seldom are the decisions to use overt military force made in the reflective manner envisioned by the nation's founders. In most instances when the United States has resorted to force, the executive branch alone ordered troops into action—in the early years to repel attacks against American soldiers or shipping, then later in a more aggressive manner (Chapter 5). Since the Second World War, the president has often used overt military force abroad with little or no consultation on Capitol Hill, including full-scale deployments during the Korean war, the naval quarantine during the Cuban missile crisis, and the sending of the Marines to the Dominican Republic, to list only a few conspicuous examples prior to the dramatic buildup of U.S. troops in Vietnam—and not to mention sundry rescue operations, show-of-force missions, and punitive strikes. That this country has declared war formally only five times in its over 200 military actions leads the conservative commentator William F. Buckley, Jr., to conclude with studied understatement that America has "some unfinished constitutional business."[12]

The invasion of the Dominican Republic in 1965 was especially troubling to members of Congress. Initially, President Johnson stated publicly that the invasion had been necessary for the "protection and rescue of Americans." Soon, though, the argument changed: the objective of the 24,000-marine invasion force was to thwart the imminent threat of a communist takeover of the island. This quick reversal, coupled with the president's lack of candor toward legislators throughout the operation, had the effect of undermining Johnson's credibility within the Congress.[13] His friendship with the Foreign Relations Committee chairman, Senator Fulbright (who had gone out on a limb to support what he believed to be a rescue operation), quickly soured.

During 1965 as well, key legislators began increasingly to express doubts about the facts of the Tonkin Gulf incident (Chapter 5). In part on the basis of research conducted by staff on the Senate Foreign Relations Committee, they suspected that reports from the executive branch at the time of the incident (August of 1964) may have misinterpreted, exaggerated, or possibly even fabricated the alleged attack by North Vietnamese patrol boats on a U.S. destroyer off the coast of Vietnam. The cauldron of distrust on Capitol Hill began to boil over. The following year (1966), Fulbright and his committee conducted nationally televised—and highly critical—hearings on America's involvement in Vietnam.

By 1969, the Senate was ready to take stronger action, passing by a vote of 70 to 16 the National Commitments Resolution. The resolution called for greater consultation between the branches *before* the executive branch entered into military and other commitments abroad, and was described by its sire, the Foreign Relations Committee, as "an invitation to the executive to reconsider its excesses, and to the legislature to reconsider its omissions, in the making of foreign policy."[14] On the heels of this resolution came the Cooper-Church Amendment of 1970, passed in the Senate in an effort to force the withdrawal of U.S. forces from their invasion into Cambodia. For the first time in American history, the Senate threatened to use its penultimate power (short of impeachment) against the president in order to curb his use of military force: the power of the purse. The amendment was worded to cut off funding for support of U.S. troops in Cambodia if the president had failed to withdraw them by July 1, 1970. President Nixon did withdraw the troops from Cambodia (as he claimed he intended to do all along), though the war in Vietnam lingered on.

This struggle between the branches for control over the war power reached a climax in 1973 with the passage of the *War Powers Resolution*. This statute, referred to by then Speaker of the House Carl Albert (D-Okla.) as one of the two most important laws passed in his long tenure on Capitol Hill,[15] placed obstacles in the way of presidential authority to commit American forces abroad without congressional approval. "No more blank checks like the Gulf of Tonkin Resolution!" declared the Congress.

The source of tension between the branches over the war power has its origins (the reader will remember from Chapter 5) in two key passages of the Constitution: Article I, Section 8, and Article II, Section 2. As a former staff director of the Foreign Relations Committee, Pat Holt, has written, "Where to draw the line between the power of Congress to declare war and the power of the president as commander in chief is one of the most controversial issues relating to the Constitution." The two articles set up the perfect conditions for a tug-of-war between the branches. When the war in Vietnam went badly and the presidency was weakened further by the Watergate scandal, Congress tightened its grip on the rope and yanked. "The War Powers Resolution, in essence," concludes Holt, "is an effort by Congress to give itself more leverage in the tug of war with the executive branch."[16]

The War Powers Resolution

The resolution, as it finally emerged for a vote in 1973 following draft after draft, was, in the words of one observer, "a complicated law in which a number of disparate strands of congressional thought were woven together."[17] The proposed statute required that the president "in every possible instance shall consult with Congress" before introducing armed forces "into hostilities or into situations where imminent involvement in hostilities is clearly indicated by the circumstances." In addition, the bill required the president to report to the Congress within forty-eight hours regarding the deployment of troops in three types of situations: when forces were sent into hostilities or into a region where "hostilities" were imminent; when forces "equipped for combat" were sent into any foreign nation; and when forces were deployed which "substantially enlarge" the number of combat-equipped U.S. troops in the foreign nation.

The resolution permitted Congress to force the withdrawal of U.S. troops from a region at any time by a concurrent resolution, that is, by a simple majority vote in both chambers—without the president's signature or possible veto. (This provision amounts to a legislative veto, critics maintain, and is therefore invalidated by the Supreme Court's 1983 *Chadha* ruling; see Chapter 6 and below).

The War Powers Resolution stipulated, moreover, that if the Congress refused to endorse the president's use of force within sixty days of receiving the initial report, the U.S. troops *had* to be withdrawn—though Congress could grant a thirty-day extension, if necessary, to ensure an orderly and safe exit. The constitutional authority of the Congress to declare war, or to enact authorizations for specific combat operations according to normal legislative procedures, remained intact.

That the law took two years to pass indicates the difficulty legislators faced in their attempts to modernize the war power. Those favoring the resolution argued for a return to a system of constitutional balance, rather than war making by the president alone. "Recent Presidents," complained a report of the Senate Foreign Relations Committee, "have relied upon dubious historical precedents and expansive interpretations of the President's authority as Commander-in-Chief to justify both the initiation and perpetuation of foreign military activities without the consent—in some instances without even the knowledge—of Congress."[18]

The chairman of the House Committee on Foreign Affairs succinctly stated what was, in his view, the central purpose of the resolution: "to restore the balance between the President and the Congress in the war-making authority by limiting the power of the President to send American Armed Forces to combat in foreign lands without congressional approval. It would restore the rightful role of Congress under the Constitution."[19] Added another legislator: "If we have learned but one lesson from the tragedy in Vietnam, I believe it is that we need definite, unmistakable procedures to prevent future undeclared wars. 'No more Vietnams' should be our objective in setting up such procedures."[20]

The proposed law had its detractors. The arch-conservative Senator Barry Goldwater (R-Ariz.) thought it would undermine relations with America's allies, who might perceive the statute as a restraint on a rapid response to threats against the collective security arrangement of the Western powers.[21] The president himself, Richard Nixon, argued that the resolution "would seriously undermine this Nation's ability to act decisively and convincingly in times of international crisis."[22] He warned that it "would give every future Congress the ability to handcuff every future President merely by doing nothing and sitting still." Especially odious to the president was the sixty-day limit, which he said would "work to prolong or intensify a crisis."[23] Nor did he look upon the concurrent resolution as a proper instrument; indeed, he declared it unconstitutional, because "the only way in which the constitutional powers of a branch of the government can be altered is by amending the Constitution—and any attempt to make such alterations by legislation alone is clearly without force."[24]

Most worrisome to liberals was the forty-eight-hour provision. At first a leading advocate of war power legislation as a means for preventing future Vietnams by executive fiat, Senator Eagleton soon turned against the resolution because of this provision. The two-day leeway given to the president made the proposal, in his view, "a dangerous piece of legislation which, if enacted, would effectively eliminate Congress' constitutional power to authorize war." The resolution had become, he feared, "an undated declaration of war."[25] At the height of the congressional debate, Eagleton declared that "every president of the United States will have at least the color of legal authority, the advance blessing of Congress, given on an open, blank-check basis, to take us to war. It is a horrible mistake."[26]

The odd coalition of conservative and liberal opponents of the resolution stemmed from an examination by the two groups of different portions of the bill. Conservatives in Congress (as well as President Nixon) had no objection to the forty-eight-hour discretionary clause, but recoiled from the limits on presidential power embodied in the sixty-day provision and the option of a concurrent resolution to force a troop withdrawal. For the liberals, the likes and dislikes were exactly reversed. Despite this odd left-right opposing coalition, however, the proponents of the resolution were far more numerous—enough even to override (in November 1973) President Nixon's veto of the proposal.

Senator Jacob Javits, the chief architect of the legislation, observed after the vote: ". . . with the war powers resolution's passage, after 200 years, at least something will have been done about codifying the implementation of the most awesome power in the possession of any sovereignty and giving the broad representation of the people in Congress a voice in it. This is critically important, for we have just learned the hard lesson that wars cannot be successfully fought except with the consent of the people and with their support. . . ." In his opinion, "At long last . . . Congress is determined to recapture the awesome power to make war."[27]

Flies in the Ointment

Since its passage, the War Powers Resolution has been dogged by controversy. Sam Nunn

Perspectives on American Foreign Policy   *10.1*

The views of three legislators on Congress and the war power:

The 535 men and women of the House and Senate have an equal responsibility with the President in a matter so crucial to the American people as war. Their collective judgment is far more likely to be right than that of the President alone.

—*Senator Jacob Javits*
R-N.Y.

Yes, the world has changed in 200 years' time. The body counts are higher in the era of high-tech warfare and superpower politics. However, that only makes adherence to constitutional principle all the more necessary, since the dying will be done by 250 million people, not just one President.

—*Senator Lowell P. Weicker, Jr.*
R-Conn.

God help the American people if Congress starts legislating military strategy.

—*Senator Richard B. Russell*
D-Ga.

Sources, respectively: Jacob Javits, "The War Powers Resolution and the Constitution: A Special Introduction," in Demetrious Caraley, ed., *The President's War Powers: From the Federalists to Reagan* (New York: Academy of Political Science, 1984), p. 3; Lowell P. Weicker, Jr., comments, "Focus on the War Powers Act," newsletter, Center for National Policy, vol. 1, 1988, p. 10; and Richard Russell, quoted by Gordon Hoxie, "The Not So Imperial Presidency: A Modest Proposal," *Presidential Studies Quarterly*, vol. 10, 1980, p. 202.

(D-Ga.), chairman of the Senate Armed Services Committee, declared flatly in 1987 that the resolution "has not worked."[28]

The *Chadha* decision raised serious legal questions about the use of a concurrent resolution to withdraw troops at any time before the sixty-day limit expired. A former counsel to the Senate Foreign Relations Committee concludes that, because of *Chadha*, this section of the resolution is now "clearly invalid."[29] Some observers inside and outside Congress continue to argue, however, that *Chadha* simply has no standing when it comes to questions of military intervention abroad, because the Court has traditionally avoided judgment on such political questions. Further, some authorities insist that *Chadha* does not apply to the resolution because—unlike true "legislative vetoes"—this statute never claimed to be delegating power to the president. The war power is shared between the branches (Chapter 5), and, from this vantage point, the concurrent resolution becomes not a legislative veto but "a useful and appropriate means for expressing congressional policy" in a domain where neither branch can claim an exclusive constitutional authority.[30]

The debate continues, but the widespread assumption on Capitol Hill is that the concurrent-resolution provision in the law may well have been vitiated by the *Chadha* ruling and that Congress would have to pass a joint resolution (susceptible to presidential veto) if it wished to withdraw U.S. troops from hostilities abroad before the sixty-day time expiration. Most authorities accept, though, the binding nature of the time requirement on the executive branch; U.S. troops would have to be withdrawn by the president after the sixty-day clock runs out, unless Congress allows a thirty-day extension—or votes to continue the war.

The ambiguous language of the statute has led to other disputes—especially over the word *hostilities*. As the renowned constitutional expert Louis Henkin has noted: "Above all, the resolution suffers gravely from a lack of any definition of 'hostilities. . . .' "[31] This flaw became a source of great consternation to some legislators in 1987–1988 when the Reagan administration placed American warships in the Persian Gulf, without reporting under the provisions of the resolution. Officials in the executive branch claimed that no report was necessary, since the ships were merely on patrol protecting U.S.–flagged Kuwaiti oil carriers. Yet, as members of Congress pointed out, U.S. ships had been fired upon and had fired back; moreover, sailors on these ships were being paid dangerous-duty pay.[32] If this situation failed to signify the presence of "hostilities," what did? (One hundred fifteen members of Congress filed suit in U.S. District Court in 1987 to invoke the War Powers Resolution; the court dismissed the suit, however, on grounds that it was a "by-product of political disputes within Congress" and, therefore, beyond the purview of the judiciary—a position upheld by the Court of Appeals on February 29, 1988.[33])

Events in the Persian Gulf were hardly the first instance of controversy regarding the proper application of the War Powers Resolution. Its uneven acceptance by presidents had already become evident in a series of earlier U.S. military operations abroad (summarized in Table 10.1). This inconsistency in the willingness of presidents to report automatically to the Congress when U.S. troops entered a region of

TABLE 10.1   KEY INTERNATIONAL INCIDENTS RELEVANT TO THE WAR POWERS RESOLUTION, 1973–1989

INCIDENT	APPLICATION OF RESOLUTION
Evacuation of U.S. citizens from Cyprus, 1974	No report
Evacuation from Da Nang, Vietnam, 1975	Report filed, NC
Evacuation from Phnom Penh, Cambodia, 1975	Report filed, NC
Evacuation from Saigon, Vietnam, 1975	Report filed, FC
Mayaguez rescue, 1975	Report filed, MC
Evacuation of U.S. citizens from Lebanon, 1976	No report
Korean "tree-trimming" incident, 1976	No report
Zaire airlift, 1978	No report
Military advisers in El Salvador, 1978–	No report
Iranian rescue attempt, 1980	Report filed, NC
Air combat over the Gulf of Sidra, 1981	No report
Peacekeeping force in Sinai, 1982	No report
Peacekeeping force in Lebanon, 1982	Report filed, MC
Peacekeeping force in Lebanon, 1982–1984	No report
Military assistance to Chad, 1983	Report filed, MC
Military aircraft for Saudi Arabia, 1984	No report
Grenada invasion, 1983	Report filed, NC
Interception of *Achille Lauro* hijackers, 1985	No report
U.S. helicopters fired on in Honduras, 1986	No report
Bombing of Libya, 1986	No report
U.S. Navy in Persian Gulf, 1987–	No report
U.S. planes repel rebels, Philippines, 1989	No report
Panama invasion, 1989	Report filed, MC

NC = no consultation with Congress; MC = minimal consultation; FC = full consultation.

hostilities—thereby starting the sixty-day time clock—rendered, in the view of one thoughtful legal authority, "largely Pyrrhic the widely hailed victory of Congress in 'recapturing' its share of the war-making power."[34]

Wrestling over the Resolution

Since the passage of the War Powers Resolution, Congress and the executive have been engaged in a prolonged wrestling match over when its provisions should be honored—with presidents periodically going so far as to declare the statute unconstitutional and, therefore, null and void (even without a test in the courts). Among the incidents listed in Table 10.1, three of the most important—the *Mayaguez* rescue operation (1975), peacekeeping in Lebanon (1982–1984), and the Grenada invasion (1983)—are examined here to illustrate the nature of the debate.

The Mayaguez Rescue   In the unsuccessful attempt to rescue American merchant sailors aboard the vessel *Mayaguez*, captured by Cambodian forces in May 1975 (see Chapter 5), President Ford failed to consult a single member of Congress in advance. Key members were simply "informed" beforehand through a brief presidential report. Representative Clement Zablocki (D-Wis.) stated at the time: "Clearly it was not the intention of the Congress [in the War Powers Resolution] to be merely informed of decisions made."[35] Senator Eagleton complained further, in disgust, that "all the President has to do is make a telephone call . . . and say, 'The boys are on the way. I think you should know.' . . . Consultation!"[36]

Moreover, the official reports from President Ford (and his successors) in compliance with the War Powers Resolution have been skimpy at best. As one study concludes: "The reports . . . are one- to two-page letters that proffer less information than might be gleaned from reading newspaper coverage of the events. Indeed, the report on the *Mayaguez* operation made no

mention of the number of casualties nor the fact that bombing of a military airfield occurred after the ship and crew were in U.S. custody."[37] For the journalist I. F. Stone, "the most important casualty of the *Mayaguez* crisis was the War Powers Resolution."[38]

Multinational Peacekeeping Force in Lebanon Another contentious series of events related to the War Powers Resolution occurred between August 1982 and February 1984. In response to a request from the Lebanese government, President Reagan in August of 1982 sent U.S. military personnel to participate in a multinational operation designed to assist the evacuation of Palestine Liberation Organization (PLO) members from this nation ravaged by civil war. Eight hundred marines joined the same number of French soldiers, plus 400 Italian troops, in the successful mission. The president duly reported this use of American forces, under the provisions of the resolution.

A month later, however, the president sent back the marines into Lebanon, this time numbering 1200 troops. Their assignment on this occasion was much more vague: to help the prospects for peace by maintaining a physical presence in Lebanon. Since the marines were bivouacked in a supposedly secure location away from the direct fighting in the capital city of Beirut, the Reagan administration argued that the "hostilities" provision in the War Powers Resolution failed to apply; no report—and, therefore, no time clock—was necessary. The murder of several marines by sniper fire in 1983 strained the credulity of this argument, and pressure mounted on Capitol Hill to invoke the resolution. The Reagan administration steadfastly refused to send a report to Congress, though, for it wanted to avoid any possible infringement on the president's flexibility as commander in chief. "We want to cooperate with the President," said the Senate Democratic leader, Robert C. Byrd (W.V.), in response, "but this is the law, and the law cannot be winked at."[39]

Yet wink the Congress did. Lamely, it decided in June of 1983 to pass a resolution on Lebanon—the *Lebanon Emergency Assistance Act*—which gave the president eighteen months to keep the troops where they were. In signing this resolution, President Reagan said: "... I do not and cannot cede any of the authority vested in me under the Constitution as President and as Commander-in-Chief of the United States Armed Forces. Nor should my signing be viewed as any acknowledgment that the President's constitutional authority can be impermissibly infringed by statute. . . ."[40] With this measure, Congress proclaimed that the clock had started (even though the War Powers Resolution requires the president to start the clock with the issuance of *his* report), then looked down at its shoes as the commander in chief brushed aside restrictions on the use of troops in Lebanon.

"Congress drove a hard bargain," concludes a constitutional scholar, with understandable sarcasm. "One wonders how its leaders emerged from the negotiations without agreeing to apologize for enacting the War Powers Resolution."[41] Senator Eagleton's appraisal of the Lebanese resolution was equally acidic: "We should face the fact that this language is a blank check to the President to do whatever he wants to do militarily in Lebanon. Cleverly worded, it is nonetheless the Lebanese Gulf of Tonkin Resolution."[42]

Then, in autumn, Reagan's "peacekeeping" mission in Lebanon unraveled. On October 23, 1983, a terrorist killed 241 U.S. marines in a suicidal truck bombing of their headquarters. This tragedy, coupled with subsequent reports on the poor security arrangements for the American troops and a revelation that the Joint Chiefs of Staff had unanimously opposed sending the marines to Lebanon in the first place, raised cries on Capitol Hill to tear up the blank check offered in the Emergency Assistance Act. When the president ordered the battleship *New Jersey* to fire upon enemy installations in Lebanon, the absence of "hostilities" claimed by the ad-

ministration became more farcical still. Faced with this rising criticism and—more tangibly—a congressional resolution calling for the "prompt and orderly withdrawal" of U.S. forces in Lebanon, the president brought the Marines home on February 7, 1984.

The Grenada Invasion   Almost as controversial as the Lebanese mission was the introduction of 1900 Army and Marine Corps personnel into Grenada on October 25, 1983—just two days after the suicide bombing of the Marine headquarters in Beirut. The purpose of this operation, ostensibly, was to rescue American students studying at the medical school in Grenada, a Caribbean island about the size of Columbus, Ohio, where conflict between rival political factions had broken out. (After the U.S. invasion, the school's administrators reported that they had anticipated no threat from the unrest.) Critics of the operation contended that the mission's real purposes were: to prevent a Cuban-backed Marxist takeover of the government; to demonstrate—against however humble an opponent—that the United States was no longer the impotent giant that some foreigners had alleged; and, most important, to divert public attention from the loss of the Marines in Lebanon.

Like the *Mayaguez* "rescue," this display of force against a weak target proved to be good politics. It boosted the president's standing in the opinion polls at the precise moment when, with the murder of so many marines placed by presidential order in a dangerous location with an ambiguous mission, it might have been expected to plummet. Evidently, the president's television charm—his much cited "Teflon" personality—had once again saved him from public opprobrium.

Nineteen Americans were killed and 144 wounded in the Grenada foray. The Reagan administration reported the use of force as required by the War Powers Resolution, but refused to acknowledge that a sixty-day clock now ran against prolonged involvement. Kenneth W. Dam, the deputy secretary of state, expressed the view of the executive branch in congressional hearings. Since it was "highly unlikely" that U.S. troops would be in Grenada longer than sixty days, he said, application of the resolution was unnecessary.[43] This assurance failed to mollify Senator Gary Hart (D-Colo.), among others.

"Frankly, I don't trust them," Hart told a reporter. "We are dealing with an Administration that is not inclined to obey the law. They can always find an excuse to stay in Grenada, and they very clearly do not want to be bound by the sixty-day limit."[44]

Through a nongermane rider to a budget bill, the Senate passed a preliminary resolution on October 28 (by a vote of 64 to 20), emphasizing that the War Powers clock had indeed started running on Grenada as of October 25; the House soon followed suit (by a vote of 403 to 23). The budget measure failed, however, and with it the Grenada rider—something of a moot point, anyway, because the administration had already begun to withdraw its troops.

A House of Cards

Attempts by Congress to play a stronger role in decisions involving the war power have, in sum, met with erratic results. Since the passage of the War Powers Resolution (and certainly before), executive-branch consultation with the Congress in advance of a military action has been sporadic at best. The record of U.S. warfare indicates that most decisions to employ overt military force have been made within the secret confines of the NSC and, before its creation in 1947, within its various analogues at the highest reaches of the executive branch.

The reports mandated by the War Powers Resolution have been inconsistent, as well as thin in content; and presidents have been reluctant to acknowledge they are being timed on their use of force overseas. The Congress itself

has often allowed the president, especially during the period from 1981 to 1986, when President Reagan enjoyed unprecedented popularity, to bend the rules of the resolution, allowing him in the Lebanese case what amounted to carte blanche—at least until the suicide attack against the Marines. Concludes one authority: ". . . in the absence of the Executive's good faith adherence to the spirit of the resolution, which the sponsors also had mistakenly expected, . . . the whole procedural edifice turned out to be a house of cards."[45] According to an experienced senator, Mark O. Hatfield (R-Ore.), the major blame for the failure of the resolution lay in a lack of "political will" in the Congress—a demand for presidential adherence to the law.[46]

In 1988, Senators Byrd and Nunn—legislators of considerable stature—declared the War Powers Resolution "broke" and offered measures to fix it. The law had failed, in their view, for several reasons:

- Presidents had been reluctant to report on their use of force, and even when they did, Congress had found it difficult to act.
- The sixty-day clock was too confining.
- The resolution failed to address the subsequent introduction of U.S. troops abroad, addressing only the initial deployment.
- The sixty-day clock allowed foreign governments and terrorist groups too much leverage over U.S. policy ("the jerks can jerk us around," said Byrd and Nunn in a joint press release).
- Congressional action could be halted by a filibuster or presidential veto, meaning that "the President, plus one-third of either the House or the Senate, could conduct a war beyond the reach of the War Powers [Resolution]."
- The resolution encouraged "confrontation rather than consultation."
- Its provisions were ambiguous, especially the term *hostilities*.
- It raised serious questions about America's "staying power in the midst of crisis."[47]

The legislators, urging their colleagues to remember that "under the Constitution the Founding Fathers gave Congress the power to declare war," offered new legislation to improve the resolution. The Byrd-Nunn proposal recommended abandonment of the sixty-day clock and a reliance on executive consultation with a panel of congressional leaders to explain the president's use of overt force abroad. The congressional leaders could then recommend to Congress an appropriate response. If legislators chose to limit or halt the use of force, the joint resolution—a majority vote in both chambers, with a subsequent opportunity for a presidential veto—would be (according to the Byrd-Nunn prescription) the appropriate instrument.

Critics were quick to denounce this retreat from a fixed-time clock. Further, some viewed the joint-resolution procedure—with its opportunity for a presidential veto (in contrast to the concurrent resolution)—as giving the executive branch too much control over war making, one of the very problems the senators had complained about themselves when introducing the bill.

A new round of discussions about the War Powers Resolution started early in 1989, with the advent of a new administration led by President George Bush. The incoming secretary of state, James A. Baker III, proposed that the Congress and the executive "agree to disagree" over the constitutionality of the resolution and move on to a "gentleman's agreement" that the branches consult together on proposed military operations. In a mood of conciliation (the "honeymoon" period enjoyed—however briefly—by new presidents), congressional leaders acknowledged flaws in the existing resolution and seemed willing to explore fresh approaches. As a sign of Congress's readiness to repair damaged relations between the branches, Speaker Jim Wright (himself soon to be deposed in a conflict-of-interest scandal) withdrew from the House docket an intelligence reform bill that would have forced the president to report on covert actions within forty-eight hours, rather than in the "timely fashion" preferred by the Reagan and Bush administrations.[48]

The Use of Nuclear Weapons

While the search continues for ways to improve the War Powers Resolution, a related issue has attracted growing attention: whether to limit the possible presidential first use of nuclear weapons. The director of the Federation of American Scientists (FAS) argued in 1984 that the president alone should not be allowed to move "the nation into the line of fire, into the war zone."[49] Rather, the Congress should establish a joint nuclear planning committee, which the president would be required to consult before ordering the first use of nuclear weapons. This proposal was not meant to undermine the authority of the president, should the United States be attacked. Under the proposal, the president would retain the right to order prompt retaliation (a second strike) if an adversary were to hit the United States with a first strike. To give the president complete discretion over the momentous decision to use nuclear weapons, though, was in the opinion of the FAS director "unnecessary, unwise, unconstitutional and unlawful."

In response to the FAS proposal, the Department of Defense rejected the contention that the president should have to consult with the Congress prior to the first use of nuclear weapons. Deterrence, said the DOD's general counsel, "rests on the policy of flexible response, which would include the use, as required, of conventional weapons, nonstrategic nuclear weapons and strategic nuclear weapons. To insure that the flexible response policy actually deters, a potential aggressor must be convinced that NATO is indeed ready to use any of the weapons it possesses, including, if necessary, nuclear weapons." Consultation with Congress, he continued, would just place an "additional procedural requirement" on first use, which would "tend to undermine NATO's deterrence policy."[50]

The nature of sophisticated weaponry in the nuclear age has appropriately led the constitutional authority Louis Henkin to wonder: "Have nuclear weapons effectively eliminated any meaningful role for Congress in decisions as to nuclear strategy? If so, our celebrated Constitution is no longer relevant for our most compelling concerns."[51] The situation may not be quite this dire; after all, Congress can still shape nuclear policy in important ways through the usual legislative process, as well as with its advice and consent for treaties (the INF Treaty, for instance), with hearings, investigations, and the like. Henkin, though, does raise vital questions about the constitutional implications of modern weaponry—particular in times of crisis.

The final segment of this chapter takes a closer look at this modern weaponry, with special attention to the foreign policy dilemmas which result from the invention of nuclear arms. The armaments of the nuclear age have clearly concentrated greater power than ever before in the office of the commander in chief—power enough to destroy the world; yet, these weapons have also had the effect of making citizens increasingly sensitive to the dangers of war making by a solitary individual. Modern weaponry underscores the virtues of shared authority, for no man or woman has the wisdom to weigh these awful choices alone; in this choice of foreign policy means, above all others, the president needs the counsel of other elected representatives.

WEAPONS OF WAR IN THE NUCLEAR AGE

Backpacks and City Busters

The United States and other major powers have three forms of military response: strategic nuclear, tactical nuclear, and conventional. The most fearful are the *strategic nuclear capabilities*, that is, those weapons able to strike the enemy from afar with massive levels of destructive

power caused by a release of nuclear energy. They include intercontinental ballistic missiles (ICBMs, which were going to be called IBMs until the International Business Machine Corporation—an American business titan already widely known by that acronym—complained to the government), submarine-launched ballistic missiles (SLBMs), and long-range bombers equipped with nuclear bombs or missiles.

The phrase *tactical nuclear capabilities* encompasses weapons that also rely on a nuclear reaction for their force, but one of more limited scope designed for relatively small targets on the battlefield. Some, though—the so-called *theater nuclear weapons*—can deliver a larger punch than the bombs dropped on Hiroshima and Nagasaki. These weapons vary in size from backpack warheads (for use by infantry, say, to stop a tank) and howitzer shells (with a range of twenty miles or so) to the NATO Lance battlefield-support missile (and its Warsaw Pact Frog-7 counterpart, with ranges of 80 and 43 miles, respectively) and the INF missiles—cruise and Pershing IIs on the American side, SS-20s and others on the Soviet side (with ranges varying from 180 to some 3400 miles). The American INF missiles had the capacity to strike the U.S.S.R. from European soil within some ten minutes; therefore, from the Soviet point of view, they were strategic weapons—a strong incentive to negotiate their elimination in the INF Treaty.

In contrast, *conventional capabilities* refers to those weapons that rely on nonnuclear technology—everything from M-16 rifles to the blast effect of chemical reactions like TNT. This distinction is somewhat artificial, however, since the effects of some advanced, high-yield conventional weapons are barely distinguishable in their heat and blast damage from low-yield tactical nuclear weapons.

The Effects of Nuclear Weapons

When detonated, nuclear weapons have multiple effects: intense heat, strong blast and high winds, radiation (which can be long-term), and severe atmospheric disturbances.

Blast and Heat   The immediate consequences of a nuclear explosion are devastating. The figures in Table 10.2, based on the assumption of a normal, clear day (twelve-mile visibility) and 80 percent of the fireball dissipated, provide a sense of the relationship between bomb yield and the effects of heat, blast, and radiation. The energy distribution of a nuclear explosion consists of 50 percent blast, 35 percent thermal energy (heat), and 15 percent nuclear radiation. Looked at from another perspective (the percentage of casualties inflicted), 50 percent of the deaths come from the release of thermal energy, 35 percent from the blast wave, and 15 percent from nuclear radiation.[52] The larger the yield of the weapon, the more important the thermal effect becomes. As shown in the table, thermal radiation remains the greatest danger at a distance from the center of the explosion (ground zero).

At or near ground zero, the largest number of casualties from the blast wave are a result of its indirect effects: collapsing buildings, flying glass, and the like. Since the primary enemy targets are usually military weapons (a *counterforce* targeting strategy) or industrial and communications centers (a city-oriented *countervalue* targeting strategy), the blast effect is important. Its destructive radius is used as the key calculation for targeting decisions, not a bomb's thermal effects.

Radioactivity   In low-yield weapons (tactical nuclear warheads, for example), radiation can be the cause of more deaths than heat or blast. The gamma rays emitted in the radiation literally tear apart the molecules of tissues as they pass through the human body; they can also produce genetic alterations if they enter the testes or ovaries. The effects of radiation are often delayed. Some cancers caused by radiation fail to appear for five years; others may lie dormant for as long as forty years.

The *rad* is the unit used to measure how much energy is absorbed by a target. A dental x-ray is equivalent to about 0.1 rad. Following an exposure to 450 rads, a human being has a 50-50 chance of dying; that is, about 50 percent of those exposed to this level of radiation will succumb.[53] For children, the elderly, and the infirm, a lesser dose can be fatal. Sheltering can be important against radiation attack; a sixteen-inch barrier of earth can reduce the radiation by a factor of ten, say, from 450 rads down to 45.[54] The short-term symptoms of various radiation doses on human beings are summarized in Table 10.3.

TABLE 10.2   THE EFFECTS OF NUCLEAR WEAPONS

YIELD	RADIUS IN MILES OF THIRD-DEGREE BURNS	RADIUS IN MILES OF 165-MPH WINDS	RADIUS IN MILES OF 500 RADS OF RADIATION
2 kT	0.58	0.55	0.57
13 kT	1.40	1.00	0.80
1 MT	8.00	4.30	1.60
20 MT	25.00	11.80	3.00

Yield in kilotons (kT) and megatons (MT). 165-mph winds are equivalent to about 5 pounds per square inch (psi) pressure above normal atmospheric pressure. (An overpressure of 3 psi is sufficient to collapse a frame house.)

Source: Professor George Rathjens, Harvard-MIT Summer Program on Nuclear Weapons and Arms Control, Cambridge, Mass., June 17, 1985.

TABLE 10.3 EFFECTS OF WHOLE-BODY RADIATION DOSES

DOSE IN RADS

Up to 150	No short term effects.
150 to 250	Nausea and vomiting within 24 hours, recovery within 48 hours.
250 to 350	Nausea and vomiting within 4 hours; symptom-free period begins in about 48 hours; symptoms reappear leading to some deaths in 2 to 4 weeks.
350 to 600	Nausea and vomiting within 2 hours. Many deaths in from 2 to 4 weeks; incapacity prolonged.
Over 600	Nausea and vomiting almost immediately. Practically 100% deaths within 1 week.
2600	Incapacitation within 1 hour.
5000	Complete incapacitation within 5 minutes. Death within a day or two.

Adapted from L. W. McNaught, Nuclear Weapons and Their Effects *(London: Brassey, 1984), p. 58. Reprinted by permission.*

Atmospheric Alterations   The *electromagnetic pulse* (*EMP*) associated with nuclear explosions would also have a profound effect on the waging of modern warfare, especially if the nuclear warheads were detonated at a high altitude. According to one specialist, "gamma rays will cause electrons to be ejected from atoms in the air thus ionising the atmosphere around the burst. This will result in disturbances of electromagnetic waves transmitted by radar and communications equipment." These atmospheric disturbances could disrupt or paralyze all communications, radar operations, and early warning systems throughout NATO, for example, in the case of a first ("preemptive") strike by the Soviet Union. "A pre-emptive strike of this nature," concludes this expert, "would be a most attractive proposition to the Warsaw Pact in the early stages of any future war."[55]

Nor can one easily dismiss the brooding omnipresence of a *nuclear winter* that could descend over the earth in the aftermath of a nuclear war. Using computer modeling, a group of American scientists have predicted dire atmospheric changes stemming from a nuclear exchange. Even a limited nuclear war could have catastrophic effects on climate if cities were targeted, they conclude, because the soot from burning buildings would rise into the atmosphere and block out the sun's rays. Many uncertainties remain in these computer-based estimates, however. Some critics believe that scientists have exaggerated the threat. Some Russian researchers even argue that nuclear blasts would, on the contrary, extinguish fires; therefore: no soot and no nuclear winter.

Scientists who have examined the computer models acknowledge, nevertheless, that a nuclear war could well bring in its wake a rapid drop in earth temperatures. The surface of the earth might freeze to a depth of one meter (making it difficult, if not impossible, to bury the dead). Food supplies would diminish; drinking water would freeze. "It is clear that the ecosystem effects *alone* resulting from a large-scale thermonuclear war could be enough to destroy the current civilization in at least the Northern Hemisphere," sums up a research team. "Coupled with the direct casualties of perhaps two billion people, the combined intermediate and long-term effects of nuclear war suggest that eventually there might be no human survivors in the Northern Hemisphere; ... the possibility of the extinction of *Homo sapiens* cannot be excluded."[56] The most reasonable conclusion to draw at this time is that no one really knows for sure what the ecological effects of a nuclear war would be. Nor is anyone likely to know in advance.

Disease   Even without a nuclear winter, the postattack conditions would be decidedly grim.

Radiation would linger, causing decreased sperm counts (among other pathologies). Medical supplies, including antibiotics, would be destroyed, and a sizable proportion of the total number of physicians and nurses would be killed or incapacitated.

Using the common baseline of a 6500-megaton attack against the United States, about half of the grain supply in this country would be destroyed immediately; and obviously, the distribution of food would be enormously difficult. In the filthy, garbage-strewn postattack environment, a recrudescence of the rat population would occur. Preceding the possible freezing of the earth would come its scorching and sterilization with the first impact of the warheads. From a psychological perspective, the population—despite some acts of heroism—would experience profound and widespread depression. The United States and the Soviet Union, in a word, would be thrown back into a "medieval setting."[57]

Star Wars

The comparative cheapness of nuclear weapons makes them attractive to military planners. A warhead costs about $1 million to produce, and an extra $2 million to $10 million will provide a delivery system, from a slow-moving cruise missile to a rocketing ICBM. These weapons represent by far the most cost-effective way to destroy cities or other targets covering wide geographic areas. The ratio of the cost of objects destroyed to the cost of the weapon is about 1000 to 1. This combination of cheapness and enormous destructive power has made the defense of cities and industrial areas, in the view of most experts, all but impossible.

The Reagan administration, however, advanced an imaginative proposal that—despite the skepticism of experts—sought to protect the United States against nuclear attack by enemy missiles. The plan, which envisioned shooting down enemy missiles in their flight with space-based laser technology, is known as the *Strategic Defense Initiative*, or *SDI* (labeled "Star Wars" by the media, after a popular science-fiction film loaded with laser guns and other electronic gadgetry). Whether such a *ballistic missile defense* (*BMD*) system would actually work became a topic of intense debate. Key scientists remained skeptical; they calculated that it would be less expensive for the Soviets to overwhelm the SDI system with hundreds of new missiles than for the United States to strengthen its defenses against the bombardment. In answer to Secretary of Defense Weinberger's rhetorical observation in 1984, "We made it to the moon; why can't we do this?" critics responded: "The moon didn't fight back!"

If SDI worked at 90 percent efficiency, over 1000 Soviet warheads would still slip through the defense—enough to make America's cities look like so many spent campfires. Even if U.S. scientists could construct an impermeable umbrella, nuclear weapons are becoming increasingly smaller in size and easier to smuggle into this country beneath a Star Wars shield. The bomb dropped on Hiroshima weighed 10,000 pounds; its equivalent today weighs about 100 pounds and could fit into the trunk of an automobile—before long, into a hatbox.

Although the Bush administration quickly expressed less of an infatuation with SDI, research moves forward nonetheless—driven in part by a constituency of physicists and engineers. The federal funding has become an almost irresistible opportunity for them to carry out basic research at the government's expense—a Manhattan Project for their generation. While the government and private scientists explore the feasibility of the Star Wars defense, the protection of the United States against a nuclear attack continues to rest upon deterrence and—at its core—a nuclear weapons triad.

Deterrence and the Triad

The appeal of SDI is understandable. If only the danger of nuclear war really could be elimi-

Perspectives on American Foreign Policy 10.2

Physicians for Social Responsibility depict a nuclear detonation in a U.S. city:

A single one-megaton thermonuclear warhead explodes on a clear day over a major U.S. city. Within 1.5 miles of ground zero, blast overpressures as high as 200 pounds per square inch (psi) crush, collapse, or explode all buildings, however strongly constructed. 600 mile per hour winds hurl debris at lethal velocities. The fireball, with temperatures exceeding 27 million degrees Fahrenheit, vaporizes everything.

All human beings within this zone immediately die. . . .

Between 1.5 and 2.9 miles from ground zero, blast overpressures range from 10 to 20 psi. All but the strongest buildings collapse. Winds reach 300 mph. The heat of the explosion evaporates aluminum siding, melts acrylic windows and causes spontaneous ignition of clothing.

50% of the population in this zone immediately dies. All exposed persons who do not die from the blast suffer third degree burns.

4.3 miles from ground zero, blast overpressures still reach 5 psi. Winds exceed 150 mph. Asphalt paving melts. Wood and fabric ignite.

8.5 miles from the center, winds continue to reach hurricane strength. Every fifth person outdoors suffers third degree burns. 70% of those outdoors suffer second degree burns.

All this within moments of detonation.

Death awaits many who survive these first few seconds. Radiation, stress, cold, hunger, and burns combine to undercut survivors' immunological systems, and in a world of spreading disease, thousands more die.

One bomb. One city. Tallahassee. Seattle. Chicago.

Whatever the target, thousands, perhaps millions, die. Many others are critically injured—with nowhere to turn. . . .

In a major attack, most of the country's physicians and medical care personnel, concentrated in major urban areas, will be killed instantly. There will be no means to transport surviving physicians to the victims, nor the victims to the physicians. And with hospitals destroyed, there will be no equipment, beds, diagnostic and X-ray facilities, blood, plasma, or drugs with which to treat the millions who lie dying. . . .

From a pamphlet distributed in 1985 by the Physicians for Social Responsibility, an organization established by U.S. physicians as a means for educating people about the likely effects of nuclear warfare which now has members from countries throughout the world.

---

nated with a supershield, hermetically sealing off the United States from external danger—like the tranquil Christmas scenes sealed inside glass paperweights! Instead, at present, the human race is forced to rely on the more fragile, if (argue SDI critics) more realistic, concept of MAD.

Robert S. McNamara, the secretary of defense in the Kennedy and Johnson administrations, once provided this elaboration on the meaning of deterrence. "The cornerstone of our strategic policy continues to be to deter deliberate nuclear attack upon the United States or its allies," he wrote. "We do this by maintaining a highly reliable ability to inflict unacceptable damage upon any single aggressor or combination of aggressors at any time during the course of a strategic nuclear exchange, even after absorbing a surprise first strike. This can be defined as our assured-destruction capability,

. . . the very essence of the whole deterrence concept." What both sides face, McNamara concluded, is "certainty of suicide to the aggressor, not merely to his military forces, but to his society as a whole."[58]

Ground-Launched Missiles   The strategic deterrent capability of the United States consists of three component parts referred to earlier, known as the *triad*: ICBMs, SLBMs, and intercontinental bombers. One of the great debates about this capability has surrounded the question of ICBM vulnerability. Soviet warheads have become sufficiently powerful and accurate to raise concern that a quick strike against America's ICBMs (which rest in underground silos located chiefly in the west and midwest) might destroy them, despite their "hardened" silo shells of thick concrete.

Various plans have been proposed to protect this "leg" of the triad. President Nixon advocated an *antiballistic missile (ABM)* system—a precursor of SDI, relying on nuclear-armed interceptors to destroy incoming warheads before they could strike American cities or ICBM silos. Even though the Soviets themselves constructed a cluster of ABMs around Moscow, U.S. legislators rejected this approach to the protection of U.S. cities as too costly and unlikely to work anyway (the same arguments now offered against the SDI proposal). By a margin of one vote, however, senators did allow the development of a limited ABM system to be built as a shield for a single ICBM site. Local opposition to the shield (viewed by citizens more as a lightning rod attracting Soviet missiles than a protection), coupled with lingering doubts about its effectiveness, led to a prompt mothballing of the ABM site soon after its construction.

During the Ford and Carter administrations, the Pentagon conceived of a "racetrack" method for reducing the vulnerability of U.S. missiles to a Soviet first strike. According to this scheme, the United States would place its new-est ICBMs (the Missile Experimental, or MX) on railroad cars. The MX would shuttle along vast tracks in the western states; each missile would be provided with twenty-three sequential hiding places so that the Soviets would never know with certainty where to strike. To complicate Soviet targeting further, several additional railroad cars would be empty. Presumably, this shell game would guarantee that some American missiles would always be available following an attack to strike back at the USSR (a so-called *second-strike capability*).

The local opposition to this racetrack plan grew rapidly. Citizens of Utah, Nevada, and surrounding states refused to have their homeland turned into high-priority targets for the Soviet Union. The ecological problems were also unsettling. Some engineers estimated that virtually all the water in the western states would be required just to mix the concrete needed for the construction of the railway hiding places— the greatest engineering project since the building of the pyramids. Moreover, critics feared that the Soviet response would simply be to build more warheads, with even larger yields, in order to saturate the entire track configuration in time of war.

The Reagan administration repudiated the racetrack concept, and weapons designers turned to new possibilities, such as the placement of the MX off American shores, concealed beneath the waves on the continental shelf. The administration, however, proved unable to settle on a basing mode for the MX. Meanwhile, legislators advocated a road-mobile missile with a single warhead, the "Midgetman," and the Air Force returned to the racetrack idea (in part because it seemed to be less costly than the Midgetman proposal). One humorist suggested, perhaps with as much credibility as various official plans, that U.S. missiles could be placed in unmarked Volkswagens on the New Jersey Turnpike.

The debate over ICBM vulnerability remains lively, with the Bush administration advocating a mix of MX and Midgetman missiles (a compromise designed to negotiate a settlement between the two weapons' proponents). This debate aside, it is unlikely that the weaknesses of a single leg in the triad would tempt the Soviets to attack; the United States could still kick back with its other two legs. Moreover, the possibility exists that, upon seeing Soviet missiles fired toward the United States, this country might launch its ICBMs immediately, thereby freeing the ICBMs from their potential tombs—a response known as *launch on attack*. America's ICBMs could be fired even earlier, in response to a strategic intelligence warning that the Soviets were about to attack (*launch on warning*).

Bombers The bomber leg of the triad has some special advantages. About 30 percent of this force is always on alert and would probably survive a Soviet first strike. Further, this is the only system that can be redirected, or even recalled, after being set on its flight path. Critics, though, feel that these war machines have become the dinosaurs of the nuclear age: large, slow-moving targets for defensive missiles and fighter planes to knock out of the air with ease. The invention of the radar-elusive Stealth bomber was meant to add credibility to this portion of the deterrent structure, but critics remain doubtful that even this expensive airplane could make it through Soviet defenses—though when an adventurous West German youth managed to land a small plane near Moscow without detection or interference, one began to wonder how capable Soviet air defenses really are!

Submarines The submarine leg is no doubt the least vulnerable portion of the triad. Hidden deep beneath the ocean's surface, *each* of America's thirty-seven nuclear submarines carries more destructive power than the combined total released during every war fought since the dawn of mankind! Moreover, they are difficult for the Soviets to locate, and even harder to attack if found. As the Soviets improve their anti-

submarine warfare (ASW) capabilities, the United States improves its deception measures to keep the submarines hidden. "Our subs look pretty invulnerable for a long time," concludes one authority.[59] The major shortcoming of this portion of the triad is the difficulty of communicating to a submarine deeply submerged, although communications engineers are making significant strides toward solving this technical challenge.

Command and Control

The subject of disseminating information and orders from decision makers to the military commanders in the field, called *command-control-communications* (C^3), raises some alarming scenarios. Computer chips have been known to fail in this nation's early-warning system, giving false signals that a Soviet attack was under way. Once what seemed to be Soviet missiles on the radar screen proved to be only a flock of swans. On another occasion, a Finnish farmer accidentally plowed through the "hot line" telephone link between the United States and the Soviet Union. (Measures have been taken to improve the security of this line.) While none of these incidents produced or happened during a crisis, they underscore the fragility of warning and communications systems upon which peace might depend. Moreover, C^3 systems are vulnerable to manipulation. Communications networks could become channels for disinformation, with Americans or Soviets trying to fool one another with false information to gain a military advantage. The networks can be jammed, too—say, with the Grateful Dead at 300 decibels.

Unhappily, the United States no longer enjoys much of a buffer of time and distance from its enemies. If a nuclear war were to commence, the first half hour would streak by like a flash of lightning. Within a minute or two, U.S. technical sensors (satellites and radar outposts) would record and transmit homeward data on the Soviet launch of ICBMs and SLBMs. Within

A port bow view of the Trident submarine *USS Tennessee*, near its home port at Kings Bay, Georgia, in 1989. (Official U.S. Navy Photograph)

ten to twelve minutes, the first Soviet SLBMs would hit the United States, continuing over the next ten minutes. Fifteen minutes later the first ICBMs would arrive. The chaos of communications under such conditions can be readily imagined.

Decapitation   A central C^3 problem is to protect U.S. command posts. According to one expert, this challenge stands as "the most significant problem of modern strategic forces. . . ."[60] One can conceive of a successful Soviet strike against the White House, the Congress, the Pentagon, and other command centers that would deprive the United States of its top leadership in time of war—a swift military stroke called *nuclear decapitation*. Headless, the body might have to surrender or submit to total destruction.

To guard against decapitation, this nation has fashioned various safeguards. One safeguard has been the establishment of DUCs (deep underground centers) where the *National Command Authority (NCA)*—that is, the top political and military leaders of the United States—can hide from the downpour of nuclear missiles. Caves have been constructed for this purpose in the mountains of Maryland, and in Colorado at NORAD (North American Defense) Headquarters near Colorado Springs. In an alert condition indicating an imminent Soviet attack or one already under way (Defense Condition One, or "DEFCON 1"), the NCA is expected to rush to predesignated locations—the backyard of the White House, for one—to be whisked away by helicopter into their mountain refuges. From within these caves, however, communications with the outside world would be difficult; moreover, likely as not, these locations could prove to be merely expensive cremation vaults.

Another possibility is to go aloft. The president has a specially equipped plane, officially known as the National Emergency Airborne Command Post, or NEACP (pronounced "kneecap"), designed to serve as a command center in time of nuclear war; but whether or not the president and his staff would have time to board the custom-built Boeing 747 is problematic. No doubt this airplane would be a top target for a surprise submarine-launched missile attack, if the Soviets resorted to a decapitation strategy. To ensure that the United States always has at least one airborne command post during time of war, the Air Force since 1961 has maintained in the skies at all times—twenty-four hours a day, 365 days a year—one or more airplanes code-named "Looking Glass," commanded by brigadier generals.

In the doctrine of nuclear deterrence, then, C^3 is a weak link. Further, insufficient thought has gone into how the United States and the Soviet Union would communicate with one another if war ever did break out. Presently, the NEACP has no "hot line" capability. Once nuclear war began and America's leaders went aloft (the Soviets have underground command facilities only), this country would have no way to end the war through negotiations. Despite the fragility of the system, decapitation remains an unlikely scenario, though, simply because it could fail; the unacceptable result might be to trigger the deterrent capabilities of the nation attacked, bringing about the destruction of both sides.

Communications Redundancy   To make a decapitation strategy riskier still for the Soviets, the budget for C^3 is being increased to build redundancy of communications into the links between the NCA and the field commanders at silo locations, in bombers, and at sea. The object is to make sure that, should one link fail, others will be available to keep the network intact. Further precautions are being taken on both sides to reduce the possibility of an accident or mechanical malfunction leading to war. Electromechanical locks, called *permissive action links* (PALs), have been placed on tactical nuclear weapons, for instance, to prevent the firing of a weapon without proper authority—say, by a deranged military officer or by a terrorist group that has stolen a bomb.

The Arsenals

Though some concern has been devoted to reducing the risk of war, the weapons arsenals on both sides remain enormous. Table 10.4 outlines the distribution of nuclear weapons across the triad.

TABLE 10.4   STRATEGIC WARHEADS: A U.S. AND SOVIET COMPARISON (1986)

	NUMBER OF WARHEADS	
WEAPON SYSTEM	U.S.	U.S.S.R.
Land		
ICBMs	2145	6420
Sea		
SLBMs	4760	2800
Sea-launched cruise missiles	A few	0
Air		
Air-launched cruise missiles	1700	400
Air-launched bombs and short-range missiles	2140	360

Source: Adapted from David P. Barash, The Arms Race and Nuclear War *(Belmont, Calif.: Wadsworth, 1987), pp. 33, 36; and data from Edward L. Warner, Rand Corporation, cited by the* New York Times, *October 16, 1986, p. 8.*

Strategic Weapons   Military experts estimate that just 300 to 500 one-megaton bombs fired by each superpower would destroy about 70 percent of the population and industrial capacities of both nations. The United States has thirty Poseidon nuclear submarines and seven new Trident models. The Poseidons carry sixteen missiles each. In eighteen of the Poseidons, the missiles are tipped with ten warheads, or MIRVs (multiple, independently targetable reentry vehicles); in twelve, the number is eight warheads. The Tridents have twenty-four missiles, each with eight warheads. The aggregate sum, then, is 5760 warheads, with a combined yield equivalent (at 100 kilotons per warhead) to some 576 megatons of TNT! Since about 60 percent of these submarines are at sea at any time, the fleet together always has some 3456 warheads aimed toward the U.S.S.R. Another 3840 hydrogen bombs and missile warheads are ready for use aboard the American fleet of 324 strategic bombers. Finally, the United States has some 1045 ICBMs with about 2145 warheads.[61]

The Soviets have a similar capacity for destruction, although they have placed their emphasis chiefly on ICBMs. Sixty-four percent of the Soviet warheads are land-based, 28 percent are submarine-based, and 8 percent are on bombers (the comparable American distribution is, respectively, 20 percent, 44 percent, and 36 percent).

Tactical Nuclear Weapons   Added to this mountain of strategic warheads are the tactical nuclear weapons. About 20,000 of them exist in the U.S. arsenal, of which some 6000 are located in Europe. The Soviets have about 12,000 tactical nuclear weapons, with roughly 3000 dedicated to the European theater. Even after the INF Treaty goes into effect in a phased withdrawal of this missile class over the next few years, the two superpowers will continue to have some 4000 smaller nuclear warheads in their respective European theaters—a subject of pending negotiations between the Bush administration and President Gorbachev (following a hoped-for arms accord reducing conventional weapons in Europe).

Conventional Weapons   While the biggest bang remains in the nuclear arsenal, the biggest bucks are spent on nonnuclear armaments. Former Secretary of Defense McNamara has explained why. "The fact that the Soviet Union and the United States can mutually destroy one another regardless of who strikes first narrows the range of Soviet aggression which our nuclear forces can effectively deter," he writes; ". . . we, and our allies as well, require substantial nonnuclear forces in order to cope with levels of aggression that massive strategic forces do not, in fact, deter."[62]

A Range of Responsibilities   Throughout the cold war, "resisting Soviet pressure to expand beyond the containment line has remained the central tenet of military strategy," state two authorities on U.S. military strategy. This objective has required an immense military establishment able to respond to "the broadest possible range of exigencies," since containment has stood traditionally as a defensive strategy for the most part, designed to meet communist advances at the time and place chosen by them.[63] With the advent of the Reagan Doctrine, however, containment took a more aggressive turn.

According to the Reagan Doctrine, "containing communism is insufficient," observes an analyst. "The Soviet Union can be challenged by 'rolling back'—undermining and overthrowing—Third World revolutionary governments." Other military experts put it this way: ". . . the Reagan administration's aggressive doctrine of *'low-intensity conflict,'* or 'LIC' as it is known in Pentagon circles, . . . represents a strategic reorientation of the U.S. military establishment, and a renewed commitment to employ force in a global crusade against Third World revolutionary movements and governments." This use of force short of full-scale war against the Soviet Union "identifies Third World insurgencies—and not Soviet troop concentrations in Europe—as the predominant threat to U.S. security; it is, moreover, an outlook that calls on the United States to 'take the offensive'—in contrast to the passive stance of 'deterrence'—to overcome the revolutionary peril."[64]

Threats against America's access to the world's vital natural resources; periodic "wars of national liberation"; terrorist attacks against U.S. military bases and diplomatic personnel; the logistical problems of maintaining armies far from these shores; the strength of the Warsaw Pact forces—each challenge relies upon a credible conventional capability. The precise size and mission of the conventional deterrent, however, continues to be bitterly disputed by laymen and specialists alike.

How Much Is Enough?   The figures in Table 10.5 provide a look at the conventional balance of forces between the NATO and Warsaw Pact nations. The American investment in conventional forces during the Reagan years was unprecedented in peacetime: an 8 to 9 percent real

TABLE 10.5   NATO AND WARSAW PACT CONVENTIONAL FORCES IN EUROPE (1989)

	NATO	WARSAW PACT
Personnel		
Active Ground Forces	2,200,000	3,100,000
Weapons		
Battle tanks	22,224	57,300
Armed helicopters	2,600	3,800
Combat aircraft	3,977	8,250
Artillery pieces	17,328	46,270

Source: Adapted from figures presented in the New York Times, *May 30, 1989, p. 6, based upon NATO estimates and the calculations of various U.S. defense experts.*

growth in defense expenditures per annum (in 1985 constant dollars)—the highest growth rate since the Second World War.[65] Annual military spending neared $400 billion in 1987, compared with $144 billion in 1980. According to a former member of President Reagan's Council of Economic Advisers, the United States at the end of the 1980s was "spending in real terms 20 percent more [on defense] than we were spending at the peak of the Vietnam War."[66] Note two other military experts: ". . . the Reagan era military buildup appears to have elevated military spending to a historically higher level than ever before in peacetime."[67]

A major push behind this buildup was the Reagan administration's severe interpretation of global threats to the United States—especially its proclivity to view U.S.–Soviet relations in zero-sum terms. Its geopolitical strategists worried that America's global eminence might be in a state of decline. Among other examples, they cited the erosion of U.S. military bases abroad, down 75 percent from Second World War levels, as well as the Soviet advantage in conventional weapons in the European theater. As the appropriate remedy, they advocate an even greater U.S. arms buildup.

Despite the record increases in defense spending during the early years of the Reagan administration, its officials continued to press for larger spending. The defense authority William W. Kaufmann has commented on the administration's estimates that "U.S. and allied forces would not be able to hold out for long against an enemy onslaught, whether by the Warsaw Pact in central Europe, by Soviet units racing down through Iran, or by North Korean armor attacking across the demilitarized zone."[68] In his view, these estimates were exaggerated and overly pessimistic, resting on the dubious assumptions that all the available Soviet firepower could be thrown against a single theater of war and that the Warsaw Pact can match NATO as a reliable fighting force. The gloom-and-doom estimates may have had more to do, in Kaufmann's opinion, with the administration's ideological fixation on the Soviet Union as an implacable enemy than with an objective analysis of U.S. security needs.

Kaufmann does acknowledge, though, the difficulty of holding off with conventional forces a Soviet conventional attack against western Europe. The chief responsibility of the secretary of defense, he concludes, "lies in determining the size and composition of the strategic nuclear forces needed to prevent Soviet leaders from having any realistic expectation of gaining an exploitable military advantage and the general purpose [conventional] forces appropriate to the *initial* defense of a *small* number of vital theaters in conjunction with allies."[69] The uncertainty surrounding the ability of the United States to deter the Soviets with conventional forces highlights the importance of the nuclear deterrent. As another respected military analyst emphasizes, "Without the restraining influence of the threat of nuclear holocaust, implicit in nuclear weapons, the likelihood of conventional war might rise dramatically."[70]

No one can dispute that large amounts of the nation's resources are devoted to military purposes. The defense budget approaches expenditures of $1 billion a day! The B-52 bomber provides one of many illustrations on the high cost of defense. "The B-52 burns 3,000 gallons of fuel an hour," states Air Force Lieutenant General Kelly H. Burke. "It costs $12,000 an hour on fuel alone."[71] The yearly operating cost of America's fleet of 241 B-52s is nearly $2 billion. More than half of America's federal taxes go into the defense budget, if one includes interest payments on the national debt incurred by past defense spending. In the 1987 Defense Department budget, sixteen proposed weapons systems cost over $1 billion each (with SDI research leading the list at $4.8 billion).

Regardless of all the impressive hardware available in today's war chest, no one is sure how much is necessary to deter real or potential enemies. "How much is enough?" has always been the central defense question. The answer depends upon one's perspective. The Pentagon is notorious for its "worst-case" analysis of the military threat. "The Army would need 54 divisions, instead of its 16, if all the worst-case analyses were followed," Kaufmann concludes.[72] Another problem is the difficulty of knowing precisely how much America's adversaries are spending on weapons and, more difficult still, for what purposes. Analysts have consistently disagreed on how to measure and interpret Soviet military expenditures.[73]

Several experts believe that the U.S.S.R. is spending even more than the United States on defense. The chairman of the U.S. House Armed Services Committee, Les Aspin, points out, though, that a sizable fraction of Soviet military equipment and personnel are directed toward the Chinese and other adversaries, not toward the United States. Moreover, the quality of troop training (coupled with a high turnover of personnel) makes the Soviet forces inferior to their American counterparts. In Aspin's opinion: ". . . a lot of statistics are abused when we talk of the Soviet military. We must put those numbers in perspective and not jump to the conclusion that the Soviet bear is ten feet tall."[74]

It is possible that no level of defense expenditures would be enough, for sometimes an enemy simply will not be deterred from aggressive intentions—Adolf Hitler, for example. Effective deterrence may depend on how crazy the opponent is, and on how much pain both sides are willing to absorb. These are inevitably matters of imprecise calculation.

Arms Control

A central conclusion to be drawn from this review of U.S. defense strategy is this: until a reliable SDI shield is constructed—and it seems unlikely that one can ever be built that would guarantee protection from a saturating storm of enemy missiles—the security of the United States will continue to rely ultimately on nuclear deterrence, what Winston Churchill called the "balance of terror." Given this situation, the objective in the view of many strategists ought to be the careful maintenance of a military balance, so that no superpower is tempted into a first strike. To be avoided is a situation where one side seems too weak, which might invite an attack by the other side. This is sometimes called the "Munich syndrome," an allusion to the time when Hitler acted out of disdain for perceived weakness in the West (Chapter 3). Equally to be avoided is a situation where one side seems too strong, which might provoke an attack by the weaker side in paranoiac self-defense—the "Pearl Harbor syndrome," as when Japan evidently acted out of fear in 1941 and struck the United States.[75]

Efforts to achieve a balance of arms—ideally at a lower level—and to reduce the risks of war are referred to as *arms control*. Advocates of arms control argue that it is better to negotiate than to fight, and that eventually real progress can be made toward the goal of a world with fewer nuclear warheads and conventional arms. They point also to the economic consequences of the superpower arms race. Both nations have each spent over $1 trillion on defense in the 1980s, squeezing budgets to wring out money for weapons instead of rebuilding their faltering industries, improving educational systems, providing improved health care, and a thousand other domestic needs.

Citizens in both countries may well wonder what the huge military expenditures have achieved. In the United States, news reports in the 1980s about $7000 coffee pots and $400 toilet seats as part of the defense budget came to symbolize the inefficiencies of Pentagon spending. According to one experienced analyst, the Department of Defense increased the budget for new missiles by 90 percent, yet the number of missiles actually bought increased only 6 percent; for aircraft, the comparable figures were 75 percent and 9 percent. "What, indeed, have they purchased with our trillion dollars?" he asks. "America's pocket has been picked, and we are only marginally stronger for it."[76]

In rebuttal, opponents of arms control point

to the meager accomplishments of superpower negotiations, despite decades of attempts to scale back on armaments. The 1963 test ban treaty, which prohibited the testing of nuclear weapons in the atmosphere, was clearly an environmental and health boon (testing above ground had led to some 5000 additional cancer deaths a year around the world caused by strontium 90 and other radioactive particles in the atmosphere); but testing continued underground and nuclear weapons became ever more powerful. Moreover, neither SALT I, SALT II, nor any other agreement (with the single exception of the INF Treaty) has managed to freeze or reverse the competition in arms between the superpowers, each only slowing it.

Belief in the efficacy of arms control assumes that leaders of the United States, the Soviet Union, and other countries can agree on a fundamental proposition: that nations have a common interest in avoiding attempts to blow each other up. While this assumption seems reasonable on the surface, many American conservatives reject it. They believe, on the contrary, that the Soviet intention is precisely to destroy the United States if it can find the opportunity. From this perspective, arms control becomes dangerous. It is a narcotic lulling the American people into a false belief that the differences between this nation and the Soviet Union can be resolved peacefully, when in fact the two superpowers continue to be engaged—despite Gorbachev's apparent friendliness—in a mortal struggle which allows no compromise. "One cannot bargain with the devil," is a standard admonition from arms control opponents. Even Henry Kissinger, the chief SALT I negotiator, warned President Reagan not to expect too much of the Soviet Union—so dramatically different from the United States in culture and ideology—in the wake of the INF agreement, regardless of the president's apparent rapport with Gorbachev. Kissinger advised Reagan "not to confuse foreign policy with psychiatry."[77]

A more moderate group, based at Harvard

University, reasons that the greatest danger that could lead to a failure of deterrence is neither excessive weakness nor strength on either side (though these conditions are to be avoided) but, rather, a sequence of events that could lead nations on an unintended stumble toward war through technical accidents and misunderstandings. As a guard against such eventualities, this group recommends improved PAL systems, the withdrawal of hair-trigger nuclear artillery in Europe, an improved hot line linkage among all nuclear powers, "hardened" (that is, less vulnerable) C^3 facilities, and better training for crisis management and prevention, among other proposals.[78]

The weapons of modern warfare raise a host of difficult problems for decision makers. Their power (some 2.5 tons of TNT for every man, woman, and child on this planet), vast number, and rapid speed of delivery have made the use of overt force a more ominous instrument of foreign policy than in earlier days. The founding fathers prudently refused to lodge the war power in the hands of the president alone; today, surely, they would feel even more strongly about the desirability of sharing this authority with the legislative branch. The War Powers Resolution states that the use of American troops abroad should rest on the "collective judgment of both the Congress and the President" [Section 2(a)]. This principle, as the constitutionalist Louis Fisher rightly observes, "is the dominant lesson of the past four decades."[79]

SUMMARY

With the invention of nuclear weapons, warfare reached a new level of potential violence. The superpowers have enough warheads between them to reduce one another's cities to rubble. Yet these weapons may well have helped to keep World War III at bay. The condition of mutual deterrence, whereby each superpower maintains a capacity to annihilate the other, creates a "balance of terror" that underlies, paradoxically, a long period of global stability between the United States and the Soviet Union. This balance is precarious, however, with command-and-control facilities representing a major point of vulnerability. Arms control negotiations have tried, with only modest success, to slow the nuclear and conventional arms race.

Given the heightened dangers of modern weaponry, the decision to use the war power has become ever more fateful. American foreign policy over the years—and dramatically in the past two decades—has witnessed an often acrimonious struggle between the executive and legislative branches over the use of military force. In its efforts to reclaim authority over the war power, Congress fashioned in 1973 a rather clumsy mechanism in the War Powers Resolution. Designed to prevent future open-ended presidential discretion over the deployment of U.S. troops into hostilities abroad (the Gulf of Tonkin scenario), the resolution has met with inconsistent results. Troubling ambiguities remain regarding its proper application. Whether (and how) presidential discretion should be limited with respect to the first use of nuclear weapons has become a further bone of contention. In this constitutional debate, the executive branch has frequently displayed a preference for either of two solutions: removal of Congress altogether from decisions about the use of force, or—since legislators are unlikely to accede to this approach—resort to the use of the war instrument through secret means in an attempt to avoid legislative debate (the paramilitary option).

KEY TERMS

military strategy
operational dimension
logistical dimension
social dimension
weapons technology
deterrence
mutual assured destruction (MAD)
war-fighting doctrine
War Powers Resolution
hostilities
Lebanon Emergency Assistance Act
strategic nuclear capability
tactical nuclear capability
theater nuclear weapons
conventional capabilities
counterforce
countervalue

rad
electromagnetic pulse (EMP)
nuclear winter
Strategic Defense Initiative (SDI)
ballistic missile defense (BMD)
triad
antiballistic missile (ABM)
second-strike capability
launch on attack
launch on warning
C^3
nuclear decapitation
National Command Authority (NCA)
permissive action links (PALs)
low-intensity warfare (LIW)
arms control

NOTES

1. Paul P. Craig and John A. Jungerman, *Nuclear Arms Race: Technology and Society* (New York: McGraw-Hill, 1986), p. 8.

2. See Norman J. Padelford and George A. Lincoln, *The Dynamics of International Politics* (New York: Macmillan, 1962), p. 434.

3. See Michael Howard, "The Forgotten Dimensions of Strategy," *Foreign Affairs*, vol. 57, Summer 1979, pp. 975–986.

4. *Ibid.*, p. 977.

5. President Ronald Reagan, news conference, Washington, D.C., October 23, 1987.

6. Richard Smoke, *National Security and the Nuclear Dilemma* (Reading, Mass.: Addison-Wesley, 1984), p. 56.

7. Bernard E. Trainor, "Another U.S. Study down the Drain?" *New York Times*, January 13, 1988, p. 22.

8. For a listing of U.S. military actions since 1945, see Barry M. Blechman and Stephen S. Kaplan, *Force without War: U.S. Forces as a Political Instrument* (Washington, D.C.: Brookings, 1978).

9. For the Weinberger list and an evaluation, see Bernard E. Trainor, "Weinberger on Persian Gulf: Cap the Chameleon?" *New York Times*, October 9, 1987, p. A20.

10. Francis O. Wilcox, "Cooperation vs. Confrontation: Congress and Foreign Policy since Vietnam," *Atlantic Community Quarterly*, vol. 22, Fall 1984, p. 271.

11. Cited in "The War Powers Act Controversy," *Congressional Digest*, November 1983, p. 276.

12. *Firing Line*, Public Television, December 20, 1987.

13. For accounts of this intervention, see William H. Blanchard, *Aggression American Style* (Santa Monica, Calif.: Goodyear, 1978), pp. 134–151; and Jerome N. Slater, "The Dominican Republic, 1961–66," in Blechman and Kaplan, *op. cit.*, pp. 289–342.

14. Pat Holt, *The War Powers Resolution: The Role of Congress in U.S. Armed Intervention* (Washington, D.C.: American Enterprise for Public Policy Research, 1978), p. 4.

15. Interview with the author, Washington,

D.C., July 15, 1975. The War Powers Resolution is often inappropriately referred to as the War Powers Act; *resolution* is the accurate word, for this statute was passed in the form of a joint resolution, distinguished from routine acts of Congress (though having the same legal weight) by the special focus of a resolution on a particular issue, as opposed, say, to the annual authorization acts for various ongoing programs in the federal government. The other key statute, in Speaker Albert's opinion, was the Budget and Impoundment Control Act of 1974. Throughout most of the war in Vietnam, Carl Albert had remained a loyal supporter of presidential ascendance over foreign policy decisions. The souring of this war, coupled with the Watergate experience, caused him to question his blind fidelity. He was particularly incensed by President Ford's use of covert operations in Angola in the aftermath of the Vietnamese war (1975). "I object to [the Ford administration's] underhanded attempts at sneaking this issue past Congress and the American people," he wrote in constituency letters, adding with a new philosophical perspective: "The Constitution gives the Congress, not the Secretary of State, the sole right to declare war and approve treaties. These are such important acts that only the entire Congress was given the authority. I will do all that I can to prevent further erosion of Constitutionally delegated Congressional authorities. This is a government run by the people, and I intend to keep it that way." [See, for example, the Carl Albert Collection, the Carl Albert Congressional Research and Studies Center Congressional Archives, University of Oklahoma, Box 1-160, Folder 7, letter to Richard G. Johnson, M.D.]

16. Holt, *op. cit.*, p. 39.

17. Cecil V. Crabb, Jr., and Pat M. Holt, *Invitation to Struggle: Congress, the President and Foreign Policy* (Washington, D.C.: Congressional Quarterly, 1984), p. 143.

18. Report No. 220, Committee on Foreign Relations, U.S. Senate, 1973, in Senate Reports, vol. 161 (no. 13017-3), p. 4.

19. Representative Clement J. Zablocki (D-Wis.), *Congressional Record* 119, October 4, 1973, p. 33038.

20. Representative Spark M. Matsunaga (D-Hawaii), *Congressional Record* 119, July 18, 1973, p. 24702.

21. See *ibid.*, p. 24532.

22. "President Nixon's Veto of War Powers Measure Overridden by the Congress," *Department of State Bulletin* 26, November 26, 1973, p. 662.

23. Holt, *op. cit.*, p. 8.

24. *Congressional Quarterly Almanac*, vol. 29 (1973), p. 907.

25. Thomas F. Eagleton, *War and Presidential Power: A Chronicle of Congressional Surrender* (New York: Liveright, 1974), pp. 221, 223.

26. *Congressional Quarterly Almanac*, vol. 29 (1973), p. 916.

27. "Congress Overrides Nixon's Veto of War Powers Bill," *Congressional Quarterly Weekly Report*, vol. 31, November 10, 1973, p. 2985; and the *Congressional Record*, November 7, 1973, pp. 36187.

28. Quoted in the *Atlanta Constitution*, November 10, 1987.

29. Michael J. Glennon, "The War Powers Resolution Ten Years Later: More Politics Than Law," *American Journal of International Law*, vol. 78, July 1984, p. 577.

30. Louis Fisher, "Why Congress Passed the War Powers Resolution," conference paper, Center for Law and National Security, School of Law, University of Virginia, Charlottesville, September 23, 1988, p. 25.

31. Louis Henkin, "Foreign Affairs and the Constitution," *Foreign Affairs*, vol. 66, Winter 1987–1988, p. 300.

32. For example: Stephen Solarz (D-N.Y.), *Firing Line*, Public Television, December 20, 1987.

33. See William P. Agee, "The War Powers

Resolution: Congress Seeks to Reassert Its Proper Constitutional Role as a Partner in War Making," *Rutgers Law Journal*, vol. 18, Winter 1987.

34. Glennon, *op. cit.*, p. 571.

35. John H. Sullivan, *The War Powers Resolution: A Special Study of the Committee on Foreign Affairs*, Committee on Foreign Affairs, U.S. House of Representatives, 1982, p. 219.

36. Statement of Senator Eagleton, *Congressional Record* (November 7, 1973), p. 36177.

37. Barbara Hinkson Craig, "The Power to Make War: Congress' Search for an Effective Role," *Journal of Policy Analysis and Management*, vol. 1, 1982, p. 324.

38. Quoted by Sullivan, *op. cit.*, p. 218.

39. *New York Times*, September 16, 1983, p. 1.

40. Crabb and Holt, *op. cit.*, p. 147.

41. Michael J. Glennon, "Some Compromise!" *Christian Science Monitor*, October 24, 1983, p. 16.

42. Crabb and Holt, *op. cit.*, p. 145.

43. *New York Times*, October 28, 1983, p. 1.

44. *Ibid*.

45. Glennon, "The War Powers Resolution Ten Years Later," p. 573.

46. Senator Mark O. Hatfield, remarks, "Focus on the War Powers Act," newsletter, Center on National Policy, Washington, D.C., vol. 2, 1988, p. 6.

47. Press release, office of Sam Nunn, May 19, 1988.

48. See the *New York Times*, February 1, 1989, p. 8; on the dispute over intelligence reporting, see Loch K. Johnson, *America's Secret Power: The CIA in a Democratic Society* (New York: Oxford University Press, 1989), Chap. 10.

49. See the *New York Times*, September 9, 1984.

50. *Ibid*.

51. Henkin, *op. cit.*, p. 303.

52. L. W. McNaught, *Nuclear Weapons and Their Effects* (London: Brassey, 1984), p. 27.

53. *Ibid.*, p. 59.

54. Professor George Rathjens, MIT, Harvard-MIT Summer Program on Nuclear Weapons and Arms Control, Cambridge, Mass., June 17, 1985; hereafter cited as the Harvard-MIT Summer Program.

55. McNaught, *op. cit.*, pp. 30, 96.

56. P. R. Ehrlich, M. A. Harwell, Peter H. Raven, Carl Sagan, G. M. Woodwell, et al., "The Long-Term Biological Consequences of Nuclear War," *Science*, December 23, 1983, original emphasis.

57. Dr. Jennifer Leaning, Harvard-MIT Summer Program, June 17, 1985. For a vivid description of the short- and long-term effects of nuclear weapons, see Jonathan Schell, *The Fate of the Earth* (New York: Knopf, 1974).

58. Robert S. McNamara, *The Essence of Security: Reflections in Office* (New York: Harper & Row, 1968), p. 52.

59. Professor Ashton B. Carter, Harvard University, Harvard-MIT Summer Program, June 18, 1985.

60. John D. Steinbruner, "Nuclear Decapitation," *Foreign Policy*, Winter 1981–1982, p. 21.

61. See David P. Barash, *The Arms Race and Nuclear War* (Belmont, Calif.: Wadsworth, 1987).

62. *Op. cit.*, p. 59.

63. Donald M. Snow and Lt. Col. Dennis M. Drew, *Introduction to Strategy*, 3d ed. (Maxwell Air Force Base, Alabama: Air Command and Staff College, 1985), p. 217.

64. See, respectively, Kenneth E. Sharpe, "The Real Cause of Irangate," *Foreign Policy*, vol. 68, Fall 1987, p. 30; and Michael T. Klare and Peter Kornbluh, "The New Interventionism: Low-Intensity Warfare in the 1980s and Beyond," in Michael T. Klare and Peter Kornbluh, eds., *Low-Intensity Warfare* (New York: Pantheon, 1988), p. 3.

65. William W. Kaufmann, Harvard-MIT Summer Program, June 26, 1985.

66. William A. Niskanen, Jr., quoted by Robert Conot, "When U.S. Defense Dollars Cost a World of Consumers," *Los Angeles Times*, December 13, 1987, sec. 5, p. 3.

67. Lawrence J. Korb and Stephen Daggett, "The Defense Budget and Strategic Planning," in Joseph Kruzel, ed., *American Defense Annual, 1988–1989* (Lexington, Mass.: Lexington Books, 1988), p. 45.

68. William W. Kaufmann, *The 1986 Defense Budget* (Washington, D.C.: Brookings, 1985), p. 28.

69. *Ibid.*, p. 57, emphasis added.

70. Bernard E. Trainor, "Cutting A-Arms: Safer or More Dangerous World?" *New York Times*, October 17, 1986, p. 5.

71. Quoted in "Defense Officials Set Expense of 100 B-1B's at $19.7 Million," *Aviation Week and Space Technology*, October 12, 1981, p. 20.

72. Harvard-MIT Summer Program, June 26, 1985.

73. See, for example, the exchange Amos A. Jordan and Robert W. Komer, two military specialists, had with Les Aspin, a member of the House of Representatives and a former military analyst, published in "Soviet Strength and Purpose," *Foreign Policy*, vol. 23, Summer 1976, pp. 32–48.

74. Les Aspin, "How to Look at the Soviet-American Balance," *Foreign Policy*, vol. 22, Spring 1976, p. 106; in contrast, see Paul H. Nitze, "Assuring Strategic Stability," *Foreign Affairs*, January 1976, p. 208.

75. In his famous *History of the Peloponnesian War*, the Greek historian Thucydides wrote: "What made war inevitable was the growth of Athenian power and the fear which this caused in Sparta" (Book One, translated by Rex Warner, London, Penguin Books, p. 49).

76. Les Aspin, quoted in *New Choices in a Changing America: The Report of the Democratic Policy Commission to the Democratic National Committee* (Washington, D.C.: Democratic National Committee, August 1986), p. 57.

77. Henry A. Kissinger, *Good Morning America*, ABC Television, December 7, 1987.

78. See Graham T. Allison, Albert Carnesale, and Joseph S. Nye, Jr., eds., *Hawks, Doves, and Owls: An Agenda for Avoiding Nuclear War* (New York: Norton, 1985).

79. *Op. cit.*, p. 23.

RECOMMENDED READINGS

Allison, Graham T., Albert Carnesale, and Joseph S. Nye, Jr., eds. *Hawks, Doves, and Owls: An Agenda for Avoiding Nuclear War* (New York: Norton, 1985). An exploration of the probabilities of nuclear war, and how to reduce these probabilities.

Barash, David P. *The Arms Race and Nuclear War* (Belmont, Calif.: Wadsworth, 1987). An excellent survey of the leading facts and issues regarding warfare in the nuclear age, richly illustrated with graphics and photographs.

Blanchard, William H. *Aggression American Style* (Santa Monica, Calif.: Goodyear, 1978). A clinical psychologist examines a wide range of U.S. responses to threats from abroad.

Blechman, Barry M., and Stephen S. Kaplan. *Force without War: U.S. Armed Forces as a Political Instrument* (Washington, D.C.: Brookings, 1978). An exhaustive examination of 215 uses of its armed forces as a political instrument by the United States between the years 1946 and 1976.

Bracken, Paul. *The Command and Control of Nuclear Forces* (New Haven: Yale University Press, 1983). A thorough look at the problems of C³.

Craig, Paul P., and John A. Jungerman. *Nuclear Arms Race: Technology and Society* (New York: McGraw-Hill, 1986). A sophisticated, technical (yet understandable) survey of nuclear weapons and their effects on modern society.

Diehl, Paul, and Loch K. Johnson, eds. *Through the Straits of Armageddon: Arms Control Issues and Prospects* (Athens: University of Georgia Press, 1987). A collection of original essays on arms control with a preface by former Secretary of State Dean Rusk.

Dyson, Freeman J. *Weapons and Hope* (New York: Harper & Row, 1984). A thoughtful, philosophic discussion of nuclear weapons by a prominent physicist.

Eagleton, Thomas F. *War and Presidential Power: A Chronicle of Congressional Surrender* (New York: Liveright, 1974). An appraisal of the War Powers Resolution by an early proponent in the Senate who later became a leading critic of the initiative.

Holt, Pat. *The War Powers Resolution: The Role of Congress in U.S. Armed Intervention* (Washington, D.C.: American Enterprise Institute, 1978). An authoritative, scholarly discussion of the War Powers Resolution by a former staff director of the Senate Foreign Relations Committee.

Kaufmann, William W. *The 1986 Defense Budget* (Washington, D.C.: Brookings, 1985). A lucid explanation of a recent defense budget by a prominent authority.

Kegley, Charles W., Jr., and Eugene R. Wittkopf, eds. *The Nuclear Reader: Strategy, Weapons, War* (New York: St. Martin's, 1985). One of the better collections of published articles on strategic issues, with a useful blend of political and technical perspectives.

Klare, Michael T., and Peter Kornbluh, eds. *Low-Intensity Warfare* (New York: Pantheon, 1988). A critical examination of the "Reagan Doctrine" and other forms of counterinsurgency and antiterrorism.

Kruzel, Joseph, ed. *American Defense Annual, 1988–1989* (Lexington, Mass.: Lexington Books, 1988). Up-to-date analyses of the Reagan administration's defense strategies and budget planning.

McNamara, Robert S. *The Essence of Security: Reflections in Office* (New York: Harper & Row, 1968). A standard, clearly written exposition on the basic tenets of American strategic doctrine, written by a former secretary of defense.

McNaught, L. W. *Nuclear Weapons and Their Effects* (London: Brassey, 1984). A technical, yet understandable, analysis of how nuclear weapons work and the destructive effects they can have.

Prins, Gwyn, ed. *The Nuclear Crisis Reader* (New York: Vintage, 1984). Another useful collection of essays, more philosophical in character than the Kegley-Wittkopf reader.

Schell, Jonathan. *The Fate of the Earth* (New York: Knopf, 1982). The most moving account yet published on the danger posed by nuclear weapons, which the author sees as fatal unless human beings "reinvent politics" and learn how to settle their disputes without the friction of nation-state rivalry.

Smith, Gerard C. *Doubletalk: The Story of the First Strategic Arms Limitation Talks.* (New York: Doubleday, 1980). An excellent recounting of the dilemmas involved in U.S.–Soviet arms negotiations, written by the principal American negotiator for SALT I.

Talbott, Strobe. *Deadly Gambits* (New York: Knopf, 1984). A close account of U.S.–U.S.S.R. arms control negotiations by a diplomatic correspondent.

TALKING INSTEAD OF FIGHTING

THE IMPORTANCE—AND UBIQUITY—OF
DIPLOMACY

THE MAKING OF INTERNATIONAL
AGREEMENTS

    The Form and Content of International
    Agreements

    Presidential Comparisons

AMERICA'S AGREEMENT PARTNERS

THE PATTERN OF AMERICAN DIPLOMACY

THE HIDDEN SIDE OF AGREEMENT
MAKING

MILITARY AGREEMENTS: SOME CASE
EXAMPLES

    Thailand

Diego Garcia

Spain

Ethiopia

Philippines

South Korea

Laos

THE DANGERS OF DIPLOMACY BY
EXECUTIVE FIAT

THE DEMOCRATIC CONTROL OF
DIPLOMACY

    The Bricker Revolt

    A Second Resurgence

DIPLOMACY'S FAR REACH

SUMMARY

11

DIPLOMACY: THE ART OF PEACEFUL NEGOTIATIONS

The use of secret intelligence agencies and the war power to achieve national objectives is, like it or not, an integral part of American foreign policy. This world of semianarchy and widespread malevolence necessitates methods that, in a more ideal setting, most people would reject as repugnant and unworthy of civilized nations. Yet, even in this world of constant unrest, the use of force (covertly or overtly) has not been the most prevalent, or even the most effective, approach to foreign affairs. Most of America's external relations have been based upon dialogues with the leaders of other countries, from informal talks to solemn negotiations and occasional high-level summit meetings between heads of state—in a word, diplomacy.

This chapter examines the use of diplomacy as an instrument of American foreign policy, particularly the means by which this nation enters into binding agreements abroad (often called the treaty power). The chapter also carries forward the book's central theme: the importance of executive-legislative relations in the conduct of foreign affairs. Just as secret intervention overseas and the use of the war power have embroiled the executive and legislative branches in conflict with one another (Chapters 8 to 10), so, too, have disagreements over the proper uses of diplomacy as well as the role of each branch in determining how, when, and with whom the United States will commit its good name and resources abroad. What might seem an arid subject has led to lively disputes within the government. Indeed, as this chapter relates, international agreements entered into by executive fiat—without legislative consultation—helped incite the "revolution" on Capitol Hill during the late 1960s and 1970s favoring a greater role for Congress in the nation's international affairs.

From left to right, President Anwar Sadat of Egypt, U.S. President Jimmy Carter, and Prime Minister Menachem Begin of Israel celebrate the Camp David peace agreement of 1978. (Carter Presidential Library)

TALKING INSTEAD OF FIGHTING

Stated more formally, *diplomacy* (from the Greek *diplomata*, or "folded documents") may be defined as "the process of representation and negotiation by which states customarily deal with one another in time of peace"; or, put more simply still by George Kennan, diplomacy is "the business of communicating between governments."[1] Former Secretary of State Henry Kissinger embellishes: "[The statesman's] instrument is diplomacy, the art of relating states to each other by agreement rather than by the exercise of force. . . ."[2] Diplomacy, adds the thoughtful former Israeli minister of foreign affairs, Abba Eban, attempts to achieve national goals "by persuasion, eloquence, inducement, threat or deterrence, and not only by physical domination and war."[3]

For the great international relations scholar Hans J. Morgenthau, diplomacy was far and away the most important power possessed by a nation. Defining the concept broadly, Morgenthau considered diplomacy to be "the formation and execution of foreign policy on all levels, the highest as well as the subordinate." It was an "art" whose purpose was nothing less than to bring "the different elements of national power to bear with maximum effect upon those points in the international situation which concern the national interest most directly." When carried out with competence, diplomacy managed to "bring the ends and means of foreign policy into harmony with the available resources of national power."[4]

As the experienced U.S. Foreign Service officer and former ambassador David D. Newsom emphasizes, once a sound foreign policy is crafted by a nation's leaders, "diplomacy can then add the needed skills of implementation in the knowledge of other cultures, the skill of negotiation, the art of persuasion, and the power to observe and report." He continues, "the policies the United States pursues . . . must, to be acceptable, be expressed and explained and defended to skeptical, distracted, and occasionally unfriendly governments and peoples abroad. This becomes the task of the American diplomat who, in a mediating role, must also explain

the realities that confront America to those in Washington who may be unready to accept the anomalies of an outside world."[5]

While the job description sounds straightforward and innocuous enough, the actual practice of diplomacy is immensely complicated with often far-reaching ramifications for the nation, however mundane this approach to foreign policy may seem in comparison with calling out the marines or unleashing the CIA. The distinguished British statesman Lord Salisbury (1830–1903) once noted that the victories of the diplomat "are made up of a series of microscopic advantages: of a judicious suggestion here, of an opportune civility there, of a wise concession at one moment and a farsighted persistence at another; of sleepless tact, immovable calmness and patience that no folly, no provocation, no blunders can shake."[6] These small moves and intricate compromises, while lacking in drama, can move a nation toward momentous—and sometimes dangerous—commitments abroad.

Few have the requisite patience, training, and genius to match the skills in "statecraft" of history's great diplomats—France's Richelieu, Mazarin, Talleyrand, and Cambon, for example; or Great Britain's Cardinal Wolsey, Castlereagh, and Canning; Germany's Bismarck; Italy's Cavour; and America's Franklin, Jefferson, Madison, Jay, and the Adamses, in the early days, and Kissinger more recently. Rather than hope for the occasional genius to guide the nation's external affairs, Morgenthau urged a "dependence upon tradition and institutions." America's institutions of diplomacy have been largely inept, in his view, with the exception of the nation's earliest years; but its traditions—especially as embodied in Washington's Farewell Address and the Monroe Doctrine (Perspectives on American Foreign Policy 3.1 and 3.2)—have provided guidance to "protect a poor diplomacy from catastrophic blunders and make a mediocre diplomacy look better than it actually was."[7]

Toward a more sophisticated use of diplomacy by the United States in the future, Morgenthau recommended nine guideposts, which he divided into "rules" and "prerequisites of compromise":

Morgenthau's Four Fundamental Rules of Diplomacy

1. Diplomacy must be divested of the crusading spirit.

2. The objectives of foreign policy must be defined in terms of the national interest and must be supported with adequate power.

3. Diplomacy must look at the political scene from the point of view of other nations.

4. Nations must be willing to compromise on all issues that are not vital to them.

Morgenthau's Five Prerequisites of Compromise

5. Give up the shadow of worthless rights for the substance of real advantage.

6. Never put yourself in a position from which you cannot retreat without losing face and from which you cannot advance without grave risks.

7. Never allow a weak ally to make decisions for you.

8. The armed forces are the instrument of foreign policy, not its master.

9. The government is the leader of public opinion, not its slave.[8]

With these principles in mind, Morgenthau believed, a nation's diplomatic initiatives offered a chance to preserve peace and to build an international community that might one day meld into a peaceful world state—a higher unifying authority to replace the divisiveness of national sovereignty. Without the "accommodating processes of diplomacy, mitigating and minimizing conflicts," however, the prospects for peace struck him as dim indeed.[9]

THE IMPORTANCE—AND UBIQUITY—OF DIPLOMACY

Officials in the Bush administration hardly had time to explore their new offices in January, 1989, before a steady stream of diplomatic problems demanded their attention. Within a fortnight of the inauguration ceremonies, Secretary of State James A. Baker III stood before a meeting of an international conference on global environmental challenges and urged collective cooperation to halt the threat of global warming caused by pollutants (the greenhouse effect). The "political ecology is now ripe for action," he told the diplomats from seventeen nations meeting in Washington.[10]

As the weeks passed, the Bush administration found its agenda increasingly crowded with a host of other perplexing international challenges inherited from previous administrations. Most of the problems defied quick solution through the assignment of secret agents or armed troops. Rather, they demanded the steady, patient attention of diplomats prepared to search tirelessly for those adjustments that might calm the conflicting interests of nations. The most intractable agenda item seemed to be, as always in recent decades, unrest in the Middle East—the site of President Carter's greatest foreign policy success (the Camp David accords bringing peace between Israel and Egypt) and President Reagan's most tragic foreign policy result (the suicide bombing of the Marine headquarters in Beirut).

In the waning days of the Reagan administration, the president authorized the beginning of a "diplomatic dialogue" with the Palestine Liberation Organization, a key faction in Middle East politics. The willingness to talk directly with the PLO for the first time in over a decade signaled a renewed determination by the United States to seek a negotiated settlement in the Middle East. Immediately, Israel expressed its "regret" over the initiative, maintaining that the PLO was an untrustworthy terrorist organization. The religious and cultural differences between Arabs and Jews in the region promised to make any hopes of a rapid settlement unrealistic. Indeed, some observers predicted that a lasting peace would never be possible, given the deep-seated differences between factions in the Middle East.

"I know it's a part of the American way of life to believe that you isolate a problem and solve it," said Britain's ambassador to the UN, "but in international politics . . . you find arrangements, rather than final solutions. There is no final solution."[11] It was now up to the Bush administration to pursue the quest for livable "arrangements" in a region of great tension.

Early diplomatic efforts by the Bush administration to improve America's rock-bottom relations with a specific country in the Middle East, Iran, soon ran afoul. The government of the Ayatollah Ruhollah Khomeini, Iran's religious leader, declared that better ties would result only when President Bush ordered the release of Iranian funds that had been frozen in U.S. banks by the Carter administration. (President Carter had ordered this impoundment in retaliation for the taking of American diplomats as hostages in Tehran during the Islamic revolution of 1979.) The ayatollah's monetary concerns illustrate the frequent interplay found between diplomacy and economic matters, the focus of Chapter 12. The bartering over the Iranian assets, and the release of additional U.S. hostages held in Beirut by a pro-Iranian "Party of God" faction, promised to be intricate and lengthy—with the situation made murkier still by the death of the ayatollah in June of 1989.

The assortment of pending diplomatic objectives facing the Bush administration seemed endless—for the pessimist, a cornucopia of bad dreams; for the optimist, a series of challenging tests for America's negotiating skills. A sample list for President Bush—beyond global ecology and problems in the Middle East—included ridding the world of chemical and biological weapons (selected as a high priority for his adminis-

tration by candidate Bush during the presidential elections of 1988); slowly opening up diplomatic ties—severed in 1975—with Angola (a Marxist-led regime, but a reliable source of oil imports for the United States); exploring the possibilities for better relations with the Libyan leader, Muammar Qaddafi, nemesis of the Reagan administration (which, according to one seasoned observer, never gave serious attention to diplomatic overtures toward either him or adversaries in Grenada, but instead preferred the use of military force[12]); working more closely with southern neighbors to encourage democracy in the western hemisphere;[13] furthering arms reductions, both conventional and nuclear; and, at home, working out with Congress how major diplomatic decisions might be shared between the branches—a primary focus of this chapter to which we now turn.

THE MAKING OF INTERNATIONAL AGREEMENTS

The United States uses three major forms of international agreements for its negotiation of commitments abroad: the treaty, the statutory agreement, and the executive agreement. Treaties are required by Article II, Section 2, of the Constitution to have the support of two-thirds of those members of the Senate present and voting (Chapter 5). On any important treaty, all 100 members are likely to be present, and so the executive branch must count on mustering at least sixty-seven votes. The statutory agreement involves legislative authority, also; but, instead of an extraordinary two-thirds approval in the Senate (difficult to achieve on contentious issues), this procedure requires an easier majority vote in both chambers—51 senators plus 219 members of the House, if every member is present and voting.

Easier still is to bypass the Congress altogether—an option many executive officials, not just Admiral Poindexter and Lieutenant Colonel North, have found appealing. Here is the attraction of the executive agreement, which by definition applies to those obligations reached with other nations by the executive branch completely void of the Senate's advice and consent or the House's counsel.

The once proud treaty procedure was, at one time, reserved strictly for the most far-reaching international agreements entered into by the United States (Chapter 5). President Franklin Roosevelt allowed a serious erosion of this bedrock constitutional authority, however, by turning to the executive agreement for commitments of great importance before and during the Second World War. The destroyers-for-bases deal with the British in 1940 symbolizes this incursion. Roosevelt's extraordinary methods in wartime provided a precedent in peacetime for additional inroads into the Senate's authority over diplomatic initiatives, from military and economic arrangements with other countries to decisions regarding (among others) transportation and communications policy.

This erosion of legislative authority over external commitments, and its implications for American foreign policy, warrant closer examination. The place to begin is with a description of America's international agreements in the nuclear age: their form, their content, and the types of nations sought out by the United States for binding associations of one kind or another.

The Form and Content of International Agreements

As discussed earlier in this book, the Vietnamese war awakened legislators and others to the dangers of excessive presidential discretion. The decline of the Senate's treaty power soon became a focus for reforms. The senators focused, first, on the change that had taken place in recent years in the *form of international agreements*. Increasingly, they argued, presidents and their officers seemed to resort to executive agreements, proclamations, and other unilateral actions as a way of circumventing the participation of legislators in the formulation of international commitments. (Even during the Eisenhower administration—well before the evasiveness of the Vietnam era—"diplomacy was conducted as often as possible to avoid formal congressional involvement," notes one authority.[14]) Particularly worrisome were the more opaque forms of the executive agreement: secret pacts entered into overseas by the White House and never revealed to the Congress, verbal "promises" and "understandings" between nations—smile-and-wink agreements never committed to paper—and a whole range of obligations sealed at lower levels of the executive branch without the knowledge of the president or even the Department of State, let alone the Congress (see Figure 11.1).

A second and related criticism focused on the *content of international agreements*. According to critics, even when the executive branch included Congress in deliberations over commitments abroad, the issues presented to legislators were substantively less important than those which the executive branch chose to keep within its own councils. Critics especially feared that foreign military compacts might be entered into by way of the executive agreement (excluding congressional participation), while less risky trade or communications arrange-

FIGURE 11.1 International agreement making: a continuum of executive discretion.

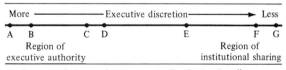

A. Secret, verbal executive agreements ("understandings," "promises")
B. Secret, written executive agreements (kept from Congress)
C. Secret verbal or written agreements (shared with select congressional committees)
D. Unclassified executive agreements
E. Statutory agreements
F. Agreements pursuant to treaties
G. Treaties

Source: Loch K. Johnson, *The Making of International Agreements: Congress Confronts the Executive* (New York: New York University Press, 1984), p. 7.

ments—say, on strawberry imports or the regulation of radio transmissions—might be presented to Congress in solemn treaty form.

To evaluate these criticisms, this chapter examines all the nonclassified American foreign policy commitments from 1946 to 1973—that is, from the beginnings of the cold war to the early stirrings of détente. This time frame is selected for scrutiny because it is the only period for which systematic data are available on the formal patterns of American diplomacy.[15] During this period, officials of the United States signed some 6000 agreements, covering a wide range of topics. In 1972, for instance, American diplomats authorized commitments with other nations on the following topics (among several others):

Television and radio facilities (Saudi Arabia)

Trade: strawberries (Mexico)

Satellite tracking station (Canada)

Whaling: international observer scheme (Japan)

Education program for agrarian reform (Philippines)

Protection of migratory birds (Mexico)

Atomic energy: cooperation for civil use (Japan)

Military assistance (Malaysia)

Air-transport services (Czechoslovakia)

Seabed arms control (multilateral)

Cultural exchanges (U.S.S.R.)

Scientific and technical cooperation (U.S.S.R.)

Weather station (Honduras)

Prevention of foot-and-mouth disease (Costa Rica)

America's international agreements can be grouped according to subject matter. Some—arguably the most important—deal with military matters: weapons systems, bases, training, supplies, arms control, and the like. Others deal with economics and trade: agreements on commerce, agricultural commodities, trademarks, taxation, debt rescheduling, economic assistance, and fishing, for instance. Three additional categories include cultural-technical agreements (encompassing education, health, cultural exchanges, scientific cooperation, environmental protection, space cooperation, and the like); transportation and communications agreements; and consular agreements, involving such matters as passports or war claims. Naturally, not all these matters are equal in rank; some deal with weather stations, others with advanced fighter aircraft. Comparisons based strictly on numbers obviously have their limits, but a brief statistical analysis of the patterns of U.S. agreements overseas is a useful place to begin, before turning to more qualitative comparisons.

Form   As Table 11.1 discloses, the overwhelming majority—almost 87 percent—of all U.S. agreements between 1946 and 1973 were statutory in form. In contrast, executive agreements and treaties account, respectively, for only 7 percent and 6 percent of all the agreements. These figures indicate that Congress has, in fact, been included in the agreement-making process; indeed, it has participated in the overwhelming majority of international agreements. The data confirm, however, that the treaty has been replaced as the official form of U.S. commitment abroad. In contrast to the conventional wisdom, though, the statutory agreement (an instrument, recall, involving both houses of Congress as well as the executive), not the executive agreement, has risen to the forefront of America's formal instruments of diplomacy.

Thus, the common argument that the form of international agreements has shifted from treaties to executive agreements, thereby ex-

TABLE 11.1   FORM OF U.S. FOREIGN AGREEMENTS BY ADMINISTRATION, 1946–1972

	ADMINISTRATION					
FORM	TRUMAN	EISENHOWER	KENNEDY	JOHNSON	NIXON	AVERAGE
Executive agreements	10.6%	5.4%	3.8%	8.0%	9.1%	7.3%
Statutory agreements	79.5	89.2	92.7	86.7	86.4	86.7
Treaties	9.8	5.4	3.4	5.2	4.5	6.0
(Number of agreements)	(1315)	(1884)	(783)	(1143)	(866)	(5991)

Entries are percentages based on numbers shown at bottom of columns. Some percentages do not add to 100, because of rounding error.

Twenty-five agreements are excluded from this table and others where appropriate because they could not be classified by form.

cluding the Congress, fails to find support in these data from the period 1946–1973. This conclusion remains unaltered when the evidence is inspected administration by administration. Even President Truman, who used the statutory agreement least often, still resorted to this form 80 percent of the time. As Table 11.1 shows, the use of treaties fell off at a nearly steady rate from Truman through Nixon.

Content   In 1946, the United States signed about 100 international agreements; by 1972, the annual volume had more than doubled as American alliances and commitments abroad spread rapidly throughout the noncommunist world. In 1946, the United States participated officially in 141 international conferences; by 1975, the number had reached beyond 800. During the same period, telegraphic communications from U.S. diplomatic posts abroad back to the Department of State increased fivefold— all figures that illustrate dramatically the exponential growth of America's global interdependence.

During this period from 1946 to 1973, the chief diplomatic interest of the United States as measured by the content of formal agreements resided in the area of economic policy and trade. About 37 percent of all the agreements fell into this category. The first Eisenhower

term marked a dramatic turning point in America's relations abroad. In 1955, this nation's pursuit of military defense pacts reached a plateau; thereafter, U.S. diplomatic activity focused increasingly (at least in the volume of official obligations) on international trade agreements—a commitment to economic interdependence which reached a high-water mark in 1962 with the efforts of the Kennedy administration to lower barriers and promote world trade. "The United States did not rise to greatness by waiting for others to lead. . . . Economic isolation and political leadership are wholly incompatible," declared the young president.[16] Kennedy sent an unprecedented bill—the Trade Expansion Act of 1962—to Congress, which gave to the White House a five-year authority to cut all tariffs by as much as 50 percent, and to reduce to zero all tariffs on commodities traded between the United States and the European Common Market.

With the exception of the Truman administration, economic agreements were consistently larger in number than any other type (during the Truman years, cultural-technical agreements predominated). The Eisenhower administration had the greatest number of economic pacts, with some 625 signed during this eight-year period; percentagewise, though, the Kennedy, Johnson, and Nixon administrations had the largest proportion of economic agreements—over 45 percent of each president's total. (Figure 11.2 displays America's international agreements by content.)

The devotion of the Truman administration to cultural-technical ties overseas can be seen in Figure 11.2: 34 percent of the international agreements signed by this administration fit into this category. This percentage is higher than for any subsequent administration and nearly surpassed the Eisenhower administration in total numbers (443 to 484), even though President Eisenhower was in office longer than his predecessor. Part of the explanation for this result no doubt relates to President Truman's

FIGURE 11.2   Trends in the content of U.S. international agreements.

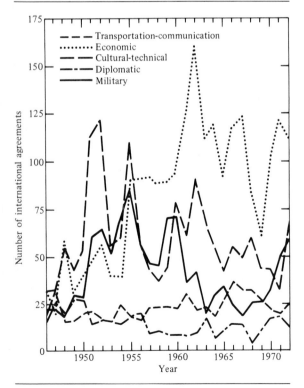

Source: Loch K. Johnson, *The Making of International Agreements: Congress Confronts the Executive* (New York: New York University Press, 1984), p. 16.

desire to bring technology to the poorer nations of the world. Not only did he dream of TVAs in the Euphrates and Yangtze valleys, but he envisioned that such programs might alleviate misery abroad as the New Deal had done at home during the great depression. "It will be the judgment of history," writes one of Truman's advisers responsible for the *Point Four* program (a key international technical assistance scheme designed during the Truman years), "that—while Roosevelt created the New Deal in America—Truman extended it to the World."[17]

Although Truman's enthusiasm for a cultural-technical approach to interdependence was difficult to surpass, subsequent administrations have devoted considerable attention to similar ties abroad. The Kennedy administration signed nearly 27 percent of all its agreements in the cultural-technical field; the Johnson administration, 23 percent; and the Nixon administration, 21 percent. For each of these administrations, cultural-technical agreements exceeded the number of military agreements. Combined, economic and cultural-technical pacts constituted almost 64 percent of America's international commitments.

The third most common type of international agreement for the United States during this period was the military pact. On average, these agreements comprised just over 19 percent of America's commitments overseas. The time of greatest expansion for U.S. military agreements came during the early phase of the cold war, as relations with the Soviet Union worsened and the United States sought to contain communism through a series of security arrangements. The Truman administration acceded to some 257 military arrangements (constituting 20 percent of all its commitments abroad), and the Eisenhower administration entered into fully 500 (26 percent of its formal international commitments). Military negotiations began to level out in the Kennedy and Johnson years—about 12 percent for each. An upward climb began once more under the next Republican president, Richard Nixon. During his first four

Perspectives on American Foreign Policy   11.1

President Truman's "Point Four" program of technical assistance to other nations

... We must embark on a bold new program for making the benefits of our scientific advances and industrial progress available for the improvement and growth of under-developed areas. ...

I believe that we should make available to peace-loving peoples the benefits of our store of technical knowledge in order to help them realize their aspirations for a better life. And, in cooperation with other nations, we should foster capital investment in areas needing development.

Our aim should be to help the free peoples of the world, through their own efforts, to produce more food, more clothing, more materials for housing, and more mechanical power to lighten their burdens.

We invite other countries to pool their technological resources in this undertaking. ... This should be a cooperative enterprise in which all nations work together through the United Nations and its specialized agencies wherever practicable. ...

The old imperialism—exploitation for foreign profit—has no place in our plans. ...

From the president's Inaugural Address, January 20, 1949, reprinted in the *Department of State Bulletin*, January 30, 1949, pp. 123–126.

---

years, he entered into some 162 military pacts and came close to matching Truman in the percentage of foreign commitments that were military in content (18 percent).

Finally, consular issues (such as international boundary disputes and the establishment of formal relations with other states), along with transportation and communications issues, have consistently drawn the least attention. On average, consular agreements comprised about 6 percent of the total during these years, and transportation and communications agreements about 11 percent.

The content of America's initiatives toward other nations has, in sum, been largely economic in character, followed by a lesser (but persistent) interest in cultural-technical and military bonds, and, last, a steady trickle of obligations dealing with transportation, communications, and consular matters.

The Interplay of Form and Content   The relationships between the three major forms of

agreements and the five policy content categories are presented in Table 11.2. Statutory agreements remain the dominant form, regardless of the agreement's policy content. The argument that the Congress has been systematically excluded from certain categories of diplomacy fails to be supported by these data. Differences across policy content do exist, however, for executive agreements and treaties. As Table 11.2 illustrates, executive agreements have been used most frequently for military and consular agreements. In contrast, treaties have been used most frequently for consular and transportation-communications policy, and least of all for military and cultural-technical policy.

In comparing policy differences within each form, then, these results lend some credence to the proposition that vital issues like military commitments have sometimes been handled through a procedure which avoided congressional participation (the executive agreement), reserving opportunities for congressional in-

TABLE 11.2   *FORM OF U.S. FOREIGN AGREEMENTS BY CONTENT AREAS, 1946–1972*

	CONTENT				
FORM	MILITARY	ECONOMIC	TRANSPORTATION-COMMUNICATION	CULTURAL-TECHNICAL	CONSULAR
Executive agreements	12.4%	4.6%	5.9%	3.7%	26.7%
Statutory agreements	84.0	88.6	84.6	93.2	60.1
Treaties	3.6	6.8	9.5	3.2	13.2
(Number of agreements)	(1146)	(2229)	(630)	(1580)	(371)

Entries are percentages based on numbers shown at bottom of columns. Thirty-five agreements, representing 0.6% of the total, were classified as "other" for content and are not shown in the table.

volvement to less critical policies. Still, one cannot ignore the large number of statutory agreements across all policy areas. Even if one were to assume that all secret executive agreements were military, the total percentage of military executive agreements would be about 30 percent. This percentage reinforces the argument that military policy seems to be more subject to executive discretion, but it does not alter the basic finding regarding the dominance of the statutory agreement—even in the realm of military policy.

Presidential Comparisons

To explore more fully the use of executive discretion in foreign affairs among the first five postwar presidents, Table 11.3 offers an "executive agreement index" (EAI) for each administration. This index is based on the proportion of

TABLE 11.3   *EXECUTIVE AGREEMENT INDEX (EAI), 1946–1972[a]*

ADMINIS-TRATION	POLICY AREA[b]					
	MILITARY	ECONOMIC	TRANSPORTATION-COMMUNICATION	CULTURAL-TECHNICAL	CONSULAR	AVERAGE
Truman[c]	0.67	0.42	0.25	0.38	0.72	0.49
Eisenhower	0.84	0.12	0.39	0.55	0.71	0.52
Kennedy	0.83	0.27	0.86	0.67	0.41	0.61
Johnson	0.88	0.52	0.26	0.46	0.71	0.57
Nixon[d]	0.74	0.77	0.53	0.66	0.58	0.66
Average	0.79	0.42	0.46	0.54	0.63	

[a] This table summarizes the use of military treaties and executive agreements only; statutory agreements, which are more numerous but less controversial, are not analyzed here.

[b] The numbers in each column represent for each administration the proportion of executive agreements compared with the total number of treaties and executive agreements EA/(T + EA). This "executive agreement index" ranges from 0 to 1; the higher the index, the greater the reliance on executive agreements for commitments abroad.

[c] Data are for 1946–1952.

[d] Data are for 1969–1973.

executive agreements (EA) among the total number of treaties (T) and executive agreements, EA/(T + EA), providing an indication of each president's degree of activism in agreement making by executive fiat. (Only the use of treaties and executive agreements is compared, since they have been far more controversial forms of international commitment than the statutory agreement.)

The data in Table 11.3 show that, across the board, President Nixon was the most aggressive in rejecting the treaty procedure, scoring the highest in the use of executive agreements. The overall pattern emerging from Table 11.3 is clear: each president—not just Nixon—relied more and more on executive agreements, at the expense of treaties, in fashioning America's formal commitments abroad. Military policy was the most susceptible to executive discretion (although all the other presidents, except Truman, surpassed Nixon in this category). For Presidents Eisenhower and Johnson, the EAI for military matters exceeded that for all other policies; and even with the remaining three presidents, the military EAI ranked second. A comparable trend of increased executive discretion over economic policy is evident in these statistics, across all five administrations.

AMERICA'S AGREEMENT PARTNERS

What countries has the United States turned to in its formal diplomacy? The nations of the world can be grouped into three broad political categories: democratic regimes, authoritarian regimes, and totalitarian regimes. *Democracies* are conceptualized as states where parties or groups compete for office in at least relatively free elections; *authoritarian regimes*—anticommunist, "right wing"—as states where political power is in the hands of a single ruler, the military, or a civilian oligarchy without the benefit of free elections; and *totalitarian regimes*—Marxist-communist, "left wing"—as

states where the Communist Party or a Marxist group holds the preponderance of political power within the society.[18]

From 1946 to 1973, the United States displayed a strong affinity for its fellow democracies—despite the limited number of these free nations. This country signed 3071 (58 percent) of its bilateral agreements with democratic regimes, 2011 (38 percent) with authoritarian regimes, and a modest 247 (5 percent) with totalitarian regimes (see Table 11.4). This ranking of agreement partners generally held across the five administrations—although the Nixon administration signed as many agreements with authoritarian regimes as with the democracies. In Table 11.4, adjustments are made to take into account the relative distribution of the three regime types in any given year. Using this control, all five administrations reveal a greater percentage of agreements with democracies than might have been expected based solely on their relative distribution in the world. The Truman and Eisenhower administrations revealed an especially high affinity toward democratic regimes, with 17 percent and 19 percent more agreements with these nations than their percentage in the international system.

What stands out most starkly from the data, though, are the very few ties between the United States and the totalitarian states—not surprising in light of the traditional antipathy in the United States toward communist regimes. America, however, did sign sixty-four agreements with the Soviet Union. While that number is large in comparison with other totalitarian states (Yugoslavia excepted), the Soviet Union nonetheless ranks below the top 20 percent of America's agreement partners. The United Kingdom, Canada, and Japan have been the primary diplomatic partners of choice for the United States. In addition, four other members of NATO have been among the principal partners, making the western European democracies high on the list of America's favorites for international negotiations (see Table 11.5). Authoritarian regimes have featured prominently

TABLE 11.4   REGIME TARGETS OF U.S. FOREIGN AGREEMENTS BY ADMINISTRATION, 1946–1972

REGIME TYPE	ADMINISTRATION				
	TRUMAN	EISENHOWER	KENNEDY	JOHNSON	NIXON
Democratic					
% of agreements	65.4[a]	61.5	55.4	53.2	45.8
% of states	48.0[b]	43.0	50.4	46.1	41.8
Difference	+17.4[c]	+18.5	+5.0	+7.1	+ 4.0
Authoritarian					
% of agreements	32.2	35.0	40.8	39.9	46.0
% of states	38.7	43.0	35.9	41.4	44.8
Difference	−6.5	−8.0	+4.9	−1.5	+ 1.2
Totalitarian					
% of agreements	2.4	3.5	3.8	6.9	8.2
% of states	13.3	14.0	13.7	12.5	13.4
Difference	−10.9	−10.5	−9.9	−5.6	−5.2
(Number of agreements)	(1120)	(1728)	(711)	(977)	(793)

[a] Entries are percentages based on numbers shown at bottom of columns. Multilateral agreements and agreements with dependent territories are not included here.

[b] The "% of states" refers to the relative distribution of democratic, authoritarian, and totalitarian regimes during each administration. To identify the relative percentage of nations within each regime category, first the number of nations in the international system for the *median* year of each administration was identified: 1949 for the Truman administration: 1957 for the Eisenhower administration; 1962 for the Kennedy administration; 1966 for the Johnson administration; and, 1970 for the Nixon administration. The following sources were used to obtain the number of independent nations in these *median* years: A. Leroy Bennett, *International Organizations: Principles and Issues* (Englewood Cliffs, N.J.: Prentice-Hall, 1980), appendix, pp. 509–514; Bruce Russett and Harvey Starr, *World Politics: The Menu for Choice* (San Francisco: W. H. Freeman, 1981), appendix B, pp. 575–583; and David J. Finlay and Thomas Hovet, Jr., *7304: International Relations on the Planet Earth* (New York: Harper and Row, 1975), pp. 24–25. The last source was particularly useful, since it contained a chronological listing of newly independent nations. As a consequence, the number of member nations for each administration from Truman to Nixon could be calculated incrementally. For each *median* year ranking, the nations were coded into the three regimes based upon the earlier regime classification. From that calculation, the percentage of nations that were democratic, authoritarian, and totalitarian in the world could be derived for each administration.

[c] A plus sign indicates that more agreements were signed with the regime type than might be expected, given the distribution of the three regime types in the international system; a negative sign indicates the converse. Professor James M. McCormick, Iowa State University, assisted in this analysis.

in America's diplomacy, too. Mexico, Peru, and Brazil in Latin America, and the Philippines, the Republic of China, the Republic of Korea, and Pakistan in Asia, have been among this nation's most favored choices for pacts. Geographically, in its selection of diplomatic partners the United States has shown a decided preference for countries on the perimeter of the communist Eurasian land mass, as well as for its neighbors in the Western Hemisphere (see Figure 11.3).

THE PATTERN OF AMERICAN DIPLOMACY

In the first quarter century of the cold war, several trends in America's formal diplomacy stand out. First, the statutory agreement was clearly the major instrument of America's international commitments. Second, despite the continuing importance of the statutory agreement, the use of the executive agreement accelerated as an instrument for military and consu-

TABLE 11.5   THE USE OF THREE FORMS OF AGREEMENT MAKING WITHIN SIX GLOBAL REGIONS

FORM	LATIN AMERICA	WESTERN EUROPE	MIDDLE EAST	AFRICA	EASTERN EUROPE	ASIA
Treaty	1.5%	5.0%	1.0%	1.6%	0.9%	2.5%
Executive agreement	4.2	9.3	2.5	4.9	18.1	8.5
Statutory agreement	94.3	85.7	96.5	93.5	81.1	89.0
(Number of agreements)	(1392)	(1563)	(600)	(307)	(227)	(1225)

Entries are percentages based on numbers at bottom of columns. Twenty-five agreements (0.5% of the total) were excluded from the analysis because Department of State classification could not be obtained. Multilateral agreements and agreements with dependent territories are not included here.

FIGURE 11.3   America's major agreement partners: twenty-seven countries most frequently targeted for bilateral pacts (the top 20 percent), 1946–1973.

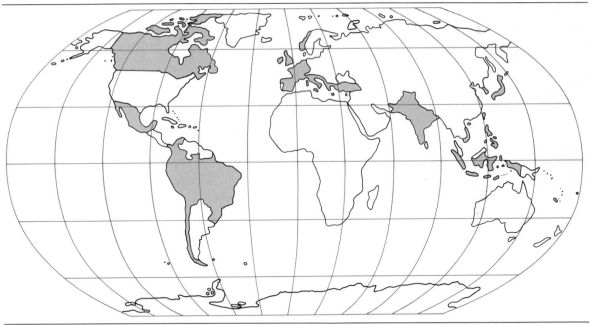

Source: Loch K. Johnson, *The Making of International Agreements: Congress Confronts the Executive* (New York: New York University Press, 1984), p. 37.

lar commitments. The first finding implies a greater *procedural* involvement by Congress in the diplomatic process than conventional wisdom suggests. This does not necessarily mean that Congress has enjoyed a genuine *substantive* involvement in the shaping of foreign policy commitments. Instead, the findings suggest only that members of Congress have been asked to give, and have given, an official green light to the vast majority of overseas commitments—most initiated by the executive branch. Whether or not the Congress had an intimate knowledge of precisely what it had approved, though, is quite a different question. Earlier studies, as well as the author's own interviews and observations, suggest that the legislative branch is often deficient on the substantive policy details of what it has approved, quite aside from its opportunities for procedural involvement.[19]

The second major finding implies that presidential discretion over selected foreign policy options has been substantial in the postwar period. While this discretion has been confined primarily to military and consular matters, the commitment of America's armed forces is obviously of great importance to this nation's external relations. The significance of executive discretion over military policy warrants further scrutiny later in this chapter.

A third major finding is that this country has tended to enter into agreements chiefly with democratic regimes—though authoritarian states have begun to rival, in number, the democracies as America's diplomatic partners. The portrait of America's alignments overseas presented here contrasts sharply with the conjectures of some recent nonempirical analyses. The widely read observations of Jeane J. Kirkpatrick (at the time, the Reagan administration's ambassador to the UN) failed, for example, to acknowledge adequately America's strong and pervasive ties to democratic states— the very hallmark of U.S. postwar diplomacy.[20] Any assessment of America's formal international commitments should underscore this attraction to kindred political and economic values overseas.

Kirkpatrick's central thesis, however, is correct: in the choice between authoritarian and totalitarian regimes as international partners, America has consistently preferred pacts of all varieties with the former. Whether this approach is morally correct, or even beneficial to this nation, is a separate matter; the fact remains that right wing autocrats have won greater favor in Washington than left wing autocrats (with their annoying ties to the Soviet Union or mainland China). The so-called *Tito gambit*, in which the United States attempted (evidently with some success) to dampen Yugoslavia's adherence to Moscow-Marxist doctrine by holding out alluring economic inducements, has been—so these data suggest— an approach attempted only in the most limited way. The United States has been more inclined to keep the Marxists at arm's length, even if this meant shoving them into the eager arms of the Soviet Union.[21] The growing American overtures toward the People's Republic of China represent the most conspicuous and important deviation from this tradition—though this warming relationship was given a cold splash in June of 1989 when PRC leaders brutally repressed prodemocracy student demonstrators, leading to U.S. protestations and strained official relations.

Kirkpatrick's distinction between "friendly" authoritarian and "unfriendly" totalitarian governments has failed to convince many foreign policy specialists who find America's flirtation with autocracies of any stripe unsavory. "It seems to me," states former Secretary of State Cyrus R. Vance, "that if you're on the rack it doesn't make any difference if your torturer is right- or left-handed."[22]

THE HIDDEN SIDE OF AGREEMENT MAKING

In a 1972 report, members of the Senate Foreign Relations Committee noted: "As the committee has discovered, there have been numerous agreements contracted with foreign governments in recent years, particularly agreements of a military nature, which remain wholly unknown to Congress and to the people. . . ."[23] Although only 7 percent of all formal U.S. commitments abroad from 1946 to 1973 were based on executive agreements, a central question remains: were there—hidden within this modest percentage—obligations of great significance? For an answer, one must turn to a more qualitative review of America's military commitments—the foreign ties that have proved to be especially controversial and costly. The placement of troops and weapons abroad, known as *forward deployment*, adds up to the most expensive portion of the U.S. military budget. Of primary interest are those military arrangements based on treaties and executive agreements because, though less frequently used, they have become for reasons discussed below far more contentious than statutory agreements.

The conventional wisdom—at least on Capitol Hill—suggests that the advice and consent of the Senate has been requested by the executive branch largely for diplomatic initiatives of little substantive importance. Senator Dick Clark (D-Iowa) once complained on the Senate floor that "the treaty form has been used for a shrimp agreement with Brazil, an agreement on the conservation of polar bears, and an agreement regarding the uninhabited coral reefs in the Caribbean."[24] Other treaties have dealt with such earthshaking matters as the recovery of lost archaeological objects in Mexico,[25] an increase in membership of the International Atomic Energy Board from 25 to 35,[26] and the international classification of industrial designs.[27]

Despite these questionable uses of the treaty procedure, research indicates that America's military treaties signed between 1946 and 1973 dealt with important, not trivial, commitments. Of the forty-one military treaties signed in these years, thirty-two (or 78 percent) involved major defense obligations. Among them were various security arrangements with Japan, the Republic of Korea, and the nations of western Europe; major arms control accords, including the nuclear test ban treaty of 1963; and postwar peace treaties with former belligerents. Nine of the treaties (22 percent) excluded from the "significant" category dealt with administrative details of major defense pacts, most notably NATO. The evidence—at any rate for defense commitments abroad during this period—fails to support the conventional wisdom; treaties have not

been completely banished from their traditional role.

When it comes to the use of executive agreements for establishing military commitments, however, Senators Fulbright, Clark, and others have been closer to the mark. Although 43 of the 142 military executive agreements dealing with military policy were routine and minor (addressing such issues as the establishment of a practice bombing range in West Germany and reciprocal air rights with Canada for rescue operations), a considerable number involved major obligations abroad. The United States entered into the following obligations partly or completely on the basis of an assertion of executive authority (usually relying upon the commander-in-chief clause of the Constitution):

- Use of the Azores air bases by the United States (1947)
- Placement of United States troops in Guatemala (1947)
- Placement of United States troops in China (1948)
- Military security in the Republic of Korea (1949)
- United States military mission in Honduras (1950)
- Broad United States military prerogatives in Ethiopia (1953)
- United States military mission in El Salvador (1957)
- United States military mission to Liberia (1958)
- United States base rights in Lebanon (1958)
- Security pledges to Turkey, Iran, and Pakistan (1959)
- Military use of the British-ruled island Diego Garcia (1966)
- Military use of Bahrain (1971)
- Agreement terminating a military and economic pact with Libya (1972)

Seventy percent (99 of 142) of these military agreements were significant enough, it seems, to have warranted closer scrutiny by the legislative branch. Several of the commitments involved the establishment of overseas bases. This has been a primary source of tension between the executive and legislative branches, as the president asserts authority under the commander-in-chief clause and the Congress sometimes resists what it perceives to be an unwise military obligation.

As illustrated in Table 11.6, the number of significant military agreements has always been greater than the number of significant treaties since the end of the Second World War. In order to estimate more precisely the extent to which significant military commitments have shifted from treaties to executive agreements, an executive agreement index is presented once more for each administration, based on the proportion of significant military executive agreements out of the total number of significant treaties and executive agreements. The index is high throughout the period 1946–1973. Clearly, most of the significant military commitments took the form of executive agreements. Although the Eisenhower and Johnson administrations were by far the most vigorous claimants for sole executive authority over military

agreement making, each of the other administrations trailed close behind.

MILITARY AGREEMENTS: SOME CASE EXAMPLES

Beyond these statistics stand a number of examples that reveal more fully the evolution of foreign military commitments entered into by executive fiat. Thailand provides one illustration.

Thailand

As mentioned in Chapter 5, Secretary of State Dean Rusk and the foreign minister of Thailand, Thanat Khoman, issued a joint statement in 1962 in which Rusk expressed "the firm intention of the United States to aid Thailand, its ally and historic friend, in resisting Communist aggression and subversion."[28] This language went far beyond the wording of the SEATO treaty, which provided only that the member

TABLE 11.6   THE DOMINANCE OF EXECUTIVE AGREEMENTS OVER TREATIES IN THE MAKING OF SIGNIFICANT MILITARY COMMITMENTS ABROAD, 1946–1972[a]

ADMINISTRATION	SIGNIFICANT MILITARY TREATIES (T)	SIGNIFICANT MILITARY EXECUTIVE AGREEMENTS (EA)	EXECUTIVE AGREEMENT INDEX EA/(T + EA)[b]
Truman	16	28	0.64
Eisenhower	6	30	0.83
Kennedy	1	4	0.80
Johnson	5	24	0.83
Nixon	4	13	0.76
Total	32	99	

[a] This table summarizes the use of military treaties and executive agreements only; statutory agreements, which are more numerous but less controversial, are not analyzed here.

[b] The numbers in this column represent for each administration the proportion of significant military executive agreements, compared with the total number of significant military treaties and executive agreements. This "executive agreement index" ranges from 0 to 1; the higher the index, the greater the reliance on executive agreements for major military commitments.

nations would "consult" in times of military peril and act to meet the common danger in accordance with their own "constitutional processes."

The end result of this joint communiqué was to convert the collective security arrangement under SEATO into a bilateral U.S.–Thai defense pact. Under the new relationship, the U.S. Military Assistance Program (MAP) for Thailand shot from $24 million in 1960 to $88 million in 1962. Further, in 1966 the two nations entered into negotiations over a secret contingency agreement (signed in 1969), which promised joint action in the event of a conventional military attack on Thailand and paid special bonuses to Thai combat troops in Vietnam (in essence, the hiring of mercenaries to fight in this civil war on America's behalf). Through communiqué and secret executive agreements, the original intent of a solemn treaty, SEATO, had been significantly altered.[29]

Diego Garcia

A report from the *General Accounting Office* (GAO, an investigative arm of the Congress) uncovered that the executive branch had bypassed the Congress on the question of using Diego Garcia—a small atoll in the Chagos Archipelago 1000 miles south of the tip of India—as a U.S. military base in the Indian Ocean. Through another secret agreement in 1966, the Department of State agreed to pay Britain's costs for its departure from Diego Garcia in order to make way for American naval and intelligence facilities. "We believe the method of financing—a technique which masked real plans and costs—was clearly," concluded the GAO report, "a circumvention of the congressional oversight role."[30]

Spain

As also came to light during the 1960s, the United States had entered into a series of secret executive agreements with Spain involving the use of its soil for military bases. This disclosure led to stormy debate in the Senate Foreign Relations Committee. Senator Fulbright failed to be impressed by the Defense Department's argument that the Armed Services Committee had been kept abreast of the secret negotiations. He sharply criticized the proclivity of the executive branch "to tell the Chairman of the Armed Services Committee, who usually is very sympathetic with these [executive] agreements, and the [Senate] Appropriations Committee," leaving more critical legislators and the public in the dark.[31]

Yet, the critics were—for the present—still a minority, and in 1970, Congress eventually deferred to the executive agreement on Spanish bases and authorized the necessary funding. In the closing days of the legislative session, however, opponents of the agreement did manage to pass the *Church Resolution*. Sponsored by Senator Frank Church (D-Idaho), it resolved that "nothing in said Agreement of Friendship and Cooperation between the United States and Spain, shall be deemed to be a national commitment by the United States."[32] Lines were being drawn for an approaching battle over the role of Congress in the fashioning of America's diplomatic relations.

When the time came for the renewal of the Spanish bases agreement five years later (1975), the insurgence in the Senate was running at full tide. Prudently, the Department of State submitted the new agreement for approval as a treaty and kept key senators and staff carefully briefed on the progress of the negotiations as they proceeded. According to a Senate staff participant, it was "a candid, open consultation."[33] These "tactics of accommodation" by the executive branch paid off with a Senate vote of 84 to 11 in favor of the treaty. Ironically, Spain also aggressively sought a treaty instead of an executive agreement; the post-Franco regime "yearned for the symbolic benediction that a solemn treaty approved by two thirds of the Senate would provide."[34]

Ethiopia

In 1960, the United States entered into another secret pact, this time to defend Ethiopia. The Eisenhower administration pledged to support a 40,000-man Ethiopian army, promised continued military assistance, and signed a statement "reaffirming" the "continuing interest [of the United States] in the security of Ethiopia and its opposition to any activities threatening the territorial integrity of Ethiopia."[35] In exchange, Ethiopian officials allowed the U.S. National Security Agency to construct and operate an intelligence collection facility at Kagnew Station in Asmara, a city in the country's northern region (from where the NSA could monitor Middle East communications). Once more, the departments of Defense and State had expanded this nation's military commitments abroad without the knowledge of the American people or their representatives in Congress.

Philippines

Like Thailand, the Philippines enjoyed (since 1952) a formal military alliance with the United States based on a treaty, in this case the *Philippines Mutual Defense Treaty*. And like the SEATO treaty, this contract with the Philippines also promised consultation and, if necessary, military protection in accordance with constitutional processes—presumably joint actions by Congress and the presidency. These assurances were evidently insufficient for Philippine President Magsaysay, who requested in 1954 a firmer guarantee of America's military shield.

In response, Secretary of State John Foster Dulles forwarded to Magsaysay a diplomatic communiqué concluding that, since U.S. military forces were already stationed in his country, "an armed attack on the Philippines could not but be also an attack upon the military forces of the United States."[36] In place of "constitutional processes," Dulles had substituted assurances of a quick American military response. President Eisenhower and a new president of the Philippines (García) reaffirmed this

"further bilateral assurance" (the State Department's euphemism) through a joint communiqué in 1953, and by an executive agreement the following year: the *Bohlen-Serrano Agreement*.[37]

The stationing of U.S. soldiers in the Philippines had been far more telling about America's defense intentions than the language of a formal treaty. As a Senate inquiry into U.S. military commitments abroad concluded in 1970, "overseas bases, the presence of elements of U.S. armed forces, joint planning, joint exercises, or extensive military assistance programs represent to host governments more valid assurances of U.S. commitment than any treaty or agreement."[38] The executive branch seemed more than willing to provide these assurances, without public debate on their merit.

South Korea

In an arrangement similar to the one struck with Thailand, the United States promised the government of South Korea in 1966 (through secret executive agreement) that it would pay for commercial consumables—tires, clothing, oil products, gas—used by its soldiers at home if Korean officials would send combat troops to Vietnam. Again, the money would be quietly siphoned out of military assistance funds, appropriated by Congress not for this purpose but for the development or purchase of new weapons.[39]

Laos

During the 1960s in Laos, the executive branch launched a wide array of secret military and paramilitary operations without any written agreements whatsoever. Everything was based on "oral understandings" which, according to a Department of State spokesman, were just as binding as written ones.[40] Among the commitments made in this fashion were the absorption of three-fourths of Laos's foreign exchange needs (including food), the loan of Agency for

International Development (AID) advisers and public road experts, and the placement of American military spotters in combat zones. A Senate subcommittee wanted to know how all this came to pass:

> Subcommittee counsel: . . . under what authority are the American personnel in Laos there?
>
> State Department spokesman: They are there under the executive authority of the President.[41]

THE DANGERS OF DIPLOMACY BY EXECUTIVE FIAT

Several lessons emerge from the partial list of examples presented above. First, U.S. military commitments abroad have often been based on the most slender reeds of authority. While the oral understandings with Laos may represent an extreme case, the other various secret letters, communiqués, and agreements in these examples also represent a foreign policy dominated by hidden bureaucrats, closed doors, and confidential covenants. Sometimes the "agreements" have been only tacit understandings, susceptible to misinterpretations. The presence of American soldiers or bases may mean more than the most elaborate and solemn parchment approved by the Senate.

"Whether or not we have such a treaty with a particular country," testified Secretary Rusk, "the presence there of a U.S. base clearly [signifies] an interest and concern on our part with the security of that country."[42] NATO provides a close illustration. The language of this treaty is ambiguous; but, with American troops stationed in western Europe, everyone understands that a Soviet attack westward would inevitably draw in the United States. It is precisely this need to protect U.S. troops stationed abroad that makes the initial commitment of defense assurances such an important decision.

Sometimes America's diplomatic obligations are stretched far beyond their original intent—a so-called *creeping commitment*.[43] This happens as executive-branch officials seek to "fill in the details" once a broad agreement is reach. As with Dulles's interpretation of the Philippines Mutual Defense Treaty, the expansion of a relationship can be considerable. These "auxiliary arrangements"—executive agreements following in the wake of treaties and statutory agreements—take on a bewildering variety of forms, including memoranda of understanding, exchange of notes, exchange of letters, technical arrangements, protocols, the *note verbale*, the *aide-mémoire*, agreed minutes, joint communiqués, joint military plans, military assistance, and the stationing of troops. Particularly difficult for legislators to monitor are *third-party agreements*, whereby the United States makes promises to another nation through intermediaries, as when American diplomats in 1980 worked through Algerian offices to negotiate the release of U.S. hostages in Iran.

These shell games, whereby Congress and the public are kept guessing about the true nature of U.S. commitments abroad, also occur outside the realm of military affairs. Secret agreements have been used by the executive branch to conduct political negotiations and to carry out intelligence operations, as illustrated respectively by the *Sinai support mission* and the use of the CIA to instigate plots and counterplots around the world.

Former Secretary of State Henry Kissinger has been widely criticized for his use of secret agreements for diplomatic purposes. Chiding him for "obsessive secrecy," Senator Henry Jackson (D-Wash.) once accused Kissinger of withholding from Congress for two years secret "understandings" reached with the Soviet Union during the initial SALT negotiations. Further, Kissinger allegedly withheld "crucial communications" on the faltering U.S.–Soviet trade talks in 1974.[44] The experienced diplomatic correspondent Tad Szulc draws a similar conclusion: "The fact is that virtually nobody—

possibly not even [Presidents] Richard Nixon and Gerald Ford—knew precisely what promises and commitments Kissinger made to foreign leaders during his eight years in power: to Mao Tse-tung and Chou En-lai, Brezhnev and Dobrynin, Le Duc Tho, Sadat and King Faisal, Golda Meir or any number of other foreign presidents, foreign ministers and ambassadors."[45]

One of the controversial "understandings" reached by Kissinger was with Israel and Egypt in 1975 over the question of a Sinai disengagement. These negotiations included the commitment of U.S. personnel to serve as monitors in a region where military hostilities might have easily resumed with little warning. The "understanding" was declared by the Department of State to be the proper exercise of executive authority, not a commitment requiring a use of the treaty procedure—though President Ford backed away from this position when congressional criticism mounted. He eventually sought legislative authority, via a statutory agreement, to implement the provisions of the accord.

As part of its paramilitary or warlike operations, the CIA has entered into many secret agreements. They have included pacts with Ukrainian guerrillas (1949–1953); Polish resistance groups (1950–1952); Albanian rebels (1949–1952); Tibetan insurgents (1953–1959); splinter groups in China and North Korea (1950–1954); and factions in Guatemala (1954), in Cuba (1961–1964), in Laos (throughout the 1960s), in Vietnam (1955–1974), and in Nicaragua (1981–1989), to recall only a partial listing from Chapter 9.

All too often, charge critics, the executive branch has bypassed the Congress, making major foreign commitments with the simple signature of a bureaucrat across the dotted line on an executive agreement, by writing a letter, or even by offering just an oral promise. The Congress has long been aware of this practice, but—until recently—its efforts to place limits on this slippery form of diplomacy have met with little success. At a Senate Foreign Relations

Secretary of State Henry A. Kissinger photographed in Egypt in 1975 during one of his many diplomatic trips to the Middle East. (UPI/Bettmann Newsphotos)

Committee hearing in 1971, Senator Fulbright observed, "We have discovered that the President does not always know best, and that, indeed, the country would be far better off today if the Congress had been more assertive in the exercise of its constitutional role, which consists at least as much in assertion and criticism as it does in subservience."[46] In response to what they perceived to be an excessive use of executive discretion in the sealing of international commitments, key legislators initiated a search for more democratic controls over American diplomacy.

THE DEMOCRATIC CONTROL OF DIPLOMACY

The concern of Senator Fulbright and his colleagues about diminishing legislative control over U.S. commitments abroad represented the second time in the postwar period that Congress had sought to trim back the conduct of diplomacy by executive fiat. The first attempt occurred in the 1950s and was unsuccessful. Led by John W. Bricker (R-Ohio), legislators in the Senate sought an amendment to the Constitution that would sharply limit both the president's authority to make international agreements and the effect such agreements would have on U.S. domestic law.

The second attempt, spearheaded by Fulbright and others in the 1970s, was partially successful and is consequently of greater importance. Led by legislators wary of presidential excesses during the war in Vietnam, this initiative had (at first) the modest goal of requiring the executive branch merely to inform Congress of those foreign pacts its officials had entered into. Subsequent attempts were made, however, to move beyond the establishment of simple reporting requirements toward greater legislative control over the substance of the agreements themselves. Here were rougher seas to cross.

The Bricker Revolt

Most troubling to Senator Bricker and his supporters was Article VI, Clause 2 of the Constitution, which reads: "This Constitution, and the Laws of the United States which shall be made in Pursuance thereof; and all Treaties made, or which shall be made, under the Authority of the United States, shall be the supreme Law of the Land; and the Judges in every State shall be bound thereby, any Thing in the Constitution or Laws of any State to the Contrary notwithstanding." To the *Brickerites*, this passage allowed the president, in effect, to add to the constitutional system by making treaties and other agreements "under the authority of the United States," which in turn would bind federal and state law. By international agreement, the president or his subordinates might impose upon the nation legal obligations that would invade the domain of power reserved to the states and, thereby, deprive the

people of rights guaranteed under the Constitution. The Bricker movement was, in a nutshell, a thinly disguised defense of states' rights, a concept dear to the conservative wings of both major parties.

Disturbing to the Brickerites were proposals before the United Nations to advance an antigenocide convention, a declaration of human rights, and other proposals, which, if adopted as treaties by the United States, would have pledged—or at least so feared the Brickerites—this country to endless interference in the domestic affairs of other countries and, more important, invited their interference in ours. Here was a paramount consideration. According to one student of the Bricker era, many southern senators dreaded that the federal government might declare desegregation in the United States by means of an executive agreement (perhaps with an African ally).[47]

As early as 1943, New Dealer devotion to the idea of a United Nations had already inflamed passions among isolationist critics on Capitol Hill—especially the instrument of commitment preferred by the Department of State. With reference to a UN Relief and Rehabilitation Administration draft agreement, the State Department informed the influential anti-New Dealer Senator Arthur Vandenberg (R-Mich.) that "the United States participation in the establishment of this United Nations administration should be through an executive agreement."[48]

Vandenberg wasted no time in reply. The draft, he said, "pledged our total resources to whatever illimitable scheme for relief and rehabilitation all around the world our New Deal crystal gazers might desire to pursue . . . [with] no interference with this world-wide prospectus as it might be conceived by Roosevelt, Lehman, Hopkins and Col. House, until that long last moment when Congress would be confronted with a 'fait accompli.' "[49]

Behind the ardent defense of states' rights and the distaste for New Dealers stood another danger perceived by the Brickerites: secret executive agreements. The memory of President

Roosevelt's hidden agreements with the Soviets during the Second World War—a bugaboo of the Republican Party since 1945—remained a central concern of the Bricker forces. "The power of the executive agreements has resulted in such catastrophes as Yalta, Potsdam, and Tehran,. . . " fumed a statement from the Wisconsin State Republican Party in 1953.[50]

Bricker introduced his amendment to curb the president's power over international agreements initially in 1951, but not until 1954 did Senate conservatives settle on compromise language which they thought would have a chance of passing. Critics of the Bricker amendment, including President Eisenhower and Secretary of State Dulles, were dismayed that the measure might actually become law. For the journalist Walter Lippmann, efforts to improve the wording of the amendment had led to several renditions that were "one and all . . . unwashed, unpeeled, uncooked, and not yet fit to be eaten."[51] The constitutional authority Professor Edward S. Corwin concluded—magisterially—that

> No such act of mayhem on the Constitution is required to meet existing perils. The Anti-Genocide Convention, the proposed Conven-

tion on Human Rights and the like are undoubtedly ill-considered proposals, but the Senate itself has the power, has it but the intestinal fortitude to use it, to administer the *congé* to all such utopian projects. Can it be that some Senators prefer to be able to invoke the Constitution as a reason for doing the sensible thing rather than face up to certain pressure groups? The Bricker proposal is really a vote of lack of confidence in the political courage and integrity of the body form which it emanates.[52]

The Brickerites, however, were not easily dissuaded. On February 26, 1954, they rallied behind a substitute amendment offered by Senator Walter George (D-Ga.), after Bricker's own tougher amendment was defeated (it required implementing legislation by *state* legislatures for all international agreements touching on questions of states' rights!). The *George amendment*, if successful, would still have represented a significant victory for the Bricker movement. It read:

> Section 1. A provision of a treaty or other international agreement which conflicts with this Constitution shall not be of any force or effect.
>
> Section 2. An international agreement other than

Perspectives on American Foreign Policy   11.2

The views of John Foster Dulles changed dramatically in opposition to the Bricker movement when he joined the Eisenhower administration. Less than a year before being appointed secretary of state, Dulles had argued before an audience of attorneys in Louisville, Kentucky:

The treaty-making power is an extraordinary power liable to abuse. Treaties make international law and also they make domestic law. Under our Constitution treaties become the supreme law of the land. They are indeed more supreme than

ordinary laws, for congressional laws are invalid if they do not conform to the Constitution, whereas treaty laws can override the Constitution. Treaties, for example, can take powers away from the State and give them to the Federal Government or to some international body and they can cut across the rights given the people by the constitutional Bill of Rights.

Quoted in *Hearings of the Committee on the Judiciary, U.S. Senate*, 83d Cong., 1st Sess., p. 862.

a treaty shall become effective as internal law in the United States only by an act of Congress.[53]

Begrudgingly, the Brickerites accepted this language as a final refuge. As one analyst notes, the George amendment drew "great appeal from the fact that it avoided the radicalism of the Bricker proposal while at the same time it satisfied the desire of many senators for greater control over the drawing up of executive agreements."[54]

At last came the moment the Brickerites had labored toward for three years. It was now or never; all their chips were on the George substitute amendment. "The last moments of the debate were both bitter and emotional," reported the *New York Times*.[55] The clerk began the slow calling of the roll. Thirty minutes later, the vote was yeas 60, nays 31. The George amendment—and the Bricker movement—had failed by a single vote.

"Spurred by the success of the Twenty-Second Amendment [limiting presidents to two terms], the foes of Presidential power launched the Bricker amendment, ... " writes Louis W. Koenig.[56] Beyond their fear of "presidential autocracy," the Brickerites—neoisolationists—were worried even more about the consequences of the "new internationalism." During a hearing on the Bricker proposal, Senator Pat McCarran (D-Nev.) burst out: "... I voted for what I consider now to be a bad treaty that I will regret probably all the days of my life ... the United Nations."[57] For the Brickerites, international agreements had become, as one witness put it during hearings, "a kind of 'Frankenstein' instrumentality, which can change and even destroy the liberties of the American people and their form of government."[58]

Could an international agreement abrogate a statute, or affect state law beyond the enumerated powers of the Constitution? With the failure of the Bricker movement, such questions would remain unanswered—at least by constitutional amendment. For this blessing, the

Eisenhower administration was deeply thankful. "This is an area to be dealt with by friendly cooperation between the three departments of government which are involved," opined Secretary Dulles, "rather than by attempts at constitutional definition, which are futile, or by the absorption, by one branch of government, of responsibilities which are presently and properly shared."[59]

The weak spot in the Dulles prescription was the phrase "properly shared." In the decade following the Bricker movement, a new congressional challenge would confront the issue of international agreements. This time the insurgents, paradoxically, would be the internationalists in the Congress, who had now come to believe that the executive branch had failed to share diplomatic responsibilities properly with the legislative branch.

A Second Resurgence

The underlying motive of the Bricker movement, suggested Senator Fulbright in 1954, was "a retreat from the world."[60] The second uprising in Congress against presidential dominance over U.S. diplomacy also displayed, ironically from the opposite end of the political spectrum, a jaded outlook on unwarranted involvement around the globe. "Come home, America!" implored one of its spokesmen, Senator George McGovern (D-S.Dak.), in a 1972 presidential campaign speech. Beware the "apostles of interventionism," warned Senator Church in one of his 1976 presidential campaign addresses critical of a hyperactive American involvement abroad. Critics quickly dubbed this fresh wave of legislative insurgents the "neoisolationists."[61]

The appellation was misleading, however. The Brickerites and the insurgents of the next generation were worlds apart in philosophy and tactics. The Brickerites opposed continued U.S. involvement in the UN and other multinational organizations ("backdoor approaches to world government," admonished a leading lobbyist for the Bricker amendment[62]), worried chiefly about undue executive power to change *domestic* law through international agreements, and sought sweeping constitutional changes for the making of international agreements.

In contrast, the neoinsurgents accepted the UN as a modestly useful forum, extolled the virtues of some other multinational entities (notably NATO, the International Court of Justice, and other collective security arrangements to protect America's vital foreign interests), worried chiefly about undue executive power to change *foreign* policy through an injudicious involvement of U.S. military personnel in regions of peripheral concern to America's future, and pursued comparatively modest reforms to limit executive discretion.

If the Brickerites were in full retreat from the world (something of an exaggeration, since even Senator Bricker recognized the value of NATO), the neoinsurgents preferred only a partial retreat—a reflection once again of the twin impulses of isolationism and interventionism that have characterized American foreign policy down through the years (Chapter 3).[63] They opposed an overextension of U.S. commitments to far-flung corners of the globe which appeared of dubious relevance to the well-being of Americans. Not even George McGovern wanted America to come home from everywhere, just from Third World backwaters where it had no business.

"Our gravest mistakes in the last twenty years have come from the assumption that we have the wealth and power to mold the world to our own liking," emphasized Senator Church in 1970, referring to the developing countries. "We don't, and the sooner we learn to impose some reasonable restraint on our own tendency to intervene too much in other people's affairs, the happier land we will have and the less burden we will place upon our own people to undertake sacrifices that are not really related to their own good or the good of the country."[64] In the 1950s, the rallying cry of the Brickerites had been "Protect states' rights!"

For the neoinsurgents, the cry was "No more Vietnams!"

Despite fundamental disagreements on policy objectives, the Brickerites and the insurgents of the Vietnam era were closely aligned in their belief in one bedrock principle: a distrust of executive discretion in foreign policy. Resist executive "encroachment," argued Senator Knowland of California, the Republican majority leader, in 1954; "Swing back the pendulum [of constitutional imbalance]!" urged Senator Church in 1970.[65] What both movements desired ultimately was not foreign policy by the executive or by the Congress, but a "constitutional balance" between the two (to employ a favorite phrase from both eras). As Stephen A. Garrett has aptly noted, these movements were "substantially focused on the necessity of reasserting the prerogatives and status of the Congress as such if that institution is to maintain its vitality as a central component of the American Constitutional system."[66]

Revolt of the Fulbright Committee   President Johnson's misrepresentations over (and eventual invasion of) the Dominican Republic in 1965, followed by increasing skepticism in the Senate about the Gulf of Tonkin Resolution, set the stage for the legislative reform of formal agreement-making procedures. In 1968, Johnson hastily requested the Senate to approve a broadly worded resolution of foreign aid for Latin America. On the eve of a hemispheric summit meeting in Punta del Este, the president sought congressional support for costly new agreements. Once burned (the Gulf of Tonkin Resolution), twice shy, the Senate Foreign Relations Committee with Fulbright at the helm refused to write another blank check and instead passed, by a unanimous vote, a substitute resolution stating that all new foreign aid initiatives in Latin American would be given due consideration in accordance with the committee's normal legislative timetable.

With this shot across the White House bow, the committee had gone beyond mere speech making in its search for an acceptable balance between the Congress and the executive branch in diplomatic affairs. The mood of skepticism on Capitol Hill had changed to outright defiance. An institutional revolution was under way.

In June of 1969, the Senate passed the *National Commitments Resolution*, which declared: "Be it resolved, that it is the sense of the Senate that a national commitment by the United States to a foreign power necessarily and exclusively results from affirmative action taken by the executive and *legislative* branches of the United States Government through means of a treaty, convention, or other *legislative* instrumentality specifically intended to give effect to such a commitment" (emphasis added). Then came the Church resolution in December 1970, regarding the Spanish bases agreement discussed earlier in this chapter.

The Case-Zablocki act   By 1972, the Senate was ready to take its biggest step ever toward tighter legislative controls over international agreements. So far, legislators had only passed resolutions—some toughly worded to be sure, but still just expressing a point of view without the force of law. Now the Senate turned to statutory remedies. Out of a sense of despair over the inability of Congress even to find out what commitments the executive branch had been making overseas (especially in Indochina), Senator Clifford Case (R-N.J.) introduced legislation to remove this blind spot. He sought to guarantee that Congress had access to information about all U.S. commitments abroad. To this end, the Senate passed the Case act by a vote of 81 to 0. Clement Zablocki (D-Wis.) introduced the same measure in the House, and six months later, the proposal passed in that chamber, too. On August 22, 1972, President Nixon—in the face of a united Congress prepared to override a veto—signed the *Case-Zablocki act* into law. The Department of State would have to report, henceforth, all international agreements to Congress within sixty days.

Hesitant and cautious in contrast with the bold initiatives of the Brickerites to amend the Constitution, the Case-Zablocki act nonetheless represented a significant step by Congress toward an institutional sharing of power over the directions of American diplomacy. As members of the Foreign Relations Committee stated in a report issued during debate on the proposal:

> the principle of mandatory reporting of agreements with foreign countries to the Congress is more than desirable; it is, from a constitutional standpoint, crucial and indispensable. For the Congress to accept anything less would represent a resignation from responsibility and an alienation of an authority which is vested in the Congress by the Constitution. If Congress is to meet its responsibilities in the formulation of foreign policy, no information is more crucial than the fact and content of agreements with foreign nations.[67]

Whatever its virtues, the imperfections of the Case-Zablocki act soon became evident. The sixty-day provision in the law, for example, permitted the executive branch to inform the Congress *after* a commitment has already been made to another country. With this late awareness of a sealed negotiation, Congress was faced with either going along with the diplomatic initiative or wrecking the arrangements by shutting off funds or otherwise barring implementation. "The reports come up here so late, we have to rely on contacts and leaks in the executive branch to find out when really important negotiations are under way," noted a frustrated Senate staff aide.[68]

More alarming still to legislators is when the executive branch fails to report at all on its international agreements. Inquiries by the researcher David J. Kuchenbecker revealed in 1978 that "few major agencies could indicate even the number of international agreements they had entered into during the previous year."[69] The most compelling evidence that something was amiss initially surfaced as part of a GAO investigation. In February 1976, a GAO report concluded that the transmission of executive agreements to the legislative branch under the provisions of the Case-Zablocki act suffered from significant omissions. The report, limited to an examination of U.S. agreements with the Republic of Korea, documented more than thirty instances since the passage of the law in which agreements had not been sent to the Congress. Several dealt with military matters, such as the joint use of Taegu Air Base and the transfer of $37.6 million worth of military equipment to Korean troops. Not only were the agreements never reported to the Congress, they were never reported to the Department of State either.[70] Clearly, government agencies— including the Department of Defense—had negotiated and transacted international agreements on an agency-to-agency basis without sufficient monitoring by State Department diplomats or legislators.[71]

In October of 1978, Congress moved to tighten the Case-Zablocki reporting requirements, adding three new statutory requirements. First, "any oral international agreements" had to be reduced to writing and submitted to the Congress. Second, all late agreements (that is, beyond the sixty-day limit) required a written presidential explanation. And third, the Department of State's control over agency-to-agency agreements was increased by mandating State Department– agency consultation before the formal signing of an international agreement. As one authority correctly concluded, Congress's patience was "clearly at an end."[72]

These changes helped improve the State Department's control over agreement-reporting procedures, and focused accountability for easier monitoring by the legislative branch. Nevertheless, the number of agreements reported late continued to be substantial in 1978 and 1979. According to the first report under the tightened provisions of the Case-Zablocki law, 132

agreements were late in transmittal to Congress during 1979. The number dropped significantly the next year, yet still summed to forty-six agreements.[73] Progress has been achieved toward compliance under the Case-Zablocki act and its amendment, but clearly problems persist even with this relatively simple reporting requirement.

The Treaty Powers Resolution   In 1976, 1977, and 1978, Senator Dick Clark (D-Iowa) offered a much stronger remedy for this problem: the *Treaty Powers Resolution*. This legislation sought to express a sense of the Senate that any "significant" international agreement should be cast as a treaty and, thus, should be submitted to members for their advice and consent. Section 4 of the resolution bore sharp teeth: if the executive failed to submit an agreement which senators had decided (by a simple resolution) should have been submitted for ratification as a treaty, then the Senate rules would declare it henceforth out of order "to consider any bill or joint resolution or any amendment thereto, or any report of a committee of conference, which authorizes or provides budget authority to implement such international agreement."[74] The money spigots would be shut off until the Senate gave its advice and consent to the agreement in dispute.

A majority of the Senate proved unwilling, however, to endorse this bold challenge to executive agreements. In retrospect, staff observers believe that the Clark proposal represented chiefly a "finger-shaking" exercise by the Foreign Relations Committee toward the executive branch.[75]

The initiative did have some effect, despite its defeat. It stimulated an exchange of letters between the chairman of the committee, John Sparkman (D-Ala.), and the assistant secretary for congressional relations at the Department of State, Douglas J. Bennet, Jr. The *Sparkman-Bennet letters* led to an understanding that, in the future, the Department of State would "inform the committee periodically, on a confidential basis, of significant international agreements which have been authorized for negotiation. . . ."[76] In turn, the committee would then advise the department on any agreement that its members would like to discuss further regarding the appropriate form of diplomacy: treaty, statutory agreement, or executive agreement. Sparkman stated that the procedures "must cover all significant international agreements . . . regardless of the executive entity involved in the negotiation or approval process." As he further stressed, his committee expected that "*consultation*—not *notification*—will occur at any time an option is opened or foreclosed to use the treaty or executive agreement form in the case of any international agreement of significance. . . ." (emphasis added). The message was clear: the less consultation from you, the more heat from us.

Two Houses Do Not Make a Home   Throughout this struggle between the Senate and the executive branch, the two houses of Congress have often been at one another's throat as well over this issue. Secretary of State Dulles ob-

served in 1953 that an "undefined and probably undefinable borderline [exists] between international agreements which require two-thirds Senate concurrence, but no House concurrence, as in the case of treaties, and agreements which should have the majority concurrence of both chambers of Congress."[77] Leading members of the Senate, however, have been prepared to fight in order to protect their prerogatives.

"If they begin now to intrude on the treaty-making power of the Senate, we are going to find ourselves in a position where we can't do anything without the House's consent," complained Senator Church, the ranking Democratic member of the Foreign Relations Committee, in 1977. "Their nibbles end up being big bites, and we are being bitten to death."[78] Yet, logically asks a senior staff aide on the House Foreign Affairs Committee: "Could the framers have intended otherwise than that the representatives of the taxpayers and citizens who must fulfill these national commitments, have a voice in this approval?"[79]

Sometimes the executive branch takes advantage of this divisiveness for its own pur-

---

Perspectives on American Foreign Policy 11.3

Senator Dick Clark on the Treaty Powers Resolution:

. . . under the existing situation, there is no balance. The President of the United States alone decides what is to be sent up as a treaty. The Senate has no choice in that whatsoever. If the President of the United States decides to send the SALT agreement to this body as a treaty, we will consider it as a treaty. If the President of the United States decides that it is an executive agreement, it will be an executive agreement. The Senate will not decide and will have no voice in that decision

except insofar as the President may decide to consult with us.

The same is true of any other international agreement. It is really, under the existing situation, the President, and the President alone, who decides whether any agreement that is signed is going to be considered by this body at all. The President can dispense with Senate advice and consent merely by calling a treaty an executive agreement. I do not see that as a fair balance.

Congressional Record, June 28, 1978, p. S10010.

poses. "The Clark Resolution would constitute a very significant and unwise interference with the role of the House of Representatives," offered a legal adviser for treaty affairs in the Department of State during the debate over the treaty powers proposal.[80]

Executive Reinterpretation of Treaties   Institutional battles over the proper approaches to diplomacy continued unabated during the Carter and the Reagan administrations. In 1977, President Carter's first secretary of state, Cyrus Vance, announced that, even though the terms of the SALT I treaty were due to expire soon, the United States would continue to honor its provisions, so long as the U.S.S.R. followed suit. The Senate Foreign Relations Committee objected to this method for reaching an arms accord as an infringement upon the constitutional requirement for the Senate's advice and consent.[81] In rebuttal, the Department of State emphasized that Vance's announcement represented simply a "policy statement," which did not legally bind the United States or the Soviet Union; as such, it did not require a formal two-thirds vote of the Senate.[82] The members of the Foreign Relations Committee grumbled, but took no further action.

One of the most heated debates between Congress and the executive branch over diplomatic procedure occurred during the Reagan years, as a result of disagreements over the meaning of the Antiballistic Missile (ABM) Treaty of 1972. Critics charged that the Department of State legal adviser Abraham D. Sofaer (pronounced "SO-fair") had given the treaty an overly permissive interpretation in 1988, in order to give the Reagan administration sufficient leeway to test and ultimately deploy in space its proposed "Star Wars" defense system. By implication, Sofaer was attempting to claim that whatever a previous administration (in this case President Nixon's) might have told the Senate about the meaning of a treaty did not necessarily bind subsequent administrations.

"It is the legal adviser, who when asked to 'legalize' short-term policy ends over constitutional means, must be prepared to say no," responded the Senate Foreign Relations Committee (controlled by a Democratic majority). "By failing to meet that standard, Mr. Sofaer has done a disservice to the [State Department's] Office of Legal Adviser."

In Sofaer's view, however, the chief executive enjoyed a constitutional right to decide on a new interpretation of a treaty—without Senate approval. "It's a close call," he opined, "but it is the President's."[83]

For members of the Senate, Sofaer's theories loomed as an unacceptable challenge to its responsibilities for treaty approval. To make its dissatisfaction clear, the Senate attached a single condition to an important arms accord before it (the INF treaty): executive testimony on its meaning, provided to legislators during hearings, would remain binding. Unwilling to see his INF hopes go up in smoke over this interbranch dispute, President Reagan muzzled the State Department's legal adviser and provided assurances to the Senate that his administration would honor all treaty interpretations offered to legislators by executive officials during the approval process. Senate consent would, in a word, be required after all before any reinterpretation of a treaty by the executive branch.

DIPLOMACY'S FAR REACH

Although the controversial operations of the CIA and the occasional landing of the U.S. Marine Corps overseas are events that capture bold newspaper headlines, the fact remains—as former Israeli Foreign Minister Abba Eban has underscored—"that most of the conflicts in the relations between states are resolved through the routines and procedures of diplomacy." One can thank the world's diplomats in large measure for the smaller number of wars that have occurred than might have been the case on this hostile globe in the absence of their talents and dedication to peace. "Diplomacy must be judged by what it prevents, not only by what it achieves," continues Eban, sharing Hans Morgenthau's hope for an eventual world government: "Much of it is a holding action designed to avoid explosion until the unifying forces of history take humanity into their embrace."[84]

Diplomacy and the agreements that result from official dialogue can carry sweeping implications for America's future. Just as skillful negotiations have often been able to prevent or limit international conflicts, so, too, have they established bonds drawing (as Washington and Jefferson feared) the United States into foreign intrigue. Often diplomacy leads to the creation of military alliances which have a direct bearing on when and where U.S. citizens will be expected to take up arms.

Diplomacy, then, has frequently been the precursor to America's overt or covert military intervention abroad. This is why, in the wake of the experiences of the war in Vietnam, legislators have come to believe that Congress has a major stake in the shaping of U.S. diplomatic initiatives. "If you've got children or grandchildren who might have to go [to war]," once observed Robert C. Byrd (D-W.Va., minority leader of the Senate at the time), "you'd feel much better with Congress being brought in, than leaving it to one man."[85] In this new spirit of involvement and sense of responsibility that settled over the Congress during the 1970s, Senator Humphrey warned Secretary of State Vance as Vance prepared to depart on a trip to the Middle East: "Don't make any commitments until you've been back here [to Capitol Hill]—not even smiling ones."[86]

Most legislators understand the distinction between "open covenants" and "covenants openly arrived at." Morgenthau has sensibly delineated between the two. "Disclosure of the results of diplomatic negotiations is required by the principles of democracy, for without it there can be no democratic control of foreign policy," he wrote. "Yet publicity for the negotiations themselves is not required by democracy and runs counter to the requirements of common sense."[87] Most Americans and their representatives in Congress appreciate the importance of privacy and secrecy in the negotiating process; but legislators also understand that democracy and the Constitution require their participation in the great decisions of war and peace that determine the fate of the American people they represent.

SUMMARY

Most international disputes are resolved not by force of arms or by secret intervention, but through diplomacy—the art of negotiations between states leading to peaceful agreements. Diplomacy is the warp and woof of American foreign policy; its presence is felt everywhere, from collective efforts to clean up global environmental pollution to the search for peaceful settlements of disputes in the Middle East, Central America, Southeast Asia, and other "hot spots" around the world.

The United States has employed three primary forms of international agreements in its formal diplomatic negotiations: the treaty, the statutory agreement, and the executive agreement. They require, respectively, a two-thirds vote of those members present in the Senate, a majority vote in both houses of Congress, and no legislative authority at all. During the period from 1945 to 1973 (for which systematic data are available), the United States used the treaty form in only 6 percent of its international agreements. Statutory agreements were the most prevalent form of formal negotiations—fully 87 percent—and the executive agreement accounted for 7 percent.

The executive agreement initially evolved to handle the many routine negotiations between nations that would only clog the legislative process if they had to be sent through committee (such as agreements regarding the protection of migratory birds). The opportunity to avoid legislative debate provided by this approach has, however, made it a form of considerable appeal to executive officials for the consummation of many significant commitments abroad. During the period 1945–1973, the Nixon administration proved to be the most aggressive in rejecting the treaty form in favor of executive agreements. Presidents have been drawn to the executive agreement especially for key military negotiations, including commitments to Thailand, Spain, Ethiopia, the Philippines, South Korea, and Laos.

In its making of agreements abroad, the United States has been consistently attracted to fellow democracies, followed by right wing authoritarian regimes and, a far distant third, left wing totalitarian regimes. The United Kingdom, Canada, and Japan have been the primary diplomatic partners of the United States.

Congress has twice attempted to curb executive discretion over diplomatic commitments: first, in a movement led by Senator John Bricker of Ohio during the 1950s and, second, as a result of outcries by "doves" in the Senate during the 1970s. The Bricker movement failed by one vote to achieve its restraints on the use of executive agreements. The efforts of the doves in the next generation partially succeeded, however, leading to the passage of the Case-Zablocki act. This important law requires executive-branch reports to the Congress on the use of all executive agreements, placing legislators in a position at least to know about these (often secret) pacts and—if they wish—to raise objections about this approach to diplomacy.

KEY TERMS

diplomacy
agreement form
agreement content
Point Four
"executive agreement index"
democratic regimes
authoritarian regimes
totalitarian regimes
procedural involvement
substantive involvement
Tito gambit
forward deployment
GAO

Church resolution
Philippines Mutual Defense Treaty
Bohlen-Serrano Agreement
creeping commitment
third-party agreements
Sinai support mission
Brickerites
George amendment
National Commitments Resolution
Case-Zablocki act
Treaty Powers Resolution
Sparkman-Bennet letters

NOTES

1. Both the formal definition and Kennan's description are from Norman J. Padelford and George A. Lincoln, *The Dynamics of International Politics* (New York: Macmillan, 1962), p. 340.

2. Henry A. Kissinger, *A World Restored* (Boston: Houghton Mifflin, 1957), p. 326.

3. Abba Eban, *The New Diplomacy: International Affairs in the Modern Age* (New York: Random House, 1983), p. 334.

4. Hans J. Morgenthau, *Politics among Nations: The Struggle for Power and Peace*, 4th ed. (New York: Knopf, 1967; first published in 1949), pp. 135–136.

5. David D. Newsom, *Diplomacy and the American Democracy* (Bloomington: Indiana University Press, 1988), pp. 23, 219. Newsom notes further that another valuable mission of the American diplomat is to help protect U.S. citizens overseas. In this capacity, he or she "is a combination of parish priest and city clerk, helping to get fellow citizens out of jail, issuing replacement passports, settling citizenship problems, handling the effects of the deceased, seeking to reunite families, and registering births" (p. 199).

6. Quoted in correspondence to the author from the British scholar-researcher Frank Adams, December 21, 1988.

7. Morgenthau, *op. cit.*, pp. 137, 139. Part of the ineptitude has come from poor presidential selection of ambassadors—often political appointees who have won their posts because of campaign contributions, rather than diplomatic expertise. This unfortunate practice has grown under Presidents Reagan and Bush. Indeed, forty-seven of the first sixty names submitted by President Bush to the Senate Foreign Relations Committee for approval as ambassadors in 1989 were political appointees—one of whom (Della Newman, a real estate broker from Seattle and chairperson of Bush's Washington State presidential campaign) told a reporter she had no interest in foreign policy. She was unable even to name the prime minister in her country of assignment, New Zealand (George Hackett, "Notorious Ambassadors," *Newsweek*, June 5, 1989, p. 26). President Bush promised that his final list of friends nominated to ambassadorial posts would be no more than one-third of the total number of slots. This would leave the record for amateur ambassadors to the Reagan administration, at 40 per cent of the total (*New York Times*, November 7, 1989, p. 6).

8. Morgenthau, *op. cit.*, pp. 540–548.

9. *Ibid.*, p. 549.

10. *New York Times*, January 31, 1989, p. 1.

11. Sir Crispin Tickell, the John A. Sibley Lecture, School of Law, University of Georgia, Athens, February 2, 1989. Abba Eban notes that diplomacy "does not offer salvation. It moves in a world in which the stakes of diplomacy are so high that even modest progress is worthy of profound respect. Imperfect solutions have to be compared with even less perfect alternatives" (*The New Diplomacy*, p. xiii).

12. Newsom, *op. cit.*, p. 160.

13. See Jimmy Carter, "Let's Use a Little Diplomacy in Panama," *Washington Post*, National Weekly Edition, April 25–May 1, 1988, p. 29.

14. Newsom, *op. cit.*, p. 41.

15. Classified and spoken agreements are excluded from these data; it is illegal to discuss the former, and no reliable records exist on the latter. A senior staff member of the House Foreign Affairs Committee estimates that about 5 to 10 percent of all international commitments are secret and deal mainly with military policy (interview, June 1974, Washington, D.C.). The data examined here come from the following sources: *United States Statutes at Large; United States Treaties and Other International Agreements; Treaties and Other International Acts Series*, numbered pamphlet copies of international agreements; and *Digest of United States Practice in International Law*, all published each year by the Government Printing Office, Washington, D.C.; plus *International Agreements Other Than Treaties, 1946–1968: A List with Citation of Their Legal Basis*, Department of State, Office of the Legal Adviser for Treaty Affairs, January 10, 1969, mimeographed, with supplemental updates. For a more complete description and analysis of these data, see Loch K. Johnson, *The Making of International Agreements: Congress Confronts the Executive* (New York: New York University Press, 1984), from which much of this chapter is drawn.

16. Quoted in Theodore C. Sorenson, *Kennedy* (New York: Harper & Row, 1965), p. 411.

17. Quoted in Alonzo L. Hamby, *Beyond the New Deal: Harry S. Truman and American Liberalism* (New York: Columbia University Press, 1973), p. 372.

18. On the distinction between authoritarian and totalitarian regimes, see Roy Macridis, *Contemporary Political Ideologies: Movements and Regimes* (Cambridge, Mass.: Winthrop, 1980), especially pp. 223–225; and Jeane J. Kirkpatrick, "Dictatorships and Double Standards," *Commentary*, November 1979, pp. 34–45. For information on the governments of different countries, see Arthur Banks, *Political Handbook of the World* (New York: McGraw-Hill, 1976), and Central Intelligence Agency, *National Basic Intelligence Factbook* (Washington, D.C.: Government Printing Office, annually).

19. See, for example, Theodore J. Lowi, *The End of Liberalism*, 2d ed. (New York: Norton, 1979).

20. Kirkpatrick, *op. cit.*, p. 44.

21. See J. William Fulbright, "Reflections: U.S. Foreign Policy since 1945," *New Yorker*, January 8, 1972, pp. 41–62.

22. Quoted in the *New York Times*, June 8, 1988, p. 5.

23. "Transmittal of Executive Agreements to Congress," Senate Report No. 92-591, January 19, 1972, pp. 3–4.

24. *Congressional Record*, June 28, 1978, p. S9996.

25. See "Transmittal of Executive Agreements to Congress," *Hearings of the Senate Foreign Relations Committee*, October 20 and 21, 1971, p. 2.

26. "Congressional Oversight of Executive Agreements," *Hearings of the Subcommittee on Separation of Powers, Senate Judiciary Committee*, April 23 and 24 and May 12, 18, and 19, 1972, p. 54.

27. "Executive Agreements with Portugal and Bahrain," *Hearings of the Senate Foreign Relations Committee*, February 1, 2, and 3, 1972, p. 4.

28. See "National Commitments," Report No. 91-129, Senate Committee on Foreign Relations, April 16, 1969, p. 28.

29. See "U.S. Security Agreements and Commitments Abroad: Laos and Thailand," *Hearings of the Subcommittee on United States Security Agreements and Commitments Abroad, Senate Foreign Relations Committee*, Part 6, 1969–1970, hereafter cited as the Symington subcommittee (after its chairman, Stuart Symington, D-Mo.).

30. See the *Washington Post*, January 25, 1975.

31. "Morocco and Libya," *Hearings of the Symington Subcommittee*, Part 9, p. 1979.

32. *Congressional Record*, December 11, 1970, p. 41167.

33. J. Brian Atwood, "Downtown Perspective: Lessons on Liaison with Congress," in Thomas M. Franck, ed., *The Tethered Presidency* (New York: New York University Press, 1981), p. 217.

34. *Ibid.*, p. 218.

35. "Ethiopia," *Hearings of the Symington Subcommittee*, Part 8, p. 1904–1905.

36. Senate Foreign Relations Committee Report, December 21, 1970, p. 5.

37. *New York Times*, April 9, 1954, p. 2. By 1983, the United States was spending close to $1 billion in aid to the Philippines for the privilege of a further five-year lease for American bases there. The Reagan administration curried the favor of Philippine President Ferdinand E. Marcos with more than cash; in 1981, Vice President George Bush praised Marcos's support for "democracy," stretching that word to the breaking point in a nation that was clearly a dictatorship, and President Reagan offered Marcos an enthusiastic welcome on his state visit to the United States in 1982. See Bernard Gwertzman, "For U.S., Global Needs Can Overshadow Human Rights," *New York*

Times, August 28, 1983, p. 1E. In 1986, Marcos was stripped of his power in a relatively bloodless revolution led by centrists who promised genuine democracy.

38. Senate Foreign Relations Committee Report, December 21, 1970, p. 20.

39. *Ibid.*, p. 9.

40. "Kingdom of Laos," *Hearings of the Symington Subcommittee*, Part 2, p. 437.

41. *Ibid.*, 433.

42. *Hearings of the Subcommittee on Preparedness, Senate Committee on Armed Services*, August 25, 1966, p. 4.

43. This phrase is from a Senate Foreign Relations Committee report, December 21, 1970, p. 4.

44. *Washington Post*, April 9, 1975.

45. *The Illusion of Peace* (New York: Viking, 1979), p. 212.

46. "Transmittal of Executive Agreements," Senate Report No. 92-591, 1972, *op. cit.*, p. 3.

47. Interview, Professor Francis M. Carney, University of California, Riverside, May 21, 1968. See, also, Stephen A. Garrett, "Foreign Policy and the American Constitution: The Bricker Amendment in Contemporary Perspective," *International Studies Quarterly*, vol. 16, June 1972, p. 201. On the key Bricker amendment vote, all but three of the twenty-two southern senators would support Bricker. For a more recent example of conservative senators reluctant to approve an antigenocide treaty for fear it might serve as a "pretext for foreign meddling in United States domestic affairs," see Martin Tolchin, "Senate Surprised on Genocide Pact," *New York Times*, September 14, 1984, p. 4.

48. Arthur H. Vandenberg, Jr., ed., *The Private Papers of Senator Vandenberg* (Boston: Houghton Mifflin, 1952), pp. 67–68.

49. Dean Acheson, *Present at the Creation: My Years in the State Department* (New York: Norton, 1969), p. 72.

50. Quoted in Henry Steele Commager, "The Perilous Folly of Senator Bricker," *The Reporter*, vol. 9, October 13, 1953, p. 16.

51. "Today and Tomorrow," *Washington Post*, February 4, 1954.

52. Edward S. Corwin, "The President's Treaty-Making Power," *Think*, vol. 19, July 1953, p. 6.

53. *Congressional Record*, February 2, 1954, p. 1103.

54. Garrett, *op. cit.*, pp. 198–199. Ironically, in light of his later views, Senator Fulbright was perhaps the most articulate opponent of the efforts to curb international agreements. "It was never intended by the Founding Fathers," he declared during the floor debate, "that the President of the United States should be a ventriloquist's dummy sitting on the lap of the Congress" (*Congressional Record*, February 2, 1954, p. 1106). Use of the war-making powers by President Johnson eleven years later would dramatically change the Senator's pro-presidency stance; see Chapter 10.

55. William S. White, "Senate Defeats All Plans to Check Treaty Powers, Final Vote Margin Is One Vote," *New York Times*, February 27, 1954.

56. *The Chief Executive* (New York: Harcourt, Brace, & World, 1964), p. 7. The Twenty-second amendment, ratified in 1951, limited the tenure of presidents to ten years.

57. *Hearings of the Committee on the Judiciary, U.S. Senate*, 82d Cong., 1st Sess., p. 145.

58. Frank Holman testifying in *Hearings of the Committee on the Judiciary, U.S. Senate*, 85th Cong., 1st Sess., p. 423.

59. *Hearings of the Committee on the Judiciary, U.S. Senate*, 83d Cong., 1st Sess., p. 828.

60. *Congressional Record*, February 2, 1954.

61. See, for example, William F. Buckley, Jr., "The CIA's $6 Million and Italian Politics," *Washington Star*, January 16, 1976.

62. Mrs. Robert Murray, coordinator of the Vigilant Women for the Bricker Amendment, *Hearings of the Senate Judiciary Committee*, 1955, p. 423.

63. The London *Economist* has noted: "At one extreme, the United States ignores the world outside the Americas because it feels it neither likes it nor needs it. At the other it plunges into the world to put it to rights" (January 21, 1984; quoted by Newsom, *op. cit.*, p. 12).

64. Interview, February 21, 1970, Washington, D.C.

65. *Congressional Record*, February 26, 1954, p. 2372; *Congressional Record*, April 30, 1970, p. 13565.

66. Garrett, *op. cit.*, p. 213.

67. "Transmittal of Executive Agreements to Congress," Senate Report No. 92-591, 1972, *op. cit.*, p. 3.

68. Interview, May 28, 1974, Washington, D.C.

69. Kuchenbecker, "Agency-Level Executive Agreements: A New Era in U.S. Treaty Practice," *Columbia Journal of Transnational Law*, vol. 18, 1979, p. 64, note 239.

70. Report of the comptroller general of the United States, "U.S. Agreements with the Republic of Korea," ID-76-20, February 20, 1976.

71. Joseph S. Nye, Jr., notes that "nearly all the major executive departments have little foreign ofices of their own. In 1973, for example, of 19,000 Americans abroad on diplomatic missions, only 3,400 were from the State Department and less than half of the government delegates accredited to international conferences came from the State Department" ("Independence and Interdependence," *Foreign Policy*, vol. 22, Spring 1976, p. 138; see, also, Raymond Hopkins, "The International Role of 'Domestic' Bureaucracy," *International Organization*, vol. 30, 1976, p. 424).

72. Kuchenbecker, *op. cit.*, p. 68.

73. Marjorie Ann Browne, *Executive Agreements and the Congress*, Issue Brief Number IB 75035, Washington, D.C.: Congressional Research Service, February 27, 1981, p. 5.

74. Senate Resolution 486, 94th Cong., 2d Sess. (1976).

75. Interviews, June 28, 1978, Washington, D.C.

76. "International Agreements Consultation Resolution," Senate Report No. 95-1171, August 25, 1978, pp. 2–3.

77. "Treaties and Executive Agreements," *Hearings of the Subcommittee of the Judiciary Committee, U.S. Senate*, 82d Cong., 2d Sess., p. 21.

78. *Hearings of the Committee on Foreign Relations, U.S. Senate*, 1977, p. 21.

79. James T. Schollaert, "A Critique of Recent U.S. Practice of International Agreements Law," paper presented at the annual meeting of the American Society of International Law, San Francisco, April 23, 1977 (mimeographed), p. 4.

80. Arthur W. Rovine, "Separation of Powers and International Executive Agreements," *Indiana Law Journal*, vol. 52, 1977, p. 428.

81. Senate Report No. 499, 95th Cong., 1st Sess. (1977).

82. See letter from Herbert J. Hansell, legal adviser of the Department of State, to John J. Sparkman, chairman, Senate Foreign Relations Committee (dated September 28, 1977), reprinted in *ibid.*, pp. 9–10 (quoting Paul Warnke, director of the Arms Control and Disarmament Agency), as cited by Michael J. Glennon, "The Good Friday Accords: Legislative Veto by Another Name?" *American Journal of International Law*, vol. 83, 1989, p. 544.

83. See Michael R. Gordon, "Legal Adviser Leaves a Trail of Furious Debate," *New York Times*, March 1, 1988.

84. *Op. cit.*, pp. 399, 401.

85. Quoted in the _New York Times_, September 21, 1983.

86. Briefing on the Middle East, Committee on Foreign Relations, U.S. Senate, February 11, 1977 (attended by the author).

87. Morgenthau, _op. cit._, p. 533.

RECOMMENDED READINGS

Beaulac, Willard. _Career Ambassador_ (New York: Macmillan, 1951). Insightful recollections on the profession by an American ambassador.

Cottam, Richard. _Iran and the United States: A Cold War Case Study_ (Pittsburgh: University of Pittsburgh Press, 1989). A revealing probe into the demise of U.S.–Iranian diplomatic relations and the ensuing consequences.

Eban, Abba. _The New Diplomacy: International Affairs in the Modern Age_ (New York: Random House, 1983). A former Israeli minister for foreign affairs, highly regarded in the diplomatic community for his intellect and thoughtful judgment, offers valuable insights into world politics and the art of peaceful negotiations.

Fulbright, J. William. _The Crippled Giant_ (New York: Random House, 1972). A searing critique of U.S. diplomacy by a leading advocate in the 1970s of an increased legislative role in the fashioning of America's external relations.

Gilbert, Amy M. _Executive Agreements and Treaties, 1946–1973_ (New York: Thomas-Newell, 1973). A descriptive review of America's use of treaties and executive agreements during a quarter century following the close of the Second World War.

Herz, Martin F. _215 Days in the Life of an American Ambassador_ (Washington, D.C.: School of Foreign Service, 1981). A frank and witty examination of diplomatic life.

Ikle, Fred C. _How Nations Negotiate_ (New York: Harper & Row, 1964). An exhaustive primer on the art of diplomatic dialogue.

Johnson, Loch K. _The Making of International Agreements: Congress Confronts the Executive_ (New York: New York University Press, 1984). A statistical and descriptive analysis of agreement making from the Truman through the Ford administration, with prescriptions designed to improve congressional monitoring of executive agreements.

Kennan, George F. _American Diplomacy, 1900–1950_ (Chicago: University of Chicago Press, 1951). Kennan traces America's place in the world from its high sense of security in 1900 to high insecurity in 1950, searching for an answer to the question: To what extent was this unfortunate transformation the fault of U.S. diplomacy?

Kissinger, Henry A. _White House Years_ and _Years of Upheaval_ (Boston: Little, Brown, 1979 and 1982, respectively). The memoirs of America's most famous scholar-diplomat and the secretary of state in both the Nixon and Ford administrations.

Kuchenbecker, David J. "Agency-Level Executive Agreements: A New Era in U.S. Treaty Practice," _Columbia Journal of Transnational Law_, vol. 18, 1979. An exhaustive inquiry by a legal scholar into the use of executive agreements by the United States.

Lake, Anthony. _Somoza Falling_ (Boston: Houghton Mifflin, 1989). An absorbing case study of American diplomacy, underscoring the clashes that arose between professional Foreign Service officers and political appointees during U.S. negotiations with Nicaraguan factions from 1978 to 1979.

Newsom, David D. _Diplomacy and the American Democracy_ (Bloomington: Indiana University Press, 1988). Written by one of America's finest ambassadors, this study provides clear insights into the relationship between diplomats and other segments of society, including legislators, the media, spies, military officers, and citizens.

Nicolson, Sir Harold. _Diplomacy_ (London: Thornton Butterworth, 1939). A brief and classic primer on the subject by one of Britain's best scholar-diplomats.

O'Brien, Conor Cruise. *The Siege: The Saga of Israel and Zionism* (New York: Simon & Schuster, 1986). A thorough look at the troubled diplomatic waters of the Middle East.

Rovine, Arthur W. "Separation of Powers and International Executive Agreements," *Indiana Law Journal*, vol. 52, 1977. A penetrating legal analysis into the use of executive agreements and Congress's response to the concomitant erosion of the treaty power.

Stennis, John, and J. William Fulbright. *The Role of Congress in Foreign Policy* (Washington, D.C.: American Enterprise Institute, 1971). Two leading legislators (both former Rhodes scholars) debate the proper limits of congressional involvement in the shaping of U.S. diplomatic initiatives.

Strang, Lord. *The Diplomatic Career* (London: Andre Deutsch, 1962). An elegantly written British view on the art of diplomacy by an experienced practitioner.

Sutherland, Arthur. "The Bricker Amendment, Executive Agreements and Imported Potatoes," *Harvard Law Review*, vol. 65, June 1952, pp. 1305–1338. A distinguished legal scholar examines the Bricker movement.

Whalen, Charles W., Jr. *The House and Foreign Policy* (Chapel Hill: University of North Carolina Press, 1982). A former member of the U.S. House of Representatives makes the case for this chamber's strong involvement in foreign affairs, notwithstanding the Senate's claims to a superior standing by virtue of the Constitution's treaty clause.

ECONOMIC GOALS: AN INTEGRAL PART OF AMERICAN FOREIGN POLICY

THE POSTWAR INTERNATIONAL ECONOMIC SETTING

TRADE AS AN INSTRUMENT OF AMERICAN FOREIGN POLICY

AMERICA'S TRADING PARTNERS—AND RIVALS

AMERICA: NO LONGER THE SOLITARY ECONOMIC BEHEMOTH

FRAGMENTATION OF THE INTERNATIONAL ECONOMIC SETTING

THE FRAGMENTATION OF ECONOMIC POWER AT HOME

THE USE OF TRADE SANCTIONS

FOREIGN AID AS AN INSTRUMENT OF AMERICAN FOREIGN POLICY

TRADE AND AID: STEPCHILDREN OF AMERICAN FOREIGN POLICY

SUMMARY

12

ECONOMIC STATECRAFT: THE INSTRUMENTS OF TRADE AND AID

Japanese automobiles at a U.S. port-of-entry. (AP/Wide World Photos)

Although the scene was Christmas day in rural Georgia, it could have been anywhere across the country. As a middle-class family sat around the Christmas tree opening presents, they began to notice how few of the gifts had U.S. labels. From Scotland came a sweater and a bottle of liquor; from West Germany, a music box, china, biscuits, and a hairbrush; from Mexico, a pair of slippers and sweets; from South Korea, stuffed animals, a sweatshirt, and a calculator; from Taiwan, a cribbage board, a running outfit, a backpack, an umbrella, a bowl, and a set of coasters; from France, wine and gourmet food; from Belgium, more sweets; from Sweden, a compass; from Hong Kong, a shirt and a doll; from England, tea; from Spain, crayons; from Japan, toys; from the Philippines, hand-carved napkin rings. A majority of the presents had been made in another country. Moreover, in the family's garage were parked two Japanese automobiles, in the den stood a Japanese TV and VCR, in the kitchen a Japanese microwave oven, and in the parlor a Yamaha piano.

One does not have to travel beyond the home place to see the challenge faced by the United States in the international marketplace. Whether or not Americans are up to this stiff competition has become one of the great issues before the nation today. The pleasant image of gifts around a Christmas tree belies the harsh economic reality confronting the United States. Since 1980, this country has suffered a series of annual budget deficits ranging from $140 to $220 billion, accumulating into a domestic government debt in 1989 of some $2.7 trillion (compared with $1 trillion in 1980). By 1992, the national debt will exceed $3 trillion.

Moreover, America's trade deficits oscillate between $130 billion and $150 billion each year. Other nations are also rapidly buying up U.S. business. In 1980, foreign claims on American assets (government bonds, stocks, real estate, companies, and so on) amounted to $0.5 trillion; today, the figure is over $1.5 trillion.[1] These conditions (and others) have created an unhealthy U.S. dependence on other nations. Accompanying this relative decline in America's economic strength has come, here and abroad, a sinking confidence in this nation's global leadership.

ECONOMIC GOALS: AN INTEGRAL PART OF AMERICAN FOREIGN POLICY

"It's no longer American foreign policy," observed a recent chairman of the Senate Foreign Relations Committee. "It's American foreign *economic* policy."[2] The chairman meant to convey the extent to which international economic issues have displaced more traditional national security and diplomatic issues (Chapters 8 to 11) on the agenda of U.S. foreign policy.

Economic issues have never been fully off the agenda, from Thomas Jefferson's concern over the interruption of American shipping by the Barbary pirates to Ronald Reagan's scolding of Japanese leaders for flooding U.S. markets with automobiles while building tariff dikes at home against American-made exports. Throughout the nation's history, the primary goal of international economic policy has been to protect and promote the commercial interests of the American people and to maintain access to those natural resources overseas important to U.S. industry and national defense.

In pursuit of its economic goals, the United States has drawn upon the various instruments of foreign policy discussed in Part 2 of this book. An important argument over the years for the buildup of a powerful navy, for example, has been to keep the sea-lanes open for American commercial interests. As the reader has seen in previous chapters, the United States has often sent in the Marines or the CIA to protect U.S. business interests abroad, as in Iran (oil), Guatemala (bananas), and Chile (copper), among other countries throughout the world—although this economic motivation has been coupled with (and usually superseded by) a po-

litical and military decision to contain communist expansion.

This chapter examines, first, the setting in which economic policy is decided—one characterized by institutional fragmentation at home and a relative decline of America's influence abroad; second, the specific instruments of economic power, from embargoes and boycotts (negative economic sanctions) to most-favored-nation rights and tariff reductions (positive economic sanctions); and, third, the role of foreign aid as an instrument of economic influence in America's relations with other countries.

THE POSTWAR INTERNATIONAL ECONOMIC SETTING

Despite the steady interest in economic questions, they have largely been relegated—until recently—to a backseat on the nation's policy agenda, behind the political and, especially, the national security issues associated with the cold war. This reduction of commercial matters to a lower status was reinforced in the immediate aftermath of the Second World War by the comparative calm that settled over international economic disputes. The *Bretton Woods agreement* of 1944 established a stable postwar monetary system for the major industrial nations in the West; and in the East, Soviet hegemony provided for a quite different, but nonetheless comparable, economic stability.

As for the developing world (lying primarily south of the industrialized nations), its members remained for the time being largely subservient to the dominant economic forces of the north. Occasionally, an economic issue would wax preeminent, as when Western leaders devoted considerable energy toward the establishment of the European Economic Community (EEC). By and large, though, as one economic specialist observes, "as a result of the establishment of agreed structures and rules of international economic interaction, conflict over economic issues was minimized, and the significance of the economic aspect of international relations seemed to recede."[3]

New Economic Worries for the United States

By the 1980s, however, the world had become more complicated. Among other changes, the dollar suffered a loss of respect as the key currency holding together the monetary arrangements of the Western nations. The financial costs of the war in Vietnam, comments Leonard Silk, a *New York Times* financial correspondent, "sealed the doom of the postwar world monetary system that had been built on a strong dollar and fixed exchange rates between the dollar, gold, and all other currencies."[4] President Johnson refused either to raise taxes as a means for financing the war or to trim back on his domestic "Great Society" program, thereby further harming the dollar through spiraling inflation at home.

Under President Nixon, the domestic inflation worsened. So did the nation's balance of payments. By *balance of payments*, economists mean (in Paul A. Samuelson's words) "the balance between export of goods and import of goods. Between gold coming in and out. Between capital loans (or 'I.O.U.'s') going in and out. Between gifts and foreign aid. And between all these taken together."[5] Under Nixon, the balance registered a deficit; that is, the difference between what the United States sold and what it bought was unfavorable, as dollars continued to pour out of this country.

Finally, in 1971, President Nixon convened an emergency international economic summit at the Smithsonian Institution in Washington, D.C. The upshot of the *Smithsonian agreement*—the "greatest monetary agreement in the history of the world," in Nixon's opinion—was for the United States to devalue the once sacrosanct dollar (by 8 percent) in an effort to restore its equilibrium and strengthen America's position as the reigning monarch of international finance (as envisaged at Bretton Woods).

Even this drastic step—dubbed the "Nixon shock," for it marred the reputation of the once almighty dollar—failed to curb the outflow, and another devaluation proved necessary in 1973 (10 percent this time). This step also failed to calm the dollar. Currencies (the West German mark, the Japanese yen, the pound, along with the dollar) now "floated" up and down in response to supply-and-demand bidding in the foreign exchange markets—a *floating world monetary system* in place of the fixed-rate system established by the Bretton Woods agreement. The comforting stability of the fixed-rate system had vanished.

Nor was the United States any longer the overwhelmingly dominant trading power it had once been in the aftermath of the Second World War. From out of the rubble of western Europe and Japan grew strong economic rivals. They flourished with help from the United States, which provided $17 billion in outright grants under the Marshall Plan (discussed later in this chapter) chiefly to bolster the countries of western Europe against Soviet aggression—augmented by the availability of cheap energy, a skilled and expanding population, modern machinery, easy liquidity and credit conditions, an enormous pent-up consumer demand, and a strong determination to succeed. In some goods, the Soviet bloc, too, was becoming a more potent industrial competitor.

A Rising Third World

Moreover, countries in the Third World were no longer simply economic pawns of the colonial powers. Some indeed had become central players in the game of global Monopoly, forming cartels to extract higher prices from wealthy industrialized nations dependent upon the import of mineral resources. The *Organization of Petroleum Exporting Countries (OPEC,* composed chiefly of Arab nations) was able, for example, to take advantage of the rising demand for oil within the major industrial powers. When war broke out in the Middle East in 1973 between Israel and the surrounding Arab states, the Arab members of OPEC instituted an oil embargo against the Netherlands and the United States. In this fashion, they hoped to bring pressure by these two nations against Israel, forcing accession to Arab demands. Further, OPEC increased the price of its oil fourfold over the next year, from about $2.10 per barrel of Persian Gulf oil in 1973 to more than $8 per barrel in 1974. The profits of OPEC in this single year alone amounted to some $70 billion—"the greatest single financial coup in history."[6]

The effects of the OPEC oil price increase have been far-reaching. Among the oil-importing nations (mainly the advanced market economies), the high prices have been inflationary. Even with the current oil glut resulting from overproduction, the United States and other Western nations have been hemorrhaging their national wealth through the purchase of oil from OPEC. The sums of money going out have far exceeded purchases by OPEC countries of Western exports, creating large trade imbalance. Ironically, oil importers must often borrow money from OPEC in order to buy more oil—and become yet more indebted. The outflow of funds exacerbated the *stagflation* afflicting the industrialized nations to one degree or another (especially during the 1970s), that is, the stifling effect of economic stagnation and high unemployment coupled with inflation. Economists uniformly agree that this "mysterious ailment" saps a nation's economic growth, but they disagree on its causes and cure. Clearly, though, a dependency on foreign oil aggravates the condition in the West. Energy alternatives that might wean the Western nations away from OPEC's oil wells remain unattractive to planners because of the environmental and safety hazards associated with coal and nuclear energy and the continuing technological limitations of solar energy.

Meanwhile, the OPEC nations have been the beneficiaries of vast—indeed virtually unmanageable—sums of money, so-called *petrodollars*. The difference between a country's total export and its total import of goods and services is referred to as the *balance on current account*.[7] The surplus earnings (the current account surpluses) of OPEC nations are considered to be in excess of $500 billion.[8] In part, this wealth has been redistributed to other nations in the form of loans and grants, though overwhelmingly only to fellow Arab and Muslim states. Some of the wealth has been used to buy important financial assets in the West, from exclusive department stores to commercial banks—another unsettling development from the perspective of Westerners worried about further Arab influence over their lives. Petrodollars have supported, as well, extravagant lifestyles for oil-rich sheikhs, including gambling boats off the coast of Saudia Arabia and top-of-the-line Mercedes automobiles used almost like disposable tissues.

The amount of petrodollars generated by the OPEC states has been so large that a significant recycling problem has arisen. Billions of petrodollars have been deposited in chiefly European banks (where they are known as *Eurodollars*) for investment purposes—"hot money," in the argot of financial speculators. Often these huge sums have been the object of rapid, often careless and destabilizing, shifts from accounts in one country to accounts in another, as speculators attempt to maximize profits according to fluctuations in currency exchanges. The various problems associated with the rise of the OPEC oil cartel have contributed substantially toward the new prominence given international economic issues on the agenda of national policymakers.

World-Class Competition

Policymakers have been further shocked out of complacency by the declining capacity of the United States to capture as much of the world market as was once the case. From the 1950s until now, the U.S. share of world production has declined from 60 percent to around 20 percent. This faltering competitiveness (or economic inefficiency) "may be the dominant economic issue of the remaining years of the 20th century," observed the Speaker of the House in 1986.[9] Beyond the sluggishness of the economy attributable to mammoth budget deficits and the volatility of the dollar stands another key retardant of U.S. competitiveness in the world marketplace: *productivity*—the amount of production per worker.

While Japanese productivity has grown at an annual rate of 8 percent since the 1960s, America's has grown at just 2.7 percent. Once the United States dominated the production of automobiles in the world, building half the total; now it manufactures only 23 percent of the total. In the past, the United States seldom ran a deficit in its foreign trade; now it shoulders the world's largest deficit. Only five years ago, the United States was the world's largest creditor; now it is the world's largest debtor—exceeding all of the developing nations in Latin America combined. Such statistics have done as much as the Nixon shock or the oil shock to turn the minds of decision makers toward economic issues.

Indeed, the constituencies of elected officials often demand greater attention to international economics, because the rise of foreign competition has usually meant the decline of some American factory or small business in Middletown, U.S.A. This chapter examines the growing significance of economics—trade and aid—to foreign policy. Here is yet another power that can be used by, and against, the United States.

TRADE AS AN INSTRUMENT OF AMERICAN FOREIGN POLICY

An examination of trade as a power in U.S. external relations must begin with a description of the setting in which trade with other nations takes place. This setting has evolved in recent decades into a much more complicated array of market relationships than was true in the immediate postwar period.

International Trading Systems

Joan Edelman Spero has outlined the three systems that make up today's global trading network: the Western system, which includes relations between North America, western Europe, and Japan; the North-South system, binding the developed market economies of the North with the struggling economies of Africa, Asia, and Latin America; and the East-West system, with its ties between the developed market economies of the West and the planned economies of the Soviet Union and the communist nations of eastern Europe.[10] She characterizes these systems, respectively, as interdependent, dependent, and independent.

Western Interdependence   The Western system is interdependent because of the high rate of interaction among the member states. These nations are drawn together by the bonds of the U.S. dollar (however weakened), common international banking practices, overarching multinational corporations (MNCs), political and military alliances, and their robust economies, among other affinities. While these nations have benefited from their relationship as a result of reliable markets, liquidity, and credit, each has become more vulnerable to external influences from other members; so close are the economic ties that a ripple in one country's economy can be felt throughout the system. The largeness of the U.S. economy has made it somewhat less vulnerable to these influences than is true for other members, but none has the kind of control over its own economic destiny that was enjoyed in earlier times.

North-South Dependence   The relationship between the market economies of the North and the developing economies of the South remains one of dependence, though less so now than during the days of colonialism (and for the few lucky nations with oil deposits the dependency bond has been reversed to some extent). The asymmetry in the relationship is readily apparent in the difference in the average gross national product (GNP) per capita between the two regions: $7317 for the North in 1977, for example, and only $573 for the South.[11] Nor does this gap seem to be closing. The dependence arises because the economic "traffic" is largely one-way: from the South to Northern markets. Moreover, countries in the South often have only one or two major export offerings; consumer demand in the North for these products (bananas or coffee, for instance) can mean economic life or death to the poorer nations.

Dependence comes, too, from the need for external capital. As the price of oil soared in the 1970s, the oil-poor Southern nations faced chronic balance-of-payments deficits. To pay their oil bills, they borrowed from the International Monetary Fund (IMF), the International Bank for Reconstruction and Development (IBRD), and other international forums designed to provide public concessional funds for poorer nations (and controlled by the Northern market economies). They borrowed as well from private commercial banks, which offered the advantage of fewer strictures imposed on the borrower. Indeed, these private banks—flush with Eurodollars in the Eurocurrency market—eagerly sought outlets for investment, as ambitious, young bank bureaucrats rushed around the globe lending out too much money too quickly ("overleveraging"), with insufficient regard for the creditworthiness of the recipients.

This pell-mell recycling of funds (chiefly petrodollars) has led to the overextension of many banks and an almost hopeless indebtedness among poorer nations to the private banks ($175 billion in 1979), not to mention the IMF and the IBRD. The total Third World debt had reached about $1.2 trillion by 1989, with the poorer nations of the South paying out a net of some $20 billion to $30 billion per year to the developed nations of the North.[12]

To resist this dependence, the nations of the South began in 1974 to express a new feeling of unity among themselves and a concomitant aggressiveness toward the North. Emboldened by the unraveling of the Bretton Woods order and by the successful muscle flexing of the OPEC oil cartel, they demanded in various forums a "new international economic order" that would more fairly disperse the riches of the North to assist developing economies in the South—a kind of global New Deal of wealth redistribution to replace northern dominance over trade.

Referring to themselves as the *"newly industrialized countries"* (NICs), some third world nations—especially in east Asia—began by the 1970s to display high growth rates, challenging the more established manufacturing countries in the West in the production of some goods. A shift was taking place in comparative advantage. The widely accepted *theory of comparative advantage*, espoused by the self-made millionaire David Ricardo in 1817, argues that each country is especially well suited to produce some good. As Silk explains:

> Each producer [nation] has a "comparative advantage" in doing what it does best—and trading for the rest. Just as a highly paid lawyer should not waste his time typing his own briefs (even if he is a better typist than his secretary) or a highly paid doctor should not paint his own house (even if he is a better and faster painter than any he can hire), a nation should concentrate on what it can do best, given its limited resources.

Or, in Samuelson's succinct expression: "International specialization pays for a nation."[13]

The NICs had proven themselves more capable of making low-cost shoes, shirts, and other goods than the industrially advanced nations; therefore, they became viable trading partners less dependent on Northern cash bailouts and strict IMF controls. Yet, while NIC growth rates soared in the 1970s and 1980s at 6 percent or better, poor African nations remained mired down at a growth rate of around 0.2 percent.[14]

So destitute are some nations that for them the theory of comparative advantage becomes a mockery. Others are so strongly dependent upon a single market for a single export (the United States, for example, is the main purchaser of Ugandan coffee) that a relationship of economic dependence threatens to rob national sovereignty of any real meaning.

East-West Independence   The East-West trade picture has been characterized by independence. Driven apart by the hostilities of the cold war, the developed market economies of the West and the planned, Soviet-dominated markets of the socialist states may as well have been, until recently, on different planets, so minimal was their commercial contact. In the late 1960s, however, the sluggish economy of the Soviet Union led its leaders to a key decision: they would have to turn more toward the West in order to stimulate their productivity through the infusion of outside technology. Symbolic of this opening to the West was a $1.5 billion deal in 1966 with Fiat, the Italian automaker, to build an assembly line in the U.S.S.R. The Nixon administration's warming overtures to Moscow, labeled *détente*, led to an invigorated American interest in greater interaction with the economies of the East bloc as well. Food exports to the Soviet Union, especially wheat and corn, rose precipitously (and currently account for about half of America's exports to the U.S.S.R.), and a wide range of other commodities began to move back and forth between the superpowers.

As Table 12.1 illustrates, commercial ties between the United States and the Soviet Union grew more or less steadily from the late 1960s onward, with the first full year of détente (1973) producing a dramatic spurt forward in trade relations. During the 1980s, economic transactions between the superpowers have fluctuated. The general trend, though, has been toward a renewed rise in Soviet exports to the United States since 1983 (following a trough in

TABLE 12.1   U.S.–SOVIET TRADE: SOVIET EXPORTS TO AND IMPORTS FROM THE UNITED STATES, FOB (IN MILLIONS OF U.S. DOLLARS)[a]

	EXPORTS	*IMPORTS*
1960	25	60
1961	24	51
1962	17	27
1963	25	28
1964	21	163
1965	34	65
1966	47	63
1967	39	63
1968	43	57
1969	61	117
1970	64	115
1971	60	144
1972	93	560
1973	186	1385
1974	235	747
1975	191	2031
1976	264	2662
1977	369	1707
1978	375	2349
1979	535	3797
1980	463	1510
1981	387	2339
1982	248	2589
1983	367	2002
1984	602	3283
1985	441	2421
1986	605	1248

[a] Official Soviet statistics; converted from rubles to dollars at the average exchange rate for each year.

Source: For 1960–1979: Vneshnyaya Torgovlya SSSR (Foreign Trade of the USSR, Moscow: USSR Ministry of Foreign Trade), *compiled by Joan Edelman Spero, in* The Politics of International Economic Relations, 2d ed. *(New York: St. Martin's, 1981), pp. 310–311. Copyright © 1981 by St. Martin's Press, Inc. Reprinted with permission. For 1980–1986, U.S. Census Bureau, U.S. Department of Commerce.*

1981 and 1982), and a decline in Soviet imports. In 1986, Soviet exports to the United States reached an all-time high of $605 million—even though President Reagan had called the U.S.S.R. an "evil empire" just three years earlier. In contrast, Soviet imports from the United States skidded downward in 1986 to their lowest level since 1974 ($1.248 billion).

In part, this ambivalent trade posture toward the Soviet Union reflects the dichotomy of views within the U.S. government over how to react toward President Gorbachev's efforts to improve the Soviet economy. The right wing of the Reagan and Bush administrations opposed efforts to aid the Soviets in their efforts to modernize their economy, for fear that a stronger U.S.S.R. will simply mean more rubles for tanks and missiles. The Republican Party's right wing also hopes that a disintegrating Soviet economy might lead eventually to an overthrow of the communist regime—or at least its dramatic reform.

More moderate elements in both administrations, especially the career diplomats, remained hopeful that Gorbachev's *perestroika* would work; they were willing to cooperate with Soviet leaders in order to improve commercial ties, believing that through increased trade the superpowers might enjoy better relations, resulting in a safer world. Whatever the hidden forces behind these trade statistics, the end result seemed to be a healthier trade balance between the United States and the Soviet Union.

A Portrait of American Trading Practices

Looking at overall world trade patterns, most of the global commercial activity resides within the Western industrialized nations. Some 42 percent of the total world exports and imports take place within the circle of these market economies alone. Over 50 percent of U.S. trade is with the other industrialized nations of the West. When these twenty-three nations turn outward beyond their own circle for commercial intercourse, their combined percentage of total world exports and imports tallies about 9 percent with the non-OPEC developing nations (113 countries), 6 percent with OPEC (13 countries), and only 3 percent with the planned economies of the Soviet bloc (12).[15]

For the United States, though, the developing world—home for three-quarters of the world's population—is a more significant trading region than these overall figures for the advanced market economies would indicate. The developing nations supply the United States with such essential resources as tin, rubber, bauxite, and oil. They also happened to represent the fastest-growing markets for the United States, accounting for more of America's exports in some recent years than Japan and the EEC (founded in 1958) combined.[16]

Despite a relative decline, the United States remains by far the single largest international trader, engaging in commercial transactions with all the countries of the world. America's imports consist primarily of consumer goods, automobiles, and fuels. Petroleum imports alone accounted for 30 percent of total U.S. imports in 1977; in 1984, though, oil imports had dropped to 17 percent of the total, as a global recession forced down OPEC oil prices, the OPEC members proved unable to hold prices high as a disciplined cartel, and other sources of oil—the North Sea among them—became available. (In 1981, Saudi Arabia, the leading OPEC producer, earned almost $100 billion in oil revenues; in 1986, just $18 billion.)[17]

While oil imports stand as the largest single deficit commodity in U.S. trade, America records significant deficits with other products as well, notably: passenger motor vehicles (the most dramatically worsening imbalance among the major classes of manufactures); wearing apparel; iron and steel; consumer electronics; nonferrous metals; footwear; trucks and buses; coffee, tea, and spices; natural gas; paper; telecommunications equipment; alcoholic beverages; toys and sporting goods; and fish. For some imports, the U.S. domestic economy provides no alternative products, as is the case presently for coffee, VCRs, and diamonds.

American exports consist primarily of food, chemicals, and machinery. These export opportunities are the lifeblood of some U.S. industries. The $216 billion worth of exports in 1984 included 4819 different product classifications, from over $7 billion worth of corn sent abroad to $2000 worth of skateboards. The United States has significant trade surpluses in several products: cereals and grains; aircraft equipment and spacecraft; oilseeds; computers; coal; scientific and engineering equipment; military arms and vehicles; construction equipment; plastic and rubber; cotton; animal feed; tobacco; power-generating equipment; organic chemicals; and pharmaceutical products.

Table 12.2 presents three snapshots, taken in 1960, 1976, and 1984, of U.S. trade relations with the rest of the world. What stands out in stark relief is the recent unfavorable balance for the United States between imports and exports in almost every part of the world. The 1984 U.S. trade deficit was, according to the U.S. Department of Commerce, "the largest in amount ever experienced by any nation."[18] In subsequent years, the deficit expanded further still (see below)—reaching over $158 billion by the end of 1987. Were it not for the $17 billion reduction in U.S. oil imports in 1986, the U.S. trade deficit would have risen to some $183 billion that year.[19]

An America in Debt

By the close of 1987, the total indebtedness of the United States abroad—counting trade and current account balances—exceeded $350 billion; by 1994, America's net foreign debt is expected to rise above $1 trillion.[20] This shift in the balance of payments to the point where America has become, for the first time since 1914, a debtor nation—that is, this nation owes more to foreigners than they owe to the United States—is attributable chiefly to a steady deterioration in American merchandise trade performance. The U.S. performance in manufactures

TABLE 12.2   U.S. TRADE BALANCES: 1960, 1976, AND 1984 (IN BILLIONS OF U.S. DOLLARS)[a]

	1960		1976		1984	
	IMPORTS	*EXPORTS*	*IMPORTS*	*EXPORTS*	*IMPORTS*	*EXPORTS*
W. Europe	$ 4.2	$ 6.3	$ 24.3	$ 32.4	$ 75.0	$ 58.0
Canada	2.9	3.6	27.5	24.1	67.0	46.0
Japan	1.1	1.3	16.9	10.1	60.0	23.0
Other E. Asia	0.9	0.9	15.0	8.6	52.0	24.0
+China	0.1	0.1	3.3	1.6	3.4	3.0
+S. Asia	0.1	0.8	1.0	1.7	3.5	3.1
	1.3	1.8	19.4	11.8	58.9	30.1
Latin America	1.3	1.5	14.0	10.1	44.0	26.0
Near East	0.3	0.8	10.0	9.2	9.0	11.0
Africa	0.5	0.8	13.5	9.0	15.0	9.0
Australia-Oceania	0.3	0.5	1.9	2.7	4.0	6.0
Soviet Bloc	0.1	0.2	0.9	3.5	2.4	4.2
Totals	$15.0	$17.0	$121.0	$115.0	$341.0	$217.0

[a] Figures provided by the Rusk Center, University of Georgia.

Sources: 1960 figures: U.S. Department of Commerce, United States Imports of Merchandise for Consumption, Calendar Year 1960, FT 120, *and* United States Exports of Domestic and Foreign Merchandise, Calendar Year 1960, FT 420 *(all customs value basis); 1976 and 1984 figures: U.S. Department of Commerce,* Highlights of U.S. Export and Import Trade, FT 990, December 1976, 1984 *(imports: CIF value basis; exports: FAS value basis).*

TABLE 12.3   U.S. TRADE BALANCES:
1985, 1986, AND 1987 (IN BILLIONS
OF U.S. DOLLARS)

PARTNER	TIME PERIOD		
	1985	1986	1987
Canada	−17.8	−14.9	−13.8
EC[a]	−20.9	−25.2	−22.9
Japan	−46.6	−59.0	−57.1
NICs	−33.3	−37.2	−44.8
OPEC	−11.2	−9.1	−13.1
Other	−0.5	−6.4	−6.3
Worldwide	−130.5	−152.1	− 158.2

[a] The European Community (EC) added two members in January of 1986. Statistics for 1985 include the original ten members, and for 1986–1987 the new composite of twelve.

Source: Adapted from U.S. Department of Commerce figures compiled in "Composition of the U.S. Merchandise Trade Deficit," International Economic Review, Office of Economics, U.S. International Trade Commission, March 1988, p. 23.

trade underwent a net negative swing of some $158 billion from 1981 to 1986.[21]

That these international trade imbalances have worsened since the close of 1984 is evident in the statistics for U.S. commercial intercourse with selected countries presented in Table 12.3. During some months of 1986, the United States—supposedly the "breadbasket of the world"—actually imported more food than it exported, a state of affairs never before witnessed during the postwar era; and with almost every important American trading partner, the merchandise trade deficit grew larger in 1986 and 1987 than it had been in 1985.

AMERICA'S TRADING PARTNERS—AND RIVALS

Among the various economic ties between the United States and the rest of the world, the most significant are the relationships with Canada and Mexico, in this hemisphere, and with the Federal Republic of Germany (West Ger-

many) and Japan beyond. While these nations are valued American allies, their growing economic prowess has led to friction in the competition for world market shares.

North and South of the Border

Canada exports more to the United States than to any other country and, in return, takes in 20 percent of all American exports—the largest two-way trading relationship in the world. The merchandise trade (exports plus imports) between the two nations totaled $125 billion in 1985. In comparison, U.S.–Japanese merchandise trade summed to only $88 billion that year, and U.S. merchandise trade with all ten members of the European Community totaled just $108 billion. South of the border, Mexico's prominence is reflected in its standing as America's fourth largest export market.

Mosel Wine and BMWs

West Germany and Japan loom as the economic giants in competition with the United States. West Germany is now the world's number one exporter. "Today we *worry* about what the Germans do," states an economic analyst. "In the 1960s, we did not. We dominated the economy and did not have to."[22]

With more than 30 percent of its GNP generated by international trade, West Germany depends heavily on an open world economy. At its foundation, the U.S.–German trading relationship rests on the exchange of American military protection against possible Soviet aggression in return for West German guarantees of U.S. access to the lucrative EEC markets for goods and investment. The importance of this trade-off was made apparent in the 1960s when French President Charles de Gaulle attempted to drive a wedge between the United States and West Germany. He argued that the French and the Germans ought to unite in common resistance to the threat of American economic domination over Europe. Fearful that such a move would severely injure the American balance of payments with Europe and trigger U.S. sentiment to reappraise its costly stationing of GIs in Europe as a buffer against the Soviets, West German officials rejected de Gaulle's overtures.

Today, the Europeans are less worried about U.S. economic dominance (or a Soviet invasion). Indeed, notes one analyst, if successful, the anticipated Single European Market (planned for 1992) "will complete the work of the original Common Market and make Western Europe the most populous, most productive, and richest industrial community on earth."[23]

The Sony-Toyota Invasion

Japan, too, is a great trading nation, closely rivaling West Germany in exports (40 percent of which come to the United States). And, as with German-American economic ties, security considerations have been at the heart of the Japanese-American commercial relationship as well—though of a different character. Japan has been allowed reasonably good access to the American market, in exchange for U.S. base rights in Japan and Okinawa.

"In contrast to the situation prevailing in Europe," writes Robert Gilpin, "the purpose of the American military base structure in Japan is not merely to deter local aggression against the Japanese; rather, it is essential for the maintenance of American power and influence throughout the western Pacific and Southeast Asia." In reference to the Korean and the Vietnamese wars, Gilpin continues: "Without access to Japanese bases the United States could not have fought two wars in Asia over the past two decades and could not continue its present role in the area. Largely because of this dependence upon Japanese bases for its strategic position around the periphery of Communist China, the United States has been willing to tolerate in a period of balance-of-payments deficit the $1.5 billion annual trade surplus Japan enjoys vis-a-vis the United States."[24] Gilpin's ob-

servations were published in 1972; by 1986 (as the reader can see in Table 12.3), the Japanese trade advantage over the United States had reached a level of $59 billion for the year!

About half of America's trade deficit with Japan stems from the sale of Japanese automobiles and auto parts to U.S. consumers. In spite of much grumbling recently over the flood of Japanese cars entering the United States—leading to the establishment of "voluntary" quotas by the Carter and Reagan administrations in an attempt to slow the tide (2.3 million vehicles in 1989, as in the previous four years)—Japan continues to enjoy an extraordinarily favorable balance of trade with the United States, as Americans swallow hard and try to remember the importance of U.S. strategic military bases on Japanese soil. The swallowing becomes more and more difficult, however, as the trade imbalance rises. In 1984, Japan's surplus with the United States practically doubled over the preceding year, achieving a 40 percent growth in exports compared with only a 9 percent growth in imports.[25] (See Figure 12.1, which traces the U.S. trade gap with Japan through the 1980s.)

FIGURE 12.1   The U.S. trade gap with Japan.

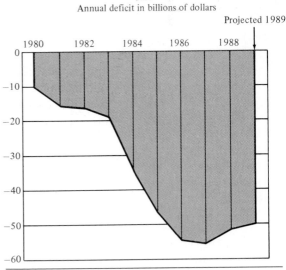

Source: Based on Commerce Department data.

Further, complain some critics, Japan absorbs little of the defense costs associated with the U.S. nuclear and conventional umbrella which protects the Japanese. If one examines the combined GNP of the most advanced industrial nations in the Western alliance (United States, France, Great Britain, West Germany, and Japan), Japan accounts for 14 percent of this total, yet pays for only 3.3 percent of the defense burden. In contrast, America accounts for 40 percent of the combined GNP and pays practically 57 percent of the defense costs for the alliance. Other close American observers of Japan note, however, that the 1 percent of Japan's GNP spent on defense sums to $30 billion—comparable to the defense expenditures of America's European allies.[26]

Protectionism versus Free Trade

Negative trade statistics, plus the loss of sales to domestic manufacturers and jobs to workers which they reflect, cause *protectionist* pressures to swell in company towns across America—that is, support for the use of government tariffs and quotas against imports in order to protect U.S. industries from foreign competition. In 1988, one of the leading presidential contenders, Representative Richard Gephardt (D-Mo.), ran chiefly on a protectionist platform; though he won only in Iowa during the delegate-selection phase of the campaign, his message had substantial support in some portions of the country hit by foreign competition. In 1989, Gephardt's colleagues in the House of Representatives selected him as their majority leader and in this capacity he continued his drumbeat against unfair Japanese trading practices. A wave of anti-Japanese sentiment—*Nippophobia*—seemed to have swept into Washington.

While in office, President Reagan had steadfastly defended a policy of *free trade* (the removal of government tariffs or other restrictions on international commercial transactions)—though,

like his successor, President Bush, he applied behind-the-scenes pressure on the Japanese and others to buy more U.S. products and cut back on their own flow of goods into the American market. Moreover, both presidents not only occasionally threatened to adopt protectionist measures if other nations continue to ignore their pleas for trade fairness, but—free-trade rhetoric to the contrary—both quietly increased American barriers to imports.

Japan was not the only target of protectionist critics. From 1980 to 1988, the percentage (by value) of goods produced within the United States that were protected by some form of nontariff barrier (a form of trade restriction defined and discussed below) rose from 20 percent to 35 percent.[27] In 1986, the United States threatened to impose a five-year import restriction on West German and Swiss machine tools, designed to limit high-technology imports from the Federal Republic by as much as 40 percent. In response, the government of West Germany stated angrily that it would join with the European Community to "assert their rights and interests" unless Washington retreated from this protectionist stance.[28] Similar disputes arose between the United States and Japan over cigarettes and aluminum products (among many other items), and with Taiwan over wine, beer, and tobacco.

President Reagan threatened to impose further import barriers against the Japanese and the Taiwanese unless they reduced their trade barriers against these U.S. products, and President Bush created a commission to conduct a full-scale review of U.S.–Japanese commercial ties. Meanwhile, on Capitol Hill, Congress passed the Omnibus Trade Act in 1988, designed to identify and trigger retaliatory steps against unfair practices among U.S. trading partners, and, in 1989, displayed growing hostility toward Japan—in Representative Gephardt's words as he campaigned in the House for the number two post, "the most closed market in the world."[29]

AMERICA: NO LONGER THE SOLITARY ECONOMIC BEHEMOTH

Although the U.S. dollar will no doubt continue to be the world's leading currency far into the future, the unraveling of the Bretton Woods system and the decline of the United States as the sole world economic superpower stand as the most important international economic developments in the postwar period. A relative decline in America's share of the international market was to be expected, as the Germans and the Japanese (among others) began to rebuild their economies. Several additional influences have contributed to this decline (which is by no means totally irreversible). Domestic economic growth could spur U.S. exports, for example; and conversely, an austerity program could reduce imports. A weakening of the dollar would also stimulate U.S. exports—though not without some negative consequences.[30]

The Muscle-Bound Dollar

One cause of the decline has been (until the mid-1980s) the overvaluation of the dollar compared with other world currencies. As the United States pumped gold and dollars into the world economic system in an effort to revitalize the enfeebled countries of Europe and Asia following the Second World War—in part so that America would have partners to trade with—this country inevitably incurred deficits in its balance of payments. The gap within the United States between the outflow and the inflow of dollars widened as the dollar—buoyed by U.S. political and economic dominance in the aftermath of the war—grew stronger and Americans took advantage of the high value of the dollar to make purchases abroad. As a consequence, U.S. trade deficits became chronic.

These dynamics led to the overvaluation of the dollar. When the value of the dollar is high, imports are encouraged and exports discouraged. Thus, the United States found it increasingly difficult to export, but to buy imports—or to travel or invest abroad—became much cheaper for Americans. This appreciation of the dollar (up 39 percent from 1980 to 1984[31]) encouraged the migration of American businesses overseas, drawn by the cheap labor and foreign assets made all the more affordable by the overvalued dollars. In 1987, the Reagan administration took steps to weaken the dollar in hopes of correcting the worst trade imbalances in the postwar era.

Sagging—and Resistant—Markets

Customary markets for U.S. exports have lagged, also. In Europe, the GNP growth rate since 1982 has been languid; and in the developing world, debtor nations have been forced to reduce their imports in order to ease their acute debt crises. In 1982 and 1983, the United States lost about $15 billion of expected trade—nearly half of the total drop in U.S. exports during this period—as the Latin American countries of Mexico, Brazil, Venezuela, Argentina, Chile, and Peru cut back on their imports of American goods. Mexico alone accounted for $8.7 billion in this drop.

Added to these difficulties have been the ongoing drain on the U.S. trade balance stemming from both the domestic consumption of foreign oil and various overseas market barriers faced by American exports. Sometimes these market barriers take the form of formal import tariffs and quotas. More often the barriers are less visible and, therefore, more insidious—so-called *nontariff barriers* (*NTBs*), including "buy national" campaigns (deeply ingrained in the Japanese), inspection requirements, customs valuation procedures, industrial and environmental standards, domestic content stipulations, distribution intricacies (Japan's system is particularly complex and antiquated), legal and language idiosyncrasies, and the like.

Some of these barriers are imposed by foreign nations in an unfair attempt to block free trade with the United States. Japan appears guilty of this charge with certain commodities, like tobacco and citrus fruits, though recent diplomatic negotiations have led to some NTB reductions. Moreover, Japan's production of some cars in the United States, along with the making under license of more U.S. products—Budweiser beer for one—in Japan, has eased this source of tension somewhat.

Other barriers U.S. businesspeople could probably overcome with additional effort, such as greater devotion to the study of Japan's distribution system and learning the Japanese language. It now borders on a cliché to note that in Manhattan at this moment hundreds of Japanese businesspeople can be found scurrying around negotiating deals in perfectly acceptable English, while probably fewer than twenty of their American counterparts are similarly engaged in Tokyo speaking the Japanese tongue. Americans could also make greater efforts to craft products having greater appeal in Japan, such as building some cars for export with the steering wheel on the right-hand side. Japanese automakers have certainly found it profitable to build left-hand-side steering wheels for the U.S. market.

The competitive edge of the United States for high-technology products is also eroding. While this nation remains the chief exporter of high-tech products, the advanced industrialized nations are closing rapidly. "Forty percent of the college graduates in Japan and West Germany are in engineering and the sciences, compared with 16 percent here," cautions one observer, adding: "In the 1970s, we generated 75 percent of new science and technology; in the 1990s, we will generate only about one third, and a majority of our effort goes into the military."[32] Moreover, the NICs in east Asia, along with Brazil, Mexico, and others, are displaying a growing competitiveness in this sector, aided by the advantage of lower labor costs.

Lower labor costs in Japan are often pointed to as one reason why their automobiles are less expensive than American automobiles; the difference in labor costs in the production of cars in the two countries is about $250 per vehicle—a victory for the American worker won over the decades through tough labor union bargaining with management. It may prove a Pyrrhic victory, though, if these higher salaries have led to a price tag on U.S. autos that alienates consumers and pushes them toward import dealerships. (The cost to the Japanese of shipping their vehicles overseas, however, would seem to offset their lower labor-cost advantage.) Other factors said to give the Japanese a competitive edge in the auto business include the more sophisticated mechanization of the Japanese assembly line, particularly the extensive use of robots for routine welding and other tasks; higher morale in the workplace as a result of careful efforts by management to nurture an esprit de corps through group calisthenics, the sharing of bonuses, less of a pay differential between management and workers, and greater job security; and lack of racial tensions among workers, unlike the animosities that occasionally flare between blacks and whites in Detroit factories.

Alliance Strains

The increasing trading strength of West Germany, Japan, and other nations once subservient to U.S. economic dominion has created serious strains in the political, military, and diplomatic bonds uniting the Western industrial powers. The foreign policy specialist Richard J. Barnet looks upon Japanese economic competition, for example, as a significantly greater threat to the future of the United States than anything the Soviet Union is doing now, or is likely to do.[33]

This nation's economic superiority in the early postwar period gave U.S. officials an advantage in their relations with other countries. In western Europe, the wealth of the United States made it possible through the Marshall Plan to assist America's allies in their efforts to rebuild their societies. With feelings of respect and appreciation for this assistance, Europeans were willing to follow America's political and military leadership. The power of trade and aid, coupled with the military protection the United States could provide against Soviet aggression, spilled over to enhance America's diplomatic power.

The leadership of the United States has been weakened further by a changing sense of security threats in Europe and in Japan. The Soviet Union is viewed as less of a danger in western Europe than was the case in the two decades following the fall of the Third Reich—particularly with Gorbachev's successful peace initiatives between 1987 and 1989 (even if the jury is still out on how genuine these overtures are). The Europeans now feel less dependent on America for protection; indeed, they have become increasingly concerned about jeopardizing their own economic fortunes by too close an adherence to every U.S. edict of noncooperation with the centrally planned economies of the Soviet bloc. In 1982, for example, the Reagan administration attempted to punish the Soviets for encouraging the imposition of martial law in Poland; the president called upon European allies to desist in their cooperation with the construction of a pipeline that would carry natural gas from the Soviet Union to Western Euope. The Europeans, energy-poor, refused; their economic vitality stood to be improved by this new source of fuel.

Nor do America's European allies appreciate the hard-line position adopted by the United States on what items the West should export to the Soviet bloc. In 1950, the Western alliance created an export-control system called the *Coordinating Committee (COCOM)*. The purpose was to establish a united stand on the control of strategic exports to communist countries; that is, to make sure that products useful for military purposes—notably sophisticated technology transfers—were banned. As Gary K. Bertsch notes, however, "determining which equipment should be prohibited involves con-siderable controversy."[34] The United States has tried to increase the COCOM list of controlled items, while its allies in Europe have tended to view this expansion as an unnecessary damper on profitable commercial opportunities in the East. The Reagan administration expressed particular concern about such products as computer equipment, robotics, gas-turbine engines, and high-grade silicon; to the Europeans, these and similar products are considered normal nonstrategic, industrial trade—and profitable.

America's allies became especially cynical about U.S. motives when the Reagan administration proved eager to drop the grain embargo against the Soviet Union (introduced by the Carter administration in the aftermath of the Soviet invasion into Afghanistan) in order to promote U.S. agricultural interests. As Bertsch concludes, "What is good for the American farmer, our allies contend, must be good for the European worker."[35]

Both sides continue to jostle among themselves and within their own countries over where to draw the line between excessive COCOM controls that impede profitable nonstrategic commerce, on the one hand, and lax controls that might provide the Soviets with advanced technology adaptable to military use, on the other hand. The hard-liners in the Reagan administration had their at-home critics; even the president's own Commission on International Competitiveness estimated that export controls cost the U.S. economy some $7.6 billion annually in lost sales.[36]

On the Japanese side of the globe, the threat of international communism has receded as well. The People's Republic of China appears far more civil in its international relations now than it did during the 1950s and 1960s—though its harsh crackdown on prodemocracy factions in 1989 lost the PRC many friends (and investors) around the world. For the people of Japan, the prospect of American protectionism looms as a more real, immediate, and potentially devastating threat than the Chinese Army.

This lessening of European and Japanese dependence on the United States for security should not be overstated. Both regions still rely upon the U.S. nuclear deterrent for their ultimate safety from a potential Soviet or Chinese attack. As the likelihood of such attacks has declined, though, the effect has been to reduce America's influence as a leader among the industrial nations.

THE FRAGMENTATION OF THE INTERNATIONAL ECONOMIC SETTING

Compared with its once dominant stature, the United States has become more isolated economically and politically as Western and nonaligned nations, large and small, display a greater self-confidence in the pursuit of their own destinies. In place of the United States as the economic "magnetic pole" for the noncommunist nations have come a plethora of organizations trying to provide leadership in this fragmented setting.

An Institutional Proliferation

Among the institutions and movements—some old, some new—which garnered increased importance as the Bretton Woods arrangements went into a decline are the:

- *International Monetary Fund (IMF).* Created by the Bretton Woods agreement in 1945, the IMF's chief responsibility has been the maintenance of international monetary stability. The resources of the IMF, contributed by members as an initiation fee, are used as a revolving fund. Its importance has been magnified in recent years as a primary hope of financial support for the developing nations.
- *General Agreement on Tariffs and Trade (GATT).* A multilateral trade treaty entered into by twenty-three nations in 1947,

GATT remains the only code of conduct for international trade accepted by most nations of the globe. Its current membership consists of eighty-five nations, with twenty-two more (developing nations) affiliated less formally and less bound by the regulations of the regime.
- *Conference on International Economic Cooperation (CIEC).* A conference of eight industrial nations, seven OPEC nations, and twelve developing nations held in several sessions from 1975 to 1977 and often referred to as the "North-South dialogue."
- *International Bank for Reconstruction and Development (IBRD, or World Bank).* Another Bretton Woods institution that remains important as a loan bank and source of technical assistance for developing nations.
- *International Development Association (IDA).* Established in 1959, the IDA is an affiliate of the World Bank designed to assist the especially needy nations with no-interest loans and a long repayment schedule (so-called soft loans).
- *Group of 77.* A collection of developing countries organized in 1964 in preparation for UNCTAD I (UN Conference on Trade and Development) in Geneva. Its membership, comprising some of the richest nations in the world (OPEC) and some of the poorest, now stands at over 120, though it has kept its original name. The Group of 77 functions as a caucus for the developing countries on economic matters in UNCTAD and various other forums of the United Nations.
- *Organization for Economic Cooperation and Development (OECD).* This organization, established in 1961, consists of twenty-two industrialized market economies of North America, Europe, and the Far East. Among its objectives are its own economic development, assistance to the Third World and the Fourth World (the very poorest nations, with per capita incomes below $200), and increased world trade.

This is only a partial listing of organizations. In addition, various nations have established (among other examples) the African Development Bank, the Asian Development Fund, the Inter-American Development Bank, a series of UNCTAD meetings, the UN Industrial Development Organization, the Food and Agriculture Organization (FAO), and, within the government of the United States, the Agency for International Development (AID) and the Overseas Private Investment Corporation (OPIC, which provides risk insurance for development projects in poorer nations). The challenge for these groups and organizations is to maintain the prosperity of the developed nations while, at the same time, bringing the fruits of modern affluence to the developing nations. This requires nothing less than an economic tide to lift all the boats of the world—a Herculean task that presently is guided more by the dreams of idealists than a carefully designed plan.

Making the job all the more difficult is the lack of harmony between countries in the North and the South, not to mention internal disagreements within each regional bloc. Even when it comes to procedures, let alone substance, sharp differences of opinion arise. The North prefers to conduct negotiations through agencies like the IMF and the World Bank, for example, while the South finds the UN General Assembly more attractive, for there it has more votes.

The Multinationals

As if national egos were an insufficient complication, the international economic system is made all the more complex by the existence of the *multinational corporations* (*MNCs*)—firms "with foreign subsidiaries which extend the production and marketing of the firm beyond the boundaries of any one country."[37] The MNCs grew up in the postwar era as a product, in part, of the global revolution in transportation and communications; it became technically possible for businesses to have ties stretching around the globe.

The effects of the MNCs have been much debated. Some observers view them positively as benign contributors to world trade, others negatively as a spearhead of imperialism. Most political economists, though, look upon the MNC as an inevitable phenomenon with some good and some bad effects. In market economies like Canada, France, and Great Britain, for instance, American-owned MNCs seem to have produced positive results in the host economy—especially in capital formation, export promotion, balance of payments, and improved access to advanced technology and management skills.[38]

But the MNCs have also cast a long shadow. Some have exhibited alarming predatory behavior, exemplified by the efforts of the International Telephone and Telegraph Company (ITT) to undermine the freely elected government of Chile under President Allende in the 1970s. The huge corporation provided funds to the CIA, recall, in hopes of stimulating a coup in Chile (Chapter 9). Some analysts argue that the MNC is rapidly replacing the nation-state as the key entity in the shaping of international economic policies, as implied in the title of Raymond Vernon's influential book *Sovereignty at Bay*.[39] Marketing decisions by corporate executives with a global perspective can become more important than the political decisions of elected representatives within an individual nation. The end result, according to this thesis, is the gradual replacement of state sovereignty with corporate power, as MNC executives reach around the world in search of market opportunities regardless of the political aspirations of national leaders. Profits supplanting politics.

According to Vernon's thesis, the MNCs will turn increasingly toward the South in search of raw materials and lower labor costs. This will lead to a partnership between the MNCs and the Third World (a *transnationalism*) benefiting both. Critics of this thesis are less sanguine, envisioning instead a new form of imperialism (the so-called *dependencia* model), in which aggressive and powerful MNCs dominate the developing world.[40] (See Perspectives on American Foreign Policy 12.1.)

A third possibility is considered more likely by Robert Gilpin: the mercantilist model. This approach, with roots in the European post-feudal period, emphasizes the nation-state as the continuing primary force in the shaping of international economic decisions. According to this view, the MNCs are powerful but less so than often touted. As Gilpin puts it, "the essence of mercantilism . . . is the priority of *national* economic and political objectives over considerations of *global* economic efficiency."[41] From this perspective, the power of the sovereign state remains the essential force in world politics.

While the mercantilist model seems the most credible, no one can deny that MNCs have further confused an already fragmented international economic regime. This fact has been illustrated vividly for U.S. officials by the Angolan civil war. In this southwest African nation, an American-owned MNC—Gulf Oil Company—has been allied with a Marxist regime based in northern Angola, the site of rich oil fields. The Marxists are locked in battle against a rebel faction operating out of the southern hinterland. At the same time the U.S. government buys 75 percent of the oil produced by the Marxist regime (making America its chief trading partner), the CIA continues to finance the anti-Marxist counterrevolutionaries!

Perspectives on American Foreign Policy   *12.1*

Harry Johnson on transnationalism (the "sovereignty-at-bay" thesis):

In an important sense, the fundamental problem of the future is the conflict between the political forces of nationalism and the economic forces pressing for world integration. This conflict currently appears as one between the national government and the international corporation, in which the balance of power at least superficially appears to lie on the side of the national government. But in the longer run economic forces are likely to predominate over political, and may indeed come to do so before the end of this decade [the 1970s]. Ultimately, a world federal government will appear as the only rational method for coping with the world's economic problems.

*   *   *

Stephen Hymer on the dependencia model:

. . . a regime of North Atlantic Multinational Corporations would tend to produce a hierarchical division of labor within the firm. It would tend to centralize high-level decision-making occupations in a few key cities in the advanced countries, surrounded by a number of regional sub-capitals, and confine the rest of the world to lower levels of activity and income, i.e., to the status of towns and villages in a new Imperial system. Income, status, authority, and consumption patterns would radiate out from these centers along a declining curve, and the existing pattern of inequality and dependency would be perpetuated. The pattern would be complex, just as the structure of the corporation is complex, but the basic relationship between different countries would be one of superior and subordinate, head office and branch office.

Quoted in Robert Gilpin, "Three Models of the Future," *International Organization*, vol. 29, 1975, pp. 37, 43–44. Reprinted by permission of the MIT Press, Cambridge, Massachusetts.

THE FRAGMENTATION OF ECONOMIC POWER AT HOME

Just as the international economic setting is now characterized by a diffusion of power, so are the U.S. domestic institutions that deal with international economic issues (as the reader would anticipate from Chapter 6). Prior to the Second World War, the Department of State was the exclusive "club" for dealing with most problems of international economics; men like Cordell Hull, Sumner Wells, and Breckenridge Long—experts in trade strategies—made the key decisions. Today, this policy-making role has become dramatically diffused; and, notes a former senior State Department official, "diffusion has led to confusion."[42]

Fission within the Executive Branch

Consider, first, just some of the institutions within the executive branch involved directly in one aspect or another of international economic policy, listed in Table 12.4. The purpose of this listing is to provide the reader with a sense of how widely dispersed the responsibilities are in the U.S. government for foreign economic policy.

As this partial listing suggests, gone are the days when a small group of State Department diplomats decided upon America's international economic policy. Writes one knowledgeable Washington observer: ". . . the machinery of American foreign policy has become so sprawling and cumbersome that no one has exclusive domain over foreign and national security policy."[43] This characterization fits external economic relations to a T.

President Reagan's secretary of state, George P. Shultz, tried to reestablish his department as the focus for decisions on international economic policy, but he met only with modest success. The fact remains that, compared with other major powers, U.S. economic diplomacy lacks institutional coherence. Instead of various government entities working together toward a common economic objective, often bureau

chieftains (in alliance with legislative leaders and outside interest groups—the "iron triangles" of Chapter 6) have their own agendas that may or may not coincide with the president's. The president and the Department of State may call for free trade, while the Department of Labor, the U.S. automobile industry, and legislators from Detroit may constitute a "subgovernment" dedicated to raising barriers against Japanese auto imports.

One leading authority on U.S. trade policy, I. M. Destler, argues that some degree of decentralization is inevitable, but which agencies should take the lead on certain issues needs to be clarified. He recommends that the special trade representative (STR) be given responsibility for trade, the Department of Agriculture for food, the Department of Energy for energy issues, Treasury for monetary matters, and State for foreign aid. "But it is much harder, . . . " he notes, "to assure that they will keep their parochialism in check. And no single department or cabinet member can exercise effective oversight of overall foreign economic policy. . . . "[44]

The result has sometimes been strong disagreements and infighting among the various agencies over appropriate policy directions. Decentralization of authority over trade policy and a struggle among executive agencies—aided and abetted by members of Congress and pressure-group leaders—has been the norm for many decisions on economic policy toward other nations, as Perspectives on American Foreign Policy 12.2, on oil-gear exports, reveals.

Fission on Capitol Hill

The Congress has grown increasingly interested in international economic issues, too, and has experienced a proliferation of committees and subcommittees competing for "turf" (authority) over this jurisdiction. As Table 12.5 illustrates, the decentralization of authority for U.S. foreign economic policy has been as rampant on Capitol Hill as it has been "downtown" in the executive branch. On top of this struc-

TABLE 12.4   INSTITUTIONAL FRAGMENTATION OVER INTERNATIONAL ECONOMIC POLICY WITHIN THE EXECUTIVE BRANCH: A PARTIAL LISTING

Each of the following entities has important responsibilities for U.S. international economic policy.

Presidential Advisory Bodies

National Security Council
Office of the Vice President
Council of Economic Advisers
Council on Wage and Price Stability
Advisory Committee for Trade Negotiations
Office of Management and Budget
Office of the Special Representative for Trade
 Negotiations (STR for short)

Department of State

Office of the Under Secretary for Economic Affairs
Office of the Under Secretary for Security
 Assistance, Science and Technology
Office of the Director of Policy Planning Staff
Regional and functional bureaus (other departments
 are also divided in this manner)
Agency for International Development
United States mission to the United Nations

Department of Defense

Office of the Assistant Secretary for International
 Security Affairs

Department of the Treasury

United States Customs Service
Office of Balance of Payments
Office of Trade and Commodity Research
Assistant Secretary of International Economic Policy
Economic Policy Group

Department of Agriculture

Office of the Assistant Secretary for International
 Affairs and Commodity Programs

Department of Commerce

Office of the Assistant Secretary for Industry and
 Trade Administration

Department of Energy

Assistant Secretary for International Affairs

Department of Labor

Office of the Deputy Under Secretary for
 International Affairs

Department of Transportation

Assistant Secretary for Policy and International
 Affairs

Other Economic Entities within the Executive Branch

Export-Import Bank of the United States
Foreign Trade Zones Board
International Bank for Reconstruction and
 Development (World Bank)
Overseas Private Investment Corporation
United States International Trade Commission

---

tural fission comes the additional fragmentation that results from 535 representatives out to protect the interests of their own constituents.

The comprehensive trade pact with Canada in 1988 illustrates how different segments of the Congress can slow—or even stop—a major in-ternational agreement. "The congressional hurdle is the major hurdle full of potential pitfalls," complained a Canadian spokesman."[45]

The causes of his frustration were evident, among them: the senators from Wyoming balked because of the pact's potential impact on

Perspectives on American Foreign Policy 12.2

Clyde H. Farnsworth of the New York Times *on a U.S. government dispute over oil-equipment exports to the Soviet Union:*

The Reagan Administration, over objections by Defense Secretary Caspar W. Weinberger, has decided to remove most controls on exports of oil and gas equipment and technology to the Soviet Union. . . .

. . . It is a victory for Commerce Secretary Malcolm Baldrige and Secretary of State George P. Shultz, who agreed that the controls were hurting American business more than the Soviet Union.

Because of the reluctance of European and Japanese suppliers to adopt similar restrictions, the Russians were getting comparable equipment anyway, these officials argued.

In welcoming the decision, Lloyd Bentsen, Democrat of Texas, the Senate Finance Committee chairman, said that more than 600 companies in 38 countries produce oilfield equipment and are not restricted by comparable export controls.

He reported that the Central Intelligence Agency had documents that most categories of equipment and technology are freely available to the Russians from these other suppliers.

The Pentagon, according to sources familiar with the discussions, held that the American equipment was of higher quality and would therefore help the Russians produce more oil and gas at lower costs. Petroleum exports account for 60 percent of Moscow's hard currency earnings.

In the Pentagon view this additional money, on top of heavy Soviet borrowing in the West, would give Moscow more to invest in weapons. . . .

. . . The principal impetus for removing the oil and gas controls came from the Petroleum Equipment Suppliers Association, representing the domestic industry, chiefly based in the Southwest, which has been hurt by depressed conditions in the oil sector.

From "Oil-Gear Export Curbs to Soviet to Be Lifted," *New York Times*, January 16, 1987, p. 26.

---

uranium miners in their state; Ohio and Pennsylvania representatives worried about provisions affecting the steel industry in their states; South Carolina legislators fussed over subsidies given to Canada's textile companies; farm-state legislators expressed similar concern over subsidized beef, wheat, potatoes, and hogs; Maine's representatives gave long speeches about subsidized fish. This important trade bill was destined to pass (both Canadians and Americans valued their close alliance too much to see it fail), but not before a host of legislators had added changes here and there—on everything from cattle and wheat to lead and zinc—in an effort to protect the interests of constituents.

Often these competing centers of power on Capitol Hill—pluralism run wild—collide with one another in their separate efforts to hold hearings, pass laws, and oversee the executive agencies. In any given recent session of Congress, one can find an array of subcommittees all holding hearings on Japanese automobile imports or some related trade controversy, with the same witnesses, the same questions, and the same answers. As discussed in Chapter 6, this can lead to a heavy surcharge on the time of top officials in the executive branch.

Congress has also shown through the passage of tough legislation that it intends to be a major player in the formulation of U.S. policy on trade and aid. Its members routinely slash

TABLE 12.5   *LEGISLATIVE COMMITTEES AND SUBCOMMITTEES WITH JURISDICTION OVER INTERNATIONAL ECONOMIC POLICY: A PARTIAL LISTING*

The Senate Chamber
Subcommittee on Foreign Agricultural Policy (Committee on Agriculture)
Subcommittee on Foreign Operations (Committee on Appropriations)
Subcommittee on International Finance (Committee on Banking, Housing and Urban Affairs)
Subcommittee on International Trade (Committee on Finance)
Subcommittee on Foreign Assistance (Committee on Foreign Relations)
Subcommittee on Foreign Economic Policy (Committee on Foreign Relations)
Regional Subcommittees (Committee on Foreign Relations)

The House of Representatives

Subcommittee on Foreign Operations (Committee on Appropriations)
Subcommittee on International Development Institutions and Finance (Committee on Banking, Finance and Urban Affairs)
Subcommittee on International Trade, Investment and Monetary Policy (Committee on Banking, Finance, and Urban Affairs)
Subcommittee on International Development (Committee on Foreign Affairs)
Subcommittee on International Economic Policy and Trade (Committee on Foreign Affairs)
Regional Subcommittees (Committee on Foreign Affairs)
Committee on Interstate and Foreign Commerce
Committee on Merchant Marine and Fisheries
Subcommittee on Trade (Committee on Ways and Means)
Ad Hoc Committee on Energy

Joint Senate and House Panels

Subcommittee on International Economics (Joint Committee on Economics)
Congressional Budget Office

---

the foreign aid budget proposed by the executive branch—often with a meat cleaver—and Congress has placed strict prohibitions on some forms of trade policy (such as the sale of advanced computers to the Soviet Union).

Among the most controversial legislative forays into the thicket of trade policy was the passage in 1973 of the *Jackson-Vanik amendment*. This law, remember, tied U.S. trade and credit for the Soviet Union to concessions on Jewish emigration (Chapter 8).[46] In a campaign backed strongly by Jewish groups throughout the country, Senator Jackson and Representative Vanik forced the Nixon administration to link U.S.–Soviet economic relations with the number of Jews allowed to leave the USSR. The administration preferred instead to pursue talks on Jewish emigration privately with Soviet leaders, so as not to disrupt détente. The Soviets resented the Jackson-Vanik attempt to exert pressure on their internal political decisions and, in defiance, reduced the flow of Jewish émigrés to a trickle.

On other occasions, the Congress has played an effective role on selected economic issues. One example is the settlement of an international financial dispute with Czechoslovakia which had stymied State Department diplomats for years.[47] Members of Congress have also steadily reminded experts in the executive branch (through hearings, letters, press releases, and various forms of oversight) that their fancy theories of international trade can have painful effects on constituents—the forgotten worker on the assembly line or in the cotton mill.

If carried to an extreme, congressional intervention can lead to a protectionist stampede ultimately detrimental to world trade—a genuine danger of the current Nippophobia. The *Smoot-Hawley tariff* of the early 1930s, which exacerbated global trade relations and contributed to the outbreak of the Second World War, serves as a painful reminder of the harmful consequences that can accompany extreme tariff rates. The executive branch meant only to raise duties chiefly on agricultural products, but pressure groups soon descended on this bill in search of protection for their narrow interests. When the law finally passed, it had elevated the average rate on dutiable goods by more than 50 percent—a record high—and included more commodities than ever before under the new tariff umbrella. Nations throughout the world retaliated against the Smoot-Hawley act by raising their own tariffs against U.S. exports. A trade war was under way.

Short of this extreme, however, someone must remind the drafters of econometric charts that behind their sweeping parabolas lie real human costs. Elected representatives of the American people in Congress, constantly in touch with citizens across the land and sensitive to the needs of average individuals (read voters), are well suited to the task of defending the interests of U.S. auto workers and citrus farmers, textile machinists and semiconductor technicians, and all the other Americans struggling against the sometimes unfair trade practices of Japan and other nations. This is an important part of a representative's role in a democracy.

THE USE OF TRADE SANCTIONS

What all these findings sum to is an international political economy much more complicated than often supposed. With the demise of the arrangements set up by Bretton Woods, the world trade system has experienced a steady disintegration; and within the United States, decisions on trade and aid have become vastly more complex as a result of a proliferation of new institutions. Despite the relative decline of this nation as a global economic force, however, America remains the leading economic power in the world and the various trade sanctions at its disposal continue to be significant instruments of U.S. foreign policy.

Economic Sticks and Carrots

Most-favored-nation (*MFN*) rights, for example, bestow upon another country the best trading relationship for their imports the United States has to offer—a form of economic reward for those nations that are considered important to American foreign policy interests and are prepared to allow the United States reciprocal trade opportunities. When PRC leaders used force against prodemocracy demonstrators in 1989 (executing several in hasty trials), some U.S. legislators called for the termination of MFN privileges for China; President Bush was unwilling to go that far, cutting off instead the sale of all American military equipment.

Embargoes are one more instrument of economic statecraft, a prohibition on exports; and *boycotts*, a prohibition against imports (or other forms of business cooperation with another country), are another. Both represent forms of economic punishment. When the Soviet military invaded Afghanistan in 1979, President Carter instituted a grain embargo against the Soviet Union. The Reagan administration subsequently lifted the embargo, when the policy proved to have little effect other than to hurt the sales of American farmers. The United States has maintained a boycott against Cuban sugar ever since its communist leader, Fidel Castro, came to power in 1959.

Blacklisting is an additional form of economic retaliation. It resorts to the establishment of a ban against business transactions with any firm that continues to trade with a nation targeted by the U.S. government for an embargo or a boycott. Now and then, pro-Israeli groups within the United States lobby for the blacklisting of American companies with high sales in Arab nations.

Another technique, *dumping*, consists of selling exports below cost, in order to undermine the exports of another nation. Japan recently agreed, under pressure from the Reagan administration, to stop dumping computer chips below cost into U.S. markets. And *preclusive buying* means purchasing commodities chiefly in order to deny them to an enemy, as when in the 1930s the United States bought weapons-grade tungsten from Spain as a means for keeping it out of Nazi hands. In November 1979, President Carter resorted to yet another economic punishment in reaction to the seizure of American hostages in Iran by young militants. He ordered the *freezing of assets* owned by Iran within the United States—more than $12 billion worth of Iranian funds lodged in American banks.

The economic analyst David Baldwin has divided these and other sanctions into the positive and negative inducements outlined in Table 12.6.

The Limits of Economic Inducements

The list in Table 12.6 seems potent. Despite the potential power these and the other induce-

---

TABLE 12.6   INSTRUMENTS OF INTERNATIONAL ECONOMIC POWER: TRADE SANCTIONS AND INDUCEMENTS

POSITIVE INDUCEMENTS	NEGATIVE SANCTIONS
Trade	**Trade**
Favorable tariffs	Embargo
Most-favored-nation (MFN) rights	Boycott
Tariff reduction	Tariff discrimination
Direct purchase	Withdrawal of MFN rights
Subsidies to exports or imports	Blacklist
Granting export and import licenses	Quotas
	License denial
	Dumping
Capital	Preclusive buying
Providing aid	
Investment guarantees	**Capital**
Encouragement of private capital	
Favorable tax measures	Freezing assets
	Import and export controls
	Suspension of aid
	Expropriation
	Unfavorable taxation
	Withholding dues to IMF and similar agencies

Source: Adapted from David A. Baldwin, Economic Statecraft *(Princeton, N.J.: Princeton University Press, 1985), pp. 41–42. Copyright © 1985 by Princeton University Press. Reprinted by permission.*

ments appear to hold, however, over the years they have proved to be of only modest importance as a means for forcing other nations to bow before America's will. Embargoes and boycotts, for instance, have often failed because other nations refused to honor them. When the United States has deprived the Soviet Union of grain, Canada, Argentina, and others have been pleased to fill the demand; and American farmers—reluctant to lose these sales—have soon clamored to remove the sanctions. Moreover, some countries will remain resistant to outside pressures, regardless of internal economic deprivations. Chinese leaders remained adamant about snuffing out all vestiges of revolutionary fervor among their young people in 1989, executing those leaders of the prodemocracy movement who could be found—despite a sharp international reaction (including threats of economic reprisal) against the regime's brutality.

Economic power is by no means useless, as the discussion of foreign aid below illustrates; but its instruments have definite limitations. One authoritative study on embargoes concludes that they have "not been notably successful except as a direct adjunct of war."[48] Baldwin's survey of many well-known attempts to use economic statecraft leads to the more guarded conclusion that sanctions work sometimes, but that policymakers and scholars still do not know enough about the subject to predict with any exactitude how and when they will work.[49]

Despite this fog of uncertainty, the United States will no doubt continue to turn at times to the use of economic inducements for its foreign policy objectives. This approach represents, at any rate, a less far-reaching and irrevocable use of power than overt or covert military force and, for that reason alone, will remain attractive to many policymakers. The rub lies in trying to make these instruments operate in light of the institutional decentralization—not to say disarray—that characterizes foreign economic policy, both at the international and the domestic level. Short of an extreme emergency forcing the country to concentrate authority as it did during the days of the depression and the Second World War, the institutional fragmentation of the economic power will continue to produce less a coherent national policy of consistent purpose than a "muddling through," as sundry agencies, pressure groups, legislative committees, and forceful personalities bring their weight to bear at various times and places when the nation responds to threats and opportunities abroad.

FOREIGN AID AS AN INSTRUMENT OF AMERICAN FOREIGN POLICY

Foreign aid may be defined as "economic and military assistance on a government-to-government level, or through government-supported agencies or programs."[50] Economic assistance, referred to by one authority as "an obvious weapon in the contest for global influence,"[51] includes direct grants, technical cooperation, and loans that are either "hard" (that is, offered at commercial bank interest rates) or "soft" (which, the reader will recall, are concessional—that is, at low interest rates). Most U.S. economic aid to the developing world has been in the form of soft loans.

Military assistance (often called *security assistance*) includes the use of military advisory groups, equipment, and defense-oriented economic support—such as funding for the construction of dock facilities and railroads. It comes in five categories: the military assistance program (MAP), which provides friendly nations with military hardware and services on a grant basis; foreign military sales, which offer the same benefits on a credit and loan basis; security support assistance—the most expensive category, designed to foster economic and political stability in regions where the United States has military bases or other security interests (as in the Philippines); military training,

---

Perspectives on American Foreign Policy   12.3

Benjamin Constant contrasting the war and the economic power:

War and commerce are but two different means of arriving at the same aim, which is to possess what is desired. Trade is nothing but a homage paid to the strength of the possessor by him who aspires to the possession; it is an attempt to obtain by mutual agreement that which one does not hope any longer to obtain by violence. The idea of commerce would never occur to a man who would always be the strongest. It is experience, proving to

him that war, i.e., the use of his force against the force of others, is exposed to various resistances and various failures, which makes him have recourse to commerce, that is, to a means more subtle and better fitted to induce the interest of others to consent to what is his own interest.

Quoted in Albert O. Hirschman, *National Power and the Structure of Foreign Trade* (Berkeley: University of California Press, 1945; expanded ed., 1980), pp. 14–15, note.

---

which provides instruction in military science within the United States to foreign soldiers; and the peacekeeping missions, which help fund United Nations forces in troubled zones like the Sinai Peninsula and Cyprus.

A Portrait of U.S. Foreign Aid

Table 12.7 depicts for one year during the Carter administration how much money the United States spent on the various forms of economic and military assistance—a total of nearly $6.8 billion. By fiscal year 1988, the sum had reached almost $20 billion, with large increases in the military assistance program under the Reagan administration.

Even though in overall dollar terms the United States is the leading provider of foreign aid in the world, its levels of assistance have been modest. "The total cost in tax dollars for all our security and economic assistance programs in the developing countries is $43.91 per person," noted Secretary of State George P. Shultz in 1983. "In contrast, we Americans spend $104 per person a year for TV and radio sets, $35 per person per year for barbershops and beauty parlors, $97 per person per year for

soap and cleaning supplies, and $21 per person per year for flowers and potted plants."[52]

Although the United States is the richest nation in the world, it usually ranks only about twelfth among the seventeen Western nations with aid programs, as measured by percentage of GNP expended; in 1987, America ranked next to last as an aid giver among the industrialized nations in terms of GNP percentage (at 0.2 percent, above only Austria's 0.17 percent; see Figure 12.2).[53]

A Pound of Containment and a Dash of Altruism

As mentioned earlier, the disparity in lifestyles between the rich and poor nations has created deep-seated resentments throughout the southern part of the globe. The economist Robert L. Heilbroner has compared the world to "an immense train, in which a few passengers, mainly in the advanced capitalist world, ride in first-class coaches, in conditions of comfort unimaginable to the enormously greater numbers jammed into the cattle cars that make up the bulk of the train's carriages."[54] In the minute it will take you to read this paragraph, twenty-

TABLE 12.7   FOREIGN ECONOMIC AND
MILITARY ASSISTANCE FOR FISCAL YEAR
1978

	(U.S. $MILLIONS)
Title I—foreign assistance	
Food and nutrition	515
Population planning and health	250
Education and human resources	76
Technical aid and energy	90
International organizations	231
American schools and hospitals	24
Contingency fund	5
Disaster assistance	19
Italy relief	25
Sahel development	50
Narcotics control	37
Foreign Service fund	21
Middle East special fund	8
Security-supporting aid	2202
UN forces in Cyprus	9
Agency for International Development expenses	213
Military assistance	220
Military training	30
Title II—military credit sales	677
Title III—other foreign aid	
Peace Corps	83
Refugee aid	53
Emergency refugee aid fund	10
Asian Development Bank	218
Inter-American Development Bank	480
International Bank for Reconstruction and Development	380
International Finance Corporation	38
International Development Association	800
African Development Fund	10
Title IV—Export-Import Bank	5471
Total	$6773

Source: Congressional Quarterly Almanac *(Washington,
D.C.: Congressional Quarterly, 1977), p. 286.*

eight children will die somewhere in the world from malnutrition and disease. With each passing minute, another twenty-eight will die—a shocking roster of 40,000 deaths of the young and innocent every day.[55] Much of this tragic loss—some 80 percent—stems from a simple lack of clean water to drink.[56]

Statistics like these and the horror they reveal touch a responsive chord in many Americans. This sense of humanitarianism—a willingness to help those less fortunate that has been an important strand in the American religious tradition—has been a steady source of support for advocates of the foreign aid program. No doubt more important still, though, has been a more self-interested motivation. As part of the containment doctrine designed to wall in international communism (Chapter 4), officials decided early in the postwar period that the United States would have to strengthen governments around the world, making them more pro-West and less vulnerable to Soviet influence.

As the diplomatic historian Dana G. Monro has put it with reference to America's own backyard, ". . . We were interested in economic development in the Caribbean because the poorer countries were not likely to have better governments [i.e., pro-Western democracies] so long as the masses of the people lived in ignorance and poverty."[57] In this spirit, President Lyndon Johnson once declared that foreign aid was "the best weapon we have to ensure that our own men in uniform need not go into combat."[58] Coupled with this central motive to immunize developing countries against communism was the further objective of gaining access into overseas markets through the admission ticket of foreign assistance.

Driven by these goals, U.S. foreign aid went from primarily private and missionary donations before the Second World War to an expanding program whose task it was to reconstruct the war-torn nations allied with the United States, strengthen other noncommunist states, and encourage development of the poor

FIGURE 12.2   Development assistance provided by the industrialized nations as a percentage of GNP, 1987.

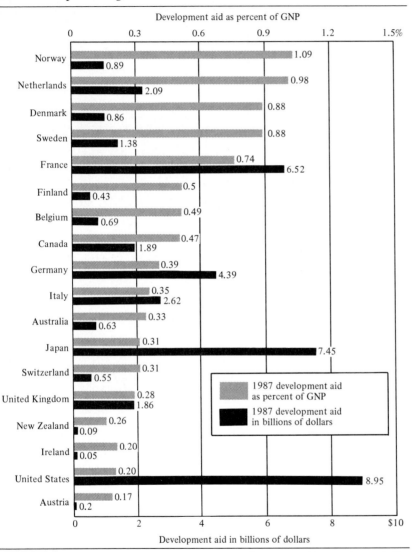

Source: U.S. Agency for International Development, "Cooperation Fosters Economic Development" *USAID Highlights*, vol. 6, Spring 1989, p. 2, based on data from the Scripps Howard News Service and reprinted from the *Washington Times*.

nations as viable markets and buffers against communist expansion. The underlying political assumption was that economic development would nurture the seeds of democracy and, once established, the democracies could stand united against communism. From 1947 to 1950,

U.S. officials earmarked most foreign aid (some $26 billion) for economic development.

During the 1950s, however, officials discarded this simplistic formula correlating economic aid and containment. Democracy had failed to take root with the celerity planners had hoped for (indeed, recall that among the nations of the world only nineteen are acknowledged to have true democratic governments[59]). The United States turned instead mainly toward military defense assistance for countries like South Korea, South Vietnam, Formosa, and the Philippines.

The Central American nation Guatemala offers an illustration. America's entire military assistance program in Guatemala from 1944 to 1953 summed to only $600,000. Then, in 1954, in the wake of a successful CIA operation to remove a president with suspected Marxist leanings (and a man who the U.S. corporation United Fruit Company feared might nationalize its banana plantations), the funding for the military assistance program soared virtually overnight to $45 million.[60]

As America's aid program unfolded in the postwar period, its key early initiatives included the Truman Doctrine and the European Recovery Program—the famous Marshall Plan—of 1947; the China Aid Act of 1948, followed by economic aid to other Asian nations in 1949 (Korea, Indonesia, Burma, Indochina, Thailand, and the Philippines) as well as, in the same year, the Point Four technical assistance program for Asia, Africa, and Latin America and the Mutual Defense Assistance Act for Europe; the Mutual Security Act for the Third World in 1951; and the Agricultural Trade Development and Assistance Act in 1954 (known widely as Public Law 480, or the "food for peace" act). The Marshall Plan remains the shining jewel among them, simply because it achieved so stunningly its objective of postwar reconstruction.

Between 1948 and 1952, America spent over $13 billion via the Marshall Plan to revive the economies of Europe (a comparable program would cost about $90 billion today). The result was a quick and robust recovery. Planners hoped this approach could become a model for American aid directed toward other parts of the world. The Marshall Plan, according to former Senator Fulbright, "created a false impression

that we could solve any problem by throwing money at it."[61] Unfortunately, few locations in the world had the prerequisites for success that Europe enjoyed, among them a skilled and experienced work force, strong productive potential, a common culture, and a readiness among leaders to work with one another.[62]

While in the 1950s the United States had turned more toward military assistance, during the 1960s (the "decade of development") it switched back to a concentration on economic assistance. Economic aid was double the amount of military aid from 1960 to 1965—just the reverse of the previous decade. The new and more altruistic emphasis was on "soft" loans over direct grants and technical aid. These loans came at a lower interest rate than loans in the private sector and allowed longer repayment schedules (and with repayment allowed in local currencies). Bickerton writes that, by 1960, soft loans had become "the single most important tool employed in the U.S. foreign aid program."[63] Among the landmarks of this period were the establishment of the Agency for International Development (AID) in 1961, providing better organizational focus within the State Department to America's foreign assistance programs; and, in the same year, the creation of two complementary programs, the Peace Corps and the Alliance for Progress (designed to strengthen the U.S. economic aid package for Latin America).

Souring on Aid

By the mid-1970s, however, pessimism about the usefulness of foreign aid had spread throughout the policy-making community in Washington. Aid had long had its critics ("the greatest give-away in history," perennially grumbled Representative Otto Passman, D-La., the powerful chairman of the House Appropriations Subcommittee on Foreign Operations[64]); but dissent against foreign assistance on Capitol Hill now became pervasive. The failure to achieve success in Indochina, despite the bil-

Peace Corps Volunteer Ann Eppler, 23, plays pick-up sticks with village children on the porch of her house in Telu, near Bo, Sierra Leone. (Courtesy Peace Corps)

lions of dollars worth of U.S. assistance pumped into that region of the world, cast a pall over the aid program soon after America's retreat from Saigon in 1975. Also, with the coming of détente in 1973–1974, the need to shore up the developing world against the Soviets seemed less imperative.

Moreover, all too often aid seemed merely to prop up dictators who siphon off funds for their own aggrandizement. Liberals on Capitol Hill decided to put a halt to aid for unsavory regimes which tortured dissidents and otherwise

violated human rights. The *Harkin amendment*, which was sponsored by Thomas Harkin (D-Iowa) and narrowly passed in 1974, placed a ban on aid to "any country which engages in a consistent pattern of gross violations of internationally recognized human rights" unless the president "determines that such assistance will directly benefit the needy people in such country and reports such determination to the Congress." The law also gave either chamber of Congress the right to override the presidential determination and, therefore, to stop the aid by a

Perspectives on American Foreign Policy   12.4

The American diplomat David D. Newsom on the Peace Corps:

Although not officially part of our assistance programs, the Peace Corps has done wonders around the world in showing people that, with the right kind of effort, things can be done. Some years ago, I was at the opening of a six-kilometer road from a village in a West African country to a main road. Before the road was built, all the products of the village had to be portaged over a narrow path fording two streams. The road was made possible because an American technician, in this case a 61-year-old former telephone lineman from Chicago, had discovered a field of castaway truck chassis and had shown how, by welding the chassis together, small bridges could be built. His was the ingenuity and the motivation. The work was that of the villagers. . . .

From David D. Newsom, *Diplomacy and the American Democracy* (Bloomington: Indiana University Press, 1988), p. 178.

---

majority vote in one house (a provision nullified by the *Chadha* decision, discussed in Chapter 6).

Later in the decade, aid critics pointed to the large foreign bank accounts held by Somoza of Nicaragua and other U.S. cronies in the Third World. And, in 1986, photos of the thousands of shoes purchased by Imelda Marcos, the wife of the deposed Philippine dictator, Ferdinand Marcos—a recipient of enormous sums of U.S. assistance—further soured aid critics. "Compared to Imelda, Marie Antoinette was a bag-lady," complained a leading member of Congress.[65]

Most important, however, were the lingering doubts that aid had much effect on a nation's development. Indeed, U.S. assistance might actually retard rather than accelerate a nation's progress, argued critics, through the establishment of an unhealthy dependency among recipients. Further, many countries to whom the United States provided aid seemed to have no compunction whatsoever against voting in opposition to U.S. objectives at the UN and in other international forums. Was foreign aid worth the cost, especially when this country had underdeveloped areas of its own where the limited resources of the taxpayer might be spent?

"I go home and see farmers' wives cry in front of me," said one midwestern legislator (who also happened to be chairman of the Appropriations Subcommittee on Foreign Operations—the key House panel on foreign assistance). "Don't tell me about the Philippines."[66]

What were the results of this expensive investment? One scholarly review of the U.S. aid program could only answer: "The impact of foreign aid remains obscure and perplexing."[67]

The Congress began routinely during the 1980s to slash aid for some nations by over 50 percent. (Those countries with effective lobbies in Washington managed to avoid the ax.) Despite the new skepticism about foreign aid, however, the total aid expenditures during the Reagan years ironically increased. This rise in spending was a result in part of the administration's emphasis on expensive military hardware sales and grants to Third World countries, as (in its first term at least) it heated up the cold war conflict with the Soviet Union throughout the world. The funding request for military grant assistance in 1988, for example, climbed

47.7 percent over the previous year—from $900 million to $1.3 billion; and spending requests for the military sales program went from $4 billion to $4.4 billion.[68] The increased spending also reflected a renewal of an interest in economic aid as a deterrent to communism; in 1984, members of the Kissinger Commission (chaired by the former Secretary of State) recommended an $8 billion economic aid program for Latin America to thwart communist takeovers.

Despite this resurgence of foreign assistance in the name of anticommunism, criticism of the U.S. aid program continues to be intense and pervasive. A widespread pessimism infuses the policy-making and academic communities over America's ability to bring about the global development once thought possible in the heyday of the Kennedy and Johnson years. One leading expert concludes, bleakly, that the "result of the recent economic disorder, thus, will most likely not be the end of Third World dependence but the creation of a new and more miserable Fourth World."[69]

Yet, can the United States afford to turn a cold shoulder to the needs of developing nations? "We need officials who care about these poor, weak nations and their peoples, officials who will show up occasionally to ask, 'What are your special problems? What can we buy from you, and what can we sell? What is it in medicine, food, education, technology that we can provide?' " writes the journalist Carl Rowan, a former U.S. ambassador. "When the automatic rifles are being fired, and artillery shells are exploding, as in El Salvador and Nicaragua, it is a bit late for the U.S. to fashion a policy."[70]

TRADE AND AID: STEPCHILDREN OF AMERICAN FOREIGN POLICY

Not everyone has been pessimistic about the use of economic power in the pursuit of U.S. foreign policy objectives. "Aside from war and preparations for war, and occasionally aside from migration," writes the economist Thomas C. Schelling, "trade is the most important relationship that most countries have with each other."[71] For Secretary of Defense Robert S. McNamara (speaking with some hyperbole), "the foreign aid program generally and the military assistance program specifically has now become the most critical element of our overall national security effort."[72]

Yet, the opinions of some prominent experts and officials to the contrary, trade and aid continue to be instruments of only secondary importance in the priorities of most foreign policy officials. The reaction of most administrations, still transfixed by the specter of communism spreading like a red stain inexorably across the globe, has been to think first in terms of covert action or overt military intervention: the powers of secrecy and war. Trade and aid have remained the neglected stepchildren of American foreign policy, for the most part ignored in the White House and other high councils. The greatest concern to American security, however, is less apt to be Suriname, Chad, Grenada, Nicaragua, or Libya than the economic well-being of Mexico, the status of America's own balance of payments, the viability of U.S. industries, the amicable settlement of trade disputes with America's great allies (Japan, West Germany, and the other industrial nations of the West), and a willingness to work toward economic improvements in the Third and Fourth Worlds—where adject poverty will continue to breed resentment and terrorism.

"Political economy is the name of the next task, not geopolitics," writes Senator and former UN Ambassador Daniel Patrick Moynihan (D-N.Y.). "This will be missed by those who do not understand that the latter derives from the former. With great respect, *they* will not be missed."[73]

SUMMARY

International economic objectives—protecting the sea-lanes for the transit of commerce, seeking foreign markets for American goods, ensuring access to valuable natural resources abroad—have always been a part of the U.S. foreign policy agenda. In the first few decades following the Second World War, the United States enjoyed an enviable position in the world: the status and wealth of an economic giant. As the ever-industrious West Germans and Japanese rebuilt their economies (with substantial assistance from Americans), the United States soon found itself less of a giant among pygmies, however, than just one strong trading nation among many. Even once-poor nations of the Third World began to emerge in the 1970s as economic powers to be reckoned with. Some—notably the Arab states—formed cartels to strengthen their control over valuable indigenous resources (oil especially); and others—South Korea and Taiwan, among them—proved capable of manufacturing and marketing competitively a range of industrial products. No longer the behemoth astride a war-wrecked globe, America now faced the challenge of rising to new competition and halting the relative decline of its commercial standing in the world.

In this new era of economic competition, the United States confronted a complicated marketplace abroad and increasing fragmentation of authority over international trade policy at home. Among nations of the Western alliance, a pattern of economic interdependence arose. On the global North-South axis, in contrast, the developing nations of the South remained largely dependent on the economic decisions of the Northern industrialized nations—though with a growing sense of their own economic potential and a rising bitterness over their lingering dependency. On the East-West axis, economic ties between the West and the Soviet bloc remained largely independent of one another; yet, even here, change was in the air with mounting pressures on both sides to improve commercial relations. Dependence, independence, interdependence—the crosscurrents tugged at one another and produced a global economic setting of vast complexity and an uncertain future.

Two trading relationships remained constant in this setting of change: Canada and Mexico remained among America's most important and reliable trading partners. Added to the list were the two new giants, West Germany and Japan, whose economic prowess has led to occasional friction with the United States over fair trading practices—especially the Japanese, accused of flooding the U.S. market with their goods while resisting American exports. The inundation of the home market with Asian goods has set loose an outcry from some groups in the United States for protectionist legislation, a movement strongly opposed by "free-traders."

America's relative decline as an international economic force has been attributed to several causes (some of which are reversible). Among them: an overvalued dollar in the postwar period (hurting U.S. exports), stagnant Third World markets, unfair protectionist practices abroad, and poor productivity at home. This decline, and the rising competition with West Germany, Japan, and other industrialized nations, has been accompanied by strains in the Western alliance. American critics have grown increasingly vocal about what they perceive to be unfair trade practices abroad and inadequate payment of collective defense costs by U.S. allies.

In place of America's postwar economic dominance has come a proliferation of new international organizations and arrangements—

the International Monetary Fund and the General Agreement on Tariffs and Trade, among a host of others—that seek, imperfectly, to provide some order in the present reign of global economic pluralism. Offering some overarching cohesion, too, are the multinational corporations. In both instances, the new structures have been the subjects of criticism: the international organizations for (among other things) failing to accommodate the needs of the poor nations, and the multinationals for (among other things) undermining—indeed, blatantly opposing—the sovereign authority of the nation-state.

At home, the proliferation of economic authority has been the rule, too, in the past two decades. Within the executive branch, cohesive, long-range economic planning has usually been the victim of institutional fragmentation and bureaucratic parochialism within the executive branch, as more and more agencies claim a role in the making of international economic policy and officials scramble to protect their interests and those of allied pressures groups. Similarly, the Congress has experienced a proliferation of subcommittees dealing with foreign economic policy, as legislators begin to realize the added importance in the modern era of international trade decisions to their own constituencies. The end result has been a federal government often unable to deal coherently with intricate trade issues.

Efforts by the United States to use economic power as an inducement to achieve its economic objectives abroad have met with mixed results; but, for the most part, the use of trade sanctions—positive and negative—has proved unsatisfactory. Other nations are simply less vulnerable to U.S. economic pressure than some policymakers have anticipated, in part because the target nation can usually find some other country willing to sell the denied goods.

Along with trade, foreign aid has been another significant instrument of America's economic statecraft. This aid has come mainly in two packages: economic assistance and military (security) assistance, with an emphasis on the latter. Although sometimes motivated by humanitarian concerns, U.S. foreign aid has been viewed by most policymakers primarily as another form of resistance to communist encroachments throughout the world—a further buttress for the containment doctrine. In the past two decades, criticism of America's aid program has mounted as scholars and government officials alike question its effectiveness. Legislators have been more willing in recent years to slash the aid budget dramatically—though military assistance continued to enjoy robust funding as part of the Reagan Doctrine to combat communism in the developing world.

Despite its obvious importance, questions of trade and aid have been relatively ignored by policymakers over the years, in favor of various political and national security issues. The new challenges to America's commercial supremacy, though, have brought forth calls for closer attention to the uses of economic power—the neglected stepchild of American foreign policy.

KEY TERMS

Bretton Woods agreement
balance of payments
Smithsonian agreement
floating world monetary system
Organization of Petroleum Exporting
  Countries (OPEC)
stagflation

petrodollars
balance on current account
Eurodollar
productivity
new industrialized countries (NICs)
theory of comparative advantage
protectionism

KEY TERMS *(Continued)*

Nippophobia
free trade
nontariff barriers (NTBs)
Coordinating Committee (COCOM)
International Monetary Fund (IMF)
General Agreement on Tariffs
  and Trade (GATT)
Conference on International Economic
  Cooperation (CIEC)
World Bank
International Development Association (IDA)
Group of 77
Organization for Economic Cooperation
  and Development (OECD)
multinational corporation (MNC)

transnationalism
dependencia model
Jackson-Vanik amendment
Smoot-Hawley tariff
most favored nation (MFN)
embargo
boycott
blacklisting
dumping
preclusive buying
asset freezing
foreign aid
security assistance
Harkin amendment

NOTES

1. For these figures and a useful discussion of their implications, see Felix Rohatyn, "America's Economic Dependence," *Foreign Affairs*, Special Issue: "America and the World, 1988/89," vol. 68, 1989, pp. 53–65.

2. Remarks, Senator Frank Church (D-Idaho), Washington, D.C., August 28, 1980.

3. Joan Edelman Spero, *The Politics of International Economic Relations*, 2d ed. (New York: St. Martin's, 1981), p. 2.

4. Leonard Silk, *Economics in Plain English* (New York: Simon & Schuster, 1978), p. 107. The Johnson administration estimated that from June 1966 to June 1967, it would have to spend $11 billion to $17 billion on the Vietnamese war; the actual figure turned out to be $21 billion for those twelve months alone, with costs continuing to rise [Stanley Karnow, *Vietnam: A History* (New York: Viking, 1983), p. 487]. On efforts by the Johnson administration to conceal from Congress and the American people the true costs of the war (and Johnson's denial of this charge), see Doris Kearns, *Lyndon Johnson and the American Dream* (New York: Harper & Row, 1976), pp. 297–298.

5. Paul A. Samuelson, *Economics*, 4th ed. (New York: McGraw-Hill, 1958), p. 632.

6. Silk, *op. cit.*, p. 115.

7. See Samuelson, *op. cit.*, p. 633.

8. Rimmer De Vries, "The International Monetary Outlook for the 1980s: No Time for Complacency," *World Financial Markets*, December 1979, p. 5, cited by Spero, *op. cit.*, p. 58.

9. Jim Wright (D-Tex.), quoted in the *New York Times*, December 15, 1986, p. 15.

10. Spero, *op. cit.*, pp. 12–18.

11. *World Economic and Social Indicators, April 1980* (Washington: International Bank for Reconstruction and Development, 1980), p. 7, cited by Spero, *op. cit.*, p. 14.

12. See the *IMF Survey*, March 17, 1980, p. 89, cited by Spero, *op. cit.*, p. 16, and Rohatyn, *op. cit.*, p. 57.

13. See, respectively, Silk, *op. cit.*, p. 64, and Samuelson, *op. cit.*, p. 651.

14. These statistics come from *World Development Report, 1979* (Washington, D.C.: International Bank for Reconstruction and Development, 1979), p. 13, as cited by Spero, *op. cit.*, p. 15.

15. These figures are cited by Thomas L. Brewer, *American Foreign Policy: A Contemporary Introduction*, 2d ed. (Englewood Cliffs, N.J.: Prentice-Hall, 1986), p. 244.

16. Warren Christopher, deputy secretary of state, "Resources and Foreign Policy," *Current Policy No. 185*, U.S. Department of State, Bureau of Public Affairs, Washington, D.C., May 28, 1980, p. 2.

17. For the 1977 figure, see Richard N. Cooper, under secretary for economic affairs, "Economics and U.S. Security in the 1980s," *Current Policy No. 158*, U.S. Department of State, Bureau of Public Affairs, Washington, D.C., March 7, 1980, p. 2; for the 1984 figure, see *United States Trade: Performance in 1984 and Outlook*, U.S. Department of Commerce, International Trade Administration, Office of Trade and Investment Analysis (Washington, D.C.: U.S. Government Printing Office, June 1985), p. 17. The figures for Saudi oil earnings come from the *New York Times*, February 12, 1987, p. 29.

18. *United States Trade 1984*, p. 49.

19. Lester C. Thurow and Laura D'Andrea Tyson, "The Economic Black Hole," *Foreign Policy*, vol. 67, Summer 1987, p. 16. In 1985, the United States imported 31 percent of its oil from abroad; by 1987, the figure had risen to 41 percent—approaching the peak of 43 percent in 1979. According to one analyst: "Ballooning oil imports were the biggest single factor in making our trade deficit worse [in 1987]" (Robert Giordano of Goldman Sachs, interviewed by Dan Corditz, *ABC News*, December 18, 1987).

20. Robert B. Reich, "The Economics of Illusion and the Illusion of Economics," *Foreign Affairs*, "Special Issue: America and the World 1987/88," vol. 66, 1988, p. 516; Rohatyn, *op. cit.*, p. 56.

21. *United States Trade 1984*, p. 12.

22. Donald Ratajcza, quoted in the *Atlanta Journal and Constitution*, January 18, 1987, p. 2-E.

23. William Pfaff, "Reflections: Where the Wars Came From," *New Yorker*, December 26, 1988, p. 83.

24. See Robert Gilpin, "The Politics of Transnational Economic Relations," in Robert O. Keohane and Joseph P. Nye, Jr., eds., *Transnational Relations and World Politics* (Cambridge, Mass.: Harvard University Press, 1972), reprinted in George Modelski, ed., *Transnational Corporations and World Order: Readings in International Political Economy* (San Francisco: Freeman, 1979), p. 72.

25. Frank D. Downing, "Japan's Global Trade Patterns: A Contribution to Trade Friction," in *United States Trade 1984*, p. 55.

26. For these arguments, see respectively Reich, *op. cit.*, p. 519, and Mike Mansfield (the U.S. ambassador to Japan from 1977 to 1989), "The U.S. and Japan: Sharing Our Destinies," *Foreign Affairs*, vol. 68, Spring 1989, p. 8.

27. Reich, *op. cit.*, p. 521; see, also, I. M. Destler, *American Trade Politics: System under Stress* (Washington, D.C.: Institute for International Economics, 1986).

28. "The Week in Germany," German Information Center, New York, December 18, 1986, p. 5.

29. Quoted by Art Pine, "'Nippophobia' Affects Making of Trade Policy," *Los Angeles Times*, April 24, 1989, sec. 4, p. 12.

30. See Martin Feldstein, "Correcting the Trade Deficit," *Foreign Affairs*, vol. 65, Spring 1987, p. 804. For a list of self-improvements that would assist a U.S. economic recovery, see Rohatyn, *op. cit.*, p. 64.

31. *United States Trade 1984*, p. 45.

32. Mortimer B. Zukerman, "What Should Make Bush Run Now," *U.S. News & World Report*, February 6, 1989, p. 70. One expert on Japan notes that "fewer than 1,000 U.S. scientists speak Japanese, while English is a

requirement for science students in Japan" (Walter Russell Mead, "Japan-Bashing, an Ugly American Tradition," *Los Angeles Times*, June 4, 1989, sec. 5, p. 2). The former U.S. ambassador to Japan, Mike Mansfield, points to hopeful new efforts toward educating Americans about Japan: ". . . in 1986 over 23,400 U.S. college students were enrolled in Japanese-language courses and . . . nearly 100 American high schools teach Japanese" ("The U.S. and Japan," p. 16).

33. Conversation with author, April 21, 1988, Cambridge, Massachusetts.

34. Gary K. Bertsch, "East-West Trade and Technology Transfer: Toward a Policy of Nonmilitary Free Trade," *SAIS Review*, vol. 4, Summer-Fall 1984, pp. 100–101.

35. *Ibid*.

36. Quoted by Gary K. Bertsch, "U.S.–Soviet Trade and the National Interest: Assessing the Costs and Benefits," in Roland S. Homet, Jr., ed., *East-West Outlook*, vol. 9, May 1986, p. 3.

37. Spero, *op. cit.*, p. 103.

38. *Ibid.*, p. 110.

39. Raymond Vernon, *Sovereignty at Bay: The Multinational Spread of U.S. Enterprises* (New York: Basic Books, 1971).

40. See Johan Galtung, "A Structural Theory of Imperialism," *Journal of Peace Research*, vol. 2, 1971, pp. 81–98; and Stephen Hymer, "The Multinational Corporation and the Law of Uneven Development," in Jagdish Bhagwati, ed., *Economics and World Order— From the 1970s to the 1990s* (New York: Macmillan, 1972), pp. 113–114.

41. Robert Gilpin, "Three Models of the Future," *International Organization*, vol. 29, 1975, p. 44, original emphasis.

42. Former U.S. Ambassador to West Germany Martin Hillenbrand, "Economic Diplomacy," lecture, University of Georgia, Athens, January 17, 1983.

43. Hedrick Smith, *The Power Game: How Washington Works* (New York: Random House, 1988), p. 570.

44. I. M. Destler, *Making Foreign Economic Policy* (Washington, D.C.: Brookings, 1980), p. 215.

45. Clyde H. Farnsworth, "Approval of Canada Trade Pact Seen," *New York Times*, May 9, 1988, pp. 21, 24, 42.

46. See Paula Stern, *Water's Edge: Domestic Politics and the Making of American Foreign Policy* (New York: Greenwood Press, 1979).

47. See Loch K. Johnson, "Legislators as Diplomats: The Czechoslovak Gold Dispute," *Journal of Legislation*, vol. 9, Winter 1982, pp. 36–51.

48. Joan Hoff Wilson, "Economic Foreign Policy," in Alexander DeConde, ed., *Encyclopedia of American Foreign Policy: Studies of the Principal Movements and Ideas*, Vol. II (New York: Scribner, 1978), p. 320.

49. David A. Baldwin, *Economic Statecraft* (Princeton, N.J.: Princeton University Press, 1985). On the failure of the trade embargo against the Sandinista government in Nicaragua instituted by the Reagan administration, see Stephen Kinzer, "Anti-Sandinistas Urge End of U.S. Embargo," *New York Times*, January 12, 1989, p. 5.

50. Ian J. Bickerton, "Foreign Aid," in DeConde, *op. cit.*, p. 372.

51. David D. Newsom, *Diplomacy and the American Democracy* (Bloomington: Indiana University Press, 1988), p. 161.

52. Bernard Gwertzman, "A Citizen Pays $43 for Aid, Schultz Says, and $35 for Hairdos," *New York Times*, February 25, 1983.

53. Charles W. Kegley, Jr., and Eugene R. Witkopf, *American Foreign Policy: Pattern and Process* (New York: St. Martin's, 1979), p. 93; for the 1987 data, see U.S. Agency for International Development, "Cooperation Fosters Economic Development," *USAID Highlights*, vol. 6, Spring 1989, p. 1.

54. Robert L. Heilbroner, *An Inquiry into the Human Prospect* (New York: Norton, 1975), p. 39.

55. *Evening News*, ABC Television, December 11, 1986.

56. Conference of Soviet-American Physicians, WETA Public Television, December 1984.

57. Cited by Wilson, *op. cit.*, p. 287.

58. Quoted by Bickerton, *op. cit.*, p. 375.

59. See Arend Lijphart, *Democracies* (Cambridge, Mass.: Harvard University Press, 1982), p. 5.

60. See David Wise and Thomas B. Ross, *The Invisible Government* (New York: Vintage, 1974).

61. Quoted by Ann Hughey, "The Lessons of the Marshall Plan," *New York Times*, June 7, 1987, p. 4-F.

62. See Gaddis Smith, "The Marshall Plan," in DeConde, *op. cit.*, p. 544.

63. Bickerton, *op. cit.*, p. 374.

64. Quoted by Bickerton, *ibid.*, p. 375.

65. Representative Stephen Solarz (D-N.Y.), quoted on *Washington Week in Review*, Public Broadcasting System (PBS), television news show, March 14, 1986.

66. Quoted by Peter Osterlund, "Congress Tightens Foreign-Aid Screws," *Christian Science Monitor*, September 18, 1986.

67. Bickerton, *op. cit.*, p. 378.

68. Joanne Omang, "$1.3 Billion More Sought in Foreign Aid Programs," *Washington Post*, December 31, 1986, p. A-13.

69. Spero, *op. cit.*, p. 176.

70. Carl Rowan, "American Ignorance," *Atlanta Constitution*, November 4, 1979.

71. Thomas C. Schelling, "National Security Considerations Affecting Trade Policy," *Williams Commission Report: Papers*, vol. 1, July 1971 (Washington, D.C.; Government Printing office), p. 737.

72. Quoted by Bickerton, *op. cit.*, p. 375.

73. Daniel Patrick Moynihan, "Reagan's Doctrine and the Iran Issue," *New York Times*, December 21, 1986, p. E-19.

RECOMMENDED READINGS

Baldwin, David A. *Economic Statecraft*. (Princeton, N.J.: Princeton University Press, 1985). An award-winning, careful analysis of the limitations of trade and aid as an instrument of foreign policy.

Bergsten, C. Fred, ed. *The Future of the International Economic Order: An Agenda for Research* (Boston: Heath, 1973). A collection of essays outlining suggestions for research which still remains a rich lode of good ideas.

Bertsch, Gary K., ed. *Controlling East-West Trade and Technology Transfer: Power, Politics, and Policies* (Durham, N.C.: Duke University Press, 1988). Essays on the advisability of increasing U.S. trade in high technology with the Soviets, among other important topics.

Bickerton, Ian J. "Foreign Aid," in Alexander DeConde, ed., *Encyclopedia of American Foreign Policy: Studies of the Principal Movements and Ideas*, Vol. II (New York: Scribner, 1978), pp. 372–379. An excellent survey of the history and problems of American foreign aid in the postwar period (one of many valuable chapters in this three-volume collection).

Cohen, Stephen D. *The Making of United States International Economic Policy* (New York: Praeger, 1977). This and the volume by Destler provide useful descriptions of the institutional fragmentation of American trade policy.

Cooper, Richard N. *The Economics of Interdependence: Economic Policy in the Atlantic Community* (New York: McGraw-Hill, 1968). A good place to begin for an understanding of U.S.–European trade relations.

Destler, I. M. *Making Foreign Economic Policy* (Washington, D.C.: Brookings, 1980). A detailed examination of Russian wheat purchases from the United States, the soybean embargo of 1973, the politics of food aid, and the legislative intricacies of passing a trade bill, among other fascinating glimpses into the formulation of U.S. trade-and-aid policy.

Gilpin, Robert. *U.S. Power and the Multinational Corporation: The Political Economy of Foreign Direct Investment* (New York: Basic Books, 1975). A look at the MNCs by one of America's most trenchant analysts of international economic affairs.

Heilbroner, Robert L. *An Inquiry into the Human Prospect* (New York: Norton, 1975). A thought-provoking examination of the deteriorating international economic system, with a special sensitivity to the perspective of poor countries.

Kennedy, Paul. *The Rise and Fall of the Great Powers: Economic Change and Military Conflict from 1500 to 2000* (New York: Random House, 1987). A best-selling historical work by an Englishman on the faculty of Yale University, with the thesis that America's military commitments have overreached this nation's ability to support them economically—a condition of "imperial overstretch."

Modelski, George, ed. *Transnational Corporations and World Order* (San Francisco: Freeman, 1979). A sophisticated set of readings on international political economy, including writings by Robert Gilpin, Raymond Vernon, Charles Kindleberger, and Johan Galtung, among others.

Samuelson, Paul A. *Economics*, 4th ed. (New York: McGraw-Hill, 1958). This classic introduction to the study of economics has several chapters on international matters, each lucidly written and illustrated.

Silk, Leonard. *Economics in Plain English* (New York: Simon & Schuster, 1978). Another excellent primer on economics, written by the chief economics correspondent for the *New York Times*—easier-going than Samuelson (though far less comprehensive), with several helpful examples drawn from the realm of international economic policy.

Spero, Joan Edelman. *The Politics of International Economic Relations*, 2d ed. (New York: St. Martin's, 1981). A superb survey of the key international economic issues, with an emphasis on North-South and East-West trade relations.

Whitman, Marina V. N. *Reflections on Interdependence: Issues for Economic Theory and U.S. Policy* (Pittsburgh: University of Pittsburgh Press, 1979). Another valuable analysis by a leading light in the study of American foreign economic policy.

Yergen, Daniel, and Martin Hillenbrand, eds. *Global Security: A Strategy for Energy and Economic Renewal* (Boston: Houghton Mifflin, 1982). A collection of essays on the oil crisis and other hazards to American security, edited by a Harvard University faculty member, Yergen, and a distinguished American diplomat, Hillenbrand.

PRUDENCE AND MORALITY

   Hard-Boiled Realism

   The Longing of Idealists

SELECTED ETHICAL DILEMMAS IN
RECENT FOREIGN POLICY DECISIONS

   Illustrations from the Second World War

   Ethics and Nuclear Deterrence

The Ethics of Strategic Intelligence

   Human Rights

CHARTING A MORAL COURSE

   Three-Dimensional Ethics

   Muscle and Morality

SUMMARY

MORALITY AND FOREIGN POLICY: ON BEING GOOD IN A BAD WORLD

PRUDENCE AND MORALITY

The second half of this book has focused on the uses of U.S. foreign policy, that is, the means selected by officials to achieve America's international objectives. This chapter looks at moral suasion as an instrument of foreign policy. It will perhaps seem odd to some readers to think of morality as a means, but the espousal of high principles by America's leaders has long exerted a strong attraction on other countries. Several foreign governments have modeled their constitutions after the U.S. Constitution, for example, because of its noble democratic ideals.

The United States has been accepted as the leader of the Western world not simply because of its economic strength or its imposing array of nuclear warheads, but in real measure from the devotion of Americans to human rights, democracy, and freedom around the globe. The Soviet Union, after all, has an impressive military arsenal, too, but its methods of autocratic rule (despite a democratic-sounding constitution) offer nothing to admire—the charisma of its newest leader, President Gorbachev notwithstanding. The United States needs friends in the world, if for no other reasons than to enhance its own security (as with NATO, for example) and opportunities for commerce. In the competition for friends, ideals matter, democratic principles matter, justice matters, a credible concern for the needs of the poor and the hungry—a majority of the world's population—matters.

Moral considerations have often influenced the course of a nation's external affairs. One tragic illustration comes from the era of nineteenth-century colonialism. King Leopold II of Belgium was accused of using unsavory means to extract larger and larger quotas of rubber from the Congo (which he had acquired as a private estate for business purposes). Africans who failed to meet the king's expected allotments became victims of atrocities. One cameraman returned to Europe with a gruesome photograph of a father in the Congo, sitting next to the hand and foot of his little girl; they had been severed by rubber sentries as a punishment for the father's failure to meet the rubber quotas for his village. Press reports on such brutalities shocked Europeans and eventually forced the king in 1908 to transfer the administration of Congolese affairs over to Belgian government authorities.[1]

This century has witnessed worldwide moral outrage over Nazi atrocities, the mass murders directed by Joseph Stalin against his opponents in the U.S.S.R., and the butchery ordered by Pol Pot in Cambodia. In 1989, a directive from Iran's religious leader, Khomeini, to kill an Indian novelist living in London (who had written a novel with passages thought by Islamic fundamentalists to be blasphemous of the Muslim faith) stirred a worldwide backlash against this extreme form of "literary criticism."

Ethical considerations have long been a part of the U.S. foreign policy agenda. Among many examples: the missionary zeal at the turn of the century sending Americans overseas (Chapter 3), President Wilson's call for open diplomacy (Chapter 3), the revulsion over CIA assassination plots that led to an executive order in 1975 prohibiting this "Godfather" approach to America's foreign objectives (Chapter 9), and the 1974 Harkin amendment on human rights (Chapter 12). The *Washington Post* journalist Bob Woodward (who became famous for helping to break the Watergate scandal) has expressed a view held by many Americans concerning the moral blindfolds of the Reagan administration:

If there's a tragic part to [CIA Director William J.] Casey, and I guess there is, it is that he ultimately didn't realize what this country is about. That we are different; that, yes, we will have an intelligence agency; yes, we will do things in secret—but those nation-defining activities, like war, can't be done in secret. That we can't go out and try to get the Saudi intelligence service to kill people we don't like, be-

cause in America we don't do that in secret, because that tells the world who we are. It tells *us* who we are.[2]

Although many Americans endorse a moral approach to foreign policy, an influential school of thought—the realists—remains skeptical about the value of ethical principles in the conduct of a nation's affairs. In their dominance over the study—and the practice—of international politics, the realists have consistently advocated prudence over morality, the capacity for war as a better protection of the national interest than the capacity for ethical judgment, the big stick before the pure heart. According to the realist school, leaders of a major power must be—foremost—tough and shrewd. "How many divisions do they have?" is a celebrated realist's query, attributed to Stalin. Here, according to the realists, is the overmastering consideration for any provident leader responsible for a nation's external relations.

Still, many students of international relations (and a large number of American citizens) are unwilling to discount the role that ethics should play in America's foreign affairs. Inis L. Claude, Jr., the thoughtful international relations scholar, notes that Americans ". . . undoubtedly place a high value on having—not merely on being thought to have—clean hands and a pure heart; the discomfort of a guilty conscience, or even of nagging uncertainty about one's virtue, is not an easy thing to bear." He attributes the unwillingness of the United States to participate in global politics before the twentieth century in part to "the dread of dirty hands."[3]

The differing worldviews of realists and idealists have contributed significantly to America's oscillation between, on the one hand, a deep involvement in world affairs and, on the other hand, a longing for a return to the innocence that accompanied isolation from other nations (Chapter 3)—though by no means do all idealists advocate moral purity through isolation. President Woodrow Wilson was a leading idealist, yet his League of Nations proposal would have thrust the United States directly into a position of global leadership.

The choice faced by foreign policy officials is rarely one of morality versus pragmatism, idealism versus realism. As Henry Kissinger has put it, "Our cause must be just, but it must prosper in a world of sovereign nations and competing wills." Arguing that sound policy has to "relate ends to means," he argues that "neither moralistic rhetoric nor obsession with pure power politics will produce a foreign policy worthy of our opportunity—or adequate for our survival."[4] This chapter explores this balancing act between ethical values and hard-nosed realism in America's foreign affairs.

Hard-Boiled Realism

Inis Claude observed in 1962 that theories of international politics were "as yet a thing of shreds and patches."[5] This condition has failed to improve much over the years since then; yet, now (as then) one group of scholars—the realists—remains convinced they have grasped the central motive force in international relations. For the realists, in the words of one of their leading lights, Hans J. Morgenthau, the "iron law" of foreign policy is "that statesmen think and act in terms of [the national] interest defined as power." In turn, power is to be understood as a nation's military strength—its capacity to inflict punishing physical violence against an adversary. To ensure that no enemy is able to assemble a military capability that could prove overwhelming, major nations must try to maintain a balance of military power—here, continues Morgenthau, was "a universal instrument of foreign policy used at all times by all nations who wanted to preserve their independence."

Those nations oblivious to this elemental fact risked imprudent behavior that could lead to their military defeat—even Carthaginian obliteration. In this sense, a nation's leaders are advised to be "objective" and "realistic." Moralism and sentimentality would have to take a back seat (if any seat at all) to the requirements of national security and military readiness.

A moral dilemma faced by British Prime Minister Winston Churchill during the Second World War provides an illustration of hard-boiled realism in action. In 1940, Royal Air Force (RAF) bombers conducted a raid against Munich at the time Hitler was visiting the city to celebrate the seventeenth anniversary of the Beer Hall Putsch—his first (and failed) attempt to gain power in Germany. Hitler escaped injury during the RAF raid, but vowed revenge for the affront. His choice of targets was the historic cathedral city of Coventry in England. British intelligence officials learned of the retaliatory attack in advance, thanks to *Ultra*, the code name for a highly secret and successful operation designed to intercept top-secret German military and diplomatic communications. Churchill's unenviable task was to decide whether to warn the people of Coventry (at least the city's leaders, doctors, and firefighters) about the impending raid—or to protect the Ultra secret.

If the prime minister failed to warn Coventry, its citizens would face the onslaught of over 500 German bombers without an opportunity to escape or ready themselves. Yet, if Coventry were warned, German intelligence agents would spot the evacuation and the increased defenses around the city; they would realize that British scientists had deciphered their communications codes. The Germans would then change to new communications channels, depriving Britain of a vital window onto Nazi operations which might be even more significant than the Coventry attack. Foremost in the mind of the realist would be the protection of Britain's military capability, the innocent lives of the men, women, and children of Coventry notwithstanding. Churchill, the realist, chose to protect Ultra. In Coventry, the human cost of the "surprise" Nazi attack was 554 citizens dead (150 charred beyond recognition), 865 seriously wounded, and some 4000 more burned or injured.[6]

For many realists, the need to be tough-minded goes beyond the establishment of an equilibrium of power among the major nations; as Claude notes, "balance of power theorists tend to put more stock in defeating aggressors by preponderant power than in deterring them by equivalent power."[7] Claude and Arnold Wolfers (among other well-regarded scholars) essentially agree with the realists' focus on the importance of the war power, but prefer an emphasis on a weapons *equilibrium* rather than superiority as a national objective.

Whether the goal is superiority or equilibrium, realists depend upon military force—active or potential, overt or covert—to maintain a semblance of balance and order amidst the anarchy of a globe comprising disparate nation-states, each with its own fears and ambitions, vulnerabilities and strengths. And it is precisely this same global anarchy, with its continual warfare and endless international intrigue, that distresses and animates the idealists in their opposition to the realist philosophy.

The Longing of Idealists

The idealists long for peace and justice in the world, not just order, and they are unimpressed by the use of military force to achieve this goal. They are critical of the realist prescriptions for two main reasons. First, the realist's concentration on order-of-battle charts, warhead counts, and the number of warships and aircraft obscures the ethical component of international politics. A sense of ethics is (or at least should be, in the view of idealists) important to a country like the United States, which professes a commitment to democracy, human rights, and the quality of life. Surely, argue idealists, America ought to stand behind a higher principle than simply "might makes right." And second, reliance on the war power has failed to bring peace. The 10 million graves around the world filled with battle casualties since 1945 offer solemn testimony to this fact, not to mention those who fall on the battlefields

of Angola, Iran, Iraq, Afghanistan, Cambodia, Nicaragua and the Horn of Africa (among other places) as this book is being written.

Despotism   A respected international journalist reports that "in Chile, there is torture every day, and at every hour of the day."[8] Here is testimony gathered by the journalist from two among the many recent victims of Chilean repression:

> The whole time, approximately sixteen days, they had me blindfolded. . . . Later, they put electrodes on my toes, knees, the tip of my penis, and on my testicles. . . . Every night, except for the last two, they made me sleep standing up. The next day, they began what became a daily routine: they would hang me and beat me. . . . (Testimony of Sergio Buschmann Silva)

> I had wounds all over my body, I couldn't control my muscles and my body was in a permanent state of spasm and shivering. . . . My lips were totally destroyed, to the point that pieces of skin were hanging and I couldn't speak properly. . . . Captain Tellez shot off four shots from a revolver and then told me there were two shots left; he made me take the revolver and test the trigger by putting it to my forehead and made me squeeze the trigger every time I answered a question negatively. . . . (Testimony of Alfredo Bruno Malbrich Baltra)

The "crime" of these two Chilean citizens was to have criticized their government. Other dissenters have been less fortunate still. In the past fifteen years, reportedly thousands of Chilean dissenters have been killed or imprisoned, and hundreds more have simply "disappeared." In the small village of Calama, far north of Santiago, a Chilean general reportedly ordered his soldiers to execute twenty-six men without a trial; their wives were warned to remain silent about these "disappearances," or else next their children would be murdered.[9]

Should these internal affairs influence the foreign policy of the United States toward

Chile? A dyed-in-the-wool realist, while not without sympathy for these victims, would likely be more concerned with the larger strategic question: Is the Chilean dictatorship a helpful buffer against Soviet encroachment into the Western Hemisphere? For the realist, the answer is apt to be yes; at least the Chilean autocrat, General Augusto Pinochet, is not another Marxist, prepared (like Fidel Castro) to invite Soviet troops into the region.

From the vantage point of the idealist, however, for the United States to maintain ties with a man like Pinochet, who has governed over a police state engaged in the brutal torture of its own citizens, is morally repugnant and unworthy of America's ideals and traditions. It makes a mockery of this nation's professed love for freedom and discredits Americans in the eyes of other countries around the world who look toward the United States as a moral leader, not just as an arsenal of imposing weaponry.

An idealist would be troubled by many other ties between the United States and unsavory regimes and groups abroad. President Reagan referred to the contras in Nicaragua as "freedom fighters" equivalent to America's own Founding Fathers; yet, independent U.S. observers have discovered shocking human rights abuses by the contras (as well as by their Sandinista opponents). In November of 1987, the New York–based Lawyers Committee for Human Rights accused the contras of "continuing gross human rights violations," including "political killings, disappearances and other serious mistreatment of civilian noncombatants."[10]

In light of the repugnant behavior of the contras, do they continue to warrant the support of the United States? Yes, realists would argue, because the contras are anticommunist; U.S. support is necessary as a barrier against the establishment of a Soviet military base in Nicaragua. No, idealists would retort, because the contras (or at least certain elements among them) are thugs whose treatment of Nicaraguan civilians is just as bad as, if not worse than, that of the Sandinistas, who seem to remain popular

in many parts of the nation. The world will judge America in part by the company it keeps, idealists maintain, and the contras are bad company.

Put another way, for America to touch pitch is to become defiled. In the end, this debate between realists and idealists (analytical labels, recall, which in reality clothe a range of views, not just two polar extremes) comes down to a balance between, on the one hand, a nation's global strategic interests—as defined in terms of military advantage—and, on the other hand, the ethical implications of a nation's commitments abroad.

In South Africa, the government's practice of apartheid is repellent to most Americans, yet the United States maintains ties with this nation's ruling whites. During the Iran-contra affair of 1986–1987, legislative investigators discovered that the Reagan administration had even sought (and obtained) covert financial support from the South African regime to help sponsor the contra war against the Sandinistas. In Equatorial Guinea, the mad dictator, Francisco Macías Nguema, murdered or forced into exile roughly one-third of his nation's citizens before, in 1976, the United States finally decided to suspend relations (one of Macías's favorite "events," which he staged periodically, was to order his guards to machine-gun political prisoners gathered in a soccer stadium, a public spectacle accompanied by the blare of pop music in the background).[11]

In Haiti during the summer of 1986, paramilitary forces linked to the government massacred 300 members of a peasant cooperative known to be critical of the regime; in 1987, as the nation approached its presidential elections, plainclothes police murdered an opposition candidate, Yves Volel. Despite these events, the $100 million U.S. aid program for Haiti continued unabated, without even a murmur of public criticism of the government by U.S. officials. On election day in December of 1987, the reign of government-condoned terror escalated to the point where voters were gunned down as they attempted to cast their ballots. Only then did the Reagan administration halt the aid program.[12]

The list of other countries with ties to the United States who have a dismal record of treatment toward their citizens is lengthy—a circumstance that causes great anguish to those concerned about the moral dimension of American foreign policy. The abuse of human beings in communist regimes is widely recognized and criticized as well—by realists and idealists. These governments, however, are largely beyond the influence of the United States; as a result, idealists are more inclined to direct their reformist zeal toward abuses in those countries where America can make a difference through its granting or denial of economic and military assistance. (The difficulties involved in these choices are examined more extensively later in this chapter.)

Systemic Evils   Equally odious to idealists as the involvement of individual nations in atrocities against their own citizens is the larger global system based on a balance of military power. No doubt the most well-known American opponent of this balance-of-power approach to world affairs was President Wilson. Not only was he an articulate critic of national selfishness (which he thought embodied the realist's worldview), but he was also a man of action determined to do something about his beliefs. Wilson sought nothing less than a sweeping reordering of the accepted method for international relations, in which, he said, "the balance was determined by the sword." In place of a precarious balance-of-power approach, he proposed a new world order based on the League of Nations.

In the balance-of-power approach, Wilson saw only an "ugly plan of armed nations, of alliances, of watchful jealousies, of rabid antagonisms, of purposes concealed, running by the subtle channels of intrigue through the veins of people who do not dream what poison is being injected into their systems."[13] Inis Claude offers this summary of *Wilsonianism*: "[Balance of power] stood, [Wilson] thought, for selfish rivalry among autocratic cliques; secret and devious maneuvering; ruthless intrigue; cynical bargaining and unconscionable bartering of helpless and innocent peoples; sacrificing the interests of peoples to the ambitions of militaristic tyrants."[14]

For Wilson, the realists had set too low an ethical standard for the United States. The son of a rural Virginia Presbyterian minister, he aspired to a higher political morality for this nation. Through a fresh system of open alliances based on collective security for all the nations of one world—not two or more worlds in jealous rivalry—the president hoped to replace competitive security with cooperative security. Individual nations would no longer be able to maneuver at will—a cherished precept for the realist—but instead would have to sublimate their selfish interests to the collective good of a peace and order based upon morality, strong antiwar values, and a willingness among all to come to the aid of any victim of aggression. "We shall now be drawn together in a combination of moral force that will be irresistible," declared Wilson. ". . . It is moral force as much as physical that has defeated the effort to subdue the world."[15]

For all his noble aspirations, Wilson seems to have been ill equipped to translate his preachings on collective security into the substance of concrete policy acceptable to other world leaders (or even his own Congress). Observing Wilson for the first time when the president traveled to Paris in 1919 for the League of Nations talks, the noted economist and essayist Lord Keynes judged him to be no match for his rival negotiators, the realists Clemenceau of France and Lloyd George of Great Britain. Whereas the European leaders were cunning and cynical, Wilson—though enjoying "a moral influence throughout the world unequalled in history"—came across as a "nonconformist clergyman . . . very bad at the game of compromise." Wilson brought to Paris ideas that were "nebulous and incomplete," thought Keynes. "He could have preached a sermon on any of them or have addressed a stately prayer to the Almighty for their fulfilment, but he could not frame their concrete application to the actual state of Europe."[16] As a result, Clemenceau and Lloyd George, with their eye for detail and their willingness to accommodate one another—a yielding repugnant to the stubborn and principled Wilson—soon controlled the proceedings.

Keynes vividly portrays Clemenceau's Old World realism here in Perspectives on American Foreign Policy 13.1—a philosophy that occupied in Wilson's mind only a place of moral revulsion.

Who had the correct view of how international affairs ought to be conducted, Woodrow Wilson or Clemenceau? With their strong religious heritage (the colonists after all braved the perils of the New World in search of religious freedom, and today, Americans are more frequent churchgoers than any other Westerners), citizens of the United States are apt to feel some empathy toward Wilson's concern for the small and powerless states so vulnerable in the balance-of-power system. Having some appeal, too, is Wilson's desire to replace the haphazard jockeying of the balance system with an organized approach to peacekeeping.

Yet, despite Wilson's uplifting rhetoric that touched people around the world who longed for a greater assurance of peace in the future, clearly the League of Nations proved a failure. As Hollis W. Barber remarks, "it was unable to cope with the political facts of international life."[17] The punishment of aggression—indeed, even attempts to define the word—proved feckless; sanctions against aggressors were minimal and tardy; the international supervision of selected colonial regions was abandoned, as were arms control measures, because nations contin-

---

Perspectives on American Foreign Policy 13.1

The realism of the French statesman Georges Clemenceau, a contemporary of Woodrow Wilson:

His principles for the Peace [of 1919] can be expressed simply. In the first place, he was a foremost believer in the view of German psychology that the German understands and can understand nothing but intimidation, that he is without honour, pride, or mercy. Therefore you must never negotiate with a German or conciliate him; you must dictate to him. On no other terms will he respect you, or will you prevent him from cheating you. . . . Nations are real things, of which you love one and feel for the rest indifference—or hatred. The glory of the nation you love is a desirable end—but generally to be obtained at your neighbour's expense. The politics of power are inevitable, and there is nothing very new to learn about this war or the end it was fought for; England had destroyed, as in each preceding century, a trade rival; a mighty chapter had been closed in the secular struggle between the glories of Germany and of France. Prudence required some measure of lip service to the "ideals" of foolish Americans and hypocritical Englishmen; but it would be stupid to believe that there is much room in the world, as it really is, for such affairs as the League of Nations, or any sense in the principle of self-determination except as an ingenious formula for rearranging the balance of power in one's own interests.

John Maynard Keynes, "The Council of Four, Paris, 1919," in *Essays and Sketches in Biography* (New York: Meridian, 1956), p. 261.

ued to feel so insecure they were unwilling to risk a cutback in weapons. National sovereignty—the realist's national self-interest—remained ascendant over experiments in international cooperation.

A generation later, the United Nations sidestepped attempts even to try the establishment of a global system of collective security. Its fifty-first article advised that conflict would have to be settled by "individual or collective self-defense," as devised by the powerful sovereign states. Nations did enter into collective security arrangements, but not of the kind Wilson envisioned; instead, NATO and other military pacts resembled more the old balance-of-power system than the Wilsonian one-world alliance for peace. These modern military alliances represent a victory of realism over idealism, pragmatism over theory, prudence over morality.

The balance-of-power system is, in sum, as Claude has put it, "for better or for worse, the operative mechanism of contemporary international politics." In light of this, he advises that "it seems more sensible to build one's hopes upon the possibility that states may be induced to accept restraint and responsibility in the pursuit of their own interest in world order, than upon the expectation that states can somehow be pressed to abdicate their roles in world affairs."[18]

Today, then, realism dominates the foreign policy of the United States and virtually every other nation. When the Reagan administration invaded Grenada, sent troops to Lebanon, bombed Libya, filled the Persian Gulf with warships, and directed semisecret wars in Nicaragua, Afghanistan, and Angola (among others), its purpose was to prevent the Soviet Union or terrorist groups from eroding America's position around the globe. The balance of power would be maintained; force and the containment doctrine would be the means to ensure the balance.

Despite this continuing preeminence of balance-of-power politics, however, morality has by no means been banished altogether from the world stage. On the scales of international politics, American leaders do weigh the problems of hunger and malnutrition abroad, the effects of weapons on civilian populations, the need to help poorer nations with their economic growth, the dangers of global pollution from the factory wastes of the industrial societies, and a good many other questions with obvious ethical components. (Recall from Chapter 4 how Robert Kennedy argued against a U.S. air strike against Cuba in 1962, on grounds that world opinion would condemn the action as immoral.)

The Marshall Plan, the Peace Corps, the 1963 test ban treaty, the Harkin amendment, among other examples, were all motivated in part by an ethical desire to improve the human condition around the world. Granted, questions of power balance dominate the calculations of policymakers; but to view their decisions strictly in realist terms would be an error. The philosophies of most policymakers—some of whom, like Presidents Wilson and Carter and Secretary of State Dulles, have displayed a strong theological bent—are typically an amalgam of realism and idealism.

The significance of ethics to international affairs can be seen further in a series of key decisions (summarized below) faced by leaders in the United States and allied nations during the modern era. The purpose of this summary is to illustrate how, in many instances, moral and "practical" considerations become inextricably interwoven in deliberations over foreign policy.

SELECTED ETHICAL DILEMMAS IN RECENT FOREIGN POLICY DECISIONS

Illustrations from the Second World War

Three decisions during the last global war caused considerable moral anguish in the high councils of government in Britain and the United States. The first case looks at British Prime Minister Neville Chamberlain's quest for peace through an agreement with Hitler.[19]

The Munich Pact   If the League of Nations represents the most conspicuous initial failure of idealism in the twentieth century, the second is Chamberlain's policy of appeasement toward Hitler. One motivation above all others seems to have impelled the prime minister toward his Faustian bargain of "peace in our time" in exchange for Nazi control over Czechoslovakia: Chamberlain's desperate hope that war in Europe could be avoided. He seemed to signal, in Hitler's view at least, that Britain longed for peace at any cost. To the German leader, this evidently meant only one thing: Chamberlain was a coward who could be bullied as the Third Reich fulfilled its territorial ambitions in Czechoslovakia, Poland, and beyond. Hitler misjudged the prime minister in an error of stupendous cost for both sides, not to mention the other nations that would soon be drawn into the conflagration.

Of interest here is the ethical dimension of Chamberlain's decision to trust the promises of the German dictator. If Chamberlain's intuition had been correct that Hitler's appetite could indeed be satiated by the Czech morsel, a great many lives would have been saved in the avoidance of war, though certainly the freedoms of Czech citizens—another moral good—would be trampled in the exchange. The idealism of the prime minister in this instance, however, appears only to have blinded him to Hitler's diabolical intentions. "It is possible to make the historical judgement," concludes a recent study, "that Chamberlain, by allowing this hatred [of war] to dominate his political action, encouraged Hitler's misjudgement, and thus contributed to the outbreak of the very war he so desperately hoped to avoid."[20] In the balancing of competing moral claims, the prime minister badly miscalculated and thus entered the ranks of historical ignominy.

Hiroshima and Nagasaki   Whether or not to use a nuclear weapon against the Japanese in 1945 was a decision laden with obvious and painful ethical implications. The atomic bomb had the destructive power to level cities, sending their civilian population—women, children, the aged—to a fiery death. Even those who survived might wish they had died quickly, because of the long-range illnesses—even possible genetic alterations—that can accompany exposure to the bomb's radioactive emissions. Yet, as in so many major foreign policy decisions, a failure to decide would have had ethical implications, too. Every week during the war in the Pacific, hundreds of American soldiers paid Nature's debt. The United States lost 75,000 soldiers on Okinawa alone. By April 1945, kamikaze raids had sunk thirty-four U.S. ships, including three aircraft carriers. An invasion of Japan would probably have incurred (according to estimates by the Joint Chiefs of Staff) several hundred thousand American casualties, as well as an even larger number of Japanese deaths— far more immediate loss of life than one atomic bomb, even two, would produce. Primarily to save as many American lives as possible, President Truman made the decision to drop his ultimate weapon on Japan.

This decision was not taken lightly. Truman, Secretary of War Henry L. Stimson, and others agonized over the dreadful implications of the new weapon. Even after Truman arrived at the decision to use the bomb, Stimson argued on moral grounds against certain targets. The government's target-selection committee had identified Kyoto, the former capital of Japan and a city of beauty and historical importance, as one potential target. The city was spared after Stimson informed Truman, in a revealing mixture of realism and idealism, that "Japan's help against Russia might be needed in the future but that if Americans destroyed this cultural shrine they would never be forgiven."[21]

Some critics question whether the use of an atomic bomb against any Japanese city was really necessary. They suggest that U.S. authorities could have told their Japanese counterparts about the weapon, then demonstrated its potency in a rural part of Japan, on an uninhabited Pacific atoll near Japan, or perhaps dropped the bomb on a flotilla of Japanese naval ships at sea. The rebuttal to these arguments is twofold. First, the United States had very few bombs and could ill afford to use one in a demonstration; moreover, the demonstration bomb might have been a dud—and a windfall for Japanese scientists to examine. Second, the Japanese were so resolute in their determination to fight down to the last soldier (in fidelity to the ancient Samurai code of the Japanese warrior class) that the Truman administration calculated it would take something as profoundly shocking as the bombing of a major city in order to convince them further resistance was futile.

Critics of the atomic bombing maintain as well that the United States should have provided a clearer warning to the Japanese about which city was to be hit, so that innocent noncombatants could have been evacuated. While in this instance no Ultra secret had to be preserved, a warning might have caused the Japanese to gather American prisoners of war in the target city as a means for deterring the bombing. The Japanese also could have alerted their meager air defenses to the impending attack, concentrating their efforts around the target city.

Less defensible than the bombing of Hiroshima was the attack, only three days later, against Nagasaki. This brief interval left precious little time for the Japanese war cabinet to assemble, consider the danger of further delay, and arrive at a declaration of surrender. The U.S. military had advanced the timetable for the bombing of Nagasaki by a few days because of approaching bad weather—hardly a satisfactory reason for extinguishing the lives of 40,000 people when a second bomb might have been unnecessary. Here was a tragic moment in American foreign policy when a heightened moral sensitivity might have saved a city bustling with human beings.

The Plight of Russian Prisoners   During the Second World War, the German Army on the eastern front captured a large number of Russian soldiers, who were then forced (or occasionally volunteered without threats) to fight against the Stalinist regime in their homeland. After the war, Soviet leaders demanded the return of these soldiers. Some members of the British cabinet balked at the demand, for they realized that the Soviet Union would deal harshly with these "traitors"—quite possibly even kill them, regardless of the circumstances under which each individual Russian came to fight in a German uniform.

In rebuttal, Foreign Secretary Anthony Eden insisted that the cabinet eschew "sentimentality"; larger issues were at stake. From Eden's realist perspective, Britain needed to maintain good relations with the Soviets, in part so that they would return British and American POWs in German territory liberated by the Red Army. Further, he argued, it was undesirable to be "permanently saddled" with Russian prisoners, some of whom, he advised, were quite unsavory types. Anyway, Eden concluded, the British had no legal or moral right to interfere in the affairs of other sovereign states.[22]

At Yalta, the Western powers accepted the reasoning behind Eden's arguments, even though the British secretary of war (among others) expressed revulsion at the idea of forced repatriation. In a secret agreement, the Yalta participants endorsed the return of all the Russians—forcibly if necessary. This agreement led to their mass exodus, often at point of bayonet, back to the U.S.S.R.—1,393,902 in two months alone during 1945. In the process, some people sure to be murdered by the Soviet authorities, and some who were not even Russians (Cossack officers, for example), found themselves swept into the net and sent eastward. Several committed suicide, including entire families, rather than fall into the hands of Soviet authorities.

The tide of moral indignation over this policy began to rise. "A high percentage of Soviet displaced persons consists of women and children," protested a British general in Austria, "against whom the use of force by British soldiers would be contrary to normal British practice. ..."[23] British Field Marshall Alexander had already expressed dismay to his government. The supreme allied commander, General Eisenhower, responded to this criticism by defining more narrowly—over the objections of the British Foreign Office—those who would be repatriated to include only former soldiers of the Red Army and individuals who had clearly collaborated with the Nazis.

In the case of the Russian soldiers, two moral goods were placed in conflict. For Western diplomats, a desire to maintain peace by mollifying the Soviet demands for a return of their soldiers; for the military commanders, who had to carry out the day-to-day removal of the Russians and were eyewitnesses to the personal tragedies inflicted by the policy, a desire to help individuals out of a terrible situation. In this instance, the plight of individuals finally won out over strategic interests—a result aided no doubt by the souring relations between the West and Premier Stalin (who himself had already broken several of the Yalta agreements) and by the expression of moral outrage from key members of the British military establishment.

Ethics and Nuclear Deterrence

As emphasized at the beginning of this book, nothing so defines the era following the Second World War as the existence of nuclear weapons. Their proliferation and stockpiling not only has led to a widespread sense of anxiety in the world about their possible use but has raised subtle yet profound ethical questions about nuclear warfare and how to guard against it (deterrence). These questions of *nuclear ethics* have passed beyond the closed doors of lofty decision councils; as revealed by mass protests in the United States, Great Britain, and West Germany, public attention to the danger of nuclear war has risen dramatically in recent years. In 1984, this issue stimulated the largest public demonstration in American history, as advocates of a nuclear freeze (the simultaneous cessation of nuclear warhead production in both the United States and the Soviet Union) rallied in the streets of New York City.

The freeze movement failed to achieve its objective, but did succeed in drawing large numbers of U.S. citizens into the nuclear debate. Across the land, in cities and small towns, people convened to discuss the freeze and related proposals, and passed freeze resolutions in their city councils—a rare excursion of local government into the realm of foreign policy. Behind these discussions and debates lay the fundamental moral question of the nuclear age: can the possession of nuclear weapons—poised in their launch tubes ready to annihilate millions of people, perhaps destroy all humanity—be justified?

Kant and the Consequentialists   One school of thought on this question argues that reliance on nuclear weapons to keep the superpowers at bay—the theory of deterrence—must be rejected, for it is patently wrong to place in jeopardy the lives of millions of noncombatant civilians.[24] This argument represents a radical break with existing policy, and in its stress on the wrongness of even the *threat* to kill—the very core of deterrence theory—it finds itself in harmony with the beliefs of Immanuel Kant, the German philosopher (1724–1804). "Do what is right though the world shall perish," admonished Kant, who more than anything cherished the moral purity of the individual. Applying the logic of this argument to deterrence, *modern-day Kantians* maintain that what one ethically cannot do—murder millions of innocent men, women, and children—one cannot *intend* to do either, with nuclear missiles ready for firing at a moment's notice; therefore, the nuclear option must be discarded altogether.

In this spirit, the theologian Paul Ramsey draws an analogy between nuclear deterrence and the tying of babies to the bumpers of automobiles during the holiday season. Under these conditions, people would presumably drive more carefully and lives would be saved—a moral good; but the method used would be so morally repugnant as to be clearly wrong and unacceptable.

A second school in Western moral tradition, the *consequentialists*, offers a different focus—on the outcome of an act, not the goodness of the individual involved. From this perspective, nuclear deterrence serves a useful purpose, despite the sword of Damocles which it suspends above humanity. Since the bombing of Nagasaki, no nuclear weapon has been fired in anger; the world has escaped the outbreak of global conflict between major powers—a third world war—quite probably as a consequence in part of the deterrent effect provided by these weapons. The existence of nuclear weapons aimed at one another has become a part of the human condition ("existential deterrence," in the phrase of one keen observer[25]), to be accepted as the price one must pay to maintain a balance of power and, thereby, thwart aggression by the major powers. For the consequentialists, the *effect* of one's decision is of overriding importance, not the purity of the decision maker.

Joseph S. Nye, Jr., argues that both the Kantian and the consequentialist traditions "express important truths."[26] But, using a vivid scenario, he illustrates how difficult decisions can be for proponents of both traditions (see Perspectives on American Foreign Policy 13.2).

In the setting presented in the scenario from Nye, would you join the ranks of the Kantians or the consequentialists? What if the stakes were raised to, say, the possibility of saving a hundred or a thousand peasants rather than one? Or, in another scenario, what if a terrorist clutched a child (perhaps your own) in one arm to protect himself, while with his free hand he gripped a plunger on an explosive device which could detonate a nuclear bomb in the heart of a metropolis, if his demands went unmet? Should one shoot through the body of the child to kill the terrorist and save the million-plus inhabitants of the city? Would Kant himself refuse?

"At some point does not integrity become the ultimate egoism of fastidious self-

---

Perspectives on American Foreign Policy   13.2

The Kantian and consequentialist schools of ethics: a hypothetical case:

Imagine that you are visiting a Central American country and you happen upon a village square where an army captain is about to order his men to shoot two peasants lined up against a wall. When you ask the reason, you are told someone in this village shot at the captain's men last night. When you object to the killing of possibly innocent people, you are told that civil wars do not permit moral niceties. Just to prove the point that we all have dirty hands in such situations, the captain hands you a rifle and tells you that if you will shoot one peasant, he will free the other. Otherwise both die. He warns you not to try any tricks because his men have their guns trained on you. Will you shoot one person with the consequences of saving one, or will you allow both to die but preserve your moral integrity by refusing to play his dirty game?

From Joseph S. Nye, Jr., *Nuclear Ethics* (New York: Free Press, 1986), p. 18, adapted from Bernard Williams, in J. J. C. Smart and Bernard Williams, *Utilitarianism: For and Against* (Cambridge, England: Cambridge University Press, 1973), p. 98.

righteousness," Nye asks, "in which the purity of the self is more important than the lives of countless others?" He notes that, in the conduct of foreign policy, the absolutist ethics of Kant "bear a heavier burden of proof in the nuclear age than ever before."[27]

One of the most thoughtful attempts to go beyond theory and hypothetical cases about nuclear war came out of the National Conference of Catholic Bishops on War and Peace, held in 1983. Following the conference, the bishops issued a pastoral letter which summed up their deliberations on the real-world moral implications of nuclear deterrence.

The Bishops' Letter   The letter written by the Catholic bishops is filled with tension, mirroring the ambivalence felt by the broader public as well toward the existence of nuclear weapons and the doctrine of deterrence.[28] At first blush, the bishops seem to break radically with the "balance of terror" (Churchill's phrase) that deterrence represents. In absolute, Kantian terms, they reject the first use by the United States of any nuclear weapons. Further, drawing on the moral principle of noncombatant immunity, they shun the use of nuclear weapons at any time against "population centers or other predominantly civilian targets" (the countervalue targeting discussed in Chapter 10). "The moral demands of Catholic teaching require resolute willingness not to intend or to do moral evil," write the bishops, "even to save our own lives or the lives of those we love."

Yet, the bishops pulled back from a complete condemnation of nuclear deterrence. In their view, "in current conditions 'deterrence' based on balance, certainly not as an end in itself but as a step on the way toward a progressive disarmament, may still be judged morally acceptable." In this brief statement, the bishops obliquely acknowledged that deterrence might have some redeeming value as a source of restraint against belligerent acts between the major powers—at least until the human race had

passed beyond the nuclear crisis in its advance toward maturity. They were unwilling, therefore, to exclude the second use of nuclear weapons against military (counterforce) targets. "The nature of that use is never spelled out," recalls one of the conference participants, "but the criteria point toward a limited second strike force targeted on military objectives."[29] Thus, the circle the bishops had begun to draw against the evils of deterrence was never fully closed; left open was "a centimeter of ambiguity."[30]

The bishops arrived at this partial endorsement of deterrence out of a commitment to one overriding moral imperative: the prevention of nuclear war. If, as seemed possible, a second-strike, counterforce strategy had helped to keep the superpowers at bay, then—as the bishops shifted from a Kantian to a consequentialist's perspective—a conditional (no first use, no countervalue) moral acceptance of deterrence might be justifiable. Barely.

The position on deterrence taken by the bishops grows out of the *just-war tradition*—a compromise between pacifism and militarism. According to this ancient philosophy of war, a nation (like a person) has the right to defend itself against the unjust use of force. "Governments threatened by armed unjust aggression *must* defend their people," stated the bishops. In its use of self-defense, however, the moral nation will follow certain limitations on its use of force. Chief among them is the *principle of discrimination*, that is, avoidance of the use of force against noncombatants (another way of expressing the idea of noncombatant immunity), and the *principle of proportionality*. This second principle requires that one's use of force be roughly equivalent in scope and magnitude to that employed by the belligerent. If the U.S.S.R. were to strike against a single American nuclear submarine, retaliation by the United States against the city of Moscow would be out of proportion; the appropriate response, according to this principle, would be a counterstrike against a Soviet nuclear submarine.

Thus the bishops came to rest on a counter-force, but not first-strike, position—though they recognized how problematic limits on nuclear war might be in the heat of battle. For the time being, however, until a more mature world order arrived, the centimeter of acceptability for nuclear weapons had to be granted.

The letter also reflected political realities within the Catholic church. The church consists of a mix of Kantian and consequentialist moral perspectives. For the American bishops to have rejected the church's consequentialist traditions would have been to venture beyond the bounds of Vatican permissibility. Moreover, papal doctrine aside, most members of the conference had reached the conclusion that a full closing of the antideterrence circle would seriously undermine the credibility of the nuclear standoff, which might in itself prove to be a dangerous moral error. Finally, the release of a pastoral letter requires a two-thirds vote of the conference and, to enhance legitimacy, tradition expects the support of some 85 percent of the membership; this meant broad support had to be achieved through compromises reached between the Kantians and the consequentialists. In this sense, the preparation of the letter was "something of a political high-wire act."[31]

The conclusions drawn by the Catholic Conference on War and Peace stirred public criticism from various quarters, including from within the church itself. An American archbishop disagreed sharply with the pastoral letter and insisted that no Catholic commander of a nuclear submarine or missile silo could morally turn the key for weapons launch under *any* circumstances.[32] French bishops maintained that the actual *use* of nuclear weapons would indeed be immoral, but—rejecting the Kantian perspective—the mere *threat* to use these weapons (deterrence) did not constitute their use; thus, according to this wing of the Catholic church, one could evidently bluff so long as one did not follow through—an odd prescription, since the act of bluffing would seem to have no

credibility if it were clear in advance that one would never go beyond the bluff itself.

Other critics pointed to the practical difficulty of distinguishing countervalue from counterforce. As Susan Okum has noted, to think of targeting simply in terms of countervalue and countersilo is a mistake; the United States, like the Soviet Union presumably, has a whole range and mix of targeting priorities, many of which overlap.[33] Some sixty U.S. counterforce targets are reputedly within the city limits of Moscow.[34]

Some observers further chastised the American bishops for failing to address the potential virtues of the Strategic Defense Initiative. In their view, strongly supported by President Reagan, a Star Wars shield represented the best moral position, for eventually (if it worked) this defense would make nuclear weapons obsolete. The SDI umbrella would at last remove the constant threat of Armageddon brought on by a downpour of strategic warheads.[35] And, from still another perspective, some remained convinced that mutual assured destruction (MAD)—the essence of deterrence—was a condition here to stay, Jesuitical exegeses and visions of impenetrable space shields notwithstanding. The atomic genie could not be stuffed back into the bottle, in the cliché, and so it had to be dealt with in realistic terms—that is, through deterrence which, so far, had worked. While immoral in the Kantian sense, MAD had the highly moral consequence of fending off a third world war.

The debate over nuclear ethics continues to be spirited—and inconclusive. So, too, is the debate over another controversial component of American foreign policy: the use of secret intelligence operations.

The Ethics of Strategic Intelligence

As discussed in Chapters 8 and 9, the United States engages in three forms of strategic intelligence operations: espionage, covert action (CA), and counterintelligence (CI). Each has a moral dimension—*intelligence ethics*—that has troubled critics of America's foreign policy.

Espionage   Today espionage is practiced around the globe by every nation that can afford a network of spies. Yet, in the 1920s, one leading American official, Secretary of State Henry Stimson, found the practice morally repugnant and ordered the Department of State to halt its cloak-and-dagger operations. "Gentlemen don't read other people's mail," he sniffed.[36] But as Stimson became increasingly wary of the dangers to the United States posed by the Axis powers, he abandoned his moral purity on this subject and encouraged the American secret service to procure the best information it could throughout the world, using whatever clandestine methods would work.

Despite its widespread practice, and the unlikelihood that any major nation will adopt the puritan attitudes of the early Stimson, much thought has been given recently within the United States to the question of whether, even in this dangerous world, some restraint ought to be practiced in the use of the "dark arts." Critics have expressed strong reservations about what they perceive to be excesses in the practice of covert action and counterintelligence, and some aspects of espionage have raised doubts as well.

On one conclusion most Americans stand in agreement: the government of the United States has a moral obligation to guard its citizens against attacks from abroad. No more Pearl Harbors. In order to honor this obligation, the government spends upwards of $13 billion a year (the reader may recall from Chapter 8) on various strategic intelligence activities. Still, in connection with this moral obligation, another ethical question arises: Should any limits be placed on the intelligence agencies in their quest for information to protect this nation? While the response of some experts (particularly within the intelligence agencies) is a resounding no, observers with a finer concern for civil liberties argue on behalf of some restraint.

The argument has both a domestic and a foreign dimension. On the domestic side, critics maintain that certain American groups and institutions ought not to be used by the CIA (or other secret agencies) for the purposes of intelligence collection. High on this "off-limits" list are the media, accorded a special status by the Constitution's First Amendment (with its bow to freedom of the press). American intelligence agencies have long been attracted to the employment of media personnel abroad, chiefly because correspondents have excellent access to foreign countries and their leaders. During the 1950s, several U.S. journalists worked secretly for the CIA.[37] This relationship has come under fire, however, as a result of the so-called new morality of the post-Watergate era.

Critics of CIA-media ties argue that it is unethical for intelligence officials to recruit U.S. media personnel for espionage operations. A newsperson on the payroll of a secret agency might no longer be able to maintain his or her objectivity—especially on intelligence-related stories. Moreover, if a reporter with newspaper (or other media) credentials were caught spying, the credibility of all U.S. correspondents overseas would be eroded—regardless of whether they were or were not intelligence "assets." The end result of a CIA-media bond, the argument continues, would be an undermining of the free and democratic press within the United States and the endangering of its reporters abroad.

In response to the vocal ethical denunciation of reporters as spies by various media associations and by the U.S. Congress, the CIA has backed away from the relationship. Internal CIA regulations now prohibit the use of accredited U.S. media personnel by the nation's intelligence agencies for the purpose of espionage (leaving American free-lance writers and all foreign journalists open to CIA recruitment).[38]

Another domestic institution attractive to the CIA is the university. Since its creation in 1947, the agency has had a wide array of connections with America's institutions of higher learning.[39]

Initially, the attraction stemmed from the teeming reservoirs which campuses represent for the recruitment of intelligence officers. Many of today's CIA officials were recruited by professors with ties to the agency who passed on the names of promising students.

As more and more foreign students came to study in the United States in the postwar period, the universities took on an added allure for U.S. intelligence officials: here was an opportunity to recruit potential foreign spies in the secure environment of the American campus, rather than overseas in the often dangerous setting of the student's homeland. Some of the foreign students might even turn out to be leaders of their native land one day. What an irresistible intelligence coup to have recruited them at an early age within the United States! The universities held still another appeal to intelligence professionals: the foreign travel of professors. As with the media, why not have selected professors carry out espionage operations while engaged in their own research abroad?

Critics object to CIA-campus relations, too. The university should be a free and open place, they maintain, not a location for secret operations, where professors observe and screen American students for intelligence jobs, where foreign students become the objects of intensive surveillance and recruitment efforts designed to turn them into traitors against their own countries, where professors are not so much objective scholars in search of truth but paid assets of the federal government, a place where cloaks replace gowns. And just as the apprehension of U.S. correspondents caught spying abroad endangers other correspondents, so, too, does the discovery of a single American professor engaged in espionage harm the reputation of all other scholars—most of whom have no ties whatsoever to an intelligence agency.

Other domestic groups have clamored for protection from use by the CIA: missionaries abroad, Peace Corps volunteers and Fulbright scholars (two groups never used by the CIA), and a long list of others who travel abroad and fear that suspected connections to the CIA will curb their freedom of movement and possibly even make them targets of terrorist groups. Not without frustration about the impairment of their agency's ability to gather information abroad, CIA directors began in 1967 and then more extensively in 1976 (in both instances in response to executive and legislative investigations) to move away from the broad use of American groups for intelligence purposes. Though many groups continue to be "fair game" from the CIA's point of view (unaccredited free-lance journalists, among them), the agency has circumscribed its role on campuses somewhat through the issuance of new internal regulations. Professors, for instance, can no longer turn over the names of American students for recruitment purposes without their knowledge and permission (it remains "open season" on the recruitment of foreign students, however).[40]

As for ethics and espionage abroad, a related set of issues concerns some observers. Should the United States suborn foreign media personnel? *Pravda*, yes; but what about the media in fellow democracies, say, reporters for the *Frankfurter Allgemeine* or *Die Zeit* in West Germany, or *Le Monde* in France? The realist would say: of course, if the CIA is clever enough to recruit reporters on the staff of these newspapers, and if the reporters can carry out espionage or propaganda assignments useful to the United States, then all to the good. The idealist, however, might demur: should not America's unwillingness to see its own reporters recruited as spies be applied as well to reporters in other democracies? On this point, the cries for reform have been considerably softer within the United States than on the question of CIA "interference" with strictly American groups, and no prohibitions regarding foreign media personnel have been adopted by the CIA.

Worrisome also for those concerned about the ethical side of American foreign policy has been the way in which the CIA trains its officers, and how they acquire assets abroad. Young American CIA recruits are taught a code that seems to eschew moral considerations, advancing instead a doctrine of dishonesty that becomes a part of the officer's tradecraft. "A man should not have too many ideals . . . " advised a U.S. intelligence manual written for the OSS, and this norm lingers on.[41]

A primary job of an American intelligence officer overseas is to persuade a local national to turn against his or her own country (Chapter 8). This in itself is an activity that stirs ethical qualms in the minds of some moralists. They find it appalling that the CIA teaches its spy handlers (U.S. case officers) how to undermine the moral fiber of other human beings, transforming foreign nationals—even within democracies—into traitors. The CIA response to this criticism rests on the premise that it seeks a higher moral good: the protection of the United States and its citizens through a wide network of spies in other lands. Moreover, no one holds a gun to a foreigner's head during the recruitment process; for money, sex, or some other reason (quite often, an ideological dislike for the existing regime), the spy enters into an arrangement with the CIA under his or her own free will.

Still, the moralist may wonder how well the CIA's treatment of its spies abroad comports with the high-minded principles so often espoused by American leaders.[42] Sometimes the U.S. intelligence agencies have recruited individuals of notably unsavory character (including former Nazis) to spy on behalf of the United States. Some intelligence documents support the spy novelist John Le Carré's image of the agent as less than human (from the viewpoint of his handler), to be used and discarded without sentimentality. "No agent should be recruited without serious thought being given to the means of disposing of him after his usefulness has ended," stated an OSS manual matter-of-factly.[43] When the United States evacuated from Saigon in 1975, left behind (according to

an account of a former CIA officer) were scores of spies who had worked secretly for the United States during the Vietnamese war, along with files that revealed their identity—sure death warrants once in the hands of the invading North Vietnamese army.[44]

Covert Action   Far more controversial has been the ethical debate over covert action, America's secret intervention into the affairs of other nations (Chapter 9). Obviously, policies involving the bribery of politicians, the planting of lies in foreign newspapers, the contamination of foreign agricultural products, dynamiting oil storage facilities, mining harbors, and the like—not to mention attempted assassinations of foreign heads of state—raise serious moral questions. Assassination is the most extreme case. Outside the bounds of overt warfare, should the government of the United States ever order its secret agencies to murder someone overseas who has become a nuisance—perhaps even a danger—to the United States?

Remember from Chapter 9 former CIA director John McCone's argument that the assassination plots against Castro during the 1960s may have been reasonable in light of the times: "Here was a man that turned over the sacred soil of Cuba in 1962 to the Soviets to plant nuclear warhead short-range missiles, which could destroy every city east of the Mississippi."[45] A veteran intelligence officer speculates further that "if Congress had been asked to vote on the assassination of Fidel Castro in the early 1960s, the measure would have passed by a least a two-to-one majority, and the person who introduced the bill would have been given a medal."[46]

Be that as it may, by 1975 the nation's leaders had decided that assassination went beyond the pale of moral acceptability for this country. Beginning with an executive order on intelligence issued by President Ford in 1975, each president has officially prohibited assassination as a policy of the United States—though, recall, the existence of this order failed to deter the Reagan administration's bombing of the home of the Libyan leader, Qaddafi, which, except for good luck on his part, might well have killed him (and reportedly did kill his adopted infant daughter and severely injured his two sons, as well as hapless patients in a nearby French hospital and other civilians).[47]

A man widely reputed to be a terrorist leader—like Qaddafi—ought to be assassinated, argue some realists (or "strategists"), before he is able to inflict damage against the United States (Qaddafi reportedly attempted, without success, to purchase a nuclear weapon from the People's Republic of China), just as, in retrospect, the murder of Hitler before he achieved power in Germany would have been a good idea. Yet, does the United States wish to become, in the words of one former senator, a glorified "godfather" (in the mob sense of the word), putting out contracts on the lives of foreign leaders?[48] Should this country use drugs and chemicals to incapacitate individuals abroad who criticize America? Should rubber gloves, gauze masks, hypodermic syringes, and lethal biological materials be instruments of U.S. foreign policy? Should the CIA manufacture electric dart guns ("noise-free disseminators") and poison darts the size of sewing needles tipped with deadly poisons ("non-discernible microbioinoculators"), for the quick and silent elimination of foreign leaders who fail to support this nation's international objectives? During the 1960s, these "shoulds" (as the reader knows from Chapter 9) were answered with a secret, un-Kantian yes by CIA officials.[49]

Even from a practical perspective (morals aside), some critics wonder how useful a policy of assassination is. If Castro had been killed, he would have been replaced most likely by his brother—no improvement at all, a man perhaps even more truculent toward the United States. As former CIA Director William Colby has observed, even the murder of Hitler would have provided no guarantee that the evils of the Third Reich could have been avoided, since next in line were men like Hermann Göring, equally criminal and immoral.[50] Further, to kill other leaders is to invite the murder of America's own chief of state, who in our open society is quite vulnerable. Assassination plots open a Pandora's box.

Beyond assassination, the stomachs of idealists turn as well over the thought of bribing foreign politicians in democratic societies and planting stories in their free media—operations that outrage Americans when carried out by foreign governments against this country. (After investigative journalists discovered that the government of South Korea was bribing U.S. legislators in the 1970s, public outcry led to an investigation and indictments.) Such practices are commonly implemented by the CIA overseas, though, in operations approved (since December of 1974) by the NSC.

Perhaps most questionable of all in the minds of critics are the moral implications of large-scale paramilitary operations, for here thousands of individuals are affected—often in the most brutal manner. Frequently, the results of the CIA's secret wars have been disastrous for those the United States has offered to help. In the end, they have often been deserted: Ukrainian émigrés left to await their deaths in Carpathian caves, the Meo tribesmen of Laos eking out an existence in Thai refugee camps, South Vietnamese intelligence agents left behind to face North Vietnamese and Vietcong interrogators, abandoned Khambas in Tibet, Nationalist Chinese in Burma, the Bay of Pigs invaders, the Kurds on the Iran-Iraq border—all, in the words of one observer, "so many causes and peoples briefly taken up by the CIA and then tossed aside like broken toys. . . ."[51]

When the United States resorts to assassination and other unsavory operations, it must hire disreputable characters to carry them out. In its efforts to murder Castro, the CIA turned to the likes of the mobsters John Rosselli, Sam Giancana, and Santos Trafficante—hardly the sort of companions George Washington, Thomas Jefferson, and James Madison would have encouraged for government officials. In one internal document, a CIA official described an agent selected for covert operations in Africa: "He is indeed aware of the precepts of right and wrong, but if he is given an assignment which may be morally wrong in the eyes of the world, but necessary because his case officer ordered him to carry it out, then it is right, and he will dutifully undertake appropriate action for its execution without pangs of conscience. In a word, he can rationalize all actions."[52]

Realists swallow twice and accept the necessity of dealing with witches ("Fair is foul, and foul is fair: Hover through the fog and filthy air") as the price Americans must pay to protect their global interests. The CIA is not the Boy Scouts of America, one former agency director has observed, nor, former Secretary of State Henry Kissinger is fond of pointing out, is it engaged in missionary work. But idealists, like Roger Fisher in Perspectives on American Foreign Policy 13.3, refuse to forget the noble principles extolled in the nation's founding documents and in the speeches of its leaders down through the years; they shake their heads at the hypocrisy which bribery, lies, and murder make of these principles.

The reader may recall the realist's injunction on covert action expressed in the Doolittle Report of 1954 (Chapter 2): "... We must learn to subvert, sabotage and destroy our enemies by more clever, more sophisticated and more effective methods than those used against us. ..." Many Americans object to this philosophy. Why does this country conduct secret wars against "leaders of small, weak countries that could not possibly threaten the United States?" asked Senator Church following his committee's investigation of the CIA in 1975.

Perspectives on American Foreign Policy   13.3

Roger Fisher, a professor of law at Harvard University, on the ethics of covert action:

Our conduct should be principled and just. Conduct that is wrong for others is wrong for us. ... Two hundred years ago we knew some "truths to be self-evident," that there were "certain unalienable rights," and that we should determine our conduct by according "a decent respect to the opinions of mankind. ..."

We do not truly seek a world in which every country dances to our tune. It is not a world in which foreign leaders are secretly in our pay, in which people who disagree with us mysteriously die or disappear. We want a world that is filled with different ideas, different goals and different values. ...

We should join the battle where we can win.

Let's compete in terms of freedom, candor, generosity and tolerance for the views of others. We are far more likely to gain world support on that battlefield than by competing for prizes in subversion, deception, bribery and illegality.

When we choose our weapons, let's choose ones we are good at using—like the Marshall Plan—not ones that we are bad at—like the Bay of Pigs. To join some adversaries in the grotesque world of poison dart-guns and covert operations is to give up the most powerful weapons we have: idealism, morality, due process of law, and belief in the freedom to disagree, including the right of other countries to disagree with ours. ...

Roger Fisher, "The Fatal Flaw in Our Spy System," *Boston Globe*, February 1, 1976.

He remarked with dismay that "no country was too small, no foreign leader too trifling, to escape our attention."[53] Influential Europeans, too, have expressed consternation over America's covert interventions. "How impoverished must a country be before it is not a threat to the U.S. government?" asks the West German author Günter Grass, with Nicaragua in mind.[54]

The powerful lure of covert action for presidents was demonstrated dramatically in the Middle East during the Carter and the Reagan administrations. Both presidents were frustrated by their inability to gain the release of American hostages captured in this region. Carter attempted a paramilitary operation to rescue hostages from the U.S. embassy in Tehran, and failed; Reagan resorted to the covert sale of arms to Iran in exchange for that country's help in gaining the release of hostages in Lebanon, with limited success and an ensuing scandal.

The two operations differed in an important respect, however. The Reagan administration never reported its covert action to Congress (as required by the Intelligence Oversight Act). The operation also involved, according to subsequent congressional investigations, a violation of other statutes (including the Export Control Act, which prohibits the shipment of weapons to nations harboring terrorists). Further (as the

An American helicopter lies in ruins after an accident in the deserts of Iran during an aborted attempt by the Carter administration to rescue American hostages held in Tehran (April 1980). (UPI/Bettmann Newsphotos)

reader will recall from earlier chapters), blocked by the Boland amendments in their attempts to finance the contras in Nicaragua through the normal appropriations process, NSC staff members sought—with the help and encouragement of high-level CIA officials—to circumvent this law by channeling the profits from the Iran arms sale to the contras. The NSC staff also raised funds for the contras through other means—the "privatization" of covert action, based on funding from wealthy Americans and foreign governments like South Africa and Brunei (Chapter 9). For critics, this episode stood as the ultimate immoral use of covert action: a secret attempt to subvert the sanctity of law and constitutional procedure upon which the freedom of this republic dearly depends.[55]

Counterintelligence The Iran-contra affair was not the first time intelligence operations had resulted in the violation of U.S. law. Another egregious instance occurred during the Nixon years, growing out of that administration's concern about counterintelligence.[56] This aspect of foreign policy is devoted to the protection of the United States against operations carried out by the KGB (the Soviet CIA and FBI combined) and other hostile intelligence services. During the war in Vietnam, both Presidents Johnson and Nixon remained convinced that leaders of the antiwar protests had to be agents of the Soviet Union, receiving funds through the KGB. The White House enlisted the CIA and its sister agencies to substantiate this hypothesis. During the Johnson presidency, the agencies reported that no evidence could be found to support the allegation of a significant Soviet connection to U.S. domestic unrest; rather, the student protesters genuinely opposed the war and were prepared to say so without help from anyone.

When President Nixon entered the White House, he refused to accept this conclusion and, in 1970, gave one of his young aides, Tom Charles Huston, authority to prepare a master spy plan directing the intelligence agencies to

examine the hypothesis once more. As the reader may remember from Chapter 9, the *Huston plan*, signed by the president, allowed the CIA and other agencies to carry out espionage operations within the United States against antiwar dissenters and radical black organizations—in violation of several laws, including the 1947 National Security Act, which prohibits the CIA from domestic operations. As the historian Theodore H. White has written, the options in the Huston plan authorized federal agents to reach "all the way to every mailbox, every college campus, every telephone, every home."[57]

When FBI Director J. Edgar Hoover complained about the illegal provisions in the Huston plan (ironically, since he himself had approved similar operations for his bureau in the past), President Nixon withdrew his approval and the scheme was abandoned—or so the White House thought. Six years later, congressional investigators discovered that, despite Nixon's rescission of the order, the CIA and other agencies continued domestic surveillance operations spelled out in the Huston plan and, more astonishing still, had in fact been carrying them out years before they had been authorized by President Nixon—a fact they never bothered to tell Huston or the president!

The agencies turned to these illegal methods of counterintelligence not out of any fear that the KGB was influencing antiwar protesters or "black power" groups, but because counterintelligence officers within the agencies sought to expand their coverage of suspected foreign intelligence officers—regardless of the fact that U.S. laws prohibited operations by the CIA at home (or by other agencies without proper warrants). As an FBI intelligence officer told a congressional investigator: "I was a Soviet specialist. I felt—and still feel—that we need technical coverage [electronic eavesdropping] of every Soviet in the country. I didn't give a damn about the Black Panthers [a radical black group of the 1960s] myself, but I did about the Russians."[58]

Counterintelligence is an important and respectable defensive arm of American foreign policy; the United States must know about, and protect itself from, clandestine operations conducted against it by hostile nations. But as revealed by investigations into the Huston plan, the misuse of counterintelligence can result in a fundamental moral perversion: the turning of secret agencies against the very citizens they were established to protect.

Human Rights

A display at the Carter Presidential Library in Atlanta proudly proclaims that "no issue was closer to Jimmy Carter than *human rights*," that is, the advancement of basic freedoms and needs—food, housing, education, health care—to which all people are entitled. A strongly religious "born again" Christian, President Carter blended his foreign policy with a larger measure of moralism than any president since Woodrow Wilson (another deeply religious man)—much of it addressed to the dignity of human beings throughout the world. The remarks of his national security director, Dr. Zbigniew Brzezinski, near the end of the administration's time in office, reveal this strong emphasis on ethics. Brzezinski explained that the purpose of the Carter administration had been to be both "compassionately and morally concerned" while at the same time "preserving a stable balance of power"[59]—the balancing act referred to by Kissinger earlier in this chapter.

Freedom and Human Dignity   In Brzezinski's view, the United States should be guided by both the power of principle and the power of military strength (though his critics maintain that, in practice, he tilted toward the latter[60]). In his writings at least, Brzezinski rejected the notion that the two were in conflict; he chastized Nixon and Kissinger for a "tendency to dismiss moral concerns in foreign policy as somehow equivalent to sentimentality." Nor did he spare the Democratic Party's "tendency

to dismiss the importance of [military] power as somehow historically irrelevant." The Carter administration, he said, had "tried as best we could on the one hand to make the United States relevant to the moral concerns of our times, to the aspirations of peoples who previously have not participated in the global political process, while at the same time revitalizing and making credible the presence of American power in a world that is very turbulent, a world which without such American power could easily slide into anarchy and growing conflict."[61]

The moral concerns of the Carter administration focused most clearly on the plight of the world's developing nations. More than ever before, the government of the United States shifted its attention toward relations with the poorer nations (the North-South global axis) instead of its usual fixation with the industrial states (East-West). The president and his foreign policy advisers often spoke of the dignity that should be accorded the former colonial powers; they stressed the rightness of majority rule for South Africa, a relationship of greater political equality between large and small nations, and a fairer sharing of the world's economic wealth.

"Human rights has been a special concern of this administration," remarked Carter's second secretary of state, former Senator Edmund S. Muskie (who succeeded Cyrus Vance in 1980). "We stand for the right of people to be free of torture and repression, to choose their leaders, to participate in the decisions that affect their daily lives, to speak and write and travel freely." In Muskie's view, military arms were insufficient to defend America's vital interests: "We must also arm ourselves with the conviction that our values have increasing power in today's world."[62]

Muskie acknowledged, however, that "there are limits on our capacity to influence affairs in other countries." The violations of human rights by powerful nations like the Soviet Union were difficult to remedy, for the United States had limited leverage. In a review of U.S.–Soviet relations, the diplomatic historian John Lewis Gaddis concluded that America has little opportunity to force changes in internal Soviet policies through trade or other inducements and sanctions; the U.S.S.R. is self-sufficient enough to endure penalties imposed by the West[63]—the same conclusion the Bush administration reached with respect to the PRC in 1989 when pondering how to react to its brutal repression against pro-democracy students.

Moreover, the resources of the United States are limited, and this nation can ill afford to fight freedom wars for every oppressed country; surely, this is a central lesson of the civil war in Vietnam. And even the dictators of small nations can be fiercely resistant to U.S. pressures for democracy; the efforts of the Bush administration, for example, to bring economic and political sanctions against General Manuel Antonio Noriega of Panama in an effort to drive him from office failed; it required controversial military invasion (December 1989). Realizing its limits, the Carter administration therefore pursued what Muskie referred to as a "practical approach," doing what it could, where it could, "holding up the banner of human rights."[64]

Dictators of the Right and Left   As a practical matter, American officials must often make a choice between support for right wing, traditional autocrats (the authoritarians; Chapter 11), on the one hand—oligarchies usually unwilling to redistribute resources in their societies and sometimes engaged in gross violations of human rights, including torture—and, on the other hand, left wing revolutionaries (totalitarians) who seek a broader sharing of resources and speak of democracy, even though they have Marxist leanings and ties with Moscow and themselves often resort to brutality. Sometimes the U.S. government has sided against the authoritarians—though rarely, with the Carter administration's backing of the revolution which took place in Nicaragua a conspicuous exception. The Nicaraguan dictator, Somoza—who for years used U.S. aid for his own enrichment and stamped out internal dissent with the harsh use of his National Guard thugs—stood as a perfect illustration of someone the Carter administration found repugnant, and in this instance, the administration could do something about it by providing political and financial support for Somoza's Sandinista opponents. Whether the successful revolution led to a better situation in Nicaragua under the rule of the Marxist Sandinistas remains a subject of heated debate. Most observers, though, have been disappointed by the failure of the Sandinistas to carry out the democratic reforms which had given force and legitimacy to their revolutionary battle cry, and in 1990, Nicaraguans voted the Sandinistas out of power.

The Reagan administration proved to be less equivocal on the choice between authoritarian and totalitarian regimes (at least in its first term): the United States must resist the latter, because of their inherently repulsive (Marxist) characteristics and their inevitable ties to Moscow. A leading spokesman for the administration offered this realist's view of Nicaragua:

> By 1967 the Soviets were writing in theoretical journals about opportunities for tying down the United States in the Western Hemisphere and rendering us less able to act in such remote places as Europe and Asia. . . . We believe it would be bad for the people of the region and bad for the United States for there to be installed one-party, Marxist-Leninist states integrated into the Soviet bloc and willing to have their territory serve as bases for the projection of Soviet military power in the hemisphere.[65]

As for ethics, according to the Reagan administration, the overriding moral consideration was to protect the hemisphere against the export of communism by Soviet-backed Sandinistas. Better a heinous right wing, anticommunist dictator than a regime in collusion with the Soviet Union.

For some thoughtful observers, this debate has had an unfortunate tendency to focus on Soviet-American strategic concerns at the expense of those who most deserve consideration: the victims of repression in the developing world. In Argentina and Chile during the 1970s, for example, hundreds of citizens who criticized their government or refused to cooperate with officials (such as reluctant physicists asked to work on the development of an atomic bomb in Argentina) simply disappeared from sight. These individuals, who came to be called the *disappeared*, were victims of government imprisonment without trial, or outright murder.

Rejecting sympathy for either right or left wing autocrats, the philosopher Michael Walzer reminds us of a different sympathy: "for the tortured dissidents, the imprisoned oppositionists, the threatened minorities, all the 'disappeared' and murdered men and women of all the tyrannies, old and new. And we don't need a political theory to explain why we should keep these people always in the forefront of our consciousness, their names on the tip of our tongues."[66]

Quality of Life   Just as disconcerting as the widespread political repression throughout the world are the staggering economic conditions under which citizens born into poor nations must live. In Haiti, a neighbor just to the south of the United States, the average income per person is less than $1 a day, one of five children dies before age five, and only 20 percent of the people have access to clean drinking water. These statistics are all too common around the globe. Alarming, too, and raising additional ethical issues, is the damage being done to the world's environment by the growth-oriented industrialized societies. Noting the stress evident already in each of the earth's major biological systems—oceanic fisheries, grasslands, forests, and croplands—an authority on global ecology argues that "if civilization as we know it is to survive, [an] ethic of accommodation must replace the prevailing growth ethic."[67]

Thus, standing next to the basic human rights of freedom and dignity, of basic nourishment and shelter, is an *ethics of ecology*. The 1986 accident at the Chernobyl nuclear plant in the Soviet Ukraine serves as a tragic reminder of how vulnerable society is to the dangers of modern technology. Cancer cases have doubled in the region near the stricken plant, and calves are now born routinely without heads and limbs. "My daughter recently got married,"

Perspectives on American Foreign Policy   13.4

Louis J. Halle on medieval knighthood as a model for American foreign policy:

The national ideal of a supremely great power like the United States should be that of the gentle knight—exemplified in medieval literature by Lancelot, by Percival, by King Arthur. The gentle knight was strong, but his strength aroused neither fear nor resentment among the people because they knew it to be under the governance of moral responsibility and in the service of the general welfare. Precisely because he was strong, the gentle knight could afford to be modest, considerate, and courteous. His strength threatened only such outlaws as themselves constituted a threat to society. Consequently, his strength was not only in his arm *but in the regard of humankind.* Wherever he went, his quiet voice represented legitimacy, speaking with its authority.

Louis J. Halle, *The Elements of International Strategy: A Primer for the Nuclear Age* (Lanham, Md.: University Press of America, 1984), p. 120, emphasis added.

said a mother who cares for pigs at a nearby tainted farm. ''What kind of grandson will I have?''[68]

CHARTING A MORAL COURSE

The purpose of the illustrations in this chapter is to remind the reader that moral questions are very much a part of foreign policy—indeed, they are ''inescapable.''[69] Since the world continues to be dominated by calculations of military strength, the perspective of the realist with its emphasis on the balancing of military power will no doubt remain the overmastering consideration in the minds of foreign policy makers—at least for the foreseeable future. The failure of military balance can produce decidedly immoral results, as humanity has learned from two world wars.

Three-Dimensional Ethics

Yet, as this chapter has tried to show, ethical issues cannot be—indeed, refuse to be—ignored. In the weighing of moral considerations, Joseph S. Nye, Jr., points out that a reliance on one-dimensional rationalizations—be they pure Kantian, pure consequentialist, or pure anything else—would be an error.[70] The ethical strands interwoven in the choices that leaders must make are more complex; policymakers (and policy analysts) must be aware of the interplay between the *motives* of decision makers, the *means* they propose, and the likely *consequences* of their choices—a *three-dimensional ethics*.

Are the intentions of policymakers worthy? Have they given careful attention to the appropriateness of their methods? Are the results acceptable? Here are key questions regarding motives, means, and consequences that must be addressed for a more reliable judgment on the moral goodness of a decision. As Nye remarks, if a child were to be killed in an automobile accident on an icy road as a well-meaning driver attempted to bring her home, the driver's inad-

equate consideration of the road conditions (facts about the means) along with the tragic consequences for the child would warrant a negative moral judgment on the driver's decision—mitigated only slightly by his worthy desire to see the child home with her parents on a cold winter night.[71]

When Nye applies his threefold categories to the ethical problem presented by the existence of nuclear weapons, he derives the following ''maxims'':

Motives

1. Self-defense is a just but limited cause.

Means

2. Never treat nuclear weapons as normal weapons.

3. Minimize harm to innocent people.

Consequences

4. Reduce risks of nuclear war in the near term.

5. Reduce reliance on nuclear weapons over time.[72]

As Nye concedes, these maxims fall short of a solution for every ethical dilemma presented by nuclear weapons; but they do provide (like the Catholic bishops' letter they closely parallel) policymakers and citizens with some guidance through this difficult age. Further, Nye's insistence on a three-dimensional ethics helps steer us away from overly simple, and therefore misleading, judgments about the appropriate moral stance on a wide range of international issues. Few of the moral issues faced by decision makers (like the rest of us mortals) are likely to be easy, and judgments are apt to remain clouded by uncertainty; nevertheless, like our understanding of personality and its effects on foreign policy, so, too, has our understanding of ethics and international affairs improved in recent years. One can hope that with the

---

Perspectives on American Foreign Policy   **13.5**

The historian Arthur M. Schlesinger, Jr., on international morality:

. . . The assumption that other nations have legitimate traditions, interests, values, and rights of their own is the beginning of a true morality of states. The quest for values common to all states and the embodiment of these values in international covenants and institutions is the way to establish a moral basis for international politics.

This will not happen for a long, long time. The issues sundering our world are too deep for quick resolution. But national interest, informed by prudence, by law, by scrupulous respect for the equal interests of other nations, and above all by rigorous decency, seems more likely than the trumpeting of moral absolutes to bring about restraint, justice and peace among nations.

From Arthur M. Schlesinger, Jr., in Robert J. Myers, ed., *International Ethics in the Nuclear Age*, Vol. 4, Ethics and Foreign Policy Series, Carnegie Council on Ethics and International Affairs (Lanham, Md.: University Press of America, 1987), p. 34.

---

growing analytical attention and sophistication will come greater wisdom.

Muscle and Morality

Few students of foreign policy would question Stanley Hoffman's observation that realism "remains the dominant paradigm in the study of international affairs."[73] The failure of the League of Nations, the naïveté of Neville Chamberlain, and other twentieth-century manifestations of idealism have tarnished this approach to foreign policy. One recent instance of misguided idealism of the kind that has given the term a bad name occurred in 1978 during the Nicaraguan civil war. Twenty-five well-groomed young Americans arrived in Managua to "pulsate peace" into the region through the chants of transcendental meditation.[74]

Yet, who would be so bold as to deny that the power of principle—the pursuit of high ideals—can hold strong sway over the opinions of human beings around the world? Clearly the speeches and often the actions of American leaders are drawn in this direction. "Should we use military power to intimidate smaller nations? Should we no longer stand up for the ideals we believe and that we share with all humanity?" asked Vice President Walter Mondale in 1980. ". . . I reject that view as naive and dangerous," he answered. "Strength without principle is weakness."[75]

SUMMARY

Considerations of military balance dominate the conduct of U.S. foreign policy, as they do the external relations of most other nations. Without the order imposed on the international system by military balance, history has shown in blood that aggressive regimes are tempted into war. The resulting chaos that accompanies military struggle represents the greatest human immorality. Yet, concern over the balance of military power—however preeminent—is not the only influence on policymakers. Moral considerations often enter into their deliberations and decisions.

The influence of ethics can be seen in a number of foreign policy decisions. With a misguided faith in the promises of Adolf Hitler, British Prime Minister Neville Chamberlain signed a worthless peace pact with the Nazi dictator, emboldening Germany to discount the British as spineless moralists who would prefer peace at all costs to war. The United States selected its targets in Japan for atomic bombing on the basis, in part, of moral considerations—though critics argue that this nation was insufficiently sensitive to ethical considerations in its hasty attack against the second target, Nagasaki. In their treatment of Soviet prisoners of war, Western leaders eventually adopted a more humane policy based on ethical considerations rather than pure balance-of-power politics.

Ethics has played a part, too, in the weighty discussions of citizens and policymakers over deterrence and the proper intended use of nuclear weapons. The American Catholic bishops, in an influential pastoral letter revealing Kantian and consequentialist ethical strains, have recommended the rejection of a first-use policy for nuclear weapons by the United States, advocating instead a strictly counterforce targeting plan.

Intelligence and human rights policies are additional items on the foreign policy agenda that have attracted moral debate. Espionage, covert action, and counterintelligence all raise serious ethical questions about what boundaries, if any, should be placed on the operations of the CIA here and abroad. And the role of the United States as a guarantor of the freedom and dignity of people around the globe has gained a high priority in the deliberations of government officials (especially during the Carter administration).

Ethics and international affairs is a topic of great complexity, and no one has a guaranteed set of rules to guide policymakers with certitude toward the best mix of prudence and morality in foreign affairs. Nevertheless, analysts have become more sophisticated in their study of this elusive subject. They emphasize the importance of three key dimensions constituting most moral choices: the motives of decision makers, their attention to means, and the consequences of their choices.

Military power continues to dominate world politics, and the other foreign policy means examined in Part 2 of this book will always be important, too. Nevertheless, ethical questions are inescapable in the affairs of nations; and, sometimes, the power of principle even prevails.

KEY TERMS

Ultra

Wilsonianism

nuclear ethics

modern-day Kantians

consequentialists

American bishops' letter

just-war tradition

principle of discrimination

principle of proportionality

intelligence ethics

the Huston Plan

human rights

the "disappeared"

ecological ethics

three-dimensional ethics

NOTES

1. See D. K. Fieldhouse, *The Colonial Empires from the Eighteenth Century* (New York: Delacorte, 1965), photo no. 38 (centerpiece).

2. Interview with Bob Woodward, *Secret Intelligence*, Public Broadcasting System (PBS), produced by KCET Television, Los Angeles, February 13, 1989.

3. Inis L. Claude, Jr., "The Common Defense and Great-Power Responsibilities," *Political Science Quarterly*, vol. 101, 1986, p. 731.

4. Quoted by Anthony Lewis, "Morality in Foreign Policy," *New York Times*, October 21, 1976, p. 39; John P. Wallach, Hearst News Service, October 21, 1976.

5. Inis L. Claude, Jr., *Power and International Relations* (New York: Random House, 1962), p. 8. For the quotes from Hans J. Morgenthau, see, respectively, *Politics Among Nations*, 3d ed. (Chicago: University of Chicago Press, 1946), p. 5, and Hans J. Morgenthau and Kenneth W. Thompson, eds., *Principles and Problems of International Politics* (New York: Knopf, 1950), p. 104.

6. On Ultra, see F. W. Winterbotham, *The Ultra Secret* (New York: Harper & Row, 1984); on the Coventry case, see Anthony Cave Brown, *Bodyguard of Lies* (New York: Harper & Row, 1975), pp. 38–44. Some authorities have suggested that the Coventry story is apocryphal; regardless, it poses a thought-provoking illustration of an entirely plausible moral dilemma for decision makers in time of war.

7. Claude, *Power and International Relations*, p. 57.

8. Jacobo Timerman, "Reflections: Under the Dictator," *New Yorker*, November 2, 1987, p. 49.

9. *Ibid.*, p. 50.

10. *New York Times*, November 18, 1987, p. 4.

11. *New York Times*, October 27, 1987, p. 6.

12. *New York Times*, November 16, 1987.

13. Claude, *Power and International Relations*, pp. 81–82.

14. *Ibid.*, p. 85.

15. Quoted by Claude, *ibid.*, p. 104.

16. John Maynard Keynes, *Essays and Sketches in Biography* (New York: Meridian, 1956), pp. 177, 179, 264, 267.

17. Hollis W. Barber, *Foreign Policies of the United States* (New York: Dryden, 1953), p. 394.

18. Claude, *Power and International Relations*, pp. 277, 284.

19. For a more in-depth examination of the three cases, see J. E. Hare and Carey B. Joynt, *Ethics and International Affairs* (New York: St. Martin's, 1982), pp. 80–100.

20. *Ibid.*, p. 99.

21. Forrest C. Pogue, *George C. Marshall: Statesman, 1945–1959* (New York: Viking, 1987), p. 19.

22. Hare and Joynt, *op. cit.*, p. 82.

23. *Ibid.*, p. 86.

24. This section draws upon lectures presented by Joseph S. Nye, Jr., and others at the MIT-Harvard Summer Program on Nuclear Weapons and Arms Control, June 1985, as well as Nye's *Nuclear Ethics* (New York: Free Press, 1986).

25. See McGeorge Bundy, "The Bishops and the Bomb," *New York Review of Books*, June 16, 1983, p. 4.

26. Nye, *Nuclear Ethics*, p. 17.

27. Nye, *ibid.*

28. United States Catholic Conference, *The Challenge of Peace: God's Promise and Our Response* (1983); see, also, Douglas P. Lackey, *The Ethics of War and Peace* (Englewood Cliffs, N.J.: Prentice-Hall, 1989).

29. J. Bryan Hehir, "There's No Deterring the

Catholic Bishops," *Ethics and International Affairs*, vol. 3, 1989, p. 287.

30. J. Bryan Hehir, lecture, MIT-Harvard Summer Program.

31. Nye, MIT-Harvard lecture.

32. *Ibid.*

33. Susan Okum, "Taking the Bishops Seriously," *World Politics*, vol. 36, July 1984, pp. 527–554.

34. Hehir, "There's No Deterring," p. 285.

35. See Keith B. Payne, "The Bishops and Nuclear Weapons," *Orbis*, vol. 27, Fall 1983, pp. 535–543.

36. Cited in Victor Marchetti and John D. Marks, *The CIA and the Cult of Intelligence* (New York: Knopf, 1974), p. 167.

37. See "The CIA and the Media," *Hearings of the Subcommittee on Oversight, Permanent Select Committee on Intelligence*, U.S. House of Representatives, April 20, 1978.

38. Loch K. Johnson, "The CIA and the Media," *Intelligence and National Security*, vol. 1, May 1986, pp. 143–169.

39. Loch K. Johnson, "Cloaks and Gowns: The CIA in the Groves of Academe," in Stephen J. Cimbala, ed., *Intelligence and Intelligence Policy in a Democratic Society* (Dobbs Ferry, N.Y.: Transnational, 1987), pp. 101–128.

40. See Loch K. Johnson, *America's Secret Power: The CIA in a Democratic Society* (New York: Oxford University Press, 1989), pp. 60–61.

41. Joseph E. Persico, *Piercing the Reich* (New York: Viking, 1979), p. 38.

42. See Johnson, *America's Secret Power*, pp. 68–69.

43. Persico, *op. cit.*, p. 39.

44. Frank Snepp, *Decent Interval* (New York: Random House, 1977), especially pp. 563–580.

45. John McCone's remarks were expressed in a press conference, U.S. Capitol, Washington, D.C., June 6, 1975.

46. The anonymous intelligence officer is quoted by Bonner Day, "The Battle over U.S. Intelligence," *Air Force*, vol. 61, May 1978, p. 13.

47. See Bob Woodward, *Veil: The Secret Wars of the CIA, 1981–1987* (New York: Simon & Schuster, 1988).

48. Frank Church, "Do We Still Plot Murders? Who Will Believe We Don't?" *Los Angeles Times*, June 14, 1983, sec. 2, p. 5.

49. For a discussion of intelligence and morality, see Ed Godfrey, "Ethics and Intelligence," *Foreign Affairs*, vol. 56, 1978, pp. 624–642; and Loch K. Johnson, *A Season of Inquiry: Congress and Intelligence* (Pacific Grove, Calif.: Brooks-Cole, 1988).

50. Author's interview, William E. Colby, Washington, D.C., March 21, 1979.

51. Ferdinand Mount, "Spook's Disease," *National Review*, March 7, 1980, p. 300.

52. U.S. Senate Select Committee to Study Governmental Operations with Respect to Intelligence Activities (the Church committee, chaired by Frank Church, D-Idaho), "Alleged Assassination Plots Involving Foreign Leaders," Senate Report No. 94-465, November 20, 1975, p. 46.

53. Senator Frank Church, "Covert Action: Swampland of American Foreign Policy," *Bulletin of the Atomic Scientists*, vol. 32, February 1976, p. 9.

54. Quoted in *The Nation*, March 12, 1983, p. 301.

55. For a series of insightful articles on the morality of U.S. covert intervention abroad, see *Ethics and International Affairs*, vol. 3, 1989, pp. 27–72.

56. See Loch K. Johnson, "National Security, Civil Liberties, and the Collection of Intelligence: A Report on the Huston Plan," in "Supplementary Detailed Staff Reports on Intelligence and the Rights of Americans," *Final Report of the Church Committee*, April 23, 1976, pp. 921–986.

57. Theodore H. White, *Breach of Faith: The Fall of Richard Nixon* (New York: Atheneum, 1975), p. 133.

58. Author's interview with an FBI counterintelligence specialist, Washington, D.C., August 20, 1975.

59. Dr. Zbigniew Brzezinski, remarks before the Platform Committee of the Democratic National Committee, Washington, D.C., June 12, 1980, mimeograph, p. 1.

60. See, for example, the depiction of Dr. Brzezinski in David S. McLellan's biography of his administration counterpoint, *Cyrus Vance* (Totowa, N.J.: Bowman & Allanheld, 1985).

61. Brzezinski, remarks, Democratic National Committee, p. 1.

62. Edmund S. Muskie, "Human Freedom: America's Vision," *Current Policy No. 208*, Bureau of Public Affairs, U.S. Department of State, August 7, 1980, p. 3.

63. See John Lewis Gaddis, *Strategies of Containment: A Critical Appraisal of Postwar American National Security Policy* (New York: Oxford University Press, 1982).

64. Muskie, *op. cit.*, p. 3; for a critical examination of inconsistencies in the approach of the Carter administration to human rights, see William F. Buckley, Jr., "Human Rights and Foreign Policy," *Foreign Affairs*, vol. 58, Spring 1980, pp. 775–796.

65. See Jeane J. Kirkpatrick, "Doctrine of Moral Equivalence," *Department of State Bulletin 84*, August 1984, p. 127; see, also, her "Dictatorships and Double Standards," *Commentary*, vol. 68, November 1979, pp. 34–45.

66. Michael Walzer, "Totalitarianism vs. Authoritarianism," *New Republic*, July 4 and 11, 1981, p. 25.

67. Lester R. Brown, *The Twenty Ninth Day: Accommodating Human Needs and Numbers to the Earth's Resources* (New York: Norton, 1978), p. 7; see, also, Jessica Tuchman Mathews, "Redefining Security," *Foreign Affairs*, vol. 68, Spring 1989, pp. 162–177.

68. Associated Press, February 16, 1989.

69. Joseph S. Nye, Jr., "Ethics and Foreign Policy," an occasional paper (Queenstown, Md.: Aspen Institute for Humanistic Studies, 1985), p. 24.

70. See Joseph S. Nye, Jr., "Superpower Ethics: An Introduction," *Ethics and International Affairs*, vol. 1, 1987.

71. Joseph S. Nye, Jr., *Nuclear Ethics*, p. 20.

72. *Ibid.*, pp. 91–131.

73. Stanley Hoffman, "The Rules of the Game," *Ethics and International Affairs*, vol. 1, 1987, p. 38.

74. Cited by Robert A. Pastor (NSC staff aide for Latin American affairs, Carter administration), "Condemned to Repetition: The U.S. and Nicaragua," public lecture, University of Georgia, Athens, November 18, 1987.

75. Walter F. Mondale, speech, Commonwealth Club, San Francisco, September 5, 1980, mimeograph, pp. 3, 5.

RECOMMENDED READINGS

Brown, Lester R. *The Twenty Ninth Day: Accommodating Human Needs and Numbers to the Earth's Resources* (New York: Norton, 1978). An analysis of the four principal biological systems on which humanity depends (fisheries, forests, grasslands, and croplands), in which the author shows that the demands at current levels of population and per capita consumption exceed the long-term carrying capacity.

Buckley, William F., Jr. "Human Rights and Foreign Policy," *Foreign Affairs*, vol. 58, Spring 1980, pp. 775–796. An examination of flaws in the human rights policies advocated by the

Carter administration, which, in Mr. Buckley's view, had reached "an almost unparalleled state of confusion."

Claude, Inis L., Jr. *Power and International Relations* (New York: Random House, 1962). An award-winning critique of the balance-of-power approach to international affairs.

Drew, Elizabeth. "A Reporter at Large: Human Rights," *New Yorker*, July 18, 1977. An insightful summary of human rights policy as it evolved in the Carter administration.

Ethics and International Affairs, vols. 1–3 (New York: Carnegie Council on Ethics and International Affairs, 1987–1989). A new journal with a focus on the moral dimension of foreign policy, including commentary by Jacques Barzun, Stanley Hoffman, Ali A. Mazrui, Joseph S. Nye, Jr., and Arthur M. Schlesinger, Jr., among others.

Hare, J. E., and Carey B. Joynt. *Ethics and International Affairs* (New York: St. Martin's, 1982). A thoughtful examination of the realist and idealist schools of foreign policy, with a number of excellent case studies on the complexity of moral questions in international relations.

Kennan, George F. "Morality and Foreign Policy," *Foreign Affairs*, vol. 64, Winter 1985–1986, pp. 205–218. Kennan advocates the morality of America minding its own business—to include the use of covert action only in the most urgent circumstances—"wherever there is not some overwhelming reason for minding the business of others."

Niebuhr, Reinhold. *The Children of Light and the Children of Darkness* (New York: Scribner, 1950). One of many social-theological works by an influential "Christian realist" who, disillusioned by Wilsonian liberalism, sought a middle

course between optimistic naïveté and cynical despair.

Nye, Joseph S., Jr. "Ethics and Foreign Policy," an occasional paper (Queenstown, Md.: Aspen Institute for Humanistic Studies, 1985). A critique in monograph form of morality and American foreign policy, based on Aspen Institute seminars; Nye relegates ethics to an important but secondary place behind balance-of-power considerations.

———. *Nuclear Ethics* (New York: Free Press, 1986). A sophisticated use of a "three-dimensional ethics" to explore moral issues raised by the existence of nuclear weapons.

Osgood, Robert E. *Ideals and Self-Interest in America's Foreign Relations* (Chicago: University of Chicago Press, 1953). A useful tracing of what the author sees as an American propensity to swing back and forth between idealism and realism in foreign affairs.

Rawls, John. *A Theory of Justice* (Cambridge, Mass.: Harvard University Press, 1971). A highly regarded book which, among other things, advocates the principles of self-determination, nonintervention, and commitment to treaty pledges as a moral guide to foreign policy.

Thompson, Kenneth W. *Morality and Foreign Policy* (Baton Rouge: Louisiana State University Press, 1980). One of many books on this subject by a leading realist who advocates a "practical morality" for America's external relations, between the poles of utopia, on the one hand, and the "war of each against all," on the other hand.

Walzer, Michael. *Just and Unjust Wars* (New York: Basic Books, 1977). A thorough analysis of the just-war tradition.

IN SEARCH OF A NEW FOREIGN POLICY

THE NECESSITY FOR BETTER CITIZEN
AWARENESS OF GLOBAL AFFAIRS

OVERCOMING THE CENTRIFUGAL
FORCES OF DOMESTIC POLITICAL
INSTITUTIONS

A WORLD BEYOND THE KREMLIN

AN END TO COMPULSIVE
INTERVENTIONISM

SUMMARY

14

AMERICAN FOREIGN POLICY IN THE TWENTY-FIRST CENTURY: A NORMATIVE EPILOGUE

With the Brandenburg Gate in the background, East and West Germans stand atop the Berlin Wall in celebration of its opening in November of 1989—an event that many saw as an ending of the cold war. (AP/Wide World Photos)

IN SEARCH OF A NEW FOREIGN POLICY

The prominence of the United States as a world power is a relatively new phenomenon. As the statesman-author George F. Kennan recalls, at the beginning of the twentieth century America's external relations remained guided by "the concepts and methods of a small neutral nation." He remembers the Department of State in the 1920s, when he began his distinguished diplomatic career, as "a quaint old place, with its law-office atmosphere, its cool dark corridors, its swinging doors, its brass cuspidors, its black leather rocking chairs, and the grandfather's clock in the Secretary of State's office."[1]

Those simple days are gone. The Department of State is now a sprawling edifice of seemingly endless hallways, government-gray desks, and thousands of harried officials—in short, a modern bureaucracy. The life of the Foreign Service officer overseas has changed dramatically, too. Seldom in earlier times were the lives of U.S. diplomats at risk. The seventy-three who died in the first 189 years of the nation's history were, in almost all cases, the victims of shipwrecks, natural disasters, or tropical diseases. Since 1965, in contrast, over eighty American diplomats have died at the hands of terrorists, including six ambassadors in the past sixteen years. In place of the once attractive prospect of living abroad—with low rents and affordable servants, villas with tennis courts and swimming pools, frond-trimmed verandas with lazy fans and trays of tax-free Scotch—today's diplomat faces the constant threat of harassment and terrorism.

Yet, just as distant countries have grown more dangerous to Americans, so have they become more important. The world is increasingly difficult to ignore: the sophisticated weapons that threaten the very existence of the human species, the trading opportunities—and barriers—that so directly affect the health of America's domestic economy, the need for continuing access to natural resources vital to in-

413

dustrial manufacturing, the vanishing rain forests, the reports of human rights abuses inflicted by corrupt dictators (who often have close ties with the United States). The early American colonists also faced enormous challenges, of course, surrounded as they were on one side by an ocean dominated by powerful, hostile navies and on the other by a vast wilderness; but today's advanced weaponry, intricate patterns of trade interdependence, and deteriorating environment have made the nuclear age an era of unparalleled risk and complexity.

At the same time, rapid advances in knowledge—from medicine and astrophysics to communications and the art of governing—encourage the hope that, with every passing year, the people of this planet are becoming better equipped to cope with the epic challenges before them. A number of shadows darken this optimism, however. As Americans approach the twenty-first century, they face four major foreign policy weaknesses that must be overcome if this nation wishes to remain a leading world power.

The first weakness is the foreign policy parochialism of U.S. citizens; the second, a disarray within the institutions of government that plan and implement foreign policy; the third, the nation's fixation on the communist threat at the expense of other dangers; and the fourth, a compulsion among most U.S. foreign policy officials toward an excessive, unwarranted intervention in the affairs of other countries. This concluding chapter—a normative epilogue—briefly addresses each of these weaknesses in hopes of encouraging a new approach to America's external affairs as we approach the next century.

THE NECESSITY FOR BETTER CITIZEN AWARENESS OF GLOBAL AFFAIRS

One of the most discouraging shortcomings in America's readiness for world leadership—

and one the reader can do something about directly—is the inadequate preparation of many young Americans to assume positions of responsibility in this nation's governing institutions, or, for that matter, even as voters to evaluate rationally the foreign policy arguments made by candidates for high office. Consider these results from recent surveys on the awareness of students in the United States about world geography—one useful index of a citizen's interest in, and understanding of, international affairs:

- 30 percent of the students at the University of Miami could not locate the Pacific Ocean on a world map.
- 25 percent of the high school students in Dallas could not name the country that lies immediately to the south of the United States.
- 50 percent of the students in Hartford could not name three countries in Africa.
- 45 percent of the high school students in Baltimore failed to shade in correctly "the United States" on a world map.
- 14 percent of the high school students in Washington could not name the large nation that borders the United States on the north.
- Nearly 50 percent of college students in a California poll could not locate Japan on a map.
- Swedes, Japanese, and Canadians are more likely to know the population of the United States than are Americans.
- 95 percent of the freshmen at a college in Indiana could not place Vietnam on a map.
- In a national sample of 18- to 24-year-olds conducted during 1988 by the Gallup polling organization in nine Western nations, Americans finished last in geographic literacy.
- Three-fourths of the Americans in this poll could not find the Persian Gulf on a world map, even though the United States had amassed a sizable flotilla of Navy ships in this waterway to guard shipping.[2]

Citizens of the United States will remain unable to evaluate, sensibly and rationally, the foreign policy decisions of their public officials unless and until they become willing to learn more about the geography, culture, and politics of other lands. Nor can this nation comfortably wear the mantle of world leadership if its citizens express ignorance of, and little interest in, world affairs.

This parochialism is hardly confined to the young. The Gallup poll cited above discovered that only half of American citizens above the age of eighteen realized that the Marxist Sandinistas and the U.S.–backed contras have been fighting one another in Nicaragua; or that Arabs and Jews were at odds in Israel. Fully one-third of the U.S. sample were unable to name a single member of the North Atlantic Treaty Organization, and 16 percent thought that the Soviet Union was a member of the NATO defense pact (created in 1949, recall, as a counter to potential Soviet expansion).

A report issued recently by the Southern Governors Association notes that only 1 percent of Americans have ever studied a foreign language, even though three-fourths of the people of the world speak a language other than English; that 10,000 Japanese, fluent in English, conduct business within the United States, while only about 900 American businesspeople—few of whom know Japanese—conduct business in Japan; that the United States is the only place in the world where scholars can earn a doctorate without any foreign language study whatsoever; and that the U.S. Foreign Service remains the only diplomatic corps which does not require its officers to achieve fluency in another language.[3] In several American universities, it is possible to earn a degree in international business without taking a single foreign language course!

Scholars, too, have seen their opportunities to learn abroad cut back. As the father of the Fulbright International Educational Exchange program in 1946, former Senator J. William Fulbright (who served a record thirteen years as chairman of the Foreign Relations Committee), has recently lamented:

> There are fewer fellowships now than there were 25 years ago. It is evident that some important political leaders in Washington have failed to recognize that the exchange program is more than just a laudable experiment, that it is also an important instrument of foreign policy, designed to mobilize human resources of intellect and judgment, just as military and economic programs mobilize physical resources.[4]

Little wonder the United States has fallen behind in international trade. Continued ignorance of foreign languages, geography, customs, economic practices, and politics seems a sure prescription for American foreign policy failures in the future, along with a decline in this nation's international standing.

OVERCOMING THE CENTRIFUGAL FORCES OF DOMESTIC POLITICAL INSTITUTIONS

A further challenge is for U.S. foreign policy officials to join together better in a spirit of comity that spreads across the branches of government, and in obedience to the law and the Constitution. Intolerable in a democracy are executive-branch subterfuges epitomized by Lyndon Johnson's hidden escalation of the war in Vietnam; Richard Nixon's secret bombing in Laos; the misuse of the CIA at home and abroad (from an alliance with the underworld in murder plots against Fidel Castro during the 1960s to the surveillance of U.S. citizens during the Vietnam era); lying to the American people (from an official distortion of events in the Gulf of Tonkin in 1964 to the illegal sale of weapons to Middle East terrorists in 1986); the improper involvement of the NSC staff, private entrepreneurs, and foreign potentates in efforts to bypass laws prohibiting covert action in Nicaragua (part of the Iran-contra scandal); the plan (which also came to light during investigations into the Iran-contra scandal) to establish an "off-the-shelf, self-sustaining, stand-alone" invisible government led by the director of Central Intelligence, completely free of supervision by members of Congress or the White House; and the many other disturbing turns away from constitutional government that have occurred in the recent annals of American foreign policy. As one astute observer of this nation's conduct has noted, "Three Presidents [Johnson, Nixon, and Reagan] have now brought an arrogance to power and a conviction of righteousness that allowed them to act as if they, not the American people, were sovereign."[5]

The representatives of the American people in Congress have the constitutional right to participate in the great decisions of war and peace, the making of international agreements, the use of trade sanctions and inducements, and the direction and control of secret intelligence agencies. "Contrary to popular belief, the powers are not separated in the foreign policy–national security area," comments the prominent constitutional lawyer Lloyd N. Cutler; "they are shared for the most part, and neither Congress nor the President can do much without the other."[6]

On its side, the Congress, too, must improve its level of competence and cooperation with the presidency in foreign affairs. The spectacle of junior members playing the role of secretary of state, off in some distant capital negotiating for this or that policy objective, must be strongly discouraged. So, too, must be the excessive duplication of foreign policy hearings and other forms of legislative oversight that create an unreasonable drain on the time and energies of officials in the executive branch, as well as sow confusion regarding which members of Congress have primary authority for helping to shape this nation's external relations. Both branches must continue to search for the proper balance between the extremes of "micromanagement" by the Congress, on the one hand, and the dangers of full executive discretion over foreign affairs, on the other hand.

"The institutional lesson to be learned . . . is not that the presidency should be diminished, but that other institutions should grow in stature," writes the political scientist Aaron Wildavsky. ". . . The people need the vigor of all their institutions."[7]

A vigorous Congress and presidency working together, vital pistons in the engine of democratic government, complementing one another through constructive criticism—here is the ideal. In 1988–1989, legislators began in this spirit to revise the War Powers Resolution, calling for the establishment of a panel of eighteen congressional leaders and key committee chairmen to consult with the president before U.S. troops were sent into hostile regions. In addition, the proposal envisioned the establishment of a "permanent consultative body" of six individuals—the Speaker of the House, the president pro tempore of the Senate, and the majority and minority leaders of both chambers—with whom the president would be require to discuss the use of all military force abroad.[8]

Partisan differences and institutional tensions will continue to interrupt the smooth functioning of the government from time to time, even under the best of circumstances when both the executive and legislative branches are trying to act in good faith and with a spirit of cooperation. The nation's founders, after all, explicitly sought to build into the Constitution checks on the use of power. The appropriate remedy when the institutions are at loggerheads over major policy initiatives is open debate before the court of public opinion, followed by a vote up or down in the Congress, a possible presidential veto, and a chance for legislators to override the veto if feelings are strong enough to muster a special two-thirds vote in both chambers.

This is the framework laid out by the Constitution—not lying to congressional committees, ignoring statutory reporting requirements, dismissing legal limitations on foreign operations, or, as also occurred during the Iran-contra episode, privatizing foreign policy through secret fund-raising outside the established appropriations process. The acrimony that arose between the branches during the Reagan era "confused our allies and emboldened our enemies," recalls Senator David Boren (D-Okla.), chairman of his chamber's intelligence committee.[9]

A WORLD BEYOND THE KREMLIN

Another troubling weakness of America's foreign policy is the continued fixation of many decision makers on the Communist Threat (often capitalized like this to make it seem all the more dire)—as if everything the United States says and does in the world must be wrapped in a banner of anti-Sovietism. Conservative groups in particular maintain a steady drumbeat of exaggerated diatribe against the U.S.S.R., directing loud and unrelenting political pressure against any American official or citizen who fails to march in lockstep with their extreme cold war views.

Recently, in Oklahoma, one right wing organization filled the radio airwaves with attacks against Representative James R. Jones, a Democrat, for raising doubts about aid to the contras in Nicaragua. Claimed the ads: "President Reagan's exactly right . . . but your Congressman, Jim Jones, doesn't see the consequences of having a communist regime only two days' driving time from Texas. . . . For America's sake, call Congressman Jones right now. . . ." A 1988 fund-raising letter from President Reagan's Political Victory Fund praised conservative senators as "the few who are strong enough to stand up to the threat of Communism and say 'No further!' " In contrast, claimed the letter, "liberals" offered only "appeasement for the Communists," and a "crippled, weakened defense." The rhetoric came straight out of the 1950s—an ongoing canonical obsession with the dangers of Soviet world conquest, a belief that Russian soldiers, like nature, abhor a vacuum and will fill every opening if

the United States fails to check their aggressiveness.

This outlook is hardly confined to extremist groups on the fringe right; high-level public officeholders of both parties and various political persuasions have echoed these shibboleths. You "cannot relax for a minute," warned the Reagan administration's secretary of defense, Caspar W. Weinberger. The United States has to hold on tightly to every area of the world, he argued, countering Soviet imperialism wherever it raises its ugly head. "If you don't deal with it, they get a foothold."[10] A deputy assistant secretary of the Air Force during the Reagan years advised a forum at the National Defense University: "The most critical special operations mission we have . . . today is to persuade the American people that the communists are out to get us. . . . If we win the war of ideas, we will win everything else."[11] Troops to Lebanon, the Grenada operation, the "secret" war in Nicaragua, an American armada in the Persian Gulf without strategy or timetable—practically all manifestations of interventionism abroad become justified as part of an anti-Soviet crusade—even as the Soviet empire crumbles.

Today, despite all the dramatic changes in the Soviet bloc, the Bush administration often seemed still locked into the old siege mentality of the cold war. The administration sought funding for 132 Stealth bombers at $500 million each. In attempted to revive generous funding for the Star Wars missile defense program. It continued to pursue a dual-track MX and Midgetman missile basing scheme. And it erected new and more powerful Voice of America propaganda transmitters around the perimeter of the Soviet Union. Yet, at the same time, the administration supported troop reductions in Europe and accelerated arms control talks, and during an address at the U.S. Coast Guard Academy in 1989, the president declared: "Our policy is to seize every—and I mean every—opportunity to build a better, more stable relationship with the Soviet Union." As events in eastern Europe and the U.S.S.R. spun forward dizzily, the Bush administration projected a cautious and ambivalent stance.

In reality, communism is less a threat to the United States today than in earlier times. Even the most recent crown-king of the cold warriors, President Reagan, seems to have accepted this view. In 1988, he retracted his characterization of the U.S.S.R. as an "evil empire"[12] and sought better relations between the superpowers, beginning with an agreement to eliminate intermediate-range nuclear weapons (the INF Treaty). One of the Democratic candidates for president in 1988, former Arizona Governor Bruce Babbitt, accurately emphasized in his campaign speeches an important new reality of global politics: "Marxism as an economic theory has been a total, unqualified flop everywhere."[13] Aware of this, other nations are now far less drawn to the "Soviet model"—or, for that matter, to the "American model." Japan, South Korea, and Taiwan—new commercial powerhouses—have become economic showcases with broad appeal throughout the developing world.

Moreover, Soviet troops have experienced far less than complete success abroad, with their most recent failure in Afghanistan, where a "pacification campaign"—the most costly Soviet military operation since the Second World War—was finally abandoned in 1989 after extensive losses in the field against the mujahedeen, the Afghan guerrilla forces.[14] This particular defeat was aided significantly by the covert supply of U.S. weapons—especially sophisticated Stinger and Blowpipe hand-held antiaircraft missiles—to the mujahedeen via a CIA paramilitary operation. Even without these modern weapons in the hands of their opponents, the war in Afghanistan had become a Vietnam-like quagmire for the Soviet military, holding little prospect for victory.

In the more than four decades since the end of the Second World War, the Soviet empire has remained quite static. Its domination has been limited to the eastern European bloc and Mongolia, and within this domain nations like East Germany, Poland, and Yugoslavia—and even the tiny states of Estonia, Latvia, and Lithuania within the Soviet Union—sorely tested the Kremlin's ability to maintain its authority, let alone consolidate other foreign ventures. Then in 1989 several eastern bloc nations declared their sovereignty, and even once-obedient Cuba has drifted further and further away from Soviet bondage. The bleak reality for the Soviet leadership is that the U.S.S.R. is bounded not by a Canada or a Mexico, but by thirteen hostile nations, not to mention the several antagonistic "republics" (states) within its own borders. Mindful of this circumstance, President Gorbachev seemed prepared to try to improve Soviet relations with its neighbors and its own states.

In the most dramatic indication of the loosening Soviet grip over its dominion, the East German government opened the Berlin Wall on November 9, 1989, allowing free passage of its citizens to the west. This event marked, according to one experienced American commentator, "the day the Cold War ended."[15]

The United States can now—belatedly—shift its attention, resources, and energy away from an overwhelming concentration on anti-

---

In Developing Countries

Every Year:

- 800,000 children die from tetanus
- 600,000 children die from whooping cough
- 2 million children die from measles
- 5 million children face handicaps as a result of preventable diseases
- More than one-fourth of the children suffer from undetected malnutrition
- Children suffer from 1 billion episodes of diarrhea

Every Day:

- 40,000 children under the age of 5 die

communism and toward other global issues of importance to the prosperity of Americans alive today and those generations to follow: international trade, world health and ecology, refugee migrations, food supplies, population control (the global population has swollen to over 5 billion inhabitants), among others. "The struggle between the Soviet Union and the West may become less central," observes David D. Newsom, "as both camps look over their shoulders at circumstances outside their experience."[16] The diminishing ozone layer protecting humans from dangerous ultraviolet solar rays, the mushrooming world population, and fair trading relations (among other challenges), hold greater potential danger to citizens of both the United States and the Soviet Union than the relatively limited number of disagreements separating the two superpowers.

One of the major problems faced by both superpowers, as former President Jimmy Carter has noted, is "the increasing disharmony and lack of understanding between rich and poor nations."[17] In the developing world, 14 million children die each year from malnutrition and disease. In sub-Saharan Africa, one-fifth of all the children never reach their fifth birthday. In Ethiopia, a famine in the early 1970s caused the death by starvation of 200,000 individuals. And while the people of the developing world remain locked in a vise of poverty and poor health, the ubiquitous media carry reports to them about the life of luxury enjoyed by Western elites—hotels in New York City costing $400 a night, Washington galas where maids fill toilet bowls with freshly chopped carnations after every flush.[18]

"We can't realistically hope to achieve security and stability," concluded the late Representative Mickey Leland (D-Tex.), chair of the House Select Committee on Hunger, "in a world where more than half a billion people exist in poverty and hunger."[19]

A shift in the focus of American foreign policy does not have to—and indeed should not—entail the total abandonment of the containment doctrine. The Soviet Union, it must not be forgotten, remains a powerful adversary. It has

Destitute children in the slums of Bangkok. (UNICEF/Marcus Halevi)

Perspectives on American Foreign Policy   14.1

The editorialist Tom Teepen on one of many challenges to U.S. foreign policy:

... About 40,000 children under the age of 5 die every day—every *day*—from undernutrition and preventable diseases. Simple diarrhea remains the leading cause of death, some 4 million annually. Polio, a fearful but distant memory in the developed world, still cripples some 200,000 kids a year around the world.

These, and other tales just as sad, can be had for the asking from the 1988 annual report of UNICEF, the international children's relief agency.

It's not as though there is nothing to be done about it. An easily used oral rehydration packet can end diarrhea for just 10 cents. Imagine that. Saving a child's life for a lousy dime. Children can be immunized against the standard menu of preventable diseases for just $5 each. The price of a movie ticket can buy life and a healthy childhood. ...

From Tom Teepen, "The Third World Is Fighting Many Plagues," *Atlanta Journal and Constitution*, February 5, 1989, p. 7-B.

---

the largest army and the most powerful warheads in the world; its capacity to destroy the United States can hardly be ignored. What it does entail, however, is a redefinition of containment—a redrawing of the blueprint for American foreign policy. The new plan must retain the prudent continuation of a strong military defense; but it should reach out more energetically and sincerely for cordial relations with the Soviet Union and other communist powers, even trying to nudge the PRC back from the dark ages to which it plunged in 1989 with its brutal crackdown against internal proponents of democracy.

A new American foreign policy should also place higher on the national agenda the goal of improved ties with the emerging nations, in joint combat against what the secretary of state in the Truman administration, George C. Marshall, understood to be the real enemies of international peace. In preparation for his Harvard commencement speech of 1947 announcing the European Recovery Program (later known as the Marshall Plan), Secretary

Marshall penciled out a reference in an early draft to "the Communist threat." The enemies he preferred to list were "hunger, poverty, desperation and chaos."[20]

If the United States can apply the salve of trade, as well as cultural and educational exchanges, in an effort to heal the sores of past enmity and befriend the world's largest Marxist nation, the PRC—as it did before the crackdown in 1989—and if the United States can carry on vigorous commerce with Angola at the very time U.S. officials criticize the presence of Cuban troops there, then surely this nation can find ways to resolve its differences with its major adversary, the Soviet Union. The objective of reducing the risk of World War III is at least worth a try at restoring the level of U.S.–Soviet friendship that once blossomed during the 1930s.

The first step is for both superpowers to slough off the siege mentality that has characterized the cold war and prevented the consideration of fresh approaches to foreign policy. Each side can try harder to empathize with the historical experiences of the other. Were they to ponder the staggering loss of life suffered by Soviet citizens during the Second World War (over 20 million fatalities), Americans might appreciate more the Soviet concern for the defense of its borders. If one minute of silence were observed for each Russian killed in this war, the silence would last for thirty-seven years. Americans might consider, too, the effect of the harsh anti-Soviet rhetoric (of the "evil empire" strain) that so often comes out of Washington, and the peril that the Strategic Defense Initiative (SDI) might hold from the Soviet point of view as part of a potential U.S. first-strike capability. On their side, Soviet citizens and their leaders might ponder more seriously the effects on Americans of their own hostile rhetoric, a vigorous arms buildup (including highly sophisticated conventional weapons), billions of rubles worth of military weaponry provided to Cuba and Nicaragua (among other nations), a ballistic missile defense system that in some respects appears to undermine the 1972 Anti-Ballistic Missile Treaty, and an extensive system of suspicious civil defense facilities.

AN END TO COMPULSIVE INTERVENTIONISM

Caught in this fixation on the Soviet Union and its capacity for external aggression, the United States has abandoned its traditional instincts of caution in external affairs, embracing instead a rash and foolish posture of compulsive interventionism abroad. Henry A. Kissinger, secretary of state for Presidents Nixon and Ford, has outlined three questions that ought to guide the rational planning of this nation's international relations: What global changes is the United States prepared to resist? What are this nation's goals? And what resources does the nation have to pursue these goals?[21] If anything should be clear from America's foreign policy experiences during this century, it is that this country cannot shape the world to its liking. The United States has neither the wealth nor

the will for such a mission; and appropriately so, for neither does it have the right.

Yet, there are those in this country who continue to believe that Americans must intervene almost everywhere around the globe, especially if the Soviets have intervened—the "zero-summers" who see the world in black and white as an arena for mortal combat between the United States and the Soviet Union. Recall the declaration of the House Armed Services Committee chairman in 1970 that America was joined in a battle "between Jesus Christ and the hammer-and-sickle" (Chapter 2). For those who share this stark view of the world, every tremor of revolution in Chad, Grenada, or Nicaragua requires a U.S. response—regardless how small the nation, how large the loss of American lives, or the drain on the federal treasury. Little wonder that the popular West German author Günter Grass asked in anguish, "How impoverished must a country be before it is not a threat to the U.S. government?" (Chapter 13).

If America is to restore its financial solvency and again become a leader in the world's trading markets, if America is to regain the respect and devotion around the globe that it once enjoyed in the early postwar period, if America is to care for its own people—with one preschool child in four now living in poverty within the United States, with its population centers facing traffic gridlock, its lakes and rivers dying from acid rain and other pollutants, its teenage pregnancy and suicide rates spiraling upward, its cities and byways awash with dangerous drugs—surely this country must adopt a more discriminating approach toward foreign intervention.

The reflections of John Bright, the nineteenth-century English critic of empire, are worth bearing in mind. "I believe, if [England], seventy years ago, had adopted the principle of nonintervention in every case where her interests were not directly and obviously assailed," he wrote, "that she would have been saved from much of the pauperism and brutal crimes by which our Government and people alike

---

Perspectives on American Foreign Policy   14.2

Former U.S. Ambassador Carl Rowan (now media commentator) on the limits of American—and Soviet—power:

. . . The United States and the Soviet Union have enough arms to destroy the world, but can never have enough to control it—not in the face of the fierce nationalism, the religious fanaticism and the suicidal rage that dominate societies that are not "super" in terms of military or industrial power.

It has taken the Kremlin nine years to learn what the United States discovered so embarrassingly in Vietnam a generation ago: that there are stark limitations to the usages of military power, even in an age of nuclear overkill, nerve gases and sophisticated espionage. . . .

. . . The lesson of Afghanistan—and Vietnam—is that no foreign policy can succeed in these times if it does not contain a large element of diplomacy . . . and a credible expression of compassion for the needs of people in the most wretched reaches of Afghanistan, Angola, Cambodia, Mozambique and similar societies.

This is a lesson not easily learned by people who think that by spending $300 billion or more a year on weapons, they have made themselves "super" and bought control of the rest of this fragile planet.

From Carl Rowan, "The Superpowers Learn a Costly Lesson," *Atlanta Constitution*, February 15, 1989, p. 15-A.

---

have been disgraced. This country might have been a garden, every dwelling might have been of marble, and every person who tread its soil might have been sufficiently educated."[22]

Beyond the financial costs lies the growing realization that Americans can exercise only a limited influence on the affairs of other nations. Our experience in Indochina provides an illustration seared in the nation's memory. Despite an enormous commitment of U.S. blood and treasure to South Vietnam—more than 58,000 GIs killed and 153,300 injured, as well as the untold numbers who continue to suffer from the effects of Agent Orange and other chemical defoliants used during the war, not to mention those with lingering psychiatric and drug disturbances—the wide range of overt and covert force used by the United States proved unable to curb the internal corruption of the South Vietnamese government or unite its army into an effective fighting force.

This book concludes not with a call, certainly, for a return to isolationism. Two world wars have taught Americans that they cannot escape from the world, however much we may wish to sometimes; like it or not, the United States is inextricably bound to the other nations of this globe. It is a call, rather, for a more discriminating foreign policy. Let the United States "intervene" first with brigades of school, hospital and home builders, with nurses and physicians, with teachers, farmers, and economists, with the diplomatic corps and the Peace Corps—and only in the most pressing situations with the CIA or the Marine Corps.

Secretary of Defense Weinberger sounded an appropriate "note of caution" during the Reagan years against the rash use of U.S. force abroad. Even though the administration often ignored his prescription, it remains a sensible checklist for future overt American interventions and bears repeating (Chapter 10):

- The military action had to involve vital national interests.
- The United States must intend to win.
- The operation had to have clear-cut political-military objectives.
- These objectives had to be subjected to a continual reassessment.
- The American people had to be in support.
- All alternatives to the use of overt force had to have been tried first and found wanting.

As for the covert use of force (paramilitary or "special" operations), this option should be rarely used and only as a last resort when America's safety is at stake. Two of the nation's leading foreign policy experts have commented on the use of covert action (Chapter 9). "The guiding criterion," advised Clark Clifford, a former secretary of defense and an author of the National Security Act of 1947, "should be the test as to whether or not a certain covert project truly affects our national security."[23]

Cyrus Vance, secretary of state in the Carter administration, similarly told a congressional committee that "it should be the policy of the United States to engage in covert actions only when they are absolutely essential to the national security."[24]

In agreement with these expressions of restraint as becoming of a mature superpower, this book closes with a call for a more patient and tolerant America, one that refuses to rush into foreign conflicts without serious thought and debate; one that realizes that the world will continue to have civil wars which must be resolved by the warring factions themselves, and seldom by outside forces; one that honors the use of diplomacy as the first step in external relations, not the employment of force and secret operations. It calls for an America that, in a wise passage from John Quincy Adams's inaugural address, "is the friend of all the liberties in the world, [but] the guardian of only her own."

SUMMARY

This book ends on a normative note, urging an improved global awareness among American citizens, a greater effort toward institutional comity between the branches on matters of foreign policy, a greater concentration on world challenges beyond U.S.–Soviet relations, and a more discriminating use of overt and covert operations abroad.

NOTES

1. George F. Kennan, *American Diplomacy, 1900–1950* (Chicago: University of Chicago Press, 1951), p. 79.

2. Reported by Lee Schwartz, "We're Failing Geography 100," *Washington Post*, December 29, 1987, p. 29; for the 1988 Gallup poll, see Connie Leslie, "Lost on the Planet Earth," *Newsweek*, August 8, 1988, p. 31.

3. *Atlanta Journal and Constitution*, November 22, 1986, p. A-6.

4. J. William Fulbright, "Fulbright Exchanges Enhance Our National Security," *Chronicle of Higher Education*, December 10, 1987, p. 104.

5. William Pfaff, "If It's 'The Public Be Damned,' the Policy Is Doomed," *Los Angeles Times*, December 18, 1986, p. 11.

6. Quoted by Stuart Taylor, Jr., "Reagan's Defenders Arguing He Can Defy Congress's Ban," *New York Times*, May 17, 1987.

7. Aaron Wildavsky, "The Past and Future Presidency," *The Public Interest*, vol. 41, Fall 1975, p. 75.

8. Susan F. Rasky, "Senators Seeking to Overhaul War Powers Resolution," *New York Times*, May 20, 1988, p. 3.

9. Quoted by Margaret Garrard Warner, "An Overture to Congress," *Newsweek*, January 23, 1989, p. 26.

10. An interview with John Hughes, "Lunch with Cap," *Christian Science Monitor*, September 12, 1986, p. 16.

11. Speech by J. Michael Kelly, reprinted in Frank R. Barnett, B. Hugh Tovar, and Richard H. Shultz, eds., *Special Operations in US Strategy* (Washington, D.C.: National Defense University Press, 1984), p. 223.

12. President Ronald Reagan, quoted on *Evening News*, ABC Television, May 31, 1988. The "evil empire" characterization came in a presidential speech of March 8, 1983.

13. Colin Campbell, "Campaign Obscured Babbitt's Expertise in Foreign Policy," *Atlanta Constitution*, February 19, 1988, p. A-6. Notes Daniel Patrick Moynihan, a Democratic senator from New York and a member of the Foreign Relations Committee: "the one enormous fact of the third quarter of the 20th century [is] the near complete collapse of Marxism as an ideological force in the world. Nothing quite so sudden or so complete has ever happened. Economic doctrines have faded, political canons have been discarded, but here was an extraordinary world view, thought to be irresistible, maintaining a hold on sectors of opinion in all the great metropolitan centers of the world—of a sudden, vanished" ("Reagan's Doctrine and the Iran Issue," *New York Times*, December 21, 1986, p. E-19).

14. See Eqbal Ahmad and Richard J. Barnet, "A Reporter at Large: Bloody Games," *New Yorker*, April 11, 1988, pp. 44–86.

15. *New York Times* correspondent Hedrick Smith, *Washington Week in Review*, Public Broadcasting System, November 10, 1989.

16. David D. Newsom, *Diplomacy and the American Democracy* (Bloomington: Indiana University Press, 1988), p. 217.

17. Jimmy Carter, "The United States Must Guide Third World toward Self-Sufficiency," *Atlanta Journal and Constitution*, December 3, 1988, p. 23-A.

18. See Thomas J. Lueck, "57th St. Loc., 2 TVs/Rm., $400/Night," *New York Times*, January 31, 1989, p. 13; Haynes Johnson, "Let Them Eat Flowers," *Washington Post*, National Weekly Edition, March 12, 1984, p. 25. The statistics on conditions in the developing world come from *AID Highlights*, vol. 3, Winter 1986, U.S. Agency for International Development, p. 2; *USAID Highlights*, vol. 4, Summer 1987, U.S. Agency for International Development, p. 1; *Evening News*, ABC Television, December 11, 1986; and Leon Dash, "Millions Face Starvation in Relentless Drought," *Washington Post*, National Weekly Edition, March 12, 1984, p. 18.

19. Quoted in George D. Moffett III, "Cuts in US Development Aid Protested," *Christian Science Monitor*, September 12, 1986, p. 8.

20. Anthony Lewis, "When We Could Believe," *New York Times*, June 12, 1987.

21. Henry A. Kissinger, "Dealing from Reality," *Los Angeles Times*, November 22, 1987, sec. 5, p. 1.

22. Quoted by Senator Frank Church, *Congressional Record*, April 29, 1971, p. 12668. Bright objected especially to the disastrous Crimean campaign.

23. Testimony, "Covert Action," *Hearings of the Select Committee to Study Governmental Operations with Respect to Intelligence Activities*, U.S. Senate, December 4, 1975.

24. *Ibid.* For an effort to provide sharper detail to the Clark and Vance prescriptions, see Gregory F. Treverton, "Imposing a Standard: Covert Action and American Democracy," *Ethics and International Affairs*, vol. 3, 1989, pp. 27–44.

RECOMMENDED READINGS

Gaddis, John Lewis. "How the Cold War Might End," *Atlantic Monthly*, November 1987. Gaddis, a diplomatic historian, suggests that we might look at the U.S.–Soviet relationship not as a cold war but as a "long peace" in which international order has been maintained for a lengthier period than ever before in modern times; includes a thoughtful agenda for ending Soviet-American hostilities.

Mann, Thomas E., ed. *A Question of Balance: The President, the Congress, and Foreign Policy* (Washington, D.C.: The Brookings Institution, 1990). An excellent compilation of articles on selected instruments of American foreign policy, including overt war, strategic intelligence, diplomacy, and trade.

White, Ralph K. *Fearful Warriors: A Psychological Profile of U.S.–Soviet Relations* (New York: Free Press, 1984). An insightful argument by a psychologist for greater empathy between the superpowers—a way out of the adversarial relationship.

APPENDIX

PREAMBLE TO THE UNITED NATIONS CHARTER, 1945

WE THE PEOPLE
OF THE UNITED NATIONS

determined to save succeeding generations from the scourge of war, which twice in our lifetime has brought untold sorrows to mankind, and

to reaffirm faith in fundamental human rights, in the dignity and worth of the human person, in the equal rights of men and women and nations large and small, and

to establish conditions under which justice and respect for obligations arising from treaties and other sources of international law can be maintained, and

to promote social programs and better standards of life in larger freedom,

AND FOR THESE ENDS

to practice tolerance and live together in peace with one another as good neighbors, and

to unite our strength to maintain international peace and security, and

to ensure, by the acceptance of principles and the institution of methods, that armed force shall not be used, save in the common interest, and

to employ international machinery for the promotion of the economic and social advancement of all peoples,

HAVE RESOLVED TO
COMBINE OUR EFFORTS TO
ACCOMPLISH THESE AIMS.

Accordingly, our respective Governments, through representatives assembled in the city of San Francisco, who have exhibited their full powers found to be in good and due form, have agreed to the present Charter of the United Nations and do hereby establish an international organization to be known as the United Nations.

THE CONSTITUTION OF THE UNITED STATES OF AMERICA

(EXCERPTS RELATED TO FOREIGN POLICY)

We the people of the United States, in Order to form a more perfect Union, establish Justice, insure domestic Tranquility, provide for the common defence, promote the general Welfare, and secure the Blessings of Liberty to ourselves and our Posterity, do ordain and establish this Constitution for the United States of America.

ARTICLE I

Section 1. All legislative Powers herein granted shall be vested in a Congress of the United States, which shall consist of a Senate and House of Representatives.

Section 2. ... The House of Representatives shall choose their Speaker and other Officers; and shall have the sole Power of Impeachment.

Section 3. ... The Vice-President of the United States shall be President of the Senate, but shall have no vote, unless they be equally divided. ...

The Senate shall have the sole Power to try all Impeachments. When sitting for that purpose, they shall be on Oath or Affirmation. When the President of the United States is tried, the Chief Justice shall preside: And no person shall be convicted without the Concurrence of two thirds of the Members present.

Judgment in Cases of Impeachment shall not extend further than to removal from Office, and disqualification to hold and enjoy any Office of honor, Trust, or Profit under the United States: but the Party convicted shall nevertheless be liable and subject to Indictment, Trial, Judgment, and Punishment, according to Law.

Section 6. The Senators and Representatives ... shall in all Cases, except Treason, Felony, and Breach of the Peace, be privileged from Arrest during their Attendance at the Session of their respective Houses, and in going to and returning from the same; and for any Speech or Debate in either House, they shall not be questioned in any other Place.

Section 7. All Bills for raising Revenue shall originate in the House of Representatives; but the Senate may propose or concur with Amendments as on other bills.

Every Bill which shall have passed the House of Representatives and the Senate, shall, before it become a Law, be presented to the President of the United States; If he approve he shall sign it, but if not he shall return it, with his Objections, to that House in which it shall have originated, who shall enter the Objections at large on their Journal, and proceed to reconsider it. If after such Reconsideration two thirds of that House shall agree to pass the bill, it shall be sent, together with the objections, to the other House, by which it shall likewise be reconsidered, and if approved by two thirds of that House, it shall become a Law. But in all such Cases the Votes of both Houses shall be determined by Yeas and Nays, and the Names of the Persons voting for and against the Bill shall be entered on the Journal of each House respectively. If any Bill shall not be returned by the President within ten Days (Sundays excepted) after it shall have been presented to him, the Same shall be a Law, in like Manner as if he had signed it, unless the Congress by their Adjournment prevent its Return, in which Case it shall not be a Law.

Every Order, Resolution, or Vote to which the Concurrence of the Senate and House of Representatives may be necessary (except on a question of Adjournment) shall be presented to the President of the United States; and before the Same shall take Effect, shall be approved by him, or being disapproved by him, shall be repassed by two thirds of the Senate and House of Representatives, according to the Rules and Limitations prescribed in the Case of a Bill.

Section 8. The Congress shall have Power To lay and collect Taxes, Duties, Imposts and Excises, to pay the Debts and provide for the common Defence and general Welfare of the United States; but all Duties, Imposts and Excises shall be uniform throughout the United States;

To borrow money on the credit of the United States;

To regulate Commerce with foreign Nations, and among the several States, and with the Indian Tribes;

To establish an uniform Rule of Naturalization, and uniform Laws on the subject of Bankruptcies throughout the United States;

To coin Money, regulate the Value thereof, and of foreign Coin, and fix the Standard of Weights and Measures;

To provide for the Punishment of counterfeiting the Securities and current Coin of the United States;

To establish Post Offices and post Roads;

To promote the Progress of Science and useful Arts, by securing for limited Times to Authors and Inventors the exclusive Right to their respective Writings and Discoveries;

To constitute Tribunals inferior to the Supreme Court;

To define and punish Piracies and Felonies committed on the high Seas, and Offenses against the Law of Nations;

To declare War, grant Letters of Marque and Reprisal, and make Rules concerning Captures on Land and Water;

To raise and support Armies, but no Appropriation of Money to that Use shall be for a longer Term than two Years;

To provide and maintain a Navy;

To make Rules for the Government and Regulation of the land and naval forces;

To provide for calling forth the Militia to execute the Laws of the Union, suppress Insurrections and repel Invasions;

To provide for organizing, arming, and disciplining the Militia, and for governing such Part of them as may be employed in the Service of the United States, reserving to the States respectively, the Appointment of the Officers, and the Authority of training the Militia according to the discipline prescribed by Congress;

To exercise exclusive Legislation in all Cases whatsoever, over such District (not exceeding ten Miles square) as may, by Cession of particular States, and the acceptance of Congress, become the Seat of the Government of the United States, and to exercise like Authority over all Places purchased by the Consent of the Legislature of the State in which the Same shall be, for the Erection of Forts, Magazines, Arsenals, dock-Yards, and other needful Buildings;

—And

To make all Laws which shall be necessary and proper for carrying into Execution the foregoing Powers, and all other Powers vested by this Constitution in the Government of the United States, or in any Department or Officer thereof.

Section 9. . . . No Money shall be drawn from the Treasury, but in Consequence of Appropriations made by Law; and a regular Statement and Account of the Receipts and Expenditures of all public Money shall be published from time to time.

No Title of Nobility shall be granted by the United States: And no Person holding any Office of Profit or Trust under them, shall, without the Consent of the Congress, accept of any present, Emolument, Office, or Title, of any kind whatever, from any King, Prince, or foreign State.

Section 10. No State shall enter into any Treaty, Alliance, or Confederation; grant Letters of Marque and Reprisal; coin Money; emit Bills of Credit; make any Thing but gold and silver Coin a Tender in Payment of Debts; pass any Bill of Attainder, ex post facto Law, or Law impairing the Obligation of Contracts, or grant any Title of Nobility.

No State shall, without the Consent of the Congress, lay any Imposts or Duties on Imports or Exports, except what may be absolutely necessary for executing its inspection Laws: and the net Produce of all Duties and Imposts, laid by any State on Imports or Exports, shall be for the Use of the Treasury of the United States; and all such Laws shall be subject to the Revision and Control of the Congress.

No State shall, without the Consent of Congress, lay any duty of Tonnage, keep Troops, or Ships of War in time of Peace, enter into any Agreement or Compact with another State, or with a foreign Power, or engage in War, unless actually invaded, or in such imminent Danger as will not admit of delay.

ARTICLE II

Section 1. The executive Power shall be vested in a President of the United States of America. . . .

Before he enter on the execution of his Office, he shall take the following Oath or Affirmation:—"I do solemnly swear (or affirm) that I will faithfully execute the Office of President of the United States, and will, to the best of my Ability, preserve, protect, and defend the Constitution of the United States.'

Section 2.   The President shall be Commander in Chief of the Army and Navy of the United States, and of the Militia of the several States, when called into the actual Service of the United States; he may require the Opinion, in writing, of the principal Officer in each of the executive Departments, upon any subject relating to the Duties of their respective Offices, and he shall have Power to Grant Reprieves and Pardons for Offenses against the United States, except in Cases of Impeachment.

He shall have Power, by and with the Advice and Consent of the Senate, to make Treaties, provided two thirds of the Senators present concur; and he shall nominate, and by and with the Advice and Consent of the Senate, shall appoint Ambassadors, other public Ministers and Consuls, Judges of the supreme Court, and all other Officers of the United States, whose Appointments are not herein otherwise provided for, and which shall be established by Law: but the Congress may by Law vest the Appointment of such inferior Officers, as they think proper, in the President alone, in the Courts of Law, or in the Heads of Departments.

The President shall have Power to fill up all Vacancies that may happen during the Recess of the Senate, by granting Commissions which shall expire at the End of their next Session.

Section 3.   He shall from time to time give to the Congress Information of the State of the Union, and recommend to their Consideration such Measures as he shall judge necessary and expedient; he may, on extraordinary occasions, convene both Houses, or either of them, and in Case of Disagreement between them, with respect to the Time of Adjournment, he may adjourn them to such Time as he shall think proper; he shall receive Ambassadors and other public Ministers; he shall take Care that the Laws be faithfully executed, and shall Commission all the Officers of the United States.

Section 4.   The President, Vice-President and all civil Officers of the United States, shall be removed from Office on Impeachment for, and Conviction of, Treason, Bribery, or other high Crimes and Misdemeanors. . . .

AMENDMENT I*

Congress shall make no law respecting an establishment of religion, or prohibiting the free exercise thereof; or abridging the freedom of speech, or of the press; or the right of the people peaceably to assemble, and to petition the Government for a redress of grievances.

AMENDMENT II

A well regulated militia, being necessary to the security of a free State, the right of the people to keep and bear arms, shall not be infringed.

AMENDMENT III

No Soldier shall, in time of peace be quartered in any house, without the consent of the owner, nor in time of war, but in a manner to be prescribed by law.

AMENDMENT IV

The right of the people to be secure in their persons, houses, papers, and effects, against unreasonable searches and seizures, shall not be violated, and no warrants shall issue, but upon probable cause, supported by oath or affirmation, and particularly describing the place to be searched, and the persons or things to be seized.

AMENDMENT XI—(RATIFIED FEBRUARY 7, 1795)

The Judicial power of the United States shall not be construed to extend to any suit in law or equity, commenced or prosecuted against one of the United States by Citizens of another State, or by Citizens or Subjects of any Foreign State.

AMENDMENT XXV—(RATIFIED ON FEBRUARY 10, 1967)

SECTION 1.   In case of the removal of the President from office or of his death or resignation, the Vice President shall become President.

SECTION 2.   Whenever there is a vacancy in the office of the Vice President, the President shall nominate a Vice President who shall take office upon confirmation by a majority vote of both Houses of Congress.

SECTION 3.   Whenever the President transmits to the President pro tempore of the Senate and the Speaker of the House of Representatives his written declaration that he is unable to discharge the powers

---

* *The first ten amendments were passed by Congress on September 25, 1789, and were ratified on December 15, 1791.*

and duties of his office, and until he transmits to them a written declaration to the contrary, such powers and duties shall be discharged by the Vice President as Acting President.

SECTION 4.   Whenever the Vice President and a majority of either the principal officers of the executive departments or of such other body as Congress may by law provide, transmit to the President pro tempore of the Senate and the Speaker of the House of Representatives their written declaration that the President is unable to discharge the powers and duties of his office, the Vice President shall immediately assume the powers and duties of the office as Acting President.

Thereafter, when the President transmits to the President pro tempore of the Senate and the Speaker of the House of Representatives his written declaration that no inability exists, he shall resume the powers and duties of his office unless the Vice President and a majority of either the principal officers of the executive department or of such other body as Congress may by law provide, transmit within four days to the President pro tempore of the Senate and the Speaker of the House of Representatives their written declaration that the President is unable to discharge the powers and duties of his office. Thereupon Congress shall decide the issue, assembling within forty-eight hours for that purpose if not in session. If the Congress, within twenty-one days after receipt of the latter written declaration, or, if Congress is not in session, within twenty-one days after Congress is required to assemble, determines by two-thirds vote of both Houses that the President is unable to discharge the powers and duties of his office, the Vice President shall continue to discharge the same as Acting President; otherwise, the President shall resume the powers and duties of his office.

INDEX

Abzug, Bella S., 222
Access agents, 206
Accountability, 142, 237
Acheson, Dean, 71, 72, 73, 75, 77, 95, 103, 105, 121, 188
Achille Lauro, 278
Active-positive, 184
Acton, Lord, 99
Adams, Frank, 333
Adams, John, 45, 49, 50, 304
Adams, John Quincy, 49, 102, 304, 423
Adams-Onís treaty, 50
Advanced International Studies Institute, 179
Afghanistan, 23, 88, 92, 179, 243, 273, 418, 422
Africa, 346
  sub-Sahara, 419
African Development Bank, 357
Agee, Philip, 225
Agency for International Development (AID), 139, 320–321, 357, 369
Agricultural Trade Development and Assistance Act (Public Law 480), 369
Agriculture, 211
Agriculture, Department of, 359
Airborne Warning and Control System (AWACS), 175
Alaska, 54
Albania, 243
Albert, Carl, 275, 298
Alexander, Field Marshall, 391
Allende, Salvador, 12, 119, 178, 220, 240, 250, 251
Alliance for Progress, 369
Allison, Graham T., 91, 300
Amateurs, 34
Amazon, 8
Ambassadors (U.S.), 34, 114, 206, 333

America, ambivalence toward world, 64, 336 n. 63
American Federation of Labor, 179
American Institute of Aeronautics and Astronautics, 225
American Israel Public Affairs Committee (AIPAC), 32, 175
American Jewish Community, 175
American Legion, 179
American Veterans Committee, 179
Amnesty International, 22
Angleton, James, 141, 208
Angola, 87, 243, 251, 258, 298, 306, 358
Antiballistic missile (ABM) system, 288
Antiballistic missile (ABM) treaty, 120, 330
Anticommunist, 253
Antigenocide treaty, 335
Anti-Soviet rhetoric, 177, 417, 420
Anti-submarine warfare (ASW) capabilities, 289
Antiwar protesters, 220
Antoinette, Marie, 371
Apartheid, 385
Appeasement, 27, 60, 235, 389
Appropriations Committee, 254
Arab nations, 364, 415
Argentina, 365, 404
Armed Services Committee, 254
Arms control, 211, 295
Arms Export Control Act, 30
Arms sales, 237
Army of the Republic of Vietnam (ARVN), 82
Arsenal of democracy, 61
Asia, 187
Asian Development Fund, 357

Aspin, Les, 144, 294
Assassination plots, 241, 248, 250, 397–399
Assets (intelligence), 206, 207
Atlantic seaboard, 252
Atrocities, 381–382, 384–385
Atwood, J. Brian, 334
Australia, 129
Authoritarian regimes, 313, 403, 404
Automobiles, manufacture of, 354
Azores, 317

B-52 bomber, 294
Babbitt, Bruce, 418
Back-channels, 219
Bad secrets, 219
Bahrain, 317
Bailey, Stephen K., 149
Bailey, Thomas A., 58, 65
Bailey, Thomas G., 65
Baker, James A., III, 282, 305
Baker, Russell, 195
Balance of payments, 343
Balance-of-power, 22–23, 187, 388
Balance on current account, 344
Baldridge, Malcolm, 361
Baldwin, David A., 18, 364, 365
Ball, George W., 261
Balkanization, 141
Ballistic missile defense, 286
Baltic states, 176
Baltra, Alfredo Bruno Malbrich, 384
Barash, David P., 300
Barber, Hollis W., 65, 387
Barber, James David, 177, 183, 184, 185, 195
Barbie, Klaus, 261
Barnet, Richard J., 95, 354
Barron, John, 231
Barsotti, Charles, 185
Bartlett, Ruhl, 35

Bashaw (of Tripoli), 26, 47
Battle of Waterloo, 49
Bauer, Raymond A., 193 n. 29, 195
Bay of Pigs, 36, 76, 77, 78, 79, 114, 226, 235, 243, 247, 248, 250, 252, 398, 399
Bealac, Willard, 337
Beckett, Thomas, 247
Begin, Menachem, 302
Behavior, leadership, 185
Beliefs, leadership, 185
Bennet, Douglas J., Jr., 328
Bennett, A. Leroy, 314
Bentsen, Lloyd, 361
Berger, Raoul, 124 n. 26, 222, 223, 231
Bergsten, C. Fred, 378
Berkowitz, Bruce D., 231
Berlin blockade, 75
Berlin Wall, 9, 77, 90, 412, 418
Bertsch, Gary K., 355, 378
Betts, Richard K., 82, 83, 216, 231
Bickerton, Ian J., 369, 378
Biden, Joseph, 148
Big-stick diplomacy, 56
Bipartisanship, 112
Bismarck, Otto von, 50, 304
Bissell, Richard J., Jr., 36
Black Panthers, 401
Blackleaf-40 (poison), 244
Blacklisting, 364
Blanchard, William H., 300
Bleckman, Barry M., 300
Blow-back, 12, 240
Bohlen-Serrano Agreement, 320
Boland, Edward P., 129, 236, 259
Boland amendments, 30, 129, 236, 258, 401
Bolivia, 150, 243
Bolshevik revolution, 62
Bomb yield, 284
Bombers, 289
Bonaparte, Napoleon, 47, 48, 49, 270
Boren, David, 417
Botulinum toxin, 244
Boxer Rebellion, 55
Boycotts, 363, 364, 365
Bracken, Paul, 301
Brady, Richard, 167, 168
Brazil, 354
Bretton Woods Agreement, 342, 343, 346
Brezhnev, Leonid I., 218, 322

Brezhnev Doctrine, 88, 90
Bribes, 240
Bricker, John W., 322
Brickerites, 323, 335
Briefings, 256
Bright, John, 421
Brown, Harold, 210
Brown, Lester, 17, 410
Brown, Seyom, 17
Brunei, 236, 259, 401
Brezezinski, Zbigniew, 27, 88, 131, 136, 147, 175, 402
Buchanan, Bruce, 195
Buckley, William, 237
Buckley, William F., Jr., 274, 410
Budget and Impoundment Control Act, 113, 114, 298
Budget battles, 213
Budget deficits, U.S., 341
Bullock, Charles S., III, 194
Bundy, McGeorge, 142
Bureaucracy, 134
Burke, Edmund, 154, 169, 181
Burke, Kelly H., 294
Burkean model of representation, 169
Burma, 398
Burns, James M., 158, 196
Bush, George:
    administration of, 130, 305, 333
    as president, 34, 90, 352
    as vice president, 236, 334
Byrd, Robert C., 279, 281, 331
Byrd-Nunn proposal, 282

Calama (Chile), 384
California State Assembly, 178
Cambodia, 83, 84, 86, 87, 163, 171, 181, 220, 225, 243, 274, 278
Cambodian incursion, by U.S., 84
Cambon, 304
Camp David accords, 302, 305
Canada, 48, 49, 85, 350, 360–361, 365, 418
Canning, George, 304
Caribbean, 367
Carnesale, Albert, 300
Carney, Francis M., 335
Carr, E. H., 18
Carter, Jimmy:
    administration of, 6, 8, 9, 13, 14, 87, 89, 131, 139, 145, 218, 220, 237, 243, 306, 363, 403

Carter, Jimmy (*Cont.*):
    as president, 4, 13, 27, 34, 62, 88, 137, 145, 150, 167, 168, 194, 211, 217, 302, 305, 388, 402
Carter Doctrine, 88
Case, Clifford, 327
Case-Zablocki Act, 327–328
Casey, William J., 142, 190, 203, 212, 217, 236, 237, 249, 256, 257, 382
Castlreagh, Viscount, 304
Castro, Fidel, 5, 12, 36, 50, 76, 77, 78, 119, 142, 177, 241, 244, 245, 246, 247, 250, 364, 385, 397, 398
Catholic bishops, letter on nuclear deterrence, 393–394, 405
Catholic Church, in Central America, 217
Cavour, Camillo Benso di, 304
Central Intelligence Agency (CIA), 147, 202, 209, 226, 236, 241, 246, 249, 254, 258, 260
    agents, 206
    assassination plots, 226, 241, 243, 248, 250, 397–399
    case officers, 206
    covert operations, 11, 12, 14, 32, 74, 141, 142, 152, 178, 226, 235, 239, 241
    creation of, 10, 114, 201
    criticism of, 398–400
    intelligence operations, 112, 322, 358, 418
    invasion of Cuba, 36, 76, 213
    media ties, 395–396
    missionary ties, 396
    organization, 205
    recruitment, 133
    sale of weapons, 226, 249
    university ties, 395–396
Central Intelligence Group (CIG), 201
Chad, 243, 278
Chadha decision, 150–152, 275, 277
Chamber of Commerce of the United States, 179
Chamberlain, Neville, 14, 27, 60, 62, 76, 235, 389, 406
Character, 37, 181
Chemical substance, 240
Chernobyl nuclear disaster, 404–405

Chesapeake, U.S.S., 49
Chiang Kai-shek, 74, 80
Chicago Council on Foreign Affairs, 64
Chief of Station (COS), 204, 206
Chile, 117, 119, 178, 240, 384, 404
China, 52, 55, 62, 78, 86, 87, 104, 130, 187, 243, 317
   coal industry in, 212
   politics in, 210
   (*See also* People's Republic of China; Taiwan)
China Aid Act (1948), 369
China card, 86
Chinese Nationalists, 14
Chou En-lai, 322
Christian Democratic organizations, 240
Christian Democratic Party, 250, 251
   in Italy, 258
Christianity, 52–53
Christopher, Warren, 130
Church, Frank, 35, 107, 112, 145, 173, 186, 230, 244, 247, 251, 259, 264, 266, 319, 325, 326, 329, 399–400
Church Committee (on intelligence activities), 241, 245, 246, 265
Church Resolution (on Spain), 319
Churchill, Winston S., 4, 62, 72, 127, 294, 383
Civil War:
   American, 6, 28, 53, 270
   Vietnamese, 5, 27, 36, 38, 111, 113, 122, 128, 133, 164, 178, 186, 225, 243
Clandestine services, 204
Clark, Dick, 252, 317, 328, 329
Clark amendment, 252, 258
Claude, Inis L., 382, 383, 384, 386, 388, 411
Claus, Santa, 72
Clausewitz, Karl von, 271
Clemenceau, Georges, 35, 57, 386, 387
Clifford, Clark J., 82, 252, 422
Cline, Ray S., 36, 231, 261
Cobra venom, 243
Cockburn, Sir George, 49
Cohen, Stephen D., 378
Colby, William E., 148, 231, 239, 248, 249, 251, 252, 253, 260, 398

Cold war, 70, 73, 251, 418
Collective judgment, 296
Colombia, 56
Colonialism, 381–382
Command-control-communications (C³), 289
Commitment by accretion, 110
Committee for the Survival of a Free Congress, 179
Committee of Secret Correspondence, 200
Committee on the Present Danger, 179
Communications redundancy, 291
Communism, 237, 261
Compartmentation, 219
Complex interdependence, 27
Comprehensive Anti-Apartheid Act, 146
Comptroller (CIA), 254
Computers, 147
Conference on International Economic Cooperation (CIEC), 356
Confidence (trust), 190
Congo, 381
Congress, 143–149, 212, 242, 260
   involvement in international agreements, 315
Congressional resolution, 104
Congressional staff, 121, 147–148
Consequentialists, 392, 394
Constant, Benjamin, 366
Constituency opinion, 169
Constitution (U.S.), 30, 89, 100, 102, 106, 113, 115, 171, 199, 238, 282, 298, 306, 317, 331, 395, 428–431
Consultation, interbranch, 329
Consumers of intelligence, 215
Consumers of knowledge, 210
Containment doctrine, 23, 253
Continental Congress, 200
Contractual secrecy, 224
Contras, 5, 30, 32, 118, 129, 142, 235
Conventional capabilities, 283
Conventional forces, 272, 293
"Cooking," of intelligence reports, 217
Cooper, Richard N., 378
Cooper-Church Amendment, 172, 274
Coordinating Committee (COCOM), 355

Coors, Joseph, 236
Carson, William R., 231
Corwin, Edward S., 99, 125, 324
Cost of weapons, 180
Costa Rica, 8
Cottam, Richard, 337
Council on Foreign Relations, 178
Counterfeiting, 241
Counterforce (countersilo) targeting strategy, 284, 394
Counterintelligence, 200, 208, 401
Counterintelligence Staff (CIS), 206
Countervalue targeting strategy, 284, 394
Country directors, 139
Coup, 249
Coventry (England), 383
Covert action, 12, 45, 199, 200, 208, 237, 239, 242, 252, 256, 258, 265
   briefings, 257
   decision process, 255
   economic, 240
   paramilitary, 241
   political, 240
   propaganda, 239
   proposals, 256
Covert Action Staff (CAS), 206, 239, 240, 249
Crabb, Cevil V., 40, 125
Craig, Paul P., 301
Cratetology, 215
Creeping commitments, 109–111
Cronin, Thomas E., 158
Cryptologists, 203
Cuba, 54, 56, 78, 133, 152, 240, 243, 245, 273, 418
Cuban-American lobby, 177
Cuban American National Foundation (CANF), 177
Cuban missile crisis, 10, 53, 68, 77, 91, 112, 132, 133, 139, 213, 274
Curator mentality, 34
Customs Bureau, 203
Cutler, Lloyd N., 416
Cyprus, 278
Czechoslovakia, 60, 73, 74, 88, 273, 363, 389

Dahl, Robert A., 39 n. 13, 173
Daladier, Edouard, 60
Dam, Kenneth W., 281
Daughters of the American Revolution, 179

Daynes, Byron W., 159
De Gaulle, Charles, 351
Decision procedures (executive branch), 254
Deep underground centers (DUCs), 290
Defense, Department of, 243, 282 (*See also* Pentagon)
Defense Condition One (Defcon 1), 290
Defense Intelligence Agency, 202
Democracy, 161, 334
Democratic Party, 402
Demoscopy, 161
Dependencia model, 357–358
Deputy Director for Administration, 204
Deputy Director for Intelligence, 204
Deputy Director for Operations, 204
Deputy Director for Science and Technology, 204
Der Spiegel, 260
Dervish warriors, 4
Destler, I. M., 158, 195, 359, 378
Destroyers-for-bases deal (*see* lead base)
Detente, 62, 347
Deterrence, 272, 293, 294
"existential," 392
Developing nations, 348, 366 (*See also* Third World)
Dexter, Lewis A., 193 n. 29
Dialogue, 216
Díaz, Porfirio, 23
Diehl, Paul, 301
Diego Garcia, 317, 319
Dien Bien Phu, 79, 94 n. 26, 130, 189
Diplomacy, 13, 34, 249, 303–304, 305, 307, 331, 423
Diplomats, 34–35
Director of Central Intelligence (DCI), 202
Director of the CIA (DCIA), 201
Directorate of Administration, 204, 207
office of security, 207
Directorate of Intelligencae, 204, 207, 254 (*See also* National Foreign Assessment Center)
Directorate of Operations, 204, 206

Directorate of Science and Technology, 204, 207, 244
Dirksen, Everett, 144
Dirty tricks stigma, 207
"Disappeared," the, 404
Disease and malnutrition, global, 8, 367, 419
Dissemination (of intelligence), 216
Divestment, 178
Dobrynin, Anatoli, 322
Doctrine of eternal privilege, 221
Dole, Robert, 129
Dollar (U.S.), overvaluation of, 353
Dollar diplomacy, 56
Dominican Republic, 165, 243, 245, 249, 273, 274, 326
Domino theory, 24–26, 37, 79, 87, 130, 236, 253
Doolittle Report, 74, 399
Douglas, William O., 14
Drew, Elizabeth, 156 n. 28, 411
Drug Enforcement Agency (DEA), 203
Drug trafficking, 177
Dukakis, Michael, 176
Dulles, Allen, 208, 246, 250
Dulles, Foster Rhea, 55, 65
Dulles, John Foster, 74, 79, 104, 105, 130, 177, 188, 189, 320, 324, 325, 329, 388
Dulles era, 86
Durenburger, David, 148
Dumping, 364
Duvalier, François (Papa Doc), 246
Dyson, Freeman J., 301

Eagleton, Thomas, 274, 276, 279, 280, 301
Eastern Europe, 418
Eaton, William, 47
Eban, Abba, 304, 330, 333, 337
Ecology, ethics of, 404
Economic covert action, 240
Economic policy, institutional fragmentation of, 360, 362
Economic power, 366
Economic warfare, 239
Economist, The (London), 336 n. 63
Eden, Anthony, 390
Edinger, Lewis J., 196
Egypt, 175
Einstein, Albert, 182

Eisenhower, Dwight D.:
administration of, 23, 73, 74, 75, 79, 245, 272, 318
as president, 24, 25, 76, 81, 94 n. 21, 104, 106, 113, 130, 133, 136, 143, 164, 165, 166, 184, 246, 320
Eisenhower Doctrine, 105
El Salvador, 212, 236, 278, 317, 372
Electoral College, 170
Electromagnetic pulse (EMP), 285
Elimination by Illumination, 241
Elliff, John, 228 n. 21
Ellsberg, Daniel, 224
Embargo, 363, 364, 365
Embargo Act, 48
Empathy, 420
"En masse" public opinion, 169, 180
Ends and means, of foreign policy, 304
Energy Department, 202, 359
International Security Affairs, 203
English, as U.S. national language, 171
Enola Gay, 3
Entente, 87
"Enterprise," The, 236
Eppler, Ann, 370
Equatorial Guinea, 385
Erikson, Erik, 92
Ervin, Sam, Jr., 101, 106, 221, 222
Espionage, 200
Estimates, 212
Estonia, 23, 418
Ethics, three-dimensional, 405
Ethics and Public Policy Center, 179
Ethiopia, 317, 320
Eurodollars, 344
European Economic Community, 180, 342, 348
European Recovery Program (ERP), 71, 369
"Evil empire," 89, 417, 424 n. 12
Executive Agreement Index, 312
Executive agreements, 108, 306, 308
Executive Committee (Ex Comm), 77, 78, 133
Executive discretion, 307, 321–322, 416
Executive fatigue, 37

Executive-legislative compact, 130
Executive privilege, 221, 223
Export Control Act, 400
Export controls, 210
Extraterritoriality, 52

F-15 jet fighter, 175
Faisal, King, 322
Falk, Richard, 40
False research, 250
Farewell Address, George Washington's, 46, 61, 107
Farnesworth, Clyde H., 361
Federal Bureau of Investigation (FBI), 202, 203, 401
Federal Communications Act, 222
Federalist, The, 30, 101, 115, 122
Federation of American Scientists (FAS), 282
Felton, John, 195
Ferebee, Thomas W., 3
Field Poll (California), 169
Figley, Charles R., 95
Finding, 254, 256
Finished intelligence, 210
Finland, 23
Finlay, David J., 314
Firepower, 270
First Amendment rights, 224, 225
First independent political success, 183
First (preemptive) strike, 285, 394
Fisher, Louis, 114, 125, 148, 150, 296
Fisher, Roger, 18, 399
Five Whales, The, 144
Flanagan, Stephen J., 231
Flexible response, 76, 272
Floating world monetary system, 343
Florida, 50
"Food for peace," 369
Forbath, Peter, 231
Ford, Gerald:
    administration of, 28, 222, 251
    as president, 62, 85, 87, 119, 167, 248, 298, 322, 397–398
Foreign Affairs, 71, 73, 178
Foreign aid, 365, 367, 368
Foreign Broadcast Information Service (FBIS), 207, 213
Foreign Intelligence Advisory Board, 202
Foreign Service, U.S., 139, 415
Formosa Resolution, 104

Forty-eight-hour provision, 276
Forward deployment, 317
Founding Fathers, 236, 335
Fourth World, 372
France, 47, 49, 50, 53, 61, 79, 114, 200
    French army, 78
    XYZ affair, 45
Franck, Thomas M., 125, 231
Franklin, Benjamin, 12, 200, 304
Free trade, 352
Freedom fighters, 236
Freeze, on nuclear warhead production, 273, 380
Freezing assets, 364
Frei, Eduardo, 250
Freudian approach, 182
Friedrich, Carl, 259
Frog-7 missile, 283
Fulbright, J. William, 105, 106, 111, 112, 125, 130, 188–189, 274, 319, 322, 325, 335, 337, 338, 369
Fulbright scholars, 396, 415
Functional analysis, 15

Gaddis, John Lewis, 71, 72, 73, 74, 91, 96, 425
Gallup Poll, 163
Galtung, Johan, 18
Gang of Eight, 254
Garrett, Stephen A., 326
Garris, Jerome, 193 n. 28
Garthoff, Raymond L., 229 n. 34
Gates, Robert M., 157 n. 46, 229
Gelb, Leslie H., 82, 83, 96
General Accounting Office (GAO), 148, 319, 328
General Agreement on Tariffs and Trade (GATT), 356
General Counsel, office of (CIA), 254
General Electric, 170
Geneva Accords, 79
Geography, U.S. ignorance of, 414–415
Geopolitical threat, 252
    geopolitics, 23, 25, 372
George III, King of Great Britain, 22, 30, 99, 100
George, Alexander L., 185, 186, 196
George amendment, 324–325
George, Lloyd, 57, 386, 387
George, Walter, 324

Gephardt, Richard, 352
Germany, 56, 57, 60, 103
    East Germany, 418
    West Germany, 350, 351, 352, 354
Giancana, Sam, 245, 398
Gilbert, Amy M., 337
Gilpin, Robert, 351, 358, 379
Global corporation, 222
Global village, 28
Glynn, Henry, 57
Godson, Roy, 231
Goldwater, Barry, 129, 257, 276
    as presidential candidate, 250
Goldwater v. Carter, 150
Good-neighbor policy, 59
Good secrets, 218, 225
Goodman, Allan E., 231
Gorbachev, Mikhail S., 63, 89, 90, 91, 295, 355, 381
Göring, Hermann, 40 n. 28, 298
Graff, Sigmund, 161
Grass, Günter, 400
Grass roots opinion, 169
Great Britain, 47, 48, 50, 52, 53, 54, 61, 108, 109, 175, 179, 200
Great Depression, 59, 102
"Great Society" program, 81, 85, 343
Greece, 71, 73, 116, 119, 176, 243, 249
Greek-American lobby, 176
Green Berets, 272
Greenfield, Meg, 39 n. 19
Greenhouse effect, 8, 305
Greenland, 103
Greenstein, Fred I., 37, 196
Gregg, Donald, 216
Grenada, 5, 163, 164, 165, 278, 280, 281, 306
Griffith, Ernest S., 158
Ground zero, 284
Group of 77, 356
Group opinion, 180
Groupthink, 36
GRU (Soviet Military Intelligence), 213
Guatemala, 74, 243, 249, 317, 369
Guinea, 252
Gulf Oil Company, 358
Gulf of Tonkin Resolution, 81, 106, 111, 122, 164, 242, 274, 326
Gwertzman, Bernard, 334

Hackett, George, 333
Haiti, 152, 243, 385–386, 404
Hale, Nathan, 198, 200
Halle, Louis J., 404
Halperin, Morton, 141, 231, 253
Hamby, Alonzo L., 65, 334
Hamilton, Alexander, 101, 125
Hamilton, Lee H., 219, 229
Hanoi, 84
Hansen, Clifford, 173
Hanson, George, 31, 148
Hard targets, 206
Harding, Warren G., 58
Hare, J. E., 411
Hargrove, Erwin C., 158
Harkin, Thomas, 370
Harkin amendment, 146, 370, 388
Hart, Gary, 86, 281
Harvard-MIT roundtable, 179
Harvey, William, 248
Hatch Act, 134
Hatfield, Mark O., 281
Hay, John, 55
Hazard, Oliver, 49
Hearst, William Randolph, 54
Heclo, Hugh, 35
Heilbroner, Robert L., 366, 379
Helms, Jesse, 148
Helms, Richard, 176, 247, 248,
    264 n. 49
Henkin, Louis, 124 n. 28, 125,
    277, 283
Heraclitus, 181
Hermann, Margaret G., 196
Hersh, Seymour M., 230, 251
Herz, Martin F., 337
Hiroshima, 3, 16, 61, 286, 389–390
Hirschman, Albert O., 366
Hilsman, Roger, 142
Hitler, Adolf, 14, 23, 24, 36, 59,
    60, 61, 62, 86, 121, 294, 383,
    389, 398
Ho Chi Minh, 79, 81
Hoepli, Nancy L., 66
Hoffman, Stanley, 18, 183, 406
Holsti, Ole, 189
Holt, Pat, 275, 301
Homo politicus, 181
Honduras, 212, 235, 236, 278, 317
Hoover, Herbert, 59, 75
Hoover, J. Edgar, 203, 260, 401
Hortalez Company, 200
Hostages, 126, 237, 400
Hostilities, 275, 277, 278
Hot line, 289, 291, 296

House Foreign Affairs Commit-
    tee, 254
Hovet, Thomas, Jr., 314
Howard, Edward Lee, 225
Howard, Michael, 271
HQ Lingual, 259
Hughes, John, 423 n. 10
Hughes-Ryan Amendment, 146,
    237, 242, 253, 257, 263
"timely fashion" provision, 254
Hull, Cordell, 359
Human intelligence (HUMINT),
    212, 213
Human rights, 221, 402–403
Humphrey, Hubert H., 34, 84,
    121, 144, 331
Hungary, 243, 273, 418
Huston plan, 260, 401–402
Huston, Tom Charles, 260, 401–
    402
Hymer, Stephen, 358
Hyperpluralism, 32, 361

Iceland, 103
Idealist approach to world affairs,
    261, 384–388
Ikle, Fred C., 337
Illicit drugs, 180
*Immigration and Naturalization Ser-
    vice v. Chadha*, 150–152,
    275–277
Imperial overstretch, 379
Imperialism, 55–56, 357
Impoundment, 113
Incursion (Cambodian), 171
Inderfurth, Karl F., 158
India, 187
Indochina, 369–370
Indonesia, 187, 243, 250
Information, 11, 147, 199
Infrastructure (CIA), 250
Inherent constitutional right, 103
Institute for Contemporary Stud-
    ies, 179
Institute for Foreign Policy Analy-
    sis, 179
Instructed delegate, 169
Insurgency and instability, 212
Intelligence, 199–227
    analysis, 200
    analysts, 215
    current, 212
    cycle, 208–209
    ethics, 394–395
    facilities overseas, 319–320

Intelligence (*Cont.*):
    human, 212, 213
    missions, 200, 208
    to please, 229
    predictive, 212
    professionals, 258
    research, 212
    tasking, 212
    technical, 213
Intelligence Committee:
    U.S. House of Representatives,
        254
    U.S. Senate, 254, 257, 258
Intelligence Oversight Act (1980),
    226, 237, 242, 254, 256, 257,
    259, 263, 400
Intelligence Oversight Board, 202,
    253
Interagency Intelligence Memo-
    randa (IIM), 216
Inter-American Development
    Bank, 357
Intercontinental ballistic missiles
    (ICBMs), 22, 26, 77, 117,
    141, 283, 288, 291, 292
Intercontinental bombers, 288
Interdict, 236
Intergovernmental organizations,
    180
Intermediate-range Nuclear Forces
    (INF) Treaty, 7, 63, 89, 211,
    273, 295, 330
Intermediate-range nuclear mis-
    siles, 162, 283
Internal Revenue Service (IRS),
    203
International agreements:
    agency-to-agency, 328
    content, 307, 310
    form, 307, 308–309
International Bank for Recon-
    struction and Development
    (IBRD), 346, 356
International Brotherhood of
    Teamsters, 174
International Business Machine
    Corporation, 283
International Development Asso-
    ciation (IDA), 356
International Labor Organization,
    180
International Monetary Fund
    (IMF), 346, 356
International nongovernmental
    organizations (INGOs), 180

International North Pacific Fisheries Commission, 180
International Olympic Committee, 180
International Telephone and Telegraph (ITT), 178, 222, 240, 357
Interventionism, 28
Iran, 30, 74, 216, 222, 249, 317
  rescue attempt, 278
  Tehran hostage crisis, 9, 131, 137, 306
Iran-contra affair, 30, 32, 38, 89, 114, 146, 148, 153, 219, 222, 238, 241, 242, 253, 254, 261, 400–401
Iraq, 243
Iron curtain, 62, 177
Iron triangles, 35, 135, 136, 154
Islam, 90
Isolation, of policymakers, 36
Isolationism, 28, 44, 55, 58, 422
Isolationists, 129
Israel, 116, 148, 175, 176, 223, 225, 236, 259, 305, 415
Italy, 103
  Christian Democratic Party, 258

Jackson, Andrew, 49, 50, 271
Jackson, Henry, 219, 321
Jackson State University, 84
Jackson-Vanik amendment (1974), 219, 220, 362
Janis, Irving L., 36
Japan, 59, 61, 143, 187, 348, 414, 417
  base rights in, 351
  defense spending by, 352
  Hiroshima, 3, 4, 16, 61, 286, 389–390
  invasion of, 4
  Kokura, 3
  Nagasaki, 3, 4, 61
  technological acumen, 354
  trade with, 350–353, 364
Japanese lobbying, 176
Javits, Jacob, 176, 276, 277
Jay, John, 45, 304
Jay Treaty, 45
Jefferson, Thomas, 12, 45, 47, 48, 49, 101, 108, 200, 304, 342
Jeffersonian Republicans, 48
Jeffreys-Jones, Rhodri, 266
Jesus Christ, 27, 131, 241

Jewish emigration, 362
Jews, 219
Johansen, Robert C., 18
Johnson, Harry, 358
Johnson, Haynes, 424 n. 18
Johnson, Loch K., 194, 230, 231, 255, 266, 301, 307, 337
Johnson, Lyndon B.:
  administration of, 83, 84, 111, 133, 219, 318, 375 n. 4
  as president, 26, 27, 80, 81, 82, 111, 119, 132, 133, 145, 162, 166, 173, 184, 242, 246, 343, 367
  as presidential candidate, 250
  as senator, 144
  as vice-president, 145
Joint Chiefs of Staff, 137, 141
Jones, Howard, 41
Jones, John Paul, 133
Jones, James R., 417
Jordan, 175
Judicial review, 149
Judiciary, 149–152
Jungerman, John A., 301
Just-war tradition, 393

KAL flight 007, 217, 220
Kalb, Bernard, 220, 240
Kampiles, William, 225
Kant, Immanuel, 391, 392–393
Kantians, 391, 392, 394
Kaplan, Stephen S., 300
Karalekas, Anne, 231, 263
Karnow, Stanley, 96, 375 n. 4
Katzenbach, Nicholas, 106
Kaufmann, William W., 293, 294, 301
Kearns, Doris, 375
Kegley, Charles W., Jr., 96, 301
Kellogg-Briand Treaty, 59
Kelly, J. Michael, 423 n. 12
Kelman, Herbert C., 41
Kennan, George F., 18, 33, 63, 66, 71, 72, 73, 139, 304, 337, 411, 413
  views on containment, 71
Kennedy, John F.:
  administration of, 5, 76, 77, 309
  as president, 10, 11, 12, 36, 78, 79, 80, 81, 94 n. 26, 113, 132, 133, 134, 143, 162, 166, 169, 181, 240, 242, 246, 248
Kennedy, Paul, 33, 379

Kennedy, Robert:
  as attorney general, 77, 133
  as senator, 84
Kent, Sherman, 215
Kent State University, 84
Keshane, Robert O., 18
Key, V. O., Jr., 162
Keynes, John Maynard, 57, 387, 388
KGB, 12, 225, 239, 244, 401
Khambas, 398
Khoman, Thanat, 318
Khomeini, Ayatollah Ruhollah, 90, 237, 306, 382
Khrushchev, Nikita, 10, 12, 77, 78, 79, 141
King, Martin Luther, Jr., 81
King George's cavalry, 240
Kinzer, Stephen, 377 n. 49
Kipling, Rudyard, 26
Kirkpatrick, Jeane J., 316
Kirkpatrick, Lyman, 216
Kissinger, Henry A., 18, 28, 37, 62, 84, 86, 94 n. 34, 219, 225, 239, 295, 304, 321, 322, 337, 383, 399, 421
Kissinger Commission, 372
Kiwanis International, 179
Klare, Michael T., 301
Kleindienst, Richard, 221
Knight, Amy W., 232
Knighthood, 404
Knowland, William F., 326
Koenig, Louis W., 325
Kohl, Helmut, 162, 181, 212
Kokura, 3
Korea, North, 75, 243, 293
Korea, Republic of South, 75, 103, 164, 217, 218, 273, 317, 320, 328, 398, 418
  1983 airliner shooting, 217, 220
  tree-trimming incident, 278
Korean War, 76, 270, 274
Kornbluh, Peter, 230, 301
Krasner, Stephen D., 41
Kruzel, Joseph, 301
Kuchenbecker, David J., 327–328, 337
Kurds (Iraq), 249, 398
Kuwait, 278
Kyoto (Japan), 389

Labor Strikes, 241
Ladd, Everett C., 173
Lake, Anthony, 337

Lake Erie, battle of, 49
Lance missile, 283
Laos, 79, 83, 87, 114, 241, 243, 250, 320, 398
Lasswell, Harold, 161, 181, 189
Latin America, 239, 249, 326, 353, 372
Latvia, 418
Launch on attack, 289
Launch on warning, 289
Law of anticipated reactions, 259
Lawrence-Livermore Laboratory, 179
Lawyers Committee for Human Rights, 385
Le Carre, John, 397
Le Duc Tho, 322
League of Arab States (LAS), 180
League of Nations, 14, 57, 58, 59, 112, 182, 183, 382, 386–388, 406
League of Women Voters, 179
Leak item veto, 258
Lebanese Gulf of Tonkin Resolution, 280
Lebanon, 164, 222, 237, 243, 273, 278, 279, 280, 317
    suicidal truck bombing, 280
Lebanon Emergency Assistance Act, 280
Lee, Robert E., 53, 270
Legislative Counsel (CIA), 254
Legislative model, 128
Legislative veto, 146, 277
Leland, Mickey, 419
Lend-lease agreement, 108–109, 307
Leopold II, King, 381
Lerche, Charles O., Jr., 66
Lerner, Michael, 196
Lethal biological toxins, 245
Letters, 171
Letters to the editor, 169
Levi, Edward H., 222
Liberals, 417
Liberia, 317
Library of Congress, 148
Libya, 119, 165, 273, 317
Lincoln, Abraham, 53, 102, 131, 152, 270
Lippmann, Walter, 145
Lithuania, 418
"Little Boy," 3
Loans, 365, 369
Lobbying, 116, 174–180

Lobbyist, 174
Lodge, Henry Cabot, 57, 58, 182
Logistical dimension (of strategy), 271
Long, Breckenridge, 359
Long, Samuel, 167
Looking Glass, 291
Los Alamos Scientific Laboratory, 179
Lottier, John, 195
Louisiana territory, 48
Low-intensity conflict (LIC), 292
Low-intensity warfare, 76
Low self-esteem, 182
Lown, Bernard, 6
LSD, 244
Lueck, Thomas J., 424 n. 18
Lumumba, Patrice, 12, 79, 119, 245
Lusitania, 56

MacArthur, Douglas, 78
McCarran, Pat, 325
McCarthy, Eugene, 84
McCarthy, Joseph, 73, 80, 115, 148
McCarthyism, 73
McCone, John, 245, 246, 247, 248
McGovern, George, 325
Machiavelli, Niccolo, 14
McKinley, William, 53, 54
McLellan, David S., 70, 75, 96, 410 n. 60
McLuhan, Marshall, 28
McMahon, John, 142
McNamara, Robert S., 78, 133, 247, 287, 288, 292, 301, 372
McNaught, L. W., 285, 301
Madison, James, 30, 48, 49, 101, 122, 141, 238, 304
Madison Group, 179
Madura-foot fungus, 244
Magsaysay, President, 320
Mail, 169
Maine (battleship), 54, 56
Malaysia, 243
Manhattan Project, 286
Manifest destiny, 26, 27, 52
Mann, Thomas E., 425
Mansfield, Mike, 377 n. 32
Manual of Navy Regulations, 133
Mao Tse-tung, 322
Marbury v. Madison, 149
Marchetti, Victor, 232
Marcos, Ferdinand E., 334

Marcos, Imelda, 371
Marine Corps, U.S., 236, 422
Market, 218
Marks, John D., 232
Marquis of Queensberry rules, 261
Marshall, George C., 71, 420
Marshall Plan, 14, 71, 75, 343, 369, 388, 399, 419
Marxism, 424 n. 13
Marxist-Leninist ideology, 23
Massachusetts Institute of Technology (MIT), 120
Massive retaliation, 76
Mathias, Charles, 247
Mauritius, 243
Maximilian, Ferdinand, 53
May, Ernest R., 232
Mayaguez, U.S.S., 87, 112, 163, 164, 165, 278, 279
Mayhew, David, 117
Mazarin, Jules, 304
Mead, Walter Russell, 377
Meany, George, 81
Media assets (CIA), 239
Mediterranean Sea, 101
Medium-range ballistic missiles (MRBMs), 77
Mega-lobbies, 177
Meir, Golda, 322
Meo tribesmen, 249, 398
Mercantilist model, 358
Mercenaries, 241
Mexico, 23, 52, 57, 102, 236, 350, 354, 418
Micromanagement, 148, 259, 416
Middle East, 88, 105, 237, 248, 305, 331
Midgetman missile, 288
MIG-21s, 215
Mikulski, Barbara, 26
Military actions, 271, 297
Military Assistance Program (MAP), 109, 318, 365
Military strategy, 270
Mill, John Stuart, 190
Miller, Warren E., 170
Mills, C. Wright, 135
Mining of piers, 241
Miskito Indians, 217
Model of constitutional balance, 129
Model of presidential deference, 170
Modelski, George, 379

Mondale, Walter, 406
Mongolia, 23
Monroe, James, 49, 50, 51, 101, 304
Monroe Doctrine, 23, 50, 51, 53, 54, 57, 64–65 n. 7, 101, 187
Monrovia, 212
Moore, Frank, 145
Morgenthau, Hans J., 18, 304, 305, 331, 383
Morse, Wayne, 106
Moss, John E., 222
Most-favored-nation (MFN), 363
Moyers, Bill, 81, 220
Moynihan, Daniel P., 87, 372, 424 n. 13
Muddling through, 365
Mueller, John E., 69, 196
Mujahedeen, 241
Multinational corporations (MNCs), 357
Multiple advocacy, 186
Munich, 235
Munich syndrome, 295
Munro, Dana G., 367
Murphy Commission, 252
Muskie, Edmund S., 402, 403
Mussolini, Benito, 60
Mutual and Balanced Force Reduction (MBFR), 211
Mutual assured destruction (MAD), 272, 287, 394
Mutual Defense Assistance Act, 369
Mutual Security Act, 369
MX missile, 135, 288
My Lai, 83, 225

Nacht, Michael, 195
Nagasaki, 3, 61, 389–390
Napoleon III, 53
Napoleonic wars, 48
Narcotics trade, 211, 252, 253
Nation, 21
Nation-state, 21
National Command Authority (NCA), 290
National Commitments Resolution, 274, 327
National Conference of Catholic Bishops on War and Peace, 393–394
National Defense University, 417
National Emergency Airborne Command Post (NEACP), 290

National Foreign Assessment Center, 254
(*See also* Directorate of Intelligence)
National Foreign Intelligence Board (NFIB), 202
National Foreign Intelligence Council (NFIC), 202
National Intelligence Estimates (NIEs), 216
National Photographic Interpretation Center (NPIC), 207
National security, 225, 226
National Security Act, 208, 242
catchall passage, 242
National security adviser, 136
National Security Agency, 202, 204, 209, 214, 222
National Security Council, 136, 201, 202, 203, 226, 253
National Security Council Directive No. 4/A, 242
Natinoal Security Council Paper No. 68 (NSC-68), 73, 272
National Security Planning Group, 254
(*See also* Special Coordination Committee)
National Security Policy Group, 202
National Strategy Information Center, 179
Nazis, 23, 61, 103, 108
Nelson-Bingham Amendment, 146
Neo-isolationists, 325
Net Assessment Group, 202
Neustadt, Richard E., 29, 158
Neutralization, 32, 248
Neutron bombs, 239
Nevada, 288
New England Federalists, 48
New Orleans, 47, 48
New York Times, 224
New York Times Co. v. United States, 152, 224, 225
New world order, 28
Newly industrialized countries (NICs), 346, 354
Newman, Della, 333
Newsom, David D., 304, 333, 337, 371, 419
Ngo Dinh Diem, 81, 245
Nguema, Francisco Macias, 385
Nguyen Ngoc Loan, 84

Nicaragua, 5, 32, 89, 114, 118, 130, 141, 142, 152, 170, 178, 212, 215, 235, 238, 243, 248, 252, 256, 258, 259, 261, 372, 385, 400, 406, 415
mining of harbors, 256
Nicolson, Sir Harold, 34, 337
Niebuhr, Reinhold, 411
Nippophobia, 352, 363
Nixon, Richard M.:
administration of, 28, 92, 120, 224, 250, 260, 343
as president, 37, 62, 87, 153, 163, 166–167, 171, 182, 183, 184, 186, 221, 240, 275, 313, 322
as Republican nominee, 84, 85
and Huston Plan, 401–402
"Nixon shock," 343
Noise, 201
Noise-free disseminator, 244
Nontariff barriers (NTBs), 353
Nondiscernible microbio-inoculator, 244
Nongovernmental organizations (NGOs):
Amnesty International, 22
World Health Organization (WHO), 22
Nonstate actors, 178
Noriega, Manuel Antonio, 258, 403
North American Defense (NORAD), 290
North Atlantic Treaty Organization (NATO), 75, 133, 180, 258, 272, 282, 293, 321, 326, 388
North, Oliver L., 31, 118, 142, 149, 157 n. 53, 220, 223, 236, 237, 259, 260, 261, 306
North Sea, 348
North Vietnamese, 83
Nuclear decapitation, 290
Nuclear ethics, 391
Nuclear Non-proliferation Act, 146
Nuclear retaliation, 272
Nuclear test ban treaty, 80, 388
Nuclear waste products, 174
Nuclear weapons, 270, 283, 294
accidents and misunderstandings, 296
effects of, 283, 284, 287
proliferation of, 6

Nuclear winter, 285
Nunn, Sam, 276, 281
Nye, Joseph F., Jr., 15, 300, 336 n. 71, 392–393, 405, 411

O'Brien, Conor Cruise, 338
O'Brien, Tim, 82
Office of Management and Budget (OMB), director of, 132
Office of Strategic Services (OSS), 82, 201, 397
Office of Technology Assessment (OTA), 147–148
Oil, 170
  embargo, 344
  imports, 348
Okinawa, 351
Okum, Susan, 394
Olney, Richard, 54
Olney corollary, 54
Oman, 243
On-site inspections, 211
One-worlders, 72
O'Neill, Thomas P., 145
Open covenants, 221, 331
Open-door policy, 55
Operation Chaos, 220, 259
Operation Magic, 201
Operation Shamrock, 222
Operational code, 185
Operational dimension (of strategy), 270
Opinion-leadership hypothesis, 165, 168
Oral briefing, 212
Oral understandings, 320
Organization for Economic Cooperation and Development (OECD), 356
Organization of American states (OAS), 132
Organization of Petroleum Exporting Countries (OPEC), 86, 210, 343–344, 346, 348
Osgood, Robert E., 411
O'Sullivan, John L., 52
Overleveraging, 346
Overseas Private Investment Corporation (OPIC), 357
Oversight, 115, 146, 319
Overt-covert action, 258
Overt military conflict, 249
Owen, Robert, 263
Oxfam America, 178
Ozone layer, 419

Paine, Thomas, 29
Pakistan, 317
Palestine Liberation Organization (PLO), 279, 305
Palestinians, 176
Palmerston, Third Viscount, 53
Panama, 36
Panama Canal Treaty, 108
Paraguay, 150
Paramilitary capability, 253
Paramilitary warfare (PM), 235, 239, 241, 423
Parasites, 241
Parry, Robert, 230
"Party of God" (Lebanon), 306
Pathet Lao, 243
Partial test ban treaty, 225
Pasha (of Tripoli), 200
Passman, Otto, 144, 369
Peace Corps, 369, 370, 388, 396, 422
Pearl Harbor, 10, 32, 61, 131, 200, 260
  syndrome, 295
Peele, Gillian, 194
Peer-group pressures, 36–37
Penkovsky, Oleg, 213
Pentagon, 135, 137–139
Pentagon Papers, 152, 224, 225
People's Republic of China (PRC), 355, 365, 398, 420
Perestroika, 5, 348
Perkins, Dexter, 54, 66
Permanent consultative body, 416
Permissive action links (PALs), 291, 296
Perry, Matthew C., 52
Pershing-II missiles, 117, 239, 283
Persian Gulf, 8, 25, 88, 273, 278, 414
Peters, Charles, 195
Petrodollars, 215, 344, 346
Pescadores, 104
Pfaff, William, 423 n. 5
Pforzheimer, Walter, 230
Philippines, 55, 63, 188, 200, 278, 320, 371
Philippines Mutual Defense Treaty, 320
Phoenix program, 248
Physicians for Social Responsibility, 180, 287
Pierce, Franklin, 52
Piers, mining of (in Nicaragua), 256

Pike Committee (on intelligence activities), 263, 266
Pinochet, Augusto, 385
Pious, Richard M., 158
Pius XI, Pope, 240
Plausible deniability, 32, 237, 238, 246
Pluralism, 32
Pogue, Forrest C., 96
Poindexter, John M., 219, 226, 237, 238, 246, 259, 306
"Point Four" (Truman), 310–311, 369
Pol Pot, 87, 382
Poland, 60, 121, 243, 389, 418
Political covert action, 240
Political economy, 372
Political Victory Fund, 417
Political warfare, 239
Polsby, Nelson, 117, 158
Polycentrism, 117
Polygraph, 207
Polk, James K., 52, 102
Pool, Ithiel de Sola, 193 n. 29
Popov, Pyotr, 213
Portuguese Timor, 211
Poseidon nuclear submarines, 292
Post-war Western Europe, 239
Postattack (nuclear) environment, 286
Potsdam, 324
Power, 181
Power motive, 182
Powers, Thomas, 232, 264
POWs, 390
Prados, John, 264, 266
Pratt, Julius W., 66
Preclusive buying, 364
President, 202, 238, 335
  first use of nuclear weapons by, 282
  power of, 133–134, 151, 152–154
  role of, 154
  as sovereign, 153
Presidential Directive No. 59 (PD 59), 273
Presidential model, 128
President's Daily Brief (PDB), 215
Press, 160
Pressure groups, 35, 116, 174–180
Principle of discrimination, 393
Principle of proportionality, 393
Prins, Gwyn, 301
Prior restraint, 223
Privatization, 31, 236, 401

Processing, 214
Proclamation of Neutrality, 45
Producer of knowledge, 210
Productivity, 345
Propaganda, 239, 253, 264
Protectionism in the United States, 13, 15, 352
Psychiatry, 295
Psycho-political process, 181
Psychohistory, 183
Public administration, 32
Public opinion, 29, 64, 73, 121, 162–173, 169
Pueblo, 165, 225
Pulitzer, Joseph, 54
Punta del Este summit meeting, 326
Purse, power of, 113, 115

Qaddafi, Muammar al, 119, 212, 220, 264, 306, 398
Quemoy, 104
Quiet option, 12, 249

Rad, 284, 285
Radio Martí, 177
Radioactivity, 284
Rain forests, 2, 8
Rally-round-the-flag hypothesis, 164
Ramsey, Paul, 391–392
Ranelagh, John, 232
Ranney, Austin, 28
Ransom, Harry Howe, 201, 232
Rapid Deployment Force, 272
Rapproachement, 45
Rathjens, George, 284
Raw information, 215
Rawls, John, 411
Rayburn, Sam, 144–145
Reagan, Ronald:
    administration of, 6, 7, 8, 13, 26, 30, 35, 37, 74, 88, 92, 114, 118, 133, 137, 139, 145, 178, 190, 213, 220, 225, 235, 241, 243, 249, 355, 363, 382, 403
    as president, 34, 62, 63, 85, 89, 90, 91, 103, 118, 119, 129, 132, 145, 146, 153, 163, 165, 167, 168, 184, 203, 207, 222, 249, 254, 264, 265, 273, 279, 295, 330, 333, 342, 352, 417, 424 n. 12
Reagan Doctrine, 89, 212, 292

Reagan revolution, 35
Realist approach to world affairs, 261, 382–384
Recruiting, of intelligence personnel, 206
Reedy, George E., 195
Refugees, 152
Rehnquist, William, 171
Replay, 12, 240
Reporting requirements, 146
Republican Party, 80
    right wing of, 348
Retroactive finding, 259
Revere, Paul, 200
Revolutionary War, 45
Reykjavik, Iceland, 89, 90
Ricardo, David, 346
Richardson, Lewis F., 41
Richelieu, Duc de, 304
Richelson, Jeffrey T., 232
Rivers, Mendel, 27
Rockefeller, Nelson, 131
Rogin, Michael, 195
Rogers, William P., 37
Rogow, Arnold, 196
Rogue elephant, 141, 246, 247, 259
Role, 33–34
"Roll-back" policy, 74
Roman Catholic Church, 180
Roman senate, 149
Roosevelt, Franklin D.:
    administration of, 149
    as president, 59, 60, 61, 102, 103, 104, 108, 109, 129, 131, 150, 307, 323
Roosevelt corollary to Monroe Doctrine, 56
Roosevelt, Theodore, 56, 102, 271
Rosenau, James N., 41
Rositzke, Harry, 232
Rosselli, John, 244, 398
Rossiter, Clinton, 125, 152
Rostow, Walt W., 81
Rovine, Arthur W., 336 n. 80, 338
Rowan, Carl, 372, 422
Rudman, Warren, 30
Rush-Bagot agreement, 49
Rusk, Dean, 11, 13, 78, 85, 86, 109, 110, 144, 145, 164, 188, 190, 242, 251, 318, 321
Russell, Richard B., 105, 106, 144, 277
Russett, Bruce, 314
Russia, 389

Russians, 187, 210, 390–391
Rustow, Dankwart A., 196

Sadat, Anwar, 302, 322
Saigon, 85
Salisbury, Lord, 304
SALT (Strategic Arms Limitation Talks), 321
Samuelson, Paul A., 343, 346, 379
Sanctions, trade, 363–364
Sandinista regime, 89, 114, 217, 235, 241
Sarbanes, Paul, 176
Satellite reconnaissance, 211
Satellites, 213
Saudi Arabia, 175, 179, 236, 259, 278, 348, 382
Schell, Jonathan, 301
Schelling, Thomas, 41, 76, 372
Schlesinger, Arthur M., Jr., 32, 81, 96, 104, 106, 125, 225, 248, 406
Schneider, Rene, 245, 251
Schollaert, James T., 336 n. 79
Second-strike capability, 288
Schumacher, Kurt, 182
Secord, Richard V., 237
Secrecy, 218
Secret Service, 203
Security assistance, 365
Self-delusion, 36
Senate Foreign Relations Committee, 104, 109, 110–111, 114, 120, 121, 125, 174, 275, 316, 326, 327, 328, 329, 330
Senior Interagency Groups (SIGs), 202
Seniority system, 144
Separation of powers, 29
Seward, W. H., 53
Seward's Icebox, 54
Shackley, Theodore, 266
Shah of Iran, 216, 243
Shapiro, Catherine R., 167, 168
Sheepdipping, 243
Shellfish toxin (saxitoxin), 243
Schultz, George P., 148, 190, 207, 219, 220, 229, 359, 361, 366
Side-payments, 145
Sierra Leone, 370
Silk, Leonard, 343, 346, 379
Silva, Sergio Buschmann, 384
Sinai, 278, 322
Singer, J. David, 41, 181

Singlaub, John, 237
Single European Market, 351
Situation Room, 215
Sixty-day clock (of War Powers Resolution), 276, 281–282
Smart, J. J. C., 392
Smith, Gaddis, 54
Smith, Gerard C., 301
Smith, Hedrick, 159
Smithsonian agreement, 343
Smoke, Richard, 272
Smoot-Hawley Tariff, 363
Snepp, Frank, 264, 266
Social dimension (of strategy), 271, 273
Sofaer, Abraham D., 330
Solar-energy group, 174
Somalia, 252
Somoza, 235, 371, 403
Sorenson, Theodore C., 94 n. 21, 94 n. 26, 132, 159, 334
South Africa, 146, 178, 236, 259, 385, 401, 402
South Vietnam, 188, 248
South Yemen, 243
Southeast Asia Treaty Organization (SEATO), 79, 80, 109, 318
Southern Governors Association, 415
Southwest Peanut Shellers Association, 174
Sovereignty-at-bay, 357, 358
Soviet Union, 62, 69, 71, 75, 78, 86, 88, 89, 91, 92, 115, 129, 139, 235, 252, 261
  aggression in Western Hemisphere, 403
  computers, 210
  invasion of Afghanistan, 243, 355
  oil pipeline, 239
  rocket fuels, 215
  tanks, 240
  trade with, 347, 361, 365
Spain, 49, 50, 54, 110, 319–320
Spanier, John, 86, 96
Spanish-American War, 26, 54, 56
Sparkman, John, 328–329
Sparkman-Bennet letters, 328–329
Special Coordination Committee (SCC), 254
  working group, 256
  (*See also* National Security Planning Group)

Special National Intelligence Estimates (SNIEs), 216
Special operations, 243
Special trade representative (STR), 134, 359
Spero, Joan Edelman, 345, 347, 379
Spotting and assessing (of intelligence agents), 206
Sputnik, 77, 164
Spykman, Nicholas J., 23
SS-20 missiles, 283
Stagflation, 344
Stalin, Joseph, 62, 70, 382, 391
Stark, U.S.S., 164
Starr, Harvey, 314
State, 21
State, Department of, 140–141, 249, 359
State Department Bureau of Intelligence and Research (INR), 202, 203
States'-rightists, 129, 323
Status quo ante bellum, 49
Statutory agreements, 108, 306, 308
Stennis, John, 338
Stewart, Potter, 224
Stimson, Henry L., 389, 395
Stinger missile, 175
Stokes, Donald E., 170
Stone, I. F., 279
Stonewalling, 222
Strang, Lord, 338
Strategic Arms Limitation Talks (SALT), 87, 211, 225, 295
Strategic Defense Initiative (SDI), 9, 180, 286, 294, 394
Strategic intelligence, 10, 120, 199, 238
Strategic nuclear capabilities, 283
Strategic warheads, 291
Subgovernments, 135
Submarine-launched ballistic missiles (SLBM), 117, 128, 283, 288, 291
Submarines, 289
Subterfuge, by the executive branch, 415–416
Sugar, 241
Supreme Court, 221
Suriname, 243
Survey opinion on the Cambodian invasion by U.S., 172
Sutherland, Arthur, 338
Sutherland, George, 150, 151

Switzerland, 353
Sycophancy, 184
Symington, James, 176
Syngman Rhee, 75
Syria, 220
Szulc, Tad, 321–322

Tactical nuclear capabilities, 283
Tactical nuclear weapons, 292
Taft, Robert A., 72, 75, 103
Taft, William Howard, 56, 102
Taiwan, 74, 104, 150, 188, 352, 418
Talbott, Strobe, 96, 301
Talleyrand, Charles Maurice de Perigord, 45, 304
Targeting (intelligence), 210
Tarzan, 83
Tasking (intelligence), 211
Tatalovich, Raymond, 159
Taylor, Maxwell D., 86
Taylor, Rufus, 201
Technical intelligence (TECHINT), 213
Technology transfer, 212
Teepen, Tom, 420
Tehran, 90, 324
Television, 20, 27–28, 84, 118–119
Tellez, Captain, 384
Tennessee, U.S.S., 290
Tennessee Valley Authority, 81
Terrorism, 211, 252, 253, 258
Tet offensive, 84
Texas, 50
Textbook presidency, 131
Thailand, 109, 188, 243, 318–319
Theater nuclear weapons, 283
Theory of competitive advantage, 346
Theory of misunderstanding, 246
Third option, 249
Third Reich, 23, 26
Third World, 343
Third World insurgencies, 293
Thompson, Kenneth W., 411
Thomson, James C., 39 n. 20
Thucydides, 14
Tiananmen Square, 9
Tibbets, Park W., 3
Tibet, 398
Tickell, Sir Crispin, 333 n. 11
Tito gambit, 316
Tolchin, Martin, 335 n. 47
Torture, Congressional Resolution Against, 177
Totalitarian regimes, 313, 403, 404

Tovar, B. Hugh, 263 n.7
Tower, John, 112, 244
Tower commission, 265
Track I and Track II (U.S. policy in Chile), 250
Trade, Western interdependence, 345; North-South dependence, 345–346; East-West independence, 347
  U.S. exports, 348–349
  U.S. imports, 348
  U.S.-Japanese, 350–352
  U.S.-Soviet, 347
  U.S. trade balances, 349–350
  U.S. trade surpluses, 349
Trade Act, 146
Trade deficits, U.S., 341, 349, 350
Trade Expansion Act (1962), 309
Trafficante, Santos, 245, 398
Transnationalism, 357, 358
Treasury, Department of, 202, 359
Treaty of Ghent, 49
Treaty of Guadalupe Hidalgo, 52
Treaty of Versailles, 57, 112, 183
Treaty power, 303, 306, 308, 329
Treaty Powers Resolution, 328–329
Treaty provision (of Article II of U.S. Constitution), 107
Treaty ratification, 124 n. 27
Treaty termination, 150
Treverton, Gregory F., 266, 424 n. 24
Triad, 288
Triangle of power, 187
Tribe, Laurence H., 115
Trident nuclear submarines, 292
Tripoli, 200
Trujillo, Rafael, 245
Truman, Harry S:
  administration of, 4, 5, 23, 73, 74, 75, 80, 148, 152, 222, 251, 272
  as president, 4, 62, 70, 72, 78, 103, 104, 113, 133, 148, 162, 166, 183, 201, 208, 310, 311, 389
Truman Doctrine, 24, 71, 369
Trustee, 168
Tuchman, Barbara, 36
Turkey, 71, 73, 78, 176, 177, 243, 317
Turner, Admiral Stansfield, 204, 211, 232, 254, 257, 265
Two-gears analogy, 117

Two-step flow of communications, 168

U-2 spy plane, 164, 165
Uganda, 347
Ukraine, 243, 398
Ultra, 383, 390
Ungar, Stanford J., 66, 158
United Auto Workers, 135
United Fruit Company, 369
United Nations, 69, 75, 112, 180, 270, 323, 325, 357, 420, 427
United Nations Charter, 61
United Nations Relief and Rehabilitation Administration, 323
United States v. Curtiss-Wright Export Corp., 149, 150, 151
United States v. Nixon, 221
United States Senate, 171
United States-Canadian trade negotiations, 162
Utah, 288

Vance, Cyrus, 88, 136, 252, 316, 330, 331, 402, 422
Vandenberg, Arthur H., 61, 188, 189, 323
Vanik, Charles, 219
Venezuela, 243
Verification, 211
Verification Panel, 202
Vernon, Raymond, 357
Veterans of Foreign Wars, 179
Videotape format (for intelligence), 212, 218
Vietcong, 27, 81, 82
Vietcong Infrastructure (VCI), 248
Vietnam, 79, 83, 84, 85, 106, 107, 109, 114, 130, 189, 243, 250, 273, 274, 276, 278, 298, 414
  war in, 5, 27, 36, 38, 111, 113, 122, 128, 133, 164, 178, 186, 225, 226, 243, 319, 375, 397, 398, 422
Vietnam era, 170, 401–402
Vietnam syndrome, 87
Vietnam War Memorial, 269
Vigilant Women for Bricker Amendment, 179
Vinson, Carol, 146
Volel, Yves, 385

Walker, John (and family), 225
Wallace, Henry, 72

Wallace, Robert, 47
Waltz, Kenneth N., 41
Walworth, Arthur, 96
Walzer, Michael, 404, 411
War of 1812, 49
War Hawks, 48
War of Independence, 12, 48, 49, 53
War power, 100, 103, 366, 383
War Powers Resolution, 134, 146, 150, 241, 256, 275, 278, 296, 298, 416
Warfare, defensive, 101
War-fighting doctrine, 273
Warnke, Paul, 336 n. 82
Warsaw Pact, 75, 293
Washington, George:
  as general, 200, 218
  as president, 45, 46, 47, 49, 107, 114, 304
Washington Post, 224
Watergate scandal, 38, 62, 85, 86, 113, 128, 143, 144, 220, 221, 222, 225, 226
Weapons, 179, 384
Weapons technology, 271
Weathermen, 85
Webster, Daniel, 143
Webster, William H., 157 n. 46, 203
Wehrmacht, 24
Weicker, Lowell P., Jr., 277
Weinberger, Caspar W., 37, 210, 219, 273, 286, 361, 417
Welch, Richard S., 119
Wells, Sumner, 359
Westerfield, H. Bradford, 15
Western imperialism, 188
Westinghouse International Corporation, 174
Whalen, Charles W., Jr., 338
Wheeler, Burton K., 61
Wherry, Kenneth, 27
White, Ralph K., 424
White, Theodore H., 131, 401
White, William S., 121
Whitman, Marina V. N., 379
Wilcox, Francis O., 125
Wildavsky, Aaron, 416
Williams, Bernard, 392
Wilhelm I, Kaiser, 36
Wilson, Woodrow, 26, 27, 56, 57, 58, 59, 102, 182, 183, 184, 221, 386, 388, 402
  Fourteen Points, 58

Wilsonianism, 14, 59, 382–383, 386–387

Wittkopf, Eugene R., 301

Wolfers, Arnold, 384

Wolsey, Cardinal, 304

Woodward, Bob, 195, 264, 266, 382

Working group (for intelligence), in Carter administration, 254

World Anti-Communist League, 237

World Bank, 356

World government, 325

World Health Organization (WHO), 22, 180

World population, 419

World War I, 26, 28

World War II, 6, 14, 24, 26, 27, 28, 61, 102, 112

Worst-case analysis, 139

Wright, Jim, 282, 345

Wright, Quincy, 41

Wyden, Peter, 94 n. 26, 96

XYZ affair, 45

Yalta, 324, 390

Yergen, Daniel, 379

Yoder, Amos, 96

Yorty, Sam, 179

Yost, Charles W., 226

Young, Andrew, 179

Young Turks (in Congress), 144

Yugoslavia, 418

Zablocki, Clement, 279, 327

Zaire, 215, 278

Zero-sum strategy, 186

Ziegler, David W., 41

Zinnes, Danna A., 41

Zimmermann, Herr, 57